FAIR TRADE, CORPORATE ACCOUNTABILITY AND BEYOND

Fair Trade, Corporate Accountability and Beyond
Experiments in Globalizing Justice

Edited by

KATE MACDONALD
University of Melbourne, Australia

SHELLEY MARSHALL
Monash University, Australia

ASHGATE

Published by
Ashgate Publishing Limited
Wey Court East
Union Road
Farnham
Surrey, GU9 7PT
England

Ashgate Publishing Company
Suite 420
101 Cherry Street
Burlington
VT 05401-4405
USA

www.ashgate.com

British Library Cataloguing in Publication Data
Fair trade, corporate accountability and beyond :
  experiments in globalizing justice.
  1. International trade--Social aspects. 2. Commercial
  policy. 3. Social responsibility of business.
  I. Macdonald, Kate. II. Marshall, Shelley.
  382.3-dc22

Library of Congress Cataloging-in-Publication Data
Fair trade, corporate accountability and beyond : experiments in globalizing justice
/ by Kate Macdonald and Shelley Marshall.
     p. cm.
  Includes index.
  ISBN 978-0-7546-7439-9 (hardback) -- ISBN 978-0-7546-9119-8 (e-book)
1. International trade. 2. Competition, Unfair. 3. Foreign trade regulation--Social aspects. I. Macdonald, Kate, 1976- II. Marshall, Shelley.

  HF1379.F343 2009
  382'.3--dc22

2009030156

ISBN   9780754674399 (hbk)
ISBN   9780754691198 (ebk)

Mixed Sources
Product group from well-managed
forests and other controlled sources
www.fsc.org Cert no. SA-COC-1565
© 1996 Forest Stewardship Council
FSC

Printed and bound in Great Britain by
MPG Books Group, UK

Contents

INTRODUCTION

PART I   INDIVIDUAL AND CIVIC ACTION THROUGH FAIR TRADE

PART II   RESPONSIBLE CONSUMERS AND CORPORATIONS

CONCLUSION

List of Figures and Tables

Figures

Tables

Notes on Contributors

Jeffrey Ballinger holds a JD (New York Law School) and is a PhD candidate (Political Science) at McMaster University, Hamilton, Ontario (abd). He has, most recently, lectured in the Department of Management, Webster University (Vienna), teaching Labor–Management Relations. Before that he was a Research Associate at the Kennedy School of Government, Harvard University. In 1993 Jeff founded Press for Change, a non-profit human rights campaign organization focusing on worker rights in the developing world. He was its director until 1999, appearing on US commercial television networks, PBS and in several foreign broadcasts and documentaries as an expert commentator on the global political economy. From 1983 to 1995 he worked in Asia for the AFL-CIO. Before that, he worked for various trade unions as an organizer, leading campaigns, boycotts and political education programmes. He has published articles in *New Labor Review*, *Social Policy*, *Brown Economic Review* and *Dissent*.

Anita Chan is a research professor at the China Research Centre of the University of Technology, Sydney. She has published widely on Chinese labour issues, rural China and Chinese youth. Her current major projects involve editing a book on Walmart in China and one on labour in Vietnam, and launching a new research project related to Chinese enterprise in comparative perspective.

Sean Cooney's research interests are international and comparative labour law, with a focus on Asia, and Chinese law. He is currently working on new approaches to improving international working standards, including an Australian Research Council-funded project on regulatory reform in China to deal with the problem of wage arrears. Sean speaks Mandarin Chinese, French and German and has published articles in major refereed law journals in the United States, China and Australia, such as the *Comparative Labor Law and Policy Journal* and *Bijiaofa Yanjiu*. He currently teaches Obligations, Chinese Law, Employment Law, and Law and Economic Development in Asia. Sean has studied at the University of Melbourne, Columbia University and National Taiwan University. He also spent several years as a lawyer practising mainly in the areas of employment and administrative law.

Claribel David, after starting a career in the finance sector, made a move to support fair trade in 1998 as the Chair of Association of Partners for Fair Trade. From 2002 to 2006 she was the Board Chair for the Filipinas Fair Trade Ventures and the Director for Finance and Advocacy for the Advocate of Philippine Fair Trade. She joined the International Fair Trade Association (IFAT) in 2003 as Treasurer and Asian Representative and took on the role of Vice President in May 2007. IFAT is a global network of 350 fair trade and support organizations in 60 countries whose mission is to improve the livelihood and well being of disadvantaged producers in the South.

Annie Delaney has worked as a union and community organizer and campaigner. She has worked for the Textile, Clothing and Footwear Union of Australia and was the founding member and driving force behind the creation of the FairWear campaign, coordinating campaigns and organizing activities with homeworkers in the garment industry. She is a participant in the

International Homeworkers Movement organization, and is currently a PhD candidate at Latrobe University, Melbourne researching homework related issues. Her areas of interest include corporate accountability, informal employment, labour organizing and the intersection of race, gender and class.

Emer Diviney works at the Brotherhood of St Laurence in the Sustainable Business Unit where she leads the BSL's work on sustainability in the fashion industry. She is the author of the *Ethical Threads* report and was responsible for managing the No SweatShop Accreditation of the BSL Hunter Gatherer Stores. Emer holds a BA (Community Development) and has worked both in Australia and overseas in the aid and development sector in the areas of education, income generation, gender and development, disabilities and health. Before working in the community sector she held management roles in the fashion industry in Australia and applies this industry knowledge to the textile and clothing industry supply chain work at the BSL. She is the Chair of the Program Advisory Committee at RMIT's Fashion, a member of the Homeworkers Code of Practice Committee, and was an International Chamber of Commerce Delegate at the World Summit on Sustainable Development.

John Howe is Associate Professor and Director of the Centre for Employment and Labour Relations Law at the Melbourne Law School. John's research is concerned with the capacity of pluralist regulatory systems to achieve socially just outcomes for working people and the unemployed. He has written extensively on various mechanisms of labour regulation, and the intersection between state-based regulation and corporate governance. John is co-editor of the book *Labour Law and Labour Market Regulation* published by Federation Press in 2006, and his book *Regulating for Job Creation* was published by Federation Press in late 2008. John is Secretary of the Australian Labour Law Association, and a member of the editorial committee of the *Australian Journal of Labour Law*.

Anna Hutchens has five years experience in researching and writing on the fair trade industry. Awarded her PhD, 'Entrepreneurship, Power and Defiance: The Globalisation of the Fair Trade Movement', in 2007, Dr Hutchens' recent research on fair trade will be published by Edward Elgar in her book *Changing Big Business: The Globalisation of the Fair Trade Movement* in April 2009. Dr Hutchens' research interests include fair trade value-chains and 'mainstreaming', Fair Trade labelling and brand companies; Fair Trade market development in the Asia Pacific region; and gender issues in the Asia Pacific region. In 2009, she was awarded an AusAid-funded Pacific Economic Postdoctoral Fellowship and an Australian Development Research Award to undertake a two-year research project to evaluate how Fair Trade value chains can be made more accessible to, and empowering for, female producers and artisans in the (Asia) Pacific region.

Chan Ka-wai headed up the China Project of Hong Kong Christian Industrial Committee for 13 years, focusing on transnational corporations and labour standards in South China. He is now the Chairperson of Labour Action China and a board member of Worker Empowerment, two prominent labour organizations in South China. Ka-wai received his theological training in Hong Kong and later received his S.T.M. on Religion and Society at the Pittsburgh Theological Seminary. Ka Wai is also active in Hong Kong's politics. He was elected Kowloon City District Councillor for 2000–2007 and became the Vice-Chairperson of the Kowloon City District Council for 2004–2008. He is now the Chief Executive of the Democratic Party in Hong Kong and is sitting on the boards of several public services.

Hyun-Seung Anna Kim is a PhD candidate in management studies at the University of Cambridge. Previously she was Marketing and Fundraising Officer at the Oxfam International Secretariat, and a member of the Oxfam International Fair Trade Working Group. Originally from South Korea, Anna is interested in learning from both the bright and dark sides of growth-oriented economic development, and exploring alternative ways to align developmental goals with social and environmental sustainability. As Oxfam School Speaker and Traidcraft Speaker she regularly speaks to young people about fair trade and development issues.

Steve Knapp is the Executive Director of the FTAANZ and of Fairtrade Labelling Australia and New Zealand (FLANZ). FTAANZ supports the development of the fair trade movement and FLANZ the market for Fairtrade labelled products. Steve was involved in the establishment of FLANZ as the regional Labelling Initiative member of Fairtrade Labelling Organizations International (FLO e.V.). He is also a board member of FLO e.V. Originally from the UK, Steve has a social and commercial business background. He was owner and managing director of a commodity trading company, a senior manager within a large corporate entity and managing director of a social enterprise support agency. He graduated from the London School of Economics and is a Master of Development Studies candidate at Victoria University Wellington.

Apo Leong was born in Macao in 1949 and completed high school in Hong Kong. He worked in a US MNC factory from 1969 to 1971. He was a local newspaper reporter from 1971 until he joined the HR Christian Industrial Committee as a labour organizer in 1974. Ten years later he joined the Hong Kong Trade Union Education centre as a trade union educator and researcher. In 1990 he took on the role of Chief Researcher for the Hong Kong Confederation of Trade Unions. From 1994 Mr Leong worked as the Executive Director of the AMRC, and from 2008 onwards as the China Coordinator.

Serena Lillywhite is Manager, Sustainable Business with the Brotherhood of St Laurence. Serena is an active corporate responsibility practitioner, researcher and advocate. She has expertise and experience in responsible supply chain management in China and Australia, business and human rights, responsible investment and corporate governance. Serena has considerable knowledge of the OECD Guidelines for Multinational Enterprises and was involved in bringing the first OECD Guidelines case in Australia. She is an adviser to the OECD Investment Committee and works with the international corporate responsibility sector. Serena works regularly with the business community to foster dialogue and multi-stakeholder approaches to ethical business practices. Serena holds a Masters in International Business from the University of Melbourne and has lived and worked in China.

Orly Lobel is an associate professor of law at the University of San Diego. She writes and teaches in the areas of employment law, administrative law, legal theory, torts, consumer law and trade secrets. Prior to coming to USD, she taught at Yale Law School and served as a fellow at the Harvard University Center for Ethics and the Professions, the Kennedy School of Government's Hauser Center for Non-Profit Research, and the Weatherhead Center for International Affairs. A graduate of Tel Aviv University Law School, she clerked on the Israeli Supreme Court and did her graduate studies at Harvard Law School. Her recent publications include 'The Paradox of "Extra-Legal" Activism: Critical Legal Consciousness and Transformative Politics', 120 *Harvard Law Review* 937 (2007) (winner of the Thorsnes Prize for Faculty Scholarship). Lobel is also the co-editor of the forthcoming Encyclopedia of Labor and Employment Law and Economics (Edward Elgar, 2009).

Kate Macdonald is a lecturer in the School of Social and Political Sciences at the University of Melbourne. Her previous positions include Fellow of Government (Global Politics) at the London School of Economics and Political Science, Research Fellow at the Centre for Applied Philosophy and Public Ethics at the Australian National University, and Research Officer at the Department of Politics and International Relations at Oxford University.

Terry Macdonald is a lecturer in Global Politics at Monash University, and has worked previously as a Research Fellow at the Centre for Applied Philosophy and Public Ethics (CAPPE) at the Australian National University, and as a Junior Research Fellow and Lecturer in Politics at Merton College, Oxford University. Her recent publications on global justice and institutional reform include the book *Global Stakeholder Democracy: Power and Representation Beyond Liberal States* (Oxford University Press, 2008).

Nic Maclellan works as a journalist and researcher in the Pacific islands. Nic has travelled extensively throughout the islands region and lived in Fiji between 1997 and 2001, working with the Pacific Concerns Resource Centre. In 2006 he worked with Oxfam International as Senior Policy Advisor on the Pacific. He has written widely on trade, labour mobility and development issues in the Pacific and is co-author of a number of books on the region, including: *La France dans le Pacifique: de Bougainville à Moruroa* (Editions La Découverte, Paris, 1992); *After Moruroa: France in the South Pacific* (Ocean Press, Melbourne, 1998); and *Kirisimasi* (PCRC, Suva, 1999).

Andrea Maksimovic worked at the Victorian Textile Clothing and Footwear Union and the Victorian Trades Hall Council in Melbourne before moving to Brussels to work for the International Trade Union Confederation. She now works for SOLIDAR, a European NGO network as the International Cooperation Coordinator, on issues such as trade, aid, labour rights and migration. SOLIDAR leads the Decent Work, Decent Life campaign, aiming to put decent work at the heart of all policy-making.

Shelley Marshall is a lecturer in the department of Business Law and Taxation at Monash University, Australia. Shelley began her career as a public interest and labour lawyer before coordinating an Australia-wide campaign to improve the conditions of homeworkers. Shelley's research interests include industrial democracy, corporate governance and development. She has conducted a number of consultancies for organizations such as Homeworkers Worldwide and the International Labour Organization concerning novel methods of regulating informal and vulnerable workers. Shelley's recent publications include the edited volume *Varieties of Capitalism, Corporate Governance and Employees* (Melbourne University Press, 2008) which she co-edited with Richard Mitchell and Ian Ramsay.

Alex Nicholls, MBA, is the first lecturer in social entrepreneurship to be appointed at the University of Oxford and became the first staff member of the Skoll Centre for Social Entrepreneurship in 2004. Nicholls' research interests range across several key areas within social entrepreneurship, including: the interface between the public and social sectors; organizational legitimacy and governance; the development of social finance markets; and impact measurement and innovation. Nicholls is widely published in peer reviewed journals and has done consultancy work for not-for-profits, social enterprises, and the UK government. He is the co-author (with Charlotte Opal) of a major research book on fair trade: *Fair Trade* (Sage, 2005). His ground-breaking 2006 edition of a collection of key papers on the state of the art of social entrepreneurship globally was published in paperback edition by Oxford University Press in 2008. He is a non Executive Director of a major fair trade clothing company.

Gordon Renouf has been Director, Policy and Campaigns, at CHOICE, the Australian Consumers Association, since 2005. He is a member of the Commonwealth Consumer Affairs Advisory Council and represents consumers in various other fora. Gordon has worked on consumer issues, legal services policy and other areas of social policy for non government organizations and as a consultant to government, NGOs and the private sector. His previous positions include Director of the National Pro Bono Resource Centre, Director of the Northern Australian Aboriginal Legal Aid Service, National Convenor of the National Association of Community Legal Centres and consumer lawyer at Redfern Legal Centre.

Anna Tucker works as a policy officer at the Department of Justice in the Victorian Government. Anna recently completed a Bachelor of Laws at Monash University, where she also completed a Bachelor of Arts majoring in Visual Culture and English. During her studies, Anna worked in various roles across the arts and law, including as a research assistant for Shelley Marshall.

Peter Utting is Deputy Director, United National Research Institute for Social Development (UNRISD), where he also coordinates the institute's programme on Markets, Business and Regulation. His edited volumes include *Reclaiming Development Agendas: Knowledge, Power and International Policy Making* (2006), and *The Greening of Business in Developing Countries: Rhetoric, Reality and Prospects* (2002). He has authored numerous articles on corporate social responsibility and business regulation.

Tim Wilson is the Director of the Intellectual Property and Free Trade Unit at the Institute of Public Affairs and specializes in IP, trade, globalization and investment policy. He is regularly published in Australian and international newspapers, including the *Wall Street Journal*, and appears on television and radio programmes including ABC1's Q&A, and Joy FM's The Spin. Tim worked as a trade and communication consultant, has advised state and federal Members of Parliament, and delivered the programme to build the logistical and policy capacity of the Vietnamese government to host APEC in 2006. Tim has a Masters of Diplomacy and Trade and a Bachelor of Arts from Monash University, studied IP at WIPO, and Global Health Diplomacy and the WTO, International Trade and Development at the Institut de Hautes Études Internationales et du Développment.

Preface

It is often lamented that academics, activists and practitioners engaged in corporate accountability and improving labour standards do not jointly reflect upon the subject of their work enough. Academics talk to practitioners when they want information and practitioners don't often have the time to step back and reflect upon the efficacy of their strategies, except in planning meetings. This book arose out of a workshop held in December 2007 which aimed at creating a new space for reflection and collaboration. Its purpose was to bring normative and empirical scholars from philosophy, law, politics and economics together with practitioners, activists, social entrepreneurs, and companies with an interest in socially responsible supply chain practices, to reflect upon the challenges confronting the goal of strengthening labour regulation, social governance and human rights in a globalizing economy, and to explore new directions for building an effective and legitimate system of global social governance.

The workshop was organized by the Centre for Employment and Labour Relations Law at the University of Melbourne and the Centre for Applied Philosophy and Public Ethics at the Australian National University, with the support of the Centre for Governance of Knowledge and Development at the Australian National University and the Fair Trade Association of Australia and New Zealand. We are especially grateful to Cameron Neil from the Fair Trade Association of Australia and New Zealand for working with us on this project. He bought together a range of fair trade 'practitioners' who shared the stories of the development of Fair Trade and critically compared those stories with the parallel development of other forms of corporate social responsibility.

We were fortunate to have funding from an Australian Research Council grant received by Govnet (The ARC Governance Research Network), from CAPPE (Centre for Applied Philosophy and Public Ethics) as well as a small grant from AusAid. This funding allowed us to fly corporate responsibility scholars, practitioners and activists from the economic South, as well as those located in Europe and North America, to Melbourne, Australia for two days of discussions.

There are people who made significant contributions to the workshop, whose efforts are not apparent in this book, but without whom the workshop, and thus the book, would not have been a success. Jessica Cotton and Charlotte Morgans provided efficient administrative support. Later, Anna Tucker and Kamillea Aghtan provided outstanding research and editing assistance. Cheryl Kernot worked hard behind the scenes to publicize the workshop. Damien Carrick of ABC Radio and Jiselle Hannah of 3CR both put together radio programs based on the proceedings that helped us shape the book. A number of people from the procurement departments of companies attended and provided insights into the difficulties of turning large flotillas of companies around so that their practices reflect new values. We are grateful to everyone who attended the workshop and shared his or her views, leading to what was often a heated and passionate conversation.

These debates about the failure of existing governance arrangements to ensure decent work and livelihoods for millions of workers and producers around the world, and the potential of new governance initiatives to reassert principles of social justice in the governance of a globalizing economy, are what drive this collection.

List of Acronyms

ACFTU	All-China Federation of Trade Unions
AMRC	Asia Monitor Resource Centre
APEC	Asia Pacific Economic Co-operation
ATNC	Asian Transnational Corporation Monitoring Network
AWATW	Asian Women at Work
AWFA	Asia Wage Floor Alliance
BSL	Brotherhood of St Laurence
CA	corporate accountability
CCC	Clean Clothes Campaign
CR	corporate responsibility
CSR	corporate social responsibility
EFTA	European Fair Trade Association
EPA	economic partnership agreement
ETI	Ethical Trading Initiative
FDI	foreign direct investment
FLA	Fair Labor Association
FLO	Fairtrade Labelling Organization
FTO	fair trade organization
GRI	Global Reporting Initiative
HWCP	Homeworkers Code of Practice
HWCPC	Homeworkers Code of Practice Committee
IFAT	International Fair Trade Association (formerly the International Federation of Alternative Trade; now the WFTO)
ILO	International Labour Organization
IOC	International Olympic Committee
ISO	International Organization for Standardization
ITUC	International Trade Union Confederation (formerly the ICFTU)
MNC	multinational corporation
MNE	multinational enterprise
MOLISA	Ministry of Labour, Invalid and Social Affairs (Vietnam)
MSI	multi-stakeholder initiative
NCP	National Contact Point (of the OECD Guidelines for MNEs)
NEWS	Network of European Worldshops
NGO	non-governmental organization
OECD	Organisation for Economic Cooperation and Development
OSHA	Occupational Safety and Health Administration
PACER	Pacific Agreement on Closer Economic Relations
PICTA	Pacific Island Countries Trade Agreement
SME	small or medium enterprise
TCF	textile, clothing and footwear

TCFUA	Textile, Clothing and Footwear Union of Australia
TNC	transnational corporation
UNCTAD	United Nations Conference on Trade and Development
UNRISD	United Nations Research Institute for Social Development
VGCL	Vietnam General Confederation of Labor
WFTO	World Fair Trade Organization (formerly IFAT)
WRAP	Worldwide Responsible Apparel Production
WTO	World Trade Organization

INTRODUCTION

Chapter 1

Social Governance in a Global Economy: Introduction to an Evolving Agenda

Kate Macdonald and Shelley Marshall[1]

Introduction

In January 2007, the UK arm of the corporate giant McDonald's announced that it would be sourcing all its coffee with a certification from the US-based non-profit organization Rainforest Alliance. 'Today's announcement … means we can offer our customers great tasting coffee that benefits coffee growers, their communities and the environment', declared Steve Easterbrook, President and CEO of McDonald's UK, in the statement accompanying the launch of the new initiative.[2] Around the same time, the then CEO of global retailing giant Walmart – the reigning poster-child of global corporate abuse in the minds of many[3] – began to embrace the language of environmental and social responsibility, littering speeches and public statements with pronouncements about the company's new-found commitment to 'Doing Well by Doing Good', which involved the introduction of several environmental initiatives and incorporation of a range of 'ethical' products – including Fairtrade certified and organic ranges of coffee – into its 'Sam's Range' of premium products.[4]

Such announcements have been met with scepticism among many who have come to associate corporate brands such as Walmart and McDonald's more closely with 'McJobs', 'Always Low Wages' or the destruction of the Brazilian rainforest to feed the huge demand for beef burgers, than with agendas of social and environmental responsibility. Despite being the subject of great controversy, the embracing of such new strategies by major businesses symbolizes a huge shift in ideas around the responsibilities of business that has occurred in the last 10 to 15 years.

Indeed, such cases of large global corporations scrambling to climb aboard the 'corporate social responsibility' (CSR) and 'Fairtrade' wagons are by no means isolated examples. All around the world – but particularly in core centres of the industrialized global North – major global corporations have been searching for new ways through which principles of corporate social responsibility can be incorporated into the way they do business; or, as some would suggest, at the very least into the way they do their public relations and marketing. Putting aside questions regarding the strengths or weaknesses of these instruments, the quick and steady growth of companies that have adopted CSR mechanisms has been impressive. By the end of 2007 the UN Global Compact, the world's largest CSR initiative, had approximately 3,600 participating companies, out of what UNCTAD estimated to be a total of 78,000 transnational corporations (TNCs) and 780,000 affiliates operating

1   The authors would like to thank Kamillea Aghtan for her wonderful research and editing assistance for this volume.
2   http://www.rainforest-alliance.org/news.cfm?id=mcdonalds [accessed: 7 April 2009].
3   As one of the world's largest and most high-profile retailers, Walmart has been the subject of widespread criticism from a range of activist groups. See for example: http://walmartwatch.com/; http://www. hatewalmart.com/; http://www.wakeupwalmart.com/.
4   http://walmartstores.com/FactsNews/NewsRoom/ [accessed: 7 April 2009].

worldwide (UNCTAD 2007, cited by Utting in this volume, Chapter 9). Increased recognition of the importance of CSR is also reflected in rising government interest, especially in Europe, expressed for example through intergovernmental initiatives such as the OECD Guidelines for Multinational Corporations, and the passing of 'ethical sourcing' legislation in a number of jurisdictions (McBarnet et al. 2007).

These developments have broadly mirrored a parallel rise and expansion in the scale and support for ethical initiatives such as the Fairtrade system that operate within the civic domain. Some such initiatives have provided institutional vehicles through which growing constituencies of concerned coffee drinkers, consumers, investors and citizens can give direct expression to their concerns regarding the conditions under which goods are produced. Others have emerged to support and/or demand responsible corporate action, as well as to promote more far-reaching agendas of justice in the domains of production and trade. In short, over the course of the last decade and a half, agendas of ethical trade and consumption, together with associated agendas of corporate responsibility and accountability have been expanding and consolidating across both 'barricades and boardrooms' throughout the world (Bendell 2004).

It would be a mistake to overstate the extent or impact of this shifting agenda with respect to mainstream corporate practice. As a proportion of international corporate numbers, very few businesses have adopted practices associated with corporate responsibility such as social auditing, joining established corporate responsibility mechanisms such as the UN Global Compact or even creating their own 'corporate codes of conduct'. Furthermore, the agenda's impact on business practices associated with labour standards or environmental sustainability has in many cases been very limited. In the same period in which corporate responsibility has gained ideational leverage, real wages for many vulnerable workers have continued to fall. In December 2007, Neil Kearney of the International Textile, Garment and Leather Workers' Federation noted that over the past 12 years real wages in the textiles sector have fallen by 25 per cent and working hours increased by 25 per cent (cited by Utting, this volume, Chapter 9).[5] Instead of shrinking, as most labour economists expected, informality in working relations increased, placing great numbers of workers beyond the reach of legally enforceable standards (ILO 2002).

Regardless of such contradictions, there is little doubt that the many social movements campaigning for global social justice (a term we shall address in greater detail later in this chapter) have made some gains in the battle over ideas. Their success in shifting this contested 'ideational space' has, in turn, presented those opposing contemporary forms of corporate power with some challenging strategic dilemmas. As the corporate responsibility and fair trade agendas mature, they have been running aground against a seemingly intractable set of new problems, leading to increasing frustration, cynicism and uncertainty about how to proceed. For example, the commercial success of fair trade has meant that the Fairtrade Labelling Organization (FLO) recently faced the dilemma of whether to license Nestlé, a company that has been the subject of a number of fierce social justice campaigns (see Hutchens in Chapter 4 of this volume; see also Baby Milk Action 2009). In such cases, popularity brings with it new strategic and moral quandaries. Other practical problems have resulted from the increasing complexity and pace of change within globally dispersed supply chains. Within supply chains new power brokers are emerging who are willing to employ previously untried tactics as means of resisting pressure from corporate responsibility activists (see Maksimovic, Chapter 13 of this volume).

---

5   Presentations made at the International Labour Organization MultiForum 07: Better Business: Managing Labour Relations for Productivity and Growth, Geneva, 15–16 November 2007 and the European Union Conference on Corporate Social Responsibility: CSR at the Global Level: What Role for the EU?, Brussels, 7 December 2007.

An even greater problem faced by activists, practitioners and policy-makers is a lack of clarity around foundational theoretical questions regarding the divisions of social and political responsibility between national governments and international institutions, and between public and private actors. Both the practical problems confronting emerging initiatives and these deeper theoretical questions that underpin them are the subject of the chapters in this collection.

It is the central contention of this book that the initiatives examined by contributing authors have in common a wish to see capitalism embedded in a set of norms that identify with discourses of '(global) social justice' of varying kinds. Such goals are fundamentally concerned with countering the perceived tendency towards the production of inequality and the commodification of labour relations associated with capitalist dynamics of accumulation. Some of the groupings examined in this book broadly accept the benefits of capitalism and are committed to working within the terms of the system. They aim at 'tweaking' it so as to share its benefits and promote more *collaborative* relations. Others seek a deeper *transformation* which would challenge the terms of the system in a number of ways. Our aim is to evaluate which strategies along such a spectrum have proven successful in relation to the promotion of social justice norms of varying kinds.

In this introductory chapter, we first outline the aims, scope and approach of the book, and its contribution to theoretical and empirical debates. We then set up our approach to understanding the problem as one of the disembedding of capitalism. We describe the shift from what has been broadly described as 'embedded liberalism' in the period following the end of the Second World War through the 'neoliberal' era and to the present, and then explore the ways in which governance initiatives of the kind examined in the chapters seek to embed an increasingly global capitalism in norms of social justice. There seem to be ever-expanding numbers and variants of governance initiatives of these kinds. To assist readers to navigate the more detailed case studies provided by contributing authors, this introductory chapter also provides a description of the main types of initiatives examined by the book. We situate variants of fair trade, corporate social responsibility and corporate accountability governance initiatives and associated activism within a collaborative/transformational spectrum.

In the final part of this chapter we lay out an evaluative framework through which the contributions of the initiatives to the embedding of social justice norms in the governance of global production and trading systems can be evaluated. 'Social justice' is an appealing and widely used term, especially among social movements. However, its meaning – particularly as a yardstick by which to evaluate the achievements of specific initiatives – is hazy. We specify what we mean by norms of (global) social justice, locating this account within both theoretical literature and broader public discourse surrounding this concept. We explain how the contribution of individual initiatives to social justice goals can be evaluated not only by documenting their direct impact on the rights of individuals, but also by assessing their impact on institutional change of more or less 'transformative' kinds. This evaluative framework then lays the basis for the synthesis and evaluation of these agendas as a whole which we present in the concluding chapter to this volume.

Aims, Scope and Approach of the Book

The central driving motivation of this book is a practical one – to address a question that has moved to the forefront of debate in recent years among both participants in and scholars of global political economy: How can production and trade within transnational supply chains be governed effectively so as to protect core human and social rights and advance broader principles of justice within a global economy?

In order to examine this core question, contributors study the potential role of a range of emerging state and non-state initiatives – broadly termed 'fair trade', 'corporate social responsibility' (CSR) and 'corporate accountability' initiatives – within agricultural and industrial supply chains. These initiatives seek to promote agendas of global social justice of various kinds by developing non-state or mixed state-and-non-state instruments of public governance within global production systems. These 'initiatives' for global social justice often have a rather ambiguous status – falling neatly into neither of the established categories of 'social movements' or 'governance institutions'. Rather, characteristics of each combine in varying and often rather fluid and ambiguous ways, seeking at times to provide an institutional framework for regulating and governing global economic relationships in their own right, and at other times more closely resembling what we would traditionally conceive of as advocacy campaigns or social movements (Keck and Sikkink 1998; Tarrow 1994).

The book examines a broad range of such initiatives, varying in the extent to which they offer means of providing public governance functions in their own right, and/or operate primarily as vehicles of ideational and institutional change within other established sites of governance. Reflecting the book's central interest in the transformative potential of initiatives of different kinds, the structure of the book is organized around groupings or categories of such initiatives. Part I examines individual and civic action through fair trade. Part II examines CSR initiatives driven by responsible consumers and corporations. Part III broadly examines workers' activist campaigns as part of wider movements for worker empowerment and corporate accountability. Part IV examines initiatives that seek to strengthen and transform the role of the state.

With reference to emerging governance initiatives of these varying kinds, authors consider a number of more specific questions:

- What are the core problems of injustice or governance failure that these initiatives seek to respond to, and how are these evolving?
- How are emerging governance initiatives within the global economy themselves evolving through an ongoing process of experimentation and adaptation?
- What outcomes are such governance initiatives achieving, in relation to both direct facilitation of rights fulfilment, and also the promotion of institutional transformation to create the structural conditions for rights fulfilment at a broader and sustained level?
- What factors determine the relative success of different initiatives in promoting these outcomes?

In view of the eclectic nature of the collection – and of the theoretical and methodological approaches underpinning different contributions – we do not claim to offer systematic or comprehensive examination of these questions. Rather, we view these as the guiding questions providing an overarching coherence to the widely varying contributions to the volume; in the concluding chapter we organize our reflections on lessons from the chapters around these questions, recognizing also that such conclusions remain reflective and exploratory in nature. Our concluding analysis focuses in particular on evaluating the strengths and weaknesses of the differing initiatives, and seeking to identify key variables on which relative success appears to hinge.

By exploring these central questions with reference to a broad range of contrasting empirical examples and from a range of disciplinary perspectives, the book seeks to contribute to contemporary policy and scholarly debates in several ways. First, the book engages with debates focused on questioning the relative merits of broadly 'collaborative' (moderate) versus 'confrontational' (radical) approaches to tackling perceived injustice. Second, it examines a set of questions about 'what works' as a basis for promoting global justice norms within a globalizing economy, relating this to the design of the institutional instruments and mechanisms through which social regulation and governance takes place. Of particular interest for our purposes are debates that interrogate the relative merits of 'soft/voluntarist' versus 'hard/legal' modes of regulation; an issue that has preoccupied many regulatory scholars over the past decade at least. Third, the book engages with contemporary debates surrounding the broader macro-institutional significance of these initiatives as new forms of social governance within a globalizing capitalist economy.

Understanding the Problem: The Disembedding of Capitalism

With these central questions and debates in view, one of the first major tasks of this book is to make sense of perceived injustices in globalized labour, production and trading regimes by examining the evolving relationship between globalizing systems of liberal market economic relations, and systems of social regulation concerned with what we define below as broadly 'social justice' oriented norms, both within and beyond nation states.

In the following sections we first define the concept of (dis)embedding before discussing the ways in which governance deficits have arisen and evolved in recent years in developed and developing country contexts.

The Concept of (Dis)Embedding

The concept of (dis)embedding provides a useful framework for understanding the operation of CSR, fair trade and corporate responsibility movements as attempts to re-embed capitalism in social justice norms. The term has been widely used by scholars who seek to understand dynamics of co-dependence between social institutions of different kinds (social, political and economic), and the apparent clustering of such patterns of inter-twined social relations in particular geographical locations.[6] Understood in this sense, the concept of 'embedding' assists analysis of how markets, supply chains and transnational business systems are constituted, influenced and regulated by actors and institutions beyond the supply chain, encompassing states, local and global markets, and more diffuse complexes of territorially bounded social institutions.[7]

---

6 The former meaning is associated with economic sociologists such as Granovetter (1985), for whom the concept of embedding is primarily concerned with understanding 'how economic action is embedded in structures of social relations, in modern industrial society'. In the latter sense, Giddens (1990, 21) uses the term 'disembedding' to refer to 'the "lifting out" of social relations from local contexts of interaction and their restructuring across indefinite spans of time-space'. The latter approach is also reflected in the use of the term by some economic geographers, who 'spatialis[e] the notion of embeddedness, which had originally been developed by economic sociologists to stress the ways in which economic processes are grounded in social relations' (Cumbers et al. 2003, 328). See also (Sassen 2002, 96; 2003, 15).

7 The concept in this sense need not be limited to concrete 'institutional forms', but can also be understood as encompassing much broader and more nebulous influences, such as those Stewart (2002, 26) characterizes as the 'macro-environment' which 'encompasses the norms and political economy prevalent in a society – that is it includes the manifold influences – economic, political and social – to which individuals and groups are subject by the environment in which they operate'.

The concept tends to take on a more critical meaning when such analysis is linked to a more systemic account of modes of embedding in particular phases or forms of capitalism, as for example in Polanyi's classic work, *The Great Transformation* (Polanyi 1944). In this book, Polanyi analysed the transition Europe experienced from a virtually unregulated market in the nineteenth century through a 'great transformation' in which the market was subordinated once again to the social norms and controls in which he suggested it had traditionally been embedded. Jessop (2001b) likewise explores different forms of social embeddedness within contemporary capitalism, seeking to understand how the coupling of wider social institutions with those of market (capitalist) economic systems assists to sustain and reproduce the capitalist system as a whole.[8]

In this critical sense, which is the way we mainly use the term, the concept of 'embedding' takes on a distinctly normative meaning, in which social embedding is regarded as a process that aspires to subordinate private relations of power operating through markets to 'social values that we can defend ethically' (Sen 2009). On this view, there are two distinct grounds on which the power relations within a capitalist economy could be said to be 'disembedded'. First, such power relations may not be effectively regulated by a consistent and explicit set of social norms of any kind. Second, such a charge may be based in a more normative claim, that the norms through which such regulation is taking place cannot be ethically justified. In order to operationalize the concept of (dis)embedding as an evaluative tool, analysis therefore needs to be anchored in both an explicit account of ethically defensible norms defining the principles on the basis of which capitalism should be regulated, and an institutional account of what it would mean for these to be effectively and consistently applied.

The evaluative analysis presented in this book is anchored in the institutional dimension with reference to the capacity of political governance arrangements (involving state as well as non-state modalities) to regulate effectively a globalizing capitalist economy on a consistent and principled basis. At the normative level, our evaluation is anchored with reference to a particular set of social justice norms (elaborated further below), which define the principled basis on which power relations and inequalities of certain kinds may be considered illegitimate, and the claim of governance initiatives to legitimately intervene to protect and promote specified rights and duties thereby justified.

Dynamics of Disembedding within a Capitalist Market Economy

It is useful to begin by laying out some of the key assumptions and propositions that underpin many critical analyses of 'disembedding' within capitalist systems of market economy. While definitions of 'capitalism' vary widely, we can point towards a number of core characteristics that a broad range of critical scholars identify with a capitalist market system (Polanyi 1944; Wood 2002). Of greatest relevance to our interest in the structure and dynamics of global labour, production and trading regimes are: (a) capitalist modes of production involving the extraction of surplus from labour; (b) market exchange; (c) geographically clustered dynamics of accumulation.

Each of these tendencies has been claimed to be associated with normatively problematic social outcomes of specific kinds. *First*, commodification of labour relations are regarded as creating the conditions under which labour (particularly under conditions of surplus labour) has weak bargaining power and is likely to be 'exploited' in relation to both wages and working conditions. *Second*, unmediated market dynamics are regarded as generating price instability in relation to

---

8   Jessop (2001b) draws on Polanyi, as well as on the French regulation approach and system theoretical accounts, all of which are interested in various ways in the social embedding of capitalism.

markets of certain kinds. *Third*, uneven dynamics of accumulation within capitalism are regarded as fuelling inequalities of social power and distributive outcomes, and contributing in some cases to wider dynamics of instability.

To these material features of capitalism (understood as a distinctive institutional system of production, exchange and accumulation) may be added a *fourth*, cultural or normative dimension. For instance, in Polanyi's account of a 'market society', informal social norms that may otherwise have acted to mediate or counter unequalizing or exploitative relationships and dynamics are regarded as being eroded through the diffusion of values that legitimize self-regarding and exploitative forms of social interaction (Polanyi 1944). On this view, distinctively capitalist norms and identities may themselves contribute to intensifying (as well as reproducing) the unequalizing tendencies of the materialist structures of a capitalist market economy.

While capitalism may make important contributions to the realization of social justice norms via its generation of economic growth, the unequalizing tendencies that are produced through capitalist processes of accumulation and wealth generation have – throughout the history of capitalism – given rise to the demand for a range of regulatory and redistributive interventions to constrain and compensate for the more negative consequences of the system (O'Riain 2000). Such embedding of the capitalist market economy in both formal and informal regulatory norms is claimed to contribute both to stability and to legitimacy within the capitalist system – both enhancing its efficiency and countering its more exploitative and commodifying tendencies.

Within a capitalist political economy, such norm-based embedding of market economic relations can take place via a range of concrete institutional regimes, not all of which are directly relevant to this book's central focus on labour, production and trading systems within contemporary capitalism.[9] Of most direct relevance are the systems of institutions governing the transnational business systems through which the relations of production and trade on which this book focuses are organized. Policy regimes relating to corporate and labour regulation are of particular relevance, as well as overarching governance regimes in the domains of international trade and investment.

During different phases of its development, and within different national and sub-national contexts, capitalism has been sustained and contained by formal and informal modes of regulation of varying kinds. The institution that has historically been charged with embedding capitalism has been the state. However the state has been floundering in its role as promoter of social justice norms during recent years.

The period from the end of the Second World War to the present is often divided into two major periods: first, a period of 'embedded liberalism' in the decades following the war, during which time obligatory limits to commodification and unbridled accumulation existed in most capitalist economies. Second, observers point to a period of 'neoliberalism', regarded as extending roughly from the early 1970s to the present – or at least until its stride was interrupted by the still unfolding 'global financial crisis' of 2008/2009 (see Krippner et al. 2004; Ruggie 1982; Wade 2008).[10] In the discussion below, we first review the post-war period of 'embedded liberalism', and then review some of the new dynamics of 'disembedding' emerging during the 'neoliberal' phase of capitalist globalization, and up to the present.

---

9   In particular, the focus of many writers on macroeconomic regimes and financial regimes as means of socially embedding capitalism is beyond the scope of most of this book's focus (for example Ruggie 1982; 2008; Wade 2008).

10   Some accounts, including many rooted in the French regulation school of political economy, add to this distinction a related one between 'Fordism' and 'post-Fordism' (Harvey 2006).

The Embedding of Capitalism by the State in the Post-war Period

During the post-war period, the state was the major underwriter of capitalist productive and social relations. Both international law and broader understandings of appropriate political practice reflected and reproduced the assumption that constraining the negative aspects of capitalism was properly dealt with almost exclusively within the national legal and political jurisdictions where impacts on specific populations occur, via the actions of the regulatory, welfare and/or developmental state. The presumption that such forms of governance should take place at the national level reflected both an idea that this was the level at which influence could be exerted on predominantly nationally oriented economies, as well as an assumption that nationally oriented political communities were the appropriate level at which social justice norms should be defined and defended (Gereffi and Mayer 2004).

In the economic North the state in the post-war period was thought to be responsible for 'social integration' – to be achieved by way of the protection and stabilization of social relations against unpredictability of fluctuating relative prices – and 'system integration' providing for stable cooperation between capital and labour at the point of production (Streeck 2009). In other words, capital operated within a nationally embedded system of protection as well as restriction.

Detailed descriptions of the specific manner in which capitalism was embedded in social norms in the post-war era of the Keynesian welfare state have been undertaken elsewhere with far more depth than we could aspire to here, and it is not our purpose to rehearse these accounts (see Jessop 2001a; Ruggie 1982). Instead, we focus on briefly reviewing some of the features of the post-war governance regime of most direct relevance to the governance of those production, labour and trading relations in which we are centrally interested.

In presenting this account, sensitivity is required to the extensive variation across contexts and over time in the extent and means through which capitalism has been facilitated and constrained by regulation of differing kinds. Throughout this period, boundaries between market and non-market transactions have been continually contested, and pressure for the rationalization of social regulation has been successfully exerted to different extents in different countries.[11] In some cases the state acts to form alliances with 'capital' to reinforce and profit from unequalizing dynamics of capitalism; in other cases it acts to counter such forms of power and promote protection of defined rights and standards of equality (Crouch and Streeck 2006). Such dynamics generate a great deal of space for variations in socio-political arrangements between different 'varieties of capitalism'. Significant differences also existed throughout this period between 'advanced' and 'developing' economies and states.

In advanced economies, various forms of social control over companies have been exercised since the rise of the company in its modern form, reflecting longstanding and evolving debates about appropriate forms and levels of regulatory control. In the period immediately after the Second World War most developed country states took on a stronger role in mediating collective bargaining relationships between labour and capital. Networks of policies and regulations that came to constitute the modern welfare state were typically underpinned by organized labour, cooperatives, credit unions and other social institutions and movements seeking to subordinate the demands of the market economy to broader social purposes (Polanyi 1944). During the 1960s

---

11   As Streeck contends, 'the pursuit of economic advantage typically takes place, and is bound to take place, in the form of improvised circumvention or experimental re-utilization of institutions and institutionalized constraints not originally conceived to support capitalist expansion' (2009, 12).

and 1970s issues related to consumer and environmental protection and human rights became more prominent, as did concerns about the power and impact of transnational corporations in developing countries, strengthening social alliances in favour of social regulation in some areas (Jenkins et al. 2002).

In many developing countries, this period was a very mixed one in respect of social regulatory agendas, and may not accurately be described as embedded liberalism. The role of the state *vis-à-vis* labour and capital varied significantly between national contexts at this time (Crouch 2005a; 2005b). For many developing countries the post-war period was one in which states engaged in severe repression of labour, often on the rationale that this was necessary for national development to proceed (Deyo 1989). The latter part of the post-war period of 'embedded liberalism' was also one in which movements to control transnational corporations were particularly strong. In the late 1960s and 1970s at least 22 developing countries passed legislation of varying kinds controlling TNC activities (Jenkins et al. 2002).

The record was also mixed from the point of view of developing country farmers. A range of price-setting mechanisms to control commodity prices played an important role in seeking to subordinate the market economy to social goals during this period. A range of international commodity agreements acted to smooth commodity price fluctuations via quota systems, while commodity boards of varying kinds operated at the national level in some countries to stabilize price fluctuations, in turn having a buffering effect on employment in some cases. On the downside, welfare regimes of the kind familiar to industrialized countries were developed in only very minimal ways in most developing economies.

Although the task of regulating capitalist market economies was undertaken primarily by individual nation states, regulation at the international level was not completely absent during this period. During the 1970s in particular there were intense debates at the international level – particularly within various UN fora – on the need to regulate corporations, and other aspects of the globalizing capitalist economy. A number of international efforts to establish codes of conduct for the activities of TNCs emerged in the 1970s.[12] However, while these were international in scope, they were seen primarily as supporting the efforts of developing country governments to regulate TNCs at the national level (Jenkins 2005). Despite a scattering of regulatory arrangements at the international level, the most important social regulatory regimes within the governmental domain therefore remained nationally bounded throughout most of this period.

The state has always been an uncertain underwriter of capitalist relations of production, and of course global production and trading systems have never been fully embedded in 'social justice norms' of the kind we define below. However, regardless of the great variation both between developed states and between developed and developing states, the spirit of the post-war period was very much dominated by a confidence in the central role of state-led intervention in pursuit of social justice and development goals – however defined and implemented in different contexts at different times.

---

12   The most comprehensive of these was the UN Draft Code of Conduct on TNCs which was developed by the UN Centre on Transnational Corporations set up in 1974. Several specialized UN agencies also developed codes covering particular aspects of TNC behaviour. These included the ILO Tripartite Declaration of Principles concerning Multinational Enterprises and Social Policy and the United Nations Conference on Trade and Development's proposed codes on Restrictive Business Practices and on the Transfer of Technology (Haufler 2001; Jenkins et al. 2002).

Globalization of Capitalist Market Economies and Evolving Dynamics of Disembedding

The dynamics of interaction between capitalist production and trading systems and state-centred institutions of public governance have evolved significantly in the course of the most recent wave of capitalist globalization, roughly encompassing the last three decades. In today's 'partially globalized' economy (Keohane 2002) markets and market actors transcend national boundaries, international trade is increasingly organized through inter-firm networks and global supply chains, and capital flows freely around the world.

Many observers now suggest that contemporary economic globalization has outstripped the capacity of national-level governmental and societal institutions to regulate markets and to compensate for undesirable effects of market transactions – to an increasing extent since the early 1970s. The post-war Keynesian welfare national state that developed in most advanced capitalist societies is now seen to be in crisis, as a result of mounting tensions generated by technological change, globalization, a range of economic and political crises and a shifting ideological landscape (Jessop 2002).

Such trends are widely claimed to be leading to regulatory and governance deficits, forming part of a wider process of contemporary 'disembedding' of globalizing capitalist markets from social justice oriented norms. Weakness of state regulatory capacity is viewed as resulting from three distinct trends.

First, state regulation has been undermined by an emerging disconnect between transnational power and national political governance. This increasing disconnect has been driven in large part by the extension of the scope of organization of production beyond the boundaries of the nation-state. The transformation of many labour intensive industries in recent decades towards increasingly globalized production systems has been widely analysed (Gereffi and Memedovic 2003; McCormick and Schmitz 2002; Ross 1997). Beginning in the 1970s and accelerating through the 1980s and 1990s, production of apparel and textiles, toys, footwear, home electronics and other consumer goods destined primarily for consumer markets in the industrialized world has spread throughout the world, with manufacturing tending to cluster in a range of developing countries (Appelbaum 2006 (draft)).[13] Such changes have been facilitated by the design of macro level policy regimes and institutions in which global production and trading relations (and associated investment regimes) are constituted, as well as by factors such as technological change, falling transport and communication costs, and rising economies of scale in certain sectors, all of which have also raised the incentives and lowered the costs of global systems of production and trade.

These changes have not been without benefits for newly industrializing countries. Participation in export-oriented production of labour intensive products has been one of the key ways in which a large number of developing countries have been able to attain comparative advantage in manufacturing, and thereby to access the opportunities such trade presents for export earnings and employment. However, such changes have also been associated with significant increases in the social power of a range of local and transnational private actors, which increasingly operate beyond the control of national governments and their populations. Such power often has significant consequences for the extent to which recognized social rights of workers and populations in the production process are protected and promoted. In particular, concerns have been voiced by many regarding the labour and environmental practices associated with the growth of global value chains in developing countries (Gereffi et al. 2005).

---

13   Around 70 per cent of global clothing exports now come from developing countries (Hale and Wills 2005, 17).

Earlier literature analysing dynamics of power within global production systems focused on the power of Northern retailers and brands within 'buyer-led' global supply chains,[14] who exercise significant influence over the terms of exchange with lower-tier suppliers (Gereffi et al. 2005; Dicken 2000). However, some more recent analyses have highlighted the rising influence of large transnational contractors, based primarily in Hong Kong, Taiwan, South Korea and China, who operate factories around the world (Appelbaum 2006 (draft)). In part, this has resulted from (internal and external) economies of scale, as production in many sectors has more often than not become organized in regional clusters. This trend has also been associated with increasing consumption in Asia. Apo Leong, Ka-wai and Tucker (Chapter 15 of this volume) estimate that companies from Hong Kong and Taiwan are now the world's largest organizers or sellers of production, obtaining contracts from Europe, the United States and elsewhere in the global North, and manufacturing products in developing countries. As the contribution by Andrea Maksimovic (Chapter 13) demonstrates, however, this changing dynamic is not merely the result of 'economic' factors; political dynamics have also come into play. In some cases Southern states have become increasingly confident in promoting their economic interests in multilateral forums.

Appelbaum suggests that the emergence of these large transnational contractors portends a dramatic shift of organizational power within global supply chains, as large factories provide a potential counterweight to the growing power of retailers. Not only does Appelbaum suggest that such trends may impact the relative power of contractors *vis-à-vis* retailers, he also suggests it may have implications for labour, both in terms of working conditions and prospects for unionization. He suggests that the increasing concentration of investment within 'giant factory complexes' (supply-chain cities) has important implications for labour struggles since such concentrated capital may prove to be both more conducive and more vulnerable to labour militancy than small, dispersed production sites.

Second, state capacity has been weakened by the increasing complexity and informality associated with post-Fordist processes of capitalist development (Harvey 1990). Such increasing complexity and informality operate to make regulation increasingly difficult in large part because the organization of production has simply become more complicated (Collins 1990). In many economies, the range and complexity of work relationships has significantly expanded. There has been a broad trend amongst firms in industrialized countries towards vertical disintegration: that is, the breaking up of large, multi-function corporations into smaller units. The outsourcing of production, or vertical disintegration, has occurred in a significant number of industries, as producers recognize that they cannot themselves maintain cutting-edge technology in every field required for the success of their product (Gilson et al. 2009). This trend has also frequently been a consequence of privatization, or part of the survival strategy employed by companies in previously sheltered industries as they have been exposed to international competition (Fenwick et al. 2008). Businesses have sought the benefits of lowering overheads and cheaper labour by passing risks and costs on to others in the supply chain. Workers have been drawn upon from unorganized or informal sectors of the labour force as well as from newly industrialized and developing economies.

The broad trend towards vertical disintegration has resulted in: (a) a proliferation of corporate forms and relations; and (b) a proliferation of people who would previously have been employed inside a firm being engaged in alternative ways, including as dependent contractors, independent contractors, employees or contractors of labour hire agencies, or as part of their own businesses

---

14   While retailers and brands are distinct, the line between these two categories of actors has become increasing blurred in many cases, as retailers such as Gap and Walmart have moved into manufacturing, creating their own private labels and manufacturing their own clothing lines, while some of the biggest brands (such as Nike, Guess and Liz Claiborne) have also moved into retailing (Armbruster-Sandoval 2005). As a result, we frequently use these terms somewhat interchangeably.

(Marshall 2006). Labour relations have become far more convoluted as the structure of labour markets has changed within both industrialized and developing economies. These changes have created problems for labour law, which has increasing difficulty in defining an 'employer' and an 'employee'; yet these remain the parties between whom the bilateral employment relationship is assumed to exist (ILO 2005).[15] As a consequence, increasing numbers of workers in both developing and developed contexts now work outside the reach of labour regulation and the social protections and welfare benefits which are most often attached to this legal relationship.

Third, such dynamics of disembedding have been compounded further by the influence of 'neoliberal' agendas, which have increasingly precipitated a shift away from state intervention oriented towards the promotion and protection of social justice norms in both developed and developing countries (Jenkins 2005; O'Riain 2000). Such agendas have underpinned the dismantling of a range of regulatory systems of the kinds outlined above. Liberal policy regimes focused on facilitating global competitiveness and coordination and delegating certain regulatory responsibilities to private actors via a broad range of instruments: labour market deregulation; decreased real wages and work-related social benefits; the privatization of public services; and new bodies of law protecting TNCs and foreign investors. In some cases, legal protections for working conditions and minimum wages were weakened.

In many countries, forceful opposition to binding industry regulation emerged in the 1980s, led by organized business interests, undermining the embryonic developments that had been made in some countries and at the international level during the preceding decade (Richter 2001, 8). More broadly, a policy climate emerged which was distrustful and even openly hostile towards the state, of 'command and control' regulation, of 'planning' and 'protectionism', and of traditional forms of trade union organization (Ruggie 1982; 2003).

This was also a time during which international commodity agreements were largely dismantled, as were marketing boards and other agencies that had previously been involved in the stabilization of commodity prices. This disbanding of collective institutions designed to facilitate price coordination was often accompanied by broader processes of both price liberalization and trade liberalization. Since their introduction, such regimes have been associated with declining social and labour protections as well as instability and fluctuations in global commodity prices.

Again, important differences between countries can be observed in relation to the extent and nature of emerging regulatory deficits. The reach of globalizing dynamics as well as the impact of neoliberal policy regimes on various forms of social regulation and redistribution have varied substantially, as mediated through a broad range of institutional, political, social and sector specific factors particular to local contexts (Hall 2007). Nevertheless, across a very wide range of contexts, contemporary processes of liberal economic globalization have had important implications for the capacity of social regulatory systems at the national level to control and/or compensate for any negative effects of market capitalist institutions.

It may be that we are currently witnessing a shift in terms of the willingness of the state to underwrite capitalist relations, as a consequence of the financial crisis of 2007–2009. Thus far there are no indications that this entails a renewed readiness to regulate relations between capital and labour. However, there is a growing emphasis upon providing price stability. It remains to be seen how these new dynamics will play out in relation to the central concerns of this book.

---

15 The 'traditional employer–employee' relationship may only have dominated labour markets numerically in industrialized countries for a short time in historical terms, in the post-war period to the early 1980s. In developing countries, these kinds of working relations never attained such dominance. Regardless of the fact that vertically integrated businesses and their corollary in the labour market – the 'employee' – may be historical anomalies, the model forms the basis of labour regulation in most countries around the world.

Searching for Solutions: Emergence and Evolution of New Governance Initiatives

In response to the kinds of perceived deficits described above, a plethora of (frequently overlapping and competing) governance mechanisms with similar aims have emerged, often seeking to govern the same subjects. Some are market- and non-state-based, whilst others are associated with multilateral or unilateral state-based international regulatory mechanisms. These initiatives are heralded by many as potential solutions to such governance deficits, in light of their performance of a range of developmental and regulatory functions that extend beyond traditional legal or statutory forms of governance.

As outlined above, one of the major analytic tasks of the book is to make sense of the emerging initiatives around agendas of fair trade and corporate accountability as progressive movements towards the development of increasingly transnational regimes of social governance. In other words, we seek to understand to what extent claims about the 'second double movement' (Gereffi and Mayer 2004; Polanyi 1944; Ruggie 2008) towards the 're-embedding' of a liberal market economy (this time at a transnational or global level) are given support by the emergence of this range of social regulatory initiatives.

In this section we examine initiatives of several kinds, the origins and key features of each of which are introduced in the following discussion. First, we briefly review the three clusters of initiatives (and their more collaborative and transformative variants), based around fair trade, CSR and campaign driven initiatives. This introduction aims to assist readers unfamiliar with these agendas to navigate more easily the sections of the book containing cases of each kind. Following this examination of different kinds of non-state initiatives, we then briefly contrast two approaches to conceptualizing the role of the state in seeking to engage with and support non-state governance initiatives of this kind; these can likewise be characterized as collaborative versus confrontational in orientation.

Emergence and Development of Fair Trade

Part I of this book deals with fair trade initiatives. The term fair trade is used extensively to refer to trading principles from a diverse range of ideological perspectives – from free traders to protectionists, to those seeking to promote forms of globalization based on principles of social justice and poverty reduction. In this book the term generally refers to the range of movements, campaigns and initiatives in this latter category, mobilizing consumers and social activists in the global North to promote principles of global trade that support marginalized producers and workers in developing countries.

The fair trade movement is typically defined in this sense as referring to a set of groups formally linked through participation in the FINE network, comprising the Fairtrade Labelling Organizations International (FLO), the International Fair Trade Association (IFAT), the Network of European Worldshops (NEWS) and the European Fair Trade Association (EFTA). In the United States the Fair Trade Federation falls under this umbrella also (Raynolds et al. 2007). These organizations seek to use North–South trade as a means of empowerment rather than one of exploitation, and thus to improve the livelihoods and wellbeing of producers via support for organizational strengthening, providing a better price and a social premium, offering stable trading relations based on principles of partnership, and promoting broader systemic change via awareness raising among consumers and broader campaigning efforts for changes in the rules and norms underpinning the liberal international trading regime. The widely cited definition of fair trade as agreed by the umbrella organization FINE is:

> Fair trade is a trading partnership, based on dialogue, transparency and respect, that seeks greater
> equity in international trade. It contributes to sustainable development by offering better trading
> conditions to, and securing the rights of, marginalized producers and workers – especially in the
> South.[16]

Understood in this sense, fair trade has emerged as an 'alternative' normative and institutional
system to organize and govern production and trade in a range of sectors.

The specific norms of 'fairness' that the fair trade system seeks to entrench within this
alternative institutional system have several dimensions. Much marketing of fair trade products
– particularly within the FLO system – tends to focus on the principle of a 'fair price' for
producers, incorporating both minimum prices (specified in relation to each particular product
line), and an additional 'social premium'.[17] Moreover, the system attempts to entrench principles
of democratic decision-making and social and environmental sustainability across all stages of the
supply chain. Participating producers must be organized within cooperatives or other organizations
with democratic, participatory structures, and must comply with a range of economic, social and
environmental standards. Buyers must comply with FLO's trade standards: as well as payment of a
minimum price and a social premium, these require provision of pre-financing if requested by the
producer group, and a commitment to long-term trading relationships.[18]

The system as a whole retains a dual character, both as an *alternative trading system*, and as a
social movement (Jaffee 2007; Smith and Barrientos 2005). The institutional core of the system is
built around its trading activities, which create 'alternative' supply-chain systems linking producer
cooperatives to not-for-profit alternative trading organizations (ATOs) based in consumer countries.
These alternative supply chains therefore operate via a relatively durable institutional structure in which
production, exchange and governance activities are all coordinated by the same sets of actors: producer
cooperatives and ATOs. This core institutional structure has loose links with a broad collection of
organizations and networks that have wider 'social movement' characteristics (Tarrow 1994).

Although the fair trade movement shares a broad range of core principles, there is a great deal
of diversity within the movement, in terms of both goals and institutional structures. Indeed, in
recent years in particular, significant forms of conflict have emerged within the system between
those with divergent visions of how best to strategically position themselves in relation to the
collaboration/confrontation divide. Such dilemmas centre around what (Jaffee 2007, 1) has referred
to as a fundamental paradox at the heart of fair trade:

> In its efforts to achieve social justice and alter the unjust terms of trade that hurt small farmers
> worldwide, fair trade utilizes the mechanisms of the very markets that have generated those
> injustices.

---

16   See http://www.eftafairtrade.org. See also Murray et al. (2003); Raynolds (2002a; 2002b); Raynolds
et al. (2004).

17   FLO certification claims to guarantee 'that every product was produced by a fair trade certified
organization which was paid the fair trade price'.

18   Details of FLO standards are available at http://www.fairtrade.net/generic_standards.html. IFAT,
which coordinates a broad range of fair trade organizations beyond the FLO system, lists nine core categories
of fair trade standards: creating opportunities for economically disadvantaged producers; transparency and
accountability; capacity building; promoting fair trade; payment of a fair price; gender equity; working
conditions; child labour; and the environment.

Such tensions have often played out in relation to the divergent orientations of the certification system within fair trade organized around the Fairtrade Labelling Organization (FLO), the less formalized system organized more loosely around what now goes by the name of the World Fair Trade Organization (WFTO; formerly IFAT), and a range of other networks or associations of fair trade organizations such as the Network of European Worldshops (NEWS) and the European Fair Trade Association (EFTA). Many talk of the FLO system as reflecting a more 'mainstream' or collaborative approach, while IFAT along with the other looser networks are seen as reflecting a more 'alternative', transformational vision.[19] Of course there is significant diversity within and between each in relation to different aspects of this divide, but this rough distinction plays some useful role nevertheless.

The tensions between alternative and more mainstream approaches may have been present throughout the history of fair trade (Raynolds et al. 2007); however, they have intensified in the context of the movement's rapid growth into new commodities, production regions and market niches. Attempts to scale up fair trade volumes have led to expanding business partnerships involving large traders, distributors, supermarkets and other mainstream retailers. This has raised questions about whether such changes are likely to erode the movement's mission of challenging the terms of liberal international trade. Such forms of evolution and expansion within the fair trade movement also present challenges for fair trade's internal governance. The desire to remain or become more responsive to Southern producers' local development agendas is in some senses in tension with the desire of some within FLO to tighten regulatory procedures in line with ISO standards, or to reform the Fairtrade business model in line with market and commercial demands. These competing pressures strain the democratic and transformative institutional capacities of the governance systems that oversee fair trade.

Emergence and Development of Agendas of CSR

As in the case of fair trade, the range of movements and initiatives encompassed under the broad umbrella of 'corporate social responsibility' initiatives share certain features and logics, but also diverge widely; this cluster of initiatives can also be roughly categorized in relation to a collaboration/confrontation divide.

The chapters in Part II of this book all deal broadly with these kinds of initiatives. While there is no commonly agreed definition of CSR, there are a number of core goals and techniques we can point to as commonly shared characteristics. Broadly, corporate responsibility refers to practices that recognize corporations as bearing some responsibilities to minimize socially or environmentally harmful practices, and to strengthen controls on human rights, social, environmental and governance related activities (Blowfield 2005; Carroll 1999; Zerk 2006). The adoption of principles of corporate social responsibility therefore involves an acknowledgement that social objectives must in some cases be given priority by corporate managers alongside profit-oriented objectives,[20] whether or not these are viewed as being complementary or in conflict – a point on which there remains much disagreement.

---

19   See for example Hutchens in Chapter 4 of this volume in relation to the distinction between FLO and IFAT; see also Low and Davenport (2005).

20   These may include considerations such as boosting sales, protecting brand, attracting and retaining talent, promoting employee productivity, reducing production costs, attracting investment.

Many definitions focus on CSR as a voluntarist agenda, encompassing only that which goes beyond legal compliance. This view is reflected in the definitions offered by key government actors such as the UK government and European Commission, as well as many business groups (McBarnet et al. 2007; Zerk 2006). Others adopt a broader definition, seeing CSR as a particular normative view of the obligations of businesses in society, which may be governed via legal as well as voluntary instruments. Such obligations are defined for example by Zerk (2006) as encompassing the responsibility of business to operate ethically and in accordance with relevant legal obligations, and to strive to minimize any adverse effects of its operations and activities on the environment, individual health and wellbeing and broader social goals. This broader definition is the one adopted for the purposes of this book, in recognition of the complex ways in which government, business and civil society interact in shaping the social, economic and legal pressures that underpin contemporary CSR movements (Fox 2004; McBarnet et al. 2007).

Specific corporate practices associated with CSR agendas may include compliance with the law and broader professional or moral codes; philanthropic or charitable work; promotion of agendas of accountability and stakeholder engagement; or broader protection or promotion of social, environmental and human rights standards built into the way the core business operations of a company are managed. In some cases broader agendas such as fairness to suppliers and customers, opposition to bribery and corruption, or issues such as responsible marketing and lobbying or internal promotion of workplace diversity can also be part of the CSR agenda (McBarnet 2007). More formal CSR practices may include codes of conduct and other sets of principles and guidelines, social and environmental management systems, Occupational Health and Safety and company-community relations, triple bottom line accounting and company sustainability reporting, internal and external monitoring and verification and stakeholder dialogues (these are surveyed in more detail by Utting in Chapter 9 of this volume). CSR continues to address domestic corporate policies such as community relations, environmental practices and diversity but its primary focus is now the conduct of global corporations, especially in developing countries. In particular, corporate responsibility for labour and human rights practices of supply-chain partners has become a central dimension of contemporary CSR (Vogel 2005).

Variation is also significant within each of these clusters of CSR activity. Corporate codes of conduct for example vary widely in their scope, in the range of standards they encompass, and in the degree of transparency and worker participation associated with processes of code design, implementation, monitoring and verification (Jenkins et al. 2002). There is also some variation in the scope of the responsibilities they encompass – whether they regard responsibilities of Northern businesses and consumers to extend simply to workplace issues related directly to the process of production of goods and services, or whether they encompass broader social and developmental responsibilities that would encompass 'the production and reproduction of labour power in the global economy' (Jenkins et al. 2002, 7). Overall, the picture is generally agreed to be one of extreme unevenness in the scope and substance of protections or benefits offered as a result of the CSR agenda (Fox 2004; Jenkins et al. 2002; Newell and Frynas 2007; Utting 2005).

Likewise, the motivations for businesses to embrace discourses and practices of corporate social responsibility – often beyond their legal obligations to do so – also vary: some are strategic, others defensive, and still others altruistic or public-spirited (Vogel 2005). This is relevant to our broader interest in exploring the tensions between relatively collaborative versus confrontational approaches, which have played out particularly importantly in relation to the question of voluntarism. On one extreme is the position of Milton Friedman, who famously declared that the only social responsibility of business is to increase its profits (1970). On the other side are those who point to the ways in which certain privileged corporate powers are conferred in law and by society to facilitate the furtherance of public purposes, suggesting that these should operate together with legitimate private purposes to underpin a more expansive notion of corporate responsibility. Among those who acknowledge at least the possibility of some coherent notion of corporate social responsibility there is a further divide between those who seek to justify such responsibilities as part of a broader, enlightened corporate self-interest – often referred to as the 'business case' for corporate social responsibility – and those who view such responsibilities as more expansive moral and legal responsibilities, at times in zero-sum conflict with private purposes and concepts of value (Zerk 2006).

In concrete terms, such differing normative views have been given expression in models of corporate responsibility of divergent kinds. At one end of the spectrum are the clusters of wholly voluntary and business-led initiatives such as individual company codes of conduct, which may include brand, retailer or in some cases factory-based codes, or industry association codes such as Worldwide Responsible Apparel Production (WRAP) in the garment sector. These stand in contrast to collaborative multi-stakeholder initiatives such as the Ethical Trading Initiative (ETI) or Fair Trade Association, which are still voluntary from a legal perspective, but which encompass more extensive input from non-profit and stakeholder groups of various kinds. These may build in broader mechanisms for enabling stakeholder participation (if not control), though they also tend to share similar limitations in scope. Further along the spectrum again are those initiatives that seek to build legal frameworks for corporate responsibility. In the UK, for example, a key player in shaping recent debates about the appropriate role of law in underpinning norms of corporate social responsibility has been an alliance of UK NGOs, the CORE (Corporate Responsibility) Coalition. Agendas of this kind that seek to find new ways for states to reinsert themselves into regulatory processes are discussed further below.

Emergence and Development of Activist Campaigns as Part of a Corporate Accountability Movement

Activist campaigns have played a central role in advancing agendas of both fair trade and corporate responsibility. They have underpinned and in many cases propelled the development of CSR movements; they continue to play an important role in monitoring and holding accountable voluntary CSR initiatives; and in many cases they have played a growing role in pressing for stronger forms of state regulation of CSR principles and programmes. The chapters in Part III of this book generally concern worker-based activist campaigns and associated grassroots organizing activities.

Such campaign-oriented approaches have emerged together with the development of social movements organized around the assertion of new principles of binding, non-discretionary corporate responsibility. Often these have been based around concerns about corporate impact on human rights and the environment, though commonly these have been directed towards asserting more expansive obligations of social or global justice. Such claims have often been linked to empirical claims about liberal, market and corporate-led globalization – in particular, claims that such globalizing processes have been associated with a secular rise in corporate power, and with the intensification of corrosive social impacts of corporate activity (Korten 1995; Starr 2000).

Such movements emerged particularly strongly during the 1990s, building on increasing organization within prominent consumer sectors such as garments and coffee, in which networks of human rights and labour activists attempted to improve working conditions and raise wages for workers in developing countries via a series of public campaigns targeting both companies and consumers in industrialized countries – particularly North America and Europe. The emergence of such campaigns can be understood as being in part a response to globalization of systems of production and trade, and the increasing perception that corporate decision-makers who were accumulating increased power should be held directly accountable for the impacts of such power on affected individuals and communities (Macdonald 2007). The emergence of such campaigns has also been underpinned by the increasing capacity of activists in the global North to communicate directly with workers in distant factories, together with broader changes in the focus of the NGO sector in the United States within the post-Cold War political context. As the agenda emerged, and was developed through the success of campaigns focused on prominent brands such as Nike,[21] an even broader range of social and political organizations became mobilized around the issue.[22]

Initiatives of this kind tend to be more confrontational in orientation, rejecting the proposition that CSR agendas can plausibly be advanced on the basis of a 'business case' alone, and seeking to generate broader forms of social influence and control over corporate activity to bring it into line with the social justice and human rights norms that such movements consider businesses have an obligation to conform to. For many, mandatory legal requirements are regarded as a distinctive and in some contexts irreplaceable form of influence over corporate behaviour, though most also recognize the constructive role that can be played by other sources of influence such as corporate culture or consumer pressure.

Nevertheless, important areas of variation exist within this broad category of activist campaigns and corporate accountability movements. Some have been more consumer and Northern brand focused, while others have been more participatory in their objectives and organizational structure. Given the frequently significant disparities between the specific priorities and capabilities of such a diverse range of non-state actors, a range of distinct campaign strategies were adopted; while some groups focused on targeting firms to reform supply-chain management practices, others engaged in research, public education or promotion of grassroots organizing among workers (Harrison and Scorse 2004; Macdonald 2007).

In recent years, many campaign-based initiatives have started to identify explicitly with discourses and agendas of 'corporate accountability' as distinct from simply corporate responsibility. This shift has tended to be associated with rising interest among activists and legal scholars in the role of more confrontational strategies, which have at times entailed the mobilization of legal mechanisms – often for purposes different from those for which they were intended – as weapons in struggles over power and values.

What Role for the State? Collaborative Engager or Agent of Corporate Accountability

Debates between 'soft/voluntarist' versus 'hard/legal' modes of regulation have important implications for the role of the state in interacting with emerging non-state governance mechanisms. The contributions in Part IV of this volume engage with such debates. As these chapters show, disputes over the appropriate role of governments and law-makers (courts, legislatures, government agencies and so on) in relation to agendas of corporate responsibility have taken place on a number of levels. Recurring through much writing on voluntary initiatives such as civic, corporate and worker-based interventions has been a recognition that initiatives keep stumbling against obstacles

---

21   One particularly influential campaign was the anti-Nike campaign begun by Jeff Ballinger (contributor to this volume), former head of the AFL-CIO Jakarta office, who founded Press for Change in 1998. This drew wide media attention, leading other groups to initiate anti-Nike campaigns of their own, thereby drawing such broader groups into organizing efforts around the sweatshop agenda.

22   These included a variety of organizations including NGOs, unions and immigrant workers, as well as a wide range of individuals and organizations coordinated through email lists, student groups and churches.

of coordination and enforcement, in the absence of a strong and supportive role of the state. A key question that tends to emerge therefore is to what extent does the state need to be 'brought back in', albeit in potentially new ways?

Relevant academic literatures suggest that a number of new agendas are developing in relation to the role of the state in underwriting corporate responsibility and accountability. Early attempts to promote ethical corporate practices by states, reflecting the influence of New Governance or reflexive regulatory theories, involved increasing uses of cooperative, 'soft law' mechanisms by the state as a substitute for its traditional 'command and control' techniques of enforcement as means of encouraging higher labour and social standards. These kinds of legal strategies are seen as being based importantly on dialogue and collaboration, as government and business seek to engage in processes of mutual learning and increase compliance via preventative and cooperative efforts (Parker 2002). Non-state actors are seen as responsible and empowered participants through all stages of the regulatory process, rather than being the resistant subjects of oppositional forms of top-down regulation. This view regards regulation as more likely to be effective if used in a manner that is responsive to and draws upon existing distributions of power and resources among economic and social actors (Howe in Chapter 18 and Lobel in Chapter 17 of this volume; Ayres and Braithwaite 1995). Partly for this reason, such models have often tended to de-emphasize worker empowerment and traditional trade union strategies.

According to this view, the challenge for government is to determine how best to try to facilitate the active involvement of private actors in public action. Businesses are offered opportunities to engage in organizational learning, and to design corporate responsibility methods that are appropriate to their own business cultures. The role of government changes from regulator and controller to facilitator and coordinator. Law becomes a process of shared problem-solving rather than an ordering activity.

A range of initiatives at national, supra-national and international levels have enabled governments to engage with CSR initiatives via non-legal or quasi-legal approaches. Voluntary or soft law mechanisms at the international level include the National Contact Points for the Organisation for Economic Co-operation and Development's Guidelines for Multinational Enterprises,[23] the Compliance Advisor Ombudsman (CAO) of the World Bank Group,[24] and the European Bank for Reconstruction and Development's Independent Recourse Mechanism (IRM) which assesses and reviews complaints about Bank-financed projects.[25] A range of other transnational initiatives have also had government involvement and support of varying kinds, including multi-stakeholder initiatives like the Ethical Trading Initiative.[26] Governments in the EU, as well as US states such as California and Massachusetts, have also promoted CSR agendas by including CSR requirements in their own procurement contracts (McBarnet et al. 2007, 43).

While these soft regulatory models have been highly influential across a range of fields, they have also attracted significant controversy. The field of labour regulation is typical in both the influence and the contestation of such approaches. Critics hold that central to the design of labour relations institutions is the idea that the parties have interests that are sometimes overlapping but

---

23 See http://www.oecd.org/department/0,3355,en_2649_34889_1_1_1_1_1,00.html [accessed: 8 May 2009].

24 This is the independent recourse mechanism for the private sector arm of the World Bank Group: see http://www.cao-ombudsman.org/ [accessed: 8 May 2009].

25 The IRM gives local groups that may be directly and adversely affected by a Bank project a means of raising complaints or grievances with the Bank, independently from banking operations: http://www.ebrd.com/index.htm [accessed: 8 May 2009].

26 See http://www.ethicaltrade.org/ [accessed: 8 May 2009].

often in conflict. Industrial relations institutions seek to remedy (if only partly) unequal bargaining power between the parties. On this basis, voluntary or 'soft law' mechanisms have been criticized for treating decent work deficits as a 'technical problem' (Murray 2001): reducing democratic political control and flattening power relations (in formal but not substantive terms) compared with traditional labour law mechanisms (Blackett 2001–2002).

While interest in soft law approaches does not seem to be waning, a greater focus within the literature more recently has been on forms of 'meta-regulation' that combine soft and hard regulatory techniques (McBarnet et al. 2007; Parker 2007). Such regulatory approaches use methods that encourage collaboration between public and private actors, but also employ more confrontational techniques such as penalties and the ability of wronged parties to bring suits against wrong-doers in order to enforce compliance with desired standards. Lobel (Chapter 17 of this volume) provides examples of these types of mechanisms in the area of occupational health and safety in the United States.

A further development surrounding questions about the role of the state in promoting corporate responsibility and accountability has been the employment of existing legal causes of action by civil society actors in inventive manners to enforce principles of responsible corporate practice. Unfair competition and false advertising legislation have been used as a basis for trying to hold companies accountable for claims made in their CSR marketing materials, such as in the Californian case *Kasky v Nike*; 45 P 3d 243 (Cal 2002). A class action aiming to enforce codes of conduct also went before the Californian courts under California's Unfair Business Practices laws; this action claimed that Walmart failed to meet its contractual duty and made false and misleading statements to the American public.[27] The US *Alien Tort Claims Act*, 28 U.S.C. 1350 of 1789, which enables civil lawsuits to be brought in the United States for extraterritorial actions 'committed in violation of the law of nations or a treaty of the United States' has also been used on a number of occasions to enforce international corporate responsibility (Vogel 2005, 168). Such claims are sometimes successful in gaining publicity and providing greater corporate transparency, partly through the 'discovery' processes by which claimants have been able to gain access to documents previously not available to the public. Nevertheless, the use of such private law mechanisms places great financial and time demands on claimants, and because of the nature of the causes of action, even where the claims are successful on their own terms, the changes required of company behaviour in legal terms remain restricted in scope.

In view of the limitations of the use of existing private law mechanisms as a basis for corporate accountability, and the governance failures discussed in earlier sections, there have been widespread calls from many promoting corporate accountability agendas to strengthen legislative and regulatory responses at national, regional and international levels. Such calls have two objectives. One is the re-formation of state-based regulation so as to better fit with post-Fordist modes of production and accumulation. On the one hand, this entails grappling with non-standard working arrangements and extending the reach of regulation outside the traditional workplace or factory, as well as providing new rights to consumers. On the other, it involves extending regulation outside national jurisdictions. The second objective, then, is to explore ways in which an international legal framework can promote stronger accountability for corporate behaviour. Efforts directed towards this goal include the ongoing field of work around John Ruggie's mandate as the UN Secretary General's Special Representative

---

27 On 13 September 2005, workers at Walmart suppliers in China, Bangladesh, Indonesia, Swaziland and Nicaragua filed a class action lawsuit in Los Angeles under California's Unfair Business Practices Act, claiming Walmart failed to meet their contractual duty and made false and misleading statements to the American public. See www.laborrights.org.

on Business and Human Rights, which is seeking to clarify the responsibilities of business under international human rights law (Human Rights Council 2007; 2008). Such agendas and debates are, however, still ongoing, and legal provisions remain both significantly limited and widely contested.

Evaluating Emerging Systems of Governance

Throughout this chapter so far, we have been making reference to the idea that the initiatives examined by this book reflect a common agenda of seeking to embed contemporary capitalism in a set of norms that identify with discourses of '(global) social justice' of varying kinds.

Activists and other social actors promoting governance initiatives of the kind in which this book is interested are often united by their shared invocation of discourses and rallying cries of 'globalizing justice'. Discourses around the concept of 'global economic justice' have been particularly common, with slogans such as 'Make Trade Fair' and 'Globalize Justice' being widely used as symbols and signposts of resistance to liberal forms of globalization.[28]

The term 'social justice' is, however, highly ambiguous and contested, and in the discussion that follows we attempt to provide a working definition of the term. This definition provides an important reference point for the evaluation presented throughout the book of the performance of these different initiatives.

Norms of Social Justice Around Which These Initiatives are Oriented

In essence, the concept of social justice refers to the fairness or justice of distributions of rights, opportunities and/or resources within a given society (Cramme and Diamond 2009, 3). Within this broad definition, there is much variety and contestation regarding the scope of burdens and benefits considered relevant to considerations of justice, and the principles of fairness or justice that should apply to the distribution of such goods. Such variation exists across both different theoretical accounts of justice and different political currents of social justice activism.[29] Despite such diversity, several key ideas tend to recur within theories and discourses of social justice.

An emphasis on provision of basic *rights* or *needs* of some kind is central to most definitions of social justice. This may refer to human rights applying globally (Kuper 2005; Pogge 2002), or to broader accounts of social entitlements associated in particular with national citizenship (Marshall 1950; Miller 1997; 1999). While the scope of rights of all these kinds is contested, categories of rights related to freedom from poverty and basic protection for labour rights are widely recognized, and of particular relevance to this book. Such a rights-oriented perspective tends to emphasize the need for social regulatory instruments to seek to alleviate poverty and increase the freedom of workers and communities to exercise meaningful control over the conditions in which they work and live.

Concern for *equality* also plays an important role in most accounts of social justice, variously referring to equality within national societies (for example between capital and labour or between different genders or ethnicities), or equality between the rich and poor in the developed and developing worlds (Cramme and Diamond 2009; Miller 1997). While debate over the

---

28   See for example: http://www.oxfam.org/en/campaigns/trade; http://www.tjm.org.uk/about.shtml; http://www.startribune.com/nation/43744977.html?elr=KArks:DCiUMEaPc:UiD3aPc:_Yyc:aUU.

29   Theoretical traditions and those associated with political and activist discourse do not map cleanly onto each other, with each borrowing in rather fluid, hybrid and often only implicit ways from one another.

question 'equality of what?' has been extensive, both equality of opportunity and equality in the distribution of broader kinds of social goods or capabilities are widely recognized in some form (Miller 1991).

While theoretical and activist-led accounts of social justice have therefore varied widely, a broad overlapping consensus can be roughly identified around these core concerns of protecting basic rights and mitigating inequality via the creation of just systems of social institutions; these concepts are at the centre of our working definition of social justice.

Ambiguity is much greater in relation to the question of the appropriate *scope* of these principles of social justice; specifically, the question of what rights (and dimensions of equality) should be extended beyond national borders? In other words, in what sense can we talk meaningfully of something called 'global social justice', as we do in this book?

Within theoretical political and philosophical debates around the issues of social and global justice, analyses of social justice and global justice have tended to be rather sharply differentiated. Theoretical interest in global justice has gained ground only in the last one or two decades, following in particular the contributions of authors such as Charles Beitz and Thomas Pogge (Beitz 1983; 1999; 2001; Pogge 2001; 2002). Much debate has subsequently focused on the question of what constitutes the appropriate scope of justice – some take the national society or political community and its basic institutions as the subject of justice, while others seek to extend principles of justice to the global domain.

Within activist discourses, such debates have not been so clearly identified. In such contexts distinctions between social and global justice have often remained rather blurred, enabling significant ambiguity to remain regarding the extent to which norms of social justice are claimed to extend to the transnational level (though there is almost universal agreement among social justice activists on at least the global applicability of human rights norms).

Although there is little agreement among global justice activists regarding which social justice norms as conceptualized at the domestic level should be extended to the transnational domain, there is at least a general agreement that some such norms (and associated responsibilities) should be so extended. Moreover, activist claims about global distributive norms are almost unanimous in characterizing such norms as having the special normative weight of justice claims, as opposed to mere claims for charitable forms of assistance (for example Bendell 2004, 5).

Our use of the term 'global social justice' throughout this book seeks to capture a sense of this prevailing ambiguity in relation to questions of scope, while also reflecting the convergence of opinion around the view that justice claims of some kinds do extend beyond the scope of the national political community. This term therefore aims to accommodate a broad range of positions regarding the scope of the social justice obligations that extend beyond the national level.[30]

What Role do these Justice Norms Play in our Overall Evaluation of New Governance Initiatives?

In order to develop a means of evaluating the performance of competing and interacting governance systems, we need some kind of organized basis for considering not only the global social justice norms they articulate, but also the specific ways in which they seek to bring about institutional

---

30   In using this term we recognize that different principles may well be held to apply in relation to social relationships of different kinds, and do not seek to assert that the difference between social and global justice is merely a question of scope – a meaning that Miller (in Cramme and Diamond [2009, 23]) associates with the popular phrase 'global social justice'. Rather, we intend the term to capture persistent ambiguity on this and other basic definitional questions.

transformation. This task is not straightforward, as we require a way of conceptualizing a meaningful 'measure' of performance which somehow captures the ambiguities and hybridities described earlier in relation to what these initiatives *are*, and what they seek to *do*. When we ask in relation to these initiatives, 'what works?', we need to be clear on precisely what they aspire to achieve, so our performance measure can encompass a suitably multi-dimensional set of criteria.

We suggest that in simple terms we can conceptualize these initiatives as adding value to the broad project of promoting a more just global economic order at three levels:

- First, they seek to contribute to more just outcomes for individuals and communities by contributing directly to the *protection and promotion of human and social rights and welfare*.
- Second, they contribute to justice as a function of the institutional design features they embody; to the extent that they operate as *power-wielding governance mechanisms* in their own right, we can seek roughly to evaluate the *fairness of the institutions they embody* (as structural channels for the distribution of benefits and burdens).
- Third, they contribute to the ultimate goal of a more just global economic order via the *processes of change they promote* and facilitate within the broader governance system in which transnational economic relations are embedded, contributing in this sense as vehicles of broader institutional change.

In some respects then, qualities of institutional structures and processes may be regarded as valued outcomes in their own right. In other respects, changes to institutional structures and processes are valued largely as a means to other ends. As we explore the central questions of this book, we therefore seek to track and critically to examine the contributions and shortfalls of these initiatives at each of these levels (if only at the schematic and exploratory level of evaluation rendered possible in view of the eclectic nature of contributions discussed above).

In order to carry these criteria through as a basis for evaluation of the impacts of the initiatives on 'globalizing justice' – that is, their contribution to embedding transnational economic relations in global justice norms – we need to elaborate further what contributions of these kinds would look like in concrete form. While analysis of documented outcomes is reasonably straightforward, the challenge of how to operationalize the institutional criteria (the second and third dimensions of change identified above) requires more elaboration. The task is complicated by the fact that specific institutional qualities that contribute to promoting justice via each of the two institutional channels identified above are often entangled and overlapping in practice.

We attempt to deal with this difficulty by identifying four major clusters of institutional characteristics that we suggest contribute in varying ways to advancing the two *institutional channels* for the promotion of global justice norms identified above. These characteristics can be roughly categorized as:

a. Institutional capacities directly to promote and protect worker and producer wellbeing;
b. Opportunities for worker and producer influence over business decision-making;
c. Capacity of institutions to promote trust and cooperation; and
d. Definitions of business, consumer and state rights and responsibilities – as embodied in and promoted by institutional arrangements – that are supportive of social justice norms.

Category a refers to the functional qualities of institutions, encompassing those technical capacities that enable particular institutional arrangements to contribute directly to protecting social justice outcomes for individuals and communities. Such capacities may include those oriented towards enhanced economic production as well as those that enhance the ability of institutions to perform regulatory or redistributive functions. Strengthening capacities of these kinds are often a major goal of 'capacity building' dimensions of governance initiatives. This category gives rise to two distinct criteria of institutional transformation that can be identified as supportive of social justice norms:

a.i   strengthening technical capabilities of governance institutions and key players within them

a.ii contributing to underlying productive capabilities of the economic system being regulated

Category b describes levels of participation or influence for workers and producers over decision-making regarding labour issues in businesses. These categories reflect themes commonly analysed within industrial democracy literature (Blumberg 1968; Coates 2003) and democratic literatures more broadly (Pateman 1970). In this literature, the right to information is an important constitutive element of deeper participation in decision-making: it is impossible to influence decisions without having information about the decision at hand. However, information in itself does not represent control. Likewise, consultation by employers with labour or producer representatives in relation to labour issues is an important step for participation but does not result in *control* over decision-making. Employers and managers can consult with employees or producers and subsequently ignore their expressed preferences. Stronger forms of participation in decision-making include codetermination, entailing the right to veto (right to reject) decisions proposed by management and propose new ones. It is important to distinguish, also, between direct participation by workers and producers and indirect participation via workers' or producers' representatives. Direct involvement can result in a greater increase in individual agency, but only where it does not undermine aggregate or collective influence over business decision-making. Based on these considerations, we have developed the following criteria as indicators of the extent to which processes of institutional change are supportive of social justice norms:

b.i   increased right of consultation for worker/producer organizations regarding business decisions

b.ii increased right of veto for worker/producer organizations over business decisions

b.iii direct opportunities for affected individuals to exercise choice/agency over business decisions

As we have seen in this introductory chapter, the building of trust and cooperation is seen by some to be one of the crucial benefits of governance initiatives (reflected in Category c). Initiatives have different focuses in relation to the parties between which trust and cooperation is built. Some concentrate on building trust and cooperation between labour/producers and capital, whereas others also seek to promote cooperation with the state. Other initiatives attempt to build strong alliances among workers (qua workers) and producers (qua producers). In light of these points, we further disaggregate Category c into the following criteria:

c.i   promotion of coordination, communication and trust between labour/producers and capital

c.ii   promotion of coordination, communication and trust between labour/producers, capital *and* government

c.iii promotion of sustainable social alliances between labour/producer organizations

Category d concerns ideational or ideological transformation regarding the perceived rights and responsibilities of business, workers, consumers and the state. Here we further disaggregate this category as follows:

d.i   challenging ideas relating to rights and responsibilities of business

d.ii   challenging ideas relating to rights and responsibilities of workers/producers

d.iii challenging ideas relating to rights and responsibilities of consumers

d.iv   challenging ideas relating to rights and responsibilities of states

These then are the concrete criteria we consider as we examine the various initiatives throughout the book, as a basis for evaluating their contributions to the project of 'globalizing justice' at the level of institutional transformation. Individual authors do not work explicitly with these criteria, though these do constitute background considerations, and we invite readers to keep these criteria in mind as they read the individual chapters. We then revisit these criteria in our concluding synthesis in Chapter 20.

One significant consequence of the diversity of the approaches taken by different authors is that the evidence generated by the volume as a whole in relation to each of these evaluative criteria is somewhat uneven. In particular, many chapters have more to say about the processes of institutional change engendered by the operation of these governance initiatives than they do about ultimate outcomes (in terms of documented labour standards, welfare provision and so on). This is certainly not true of all chapters, and we draw out findings regarding outcomes for individuals and communities where possible. However, much analysis does focus on the second and third dimensions, and this is reflected in the attention we give to these different dimensions in our concluding synthesis.

Globalizing Social Justice Norms and the Collaboration/Confrontation Debate

All the initiatives examined in this volume seek to bring about outcomes for individuals and communities that are more in line with the social justice norms they identify. Where they differ is in relation to both strategies and objectives concerning broader features of institutional change.

The institutional focus of the criteria established above enables us to engage directly with the question of how such institutional change is achieved. In particular, we are interested in examining the extent to which different initiatives tend to operate within and reinforce the terms of the prevailing system (via 'collaborative' approaches), or to challenge these prevailing terms (via more 'confrontational' or 'transformative' approaches). We consider the extent to which a given initiative (as a vehicle of institutional change) challenges the system by considering both its stated ends, and the means that it adopts. Generally, a more transformative approach is more likely to:

- challenge the legitimacy of existing distributions of rights and duties (between workers/ producers, businesses, consumers and governments) within the design of the system;

- challenge social power relations embedded within institutional arrangements, via pursuit of strategies that seek to shift underlying balances of social power;
- pursue change via working outside accepted rules and procedures associated with established institutions.

At the other end of the spectrum, those seeking change 'within the terms of the system' are more likely to accept the legitimacy of prevailing distributions of roles and responsibilities (rights and duties) and/or prevailing power relations, and seek – via established rules and processes – to promote desired social justice outcomes by enhancing the capacity of the institutional system as a whole to promote and protect these desired outcomes.

The different initiatives examined by this book combine these objectives and strategies in varying ways. Each initiative – as a vehicle of transformation – targets different features of the existing governance system, and also utilizes different combinations of broadly 'collaborative' or 'confrontational' strategies in seeking to bring about institutional change of particular kinds. Thus, while the framing of this debate begins from the simple contrasting 'images' of collaborationist versus confrontational stances outlined above, our analysis also seeks to unbundle and disaggregate these overly tidy categories where necessary.

Together, the chapters that make up this volume present a very wide variety of views and canvass a broad range of issues and cases. All speak in some way to overarching debates about the objectives and strategies of these experiments in globalizing justice, and their potential contribution to the broader project of re-embedding a globalizing market economy within an emergent set of norms around the agenda of global social justice. This volume as a whole is presented as a contribution to this ongoing debate.

References

Appelbaum, Richard (2006; draft), 'Giant retailers and giant contractors in China: emergent trends in global supply chains', working paper prepared for Princeton University Conference, Observing Trade: Revealing International Trade Networks, 9–11 March 2006.

Armbruster-Sandoval, Ralph (2005), *Globalization and Cross-Border Labor Solidarity in the Americas: The Anti-Sweatshop Movement and the Struggle for Social Justice* (New York and London: Routledge).

Ayres, I. and Braithwaite, J. (1995), *Responsive Regulation: Transcending the Deregulation Debate* (New York: Oxford University Press).

Baby Milk Action (2009), Baby Milk Action website: http://www.babymilkaction.org/action/nestlefairtrade.html [accessed: April 2009].

Beitz, Charles (1983), 'Cosmopolitan ideals and national sentiment', *Journal of Philosophy* 80(10).

—— (1999), 'International liberalism and distributive justice: a survey of recent thought', *World Politics* 51(2).

—— (2001), 'Does global inequality matter?', *Metaphilosophy* 32(1/2).

Bendell, J.B. (2004), 'Barricades and boardrooms: a contemporary history of the corporate accountability movement' (Geneva: UNRISD).

Blackett, Adelle (2001–2002), 'Global governance, legal pluralism and the decentered state: a labor law critique of codes of corporate conduct', *Indiana Journal of Global Legal Studies* 8: 401–48.

Blowfield, Michael (2005), 'Corporate social responsibility: reinventing the meaning of development?', *International Affairs* 81(3).

Blumberg, Paul (1968), *Industrial Democracy: The Sociology of Participation* (London: Constable).

Carroll, Archie (1999), 'Corporate social responsibility: evolution of a definitional construct', *Business and Society* 38(3).

Coates, Ken (2003), *Workers' Control: Another World is Possible* (Nottingham: Spokesman Books).

Collins, Hugh (1990), 'Independent contractors and the challenge of vertical disintegration to employment protection laws', *Oxford Journal of Legal Studies* 10(3): 353–80.

Cramme, Olaf and Diamond, Patrick (2009), *Social Justice in the Global Age* (Cambridge: Polity Press).

Crouch, Colin (2005a), *Capitalist Diversity and Change: Recombinant Governance and Institutional Entrepreneurs* (Oxford: Oxford University Press).

—— (2005b), 'Models of capitalism', *New Political Economy* 10(4): 439–56.

—— and Streeck, Wolfgang (eds) (2006), *The Diversity of Democracy: Corporatism, Social Order and Political Conflict* (Cheltenham and Northampton, MA: Edward Elgar).

Cumbers, Andres, MacKinnon, Danny and McMaster, Robert (2003), 'Institutions, power and space: assessing the limits to institutionalism in economic geography', *European Urban and Regional Studies* 10(4).

Deyo, Frederic (1989), *Beneath the Miracle: Labour Subordination in the New Asian Industrialism* (Berkeley, CA: University of California Press).

Dicken, Peter (2000), 'A new geo-economy', in David Held and Anthony G. McGrew (eds), *The Global Transformations Reader: An Introduction to the Globalization Debate* (Cambridge: Polity Press).

Doh, Jonathan (2006), 'Global governance, social responsibility and corporate-NGO collaboration', in Sushil Vachani (ed.), *Transformations in Global Governance: Implications for Multinationals and Other Stakeholders* (Cheltenham: Edward Elgar).

Fenwick, Colin, Howe, John, Marshall, Shelley and Landau, Ingrid (2008), 'Labour and labour related laws in small and micro enterprises: innovative regulatory responses', ed. SEED (Geneva: International Labour Organization).

Fox, Tom (2004), 'Corporate social responsibility and development: in quest of an agenda', *Development* 47(3): 29–36.

Friedman, Milton (1970), 'The social responsibility of business is to increase its profits', *New York Times Magazine*, 13 September, 32–3, 122, 124, 126.

Gereffi, Gary, Humphrey, John and Sturgeon, Timothy (2005), 'The governance of global value chains', *Review of International Political Economy* 12(1).

Gereffi, Gary and Mayer, Frederick W. (2004), 'The demand for global governance', Terry Sanford Institute of Public Policy Working Paper, Duke University.

Gereffi, Gary and Memedovic, Olga (2003), 'The global apparel chain: what prospects for upgrading for developing countries?'. [Online]. Available at: http://www.inti.gov.ar/cadenasdevalor/ApparelUNIDOnew2Feb03.pdf [accessed: August 2004].

Giddens, Anthony (1990), *The Consequences of Modernity* (Cambridge: Polity Press).

Gilson, Ronald, Sabel, Charles and Scott, Robert (2009), 'Contracting for innovation: vertical disintegration and interfirm collaboration', *Columbia Law Review* 109.

Granovetter, Mark (1985), 'Economic action and social structure: the problem of embeddedness', *American Journal of Sociology* 91(3).

Hale, Angela and Wills, Jane (2005), *Threads of Labour: Garment Industry Supply Chains from the Workers' perspective* (Oxford: Blackwell).

Hall, Peter A. (2007), 'The evolution of varieties of capitalism in Europe', in Bob Hancke, Martin Rhodes and Mark Thatcher (eds), *Beyond Varieties of Capitalism: Conflict, Contradictions and Complementarities in the European Economy* (Oxford: Oxford University Press).

Harrison, Ann and Scorse, Jason (2004), 'Moving up or moving out? Anti-sweatshop activists and labour market outcomes', NBER Working Paper No. w10492 (May 2004).

Harvey, David (1990), *The Condition of Post-Modernity: An Enquiry into the Origins of Cultural Change* (Oxford: Blackwell).

—— (2006), *The Spaces of Global Capitalism* (London and New York: Verso).

Haufler, Virginia (2001), *A Public Role for the Private Sector: Industry Self-Regulation in a Global Economy* (Washington, DC: Carnegie Endowment for International Peace).

Human Rights Council (2007), 'Business and human rights: mapping international standards of responsibility and accountability for corporate acts', in A/HRC/4/035, United Nations Human Rights Council.

—— (2008), 'Promotion and protection of all human rights, civil, political, economic, social and cultural rights, including the right to development; protect, respect and remedy: a framework for business and human rights', in *Report of the Special Representative of the Secretary General on the Issue of Human Rights and Transnational Corporations and Other Business Enterprises*, John Ruggie, United Nations Human Rights Council.

ILO (2002), *Decent Work and the Informal Economy*, International Labour Conference, 90th Session, Report VI (Geneva: ILO).

—— (2005), *The Employment Relationship*, International Labour Conference, 95th Session, Report V(I) (Geneva: ILO).

Jaffee, D. (2007), *Brewing Justice: Fair Trade Coffee, Sustainability and Survival* (Berkeley, CA: University of California Press).

Jenkins, Rhys (2005), 'Globalization, corporate social responsibility and poverty', *International Affairs* 81(3).

—— Pearson, Ruth and Seyfang, Gill (2002), *Corporate Responsibility and Labour Rights: Codes of Conduct in the Global Economy* (London: Earthscan).

Jessop, Bob (2001a), 'Regulationist and autopoieticist reflections on Polyani's account of market economies and the market society', *New Political Economy* 6(2): 213–32.

—— (2001b), 'The social embeddedness of the economy and its implications for economic governance'. [Online]. Available at: http://www2.cddc.vt.edu/digitalfordism/fordism_materials/jessop2.htm [accessed: December 2008].

—— (2002), *The Future of the Capitalist State* (Cambridge: Polity Press).

Keck, Margaret E. and Sikkink, Kathryn (1998), *Activists Beyond Borders: Advocacy Networks in International Politics* (Ithaca, NY and London: Cornell University Press).

Keohane, Robert (ed.) (2002), *Power and Governance in a Partially Globalized World* (London and New York: Routledge).

Kirton, John J. and Trebilcock, Michael J. (eds) (2004), *Hard Choices, Soft Law: Voluntary Standards in Global Trade, Environment, and Social Governance* (London: Ashgate).

Korten, David C. (1995), *When Corporations Rule the World* (Aldershot: Earthscan).

Krippner, G., Granovetter, M., Block, F., Biggart, N., Beamish, T., Hsing, Y., Hart, G., Arrighi, G., Mendell, M., Hall, J., Burawoy, M., Vogel, S. and O'Riain, S. (2004), 'Polanyi symposium: a conversation on embeddedness', *Socio-Economic Review* 2.

Kuper, Andrew (ed.) (2005), *Global Responsibilities: Who Must Deliver on Human Rights?* (New York: Routledge).

Low, William and Davenport, Eileen (2005), 'Postcards from the edge: maintaining the "alternative" character of fair trade', *Sustainable Development* 13.

Macdonald, Kate (2007), 'Public accountability within transnational supply chains: a global agenda for empowering Southern workers?', in Alnoor Ebrahim and Edward Weisband (eds), *Forging Global Accountabilities: Participation, Pluralism and Public Ethics* (Cambridge: Cambridge University Press).

Marshall, Shelley (2006), 'An exploration of control in the context of vertical disintegration, and regulatory responses', in Chris Arup, John Howe, Richard Mitchell and Anthony O'Donnel (eds), *Labour Law and Labour Market Regulation: Essays in the Construction, Constitution, and Regulation of Labour Markets and Work Relationships* (Sydney: Federation Press).

Marshall, T.H. (1950), *Citizenship and Social Class and Other Essays* (Cambridge: Cambridge University Press).

McAdam, Doug, Tarrow, Sidney and Tilly, Charles (2001), *Dynamics of Contention* (Cambridge: Cambridge University Press).

McBarnet, Doreen (2007), 'Corporate social responsibility beyond law, through law, for law: the new corporate accountability', in Doreen McBarnet, Aurora Voiculescu and Tom Campbell (eds), *The New Corporate Accountability: Corporate Social Responsibility and the Law* (Cambridge: Cambridge University Press).

—— Voiculescu, A. and Campbell, Tom (eds) (2007), *The New Corporate Accountability: Corporate Social Responsibility and the Law* (Cambridge: Cambridge University Press).

McCormick, Dorothy and Schmitz, Hubert (2002), 'Manual for value chain research on homeworkers in the garment industry', Sussex: Institute of Development Studies, Women in Informal Employment Globalizing and Organizing.

Miller, David (1991), 'Theories of social justice', *British Journal of Political Science* 21(3): 371–91.

—— (1997), 'Equality and justice', *Ratio* 10(3).

—— (1999), *Principles of Social Justice* (Cambridge, MA: Harvard University Press).

Murray, Douglas, Raynolds, Laura and Taylor, Peter Leigh (2003), 'One cup at a time: poverty alleviation and fair trade coffee in Latin America'. [Online: Colorado State University]. Available at: http://www.colostate.edu/Depts/Sociology/FairTradeResearchGroup [accessed: April 2005].

Murray, Jill (2001), 'The sound of one hand clapping? The "ratcheting labour standards" proposal and international law', *Australian Journal of Labour Law* 14.

Newell, Peter and Frynas, George (2007), 'Beyond CSR? Business, poverty and social justice: an introduction', *Third World Quarterly*, special issue on 'Beyond CSR? Business, Poverty and Social Justice' 28(4): 669–81.

O'Brien, Robert (2000), 'Workers and world order: the tentative transformation of the international union movement', *Review of International Studies* 26: 533–55.

—— Goetz, Anne Marie, Scholte, Jan Aart and Williams, Marc (2000), *Contesting Global Governance: Multilateral Economic Institutions and Global Social Movements* (Cambridge: Cambridge University Press).

O'Riain, Sean (2000), 'States and markets in an era of globalization', *Annual Review of Sociology* 26: 187–213.

Parker, Christine (2002), *The Open Corporation: Effective Self-regulation and Democracy* (Cambridge: Cambridge University Press).

—— (2007), 'Meta-regulation: legal accountability for corporate social responsibility', University of Melbourne Legal Studies Research Paper.

Pateman, Carole (1970), *Participation and Democratic Theory* (Cambridge: Cambridge University Press).

Pogge, Thomas (ed.) (2001), *Global Justice* (Oxford: Blackwell).

—— (2002), *World Poverty and Human Rights: Cosmopolitan Responsibilities and Reforms* (Cambridge: Polity Press).

Polanyi, Karl (1944), *The Great Transformation: The Political and Economic Origins of Our Time* (Boston, MA: Beacon Press).

Raynolds, Laura (2002a), 'Consumer/producer links in fair trade coffee networks', *Sociologia Ruralis* 42(4).

—— (2002b), 'Poverty alleviation through participation in fair trade coffee networks: existing research and critical issues'. [Online]. Available at: http://www.colostate.edu/Depts/Sociology/ FairTradeResearchGroup/doc/rayback.pdf [accessed: April 2005].

—— Murray, Douglas and Taylor, Peter Leigh (2004), 'Fair trade coffee: building producer capacity via global networks', *Journal of International Development* 16.

Raynolds, L., Murray, D. and Wilkinson, J. (2007), *Fair Trade: The Challenges of Transforming Globalization* (London and New York: Routledge).

Richter, Judith (2001), *Holding Corporations Accountable: Corporate Conduct, International Codes and Citizen Action* (London and New York: Zed Books).

Ross, Andrew (1997), *No Sweat: Fashion, Free Trade, and the Rights of Garment Workers* (New York and London: Verso).

Ruggie, John (1982), 'International regimes, transactions and change: embedded liberalism in the postwar economic order', *International Organization* 36(2).

—— (2003), 'Taking embedded liberalism global: the corporate connection', in David Held and Mathias Koenig-Archibugi (eds), *Taming Globalization: Frontiers of Governance* (Cambridge: Polity Press).

—— (ed.) (2008), *Embedding Global Markets: An Enduring Challenge* (Aldershot: Ashgate).

Sassen, Saskia (2002), 'The state and globalisation', in Rodney Bruce Hall and Thomas J. Biersteker (eds), *The Emergence of Private Authority in Global Governance* (Cambridge: Cambridge University Press).

—— (2003), 'The participation of states and citizens in global governance', *Indiana Journal of Global Legal Studies* 10(1): 5–28.

Sen, Amartya (2009), 'Capitalism beyond the crisis', *New York Review of Books* 56(5).

Smith, Sally and Barrientos, Stephanie (2005), 'Fair trade and ethical trade: are there moves towards convergence?', *Sustainable Development* 13.

Starr, A. (2000), *Naming the Enemy: Anti-corporate Movements Confront Globalization* (London: Zed Books).

Stewart, Frances (2002), 'Macro-micro interactions in a dynamic context', in J. Heyer, Frances Stewart and Rosemary Thorp (eds), *Group Behaviour and Development: Is the Market Destroying Cooperation?* (Oxford: Oxford University Press).

Streeck, Wolfgang (2009; forthcoming), *Re-Forming Capitalism: Institutional Change in the German Political Economy* (Oxford: Oxford University Press).

Tarrow, S. (1994), *Power in Movement: Social Movements, Collective Action and Politics* (Cambridge: Cambridge University Press).

Utting, Peter (2005), 'Rethinking business regulation: from self-regulation to social control', in UNRISD Technology Business and Society Programme Paper Number 15. Geneva: UNRISD.

—— (2006), 'Corporate social responsibility and equality', in Summary of presentation for the UNRISD – Sida/SAREC Workshop on Social Policy and Equality, 21–22 February 2006, Buenos Aires, Argentina (Geneva: United Nations Research Institute for Social Development).

Vitt, Judith (2007), 'From conflict to collaboration: NGOs and businesses', *CSR Asia Weekly* 3(51). Available at: http://www.systain.de/Website/Downloads/Dokumente/csrasiaweeklyvol3week51.pdf [accessed: February 2008].

Vogel, David (2005), *The Market for Virtue: The Potential and Limits of Corporate Social Responsibility* (Washington, DC: Brookings Institution Press).

Wade, Robert (2008), 'Financial regime change?', *New Left Review* 53(September–October).

Wood, Ellen Meiksins (2002), *The Origins of Capitalism: A Longer View* (London: Verso).

Zerk, Jennifer (2006), *Multinationals and Corporate Social Responsibility* (Cambridge: Cambridge University Press).

PART I
Individual and Civic Action Through Fair Trade

Chapter 2

Fair Trade at the Centre of Development

Steve Knapp

No single change could make a greater contribution to eliminating poverty than fully opening the markets of prosperous countries to the goods produced by poor ones.

Kofi Annan, Secretary General of the United Nations[1]

The basic objective is to combine the great benefits of trade to which many defenders of globalisation point, with the overarching need for fairness and equity which motivates a major part of the anti-globalisation protests.

Amartya Sen, Honorary President of Oxfam[2]

Introduction

Trade is one of the most powerful factors linking our lives and is a source of unprecedented wealth creation. Yet international trade presents a paradox, as the prosperity created coincides with deepening mass poverty and inequality. The rules that govern international trade are not currently structured in a way that respects the needs and interests of the poor. Rather, these rules are largely determined by, and protect the interests of, the wealthy and powerful players in the market. However, it is increasingly being recognized that trade, if structured differently, could have the potential to reduce world poverty dramatically.

In view of these challenges, the aim of this chapter is to identify the multiple levels at which the Fairtrade system supports goals of rural income generation, empowerment, poverty reduction, social development and democratic decision-making, via the creation of a fair system of international trade. The opportunities opened up to poor producers by means of their participation in this system are contrasted to the barriers to development that many marginalized producers face as a result of their integration within the wider system of international trade, in which goals of trade liberalization and goals of development all too often operate at cross-purposes.

In developing this argument, this chapter draws on specific examples from the Asia-Pacific region to illustrate the impact of Fairtrade relationships established between Asia-Pacific producers and consumers in Australia and New Zealand, which have been coordinated by the institutional vehicles of the Fair Trade Association of Australia and New Zealand (FTAANZ) – a member of the International Fair Trade Association (IFAT) (now the World Fair Trade Association) – and Fairtrade Labelling Australia and New Zealand (FLANZ) – a member of Fairtrade Labelling Organizations

---

1 Quoted in NZAID, *Trade Can Reduce Poverty*, available at: http://www.nzaid.govt.nz/library/docs/nzaid-trade-can-reduce-poverty.pdf.

2 From Amartya Sen's foreword in Kevin Watkins and Penny Fowler, *Rigged Rules and Double Standards*, Oxford: Oxfam, 2002.

International (FLO). Analysis of regional developments are situated within a broader evaluation of both the wider international trade and development regimes inside of which these regional systems of trade operate, and the Fairtrade Labelling system's own structure of international governance.

Trade, Aid and Development: The Failings of the Existing International System

Before exploring some of the major contributions of Fairtrade to developmental goals, this chapter briefly identifies those features of existing arrangements that most directly undermine the potential of the international trading system in its current form to promote goals of poverty reduction and social development.

The Potential of International Trade to Tackle Problems of Global Poverty

Some 1.2 billion people in the world are estimated to live in 'dollar poverty', consuming less than one dollar per day (IFAD 2001, 15). With increased and worsening inequality, many poor people and underdeveloped regions are being left behind. In turn, rising inequality slows the rate at which economic growth is converted into poverty reduction. Using a headcount ratio, about two fifths of the population in South Asia was below the poverty line in 1998 (IFAD 2001, 40). Poverty incidence was higher in South Asia than in any other region of the world, except sub-Saharan Africa, and the region accounts for 44 per cent of the total poor (IFAD 2001, 15). Over 70 per cent of the world's poor, the majority of whom are women, are now rural and projections suggest that this figure will still be over 60 per cent in 2025. In Asia and the Pacific region, poverty is disproportionately concentrated to the extent that 80–90 per cent of the poor live in rural areas in all the major countries of the region (IFAD 2001, 18).

In confronting such problems of global poverty – concentrated particularly in rural populations – the international trading system holds considerable potential to offer pathways towards rural income generation and development. The forces of globalization have driven increases in world trade, and transfers of technology and movement of information have created incredible opportunities for certain sectors of society in both developed and developing countries.

Yet the opportunities offered by an expanding system of international trade are currently being captured disproportionately by rich, industrialized countries. While developed countries export goods worth approximately US$6,000 per capita each year, in developing countries the average is US$330 per capita, and in low-income countries less than US$100 per capita. Least-developed countries (LDCs) – a grouping that includes several Pacific countries – account for less than 3 per cent of world trade, despite comprising 40 per cent of the world's population (World Bank 2001).

One means by which trade could benefit low income countries would be for those countries to increase their share of earnings from world exports. If developing countries were to increase their share by just 5 per cent, this would generate around US$350 billion in additional income – seven times as much as they receive in aid from the developed world. Regionally if Africa, East Asia, South Asia and Latin America were each to increase their share of world exports by 1 per cent, the resultant gains in income could lift 128 million people out of poverty (a reduction of 12 per cent) (World Bank 2001).

Obstacles to Development Confronting Rural Producers

Despite the potential of international trade to confront problems of global poverty, the framework of the current economic model through which global economic interconnections have been promoted has tended to produce non-inclusive capitalism and economic growth. The advance of globalization has created a range of new opportunities such as: fostering increased linkages between countries; expanded trade, increased financial and information flows; and the rapid development of new technologies, markets, managerial know-how and financial investment capacity. However, some aspects of globalization – such as the organization of the current international trading regime – have compounded associated problems of global poverty and disenfranchisement, implying that globalization as a whole is failing to achieve its promised benefits to the poor. Instead, many marginalized people are experiencing increased insecurity and threatened livelihoods.

The obstacles confronting rural producers within contemporary processes of globalization exist at a number of levels, resulting from features of the local development environment (in producing countries and regions themselves), the international trading system, and international aid and development policy.

At the local level, the shortages of skills and capital experienced by many producers along with a lack of opportunities to add value and diversify production are major problems. As a result, many domestic, particularly rural, producers in developing countries are unable to compete in the globalized market-place in the short term. However, not only are they immediately disadvantaged by the lack of investment capital, business skills and access to markets, but the factors of production that these marginalized producers depend upon are generally non-transferable, having often been the source of livelihood for generations. Hence the prospects for redirecting their productive resources to more efficient economic activities generally do not exist and in many areas of the world this has resulted in rural farmers losing their land assets and being forced to migrate to urban areas.

Producers also face a number of barriers within the international trading system. One major obstacle is instability and price fluctuations in global markets combined with a downward trend in world prices. While all producers of commodity products are exposed to risk from price fluctuations and volatile markets, those in developing countries are more vulnerable, particularly where commodity prices have fallen below their cost of production. Faced with fluctuating and falling world prices they can become ensnared in a cycle of debt, poverty and deteriorating livelihood opportunities, and the lack of access for small farmer producers in developing countries both to markets and to market information contributes further to these difficulties.

Even in a climate of higher and rising commodity prices, small farmer producers do not necessarily receive the benefits of higher price levels. The increase in availability of small farmers' produce during harvest periods means that farm gate prices tend to remain low. Because farmers lack the capital and market information to take advantage of price movements, it is the traders and middlemen in the supply chain, rather than the farmers themselves, who generally capture the profits from price speculation during periods of high or rising agricultural commodity prices.

As a result of these challenges, poor agricultural producers continue to occupy a highly vulnerable position within the existing system of international trade; these features of the international trading system amplify the significant developmental barriers many such producers already face at the local and national levels.

Intensifying such problems further is the existing lack of policy coherence between those institutions governing the international trading system and those operating in the sphere of international development. Policies designed to further goals of poverty reduction and social development promoted by aid and development agencies are in many ways being undermined by the application of rules that often distort patterns of international production, trade and pricing to the advantage of large transnational companies and to the disadvantage of marginalized producers and workers in the South.

Another major obstacle arising from existing features of the international trading system has been the ongoing implementation of subsidies and protection in the industrialized world. Average agricultural tariffs are in the region of 60 per cent whereas industrial tariffs are rarely greater than 10 per cent (World Bank 2001, 67). Trade barriers imposed by rich countries are especially damaging because they target the goods that the poor produce: labour-intensive agricultural and manufactured products. In contrast, total subsidies to domestic farmers in the EU and United States total more than US$1 billion per day (World Bank 2001). These subsidies accrue to the wealthiest farmers, finance massive environmental damage and generate overproduction that is dumped on world markets to the extent that the agricultural superpowers export at prices that are less than one third of their production cost. This serves to drive down global prices, destroying smallholder agriculture and local economies.

In 2004, a report to the Secretary General of the United Nations by the UN Development Programme stated that the importance of agriculture in reducing poverty creates an urgent need for developing reform initiatives towards the elimination of trade-distorting subsidies which benefit agricultural producers in developed markets (CPSD 2004). The World Bank and other development institutions also acknowledge that many developing countries are still unable to realize their comparative advantage in agricultural production because farm subsidies and agricultural trade policies in industrial countries depress world prices for farm products (DFID et al. 2002). Some of the world's poorest farmers are, in effect, competing against the world's richest treasuries. Ironically, this is ultimately financed by taxpayers and consumers in the developed world.

At the same time as international trading rules create multiple barriers to development, the system of international development aid is charged with promoting goals of poverty reduction, capacity-building and export promotion. While the development aid system makes some contributions to the advancement of these objectives, its efforts are significantly weakened by its lack of commitment both to the agricultural sector and to goals of producer control and empowerment. They are also undermined in many cases when they fall into conflict with the operation of the international trading system.

In an attempt to address this incoherence in national policies, in December 2005 the World Trade Organization (WTO) Ministerial Declaration in Hong Kong committed to take actions to encourage 'Aid for Trade' initiatives. However, there was no clear definition and there remains very little agreement on what 'Aid for Trade' actually entails. The New Zealand Agency for International Development (NZAID) is recognized as initiating one of the more progressive 'Aid for Trade' programmes and is ranked first out of 22 in the trade component of the Commitment to Development Index 2008 compiled by the Center for Global Development (CGD 2009). As a smaller country with little or no trade barriers, New Zealand's policy approach perhaps benefits from encountering less pressure from vested commercial interests in the outcomes of trade negotiations that can also benefit trade development than is experienced by other OECD countries.

In its policy statement, 'Harnessing International Trade for Development', NZAID acknowledges many of the issues highlighted above and underlines the need for economic and governance factors to be set in place, including policy and regulatory frameworks that ensure the benefits of trade reach those most affected by poverty and disadvantaged by current trade structures. The statement also identifies internal constraints for developing countries, particularly in the Pacific, relating to deficiencies in market information, business skills and domestic infrastructure, and, consequently, to a lack of access to markets that cover small producers' costs of sustainable production (NZAID 2003).

One major weakness of existing development policies lies in the neglect of the agricultural sector. While agriculture is the primary source of livelihood for the rural poor, international financing for agricultural development declined by nearly 40 per cent from 1987 to 1998 (World Bank 2001). In recent years, only about 3.5 per cent of total overseas development assistance (ODA) has been devoted to agricultural development (World Bank 2007, 41). Additionally, there is considerable evidence that government and ODA has tended to favour the urban areas, the more productive lowlands, export crops, and industrial and manufacturing establishments (World Bank 2007, 40–41). In the process, policies have, often unwittingly, developed inbuilt bias against poor rural households and disadvantaged areas such that their deprivation has been entrenched.

Furthermore, development aid has tended to fund projects on the basis of outside experts deciding what is best for marginalized farmers and imposing predefined agri-business solutions on them. In this way, development engagements with the rural poor often fail to approach them with appropriate respect for their knowledge, beliefs and practices. Such efforts therefore fail to take sufficient account of the fact that a key element of human dignity for any individual as well as of the empowerment of rural communities is for those individuals and communities to retain control over the major decisions that affect their welfare. The lack of emphasis placed on promoting producer empowerment and control over institutional rules and policy priorities is also reflected in the weakness of democratic decision-making within the overarching rule-making institutions that govern prevailing international trade and development regimes.

Even to the extent that existing development policies are able to promote local capacity-building and development despite their weaknesses, a troubling disconnect remains between the priorities, institutions and policies in place in the overlapping arenas of trade and aid. Hence this lack of policy coherence limits the effectiveness of trade in promoting sustainable development. While a considerable amount of ODA is spent on strengthening trade and export capacities of developing countries, trade rules and negotiations often seek to restrict developing countries' access to developed countries' markets, the result being that developing countries' domestic markets are opened up to subsidized overproduction from the developed world, undermining local competition. Moreover, when developing countries export to rich countries they face tariff barriers four times higher than those encountered by rich countries. This costs them US$100 billion per year – twice as much as they receive in aid (World Bank 2002, 53). Developed countries even continue to export military goods to countries where conflict is the main factor restricting development.

The current structures governing international trade are not benefiting the poor and ODA is not solving the problem. Investing more in the rural poor is necessary, but understanding how to do so effectively is now crucial. Fostering a greater understanding among Northern publics, in whose names these trade and development policies are being pursued by their elected governments, is also of paramount importance.

The Fairtrade Response

While the fair trade movement as a whole encompasses a range of different actors, organizations and strategies – as discussed in other chapters in this volume – the focus of this chapter is on verified forms of fair trade and, more specifically, the certification and labelling dimensions of the fair trade movement. The principal organizations carrying out such work are FLO, an international product labelling and certification body, and IFAT, a network of trading partners that self-assess against a set of internationally agreed standards for fair trade organizations (FTOs).

The fair trade movement has grown from the successes and failures of the past relating primarily to development aid, subsidies, governmental support and non-governmental organization (NGO)-based solutions, and the emergent realization that while these initiatives have relevant roles to play, it is private entrepreneurship and trade which should be supported as the main means to eradicate poverty. Yet while the importance of entrepreneurship and trade to economic development cannot be overemphasized, it cannot take the form of a free trade free-for-all; rather, it must be promoted by building entrepreneurial skills and trade links that directly benefit the poor. Hence the fair trade movement endorses a market-based model of international trade which ensures the payment of a fair price as well as certain social and environmental standards and investment in local communities.

Fairtrade offers just such a mechanism of trade linkages and capacity-building directed at the poor and disadvantaged people who produce the commodity products consumed and used by rich countries every day. Its strategic intent is to work with producers that are disadvantaged and marginalized by conventional trade, including smallholder farmers and workers, in order to enable them to move from a position of vulnerability to one of security and economic self-sufficiency. It also aims to empower them to become stakeholders in their own organizations and to play a wider role in the global arena. Via these means, the overarching goal of Fairtrade is to achieve greater equity in international trade and therefore realize growth and stability for both individual workers and producers and their communities. Within this framework, Fairtrade facilitates change in the local political structure by supporting people to organize and, thus, provide a stronger voice to the poor.

The Fairtrade Labelling system uses standard setting, supply-chain certification, product labelling and the raising of consumer awareness to deliver development benefits at the producer level. The certification system focuses on agricultural commodity product exports from developing countries to developed countries, most notably coffee, cocoa, tea, bananas, honey, cotton, wine and fresh fruit, among others (see, for example, FLO 2008a).

FLO consists of 20 Labelling Initiatives that, together with FLO e.V., license the international FAIRTRADE Mark, or its equivalent, to businesses and enable Fairtrade labelled products to be available in more than 60 consuming markets (FLO 2008a, 11). By the end of 2007 there were more than 632 certified producer organizations in 58 developing countries coming together into three regional producer networks representing Latin American, African and Asian producers (FLO 2008a, 21, 3). FLO e.V. is the umbrella organization based in Bonn, Germany, that establishes the Fairtrade standards in consultation with producers and other stakeholders.

The FLO Fairtrade standards consist of two parts: generic standards that apply to the small farmer, hired labour or contract production situations; and product specific standards that include the minimum price and Fairtrade investment premium levels for each product. FLO-CERT is a wholly-owned subsidiary of FLO e.V. and an independent certification body. The first certification system for development to be accredited to ISO 65, FLO-CERT certifies producers' and traders' compliance with Fairtrade standards throughout the supply chain. This provides an independent third-party certification and a guarantee to consumers that any product carrying the FAIRTRADE Mark has been produced and traded to international Fairtrade standards.

The guarantee of the FAIRTRADE Mark has enabled Fairtrade products to move out of specialist retail outlets and into mainstream markets. This means that mainstream retailers and food manufacturers can sell Fairtrade certified product lines alongside conventional products, giving consumers the choice to support Fairtrade without going out of their way to purchase from specialist outlets. Mainstreaming has driven a huge growth in the sales of Fairtrade certified products worldwide. In 2007, Fairtrade certified sales amounted to approximately €2.3 billion worldwide, reflecting a 47 per cent year-on-year increase (FLO 2008a, 13). While this represents less than one hundredth of a percentage point of world trade in physical merchandise, Fairtrade products generally account for 0.5–5 per cent of all sales in individual product categories in Europe and North America. In 2007, over 1.5 million disadvantaged producers worldwide were directly benefiting from fair trade while an additional 7.5 million benefited from infrastructure and community development projects funded through Fairtrade premiums (FLO 2008a, 21).

IFAT is a global network of FTOs. The Northern IFAT members were the pioneers of fair trade marketing in most developed country markets: the European Fair Trade Association; the Network of European Worldshops; Traidcraft; GEPA; and Altromercato. Strong supporters of the FAIRTRADE Mark and the certification system, these organizations have also invested in the establishment of their own fair trade brands. In recent years, however, some IFAT members have become concerned that fair trade principles are being redefined by a label on a packet and question the commitment of many commercial companies that could be perceived to be jumping on the Fairtrade bandwagon. All IFAT members are FTOs and, as such, have fair trade principles at the heart of their operations; they trade exclusively in either FLO Fairtrade certified products or fair trade goods produced by fellow IFAT members in the South.

The following discussion examines, in turn, the various ways in which the Fairtrade certification and labelling system tackles obstacles to poverty reduction and social development faced by marginalized producers and workers. The activities of Fairtrade are shown to bring about positive change at several levels: by promoting social development and strengthening skills and institutions within producer communities; by building international trading relationships based on fairer and more supportive terms of exchange; and by developing international governance arrangements within the Fairtrade certification and labelling system itself that respects principles of producer empowerment and control. At each of these levels, the Fairtrade system promotes further developmental patterns of production and trade which, at the same time, gives producers greater control over the processes of institutional decision-making that impact so significantly on their basic livelihoods.

Fairtrade Strategies at the Local Level: South Asia and the Asia-Pacific Region

The barriers to development encountered by marginalized producers in the Asia-Pacific region reflect closely the kinds of challenges and obstacles outlined above. As in many other locations of agricultural production in which the Fairtrade system operates, most of the rural poor targeted by the Fairtrade system lack basic amenities such as a piped water supply, sanitation and electricity. Their access to credit, inputs and technology is severely limited. Constraints – including lack of information about markets, of business and negotiating experience, and of collective organization – deprive them of the power needed to interact on equal terms with other, generally larger and stronger market players. Such barriers can also undermine their capacity to add value and diversify production. Cultural and social distance and discrimination are other factors that may also, at least partly, exclude poor farmers from markets. Furthermore, low levels of social and physical infrastructure increase vulnerability to malnutrition and disease, especially in the mountainous and most remote areas of the region.

Small island developing states (SIDS) in South East Asia and the Pacific[3] face their own particular challenges. SIDS in the region struggle economically due to limited land size, population and resource bases. Their lack of human and institutional capacities have weakened their international

---

3   Listed by the UN Office of the High Representative for the Least Developed Countries, Landlocked Developing Countries and Small Island Developing States (see UN-OHRLLS 2009).

competitiveness and marginalized their economies in international trade. Additionally, increased instability in agricultural exports and dependence on food imports threaten food security.

Sources of revenue are limited, with most SIDS relying heavily on subsistence agriculture and being highly dependent on ODA and remittances. These states are physically remote and isolated and, as such, any export trade is dependent on expensive transport providers. This raises the price of imports and exports, even for trade within individual multi-island states. This also makes public administration difficult and expensive.

Remoteness discourages foreign producers and service providers, and the domestic markets may be too small to support more than one producer. Small size and geographic location work together to exacerbate certain difficulties, such as the disproportionate impact of climate change upon these countries – from economic losses as a result of reduced agricultural yields to loss of mangrove forests due to rising sea-levels (UNFCCC 2007, 4–5). Inhabitants of some islands have been forced to relocate to other islands or to new countries (see UNFCCC 2007). These are the world's first climate change refugees.

Although SIDS tend to score relatively well on some development indicators, such as education and health, more poverty exists than their per capita income would suggest. Their lack of economic diversification, import dependence and susceptibility to natural disasters render them particularly vulnerable (UN-OHRLLS 2009). Almost all of the states classified as most vulnerable to climate change are small states and about two thirds of these are islands.

FLANZ already addresses a number of enquiries from producer groups in these countries interested in accessing the Fairtrade certification system in addition to those from trading companies interested in sourcing Fairtrade certified products from SIDS in the region. With Fairtrade's mission being to 'focus on producers who are disadvantaged by unpredictable trade conditions and economic injustice' (FLO 2008c, 6), in 2008 the FLO Board extended Fairtrade standards and pricing to cover SIDS in South East Asia and the Pacific at the request of FLANZ.

In terms of product volumes and number of direct producer beneficiaries, SIDS in South East Asia and Oceania only represent a fraction of the overall impacts of the international Fairtrade system. Consequently, a 'light touch' approach from the Fairtrade system is necessary to ensure minimum cost implications and maintain a positive cost-benefit ratio for SIDS in the region.

A further challenge is presented by producer group structures in the region. Fairtrade seeks to work with a diverse range of producer group operations; not all producer organizations in the South fit into FLO's definitions of small farmer, hired labour or contract production scenarios. Farming groups in these countries are essentially extended families and clans working under a system of relationships and respect. The concept of democratic organizations is not necessarily applicable to these existing social structures and Fairtrade recognizes that the system needs to be able to adapt to suit local contexts rather than imposing systems and structures that require producers to compromise their traditions in order to join the Fairtrade system. FLO's new strategic approach enshrines these principles in the White Paper's first guidelines for optimizing the Business Model: 'FTL should enable producers to design diverse development patterns, fitting each specific context and respecting local cultures' (FLO 2008b).

Despite the obstacles, there are a number of Fairtrade certified producers operating in the region who provide apt examples of the specific challenges facing producers in South East Asia and Oceania.

In terms of physical remoteness, The Crater Mountain Cooperative in the Mount Hagen conservation area in Papua New Guinea (PNG) faces extreme challenges. The cooperative, consisting of some 2,000 coffee farmers, obtained its initial Fairtrade certification in 2003. The producers are extremely remote and isolated; the only available way to transport their coffee to markets is by air at an additional cost of approximately 50 cents/lb. Consequently, it takes the cooperative up to two months to move sufficient amounts of coffee out of the area in order to fill a single container for export. As a result of these challenges, the group has been unable to secure enough Fairtrade orders to cover their certification costs and have been unable to renew their certification.

The Highlands Organic Agricultural Cooperative (HOAC), also in Papua New Guinea, obtained Fairtrade certification in 2004. There are currently 2,600 registered farmers living amongst 32 village communities spread over 500 square kilometres in the Purosa valley region. These growers support about 12,000 family members and, with interest growing, it is expected that a further 2,000 growers will sign up with HOAC over the next two years. The HOAC/Fairtrade members all tend small plots of coffee and individually process it following organic and sustainable agricultural practices. Central processing facilities for cherry coffee have not been built due to the long distance that must be travelled between villages.

The cooperative has recently invested some of its Fairtrade premium in acquiring a piece of land in Okapa intended to be used for central collection and the processing of cherry coffee. The effectiveness of this facility, however, will depend on business development training support combined with infrastructure and road improvements. Road access from Goroka, the main Highlands coffee processing centre, to Okapa junction is normally open but the smaller feeder roads can only be serviced by tractor and trailer or on foot by people carrying small quantities of parchment coffee on their back for one or two days. These constraints limit the development potential of the area.

Fairtrade certification has brought the growers together in a common cause of development through self-help. As such, they are making their best efforts to introduce community responsibility for minor road maintenance across different clan areas. Furthermore, before their Fairtrade certification, coffee was the only cash crop for these farmers. The Fairtrade premium has been utilized to dilute their reliance on coffee and broaden their livelihood options to other Fairtrade and organic, certifiable crops for export such as spices and honey; the cooperative recently applied for Fairtrade certification for honey (FTAANZ 2008, 16–17).

Mountain Fruits (Pvt.) Ltd, a Fairtrade certified producer in the mountainous Northern Areas of Pakistan, processes and exports dried apricots on behalf of a group of 2,000 physically, economically and politically isolated farming families in the Karakoram Mountains. Since Partition in 1947, the Northern Areas have been administered by Pakistan as part of the disputed territories of Jammu and Kashmir. The complex political situation means that the population has no official constitutional status or political representation and does not enjoy the fundamental legal, political and civil rights of other citizens.

Due to lack of government investment and infrastructure, this remains one of the most disadvantaged and neglected areas of Pakistan. The farming communities are extremely poor; however, the high altitude and harsh environmental conditions of extremely cold winters and short, intensely hot summers, combined with irrigation from glacial melt waters, produce beautifully flavoured fruits. Unfortunately, because of the lack of infrastructure, most of the fruit perishes or is sold cheaply in local markets.

Mountain Fruits have provided training and introduced simple technological improvements to the drying and harvesting processes in order to meet internationally accepted standards. This has enabled the group to secure export contracts and Fairtrade premium markets, in turn allowing it to invest in the continual improvement of product quality and enabling producers to diversify into markets for other dried fruits and nuts. In 2005, the Mountain Areas Fruit Farmers' Association received their first Fairtrade premiums and, in consultation with Mountain Fruits, came together to decide how they would invest in projects that benefit the farmers, their families and their communities (Fairtrade Foundation 2007).

Women in Business Development Inc. (WIBDI) in Samoa has been active in organizing the region's small farmers to obtain organic certification and form a collective association. WIBDI is seeking Fairtrade certification for the farmers' production of bananas, coconut oil and cocoa, with the potential for diversification into other fresh fruits and value added products such as dried fruits and juices (see WIBDI 2008). Small Pacific islands like Samoa face the added challenges of extreme distance from consuming export markets and of obtaining any production economies of scale. Even with a simple and cost effective extension of Fairtrade standards, pricing and certification to cover these products, the risk remains that these challenges will continue to marginalize the farmers; this is even so within the Fairtrade system itself, as any product from the Pacific islands can be produced at lower cost in other parts of the developing world. In order for Fairtrade to be effective, the origin story and social marketing of Pacific island products will be paramount in obtaining niche and premium prices that cover their costs of production, transportation and producer development needs (see WIBDI 2008). The Fairtrade certification framework will then be able to ensure that the benefits are applied in an effective way in order for producers to work towards defining and meeting their own development needs.

Because of the variety of developmental obstacles confronted by many producers in South East Asia and the Pacific at the local level, Fairtrade promotes local developmental processes via a range of mechanisms. These strategies share a common goal of assisting disadvantaged producers to access international markets, and to improve their productivity.

Some specific ways in which these goals are promoted include the development of local entrepreneurial skills and organizational capabilities, via supporting processes of skill development, organizational capacity-building, diversification and democratic governance at the local level. Not only do such strategies directly target poverty, they also facilitate investment in wider social development processes and the ongoing strengthening of both production capacity and quality and market access among marginalized producers.

These are the kind of initiatives that aid should be supporting. The sustainable development of village-based economic activity combined with strategic, higher level investment in institutions and infrastructure create an enabling environment for enterprise to flourish. Small-scale savings and loans schemes combined with income generating activities introduce the monetary economy to villages and encourage savings and investment. Enterprise loan schemes and business support services in turn encourage small enterprise and increases in local economic activity.

Small savings and loans schemes are a common feature of Fairtrade certified producers, particularly in relation to empowering women's financial position within the community. Mountain Fruits in Pakistan manages a women's micro-credit scheme. In 2001, WIBDI began an income generation and microfinance project linked to traditional fine mat-weaving projects, giving many Samoan women the opportunity to learn new skills, particularly business and financial skills that have supported the development of a local industry (see WIBDI 2008).

Liberation Foods CIC is an FTO based in the UK with a business model that further enhances producer ownership and empowerment along the value chain. Over 22,000 smallholder producers in Latin America, Asia and Africa own a collective share of 42 per cent of the company (Liberation n.d.). Liberation enhances the Fairtrade model by bringing producer ownership and control up the supply chain to include the role of the importer through a farmer-owned retail brand. Smallholder producers are empowered and involved at board level, ensuring that their interests are represented and their profits are maximized. Through Liberation's supply chain, farmers in effect sell directly to the retailers in Europe (Liberation n.d.).

The Fair Trade Alliance in Kerala (FTAK) in India is a Fairtrade certified producer of cashew nuts and a part owner of Liberation Nut; one of their farmer members has a seat on Liberation's board of directors. In recent years, development gains in the state of Kerala have been threatened by the fall in the prices of agricultural commodities, especially of the cash crops on which a majority of the Kerala farmers now depend. FTAK has secured export markets through Liberation under Fairtrade terms and a FTAK representative reports that, with the sense of ownership of the Liberation brand, farmers have an increased commitment to the quality of their product as they are now effectively sellers. FTAK has also been able to promote farmer diversification into a range of spices that are also covered by their Fairtrade certification (*Tomy Mathews* 2008).

With HOAC assisting them to organize, farmers in remote Eastern Highlands Province of PNG are seeking political representation. They nominated their chairperson to run for the Okapa seat at the 2007 national parliamentary elections; although he did not win, the fact this community member became a candidate was considered a success by the local district. This achievement was the result of HOAC's organization and its commitment to bring the farmers' problems to the attention of the government (FTAANZ 2008).

Fairtrade also promotes processes of social development via institutional channels that seriously undertake the goal of empowering producers to control the processes of decision-making that impact on their lives. Another example of such processes of democratic institution-building at the local level is the Small Organic Farmers' Association (SOFA) in Sri Lanka, which was founded in 1997 by 183 tea growers unable to cover their cost of production individually with the price they were paid for their product (Bio Foods 2008). SOFA's membership has since swelled to over 2,000 families and some 30,000 dependants in the production chain (Samath 2007). It is presently a fully-independent farmer organization managed by its own board, elected from the cooperative members (a requirement for Fairtrade certification). Organizing into a democratic structure and becoming members of the Fairtrade system has helped the farmers within SOFA to negotiate collectively sustainable, fair and long-term contracts.

These strategies – building the organization of farmers into democratic structures; encouraging effective participation in community forums; promoting measures to curb bad agricultural practices; promoting high environmental standards; ensuring fair and stable prices for products; and supporting local community development projects – are key to the sustained reduction of rural poverty, provided the benefits of this growth are broad-based. By supporting and encouraging these multiple strategies at the local level, the Fairtrade system promotes the empowerment of marginalized producers in developing countries, thereby directly supporting processes of poverty reduction and social development and often spurring growth in the rural non-farm sector through the multiplier effects of local economic development.

The application of a robust certification system in order to ensure that these strategies are being applied effectively at the local level upholds the integrity of the Fairtrade system. Certification combats corruption by requiring continual transparency in financial flows down through the supply chain from consumer to farmer and the maintenance of product traceability in the opposite direction. At the local level, certification ensures the broad distribution of the benefits derived from Fairtrade to farmers and workers who are disadvantaged in conventional trade arrangements.

Fairtrade Activities within International Markets and Supply Chains

These multiple contributions by the Fairtrade system to social development at the local level would not be possible without the positioning of these activities within a broader system of Fairtrade certified markets, supply chains and governance arrangements at the international level, which are themselves based around principles of fairness and producer empowerment.

The Fairtrade system's international organizational architecture is therefore critical to the effective functioning and impact of the system as a whole. Through this, functions of trading, marketing, governance, administration, capacity-building and technical assistance are able to be performed in accordance with fair trade principles. The overarching structure of FLO, at the heart of the system's standard setting and governance functions, is discussed further in the following section. Here, discussion focuses on the important functions of FLO's national and regional Fairtrade Labelling Initiatives through examination of the activities of two closely related organizations in the Asia-Pacific region – the Fair Trade Association of Australia and New Zealand (FTAANZ) and Fairtrade Labelling Australia and New Zealand (FLANZ).

FTAANZ was established in 2003 to unite the growing number of parties interested in promoting fair trade awareness in Australia and New Zealand. Currently, coffee, tea, chocolate, cocoa, rice, quinoa, sportsballs and, more recently, cotton products bearing the FAIRTRADE Mark are currently available to Australian and New Zealand consumers (FLANZ 2009). FTAANZ also adopts a broad view of strategic goals for fair trade development in the neighbouring Pacific region in order to facilitate linkages between producers and fair trade markets.

FLANZ was formed in 2005 as the regional Labelling Initiative member of FLO and, as such, has the exclusive right to license the FAIRTRADE Mark in Australia and New Zealand. FLANZ's role is to develop supply chains and markets and increase sales of Fairtrade certified products, thereby representing Fairtrade producers' interests and products in Australia and New Zealand markets.

There are more than 30 different Fairtrade certified producer groups and many other producer groups from the IFAT network now supplying products in Australia and New Zealand markets. By 2009, more than 160 Australian and New Zealand businesses were participating in the Fairtrade Labelling system as 'licensees' (FLANZ 2009). In addition to this, there are two large trading IFAT members, Trade Aid in New Zealand and Oxfam Shop in Australia. The sales of Fairtrade certified products grew from just AU$200,000 in retail sales in 2003 to over AU$30 million in 2008 (FLANZ 2009). Sales of IFAT fair trade products have also grown: for example, Trade Aid announced retail sales of over NZ$6.5 million in the 2007–2008 financial year (Trade Aid 2008).

Although the Australia and New Zealand market has been one of the fastest growing in the world for Fairtrade certified products (FLO 2008a), consumer awareness and spend per capita still has a long way to go to catch up with parts of Europe and the United States. Moxie Design Group, a market research company in New Zealand, categorized New Zealand consumers as 'solution seekers' who are looking for solutions to the world's problems (Moxie Design Group Limited 2008, 4). Parallels can drawn between the results of this research and New Zealand consumers' fast-growing support for Fairtrade. Trailing Europe and the United States as Fairtrade consuming countries, the region is also behind in terms of Fairtrade certified producer organizations. Developing countries in South East Asia and Oceania comprise a very small proportion of the total number of Fairtrade certified producer organizations worldwide. This includes only a small number of coffee producers in Indonesia and PNG; the region remains underrepresented in the global Fairtrade system.

How then are FTAANZ and FLANZ contributing to processes of development, poverty reduction and increased social and global justice within the Asia-Pacific region? FLANZ operates within the overarching structure of the FLO system to promulgate and administer FLO standards, so as to promote the expansion of the Fairtrade Labelling system in national consumer markets and to support skill development and capacity-building among producer organizations in the region. These activities can be divided into three major elements: consumer-facing, business-facing and producer-facing forms of activities.

The *consumer-facing* aspects of the FTAANZ and FLANZ work focuses on building support, raising awareness and thus creating increased markets for Fairtrade products. This involves a marketing factor targeted at increasing fair trade sales, as well as a broader public education component directed towards improving public awareness in the industrialized North of barriers to development and the role of the international trading system in compounding these barriers.

Products are marketed with the message that they support the sustainable development of small farmers and workers in the South and, in the Pacific context, in island village communities. Consumers in Australia and New Zealand appear willing to support broad global development initiatives and express a keen interest in local and regional development. Current shared agendas for peace and security in the region, substantial national government aid, the existence of significant ex-patriot communities from Asia and the Pacific living in Australia and New Zealand, and an appreciation of the interlinked histories and future joint development prospects can be seen to provide persuasive grounds for the support and development of more sustainable Fairtrade products originating from the region.

Consumers must feel secure in the fact that in their support for a market-based system like Fairtrade actually delivers its promised benefits to the producer communities. The Fairtrade Mark, backed up by the development approach of minimum and progress standards and the transparent application of a robust certification system provides this important guarantee. However there is an identified need for the Fairtrade Labelling system to generate verifiable impact data that can be fed back to the consumer-facing aspects of the system.

In turn, the impact of Fairtrade is only possible through the significant and growing consumer demand for Fairtrade labelled products that has been driven by advocacy work in developed countries aimed at drawing attention to the production and trading conditions that disadvantage the poor in the developing world.

The *business-facing* aspects focus on expanding access to consumer markets through the promotion of improved business awareness and participation. Fairtrade initiatives support the development of long-term partnerships between producers in developing countries and importers in developed countries. Importers share market information and support producers in supplying products at sufficient quality to meet market demand. This enables Fairtrade consumers as well as individual businesses to contribute to poverty reduction and social development for marginalized producers via support for the fostering of enhanced trade links and the promotion of terms of exchange that are more advantageous towards marginalized workers and producers living in conditions of poverty.

Businesses are increasingly recognizing the need for ethical purchasing policies and support of Fairtrade to play a key part in their corporate social responsibility agendas. Retailers and high volume brand names, particularly in the UK, have moved beyond viewing Fairtrade as a marketing opportunity towards a deeper level of commitment. Support for Fairtrade thus forms part of a wider strategy that positions the businesses of these retailers and brand names as supporters of ethical and sustainable initiatives. This presents considerable opportunities for Fairtrade Labelling to increase significantly its engagement with businesses in order to further the interests of marginalized producers.

The *producer-facing* dimension of the Fairtrade Labelling system is generally coordinated through FLO and a network of in-country liaison officers. In the future, the Fairtrade system aims to deliver additional value to producers by enabling them to set their own objectives within the Fairtrade standards, with the role of liaison officers becoming that of supporting producers in achieving these objectives.

An important element of the FTAANZ's producer-facing activities is the function of fostering the regional linkages between producer groups in South East Asia and Oceania. The region must invest in expanding its domestic markets by encouraging small enterprise and village-based economic activity; it needs to develop trade links between the islands; and it should seek to establish niche markets for Pacific-specific products based on accurate information on target export markets. The Fairtrade system is able to address each of these needs. With its broad-based and cross-sectoral membership and its international affiliation with both major fair trade bodies – FLO and IFAT – FTAANZ is working with businesses and NGO partners to promote awareness, to grow the market and to conceive, facilitate and implement producer development and market linkage activities in the region.

Evolution of the Fairtrade Governance Model at the International Level

In order to perform all these functions at the local, regional and international levels, it is important that the Fairtrade Labelling system's own governance system has the institutional capacity to perform these multiple functions efficiently and dynamically in response to changing social and market pressures, as well as to facilitate processes of decision-making that are legitimate and accountable and enable meaningful participation and control to be extended to Fairtrade certified producers and their organizations. As in any complex organizational system, balancing these goals of efficiency and accountability is an ongoing challenge that the international Fairtrade system continues to address.

As part of the Fairtrade Labelling system's wider strategic review process, its own international governance system has been going through a process of high-level review and reform. These reforms are directed towards improving two central goals of the governance system: developing the Fairtrade system's business model and strategic management towards a single global Fairtrade system; and enhancing the system's responsiveness and accountability to agendas and preferences of the marginalized producers themselves.

Before examining the current processes of governance reform, it is useful to review briefly the existing governance arrangements operating within the Fairtrade system at the international level. FLO e.V. operates under a multi-stakeholder governance model that has developed significantly over the last two years. Now an international organization covering most regions of the world, Fairtrade Labelling began with the Max Havalaar Foundation in the Netherlands in the 1980s (FLO 2006). With support from development NGOs such as Solidaridad and Oxfam the Fairtrade Labelling network grew, and similar Fairtrade Labelling Initiatives emerged across mainland Europe, the UK, the United States, Japan and most recently Australia and New Zealand. These involved essentially the same systems and principles, but were branded Max Havalaar, Transfair or Fairtrade depending on the country and the scheme implemented (FLO 2006).

These related but autonomous organizations came together to form FLO in 1997 and have since worked collaboratively to harmonize and standardize the Fairtrade Labelling model into a global system (FLO 2006). The need for harmonization across international markets was deemed necessary to achieve Fairtrade's ambitions of scale and impact. Increased engagement from transnational companies looking for a global Fairtrade product certification system accelerated the process. At the same time, drawn by the success of Fairtrade, other labels entered the market for ethical certification; Fairtrade risked losing market share to less demanding systems such as Rainforest Alliance and Utz Kapeh which were able to offer a single certification for global markets but lacked the development and empowerment aspects of the Fairtrade system. Large industry players began to doubt whether Fairtrade could move to scale and certify the volumes they were working with. Furthermore, both industry and Labelling Initiatives were becoming frustrated with seemingly unnecessary complexities such as individualized licensing agreements, fee structures and labels that were required for different national Fairtrade markets.

At this time, FLO's only members and sole owners were Labelling Initiatives, essentially marketing organizations engaging with mainstream commercial businesses in their individual national markets. The wider fair trade movement was becoming increasingly critical of FLO for becoming overly market-driven, seeming to pander to big business while losing touch with producer interests and its original mission. Conflict with IFAT and the wider fair trade movement reached a peak during the Fairtrade Foundation UK's negotiations with and resulting licensing of 'Brand X' and Fairtrade certification of a single Nestlé coffee product, 'Partners' Blend', in 2006. Cracks were beginning to show in the form of: FLO's threatened split from IFAT as well as the wider fair trade movement; increased competition from other ethical labelling systems with lower standards and easier entry criteria; producers' growing distrust of the intent and direction that market-driven Labelling Initiatives were taking; increasing volume demands from the market; and growing conflict with producers over hired labour plantation production displacing the benefits and market access from the small farmer producers that Fairtrade was initially designed to support.

How then are current processes of governance reform seeking to address these issues to strengthen the system's business model and increase the accountability of its overarching decision-making systems while striking an appropriate balance between the need for grassroots participation and for efficient and dynamic decision-making structures within the organization as a whole?

Bolstering the global business model of the Fairtrade system with a clear strategic direction and agreed objectives is an important way to improve its efficiency and competitiveness as well as to strengthen its capacity to respond flexibly and dynamically to changing market and social trends. Managing the system's rapid market growth while retaining the integrity of its social agenda is one particular challenge these reforms seek to address. The changing role of Fairtrade in the context of rising commodity prices, the threats of climate change, crisis in financial markets and a major global economic turndown is an urgent strategic issue to be tackled.

Another important feature of the Fairtrade system's international governance arrangement is its capacity to extend control to participating producers, thereby entrenching principles of producer empowerment within the system's own internal governance system. The reforms undertaken in recent months have contributed in some significant ways to advancing this goal.

In November 2006, FLO members voted unanimously to adopt a new Constitution that enables networks of Fairtrade certified producers to become full members and co-owners of FLO (FLO 2007). A multi-stakeholder Board of Directors in charge of all matters relating to the association was also established by the new Constitution. The FLO Board now consists of 13 directors selected as representative of Fairtrade Labelling's stakeholder groups. The Board is comprised of five directors nominated by the Labelling Initiative members, four nominated by the Fairtrade certified producer organizations from the producer network members (with at least one each from Latin America, Africa and Asia), two nominated by Fairtrade registered traders and two who are independent of members, traders and producer interests, with a preference for one of these externals to be the chair (see FLO 2008a, 6). Formally, the directors act in the interests of the association as a whole rather than the stakeholders they represent. In practice, however, this is not always possible. The association's governance structure attempts to balance the need for: providing a platform for all stakeholders' involvement; developing clear strategic direction; and delivering the speedy decision-making required to operate in a competitive global environment.

With a new governance structure, increased participation in Fairtrade Labelling governance and standard setting by representatives from Fairtrade certified producer organizations, and an independently-established and ISO65-accredited inspection body, FLO-CERT, in 2007, FLO embarked on an in-depth and widely consultative strategic review process. This review was designed to address the extant problems in the system and, in a consultative and participatory manner, build consensus to determine the future direction and new business model for Fairtrade Labelling globally. This process began with a 'Green Paper' that, through broad consultation, compiled the range of positions and opinions, set out the current state of the association and presented a number of critical issues that needed to be addressed. The Green Paper was finalized and endorsed by the association's General Assembly in May 2007. This was succeeded by a White Paper defining a set of strategic options in relation to the Fairtrade context and critical issues. The contents of this paper were approved by the General Assembly one year later and work progressed in defining a new business model for FLO that would detail a system architecture best able to deliver on the association's agreed strategic objectives.

However beautifully designed a strategy may be, the devil is in the implementation. The new 'FTL Business Model' was presented to the General Assembly in December 2008 with a proposed two year period of change and implementation. The intention of the new model is: to move from a loose association of members with common interests to a single global system of Fairtrade; to progress from a system of certification that is based on control and meeting standards to one that focuses on enabling producer development via empowerment; to broaden, deepen and strengthen impact by scaling up the system; and to be a social enterprise that is a global movement for change, deriving its authority from its ownership and governance structures.

In order to achieve this, the Fairtrade Labelling system needs to design a global governance and financial model that can adequately deliver the ambitions of the business model and can take Fairtrade Labelling into the future. The governance model will need to balance transparency and legitimacy in the decision-making process with the ability to move quickly within a fast-changing market environment. This is particularly relevant given the current crisis in financial markets that will inevitably impact on commodity prices and producer livelihoods. If Fairtrade Labelling can remove unnecessary bureaucracy from its governance systems and set clear strategic objectives with measurable performance indicators rather than attempt to control all the technical aspects of the trade relationship, it is possible that the system can achieve these governance aims. It is important for Fairtrade to continue to empower the producers' position within the governance model in order for producers to become truly active participants rather than the passive beneficiaries of the Fairtrade system.

Conclusions

This chapter has presented a broad overview of some of the most important strategies through which the Fairtrade system tackles the various barriers facing marginalized producers in the developing world who seek to promote processes of development within their communities. The challenges facing agendas of local development were shown to exist at several levels, resulting from features of the local development environment, the international trading system and international aid and development policy.

In response, the Fairtrade system attempts to support and promote the development prospects of marginalized producers by building a multilevel strategic approach that is capable of tackling development obstacles at their roots in each of these levels. The contribution of the Fairtrade system to *local* processes of capacity-building were illustrated with reference to a number of examples from the South Asia and Asia-Pacific regions, in which both enhanced market access and the provision of Fairtrade premiums has enabled producers: to invest in infrastructure and training activities in order to increase their productivity; to develop local entrepreneurial skills and organizational capabilities; and to strengthen democratic governance at the local level.

Such local development processes were shown to be embedded at the *international* level within an overarching structure of Fairtrade markets, supply chains and governance institutions that are themselves based on principles of fairness and producer empowerment. These components of the system serve to build support for Fairtrade products and for broader agendas of trade justice among consumers and a wider public; to strengthen support for, commitment to and participation in Fairtrade markets among supply-chain businesses such as importers, retailers and retail brands; and to reinforce regional linkages between producers that can, in turn, feed positively into both producer development and market linkage activities with particular reference to producers in the Asia-Pacific region.

At all these levels, the Fairtrade system works to develop a joined-up strategy for promoting development – through, rather than in spite of, the international trading system. Forging such an approach often demands a delicate balancing act, not least because the Fairtrade system faces multiple constraints from features of the global political economy that are beyond its reach, such as competitive pressures in global markets and protectionist policies in many countries that import the products of developing country farmers. While, on the one hand, the Fairtrade system can seek to circumvent or substitute for failings in the 'mainstream' trading system, there are, on the other hand, some ways in which it is forced to operate within the constraints imposed by this wider environment.

It is within the context of this extensive challenge that it is possible to best understand the central logic of the Fairtrade Labelling system's strategic approach: the advancement of a joined-up approach to development and trade justice which attempts to embed goals of poverty reduction, social development and democratic governance at the centre of the international trading system, and thereby to help realize the full potential of the international trading system to promote agendas of both economic development and social justice. The Fairtrade Labelling system's new business model is designed with this ambition: to take Fairtrade firmly into the mainstream with the scale and integrity to redefine global business objectives in order to achieve broad-reaching development and empowerment through trade.

References

Bio Foods (Pvt.) Ltd (2008), *Bio Foods (Pvt.) Ltd – Sri Lanka: Producers*. [Online: Bio Foods (Pvt.) Ltd]. Available at: http://www.biofoodslk.com/sofa.html [accessed: 28 April 2009].

Center for Global Development (CGD) (2009), *Commitment to Development Index 2008*. [Online: CGD]. Available at: http://www.cgdev.org/section/initiatives/_active/cdi/ [accessed: 27 April 2009].

Commission on the Private Sector and Development (CPSD) (2004), *Unleashing Entrepreneurship: Making Business Work for the Poor*. Report to the Secretary-General of the United Nations (New York: United Nations Development Programme).

Department for International Development (United Kingdom) (DFID) et al. (2002), *Linking Poverty Reduction and Environmental Management: Policy Challenges and Opportunities* (Washington, DC: International Bank for Reconstruction and Development and World Bank).

Fair Trade Association of Australia and New Zealand (FTAANZ) (2008), *Fairtrade Development in Papua New Guinea: Linking Producers in Asia Pacific with Traders in Australia and New Zealand*, Fairtrade Feasibility Study in PNG (Australia and New Zealand: FTAANZ).

—— and Fairtrade Labelling Australia and New Zealand (FLANZ) (2007), *Annual Report 2006/7* (Australia and New Zealand: FTAANZ).

Fairtrade Foundation (2007), *Mountain Fruits, Pakistan*. [Online: Fairtade Foundation]. Available at: http://www.fairtrade.org.uk/producers/dried_fruit/mountain_fruits_pakistan/ [accessed: 27 April 2009].

Fairtrade Labelling Australia and New Zealand (FLANZ) (2009), *Retail Fairtrade Sales Figures* (Melbourne: FLANZ).

Fairtrade Labelling Organizations International (FLO) (2006), *FLO International: About Fair Trade*. [Online: FLO]. Available at: http://www.fairtrade.net/about_fairtrade.html [accessed: 29 April 2009].

—— (2007), *Annual Report 2006/07: Shaping Global Partnerships* (Bonn: FLO).

—— (2008a), *Annual Report 2007: An Inspiration for Change* (Bonn: FLO).

—— (2008b), *FTL Strategic Review White Paper, Emerging Business Model – Next Steps*, presentation to FLO General Assembly, 23 May 2008.

—— (2008c), *Strategic Review White Paper* (Bonn: FLO).

International Fund for Agricultural Development (IFAD) (2001), *Rural Poverty Report 2001: The Challenge of Ending Rural Poverty* (Oxford: Oxford University Press).

Liberation (no date), *Liberation Nuts: About Us*. [Online: Liberation]. Available at: http://www.chooseliberation.com/about_us/ [accessed: 28 April 2009].

Moxie Design Group Limited (2008), *An Overview on the Growing Global Market and Consumer Base for Sustainable Products and Services* (Wellington: Moxie Design Group Limited).

New Zealand Agency for International Development (NZAID) (2003), *Harnessing International Trade for Development* (Wellington: NZAID).

Samath, F. (2007), 'Lankan speaks to the world on small farmers', *The Sunday Times (Sri Lanka)*, 4 November 2007. Available at: http://sundaytimes.lk/071104/FinancialTimes/ft339.html [accessed: 28 April 2009].

Tomy Mathews from Kerala, India, Talks about Liberation and Fairtrade (2008). [Video]. (London: Liberation Foods CIC). Available from: http://www.youtube.com/user/LiberationFoods [accessed: 28 April 2009].

Trade Aid (2008), *Trade Aid Annual Review 2007/08* (Christchurch: Trade Aid).

United Nations Framework Convention on Climate Change (UNFCCC) (2007), *Vulnerability and Adaptation to Climate Change in Small Island Developing States: Background Paper for the Expert Meeting on Adaptation for Small Island Developing States* (Bonn: Secretariat of the UNFCCC). Available at: http://unfccc.int/files/adaptation/adverse_effects_and_response_measures_art_48/application/pdf/200702_sids_adaptation_bg.pdf [accessed: 27 April 2009].

United Nations Office of the High Representative for the Least Developed Countries, Landlocked Developing Countries and Small Island Developing States (UN-OHRLLS) (2009), *List of Small Island Developing States*. [Online: UN-OHRLLS]. Available at: http://www.un.org/special-rep/ohrlls/sid/list.htm [accessed: 28 April 2009].

Women in Business Development Inc. (WIBDI) (2008), *About WIBDI: Introduction*. [Online: WIBDI]. Available at: http://www.womeninbusiness.ws/About/tabid/2871/language/en-US/Default.aspx [accessed 28 April 2009].

World Bank (2001), *Global Economic Prospects and the Developing Countries 2001* (Washington, DC: International Bank for Reconstruction and Development and World Bank).

—— (2002), *Globalization, Growth, and Poverty: Building an Inclusive World Economy*, Policy Research Report (Washington, DC: International Bank for Reconstruction and Development and World Bank).

—— (2007), *World Development Report 2008: Agriculture for Development* (Washington, DC: International Bank for Reconstruction and Development and World Bank).

Chapter 3
Developing Markets, Building Networks: Promoting Fair Trade in Asia

Claribel B. David and Hyun-Seung Anna Kim

Mixing business with community development is a formidable task, but to the poor of Asia, Africa and Latin America it provides an accessible way to enjoy fuller meals, keep girls and boys in school, and replace rusty kerosene lamps.

Self-help economic activities – including the production and export of handicrafts and food items – started in the 1940s and continue to address issues of joblessness and insufficient income suffered by members of blighted agricultural and urban communities in many underdeveloped economies. Such economic activities have had a significant impact on the quality of life experienced by thousands of households and communities at varying stages of development.

Sustained over five decades, these small, community-based livelihood projects have, as a matter of practical necessity, bonded together to become major players in a movement known as 'fair trade', which has become an important strategy in the struggle against poverty. The slogan 'TRADE NOT AID' expresses the core conviction propelling the fair trade movement: it seeks to create *independence* rather than the dependency that can emerge as a major weakness of aid programmes.

The fair trade market has emerged as an alternative global market that brings together disadvantaged producers in developing countries and traders and other buyers in developed countries. Today, it is estimated that 7.5 million people in Africa, Asia and Latin America benefit from fair trade (FLO 2008). These include producers and farmers organized in smallholdings, as well as homeworkers and workers in the informal sector – that is, in small and medium enterprises, tea estates and plantations. Fair trade producers work in partnership with more than 200 importing organizations in Europe, to develop and sell products to consumers through more than 2,800 World Shops and 56,000 supermarkets (Krier 2005). There are also more than 150 organizations conducting fair trade business in North America and the Pacific Rim, including both non-profit and for-profit companies (FTF 2005). In Europe alone, more than 100,000 volunteers are involved in fair trading operations, most of whom are within the World Shop network (Krier 2001).

Throughout the history of fair trade, Asia has been viewed primarily as a producing region, supplying food products and crafts to the global fair trade market. With over 650 million people living on less than one dollar per day (World Bank 2007) and 882 million undernourished people in this region (Asia 2015 2006), the image of poor producers in Asia has been easily marketed to the affluent, well-educated and ethical consumers in the geopolitical North. Mirroring this is the common representation of fair trade as a system of trading relation between the global North and the South. According to this view, fair trade essentially involves 'the option of paying higher prices for imported goods so that developing world producers can have a decent standard of living' (Witkowski 2005, 22).

However, examples of domestic fair trade markets can be found both within the North (Crowell 2006; Crowell and Sligh 2006; Jaffee, Kloppenburg and Monroy 2004) and within the South

(Jaffee, Kloppenburg and Monroy 2004; Redfern and Snedker 2002). Attempts to explore South–South fair trade opportunities have also taken place in Asia, Africa and Latin America (Otero 2007; Redfern and Snedker 2002). In Asia, a fair trade market exists in a number of countries including Bangladesh, India, South Korea, Hong Kong, Singapore, Taiwan, Vietnam and the Philippines (Kim 2007), generating a number of success stories, some of which will be discussed further below (see also Quelch and Laidler 2003; Redfern and Snedker 2002). In addition to extending market opportunities to economically disadvantaged producers, new market development in Asia has broader implications for the concept of fair trade (Kim 2007).

During the past few years, a number of fair trade organizations have begun developing both domestic and international fair trade markets in Asia, as well as providing support to producers in the region. While not separate objectives given that the ultimate goal of new market development is providing opportunities for producers, this new approach has generated some distinctive fair trade activities in the region, such as consumer awareness campaigns to promote fair trade in domestic markets.

This chapter examines the evolution of both the domestic and international dimensions of fair trade activities in Asia, focusing particularly on the potential benefits of these approaches as means of leveraging a broader impact. This chapter has three main objectives. First, it seeks to demonstrate that domestic and regional approaches to fair trade can represent an effective market development strategy by localizing 'marketing mix'[1] and taking advantage of the geographical proximity between producers and consumers. Second, it aims to present the unique developmental impacts of domestic and regional fair trade in Asia resulting from the system's intensive support for the craft sector, as well as the closer forms of producer participation that it offers. Finally, the chapter attempts to highlight the role of domestic and regional fair trade networks in realizing these opportunities. The evolution of domestic and international fair trade activities in the Asian region are discussed in turn, followed by analysis of the specific case studies of the Asia Fair Trade Forum (AFTF) and a related set of country networks in Asia.

Domestic Fair Trade in Asia

Domestic fair trade markets in the Asian region can be found in a number of producing countries in Asia, including Bangladesh, India, the Philippines, Nepal, Sri Lanka, Vietnam, Bhutan and Thailand.[2] For example, Bangladesh has developed a considerably large domestic fair trade market; 35 per cent of the country's annual fair trade turnover derives from its domestic market (ECOTA 2006). The fair trade organization Aarong is a particularly well-known success story with its Tk 1.7 billion (US$24.7 million) turnover (BRAC 2007), but there are many more Bangladeshi fair trade organizations engaged in domestic activities, including Kumudini Handicraft, Heed Bangladesh, Aranya Crafts Ltd, Mennonite Central Committee and YWCA Craft Centre. The domestic sales proportions of a selection of Bangladeshi fair trade organizations are presented in Table 3.1.

---

1   'The set of marketing tools the firm uses to pursue its marketing objectives' (Kotler and Keller 2006, 19). McCarthy identified four major parts of a marketing mix, known as 'four Ps': Product, Place, Promotion and Price (Perreault and McCarthy 2005). There are also different classifications of marketing variables, for example 'Seven Ps' of services marketing (Booms and Bitner 1981).

2   In this chapter, the domestic fair trade market is defined as a market where fair trade goods and services produced in one country are sold to consumers in the same country.

Table 3.1   Bangladeshi fair trade organizations engaged in domestic activities

Organization	Number of artisans	Proportion of sales by market	
		Export market	**Domestic market**
Aranya Crafts Ltd	250	25%	75%
BRAC – Aarong	36,000	6%	94%
Charka Handicrafts	700–800	40%	60%
Folk International	200	30%	70%
GUP Batik and Handicrafts	300	20%	80%
Heed Bangladesh	11,000	90%	10%
Kumudini Handicraft	25,000	40%	60%
Mennonite Central Committee	900	93%	7%
Polle Unnayan Prokolpo (PUP)	476	20%	80%
Young Power in Social Action (YPSA)	50	0%	100%
YWCA Craft Centre	450	90%	10%

Source: ECOTA 2006.

Although domestic fair trade is still a fledgling concept in other Asian countries, noteworthy initiatives have emerged – most notably in India and the Philippines. For example, 'Making Trade Work for the Poor: Promoting Fair Trade in India (PROFIT)' is an ongoing project initiated in early 2006 in partnership with International Resources for Fairer Trade in India, Traidcraft UK, the EU and Belgian Technical Cooperation. PROFIT aims to launch fair trade products in Mumbai and Hyderabad with its own fair trade label 'Shop for Change' in 2009. This will be an important test for the future of domestic fair trade in India. In the Philippines, the organization Advocate of Philippine Fair Trade, Inc. is leading a consumer awareness campaign (CITEM 2007), while generating 30 per cent of its sales from the domestic market through its trading arm, Filipinas Fair Trade Ventures Circle Inc. (Kim 2007).

The following discussion analyses the strategies through which these organizations have sought to develop domestic fair trade markets in Asia, offering localized products with locally adapted messages to target consumers. It also identifies intervening factors which mediate the success of such strategies. Geographical proximity between producers and consumers is particularly significant, leading in some cases to innovative pricing and distribution models able to appeal to a wider public – including low-income consumers. This analysis also outlines the potential benefits of developing a domestic fair trade market for small producers and artisans in this region, by supporting the craft sector, expanding the fair trade market and thereby creating more opportunities for producers.

Products – Supporting the Craft Sector in Asia

The Asian region is a major supplier of crafts for the global fair trade market. Approximately 80 per cent of the fair trade products sold in Asian countries are non-food items (Kim 2007).[3] There is almost no other fair trade product category apart from handicrafts in Bangladesh and the Bangladesh-based ECOTA Fair Trade Forum[4] explicitly focuses on crafts only. Handicrafts also

---

3   In contrast, global fair trade sales are highly dominated by food items (Nicholls and Opal 2005).

4   A national fair trade networking body. ECOTA stands for 'Effort for Craft Organizations Trading Advancement'.

command the largest share in the Philippine market, comprising over 80 per cent of sales and far overwhelming sales of food items such as dried fruits and fruit juice (Kim 2007). In the Indian market, while special attention has been given to the huge potential of fair trade tea in the domestic market, textiles and non-food items also play a significant role in ongoing pilots.

Although the impressive growth of the global fair trade market in recent years can be attributed largely to the food sector, the handicraft sector has unique economic and social significance. Handicraft producers and artisans are mostly homeworkers operating in informal economies where wages and incomes are low, working conditions are difficult and social benefits are almost non-existent. Many of these artisans are women; due to their lack of education and capital, these female artisans often rely on craftwork as one of the few viable options for income generation. Furthermore, craftwork is compatible with their domestic responsibilities because they can engage in production at home while taking care of their children. Research shows that craft participation often has a positive impact on women's empowerment, particularly at the household level (Littrell and Dickson 1999). For producers who are primarily engaged in farming, craftwork provides a much-needed supplemental income between planting and harvesting seasons. As such, craft production remains a practical strategy for poverty alleviation.

It can be argued that the current product mix has emerged in response to supply-side driven initiatives rather than reflecting the requirements of local market demand. However, some examples demonstrate the success of such products in domestic Asian markets: for example, fair trade handicrafts have successfully penetrated the Bangladeshi market, where they are positioned as cultural products which support traditional skills and the 'spirit' of Bangladesh. The importance of the optimal product mix attracting local consumers has also been recognized by those such as the PROFIT team in India, who have considered a wider range of product lines – from tea and textiles to rice, coffee, jams and marmalades – in order to meet various consumer needs and maximize the effects of advertising and promotion.

By providing opportunities to support the craft sector effectively, the current product mix in domestic Asian fair trade markets appears to be a very promising marketing proposition, capable of generating additional benefits for small producers and artisans in Asia.

Pricing – Fair Trade at the Base of the Pyramid?

As is also often the case in the Northern market, fair trade products are sold at a premium price in many domestic markets in Asia; they are considerably more expensive than mainstream products in Bangladesh and around 30 per cent more expensive than low-end, non-fair trade products in the Philippines (Kim 2007). This significantly limits their target customer group to middle- or upper-middle-income consumers. The high price is due mainly to a lack of economies of scale and is therefore sometimes regarded as inevitable in the context of current sales levels.

However, innovative approaches exist for marketing fair trade products at competitive prices, such as direct farmer-consumer sales models in India. The 'Just Change' group trades in tea, rice, pepper, coconut oil and soap by directly linking communities such as the Orissa farmers, Tamil Nadu Adivasis and Kerala women's credit unions (Thekaekara 2006). In Tamil Nadu, the 'Uzhavar Sandhai' (farmers' market) system supplies vegetables and fruits to local consumers at an affordable price through direct sales while ensuring a fair price for producers (Kallummal and Srinivasan

2007). If this strategy proves to be scalable, fair trade products can potentially be offered to a much wider consumer pool, including consumers at the base of the economic pyramid (BoP).[5]

It is too early to predict whether this model is feasible on a larger scale; at present the boundary of direct sales is often limited geographically in order to be cost-effective for local organizations. Nevertheless, such initiatives serve to explore the possibility of fair trade products delivering benefits for both poor consumers and poor producers. Experience to date suggests that further exploration of the base of the pyramid fair trading strategies, comprising direct sales, effective supply-chain management and innovative distribution channels, is a potentially fruitful strategy to be further explored in Southern markets.

Distribution Channels – Challenges and Opportunities

The eight outlets and a large number of retail shops established by the fair trade organization Aarong stand testament as one of the most successful examples of fair trade distribution channels established in a domestic fair trade market. Other Bangladeshi and Indian organizations operate shops in large cities. However, it can be very difficult and expensive for fair trade organizations to serve a large number of customers through purely their own retail shop networks. Developing multiple distribution channels is a considerable challenge for many domestic market players.

There are ongoing attempts to establish multiple channels, by engaging mainstream players in the private sector or by exploring new channels including on-line sales. Although it may be more challenging to supply handicrafts or textiles to mainstream retailers compared with food items, some of the traditional retailers in this region are gradually engaging with fair trade. One Indian fashion retailer[6] with over 80 Indian and a few international stores, is interested in fair trade clothing and fashion crafts as well as exploring a potential partnership with the Shop for Change project. Asia Fair Trade Forum is also actively supporting the development of e-commerce within its member organizations.

Another potential opportunity is increased cooperation with other social initiatives. In many South Asian and South East Asian countries, a large number of poverty alleviation and development programmes interact with each other. For example, Aarong is a trading arm of the Bangladesh Rural Advancement Committee (BRAC), the largest NGO in Bangladesh with a huge microfinance initiative. Therefore, fair trade and microfinance programmes are integrated into their operation and fair trade producer groups are supported by 'advance credit'. This kind of partnership can create positive synergy effects, including the development of innovative local distribution channels. Many NGOs have a broad outreach in rural areas through their programmes, which could be re-organized as direct distribution networks. Successful examples of direct distribution in rural areas can be found from some private sector companies targeting the base of the pyramid market (Prahalad 2004). Likewise, Grameen Bank borrowers demonstrated that they can be valuable customers for each other's small businesses (Bornstein 1997). In addition to developing corporate partnership and government support, collaboration within the social sector needs to be considered and actively encouraged.

---

5   In this chapter, the 'base of the pyramid (BoP)' refers to the four billion people living on less than two dollars per day. The market potential at the base of the pyramid has been examined in the management literature, including: Prahalad (2004); Prahalad and Hart (2002); and Hart (2007).

6   The names of specific companies are not disclosed in this chapter, because ongoing discussions between fair trade organizations and such companies have not yet led to specific partnership agreements.

Promotion – Locally Adopted Messages and the Notion of 'Fairness'

The key messages used to promote fair trade products in the domestic market are often very different from the messages used in advanced economies. Fair trade handicrafts have been associated with the cultural identity in Bangladesh, while 'Buy Local, Buy Fair' is the campaigning slogan in the Philippines. Overall, domestic marketing tends to focus on supporting local businesses and the high quality of fair trade products, rather than directly highlighting issues of poverty.

Furthermore, findings of consumer research in Bangladesh, India and the Philippines suggest that local consumers may perceive the notions of 'fairness' differently from many Northern consumers. For example, after decades of numerous aid and development programmes in India, few people are genuinely excited about the idea of poverty alleviation itself; issues of poverty commonly receive attitudes of cynicism, scepticism and indifference. Indian consumers tend to respond much more strongly to specific issues, such as child labour. In response to this recognition, campaigns by 'Shop for Change' have focused on specific issues and tangible outcomes.

In addition, consumers in many Asian countries pay significant attention to fairness for consumers as well as for producers, for example in health-related environmental issues. While factors such as these have also been part of the fair trade message in many Northern markets, consumers in Asian producing countries tend to express greater concern about a wide range of product attributes and are unwilling to compromise fairness for consumers for the sake of fairness for producers (APFTI 2005; IRFT 2005).

Regional Fair Trade in Asia

Despite Asia's relatively small share in the global fair trade market, three types of international fair trade can be observed in this region. First, some fair trade products are sourced from developing countries throughout the world and sold in Asian buying countries – for example, Peruvian coffee in Singapore. Second, a fair trade market exists between buying countries and producing countries in Asia, such as banana chips produced in the Philippines and sold in Hong Kong. Third, an initiative known as South–South fair trade has developed fair trading links between producing countries in Asia, such as handicrafts made in Sri Lanka and sold in India.

The focus of this section lies on the second and third cases, as inter-country but intra-regional fair trade. However, these activities, especially the first and second forms, are often integrated and complementary in practice. With a few exceptions of organizations wholly dedicated to regional fair trade, most fair trade organizations in Asian buying countries deliberately market products sourced from different regions. This is partly because of the promotional benefits, but primarily due to the complementary product features, such as consumer interest in coffee or crafts from different cultures. Thus the purpose of this analysis is not to argue for the superiority of exclusively regional fair trade, but rather to recognize the potential *additional* benefits of these activities, ranging from building a closer relationship and increasing operational efficiency to creating an attractive consumer proposition by offering localized products and promoting the development of neighbour countries.

Emerging Buying Countries and Regional Partnerships

Japan has a relatively long history of fair trade going back to the early 1990s, and is the only Fairtrade Labelling Organizations (FLO) member country in Asia. However, since the early 2000s, fair trade markets have been developed in a number of emerging buying countries, namely Hong Kong, Singapore, South Korea and Taiwan. As mentioned above, fair trade products sold in these countries are not exclusively sourced from Asian producers, but some particularly well-developed partnerships between buyer and producer organizations have arisen in Asia.

One example of this is the partnership between three organizations, Nepali Bazaro in Japan, Beautiful Store in South Korea and a coffee producers' cooperative in Gulmi district, Nepal. Nepali Bazaro is a specialized fair trade producer development body, having organized, supported and monitored 52 producer groups in Nepal for the last 20 years. It is wholly dedicated to its exclusive partnership arrangement with Nepalese organizations; most members speak Nepali and visit Nepal once a month.

When Beautiful Store, a well-known NGO and a pioneer of fair trade in South Korea, decided to launch the fair trade coffee product line, it did not have the capacity to develop a new partnership with producers. Nepali Bazaro – which in fact had an oversupply of coffee beans at that time – therefore assisted by linking Beautiful Store with their partner in Gulmi district. In 2006, Beautiful Store launched a fair trade coffee brand 'A gift from the Himalayas' in the Korean market. Producers in Nepal now supply beans to both Korean and Japanese organizations at a fair price, and 10 per cent of revenue from the sales of 'A gift from the Himalayas' funds development projects for producers (Kim 2007).[7]

Although the success of this partnership cannot be attributed solely to geographical factors, it suggests some additional benefits to intra-regional strategies of networking, especially as a basis for facilitating communications and building close relationships. Direct contact between organizations in order to coordinate and finance is simpler; the smaller time difference existing at the regional level facilitates real-time phone and email communications. Arguably, the one-country focus of Nepali Bazaro enables this organization to build a partnership based on greater understanding, mutual respect and human relationships, such as that enabled by the learning of a local language. Similarly, there are other examples of Asian fair trade organizations adopting a strategic focus on a specific country, such as the Japan–Bangladesh Cultural Exchange Association. Such regional fair trade approaches may bring opportunities to expand the scope of fair trade markets while maintaining a human face.

Operational efficiency may also be increased through regional trade. For example, in theory, shipping costs should be lower in regional markets compared to those in global markets. In practice this is not always the case due to the low volume of trade in regional markets. Nevertheless, in many cases the development of domestic and regional markets enables such opportunities to be effectively captured to the extent that they are available.

Another important aspect of intra-regional fair trade is its distinctive implications for consumers, as compared with inter-regional fair trade. It is difficult to evaluate whether consumers have different perceptions about products from Asian countries compared with those from Africa or Latin America. Some may perceive them equally – simply as fair trade products from poor countries, however, this may not always be the case and important lessons can be learned from monitoring the market's reaction. For example, the experience of Oxfam Hong Kong demonstrates that people in Hong Kong tend to respond strongly to the plight of those in mainland China. Accordingly, a number of initiatives to market Chinese fair trade products such as tea and handicrafts have been developed in Hong Kong. Similarly, in response to the special concerns of many South Korean people for poverty in North Korea, the organization Korea Food for the Hungry International is now selling fair trade soya bean paste and soy sauce produced in North Korea Korea (*Kyung Hyang* 2008).

---

7   Choong-Seop Shin, email communication, 4 February 2009.

In addition, the close partnership between buying organizations and producing organizations in the same region may provide opportunities for localized product offerings.[8] In Hong Kong, most fair trade products are currently imported from European fair trade companies (such as Cafédirect, Traidcraft and Clipper), giving rise to potential problems in matching consumer tastes between the two regions. In contrast, Fair-and-Healthy and its Philippine producer partner have developed Ginger Chews for the Hong Kong market; this has now become a star product among their sales items (Becker 2006). Furthermore, the direct and close relationship between such organizations strengthens the fair trade message, enabling greater emphasis on the issue of respect for producers, as is evident from the name of the coffee product in South Korea: 'A gift from the Himalayas'.

The location of the producer organization is unlikely to be the critical decision-making factor for many fair trade organizations in Asian buying countries – its additional benefits should not be over-exaggerated. Yet there remains significant value in recognizing and further exploring such models in order to better realize the potential benefits of such regional activities.

South–South Fair Trade to Create Win–Win Scenarios

Another notable initiative in this region is international fair trade between producing countries, also known as South–South fair trade. It is probably the least developed form of the fair trade market at the present time, but its potential as a means to expand the whole fair trade market has been recognized by a range of observers (Redfern and Snedker 2002; Nicholls and Opal 2005; Otero 2007). One example of such an initiative is the fair trade shop 'Karigar' in Mumbai, operated by Asha Handicrafts, which sells crafts from the Philippines and Sri Lanka. Likewise, Viator Bangladesh has a trading partnership with a Nepali organization, and Bangladeshi textile producers import organic cotton from India. All of these are very small initiatives, but have the potential to be explored fruitfully further. Above all, they demonstrate the importance of finding and promoting complementary products.

Fair trade organizations and networks such as the AFTF (discussed in greater detail in the following section) have invested significant efforts in exploring opportunities for South–South fair trade. To develop the international fair trade market in Asia, the role of regional networks is of particular importance. In addition to a positive impact on market growth, such networks can have some influence over regional trade policy. As the market develops over time, the AFTF may well be able to play a more active role in this area as a collective voice.

Reconciling the Tension between Local Support and International Fair Trade

Tensions between different ethical consumption initiatives – such as organic food, fair trade food and local food – exist in many international markets, reflecting competitive dynamics that often characterize the relationship between these differing schemes. For example, the argument for encouraging consumer purchases of local foods – often in place of competing products sourced

---

8   The importance of local and regional approaches has been emphasized in the marketing literature, although not in the context of fair trade. One outstanding argument can be found in the term 'Glorecalization' – that is, Globalization of Value, Regionalization of Strategy and Localization of Tactic. This picture of Consistent Global Value (Brand, Service and Process), Coordinated Regional Strategy (Segmentation, Targeting and Positioning) and Customized Local Tactic (Differentiation, Marketing Mix and Selling) is certainly applicable to fair trade marketing in Asia, by offering localized marketing mix based on the regional positioning strategy, while maintaining the global value of fair trade. For more details and examples of 'Glorecalization', see Kotler, Kartajaya and Huan (2006).

internationally within the fair trade system – has received significant support from many concerned with the issue of 'food miles' and related concerns for the environment and local farmers (*Economist* 2006).

Such conflicts between local producer and international fair trade markets are likewise present in Asia. The issue has been particularly prominent in South Korea, where local farmers are widely perceived as a marginalized group in Korean society and the victims of globalization and free trade (see, for example, Vidal and Munk 2003). One newspaper editorial criticized the fair trade movement in South Korea, remarking: 'our country's farmers are experiencing major difficulties … and their plight is no less important than that of Third World producers' (*Hankyoreh* 2007).

Although most South Korean fair trade organizations import food consisting of ingredients which cannot be grown on the Korean peninsula, such as coffee, sugar and olive oil, there are some cooperatives or other organizations that fundamentally oppose all sorts of imported foods. The arguments of such groups are often presented in highly emotional terms. The issue is also important in the context of South–South trade, as many fair trade organizations and the public in producing countries are deeply concerned about local development and therefore the idea of importation may not be welcomed.

However, examples of functioning cooperation between these different initiatives do exist. For example, Doo-rae Co-operatives in South Korea promotes a wide range of local food products but also imports fair trade food items if they cannot be grown in Korea, such as sugar and olive oil (Kim 2007). Fairtrade.sg in Singapore also promotes buying local if possible and buying fair trade if not (Fairtrade.sg 2006). Beautiful Store launched coffee cookies, in partnership with 'We Can', a social enterprise which employs the disabled. This project aims to support both local producers and coffee producers in Nepal, by using Korean ingredients (flour, eggs and butter) in combination with imported coffee.

These initiatives have important implications for the expansion of the fair trade concept and have the potential to appeal more strongly to customers in Asian markets. Moreover, if other conditions remain the same, a regional approach is likely to provide an effective basis for reconciling tensions between support for local producers and for the international fair trade system.

The Asia Fair Trade Forum (AFTF)[9]

Mindful of the various considerations discussed above – in particular the desire to support the craft sector and develop fair trade in Asia – a group of Asian fair trade producers, traders and business support organizations banded together in March 2001 to form the Asia Fair Trade Forum, an NGO network aiming to contribute to the sustainable development of disadvantaged producers in the region by offering market access, creating a platform for skills development, technology transfer and access to information, and promoting fair trade practice in the region.

---

9   This chapter focuses primarily on IFAT organizations in Asia (AFTF and its members), rather than FLO members and their network in this region (Network of Asian Producers; NAP), for several reasons. First, AFTF has implemented a wide range of activities since its inception in 2001 (Rao 2008), whereas NAP was founded in 2005, only became a full member of FLO in 2007 and is therefore currently at an early stage of its development (NAP 2007; FLO 2008). Second, AFTF has been more active in promoting domestic and international fair trade in the Asian market, which is the focus of this chapter. However, it is worth noting that NAP is currently planning various activities in this region, including market development in Asian countries.

Presently, the AFTF has a membership roster of 95 social enterprises, cooperatives and confederations from 14 countries: Bangladesh, Cambodia, China, India, Laos, Nepal, the Philippines, Indonesia, Sri Lanka, Thailand, Vietnam, Timor Leste, Pakistan and South Korea.[10] Ninety per cent of members are in the craft sector and 10 per cent are small food producers.[11] These members in turn work with thousands of grassroots artisans, workers and farmers. The AFTF was the first regional chapter of IFAT – now the World Fair Trade Organization[12] – which is a global network of Fair Trade organizations in Africa, Asia, Latin America, Europe, North America and the Pacific Rim.

This section examines key achievements and challenges of the AFTF, paying particular attention to the Forum's efforts to develop domestic and regional fair trade activities. The AFTF and other fair trade networks have played a significant role in developing fair trade in Asia, where there is very little direct involvement from the mainstream private sector or the government.

Core Programmes and Achievements – Market Access, Capacity-building and Advocacy

In order to support small producers and artisans in Asia, the AFTF operates three core programmes: market access; capacity-building; and advocacy. The scope of these programmes is not limited to promoting fair trade markets within Asia. Through its capacity-building programmes – including activities ranging from product development and design training to e-commerce workshops – the AFTF aims to upgrade the competency of fair trade companies in Asia to compete in both global and regional markets. However, some of the Forum's programmes particularly address the goal of market development in Asia – this is especially true in the case of market access and advocacy.

Exemplary of a market access programme, the Asia Fair Trade Pavilion links producers with mainstream buyers through the participation of both in a range of trade fairs located in the Asian region. This initiative represents a valuable opportunity to present an exciting blend of fair trade products from different Asian countries in one marketplace, and therefore to give fair trade products visibility in the Asian mainstream market.

Likewise, the Asia Fair Trade Pavilion has been participating annually since 2002 at the Bangkok International Gift Fair (BIG). This has enabled its members to expand their client base – which has traditionally been concentrated in Europe and North America – to include commercial buyers from countries in the Asian region such as Japan, South Korea, Thailand and Singapore. In December 2005, the AFTF jointly organized the Hong Kong Fair Trade Fair and Symposium, coordinated parallel to the WTO Hong Kong Ministerial Conference and attracting attention from a large number of Hong Kong residents as well as WTO delegations from around the world. In 2007, the Pavilion participated for the first time in a food exhibition as part of the Hong Kong Food Festival.

Participating in trade fairs enables the AFTF members to create new buyer contacts, book sales orders, assess competition and obtain a better overall feel of the market. Equally important, the

---

10   Source, http://www.asiafairtradeforum.com/EN/ournetwork.html [accessed: 15 November 2008]. The latest information on the number of member organizations was checked through email communication between Anna Kim and Maiden R. Manzanal, Regional Program Manager at Asia Fair Trade Forum, 24 November 2008.

11   Eighty-five members are currently working on non-food items and 10 organizations are working on food products (Maiden R. Manzanal, email communication, 24 November 2008).

12   IFAT (formerly International Fair Trade Association) changed its name at the Annual General Meeting in October 2008. Source: http://www.ifat.org/index.php?option=com_content&task=view&id=863 &Itemid=1 [accessed: 15 November 2008].

Asia Pavilion operates as a powerful advocacy tool for creating awareness of fair trade among commercial buyers and consumers. When selling products, the members tell powerful stories about how fair trade puts food on the table and sends children to school.

AFTF is also running specialized advocacy programmes to promote fair trade in the Asia region. Traditionally, fair trade has been export-oriented – Southern producers exporting to Northern buyers. However, the AFTF is committed to realizing the potential of developing domestic markets for fair trade, and to the related goal of promoting South–South trade. This is evident from such AFTF projects as its 'Consumer Campaign to Develop Domestic Markets for Fair Trade in Asia', launched in October 2005, in the Philippines in partnership with the Philippine Fair Trade Forum (see AFTF 2005). Further, through the unique networking opportunities enabled by trade fairs, the AFTF is building partnerships with other like-minded organizations that perform advocacy work in their countries. For example, the 2005 Hong Kong Fair Trade Fair generated a significant level of interest amongst local residents, leading Oxfam Hong Kong to develop a joint project with the AFTF entitled 'Tapping the Potential of Fair Trade in Hong Kong'. Together, they have successfully sponsored two conferences, with the participation of the local business sector, and have collaborated on a consumer awareness campaign in Hong Kong, drawing on Oxfam Hong Kong's impressive campaign capability.

The AFTF's capacity-building programme likewise aims to support producers in their efforts to compete in a global marketplace – including, but not limited to, Asian markets. Its particular focus on the craft sector, exemplified by *inter alia* its provision of design training, further illustrates the capability of regional networks in meeting specific needs confronting a region. Through the Asia Fair Trade Centre for Learning, a resource centre created in 2003, the AFTF has also run business scans, trainings and workshops on a diverse range of topics such as product development and design, financial planning and management information systems (marketing planning and e-commerce).

Governance – Heeding the Voice of Producers

The highest decision-making body in the AFTF is the Annual General Assembly of members that approves constitutional matters and strategic directions. The Governing Board, composed of nine country representatives, is the Forum's policy making body and is responsible for the overall management of AFTF affairs. Members in each individual country elect their representatives, who in turn elect from among their country's ranks a set of officers. A small secretariat is based in the Philippines and implements AFTF programmes and activities.

Compared with the global fair trade networks, often driven by Northern organizations and composed of only a limited amount of Southern representation, the AFTF provides a strong basis for producers' involvement in governance. Yet this heavy focus on the participation of producer organizations may hinder some buyer organizations in their efforts to join the network. This issue must be further open to adaptation, in order to find a balance between producer participation and organizational effectiveness that is appropriate to the current role of the AFTF, particularly as it works to manage its ongoing processes of development. As the AFTF grows in terms of both membership and the complexity of its programmes, an appropriate governance and leadership structure must evolve that is strong and dynamic, whilst also democratic and transparent.

Overcoming Challenges – Towards a Network of Networks

In the midst of its achievements, the AFTF faces considerable hurdles. In addition to the challenge of managing the Forum's increasing number of members, the large disparity in the size of members raises difficulties in promoting the interest of all member parties. For example, the organization needs to bring its stronger members to trade fairs – who are ready to meet the demands of the mainstream market – together with the small members who are only beginning to build capacity.

In some respects, however, such disparities can also offer opportunities for the creation of synergies among members in order to upscale production capacity. Significant factors contributing to the weak market competitiveness of fair trade craft producers are low production capacities and high production costs. Yet because the Forum's various members export individually to common markets, an opportunity exists for the AFTF to provide a platform for members to work together for the purpose of creating synergies and economies of scale.

The goal of promoting such synergies is high on the AFTF agenda. As a method to address this challenge, the AFTF is supporting and cooperating with other fair trade networks in Asia. In particular, strengthening country networks is essential in meeting the logistical requirement of delivering services region-wide. The country networks in India, Bangladesh, Nepal and the Philippines are well-developed and the AFTF plans to provide increasing levels of support to the nascent networks in Thailand, Indonesia, Laos and Cambodia. In many respects, however, the goal of promoting increased cooperation and productive synergies between producers remains a major challenge which is yet to be fully explored.

Other Fair Trade Networks in Asia

Country Networks – Local Support and Domestic Market Development

As mentioned above, fair trade networks also exist in a number of individual Asian countries. Examples of country networks include the ECOTA Fair Trade Forum in Bangladesh, the Fair Trade Forum – India, the Fair Trade Group Nepal, the Philippine Fair Trade Forum, the Sri Lanka Fair Trade Forum and the Thai Fair Trade Forum.

The experience of the AFTF demonstrates how difficult it is for regional networks of this kind to coordinate activities which reach all their member organizations, especially through one-to-one interventions. With an expanding membership which involves 95 members to date, it is probably unrealistic to expect that the AFTF can support all of its members individually. Given such constraints, it is critical for the AFTF to strengthen country networks so that these can provide local and individual support while the AFTF continues its collective interventions at the regional level. In the long term, this division of labour between regional and country networks could further be useful for promoting effective market development in the Asian region: country networks could focus on domestic market development in their own countries while the AFTF takes the lead developing intra-regional fair trade including South–South trade initiatives.

Although the main activities and organizational capacities of country networks vary from network to network, some individual networks have already taken initial steps to develop domestic fair trade markets, via activities ranging from market research and consumer awareness campaigns to developing local labels and identifying distribution channels (AFTF 2005; APFTI 2005; ECOTA 2007b; IRFT 2005; IRFT 2006). The ECOTA Fair Trade Forum is currently prioritizing goals of domestic market development, rather than expansion of export markets, following the recent success of domestic fair trade in Bangladesh. If these attempts lead to reasonably successful outcomes, this may have broader implications for the global fair trade movement, by demonstrating the significance of emerging local and regional fair trade dynamics and opportunities.

Network of Asian Producers

The Network of Asian Producers (NAP) is a multi-stakeholder body comprising representatives of producer organizations, joint bodies, small farmer organizations and promoting bodies who are certified by or registered with the Fairtrade labelling system operated by FLO International. At present, it has 96 members from 12 countries: India, Sri Lanka, Pakistan, Nepal, China, Vietnam, Thailand, Laos, Indonesia, East Timor, Papua New Guinea and the Philippines (NAP 2007).[13] NAP is one of the three producer networks that became full members of FLO in 2007; African Fairtrade Network (AFN) and Coordinadora Latinoamericana y del Caribe de Comercio Justo (CLAC) are the others (FLO 2008). As FLO mostly certifies food and agricultural products, all the current NAP members are engaged in food or agricultural production, not handicrafts (Mohan 2008, interview).

Although the network is currently at its initial stage of planning and development, there are some noteworthy plans. In addition to the role of presenting a producer voice within FLO and reinforcing mutual learning across the network, NAP aims to facilitate processes by which members can start marketing within their own countries and across other participating Asian countries (NAP 2007). It also explores opportunities for collaboration with existing initiatives, for example Shop for Change in India (Mohan 2008, interview).

The activities of NAP in the future, especially if these can be strengthened through the collaboration with AFTF and other networks in Asia, may bring more opportunities for fair trade market development in Asia, across food and non-food products.

Informal Networks and Communities – Making Friends, Finding Partners

Some fair trade networks in Asia exist as informal communities, both within and between countries, especially in the case of emerging buying countries such as Hong Kong, Singapore and Taiwan. One such community is Fairtrade.sg – a collective of various individuals and organizations involved in promoting fair trade in Singapore. Singaporean and Taiwanese NGOs have also participated in fair trade seminars and events in Hong Kong, enabling them to share information and experiences in ways that can support their initial market development.

Most of these initiatives are currently at the stage of information sharing, but attempts have also been made to achieve operational efficiency through collaboration. An interesting potential direction for future collaboration come from a feasibility study recently conducted into the possibility of having a Hong Kong-based fair trade distribution centre. Through cooperation between fair trade organizations, this initiative would potentially be able to reduce high shipping costs currently facing many fair traders. Although the study concluded that the volume currently traded by the Hong Kong fair trade community is insufficient to break even in such a venture, this opportunity can be investigated further. The initial research studied not-for-profit organizations only, excluding supermarket chains and mainstream players within fair trade markets (Begbie and Wu 2007). Similar opportunities could

---

13   Among 95 member organizations, 47 members are in India and 19 members are in Sri Lanka (NAP 2007). There are also country networks functioning in these two countries: Indian Fair Trade Initiative and Sri Lanka Consultative Body (FLO 2007).

be also explored as potential means of achieving more efficient management in other countries, via strengthened partnership with fair trade organizations and companies.

Collaboration beyond Fair Trade Networks – Public, Private and Social Sector

As can be seen from the above examples, current efforts to build fair trade networks in Asia mostly remain limited to dedicated fair trade organizations and NGOs. However, these networks are also striving to cooperate with other organizations, including private sector companies, not-for-profit organizations specializing in other areas and the government.

In India, the PROFIT team is actively developing private sector partnerships with both multinationals and local retailers. Local shops and cooperatives are generally supportive of fair trade and some large corporations are presently interested in engaging with fair trade, including one Indian subsidiary of a consumer goods multinational company. A major Indian fashion retailer is also currently exploring the possibility of establishing such a partnership. This company has previously marketed traditional crafts sourced from villages and regards support for rural employment as an important source of social and economic value creation. If successful, this partnership will be a noteworthy example of matching corporate values with the fair trade concept in South Asia by means of supporting traditional skills, cultural identity and local economy.

BRAC-Aarong's integrated microfinance and fair trade programme also presents a strong case for collaboration between fair trade organizations and other social initiatives. As discussed above, there are many ways to maximize the available resources of existing poverty alleviation and development agendas, ranging from microfinance programmes for producers to the establishment of outreach networks for promotion and distribution.

Although local, regional and national governments have provided little support for fair trade initiatives in Asia to date, some fair trade organizations are working to gradually increase both government awareness and support for fair trade activities. For example, ECOTA Fair Trade Forum is currently conducting advocacy work in order to press the government to establish a policy to support handicraft production in Bangladesh.

Conclusion

This chapter has examined domestic and regional fair trade in Asia, its developmental impacts and its effectiveness as a development strategy that goes beyond the conventional concept of fair trade as simply a system of international trade between the global North and South. The creation of a unique marketing mix, the introduction of cultural products, innovative pricing and distribution models and locally adapted promotion messages have all been important means through which local and regional approaches to fair trade have achieved success in several Asian markets. Moreover, this has demonstrated their wider potential as an effective new market development strategy for the fair trade movement. Such approaches are also equipped to take advantage of the geographical proximity between producers and consumers, enabling the expansion of strategies such as direct sales. Furthermore, the local and regional approach can bring additional social benefits to producers in Asia, for example by supporting women within the craft sector – this provides a basis for establishing more humane relationships between buying and producing organizations that go beyond the terms of a simple business partnership, and it can further strengthen producer participation in the governance of fair trade networks.

Throughout this chapter, particular attention has been given to the role of the Asia Fair Trade Forum and a range of fair trade networks based in individual countries as means of developing new markets and promoting fair trade in Asia. In this region, there are currently few state-driven or corporate governance mechanisms to make trade fairer for small-scale producers, and the civic initiatives represented by such networks have therefore played a critical role in the development and promotion of fair trade principles. Over time, the activities of such organizations and networks may draw increasing attention from other social actors, within both the private and public sectors.

It is not easy to predict the future of fair trade in Asia, but its significant potential should be recognized and further explored. The current fair trade activities driven by Asian organizations adhere very closely to the concept of self-development or 'Trade not Aid', and have the potential to link effectively producers and consumers in this region in ways that offer mutual benefits. There is no doubt that this approach also has implications for the development of similar initiatives in Africa and Latin America.[14] Such initiatives represent important experiments in promoting fair trade which demand both more attention and increased support from researchers and practitioners within the field of international development and fair trade communities.

Acknowledgements

This chapter is based on two unpublished papers: a paper presented by Claribel David to the Fair Trade, Corporate Accountability and Beyond: Experiments in Globalising Justice Conference (2007), and a master's dissertation by H.-S. Anna Kim (2007).

Specific examples of Fair Trade activities in Asian countries were largely drawn from interviews between H.-S. Anna Kim and the following informants (job titles and organization names as of the interview dates):

- Claribel David, board member, Advocate of Philippine Fair Trade, Inc. (APFTI), Filipinas Fair Trade Ventures Circle Incorporated (FFTV), Asia Fair Trade Forum (AFTF) and International Fair Trade Association (IFAT), the Philippines, 4 July 2007.
- Hang-Soon Lee, Fair Trade Product Development Officer, Beautiful Store, South Korea, 19 July and 8 August 2007.
- Maveen Pereira, Program Manager for South Asia, Traidcraft Exchange, 24 July 2007.
- Arshad Hossain Siddiqui, Director, ECOTA Fair Trade Forum, Bangladesh, 2 August 2007.
- Arun Raste, Director, International Resources for Fairer Trade (IRFT), India, 6 August 2007.
- Miranda Yip, Campaigns Officer, Oxfam Hong Kong, Hong Kong, 13 August 2007.
- Jared Tham, steering committee member, Fairtrade.Sg, Singapore, 22 August 2007.
- Binod Mohan, Chairman, Network of Asian Producers (NAP), India, 23 November 2008.

Many people also shared critical information through email communication, including: Josh Begbie (Crossroads International, Hong Kong), Ronald Lagazo (APFTI, the Philippines), Maiden R. Manzanal (AFTF, the Philippines), Seth Petchers (Shop for Change, India) and Choong-Seop Shin (Beautiful Store, South Korea).

---

14   Most notably, there are national labelling initiatives in Mexico and South Africa: Comercio Justo México and Fair Trade South Africa. Both are associate members of FLO International. http://www.fairtrade. net/labelling_initiatives.html [accessed: 11 December 2008].

We would like to thank the following people for their valuable comments and suggestions: Nigel Walsh (Oxfam Australia), Margaret Carr (Oxfam Ireland), Fernando Contreras (Intermón Oxfam, Spain) and Frank Mechielsen (Oxfam Novib, the Netherlands). The authors are solely responsible for any remaining errors.

Disclaimer

The research conducted by H.-S. Anna Kim is independent of her work at the Oxfam International Secretariat. The views of Anna Kim expressed in this chapter do not represent those of Oxfam International.

References

Advocate of Philippine Fair Trade, Inc. (APFTI) (2005), 'Project fair: a qualitative study on fair trade', unpublished market research report (Quezon City: APFTI).

Asia 2015 (2006), *Asia 2015 Fact Sheet*. [Online]. Available at: http://www.asia2015conference. org/pdfs/Asia%202015%20launch%20fact%20sheet%20170106%20-%20updated.pdf [accessed: 9 September 2008].

Asia Fair Trade Forum (AFTF) (2005), *A Consumer Campaign to Develop Domestic Markets for Fair Trade*, paper to the IFAT International Conference, Quito, Ecuador, May. Available at: http://www.ifat.org/index.php?option=com_docman&task=cat_view&gid=93&Itemid=109 [accessed: 9 September 2008].

Bangladesh Rural Advancement Committee (BRAC) (2007), *BRAC Annual Report 2006* (Dhaka: BRAC Public Affairs and Communications). Available at: http://www.brac.net/downloads_ files/BRAC_Annual_Report_2006.pdf [accessed: 9 September 2008].

Becker, F.M. (2006), 'My heart sees their hearts', *Oxfam Magazine (Oxfam Hong Kong)* 2: 11–12.

Begbie, J. and Wu, S. (2007), 'Investigating the possibility of having a Hong Kong fair trade distribution centre', unpublished research paper (Hong Kong: Crossroads International).

Booms, B.H. and Bitner, M.J. (1981), 'Marketing strategies and organization structures for service firms', in J.H Donnelly and W.R. George (eds), *Marketing of Services* (Chicago, IL: American Marketing Association), pp. 47–52.

Bornstein, D. (1997), *The Price of a Dream: The Story of the Grameen Bank* (Chicago, IL: University of Chicago Press).

Centre for Education and Communication (CEC) (2006), 'Consumer reactions to the concept of socially responsible and environment friendly brands of tea', unpublished market research report (New Delhi: CEC).

Centre for International Trade Expositions and Missions (CITEM) (2007), *Success Stories: Advocate of Philippine Fair Trade, Inc. – Saving the World through (Responsible and Equitable) Trade*. [Online]. Available at: http://www.citem.com.ph/print_ssstories.asp?idpg=17 [accessed: 9 September 2008].

Crowell, E. (2006), 'Bringing fair trade home', *Cooperative Grocer* 127. [Online]. Available at: http://www.cooperativegrocer.coop/articles/index.php?id=697 [accessed: 9 September 2008].

—— and Sligh, M. (2006), 'Domestic fair trade: for health, justice and sustainability', *Social Policy* 37(1): 5–8.

Economist (2006), 'Voting with your trolley', *The Economist* 381(8507): 73–5.

Effort for Craft Organizations Trading Advancement (ECOTA) (2006), *ECOTA Members Organizations' Portfolio* (Dhaka: ECOTA Fair Trade Forum).

—— (2007a), *Fair Trade in Bangladesh 2005–2006* (Dhaka: ECOTA Fair Trade Forum).

—— (2007b), 'Speak out for fair trade', unpublished market research report (Dhaka: ECOTA Fair Trade Forum).

Fair Trade Federation (FTF) (2005), *The Fair Trade Federation 2005 Report: Fair Trade Trends in North America and the Pacific Rim*. Available at: http://www.fairtradefederation.org/ht/a/ GetDocumentAction/i/278 [accessed: 15 November 2008].

Fairtrade.sg (2006), *Fair Trade and You*, presentation to the One Degree Asia event, Singapore, 25–9 July. Available at: http://villagexchange.org/fta_onedegree.ppt [accessed: 9 September 2008].

Fairtrade Labelling Organizations International (FLO) (2007), *FLO Newsletter* September (Bonn: FLO International). Available at: http://www.fairtrade.net/308.html [accessed: 15 November 2008].

—— (2008), *An Inspiration for Change: Fairtrade Labelling Organizations International Annual Report 2007* (Bonn: FLO International). Available at: http://www.fairtrade.net/uploads/media/ FLO_AR2008.pdf [accessed: 15 November 2008].

Hankyoreh (2007), 'Fair trade movement gaining momentum', *The Hankyoreh*, English edition, 4 April. Available at: http://english.hani.co.kr/arti/english_edition/e_editorial/200772.html [accessed: 9 September 2008].

Hart, S.L. (2007), *Capitalism at the Crossroads*, 2nd edition (Upper Saddle River, NJ: Wharton School Publishing).

International Resources for Fairer Trade (IRFT) (2005), 'Qualitative study to understand the possibilities of promoting fair trade', unpublished market research report (Mumbai: IRFT).

—— (2006), 'Qualitative study to understand the possibilities of promoting fair trade in tea and textiles', unpublished market research report (Mumbai: IRFT).

Jaffee, D., Kloppenburg, J.R. and Monroy, M.B. (2004), 'Bringing the "moral charge" home: fair trade within the North and within the South', *Rural Sociology* 69(2): 169–96.

Kallummal, M. and Srinivasan, K.S. (2007), *Meeting Local Demands for Vegetables and Fruits – The Dynamics of Farmers' Market: A Case Analysis of Uzhavar Sandhai of Tamil Nadu* (New Delhi: Make Trade Fair Campaign).

Kim, H.-S.A. (2007), 'Market potential of domestic and international fair trade in Asia', MBA dissertation, Judge Business School, University of Cambridge.

Kocken, M. (2003), *Fifty Years of Fair Trade* (Culemborg: IFAT).

Kotler, P., Kartajaya, H. and Huan, H.D. (2006), *Think ASEAN! Rethinking Marketing toward ASEAN Community 2015* (Singapore: McGraw-Hill Education [Asia]).

Kotler, P. and Keller, K.L. (2006), *Marketing Management*, 12th edition (Upper Saddle River, NJ: Prentice Hall).

Krier, J.-M. (2001), *Fair Trade in Europe 2001: Facts and Figures on the Fair Trade Sector in 18 European Countries* (Maastricht: European Fair Trade Association). Available at: http://www. european-fair-trade-association.org/efta/Doc/FT-E-2001.pdf [accessed: 15 November 2008].

—— (2005), *Fair Trade in Europe 2005: Facts and Figures on Fair Trade in 25 European Countries* (Brussels: Fair Trade Advocacy Office). Available at: http://www.worldshops.org/ downloadc/26776_FairTradeinEurope2005.pdf [accessed: 15 November 2008].

Kyung Hyang (2008), 'Are you an ethical consumer?', *Weekly Kyung Hyang*, 4 March. Available at: http://newsmaker.khan.co.kr/khnm.html?mode=view&code=114&artid=16975&s_code=ne 004 [accessed: 31 October 2009].

Littrell, M.A. and Dickson, M.A. (1999), *Social Responsibility in the Global Market: Fair Trade of Cultural Products* (London: Sage).

Network of Asian Producers (NAP) (2007), 'The network of Asian producers status report', paper presented to the Fairtrade Labelling Organization (FLO) General Assembly, 25 May.

Nicholls, A. and Opal, C. (2005), *Fair Trade: Market-Driven Ethical Consumption* (London: Sage).

Otero, A.I. (2007), *À la recherche d'un commerce équitable Sud-Sud: quelles opportunités?* [Looking for a South-South Fair Trade: What Opportunities?], paper presented to the 2007 World Social Forum, Nairobi, Kenya, 20–25 January 2007. Available at: http://fairtrade.socioeco.org/en/documents.php#list_docs_id_doc_7611 [accessed: 9 September 2008].

Perreault Jr. W.D. and McCarthy, E.J. (2005), *Basic Marketing: A Global-Managerial Approach*, 15th edition (New York: McGraw-Hill).

Prahalad, C.K. (2004), *The Fortune at the Bottom of the Pyramid: Eradicating Poverty through Profits* (Pennsylvania: Wharton School Publishing).

—— and Hart, S.L. (2002), 'The fortune at the bottom of the pyramid', *Strategy and Business* 26: 54–67.

Quelch, J. and Laidler, N. (2003), *The BRAC and Aarong Commercial Brands*, Case 9-504-013 (Boston, MA: Harvard Business School Publishing).

Rao, A.S. (2008), 'Review of AFTF: through the looking glass', unpublished report for AFTF strategic planning (Quezon City: Asia Fair Trade Forum).

Redfern, A. and Snedker, P. (2002), *Creating Market Opportunities for Small Enterprises: Experiences of the Fair Trade Movement*, SEED Working Paper 30 (Geneva: International Labour Organization).

Thekaekara, S. (2006), 'Linking hands', *The Guardian*, 8 March, 9 (Society News and Features). Available at: http://society.guardian.co.uk/societyguardian/story/0,1725463,00.html [accessed: 9 September 2008].

Traidcraft UK (2006), 'Marketing and distribution dynamics: a survey – Bangalore, Delhi and Pune', unpublished market research report.

Vidal, J. and Munk, D. (2003), 'Farmer who got a hearing by paying the ultimate price: Korean who killed himself at WTO talks had written article telling of peasants' ruin', *The Guardian*, 12 September, 19. Available at: http://www.guardian.co.uk/wto/article/0,1040297,00.html [accessed: 9 September 2008].

Witkowski, T.H. (2005), 'Fair trade marketing: an alternative system for globalization and development', *Journal of Marketing Theory and Practice* 13(4): 22–33.

World Bank (2007), *Global Economic Prospects 2007: Managing the Next Wave of Globalization* (Washington, DC: The International Bank for Reconstruction and Development and World Bank).

Chapter 4

Mainstreaming Fair Trade:
Fair Trade Brands and the Problem of Ownership

Anna Hutchens

Fair trade has undergone exponential growth in recent years, thanks largely to the expansion of Fairtrade certified food products in mainstream distribution and retail channels. However, mainstreaming-as-product certification has provoked considerable controversy and represents a major challenge for the system of Fairtrade certification. For some, major firms represent an unbeatable opportunity for market growth and producer-level impact. According to this view, so long as the product undergoes certification, any firm – from Nestlé to fair trade organizations (FTOs) – can and should be encouraged to promote fair trade. For others, mainstream food companies' participation in the Fairtrade certification system is 'bastardizing' fair trade principles (Barrientos, Conroy and Jones 2007) and jeopardizing the market's long-term sustainability.

As the fair trade system has matured, several relatively distinct approaches to developing fair trade markets have emerged. At one end of the spectrum there are fair trade brands such as Cafédirect and Divine Chocolate, which enable producers to share in the value created through branding by means of co-ownership models. These can be contrasted with standard Fair Trade Organizations – such as many of those governed by Fairtrade Labelling Organizations International (FLO) – which attempt to more equitably distribute profits along the supply chain but tend not to share ownership and control over the business with producers to such an extent. The potential for standard fair trade organizations to promote social change within global agri-food markets is further challenged by their increasing dependence upon corporate buyers who have tended to promote more minimalist models of fair trade. Such corporate models can in turn be distinguished depending on the extent to which corporate buyers are sympathetic to more expansionist fair trade goals.

This chapter evaluates the differential extent to which each of these models promotes forms of social change that enhance the business position of small producers, thereby supporting wider goals of social development. Overall, it is argued that fair trade offers the possibility of redressing declining terms of trade between commodity producers in agricultural markets and retailers both by the facilitation of 'upgrading' and by challenging the power relations of agricultural supply chains. However, significant variations between the developmental potential of these differing models are also identified. Farmer-owned fair trade brands are shown to empower producers more effectively than standard certification models of fair trade by giving producers greater control in international food companies and trading relationships. Such models are therefore shown to offer a more sustainable and strategic approach to realizing social change in global agri-food markets. This analysis draws on empirical data from research conducted from April to July 2005, drawing primarily on interviews with practitioners within the fair trade movement (see Hutchens 2009).[1]

---

1 Data were gathered in over 60 semi-structured interviews (either face-to-face or by phone) with practitioners in the fair trade movement. Interviewees were based primarily in Europe and the United States and included individual FTOs, IFAT Executive Committee members, National Initiative/FLO staff and board

Evolution in the Global Food Industry: From Commodity-based to Brand-based Markets

The emergence and expansion of the fair trade system has been fuelled by increasing concern about declining terms of trade facing agricultural commodity producers. While developing economies remain highly dependent upon agricultural production, prices have tended to become less favourable for producers, with profits increasingly passing to 'brands' and 'retailers'. This section of the chapter briefly outlines the structure of contemporary agricultural trade relations, drawing on insights from global value chain analysis to help to illuminate the ways in which fair trade can contribute to social change and the transformation of power relations in global agricultural supply chains.

Agriculture is vital for advancement in most developing countries which are not oil or mineral rich (IFAD 2001; Mellor 2001). It is the backbone of survival for 1.2 billion living in poverty who are based in rural areas and work as either small-scale farmers or workers (UNDP 2005, 129). Acknowledging the contribution of rural agriculture to the alleviation of rural poverty, Robert Zoellick, the head of the World Bank, notes that 'growth in agriculture is 4 times more effective at raising incomes of the extreme poor than growth in any other sector' (*Japan Today* 2007). Despite its potential, the modern history of global agriculture tells a story of increasing poverty and disempowerment for small-scale rural producers. The first two thirds of the twentieth century were dominated by a system of agro-industrial development based on Fordist mass production of undifferentiated products for consumption in Western markets. Processes of globalization in the latter part of the twentieth century in the global food industry have encouraged corporate concentration, strengthening the influence of global retailers and brand manufacturers over producers in global supply chains (Vorley 2003; Heffernan, Hendrickson and Gronski 1999).

This transition has produced new forms of social organization. Increasingly, producer-driven[2] markets have been replaced by global 'buyer-driven'[3] supply chains in which buyers lead centrally coordinated but internationally dispersed production networks, setting the terms and conditions of production (for example, geographical source, market price and production timeframes) (Gereffi 1994). Global *value* chain (GVC) analysis (also known as global commodity chain [GCC] analysis) accounts for the shifting distribution of fortunes and organizational processes that have characterized post-Fordist markets. GVCs refer to the entire cluster of productive units in commodity production networks, each one commanding a value that is indirectly proportional to the level of competition at that stage of production. Highlighting issues of market coordination and entry barriers, GVCs offer a useful framework for considering the modern political economy of international trade as shaped heavily by lead firms' organizational strategies for market governance (Gibbon and Ponte 2005).[4]

---

members, conventional traders and global brand companies, politicians and policy-makers, producers as well as civil society network members. All other quotes and references included in the analysis derive from existing research and are cited as such.

2   Producer-driven chains are coordinated by large transnational manufacturers and predominate in capital- and technology-intensive industries such as the automobile and airline industries (Gereffi 1994).

3   Buyer-driven commodity chains predominate in labour-intensive sectors where production functions are typically outsourced and market information, product design and marketing/advertising costs set the barriers to entry for would-be lead firms (Gereffi 1994).

4   A variety of forms of governance exist in value-chains, not only buyer-driven and producer-driven but also modular, relational and captive chains (Gereffi, Humphrey and Sturgeon 2005). *Modular* chains involve codification, enabling the segmentation of production chains, relatively independent suppliers and frequent transactions. *Relational* chains are characterized by solidarity, trust and cooperation and even

Studies of agricultural supply chains show that this shift towards 'buyer-driven supply chains' has also led to a migration of the value of international trade away from tangible assets towards intangible assets (Gereffi 1994; see also Piore and Sabel 1984). As Interbrand explains:

> For much of the twentieth century, the vast majority of a company's assets were tangible – real estate, plant, facilities, equipment, inventory, stock investments and cash. ... Today, the intangible assets of the firm are frequently the most valuable ... particularly the company's trademarks or brands ... brands are now among a company's most valuable assets and represent the 'engines' of corporate growth, future success and ongoing profitability. (Interbrand, cited in Pritchard 1999)

As a consequence of such changes, intangible assets such as brand recognition now often contribute more to the value of a product than labour and raw materials.

While brands have become the 'engines' of corporate profitability in the food industry at the retail end of the market, agricultural commodity production has steeply declined in market value (Robbins 2003). For instance, in the cocoa industry, despite the rising value of chocolate in a global market worth US$75 billion in sales a year, the world market price for cocoa has fallen by 50 per cent since 2003 (Vorley 2003, 50). Similarly, in the coffee sector between 1975 and 1993, the world market price for coffee dropped by 18 per cent but the consumer price increased by 240 per cent (Morisset 1997).

This decline in prices and profitability for producers has created an imperative to seek greater value through supply-chain 'upgrading'. Value chain analysis suggests that market actors at low-value ends of the production chain can improve their position by 'upgrading' to high-value units of production where fewer competitors exist (see for example Kaplinsky 2006). Upgrading involves establishing 'rents' which enable firms to 'insulate themselves from competition by taking advantage of, or creating, barriers to the entry of competitors' (Kaplinsky 2006, 357). To improve their competitiveness, firms seek out ways to protect rents from competition. Intellectual property offers a powerful legal tool for rent-protection. Own-brand manufacturing is the most lucrative form of (functional) upgrading in the competitive process because the trade mark rights that underpin brands offer *ongoing* protection from imitation.[5] This poses a decisive barrier to entry for would-be competitors and contributes to anti-competitive markets (Lunney 1999; Bain 1956; Economides 1988).[6]

A Contemporary History of 'Mainstreaming' Fair Trade in Consumer Markets: Product-certification and Fair Trade Brand Companies

The fair trade system as a whole seeks to confront the barriers to development created by the changes in global value chains described above by offering market access to the most disadvantaged producers in developing countries on terms that favour their interests. Pioneered by Oxfam and other alternative trading organizations in Europe and the United States until the 1980s, fair trade has since become a much broader and more complex market phenomenon in its pursuit of larger

---

power distribution throughout the chain. In *captive* chains, producers are closely controlled by retailers and processors through contractual agreements.

5   This is unlike other forms of intellectual property such as copyright and patents that offer only a temporary monopoly.

6   For instance, of the 16,000 products that are launched on the US market each year, 95 per cent are launched as brand extensions of existing brands (Murphy, cited in Lury 2004, 71).

'mainstream' markets for small-scale producers (Tallontire 2000; 2006; Kocken 2003; Low and Davenport 2005; Litrell and Dickson 1999; Raynolds, Murray and Wilkinson 2007).

Before evaluating the relative potential of varying models of fair trade as means of promoting social change in global agri-food markets, it is helpful to outline briefly the key distinguishing features of these models and to situate them within the evolution of the fair trade movement as a whole.

The Standard FTO System and the Increasing Involvement of Corporate Buyers

Formalized by the organization 'Max Havelaar' in 1989, the Fairtrade certification system quickly spread among sister organizations across Europe under the name of Max Havelaar and 'Transfair'. In 1997, this organizational cluster established the FLO and, in 2002, created the independent auditing arm FLO-CERT. Today, the FLO is the worldwide standard-setting and certification organization for labelled Fairtrade. FLO's vision is to see that 'wherever and whenever applicable and possible, production and trade takes place under Fairtrade conditions and, in all other situations, Fairtrade standards are a reference for efforts to improve the conditions of the world's production and trade' (FLO 2004). The Fairtrade system offers producers a 'fair wage' together with a social premium for development projects. Consisting of FLO e.V. and FLO-CERT, FLO has three responsibilities: setting the international Fairtrade standards (see Table 4.1); product certification and trade auditing; and producer support services.

Table 4.1   Fairtrade labelling criteria for Fairtrade certified traders

Trader criteria
A price covering the cost of production
A social premium for development purposes
Advance payments to assist farmers during pre-harvest periods
Long-term contracts with producers to enable long-term production planning
Long-term trading relations to allow stable and sustainable production and planning

The growth of Fairtrade certified product markets internationally has been rapid. Global sales are valued at over US$1.4 billion, a small share of market trade made remarkable by a growth rate of 50 per cent (Murray and Raynolds 2007, 8; see also Krier 2005, 7). In mainstream distribution channels, sympathetic cooperative retailers and health food stores such as the UK's Fresh and Wild and The Cooperative Group (the Co-op) were the first to offer Fairtrade products in mainstream distribution channels. The Co-op converted all of its own-label coffee and chocolate to Fairtrade in 2002 and 2003 respectively. Similarly, the US retailer 'Wild Oats' converted all of its own-label coffee to Fairtrade in 2002 and now stocks a range of other Fairtrade products (Nicholls and Opal 2005, 193, 146).

The involvement of more traditional corporate retailers in national markets has fast-tracked the growth and variety of Fairtrade product markets,[7] providing the fair trade movement with significant market access. Supermarkets in fact account for 56,700 of the 78,900 'points of sale' for Fairtrade products in 25 European countries (Krier 2005). In Switzerland, the two national

---

7   Products include not only coffee but also tea, rice, sugar, cocoa, fresh fruit, juices, honey, spices and nuts, sports balls, wine and flowers.

retailers Migros and the Co-op offer own-label Fairtrade products in ten and nine different own-label product groups respectively (Nicholls and Opal 2005, 196). Migros' turnover of Fairtrade products accounted for 40 per cent of the total sales of Fairtrade in Switzerland in 2002 (Nicholls and Opal 2005, 196). In a more minimalist fashion, brand manufacturers such as Nestlé, Procter and Gamble, Kraft, Starbucks, Dole and Chiquita have more recently begun to move into the Fairtrade system, sometimes following concerted pressure from fair trade activists and consumers.

However, in spite of the opportunities for market growth created by the expanding involvement of corporate traders and buyers within the fair trade system, many FTOs within the fair trade system have been critical of such increased corporate participation, regarding it as creating significant pressures for the dilution of fair trade values and standards. Such fair traders have therefore attempted to organize their fair trade activities in ways that operate more independently from corporate influence and promote more expansive fair trade principles.

FTOs of this kind tend to regard conventional traders selling a few Fairtrade products – largely in response to consumer pressure – as falling well short of the broader principles and ethos of fair trade. Such FTOs share the more expansive vision of fair trade encapsulated in the International Fair Trade Association (IFAT) standards for FTOs. Throughout the institutional development of the Fairtrade certification system, FTOs of this kind have remained a vital force and undergone their own regional and international institutional development (Nicholls and Opal 2005; Raynolds and Long 2007).[8] As seen in Table 4.2, such FTOs adhere to more demanding standards than some others currently participating in more reductionist, corporate-dominated fair trade relationships.

Table 4.2   Standards for fair trade organizations (FTOs)

Standards for fair trade organizations (FTOs)
1. Creating opportunities for economically disadvantaged producers: supporting the poorest producers
2. Transparency and accountability: dealing fairly and openly with trading partners
3. Capacity-building: developing the skills of producers and creating opportunities for trading their products
4. Promoting fair trade: telling as many people as possible about fair trade and informing customers concerning from where products have come
5. Payment of a fair price: ensuring that producers receive a fair price for their products
6. Gender equity: providing equal pay and opportunities for women and men
7. Working conditions: ensuring that producers are working in a healthy and safe place
8. Child labour: ensuring that the United Nations *Convention on the Rights of the Child* is respected
9. The environment: ensuring that materials used in production and packing do not damage the environment

Source: IFAT 2008.

---

8   IFAT was established to represent the global association of FTOs in 1989. Further development of regional networks then occurred (especially in the North), including the European Fair Trade Association (EFTA) (a network of 11 fair trade importers across Europe) in 1990; and in 1994 both the US Fair Trade Federation (FTF) (a national association for fair traders) and the Network of European World Shops (NEWS!) (a network of 15 national World Shop associations across 15 European countries).

The Emergence of the FTO Brand Company Model

While FTOs have traditionally been found only in alternative/niche markets, in the 1990s a number of pioneers within the FTO community developed an alternative approach to 'mainstreaming' fair trade with a 'new' kind of FTO that transformed the traditional non-profit FTO into a for-profit company structure. Exploiting commercial and legal tools of marketing and branding, the FTO brand model effectively transported the 'expansionist' version of fair trade into a *mainstream* commercial setting in a form capable of competing successfully with other firms. More important, the FTO brand pushes the FTO model of fair trade to new limits by providing small-scale farmers greater ownership over the process of international trading and in the company structure. Former Director, Fair Trade NGO, USA described the limits of the FTOs in the following terms:

> Some of the [fair trade] companies – like Divine Chocolate Ltd. and Equal Exchange – those are great models, but that's not the norm in the fair trade world …

On the other hand, the CEO of a Fair Trade brand company in the UK suggested that part of the success of the company was derived from adopting a 'branded' approach:

> our [company's] success comes quite heavily down to the fact that we've taken a *branded* route, so the Fairtrade products from Cafédirect and Divine Chocolate are coming from companies that specialize in the commodity that they're dealing in and are coming to the market with a *brand* … that's quite distinct from … [FTOs that are] coming to the market with a *chocolate* … [which is] much harder to crack. You get your initial core supporters – obviously people interested in development are Oxfam supporters – but if you actually want to break it wider than that [market], then you actually need to have something that communicates something with the broadest range of the population.

AgroFair, a farmer-owned banana and fresh fruits company, is an important example of an FTO brand company. Spread across Ghana, Ecuador and Costa Rica, AgroFair fruit farmers and cooperatives own 50 per cent of AgroFair's shares and profits, the other half of which is held by its NGO and ethical investor partners (AgroFair 2006a; 2006b).[9] New growers are offered company shares after a period of 12 months of trading with AgroFair. AgroFair producers gain direct experience and skills in value-added activities such as sales and marketing.[10] This novel enterprise has had substantial success, particularly in the banana sector (its first product) with the Swiss retailer, Co-op, which sells 100 per cent of its bananas as Fairtrade.[11] In 2004, AgroFair's turnover increased by 47 per cent to €37.6 million, up from €25.6 million in 2003. In 2006, the company grew a further

---

    9   AgroFair's NGO and ethical investor partners include Twin, CTM Altromercato, Solidaridad, VIVA Trust and Triodos Innovation Fund (AgroFair 2006a).
    10   AgroFair's FTO partners take responsibility for the day-to-day operation of sales and marketing in European, UK/Ireland and Italian markets. In 2006, AgroFair's Oké-labelled bananas gained access to marketing and distribution in the United States through a new fair trade company called Oké USA. Oké USA is owned by AgroFair, Equal Exchange (US pioneer in fair trade coffee) and Red Tomato (Boston-based non-profit organization that helps family farmers in New England to access markets, founded by the co-founder of Equal Exchange). AgroFair farmers benefit from this ownership structure through ownership of company equity in addition to fair trade minimum prices and premiums.
    11   As a consequence, Co-op now sells more Fairtrade bananas than any other supermarket retailer worldwide (AgroFair 2004, 4, 24).

40 per cent, with a turnover of €62 million and a share dividend of €236,000 (half of which has gone to producers).

Cafédirect is another FTO brand. Founded in the UK in 1991, Cafédirect is the UK's 'largest 100 per cent Fairtrade hot drinks company, the fifth largest coffee brand and the sixth largest tea brand' (Cafédirect 2008, 4). Cafédirect's mission is to be the 'leading brand which strengthens the influence, income and security of producer partners in the south and links them directly to the consumer' (Cafédirect 2004, 24). The company works with 33 fair trade producer organizations in 11 countries, representing over a quarter of a million tea, cocoa and coffee producers. To date, the company has pursued its mission with remarkable success; it has expanded from offering one coffee product in 1991 to now selling 41 products ranging from drinking chocolate to gourmet and specialty coffees and teas. Cafédirect's turnover was £22.3 million in the (financial) year 2007 (Cafédirect 2008, 1). As part of a reorganization of Cafédirect's ownership structure and capital venture, since 2003 Cafédirect producers have held 5 per cent of the company's shares and have board representation (Cafédirect 2004).[12]

A final example is Divine Chocolate Ltd, set up in 1997 primarily between Twin Trading and the Ghanaian cocoa cooperative, Kuapa Kokoo.[13] Kuapa Kokoo producers have board representation and co-own the brand: 33 per cent since 1997 and 45 per cent since 2006.[14] Divine's mission is multiform: to 'take a quality affordable range of Fair Trade chocolate bars into the UK mainstream chocolate market'; and to 'pay a Fair Trade price for all the cocoa used in the chocolate sold' (Divine Chocolate Ltd 2007). Positioned consciously among other normal 'mainstream' chocolate bars in terms of price, quality and availability, Divine aims to 'raise awareness of fair trade issues among UK retailers and consumers of all ages' and 'be highly visible and vocal in the chocolate sector and thereby act as a catalyst for change' (Divine Chocolate Ltd 2007). Competing directly with major firms in the UK chocolate industry such as Cadbury and M&M/Mars, Divine Chocolate is available in 5,000 stores in the UK, including Sainsbury's, the Co-op and Tesco supermarkets. It has also experimented with private, own-label ventures with the UK's Co-op (for its entire own-brand chocolate) as well as Starbucks for all its own-brand chocolate. In 2003, the company reached profitability and has continued to do so year on year. In 2006, with 18 per cent growth, the company received a post-tax profit of over £450,000 and in 2007, after 10 years of business, the company issued its first dividend of £500/share (Martyn 2007).

---

12   Following Cafédirect's recent restructure of its corporate governance model, producers own 5 per cent of shares, 40 per cent are 'guardian shares' divided among Cafédirect's founders (Equal Exchange, Twin Trading, Oxfam and Traidcraft) and the rest are owned by the public, whose ownership is limited to no more than 3 per cent of shares and who have limited voting rights (see Cafédirect 2004; see also Nicholls and Opal 2005).

13   Other investors and/or partners included The Body Shop, SNV, Comic Relief, the UK Department for International Development, the International Cocoa Organization and Christian Aid (Tiffen et al. 2004, 24). Until July 2006, The Body Shop held ownership of 14 per cent of shares, and Kuapa Kokoo 33 per cent. The Body Shop donated its shares to Kuapa Kokoo which now owns 47 per cent of the company.

14   In 2006, The Body Shop, a founding partner and shareholder in Divine, decided to donate its shares to Kuapa Kokoo.

Contrasting and Evaluating These Differing Models

Figure 4.1 identifies a range of approaches to fair trade currently operating within the system as a whole. Each stylized 'model' of fair trade varies along a spectrum of differing degrees of trader commitment and contribution to fair trade principles.

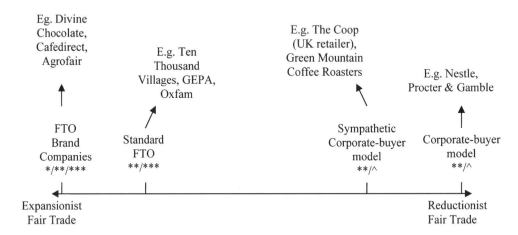

Figure 4.1   Typology of trader-participation in fair trade/Fairtrade markets

Notes: * Producer brand co-ownership in specialized-product, ** FLO Label, *** FTO Mark/meet FTO standards, ^ Corporate buyer-owned brand.

This chapter is particularly interested in exploring the implications of these differing strategies of fair trade mainstreaming. The clearest contrast exists between Fairtrade certification models (encompassing FTOs operating via both independent retail channels and relationships with corporate buyers) and the farmer-owned fair trade brand model. Certification and fair trade company branding are not necessarily mutually exclusive, since product certification is common to all companies. However, brands co-owned by small-scale farmers are unique to the FTO brand company model.[15]

Based on the movement's experience with expanding fair trade in European and US food markets via certification and FTO brands, the following discussion evaluates how effectively each of these approaches empowers producers and moves conventional firms towards a more expansive model of fair trade.

---

15   Some suggest that the certification logo itself is a 'brand' in that it adds value to a product. While true, the certification label does not offer exclusivity of ownership and disproportionate remuneration to producers in the way that farmer-owned brands do. In fact, the value of the Fairtrade 'logo' is severely diluted by multinational corporations' [MNCs] subversion of it to no more than one of their subsidiary brands, and as this chapter shows, the remuneration of 'value' in the Fairtrade value chain remains disproportionately in the hands of corporate buyers.

Mainstreaming Fair Trade via Product Certification

As noted above, the Fairtrade system requires that both higher-than-market commodity prices and a social premium be paid to Fairtrade producers. On the one hand – assuming Fairtrade-registered producers actually have a trader to whom they can sell (Doppler and González Cabañas 2006) – these sources of revenue provide some degree of financial security, especially in the volatile markets of tropical agriculture. The premiums provide for investment in community development projects such as housing, schools, roads, health clinics and medicines. On the other hand, however, producers' remuneration and status remains tied to *commodity* production – a low-value activity in the context of the current configuration of agricultural trade.

> [F]or cocoa farmers … the dollar value of cocoa in a bar of chocolate that costs 1 dollar is about *eight cents*. So you can be paying a cocoa grower a fair wage with respect to the local market, but [the producer] is not actually able to capture the value that their labour has directly and indirectly generated because all the value happens further down in the supply chain – it's in the brand. (Former Fair Trade programme manager, the Co-op, USA)

The point here is that while the price and premium may make for a 'fair' wage for producers, it remains a very low share of the overall value that is being captured within the chain. In the context of declining prices for primary commodities, the potential for development and poverty-reduction through production of primary commodities remains limited. As Wilkinson and Mascarenhas (2007, 129–30) propose, '[r]ather than maintaining colonial-based practices of simply exporting raw material, producers must be able to increase their technical and marketing knowledge and strengthen their position in alternative and conventional markets if Fair Trade movement goals are to be achieved'.

This weakness in the certification system is difficult for FLO and its constituent National Initiatives (NIs) to rectify, in part as a result of the seldom addressed issue of the FLO's funding model,[16] which is based on conventional market power structures. The FLO's national administrators, the NIs, award licenses to firms to use the Fairtrade label provided that those firms make and maintain a contractual commitment to abide by trader criteria (see above). License fees are paid to NIs and are a key revenue source for them and for the FLO – particularly in their attempt to achieve financial independence and sustainability. These fees are calculated as a percentage of a firm's overall market share, sales or volumes (depending on the NI's particular fee structure). Thus, by virtue of their enormous market share, volumes traded and sales made, the largest mainstream firms such as Starbucks or Chiquita represent NIs' largest revenue-raisers, regardless of how little Fairtrade volume they stock or sell. Dependent on the largest market players for mainstream market access and funding, NIs are both encouraged to collaborate with these traders – who have a dominant commercial-orientation rather than a Fairtrade one – and are rewarded for increasing market volumes rather than for ensuring that market value is returned to producers.[17]

---

16 An extended and complete version of the FLO's funding model is analysed in Hutchens (2009), in which the issue of producer certification fees is addressed.

17 For instance, the total revenue of Max Havelaar Switzerland derives from license fees, in the case of the Fairtrade Foundation UK, it is 85 per cent.

... one of the major problems with the 'greenwashing question' is that FLO and Transfair USA refuse to address it publicly. Their ... reasoning is obvious: these companies doing the damage provide most of the cash for their operating budgets. (Fieldwork interview notes)

[I]t's not all about volume and signing up more MNCs [multinational corporations]; there's something else. Signing up more companies doesn't address ideological issues ... FLO needs to push companies not just to address the price issue, but fundamental issues of inequality in the supply chain ... that's tough because it's easy to ask a company to write a cheque, but to hand over power, I think that's where the challenge lies. (Fair Trade coffee programme manager, international NGO)

[Fair trade] is something that has been boiled down to 'Fairtrade means producers get a fair price'. But in actuality, it's about almost everything *but* that ... [fair trade] is actually not about what you're paying so much as the fact that you are engaged in direct, long-term relations with producers, where the objective is to maximize benefits going back to the most vulnerable people in the supply chain in ways that challenge the existing terms of trade. So it's really process-oriented, it's really a long-term project ... that's not something that you can easily do by saying 'yep here's your seal and put it on your bag and pay 1.26 and be done with it'. ... Even though you can get people to pay a better price when you get these large corporations on board ... what you *lose* is ... the *power* of what *could* come if they really understood what they were buying into ... if you could really get Procter & Gamble to understand that it's not just about paying a Fairtrade price, it's about developing long-term relationships, it's about really investing in these communities, it's about seeing the sustainability of *your* business being tied to the sustainability of *their* business ... [then] we'd have a much different story to tell. (Former Fair Trade programme manager, the Co-op, USA)

The cost of this incentive structure is political. It has entailed an ongoing decline in: the certification system's focus on market access for marginalized small-producers as well as principles of *direct* trader-producer relations; investment in capacity-building (which enables producers to upgrade beyond commodity production); *long-term* business partnerships; and political advocacy for trade justice (see Bezençon and Blili 2006). The FLO's decision to begin certifying large-scale commercial farms and plantations has enabled MNCs to maintain their standard supply-chain structures (Renard and Pérez-Grovas 2007, 150),[18] even though MNCs' existing suppliers are not the most exploited or marginalized producers, nor in greatest need of capacity-building and technical assistance.[19] This aside, it is only companies that actually put the Fairtrade label on their product who are required to make contractual commitments to Fairtrade. This means that retailers – whose own-label Fairtrade goods represent a significant portion of Fairtrade sales but who outsource packing and labelling functions – are free to pursue a largely commercial agenda in Fairtrade

---

18   Despite an agreement with the FLO producer-members that certification of plantations would be exclusive to plantation-only commodities and not for commodities produced by small-producers (such as tea), the FLO has begun doing so in increasing amounts. This has been the case with bananas and tropical fruits (see Raynolds 2007; Wilkinson and Mascarenhas 2007; Renard and Pérez-Grovas 2007).

19   Vorley (2003, 14–15) notes three types of 'rural world': the 'globally competitive' world of producers who work within consolidated supply chains; the 'shrinking middle' sector, who provide residual supply to global buyers on diminishing terms of trade; and the population of 'fragile livelihoods' who are unskilled, low-waged, uneducated labourers (often migrant) who work as urban and rural casual labour. Suppliers of large MNCs can be located in the first tier of producers in rural agriculture, hence certification of their operations comes at the cost of the second and third tier suppliers who suffer continued marginalization and poverty.

production networks. It has been suggested that some retailers are switching between Fairtrade producers, abandoning relationships with producer groups, buying the cheapest Fairtrade produce available and, in so doing, threatening the system's capacity to offer developmental benefits to producers (Barrientos and Dolan 2006, 18; see especially Barrientos and Smith 2007).

While a few 'sympathetic' retailers and businesses participating in the Fairtrade system have sought to distinguish themselves from more opportunistic MNCs by making demonstrable commitments to Fairtrade markets and producers (albeit circumscribed by dominant market prerogatives and principles) (Barrientos and Smith 2007; Murray and Raynolds 2007), they are an exception to the norm.[20] Moreover, they gain no competitive advantage by doing so. They may even be pushed out of the market since the FLO's move towards ISO 65 accreditation (international standards for product certification bodies) binds the FLO to a principle of non-discrimination for traders or producers irrespective of their motives and practices in the Fairtrade system (Barrientos and Smith 2007). The certification system is not only limited in scope for producer empowerment in global agricultural markets, but is also having a largely limited effect on the 'business as usual' practices of dominant traders. These shortcomings derive from both the system's *neglect* of the sources of political inequality in brand-based markets and its *dependence* on this power structure for market access and scale.[21]

Mainstreaming Fair Trade: Fair Trade Brands

Unlike conventional traders in the FLO's system whose 'commitment' to fair trading in many cases amounts to paying a Fairtrade price and social premium, fair trade brand companies, like many FTOs operating independently from corporate buyers, preserve the integrity of trading principles. These include direct and short supply chain relations, a focus on small-scale producers and capacity-building and technical assistance in high-value areas of international business.

One unique feature of the FTO brand is its corporate governance structure: producers are not only the growers/suppliers for fair trade brand companies, but also company directors and shareholders. Greater economic security flows from this in terms of securing not only Fairtrade minimum prices and premiums for commodity production, but also the added-value derived from greater ownership in business and trading processes and (legally) in brand equity. For example, Divine Chocolate's farmer cooperative Kuapa Kokoo received £1,025,000 in Fairtrade premiums between 1993 and 2001. While this has been a valuable income stream for community and business investment, more secure financial gains have come from an additional source: their 45 per cent ownership share of the company (Kyere and Neil 2006). At current market prices, Divine Chocolate is worth some £1,833,333, which returned to Kuapa Kokoo a dividend of £47,352 in 2007 (including ordinary shares and interest on preference shares) (Martyn 2007). Fair trade brands were in fact developed to offer greater control and value to producers in international business partnerships – in other words, to address the 'limits' of the certification system.

---

20   Barrientos and Smith's (2007, 118, 120) research on retailers' participation in the Fairtrade system exposes significant differences between retailers' levels of commitment and contribution to Fairtrade principles. It also determines that FLO-CERT will be unable to discriminate in favour of 'best' practice amongst traders if it seeks ISO 65 certification.

21   These are not the only limitations to empowering small-producers. An additional problem or barrier to entry into the Fairtrade system for small-scale producers is the fees they are now required to pay to FLO-CERT to become certified. The FLO's governance structure has historically posed significant obstacles to producers' attempts to exercise greater influence over the market processes affecting them (see especially Chapter 5 in Hutchens 2009).

[The brands] were designed to achieve a few things. One was – when we started Cafédirect, it was designed to give small-scale producers who had really worked *hard* to learn how to access the market, somebody to sell to, someone to call their own. … Because you know that old adage 'you can lead a horse to water but you can't make it drink'? The thing about Transfair and the trade-marking models … [is that] the [Fairtrade] label made it possible for conventional companies to buy directly from small farmers and get some kind of reward for that … but it didn't make [conventional companies] *do* [fair trade] with many small-farmer organizations, especially the weaker ones with which they just didn't want to get involved. They tended to pick the ones that were more capable, more able. And that's not very developmental. … And I realized quite early on that [the brand] was where you made money. (Fair Trade pioneer, USA)

[Y]ou can be paying a cocoa grower a fair wage with respect to the local market, but [the producer] is not actually able to capture the value … because all the value happens further in the supply chain – it's in the brand. Companies like the Day Chocolate Company [Divine Chocolate Inc.] in the UK which sells Divine Chocolate is one third owned by the farmers that grow it. So they get the value from the Fairtrade premium and they get the value of the *brand*. … Fairtrade will only be successful and sustainable if it can adapt and respond to *emerging* difficulties that producers face. (Former Fair Trade programme manager, the Co-op, USA)

Because of their co-ownership models, FTO brands prioritize producer capacity-building as an important investment. In fact, the challenge fair trade brands pose to conventional firms in highly concentrated markets – including those selling Fairtrade certified products – is a capacity to operate thriving commercial enterprises that explicitly strengthen small producers' business capacity in the marketplace. For instance, as part of its 'Gold Standard Fair Trade policy', Cafédirect invested 86 per cent of its working capital into producer support ventures in 2006 (£574,000 in 2004–2005) (Cafédirect 2006). Similarly, Divine Chocolate has invested an increasing amount of its revenues into technical assistance, from £23,876 in 2002 to £331,486 in 2006 (Martyn 2007).

With the traditional players you can see a trend: western companies are integrating the supply chain, getting closer and closer to the global South. They do not focus only on selling bananas – they also dominate production and logistics. What AgroFair is doing can be called 'reverse supply chain integration': the Third World producer is integrating the supply chain in his own interest. The producer is dedicated not only to growing product, but to organizing logistics, and having at the same time a voice and vote in the sales strategy. In contrast to normal opinion, AgroFair has shown that involving Third World producers in business structures, making them co-responsible for the marketing strategy, is a viable aspiration. (Cited in Nicholls and Opal 2005, 91)

The entry of these business model innovations into their respective industries has demonstrated the 'viability' of operating competitive commercial enterprises that explicitly hand market power, skills, revenues and ownership to small-producers. These organizational principles and practices for farmer-empowerment remain unique to fair trade brands, and offer forms of competitive advantage that fair trade brand companies are deliberately using to engage in direct competition with established brands and catalyse industry transformation (see Figure 4.2). This has forced conventional industry members to address the issue of fair trade in their own operations, albeit not to such a radical extent as within farmer-owned fair trade brand companies.

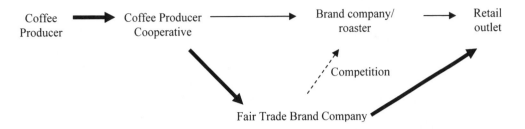

Figure 4.2   The evolution of fair trade models: Certification to brand companies
Source: Hutchens 2009.

Certification and Brands as Modes of Market Engagement: The Prospects for Social Change

The above discussion has demonstrated the clear advantages of fair trade brands over Fairtrade product certification as means of enabling producer empowerment and poverty alleviation in mainstream markets. Yet how do they compare in their capacity to bring about systemic change? This question involves recasting each model as a different type of institutional engagement and understanding its institutional effects. Regulatory scholars tell us that different social actors engage in different ways with institutions when seeking change (Braithwaite 2009) – two types of institutional engagement of particular relevance to the fair trade movement being 'resistance' and 'game-playing' (Hutchens 2009). Resisters are located within capitalist institutions and discourses and seek to change the regulatory system for the better. Their role in the process of social change is to work to institutionalize innovative yet marginal ideas of others by collaborating with institutional actors. This makes resistance vulnerable to institutional 'capture' (Ayres and Braithwaite 1992). In contrast to strategies of resistance, game-players ignore and transcend existing regulatory codes, inventing new rules and institutions in order to radically transform the prevailing system. They are much more difficult to capture. Rather, when resisters become captured, game-players re-innovate to continue promoting their aim of structural freedom.

Portrayed in this way, the FLO/NIs identify with the role of resistance. They are seeking to institutionalize Fairtrade certification by enrolling the support of their institutional allies – dominant retailers and manufacturers, adapting and compromising the model to do so. While seeming 'allies' to Fairtrade growth, MNCs are engaged in 'symbolic' imitation of Fairtrade – stocking minimal amounts of Fairtrade to associate the company with Fairtrade's value. This gives the pretence of having adopted Fairtrade ethics but actually functions to subvert the Fairtrade logo to a subsidiary brand of the MNC and control Fairtrade's market development in their interests. This strategy ensures that the Fairtrade symbol does not eclipse their own brand logo in consumers' purchasing decisions (Hutchens 2009).[22]

> I really think it is important what companies say: they see the value of their product in their *brand*, not in the [Fairtrade] label. But the certification schemes of the niche markets, Rainforest and Utz Kapeh and Fairtrade … they are building their marketing aspects on labelling a *product* … I mean, imagine you go to a supermarket shelf and you see the product of Sara Lee and Nestlé and Kraft

---

22   A popular example of symbolic imitation to capture the Fairtrade system is Nestlé's 'Partner's Blend' (launched in the UK in 2004), which amounts to less than 0.1 per cent of Nestlé's total volume (see North 2006).

... all standing close to each other, and they all have the [Fairtrade] label on the product ... [from the consumer's viewpoint] there's no credibility in the brand then ... consumers will assume that a product that has been labelled has a very high value ... [and that the label] is *the value* of the product. ... This is important to understand why the companies did not go for certification and labelling, and why they do not have an interest to transfer one of the existing certification systems to the mainstream. (Coordinator, International Initiative for Sustainable Coffee)

[I]f you have three coffee roasters – all of whom deliver Max Havelaar coffee – but you cannot as a consumer distinguish the three from each other, then those roasters are not [going to be] interested at all in the Max Havelaar brand because they're investing in their competitor. (Fair trade pioneer, the Netherlands)

The frontrunners of the fair trade brand movement identify with the role of game-playing. They respond to the structural and administrative weaknesses in the FLO – and MNCs' capture of Fairtrade – with new business models that offer more independent and genuine pathways of empowerment for small producers. Farmer-owned brand companies have in fact posed a more challenging threat to the traditional business power structure defined by Northern corporate ownership than the certification model. Democratizing this power structure in favour of small-producers represents a paradigmatic shift for conventional corporate organization and philosophy. Not surprisingly, conservative brand companies have promoted the view that farmer-owned fair trade brands are 'unviable' for mainstream business. This is the political battle that remains on the movement's horizon: influencing the restructure of conventional ownership models in international business and assets around the principle of producer co-ownership. While MNCs can evade this political challenge within the FLO's system and simply pay a marginally higher price to agricultural producers, fair trade brands' increasing success with consumers will make business model evolution necessary for conventional MNCs to survive in the market.

The future I see ... is with these new ways of doing business that we're creating in the fair trade movement and with farmers, with new ownership structures of getting value back to poor farmers and poor communities and workers. ... Are [conventional] companies going to genuinely change because [fair trade] is the way to do business, or are they going to become the dinosaurs of the future? Are they part of the new way of doing business ... or do we slowly ... *push* the boundaries and take consumers with us. ... In that situation, the *market* forces people to change or to exit. (Fair trade pioneer, UK)

Conclusion: Mainstreaming Producer Ownership

Several lessons can be gathered from the international experience in mainstreaming fair trade within the context of post-Fordist agricultural markets. First, the Fairtrade certification system is in urgent need of strengthening, in particular in its operational and strategic management of corporate-buyer participation. Second – reflecting the key insight of this chapter – farmer-owned fair trade brands offer greater scope for producer empowerment and reward in global value-chain structures. As an approach to influencing conventional institutions, this tool is also more sustainable and strategic than certification, representing a model that conventional traders should arguably aim to replicate so that Fairtrade standards are ratcheted up, not down.

However, very few brands exist within the fair trade movement (especially outside of Europe) and, relative to public awareness about Fairtrade certified products, their added-value is inadequately recognized. If the movement is to prove commercially sustainable and have political integrity in the process of 'mainstreaming' in the future, fair trade brands will need to assume a greater place in fair trade research, capacity-building and public education/marketing, and the movement will need to give greater space among the ranks of its leadership to its entrepreneurial pioneers.

References

AgroFair (2004), *The Oke Impact: 2004 Annual Report* (Barendrecht: AgroFair Europe B.V.). Available at http://www.agrofair.nl/upload/File/AgroFair_Annual_Report_2004_secure_ENG. pdf [accessed: 6 September 2008].

—— (2006a), *AgroFair the Better Fruit Company: Profile: Structure*. [Online]. Available at: http://www.agrofair.nl/pages/view.php?page_id=320 [accessed:6 September 2008].

—— (2006b), *The Oke Impact: 2006 Annual Report* (Barendrecht: AgroFair Europe B.V.). Available at: http://www.agrofair.nl/upload/File/AgroFair_Annual_Report_2006_secure_ENG.pdf [accessed: 6 September 2008].

Ayres, I. and Braithwaite, J. (1992), *Responsive Regulation: Transcending the Deregulation Debate* (New York: Oxford University Press).

Bain, J. (1956), *Barriers to New Competition: Their Character and Consequences in Manufacturing Industries* (Cambridge, MA: Harvard University Press).

Barrientos, S., Conroy, M. and Jones, E. (2007), 'Northern social movements and fair trade', in L. Raynolds, D. Murray and J. Wilkinson (eds), *Fair Trade: The Challenges of Transforming Globalization* (New York: Routledge), pp. 51–62.

Barrientos, S. and Dolan, C. (2006), 'Transformation of global food: opportunities and challenges for fair and ethical trade', in S. Barrientos and C. Dolan (eds), *Ethical Sourcing in the Global Food System* (London: Earthscan).

Barrientos, S. and Smith, S. (2007), 'Mainstreaming fair trade in global production networks', in L. Raynolds, D. Murray and J. Wilkinson (eds), *Fair Trade: The Challenges of Transforming Globalization* (New York: Routledge).

Bezencon, V. and Blili, S. (2006), 'Fair trade channels: are we killing the romantics?', *International Journal of Environmental, Cultural, Economic and Social Sustainability* 2(1): 187–96.

Braithwaite, V. (2009), *Defiance in Taxation and Governance: Resisting and Dismissing Authority in a Democracy* (Cheltenham: Edward Elgar).

Cafédirect (2004), *Cafédirect plc Annual Report and Accounts 2003–04* (London: Cafédirect). Available at: http://www.cafedirect.co.uk/pdf/annual_reports/Annual_Report_2003-2004.pdf [accessed: 6 September 2008].

—— (2006), *About Us*. [Online]. Available at: http://www.cafedirect.co.uk/about/index.php [accessed: 16 November 2007].

—— (2008), 'Onward and upward: increased profitability and social impact, new chief executive for Cafédirect', press release, 5 February (London: Cafédirect).

Dicum, G. and Luttinger, N. (1999), *The Coffee Book: Anatomy of an Industry from Crop to the Last Drop* (New York: The New Press).

Divine Chocolate Ltd (2007), *Divine Chocolate: Inside Divine Chocolate*. [Online]. Available at: http://www.divinechocolate.com/about/inside-divine.aspx [accessed: 6 September 2008].

Doppler, F. and González Cabañas, A.A. (2006), 'Fair trade: benefits and drawbacks for producers', *Puente @ Europa* 4(2): 53–6.

Economides, N. (1988), 'The economics of trademarks', *Trademark Reporter* 78: 523–39.

Economist (2007), 'Thinking out of the box: how African cocoa-growers are moving upstream into chocolate', *The Economist*, 7 April, 65. Available at http://www.economist.com/business/displaystory.cfm?story_id=8966366 [accessed 6 September 2008].

Fairtrade Labelling Organizations International (FLO) (2004), *Shopping for a Better World: Annual Report 03/04* (Bonn: FLO). Available at: http://www.fairtrade.net/fileadmin/user_upload/content/AR_03-04_screen_final-1.pdf [accessed: 16 October 2008].

Gereffi, G. (1994), 'The organisation of buyer-driven commodity chains: how U.S. retailers shape overseas production networks', in G. Gereffi and M. Korzeniewicz (eds), *Commodity Chains and Global Capitalism* (Westport, CT: Praeger).

—— Humphrey, J. and Sturgeon, J. (2005), 'The governance of global value chains', *Review of International Political Economy* 12(1): 78–104.

Gibbon, P. and Ponte, S. (2005), *Trading Down: Africa, Value Chains, and the Global Economy* (Philadelphia, PA: Temple University Press).

Goodman, D. and Redclift, M. (1991), *Refashioning Nature: Food, Ecology and Culture* (New York: Routledge).

Grievink, J. (2003), 'The changing face of the global food industry', paper presented to the OECD Conference on Changing Dimensions of the Food Economy, The Hague, the Netherlands, 6–7 February.

Heffernan, W., Hendrickson, M. and Gronski, R. (1999), *Report to the National Farmers Union: Consolidation in the Food and Agriculture System* (Washington, DC: National Farmers Union). Available at: http://www.foodcircles.missouri.edu/whstudy.pdf [accessed: 6 September 2008].

Humphrey, J. and Schmitz, H. (2002), *Developing Country Firms in the World Economy: Governance and Upgrading in Global Value Chains*, INEF Report 61/2002 (Duisburg: INEF-University of Duisburg).

Hutchens, A. (2009), *Changing Big Business: The Globalisation of the Fair Trade Movement* (Cheltenham: Edward Elgar).

International Federation for Alternative Trade (IFAT) (2008), *10 Standards of Fair Trade*. [Online: IFAT]. Available at: http://www.ifat.org/index.php?option=com_content&task=view&id=2&Itemid=14 [accessed: 16 October 2008].

International Fund for Agricultural Development (IFAD) (2001), *Rural Poverty Report 2001: The Challenge of Ending Rural Poverty* (New York: Oxford University Press). Available at: http://www.ifad.org/poverty/index.htm [accessed: 6 September 2006].

Japan Today (2007), 'World Bank puts agriculture at heart of poverty fight', *Japan Today*. [Online, 22 October]. Available at: http://www.dev-zone.org/downloads/World%20Bank%20puts%20agriculture%20at%20heart%20of%20poverty%20fight.doc [accessed: 16 October 2008].

Kaplinsky, R. (2006), 'How can agricultural commodity producers appropriate a greater share of value chain incomes?', in A. Sarris and D. Hallam (eds), *Agricultural Commodity Markets and Trade: New Approaches to Analyzing Market Structure and Instability* (Cheltenham: Edward Elgar).

Klein, N. (2000), *No Logo: Taking Aim at the Brand Bullies* (New York: Picador).

Kocken, M. (2003), *Fifty Years of Fair Trade* (Culemborg: IFAT).

Krier, J.-M. (2005), *Fair Trade in Europe 2005: Facts and Figures on Fair Trade in 25 European Countries* (Brussels: Fair Trade Advocacy Office).

Kyere, E. and Neil, C. (2006), 'Trade in the global village: harnessing and building capacities through fair trade', seminar presentation for the Fair Trade Fortnight 2006: The Regulatory Institutions Network (REGNET), Canberra, Australia, 11 May 2006.

Litrell. M. and Dickson, M. (1999), *Social Responsibility in the Global Market: Fair Trade of Cultural Products* (Thousand Oaks, CA: Sage).

Low, W. and Davenport, E. (2005), 'Postcards from the edge: maintaining the "alternative" character of fair trade', *Sustainable Development* 13(3): 143–53.

Lunney, G.S., Jr (1999), 'Trademark monopolies', *Emory Law Journal* 48(2): 367–487.

Lury, C. (2004), *Brands: The Logos of the Global Economy* (Oxford: Routledge).

Martyn, T. (2007), 'Capturing the intangible: accessing marketing rents through farmer-own brands', Masters dissertation, London School of Economics.

Mellor, J.W. (2001), 'Background paper: reducing poverty, buffering economic shocks – agriculture and the non-tradable economy', in *Roles of Agriculture Project Expert Meeting Proceedings: First Expert Meeting on the Documentation and Measurement of the Roles of Agriculture in Developing Countries* (ROA Project Publication No. 2) (Rome: Food and Agriculture Organization [FAO]). Available at: ftp://ftp.fao.org/es/esa/roa/pdf/EMP-E.pdf [accessed: 6 September 2008].

Morisset, J. (1997), *Unfair Trade? Empirical Evidence in World Commodity Markets over the past 25 Years* (Washington, DC: World Bank).

Murray, D. and Raynolds, L. (2007), 'Globalization and its antinomies: negotiating a fair trade movement', in L. Raynolds, D. Murray and J. Wilkinson (eds), *Fair Trade: The Challenges of Transforming Globalization* (New York: Routledge).

Nicholls, A. and Opal, C. (2005), *Fair Trade: Market-Driven Ethical Consumption* (London: Sage).

North, R. (2006), *On Fair Trade 'Fig Leaves': Equal Exchange Speaks Out on Abuse of the Fair Trade System*, USFT listserv. [Online]. Edited version available at *The Wedge Newsletter*: http://www.wedge.coop/newsletter/article/630.html [accessed: 6 September 2008].

Oxfam International (2002), *The Coffee Report – Mugged: Poverty in Your Coffee Cup* (Oxford: Oxfam International). Available at: http://www.oxfam.org.uk/what_we_do/issues/key_papers.htm [accessed: 6 September 2008].

—— (2004), *Trading Away Our Rights: Women Working in Global Supply Chains* (Oxford: Oxfam International). Available at: http://www.oxfam.org.uk/resources/policy/trade/downloads/trading_rights.pdf [accessed: 6 September 2008].

Piore, M. and Sabel, C. (1984), *The Second Industrial Divide* (New York: Basic Books).

Pritchard, B. (1999), 'Switzerland's billabong? Brand management in the global food system and Nestlé Australia', in D. Burch, J. Goss and G. Lawrence (eds), *Restructuring Global and Regional Agricultures: Transformations in Australasian Agri-food Economies and Spaces* (Aldershot: Ashgate), pp. 23–40.

Raynolds, L. (2007), 'Fair trade bananas: broadening the movement and market in the United States', in L. Raynolds, D. Murray and J. Wilkinson (eds), *Fair Trade: The Challenges of Transforming Globalization* (New York: Routledge), pp. 63–82.

Raynolds, L. and Long, M. (2007), 'Fair/alternative trade: historical and empirical dimensions', in L. Raynolds, D. Murray and J. Wilkinson (eds), *Fair Trade: The Challenges of Transforming Globalization* (New York: Routledge).

Raynolds, L., Murray, D. and Wilkinson, J. (eds) (2007), *Fair Trade: The Challenges of Transforming Globalization* (New York: Routledge).

Raynolds, L. and Wilkinson, J. (2007), 'Fair trade in the agriculture and food sector: analytical dimensions', in L. Raynolds, D. Murray and J. Wilkinson (eds), *Fair Trade: The Challenges of Transforming Globalization* (New York: Routledge).

Redfern, A. and Snedker, P. (2002), *Creating Market Opportunities for Small Enterprises: Experiences of the Fair Trade Movement*, SEED Working Paper 30 (Geneva: International Labour Organization).

Renard, M.-C. and Pérez-Grovas, V. (2007), 'Fair trade coffee in Mexico: at the centre of the debates', in L. Raynolds, D. Murray and J. Wilkinson (eds), *Fair Trade: The Challenges of Transforming Globalization* (New York: Routledge).

Robbins, P. (2003), *Stolen Fruit: The Tropical Commodities Disaster* (New York: Zed Books).

Schumpeter, J. (1934), *The Theory of Economic Development: An Inquiry into Profits, Capital, Credit, Interest and the Business Cycle* (Cambridge, MA: Harvard University Press).

Talbot, J.M. (1997), 'Where does your coffee dollar go? The division of income and surplus along the coffee commodity chain', *Studies in Comparative International Development* 32(1): 56–91.

Tallontire, A. (2000), 'Partnerships in fair trade: reflections from a case study of Cafédirect', *Development in Practice* 10(2): 166–77.

—— (2006), 'The development of alternative and fair trade: moving into the mainstream', in S. Barrientos and C. Dolan (eds), *Ethical Sourcing in the Global Food System* (London: Earthscan).

Tiffen, P., MacDonald, J., Mazmah, H. and Osei-Opare, F. (2004), 'From tree-minders to global players: cocoa farmers in Ghana', in M. Carr (ed.), *Chains of Fortune: Linking Women Producers and Workers with Global Markets* (London: Commonwealth Secretariat).

United Nations Development Program (UNDP) (2005), *Human Development Report. International Cooperation at a Crossroads: Aid, Trade and Security in an Unequal World* (New York: UNDP).

Vorley, B. (2003), *Food, Inc.: Corporate Concentration from Farm to Consumer* (London: International Institute for Environment and Development).

Wilkinson, J. and Mascarenhas, G. (2007), 'Southern social movements and fair trade', in L. Raynolds, D. Murray and J. Wilkinson (eds), *Fair Trade: The Challenges of Transforming Globalisation* (New York: Routledge).

Chapter 5
What Gives Fair Trade its Right to Operate? Organizational Legitimacy and Strategic Management

Alex Nicholls

Introduction

As is common with many charitable or social purpose organizations, the heart of the fair trade movement appears to carry an implicit assumption that its objectives and processes give it a legitimate right to operate as a distinct model of social justice and development. The roots of the movement in trade justice campaigning, advocacy and faith groups have lent weight to this assumption, since they carry a normative moral and political authority consistent with the stated aims and achievements of fair trade.[1] Most scholarly literature analysing fair trade shares this view and bases its theory and research on an untested assumption that fair trade offers a legitimate model for producer empowerment and economic development.[2] Despite some criticisms of specific aspects of the model – notably its economics (LeClair 2003; Maseland and de Vaal 2002; Booth and Whetstone 2007), impact (Berlan 2004) and marketing (Hudson and Hudson 2003; Wright 2004; Goodman 2004; Dolan 2007) – fair trade continues to enjoy widespread popular support and is a growing consumer-driven market trend in the North (Nicholls 2007).

However, the exponential growth of fair trade as a consumer-driven model of economic development has created both internal and external structural tensions that could threaten its continued success (Nicholls and Opal 2005; Raynolds and Wilkinson 2007). With the expansion of fair trade from an activist-based campaigning movement to a market-driven trend in ethical consumption, two models of fair trade have emerged: first, a non-certificated, community-facing, advocacy and market-linkage model that is represented by the International Fair Trade Association (formerly IFAT, now the World Fair Trade Organization: WFTO); second, a certificated, market-facing, commercial model that is represented by the Fairtrade Labelling Organizations International (FLO). In essence, these models diverge as push and pull supply chain approaches – the former is committed to growing the supplier base whilst the latter aims to grow the market (Nicholls and Opal 2005). These strategic differences can sharply divide fair trade. For example, the FLO's decision to certify Nestlé's Partner's Blend coffee as fair trade was widely condemned by activists who had long campaigned against the company (Thaekekara and Thaekekara 2007).

Just as the internal integrity of the movement is under stress, so too is its external legitimacy being called into question. As fair trade has entered the mainstream in many countries it has come under increasing scrutiny from the media and the public. Questions concerning its impact and methods are thus beginning to emerge (Barrientos 2000; LeClair 2002; Lindsey 2004; Booth and

---

1   Barratt Brown (1993); Ransom (2001); Nicholls and Opal (2005); Raynolds, Murray and Wilkinson (2007).

2   See, for example, Strong (1996; 1997); Bird and Hughes (1997); Littrell and Dickson (1997); Renard (1999; 2003); Tallontire (2000; 2002); McDonagh (2002); Nicholls (2002; 2004); Raynolds (2002); Davies and Crane (2003).

Whetstone 2007). The relative paucity of impact studies has also served to undermine the credibility of fair trade's claims[3] and recent ethnographic research explicitly questions them (Berlan 2004; 2008). The pressing nature of such challenges confronting the fair trade movement underscores the timeliness of this chapter's central goal: to undertake a rigorous assessment of how the legitimacy of fair trade is actually configured and how managers' current action relates to this process.

It is widely accepted that organizational legitimacy is a socially constructed phenomenon. Furthermore, it is an exogenous construct: namely, legitimacy only exists in the aggregated perceptions of actors external to an organization. Thus, organizations do not 'own' their legitimacy; rather, it is conferred upon them by others' judgements of their actions. An organization's public mandate to act is based upon these perceptions of its organizational legitimacy, and without such a source of legitimacy it will not be able to access the resources (such as finance, customers and staff) needed for its ongoing survival. In this sense, legitimacy may simply be defined as *the congruence, in multiple stakeholder judgements, of an organization's perceived actions with their expectations of its performance*.

In conventional businesses, legitimacy typically rests on fulfilling legal and fiduciary responsibilities to maximize value creation for the business's owners. In developed economies, society grants firms legitimacy on the basis of how well they conform to a profit-generating capitalist model of wealth creation within private ownership (although there are some regional differences in places such as China). However, for third sector organizations, such as not-for-profits, charities and social enterprises, society grants legitimacy based upon their ability to deliver public benefit above and beyond that generated by the state and private sectors. Social enterprises – organizations that have a social mission but are also profit generating (typically creating *blended value* [Emerson 2003]) – sit at the intersection of these two strands of legitimacy theory (Nicholls 2005; 2006). As a social enterprise, fair trade is also located at the meeting point of financial and social value creation and finds itself at the confluence of legitimacy judgements driven both by its resource seeking strategies and its accountability structures.[4]

It is proposed here that managing these diverse legitimacy judgements as well as the constituent populations that make such judgements presents a major challenge to the progress of fair trade. This research specifically aims to highlight how fair trade's right to operate can better be understood as part of a legitimating process largely external to it and to determine the most effective strategic pathways to both preserve and enhance fair trade's current legitimacy (see Nicholls 2009).

This chapter uses a neo-institutional framework within organizational theory to analyse the legitimacy of fair trade and to explore the assumptions underpinning its right to operate as a social enterprise.[5] The chapter falls into three parts. First, it develops an analytic model of the organizational legitimacy process in fair trade. Second, the model is used to reflect upon actual managerial action within fair trade organizations based on analysis of a sample of qualitative interviews. Finally, conclusions and recommendations are drawn from the analysis. Two specific research questions are addressed, corresponding respectively with the first and second parts of the chapter:

---

3   However, see also Blowfield and Gallet (2000); Nelson and Galvez (2000); Kocken (2002); Ronchi (2002; 2003).

4   See Dart (2004), for an analysis of how these are generating dynamic tensions in social enterprises generally.

5   For other examples of the application of this framework, see: Meyer and Rowan (1977); Meyer et al. (1978); Meyer et al. (1981); DiMaggio and Powell (1983; 1991); Meyer and Scott (1992); Suchman (1995); Dart (2004); Nicholls (2006).

1. What are the factors that contribute to building perceptions of organizational legitimacy in fair trade?
2. How effectively does current managerial action build and maintain perceptions of fair trade's organizational legitimacy?

This chapter suggests that there is some disjunction between theory and practice in the building and maintenance of fair trade legitimacy. This is particularly the case in regard to identifying the strategic importance of competing legitimating judgements of the movement. Analysis also reveals that, as a consequence of this, some elements of fair trade's ideal type of legitimacy – that is, its political dimension of advocacy and campaigning – is undervalued in current management thinking. Such legitimacy 'gaps' may well have serious consequence for fair trade's overall legitimacy and public trust over time.

Methodology

The analysis presented in this chapter draws on a combination of theoretical literature, qualitative interviews with organizational actors internal to the fair trade movement and an examination of public discourses generated by fair trade organizations.

The first research question is addressed by developing a tripartite model of the legitimating process, drawing upon a range of theoretical literature, notably neo-institutionalism, accountability theory and the growing body of multi-disciplinary fair trade research in management, social geography and not-for-profit journals.

The second research question applies this tripartite model to an analysis of qualitative interview data.[6] This analysis centres upon a group of 14 semi-structured interviews with internal actors – typically the CEO or another senior manager – which were carried out by the author over three months in 2007. Participant organizations included a major fair trade wholesaler, a national labelling initiative, a financial provider to fair trade organizations and a number of related third sector organizations and social enterprises. Pilot interviews were carried out with three of the organizations to test and refine the theoretical concepts explored in the subsequent interviewing.

Interviews were organized around a series of topics, related questions and probes drawn from the existing literature on organizational legitimacy. The questions specifically addressed the perceptions of different actors (both within and outside the movement) regarding Fair Trade's right to operate. They also considered how perceptions of fair trade's organizational legitimacy are configured with reference to subjective constructs such as reputation and trust. In the absence of any previously published research on perceptions of fair trade legitimacy, the main objective of these interviews was exploratory.

All interviews were recorded and transcribed. Analysis of the data involved three processes. First, transcripts and notes were read and reread for familiarization with the data. Second, a more detailed and systematic analysis was carried out to identify cross-sectional themes. NVivo2 was used to perform the full coding of the data. As themes emerged, further analysis of the data

---

6 A qualitative approach was adopted given the nature of the research questions, which are concerned with the perceptions of actors engaged with fair trade. This reflected both the contextual and exploratory concerns of the research (see Miles and Huberman 1994; Ritchie 2003). Whilst there are differing ontological and epistemological perspectives aligned with qualitative research methods (Lincoln and Gubba 2000; Schwandt 2000), the use of such an approach here was decided upon on grounds of interpretivism and pragmatism (Ritchie 2003).

developed more refined sub-themes as 'tree-nodes'. Data nodes were examined in combination as well as by theme to explore various dimensions of the responses. These inductively derived nodes were also mapped against each element of the tripartite legitimacy model during the analysis of the data.

The design of the research presented in this chapter can be best understood with reference to its position within a broader and ongoing research project. The data analysed here was collected during the first stage of a three-stage research process focused on the perceptions of actors internal to the fair trade system. Stage two of the research will focus on producers and other dependent external actors and stage three will explore the views of customers and other key external stakeholders.

Because the available interview data relates only to perceptions of actors internal to fair trade organizations, it is complemented by an additional data set derived from a content analysis of public statements made by key fair trade organizations, in which the unique qualities of fair trade are identified and justifications for its right to operate are publicly articulated. In a sense, this discourse data set acts as a proxy for other third party data from stakeholders beyond fair trade wholesalers and retailers by providing a synthetic 'systems of relationship' response to legitimating action – namely, the response that the fair traders expected to elicit from others by their strategic actions. Analysis of this second data set therefore allows a comparative analysis to be made between the public and private strategic positioning of fair trade's legitimacy; this comparison plays an important role in illuminating the analytic insights of the tripartite model of legitimacy.

Organizational Legitimacy in Fair Trade

To answer the first research question, this section develops a new conceptual model of the legitimation process and then applies it to the case of fair trade. The tripartite model of organizational legitimacy presented here is intended as a diagnostic and analytic rather than a prescriptive tool: that is, it does not aim to tell managers what to do to build legitimacy; rather, it aims to help them better understand how to think about the legitimation process. Consequently, it provides an artificially linear representation of the complex legitimating processes surrounding an organization or movement. Nevertheless, it aims to have heuristic analytic and descriptive value.

In essence, this model does two things. First, it provides a macro-framework through which managers can better grasp the structure of the processes through which legitimacy can be acquired, strengthened, or undermined. This is important because it draws attention to the central relationship between what managers *do*, how this is *perceived* by an array of external stakeholders, and patterns of legitimacy that result. Second, it offers managers a nuanced set of tools for analysing the relationship between different sources of legitimacy, and the perceptions of different sets of stakeholders. If these come into conflict – as they almost always do at some point in an organization's development – the strategic imperative is to discern which legitimacies matter most within an operational context and, therefore, how best to weight strategic action in relation to these multiple, interconnected determinants of legitimacy. The tripartite model suggests that legitimacies accrue as a result of aggregated stakeholder perceptions (systems of relationships) of organizational actions and qualities (legitimating competences): stakeholder perceptions act as a lens transforming and distorting actions and qualities into forms of organizational legitimacy, rather than these perceptions having any innate legitimacy of their own. The critical insight here is, therefore, that legitimacy is the product of contested perceptions amongst external – and not equally weighted – actors.[7]

Within neo-institutionalist theory,[8] an extensive body of literature examining the construction of legitimacy in organizational settings has accumulated over more than 30 years of scholarship (Dowling and Pfeffer 1975; Pfeffer and Salanick 1978; Suchman 1995). Neo-institutionalist scholars suggested that key external actors confer legitimacy in accordance with an organization's congruence with the rules and norms of a superordinate societal system (Parsons 1960; Maurer 1971; Ashford and Gibbs 1990; Hybels 1995). This approach draws its theoretical heritage from wider sociological discussions which give primacy to structure over agency in the context of power structures and constraints on organizational action (Marx 1991 [1867]; Weber 1978; 2004; Giddens 1984) and is sometimes characterized as a constraining process of isomorphism (DiMaggio and Powell 1983; Deephouse and Carter 2005). Alternatively, more recent work has taken a more cognitive turn, suggesting that legitimacy processes are largely interpretive (Meyer and Scott 1992; Elsbach 1994; Thomas 2005) and can be strategic (Rao 1994; Neilsen and Rao 1987; Lounsbury and Glynn 2001). Research on institutional innovation has added a political level of analysis that presents the construction of legitimacy as a consequence of the interplay between competing institutional logics. This gives greater emphasis to agency theory, highlighting the role and impact of independent action within an institutional setting (Friedland and Alford 1991; Stryker 2000; Galvin, Ventresca and Hudson 2004).

A second stream of scholarship in voluntary sector and not-for-profit management literature considers organizational legitimacy specifically in a social sector context. In this work, legitimacy is explicitly linked to accountability, transparency and recognition of the stakeholder voice (Edwards and Hulme 1995; Edwards 1999). This can be contrasted with more structuralist and static perspectives of neo-institutional theory that often marginalize the significance of individual actors, refuse to acknowledge variations in the cognitive models of legitimacy across stakeholders, and fail to account for the influence of power structures of elites in shaping legitimating choices (Lister 2003; see also Lukes 2005). In not-for-profit literature, legitimacy is also recognized as having a moral (Atack 1999) as well as a strategic (Hudson 2000; Dart 2004) dimension: the key observation here is that accountability and (demonstrable) relevance must be at the heart of any successful legitimacy process (Edwards 1999).

These two streams of research into organizational legitimacy reveal a number of common themes:

1. Establishing and maintaining organizational legitimacy should be a core management function.
2. Perceptions of organizational legitimacy are fluid and dynamic and thus need a sophisticated analytic framework to be understood.
3. The landscape of organizational legitimacy is made up of multiple perspectives that may be in conflict and should be weighted in terms of their relative strategic importance.
4. Perceptions of organizational legitimacy are built upon judgments of specific actions, behaviours and features of the focus organization and, as a result, have a strategic dimension.
5. Building organizational legitimacy is a function of accountability to stakeholders and can be seen as a measure of performance (see Nicholls 2008).

---

7   See also Nicholls (2008), in terms of legitimacy as a performance variable.
8   See, for example, Meyer and Rowan (1977); Meyer et al. (1978); Meyer et al. (1981); Zucker (1977). See also Jepperson (2002) and Scott (2008) for overviews.

The tripartite model developed here builds on Hybels' (1995) assertion that the resource-based and cognitive traditions within neo-institutionalism can be reconciled to develop a new analytic model of organizational legitimacy (see also Suchman 1995). Namely, that organizational legitimacy is the product of the interaction between differentiated and individualized cognitive frames and patterns of similarity and difference between organizations and superordinate social systems, with the former effectively filtering the latter. The structurationalist approach used here also acknowledges the contribution of social movement theory in its analysis of the mobilization of action frames to reconstitute societal perceptions of action and values (Davis et al. 2005).[9]

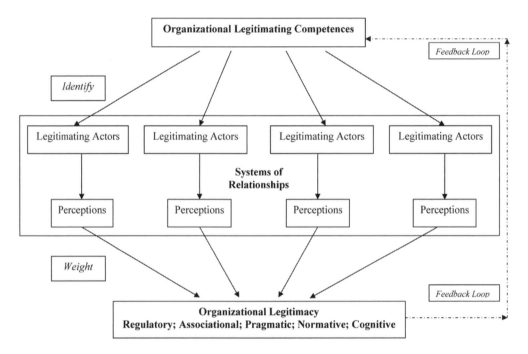

Figure 5.1   A model of organizational legitimacy

The legitimacy model has three core elements (see Figure 5.1): *legitimating competences* (organizational actions, behaviours and properties, that is, the 'objective' features of what organizations and managers *do*); *systems of relationships* (stakeholder perceptions of these actions, behaviours and properties, that is, the subjective interpretation of these, as filtered through the perceptions of a particular configuration of organizational stakeholders); and a *legitimacy typology* (different categories of legitimacy accruing from the interaction of these perceptions).

---

9   See also Hargrave and Van der Ven (2006), for an interesting comparison of social movements and institutional innovation.

Legitimating Competences

The first element of the analytic model draws upon the resource-based tradition of research in strategic management literature. The resource-based view of the firm was given a concrete focus by the concept of core competences (Prahalad and Hamel 1990; Mahoney and Pandian 1992; Teece, Pisano and Shuen 1997). In essence, these were unique organizational capabilities and processes that were hard to imitate and which therefore represented a source of potential competitive advantage. Core competences act as path-dependent assets and sources of innovation. Drawing upon this approach, neo-institutional literature explicitly cited legitimacy (as a conferred status) as a firm-specific resource (Terreberry 1968; Dowling and Pfeffer 1975; Pfeffer and Salanick 1978; Hybels 1995).

Here the concept of *legitimating* competences is proposed to represent any action, resource, attribute or property associated with an organization (or is perceived to be associated) that plays a material role in influencing stakeholders' perceptions of its legitimacy. These include the type of competences acknowledged in existing management literature (that is, specific actions, strategies, capabilities or processes), but also takes into account cognitive elements such as values and mission statements, stories and characters, and myths and histories.[10] An organization's legitimating competences come in many forms, but research to date (see, for example, Suchman 1995; Jepson 2005; Nicholls 2008) suggests that at least nine categories are significant (see Table 5.1).

Table 5.1   Legitimating competences

Legitimating competence	Strategic action
Organizational agency	
Expertise and skills	Employ high quality staff Manage efficiency Build quality control systems
Public support	Build relationships with target markets Build market share Build brand constituency
Performance impact	Develop a range of metrics Formalize and codify operations
Organizational assets	Use regulated audit mechanisms Build resource networks
Individual integrity	Align CEO reputation with cultural norms of probity, independence and objectivity
Accountability systems	Negotiate decision-making with stakeholders and build transparency
Institutional fit	
Alignment with principles	Build mission objectives around normative values appropriate to the organizational type and sector
Cultural resonance	Align organizational values, symbols, myths and narratives with appropriate cultural norms
Longevity	Build consistent performance over time

---

10   These can include, for example, symbolic systems, cultural norms, 'rational myths' and narratives, and social rules noted in Meyer and Rowan (1977, 341–3); Rao (1994); Neilsen and Rao (1987); Lounsbury and Glynn (2001).

Legitimating competences can be divided into two groups: those that are the result of organizational agency and can be internally generated by the strategic management of competing institutional logics; and those that are the result of building an institutional fit between the organization and the larger societal structures and norms to which the organization must adapt and seek 'frame' alignment. The first six competences can be categorized as internal/organizational and the remaining three as external/institutional. The strategic implication of this division is that the former six can accrue as a result of perceptions of independent organizational actions and behaviours, whereas the other three require the organization to shape its strategy dependent upon, and in conformity to, existing institutional structures (see further, Suchman 1995).

As a market driven model, the legitimacy of the fair trade movement generally is based upon its cultural resonance with the growth of ethical consumption over the last ten years. This has been demonstrated by its increased public support and exponential sales increase (see Nicholls 2007). This is underpinned by public trust in its performance impact, expertise and skills. For certified fair trade, accountability systems (namely the Fairtrade mark) are a further important legitimating competence. Ultimately, fair trade's legitimation, and thus its overall success, is dependent on maintaining public trust in its ability to translate retail sales into its key objectives of economic development and empowerment.

Systems of Relationships

The second element in the legitimacy model draws upon conceptualizations of legitimacy in both the neo-institutional and not-for-profit literatures to represent the interpretive dimension of the legitimating process. It is proposed that organizational legitimacy accrues from the aggregation of multiple stakeholder *perceptions* of legitimating competences, rather than the competences themselves. Such perceptions reflect both how stakeholders relate to the focus organization and how their own frames of reference shape their perceptions of the legitimating competences. Furthermore, both factors are influenced by wider societal and peer group norms, interactions and cognitive frames. These complex patternings are characterized as *systems of relationships*.

Despite widespread acknowledgement of the strategic value of appropriating resonant (exogenous) cultural symbols as part of an organization's legitimating project (Rao 1994; Neilsen and Rao 1987; Lounsbury and Glynn 2001), much neo-institutional thinking assumed that the agency within the legitimating process lay with the organization itself. Friedland and Alford (1991), Stryker (2000) and Galvin et al. (2004) problematized this analysis by contextualizing the appropriation of symbolic resources within a contested political process that embodied competing ideologies and dissonant points of view. However, the analytic focus – as might be expected from neo-institutionalists – still ultimately lay with structures rather than agents. An alternative reading is provided by the not-for-profit literature's focus on stakeholder accountability as the key determinant of organizational legitimacy via the role of individual agency, the impact of stakeholder voice and processes of empowerment (Edwards and Hulme 1995; Edwards 1999; Lister 2003). Systems of relationships attempts to capture these two conceptual positions, namely that legitimacy is the product of finding equilibrium across multiple competing perceptions of an organization within which individual stakeholders are the key determinants of meaning. The concept of systems of relationships thus aims to integrate structure (cultural context) and agency (individual perceptions) in a mode that translates organizational legitimating competences into enduring legitimacies.

A systems of relationships analysis allows an organization to weight strategically varying stakeholder judgements in terms of their value and significance concerning its right to operate. For example, a not-for-profit development organization working in Africa may have to decide whether the legitimating judgements of its donors, beneficiaries, governments or the media are most important for its ongoing survival and adapt its legitimating competences accordingly. Similarly, a fair trade organization will need to weigh up, and perhaps offset, the different legitimating perceptions of launching a new partnership with a commercial company across its customers, producers, activist base, government, competitors and others. A careful analysis of this legitimacy ecosystem should ensure that strategic planning will not diminish overall organizational legitimacy and its perceived right to operate. This is not an easy task, but it is of considerable strategic importance.

Since the strategic purpose of fair trade – clearly stated in all its public statements – is the development and empowerment of producers, the perceptions and opinions of these stakeholders would be expected to sit at the top of the hierarchy of systems of relationships. As a market-driven model, consumers are also of great significance as key stakeholders, though of secondary importance to producers within the rhetoric of fair trade. Other relevant systems of relationships here include the media's perceptions (given fair trade's limited advertising budget), investors (either charitable groups or 'social' investors such as Cafédirect's shareholders) and government (for example, in the debate concerning whether fair trade should have a legal definition).

Legitimacy Typology

Research to date has identified five categories of legitimacy judgements that can be presented as a legitimacy typology (see Table 5.2) (Suchman 1995; Jepson 2005; Nicholls 2008). Importantly, each of these five types can carry a different value or 'weighting' within a strategic hierarchy, moving from regulatory to cognitive (see Table 5.2). Accruing regulatory legitimacy may be largely interpreted as involving 'hygiene' factors without which an organization cannot function and is, therefore, of limited strategic impact. On the other hand, gaining high levels of cognitive legitimacy demonstrates that an organization is not only firmly embedded in the wider institutional structure of society, but that it may well be actively involved in defining and shaping such cognitive structures. High levels of cognitive legitimacy are of considerable operational value since they are likely to support long-term resource acquisition and organizational longevity. For example, the cognitive construct of 'a charity' has extremely powerful legitimating value, since it has been particularly represented for over 100 years as a special (that is, tax avoiding) public benefit organization. Consequently, any new organization identifying itself as a charity can automatically accrue significant cognitive legitimacy even without proving its performance at the time (though

Table 5.2   A typology of organizational legitimacy

Type	Regulatory	Associational	Pragmatic	Normative	Cognitive
Descriptor	Legal	By association	Appealing to self interest	Expected of others	Consistent with worldview
Basis of judgement	Compliance with relevant legal requirements and regulations	Association with other entities that are already perceived to be legitimate and/ or powerful	Ability to meet the direct needs and interests of specific stakeholders making the judgement	Acting in ways that are consistent with stakeholders' expectations of how such an organization should act towards others	Fitting into conceptual categories that stakeholders habitually use to understand the world around them

it should be noted that this legitimacy can decay over time if contradictory perceptions begin to form across stakeholder groups). It is also worth noting, however, that the higher hierarchical legitimacies are also *ipso facto* often the hardest to manage strategically.

By analysing the relationship between relevant systems of relationships and the legitimacy typology, an organization can begin to map out the judgements that are of most strategic value to its continued operational success. One insight of this analysis is that conventional strategic thinking may be challenged. For example, while the judgements of customers (and donors) may be given operational precedence, deeper and more valuable legitimating judgements may lie with beneficiaries, the media or government. If this is the case then, over time, the organization's aggregate legitimacy may decline with fatal consequences. Something of this process can be seen in the increasingly diminishing returns experienced by many corporate social responsibility (CSR) initiatives. Thus, a portfolio of aggregated legitimating judgements can be developed which coordinates legitimating competences to accrue the best mix of systems of relationships in the most effective manner in order to underpin an organization's continued right to operate. This will typically be far more than just a marketing exercise, since key systems of relationships may well be formed by direct personal experience of organizational behaviour and judgements will thus be made on actual – rather than perceived – performance.

With respect to the typology, while fair trade has focused on building associational legitimacy via a range of celebrity endorsements, as well as addressing pragmatic legitimacy via improved quality control and premium price marketing (see Nicholls and Opal 2005), it is differentiated by its normative and cognitive legitimacies. Fair trade can only flourish in the context of both public trust in its ability to deliver impacts that are not directly apparent to the consumer – that is, its normative legitimacy (see Nicholls and Alexander 2006) – and in a societal landscape in which its objectives are held to be consistent with a widely acknowledged 'worldview' of how consumption can effectively be linked to development (its cognitive legitimacy). In recognition of this, fair trade has established a set of discourses justifying its right to operate which represent an ideal type of normative and cognitive legitimacies. A content analysis of such statements reveals how such an ideal type can be deconstructed with respect to the legitimacy typology.

In 2001, FINE – a collaborative body bringing together the four leading organizations behind the international fair trade movement[11] – agreed, for the first time, a joint definition of the term 'fair trade':

> Fair Trade is a trading partnership, based on dialogue, transparency and respect, that seeks greater equity in international trade. It contributes to sustainable development by offering better trading conditions to, and securing the rights of, disadvantaged producers and workers – especially in the South. Fair Trade organizations (backed by consumers) are actively engaged in supporting producers in awareness raising and in campaigning for changes in the rules and practices of conventional international trade.

> Fair Trade's strategic intent is:

> •   Deliberately to work with marginalized producers and workers in order to help them move from a position of vulnerability to security and economic self-sufficiency;

---

11   These are: the Fair Trade Labelling Organizations International (FLO), the International Fair Trade Association (formerly IFAT, now the World Fair Trade Organization: WFTO), the Network of European World Shops (NEWS), and the European Fair Trade Association (EFTA).

- To empower producers and workers as stakeholders in their own organizations;
- Actively to play a wider role in the global arena to achieve greater equity in international trade. (FLO 2006)

The individual mission statements of the FINE members and other high profile fair trade organizations (such as TransFair USA and Cafédirect) support this statement but also extend it.[12] An analysis of these public definitions of fair trade and its purposes reveals a number of common words and phrases which can be clustered around three discourses: process focus, political focus and economic focus (see Table 5.3).

Table 5.3   Legitimating discourses in fair trade public statements

Discourse cluster	Key word	Organization
Process focus	Partnership	FINE
	Dialogue	FINE
	Transparency	FINE
	Respect	FINE; FTF
	Equity	FINE
Political focus	Rights	FINE
	Empowerment	FINE; TransFair USA; IFAT; Cafédirect
	Campaigning	FINE; FLO
	Raising awareness	FINE; FLO
	Justice	IFAT
Economic focus	Trade	FINE; FLO
	Development	FINE; IFAT; Cafédirect
	Business skills	TransFair USA; FTF
	Sustainability	FINE; IFAT; TransFair USA; FTF

While there is some variation around how these statements position individual organizations – for example, FLO highlights certification, IFAT emphasizes trade justice, TransFair USA stresses business development – there is a broad consensus across the three discourse clusters. Essentially, these three discourses represent the distinct value proposition that fair trade offers to society: namely, how it operates (process), why (political) and with whom (economic). This complex proposition is used to justify fair trade's right to operate and, in terms of its public benefit, is designed to give it a social mandate to address development issues in a new way that is differentiated from other, more conventional, approaches followed by NGOs, governments and other transnational bodies.

---

12   For instances of this, see: the FLO website at http://www.fairtrade.net/about_us.html and http://www.fairtrade.net/introduction.html; the IFAT website at http://www.ifat.org/index.php?option=com_frontpage&Itemid=1, http://www.ifat.org/index.php?option=com_content&task=blogcategory&id=8&Itemid=5 and http://www.ifat.org/index.php?option=com_content&task=view&id=1&Itemid=13; the TransFair USA website at http://transfairusa.org/content/about/overview.php and http://transfairusa.org/content/about/mission.php; the Fairtrade Foundation website at http://www.fairtrade.org.uk/includes/documents/cm_docs/2008/a/accounts2006.pdf; and the Cafédirect website at http://www.cafedirect.co.uk/our_business.

These three discourse clusters represent fair trade's self-legitimation in normative and cognitive terms. The suggestion is that fair trade derives its right to operate by operationalizing key stakeholder perceptions of its unique ability to deliver economic development and political empowerment to producers.

Current Legitimating Strategies in Fair Trade

The tripartite model suggests that fair trade's legitimacy rests upon managers strategizing the process by which its legitimating competences are interpreted by key stakeholders. The next section analyses interview data to compare actual legitimating practices against the theoretical assumptions above.

The majority of the respondents seldom discussed legitimacy in their organizations explicitly. When the concept was introduced for discussion in the interviews, respondents typically acknowledged that they were uncertain as to how to configure their own legitimacy. This seemed largely to be a consequence of unfamiliarity with the construct in operational and strategic contexts. There was an overall perception that legitimacy was a complex, socially constructed phenomenon that was not central to management thinking. As a consequence, no respondents conceptualized legitimacy as a product of stakeholder perceptions of organizational action or understood it to be largely exogenous.

When specifically asked to define organizational legitimacy, the notion was typically related to issues of accountability and responsiveness:

> I suppose I equate the word legitimacy as a mixture of being accountable to a constituency and transparency, being open about what you are doing, about what you've got to do, how you're trying to do it. (Interviewee 5)

However, this demonstrates a very limited, unidirectional view of accountability that does not acknowledge the opinions or feedback of stakeholders and, therefore, diminishes the strategic importance of their perceptions.[13]

Respondents recognized the strategic significance of the more familiar notions of trust, reputation and credibility for building a 'mandate' to operate (Interviewee 12). Deeply held values and a clear social mission were seen as important in terms of building trust and reputation in order to demonstrate 'authenticity' (Interviewee 11). Most respondents appeared to be aware of the need to manage their reputation strategically and some even had formalized procedures and mechanisms for dealing with it. These most commonly took two forms: using the media and public relations; and focusing on building relationships with important stakeholders, often based around key individual contacts and sometimes involving the personal engagement of a CEO/senior manager. Again, the focus was largely on internal systems as the drivers for legitimating constructs such as trust, rather than on better understanding external cognitive frames and perceptions.

These results suggest that managers within the fair trade movement lack an analytic framework through which they can, first, understand how their organizational legitimacy is constructed and, second, manage it effectively. Furthermore, it is clear that by giving precedence to reputation management strategies based on PR rather than stakeholder engagement, interviewees conceived of their right to operate largely in terms borrowed from CSR and the commercial world. Such an

---

13   For further reading, see the criticisms of NGO accountability in Edwards (1999).

approach suggests a drift away from more typical third sector discourses on trust and reputation that focus on accountability to beneficiaries and performance impact.[14]

Legitimating Competences

Despite a lack of clarity concerning the boundaries of organizational legitimacy, the role of stakeholder perceptions in its construction, and its relationship to fair trade's right to operate, respondents identified a number of antecedents that they felt were important for their organizational reputation and credibility. As the independent variables upon which strategies for reputation were built, these correspond largely to the legitimating competences noted above.

Of those competences that have been identified elsewhere (Nicholls 2008), interviewees explicitly mentioned: expertise and skills; public support; individual integrity; accountability systems; alignment with principles; cultural resonance; and longevity. Conversely, there was little evidence of focus on: performance impact; or organizational assets.

The absence of performance impact from the discussions suggests a skewed strategic perspective on the importance of beneficiaries and their experience of fair trade. This is further highlighted by the acknowledgement that shaping accountability systems appropriate to the fair trade model seemed to present a particular challenge:

> We don't say: 'Who are we going to upset?' We look at it ourselves, taking all that information and come up with a conclusion, and then we go back to those people and say: 'This is our conclusion. You may not like it but these were the reasons'. ... And, by the way, there have been times when we've forgotten to tell people what we've done and we get a phone call, and I realise, it is important to people. You didn't realise, but it is important. (Interviewee 14)

In one case, this accountability challenge was explicitly linked to organizational legitimacy:

> Probably the most valid arguments were actually about legitimacy, in that the national members of FLO like ourselves felt that we already had a number of streams of accountability back to consumers, development organizations, government in many cases and so on, whereas the producers had a much narrower field of networks made up of organizations who actually had a commercial interest. They are also operators as well as beneficiaries of this system. And so there were a lot of questions about how that could work. Ultimately we just had to make progress on that, because it was affecting our legitimacy if the producers were not involved in the decision-making. Even on that point, there wasn't total consensus, not just in terms of the internal power issues but even the cultural issues. Several of the countries said to me that they thought it was very odd that the beneficiaries of the project should be involved in the governance. (Interviewee 12)

Respondents highlighted the need for participation and the value of a strong membership base, but were less clear about how these aspects of operational accountability might be translated into performance models and analysis. This suggests that there could be dissonance between stakeholder engagement strategies and front-line effectiveness under conditions of heightened external scrutiny and scepticism, which could pose a potential threat to organizational legitimacy.

---

14   However, these too have been heavily criticized (see Edwards and Hulme 1995).

Systems of Relationships

A number of respondents demonstrated that they understood the stakeholder landscape in which they operated. For example, one interviewee stated:

> When we first started there were four major stakeholders groups, one was the producers, one was the founders – the original you could say shareholders – one was the employees, and one was the consumers. (Interviewee 13)

There was also evidence that organizations understood that this was not a static landscape, as Interviewee 13 went on to note:

> As we've grown we've got other opinion formers interested in what we do, so they've added to our group of stakeholders. So it's not just those four primary ones, there are others that have started to emerge. … [W]e've embraced more of the financial world … [a]nd I realised there was a whole group of people who saw [the organization] almost as a family and wanted to share their views.

Respondents also demonstrated that they understood that stakeholder perceptions varied and were important:

> It's about how you match up to people's expectations, and in some sense people's expectations are not entirely within your control. It's a real problem. It's about perceptions, but the perception has its own reality. … But this wider public perception of what we do is probably the biggest factor in all this. If we haven't got that, then the value of what we do just becomes discredited. (Interviewee 12)

There was also some acknowledgement that different perspectives could be in conflict, which was a strategic issue, but this was presented from a fatalistic rather than strategic perspective:

> So we obviously didn't satisfy everyone but you are never going to do that, and I think what we were trying to do is say, 'we've gone through an honest process here'. (Interviewee 11)

Respondents were also aware of the difficulties involved in engaging their key beneficiaries, but did not demonstrate a clear sense of the legitimating structure of their stakeholder landscape. For example, the acknowledgement that there had been a tendency to over-focus on Northern markets rather than Southern producers was cast as an accountability rather than mission-performance failure:

> I think we've realised over the last couple of years that we've somehow fallen into a trap where fair trade is something that people in the North do to people in the South rather than do with them, and we're actually trying to change that. (Interviewee 12)

Interviewees saw an important distinction between core supporters of fair trade ('activists') and other stakeholders. This was typically cast in terms of the activists' deeper understanding of, and commitment to, the fundamental social justice foundations of fair trade. For example, one respondent noted that activists were at the heart of fair trade, informing and driving the model:

> We've probably got the situation where a large number of people don't fully understand what we do, but they accept that we're a good thing. And there's a smaller group of committed activists, with whom we have a deeper dialogue about what we do and the challenges we face, and they feed back to us as whether they think we should be doing more – more of what we currently do, or even things that we don't currently do. (Interviewee 12)

In terms of conflicts across legitimating perspectives/systems of relationships, respondents were sensitive to the potential issues surrounding the move towards 'mainstreaming' fair trade. This was expressed in terms of how activists' perceptions of fair trade could be compromised by closer relations with conventional 'big' business. However, it was also clear that respondents generally repudiated activist objections, even seeing such conflict as a sign of a larger strategic success:

> The activists don't trust big business from feedback we've had from our own research – the fact that we're working with Starbucks means that people give us a bit more credibility in coffee, because Starbucks are seen as experts in coffee. (Interviewee 14)

Alternatively, respondents felt that activists' objections would diminish over time, presumably as a consequence of the demonstrably positive effects of mainstreaming:

> There's also a concern about becoming part of the Establishment. The momentum is very much driven by activists in this area, and they share the mission, but there's something about being an activist movement that in a way they like to see themselves as outsiders. I think when people start to lose interest that's when the battle's been won because it's become part of the mainstream. (Interviewee 12)

Despite being aware of the conflicts in stakeholder perceptions which arise from mainstreaming fair trade, there was no evidence that respondents had developed a strategic analysis of how to manage such potential disruption to their legitimating processes, nor that they fully understood how disruptive this could be. Furthermore, there was no clear evidence that producers' perceptions and opinions were given strategic priority over other stakeholders' views or, indeed, that managers conceived of producers' perceptions as being significant. This is in direct contradiction to the best practice for building and maintaining fair trade's overall legitimacy suggested by the tripartite model.

Legitimacy Typology

With respect to the legitimacy typology, all five identified types were mentioned in the course of the interviews, though no one interviewee cited all of them. In addition, a new category of 'individual legitimacy' – broadly defined as external perceptions of an individual's integrity and track record – emerged as significant. This new category highlighted the contribution of a senior manager/ CEO's personal integrity and reputation to building trust and reputation in their organization across stakeholders (see Figure 5.2), for example:

> ... the classic thing is they don't really understand what the hell it is you do, but if they like you, they will support you. (Interviewee 7)

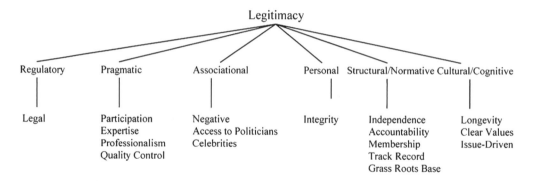

Figure 5.2   Legitimacy tree nodes

The importance of the Fairtrade certification mark emerged in a number of comments, particularly as part of an organization's normative legitimacy. However, respondents were sometimes wary of any conflict between the demands of certification and their fundamental mission. This suggests a keen awareness of the need to anchor all action in the mission first and foremost:

> We said OK this accreditation means we have some independent checks: we're transparent, we're consistent, we've got quality control procedures, all of that to do. What we don't want is a straight jacket that is managing the process but losing sight of the objectives. (Interviewee 12)

With respect to the three normative discourses of fair trade noted above the data gave mixed results. During discussions about organizational legitimacy, respondents mentioned a number of the key features of the process focus which were set out in public statements defining fair trade. The distinctiveness of how fair trade operates was articulated in an organizational vision that explicitly articulated strong ethical or social norms as the foundation for actions and activities. Central to this was a sense of the importance of the underpinning values upon which fair trade operations are built, often expressed in organizational mission or vision statements. 'Partnership' emerged as a key guiding value, as well as 'equality' across stakeholders. However, this was largely framed in operational terms as a reconfiguration of the supply and value chain, rather than as a strategic management objective for the organization itself and its legitimacy. For example:

> The values we try to adhere to in fair trade generally … would be about respect, transparency, dialogue, working as a partnership, and collaboration rather than competition between different power elements. (Interviewee 14)

Elsewhere the power relationships between producer and purchaser were more explicitly acknowledged as a matter of communication, transparency and openness, rather than legitimacy:

> We have a whole set of values, one of which is respect, one is integrity, one is about being fair to everybody … And the other value we have … it's about partnerships and being equal with each other. You know, it's about listening and hearing rather than just being talkative. (Interviewee 13)

However, it was also acknowledged that building good channels of communication was both difficult and time consuming:

It's been interesting that you need to take the time to do the communication, and communication doesn't mean once it means constantly. I would say most of my job is about talking, because you've got to reinforce these things constantly. And I don't think it's easy. (Interviewee 14)

With respect to producers, one respondent was open about process failures in accountability mechanisms:

I think that that is one area that has been very weak and it's very challenging. It's been difficult because the structure that we adopted back in 1997 when the various labelling organizations that were around set up FLO, that FLO would focus on the work with producer placing and the local initiatives would be market facing. It had a number of advantages: it meant we could focus on building them up, which was definitely what the producers wanted and what we needed to do ... What we lost was any sort of dialogue of the market context with the producers, so they understood. (Interviewee 12)

The importance of open communication and dialogue within effective governance structures was also acknowledged:

We have a producer business unit, which we also call the producer services unit, and we've invested in having people on the ground in developing countries who can liaise so that they understand more about it. ... [W]e've created our own producer relations team ... it's about having a dialogue with producers so that they know more about the market, and we can then take their views into account ... informed views about what's happening. And also changes in governance. So obviously we're revising the constitution and bringing in producers organizations as members along with the national initiatives. (Interviewee 12)

Whilst partnerships, dialogue and transparency emerged as significant legitimating factors within the fair trade process, respect and equity were less apparent. This suggests an overemphasis on internal legitimating competences rather than external systems of relationships and the interaction between them. In practical terms, this implies a lack of focus on the producer's voice and representation in strategic planning, which is reinforced with reference to the second discourse cluster. Indeed, there is little acknowledgement that the producers themselves are the critical element in establishing fair trade's normative and cognitive legitimacies and that, as a consequence, their voice should be central to strategic planning.

The interview data also included references to the economic focus of fair trade – namely, the 'with whom' that makes the model distinctive. The most common observations concerned: quality control; effective branding and marketing; and producer capacity development. A number of respondents highlighted the importance of marketing and branding to their economic mission, often in terms of bringing fair trade more into the mainstream:

I felt that people had a stigma and we were never going to move it unless we started in some respects doing mainstream marketing. So we were using mainstream tools. And the other thing was to move it from a 'we' message to a 'me' – you're going to enjoy something out of this rather than you're just giving money for this good cause. So we tried to get people emotionally attached to the product, so they're going to get something out of it instead of just paying more. (Interviewee 14)

Improving the quality of products was also seen as significant, though this was sometimes seen as having 'soft' as well as 'hard' benefits:

> It is about being trusted and respected. It's around those areas, and also the quality of the product as well, so you get the 'me' in there. … But I would say the trust and the respect is greater than the quality. (Interviewee 14)

One respondent mentioned fostering new and more empowering trade relationships, but this was in the context of quoting a mission statement rather than a broader reflection on organizational legitimacy:

> The original mission of [the organization] was … to maximize the security and empowerment of farmers … and we added in 'to be the leading brand' to strengthen the influence, empowerment, and security of farmers in the South and also link them with consumers. (Interviewee 13)

Similarly, another interviewee referred to a vision statement in order to set out the organization's development objectives in terms linking economic development with enhanced living standards:

> Well, our vision is officially a world in which everyone is able to provide for themselves, their families and their communities through their work with dignity. (Interviewee 14)

Interviewees did not mention sustainability in relation to the economic objectives of fair trade. This suggests a narrow view of development focussed on individual producers rather than the wider community or planet as a whole. This perhaps reflects the roots of the fair trade model in poverty alleviation rather than environmental campaigning.

While there was evidence in the interview data of attention to both the process and the economic elements of fair trade's legitimating discourses, the third cluster focusing on politics (the 'why' aspect of fair trade) was entirely absent. Respondents did not explicitly talk about the political dimension of the larger fair trade discourse either in terms of formal or informal processes and actions. None explicitly mentioned trade justice, campaigning or raising awareness of relevant political issues. The issue of producer rights and empowerment were largely acknowledged as a matter of process (see above) in supply chain relationships or in organizational transparency. When prompted, one interviewee considered the question of how power relationships might play out between Southern producers and their Northern fair trade buyers and appeared to recognize that this may be an issue:

> That's interesting. That's a really interesting one. I've never felt there was a power relationship. … Usually, when I go and meet producers, or they come here … there are usually things they want to tell us about … and the conversations we have are not about power, you know – they're about this is what's happening and what can we do and it's the way you present it as well, it's really important. (Interviewee 14)

The absence of a political dimension in these accounts of organizational legitimacy should be seen as significant in analysing how fair trade organizations in the North understand the systems of relationships through which their legitimacy is constructed as well as the relationship between their public statements of the ideal type of fair trade legitimacy and the actual process of building normative and cognitive legitimacy.

Reviewing Key Findings

The interview data reviewed here suggests that respondents variously understood the key elements of the organizational legitimacy model presented in Figure 5.1. There is good evidence that respondents could articulate a vision of their legitimating competences. This was largely in terms of communication with stakeholders and, to a lesser degree, accountability to producers. However, some important legitimating competences were absent from the discussion, most notably performance impact. Furthermore, there was no clear evidence that any single organization/ interviewee understood the model holistically or connected the key elements into a legitimating process (see Table 5.4). As a result, the strategic management of organizational legitimacy, where it was considered as an issue at all, was largely reduced to a matter of either PR and marketing, or the personal reputation and actions of a senior manager/CEO. What is most striking from this data is how respondents effectively marginalized the views and perceptions of producers and activists in their legitimacy strategies. Significantly, interviewees failed to pay any attention to the political and campaigning ambitions of the movement, which is of particular relevance in terms of the three discourse clusters that currently define fair trade's normative and cognitive legitimacy.

Concerning systems of relationships, respondents could identify key stakeholders and recognized that their perceptions may differ and even be in conflict. However, there was less clarity about how to weight competing legitimacy perceptions or how to manage them effectively. The strategic management of organizational legitimacy did not appear to be a recognized managerial task. While some respondents appeared to be concerned about the maintenance of organizational legitimacy, they lacked both the conceptual clarity as to how this may be approached and the analytic tools to bring it about. Respondents communicated the importance of stakeholder opinions and key relationships, but this was typically viewed managerially as something to be controlled from within the organization. This was underlined by the lack of references to performance impact when discussing legitimating competences, since the effective measurement of performance impact requires active engagement with beneficiaries' needs and feedback (Nicholls 2008). Similarly, the importance of the individual legitimacy of senior managers/CEOs within the legitimating process highlighted a reliance on internal resources to control, rather than react to, external stakeholder input.

Table 5.4   Data summary for legitimacy typology

Type of legitimacy	Respondent	Example comment
Regulatory	1, 3, 5, 6, 7, 8, 9, 10, 11, 13	I think we were the first bank in Europe to actually get the ISO 14000, ISO 14001. (Interviewee 11)
Associational	1, 2, 3, 4, 5, 6, 7, 8, 9, 10, 12, 14	If we took a lot of money from Tesco, they would think we'd gone soft. (Interviewee 2)
Pragmatic	1, 2, 3, 4, 5, 6, 8, 9, 10, 11, 13, 14	It's around … the quality of the product as well, so you get the 'me' in there. (Interviewee 14)
Normative	1, 3, 5, 6, 7, 8, 9, 10, 11, 12, 13, 14	I think being open. I think, as I was saying earlier, telling people what you're doing and why you're doing it is very key. (Interviewee 14)
Cognitive	2, 3, 4, 6, 7, 8, 9, 10, 11, 12, 13, 14	We've probably got the situation where a large number of people don't fully understand what we do, but they accept we're a good thing. (Interviewee 12)
Individual	2, 3, 4, 6, 7, 9, 10, 11, 12, 13, 14	Well, everything has been based on me … not just the legitimacy thing. (Interviewee 10)

Interviewees mentioned all of the categories of legitimacy identified in the legitimacy typology at some point, although none understood it as a conceptual framework. The relationship between different types of legitimacy was not clearly understood. For example, there was no evidence that respondents grasped that perceptions of normative and cognitive legitimacy were of greater strategic value than pragmatic judgements. Respondents also added 'individual' legitimacy as a new category of legitimacy.

When compared against the three discourse clusters identified in the main public statements concerning fair trade, it appeared that respondents focused largely on process issues with a lesser concern for economic development. A focus on the political aspect of fair trade was almost entirely absent. Regarding key process issues (that is, how fair trade operates), respondents' comments matched the public statements closely with transparency and accountability, with good communication (cast as 'dialogue') often emerging as particularly significant. Economic factors (that is, whom fair trade helps) were described by interviewees in terms of how fair trade organizations can help producers improve quality control and capacity development – namely, as interventions rather than empowerments.

The absence of any meaningful discussion of the stated political objectives of fair trade (aside from quoting mission statements) is striking. This may be explained by a number of factors. First, the majority of the interviewees worked in customer-facing fair trade organizations for whom market development has become the key strategic objective, which generates a bifurcated fair trade movement where 'activists' are separated from the commercial fair trade firms and allotted the political campaigning. Second, and perhaps more significant, it could be that the social justice roots of the fair trade movement are largely being left behind as it becomes established in the mainstream. Either way, this disjunction between managerial priorities and public statements concerning fair trade's right to operate in terms of legitimation may well threaten its integrity with key stakeholders (that is, activists and grass-roots supporters) who embody a crucial element of the fair trade model to the wider public. Without a campaigning political core, fair trade may simply become an alternative supply chain model whose claims of special impact and effectiveness are already under scrutiny.

Such concerns are consistent with recent theoretical perspectives on fair trade which suggest that mainstreaming represents a movement away from a values-based model of alternative trade towards co-option by the neo-liberal market. The public discourses around fair trade then become symbolic devices that obfuscate this change by appealing to normative notions of its impact and performance disconnected from empirical evidence or beneficiary voice. This parallels criticisms of the commoditizing language used by many development actors focusing on the 'Third World' (Escobar 1995). In light of this, key elements in the successful move of fair trade into the mainstream – FLO standards and the Fairtrade mark – can be seen as technocratic departures from its original core values of mutuality and partnership towards a depoliticization of the movement's radical agenda and the facilitation of its capture by the dominant logic of the corporation (see, for example, Ferguson 1994; Blowfield and Dolan 2008).[15] Indeed, the mainstreaming of fair trade could also be seen as a legitimation process for the neoliberal market model itself – softening its sharper contours for a more 'ethical' public (see, for example, Harriss 2002). Recent work by Michael Edwards (2008) on 'philanthrocapitalism' has come to similar conclusions.

In summary, by applying the tripartite legitimacy model to interview data, several significant strategic gaps in legitimating processes can be identified. First, interviewees did not grasp that legitimacy is a socially constructed phenomenon based around exogenous perceptions of

---

15   This also parallels Dart's (2004) analysis of the rise of social enterprise.

organizational action. As a consequence, little attention was paid either to the larger cognitive frames in which fair trade sits and upon which it draws (most significantly, the social justice movement) or to the challenges presented by conceptualizing differing systems of relationships. Second, and related to this, respondents did not demonstrate an understanding of the strategic significance of identifying and balancing competing legitimacies and legitimating judgement across systems of relationships. Third, interviewees had a largely managerialist view of the legitimating process, seeing it as a function of marketing rather than a core strategic issue. Finally, as has already been noted, the data showed a disregard for the political dimension of the fair trade model that, effectively, marginalized producer voice and representation and gave priority to engagement with the likes of Nestlé rather than other NGOs.

Conclusions

The development of a fair trade 'brand' has been carefully nurtured over recent years with its key brand values communicated by the three discourses set out above. Fair trade actors have clearly grasped the need to act as 'cultural entrepreneurs' (Lounsbury and Glynn 2001) in order to legitimate their model through established institutional myths around social justice, international development and the war on poverty. Thus, the political and social justice dimension of fair trade as an alternative trading mechanism represents perhaps its key 'rational myth' (Meyer and Rowan 1977) that provides an important cognitive frame for its right to operate to the public at large. It is surprising then that the data analysis in this chapter suggests that fair trade is in some danger of becoming dislocated from these institutional narratives and cultural norms.

As a market-driven model of economic development, consumers will largely determine the ongoing success of fair trade. While respondents clearly stated that they felt that perceptions of pragmatic legitimacy – in the form of good quality control and effective branding – were important tools for approaching the consumer market, fair trade's right to operate ultimately resides in perceptions of its normative and pragmatic legitimacy. This perception is that fair trade helps the poorest producers experience greater trade justice and thus improves their livelihoods and develops their local economy; consumers must believe that this is actually the product of their purchase decisions for the model to prosper (see Nicholls and Opal 2005; Nicholls and Alexander 2006). As such, fair trade is particularly vulnerable to any attack that undermines its credibility or reputation.[16] The main defence against such an attack is currently to mobilize the individual integrity of a CEO/senior manager to counter any negative publicity. However, such a strategy may well have diminishing returns over time.

Continued growth presents two further challenges to fair trade's organizational legitimacy. To date, the two main strategies for increasing fair trade's impact have been product diversification and growing market share (Nicholls 2002; 2004). Each presents potential threats to organizational legitimacy. With certified products, diversification requires new standards and new monitoring mechanisms. As one interviewee noted:

> The more we do and the more products we have – we're looking at more categories, mining and extractive industries, tourism, all sorts of areas – the potential for fault-lines that could damage credibility have grown probably exponentially in a complicated system. So that's a concern. (Interviewee 12)

---

16   See Jepson (2005) for the corollary in development NGOs.

However, perhaps the biggest legitimacy challenge lies in mainstreaming fair trade. Fair trade locates its roots in an unusual combination of political activists and religious faith-based groups – both embody strongly held beliefs and clear value systems. The presence of such groups within fair trade generates significant normative and cognitive legitimacy. Yet in order to grow commercially, fair trade has increasingly engaged with market actors, from ethical consumers to supermarkets and, more recently, multi-nationals such as Nestlé. Whilst this has paid off handsomely in terms of growing sales, it is as yet unclear how this may be affecting the legitimating perceptions that underpin the model's right to operate.

Fair trade has proved to be one of the most compelling marketing and retail success stories of the past ten years. Yet its commercial success has been based not only on its products' quality and features, but also on their legitimacy to consumers as an example of a new model of market-based development for poor producers. Consequently, the single most important attribute of a fair trade product is its organizational legitimacy.

This exploratory research has used a new analytic model of organizational legitimacy to examine how key internal fair trade actors understand where the basis of their right to operate lies. It has become clear that while respondents were sensitive to the importance of perceptions of their legitimacy across different stakeholder groups, they lacked a conceptual framework with which strategically to manage these perceptions. As a consequence, organizational legitimacy was generally poorly understood and the impact of conflict across legitimating actors' perceptions was underestimated. This was exemplified in the tendency of respondents to depoliticize the fair trade model, despite signing up to public statements which highlighted its campaigning elements.

The model of organizational legitimacy presented here offers a framework by which fair trade actors can better conceive of their legitimation processes and, as a result, develop strategic approaches towards them. As fair trade sales continue to grow, the threats and opportunities that this model highlights are likely to become more significant such that a failure to put organizational legitimacy at the strategic heart of future planning may well prove highly problematic.

References

Ashford, B. and Gibbs, B. (1990), 'The double-edge of organizational legitimation', *Organization Science* 1(2): 177–94.

Atack, I. (1999), 'Four criteria of development NGO legitimacy', *World Development* 27(5): 855–64.

Barratt Brown, M. (1993), *Fair Trade: Reform and Realities in the International Trading System* (London: Zed Books).

Barrientos, S. (2000), 'Globalisation and ethical trade: assessing the implications for development', *Journal of International Development* 12(4): 559–70.

Berlan, A. (2004), 'Child labour, education and child rights among cocoa producers in Ghana', in C. van den Anker (ed.), *The Political Economy of Slavery* (New York: Palgrave Macmillan), pp. 158–78.

—— (2008), 'Making or marketing a difference? An anthropological examination of the marketing of fair trade cocoa from Ghana', *Research in Economic Anthropology* 28: 171–94.

Bird, K. and Hughes, D. (1997), 'Ethical consumerism: the case of "fairly-traded" coffee', *Business Ethics: A European Review* 6(3): 159–67.

Blowfield, M. and Dolan, C. (2008), 'Stewards of virtue? The ethical dilemma of CSR in African agriculture', *Development and Change* 39(1): 1–23.

Blowfield, M. and Gallet, S. (2000), *Ethical Trade and Sustainable Rural Livelihoods – Case Studies: Volta River Estates Fair Trade Bananas Case Study* (Kent: Natural Resources and Ethical Trading Programme). Available at: http://www.nri.org/NRET/csvrel.pdf [accessed: 2 November 2008].

Booth, P. and Whetstone, L. (2007), 'Half a cheer for fair trade', *Economic Affairs* 27(2): 29–36.

Dart, R. (2004), 'The legitimacy of social enterprise', *Nonprofit Management and Leadership* 14(4): 411–24.

Davis, G., McAdam, D., Scott, W. and Zald, M. (2005), *Social Movements and Organization Theory* (Cambridge: Cambridge University Press).

Davies, I. and Crane, A. (2003), 'Ethical decision making in fair trade companies', *Journal of Business Ethics* 45(1): 79–92.

Deephouse, D.L. and Carter, S.M. (2005), 'An examination of the differences between organizational legitimacy and organizational reputation', *Journal of Management Studies* 42(2): 329–60.

DiMaggio, P. and Powell, W. (1983), 'The iron cage revisited: institutional isomorphism and collective rationality in organizational fields', *American Sociological Review* 48(2): 147–60.

—— (1991), 'Introduction', in P. Di Maggio and W. Powell (eds), *The New Institutionalism in Organisational Analysis* (Chicago, IL: University of Chicago Press), pp. 1–40.

Dolan, C. (2007), 'Market affections: moral encounters with Kenyan fair trade flowers', *Ethnos* 72(2): 239–61.

Dowling, J. and Pfeffer, J. (1975), 'Organizational legitimacy: social values and organizational behavior', *Pacific Sociological Review* 18(1): 122–36.

Edwards, M. (1999), 'Legitimacy and values in NGOs and voluntary organisations: some sceptical thoughts', in D. Lewis (ed.), *International Perspectives on Voluntary Action* (London: Earthscan), pp. 258–67.

—— (2008), *Just Another Emperor? The Myths and Realities of Philanthrocapitalism* (New York: Demos).

—— and Hulme, D. (1995), 'Introduction: NGO performance and accountability', in M. Edwards and D. Hulme (eds), *Beyond the Magic Bullet: NGO Performance and Accountability in the Post Cold War World* (London: Earthscan), pp. 1–20.

Elsbach, K. (1994), 'Managing organizational legitimacy in the California cattle industry: the social construction and effectiveness of verbal accounts', *Administrative Science Quarterly* 39(1): 57–88.

Emerson, J. (2003), 'The blended value proposition: integrating social and financial returns', *California Management Review* 45(4): 35–51.

Escobar, A. (1995), *Encountering Development: The Making and Unmaking of the Third World* (Princeton, NJ: Princeton University Press).

Fairtrade Labelling Organizations International (FLO) (2006), *FLO International: About Fair Trade*. [Online: FLO]. Available at: http://www.fairtrade.net/about_fairtrade.html [accessed: 10 November 2008].

Ferguson, J. (1994), *The Anti-Politics Machine: 'Development', Depoliticization, and Bureaucratic Power in Lesotho* (Minneapolis, MN: University of Minnesota Press).

Friedland, R. and Alford, R. (1991), 'Bringing society back in: symbols, practices and institutional contradictions', in P. DiMaggio and W. Powell (eds), *The New Institutionalism in Organisational Analysis* (Chicago, IL: University of Chicago Press), pp. 232–63.

Galvin, T., Ventresca, M. and Hudson, B. (2004), 'Contested industry dynamics. new directions in the study of legitimacy', *International Studies of Management and Organisation* 34(4): 56–82.

Giddens, A. (1984), *The Constitution of Society* (Berkeley, CA: University of California Press).

Goodman, M. (2004), 'Reading fair trade: political ecological imaginary and the moral economy of fair trade foods', *Political Geography* 23(7): 891–915.

Hargrave, T. and Van der Ven, A. (2006), 'A collective action model of institutional innovation', *Academy of Management Review* 31(4): 864–88.

Harriss, J. (2002), *Depoliticizing Development: The World Bank and Social Capital* (London: Anthem Press).

Hudson, A. (2000), 'Making the connection: legitimacy claims, legitimacy chains and Northern NGOs' international advocacy', in D. Lewis and T. Wallace (eds), *After The 'New Policy Agenda'? Non-Governmental Organisations and the Search for Development* (London: Kumarian Press), pp. 89–99.

Hudson, I. and Hudson, M. (2003), 'Removing the veil: commodity fetishism, fair trade, and the environment', *Organization and Environment* 16(4): 413–30.

Hybels, R. (1995), 'On legitimacy, legitimation, and organizations: a critical review and integrative theoretical model', *Best Papers Proceedings – Academy of Management Journal*, 241–5.

Jepperson, R. (2002), 'The development and application of sociological neoinstitutionalism', in J. Berger and M. Zelditch (eds), *New Directions in Contemporary Sociological Theory* (New York: Rowman and Littlefield), pp. 229–66.

Jepson, P. (2005), 'Governance and accountability of environmental NGOs', *Environmental Science and Policy* 8(5): 515–24.

Kocken, M. (2002), *The Impact of Fair Trade* (Maastricht: European Fair Trade Association).

LeClair, M. (2002), 'Fighting the tide: alternative trade organizations in the era of global free trade', *World Development* 30(6): 949–58.

—— (2003), 'Fighting back: the growth of alternative trade', *Society for International Development* 46(1): 66–73.

Lincoln, Y. and Gubba, E. (2000), 'Paradigmatic controversies and emerging confluences', in N. Denzin and Y. Lincoln (eds), *The SAGE Handbook of Qualitative Research* (Thousand Oaks, CA: Sage), pp. 163–89.

Lindsey, B. (2004), *Grounds for Complaint? 'Fair Trade' and the Coffee Crisis* (London: Adam Smith Institute).

Lister, S. (2003), 'NGO legitimacy: technical issue or social construct', *Critique of Anthropology* 23(2): 175–92.

Littrell, M. and Dickson, M. (1997), 'Alternative trading organizations: shifting paradigm in a culture of social responsibility', *Human Organization* 56(3): 344–56.

Lounsbury, M. and Glynn, M. (2001), 'Cultural entrepreneurship: stories, legitimacy, and the acquisition of resources', *Strategic Management Journal* 22(6–7): 545–64.

Lukes, S. (2005), *Power: A Radical View*, 2nd edition (Basingstoke: Palgrave Macmillan).

Mahoney, J. and Pandian, R. (1992), 'The resource based view within the conversation of strategic management', *Strategic Management Journal* 13(5): 363–80.

Marx, K. (1991 [1867]), *Capital: A Critique of Political Economy*, trans. B. Fowkes (London: Penguin Classics).

Maseland, R. and de Vaal, A. (2002), 'How fair is fair trade?' *De Economist* 150(3): 251–72.

Maurer, J.G. (1971), *Readings in Organization Theory: Open-System Approaches* (New York: Random House).

McDonagh, P. (2002), 'Communicative campaigns to effect anti-slavery and fair trade: the cases of Rugmark and Cafédirect', *European Journal of Marketing* 36(5–6): 642–66.

Meyer, J. and Rowan, B. (1977), 'Institutionalised organisations: formal structure as myth and ceremony', *American Journal of Sociology* 83(2): 340–63.

Meyer, J. and Scott, W. (1992), 'Centralization and the legitimacy problems of local government', in J.W. Meyer and W.R. Scott (eds), *Organizational Environments: Ritual and Rationality* (London: Sage), pp. 199–215.

Meyer, J., Scott, R., Cole, S. and Intili, J. (1978), 'Instructional dissensus and institutional consensus in schools', in W.M. Meyer (ed.), *Environments and Organizations* (San Francisco, CA: Jossey-Bass), pp. 290–305.

Meyer, J., Scott, R. and Deal, T. (1981), 'Institutional and technical sources of organizational structure: explaining the structure of organizations', in H. Stein (ed.), *Organization and the Human Services* (Philadelphia, PA: Temple University Press), pp. 151–78.

Miles, M. and Huberman, A. (1994), *Qualitative Data Analysis: An Expanded Sourcebook*, 2nd edition (Thousand Oaks, CA: Sage).

Neilsen, E. and Rao, H. (1987), 'The strategy-legitimacy nexus: a thick description', *Academy of Management Review* 12(3): 523–33.

Nelson, V. and Galvez, M. (2000), *Social Impact of Ethical and Conventional Cocoa Trading on Forest-dependent People in Ecuador* (Kent: Natural Resources and Ethical Trading Programme).

Nicholls, A. (2002), 'Strategic options in fair trade retailing', *International Journal of Retail and Distribution Management* 30(1): 6–17.

—— (2004), 'New product development in fair trade retailing', *Service Industries Journal* 24(2): 102–17.

—— (2005), 'Social entrepreneurship', in S. Carter and D. Evans-Jones (eds), *Enterprise and Small Business: Principles, Practice and Policy*, 2nd edition (Harlow: Financial Times and Prentice Hall), pp. 220–42.

—— (2006), 'Introduction: the meanings of social entrepreneurship', in A. Nicholls (ed.), *Social Entrepreneurship: New Paradigms of Sustainable Social Change* (Oxford: Oxford University Press), pp. 1–36.

—— (2007), *What is the Future of Social Enterprise in Ethical Markets?* Office of the Third Sector think piece (Canberra: Cabinet Office, Office of the Third Sector). Available at: http://www.cabinetoffice.gov.uk/third_sector/Research_and_statistics/social_enterprise_research/think_pieces.aspx [accessed: 30 October 2008].

—— (ed.) (2008), *Social Entrepreneurship: New Models of Sustainable Social Change* (Oxford: Oxford University Press).

—— (2009), 'Capturing the performance of the socially entrepreneurial organisation (SEO): an organisational legitimacy approach', in J. Robinson, J. Mair and K. Hockerts (eds), *International Perspectives on Social Entrepreneurship Research* (Basingstoke and New York: Palgrave Macmillan) pp. 27–74.

—— and Alexander, A. (2006), 'Rediscovering consumer-producer involvement: a network perspective on fair trade marketing in the UK', *European Journal of Marketing* 40(11/12): 1236–53.

Nicholls, A. and Opal, C. (2005), *Fair Trade: Market-Driven Ethical Consumption* (London: Sage).

Parsons, T. (1960), *Structure and Process in Modern Society* (Glencoe, IL: Free Press).

Pfeffer, J. and Salanick, G. (1978), *The External Control of Organizations: A Resource Dependency Perspective* (New York: Harper Row).

Prahalad, C.K. and Hamel, G. (1990), 'The core competence of the corporation', *Harvard Business Review* 68(3): 79–91.

Ransom, D. (2001), *The No-Nonsense Guide to Fair Trade* (London: New Internationalist Publications).

Rao, H. (1994), 'The social construction of reputation: certification contests, legitimation, and the survival of organizations in the American automobile industry: 1895–1912', *Strategic Management Journal – Special Issue: Competitive Organizational Behavior* 15: 29–44.

Raynolds, L. (2002), 'Consumer/producer links in fair trade coffee networks', *Sociologia Ruralis* 42(4): 404–24.

—— Murray, D. and Wilkinson, J. (eds) (2007), *Fair Trade: The Challenges of Transforming Globalization* (New York: Routledge).

Raynolds, L. and Wilkinson, J. (2007), 'Fair trade in the agriculture and food sector: analytical dimensions', in L. Raynolds, D. Murray and J. Wilkinson (eds), *Fair Trade: The Challenges of Transforming Globalization* (New York: Routledge), pp. 33–48.

Renard, M.-C. (1999), 'The interstices of globalization: the example of fair trade coffee', *Sociologia Ruralis* 39(4): 484–500.

—— (2003), 'Fair trade: quality, market and conventions', *Journal of Rural Studies* 19(1): 87–96.

Ritchie, J. (2003), 'The applications of qualitative methods to social research', in J. Ritchie and J. Lewis (eds), *Qualitative Research Practice: A Guide for Social Science Students and Researchers* (London: Sage), pp. 24–46.

Ronchi, L. (2002), *The Impact of Fair Trade on Producers and Their Organizations: A Case Study with Coocafé in Costa Rica*, Prus Working Paper No. 11 (Brighton: University of Sussex). Available at: http://www.sussex.ac.uk/Units/PRU/wps/wp11.pdf [accessed: 2 November 2008].

—— (2003), *Monitoring Impact of Fair Trade Initiatives: A Case Study of Kuapa Kokoo and the Day Chocolate Company* (London: Twin).

Schwandt, T. (2000), 'Three epistemological stances for qualitative inquiry: interpretivism, hermeneutics, and social construction', in N. Denzin and Y. Lincoln (eds), *The SAGE Handbook of Qualitative Research* (Thousand Oaks, CA: Sage), pp. 189–213.

Scott, W.R. (2008), 'Approaching adulthood: the maturing of institutional theory', *Theory and Society* 37(5): 427–42.

Strong, C. (1996), 'Features contributing to the growth of ethical consumerism: a preliminary investigation', *Marketing Intelligence and Planning* 14(5): 5–13.

—— (1997), 'The problems of translating fair trade principles into consumer purchase behaviour', *Marketing Intelligence and Planning* 15(1): 32–7.

Stryker, R. (2000), 'Legitimacy processes as institutional politics: implications for theory and research in the sociology of organizations', *Research in the Sociology of Organizations* 17: 179–223.

Suchman, M. (1995), 'Managing legitimacy: strategic and institutional approaches', *Academy of Management Review* 20(3): 571–610.

Tallontire, A. (2000), 'Partnerships in fair trade: reflections from a case study of Cafédirect', *Development in Practice* 10(2): 166–77.

—— (2002), 'Challenges facing fair trade: which way now?', *Small Enterprise Development* 13(3): 12–24.

Teece, D., Pisano, G. and Shuen. A. (1997), 'Dynamic capabilities and strategic management', *Strategic Management Journal* 18(7): 509–33.

Terreberry, S. (1968), 'The evolution of organizational environments', *Administrative Science Quarterly* 12(4): 590–613.

Thaekekara, M. and Thaekekara, S. (2007), *Social Justice and Social Entrepreneurship: Contradictory or Complementary?* (Oxford: Skoll Centre for Social Entrepreneurship).

Thomas, T. (2005), 'Are business students buying it? A theoretical framework for measuring attitudes toward the legitimacy of environmental sustainability', *Business Strategy and the Environment* 14(3): 186–97.

Weber, M. (1978), *Economy and Society: An Outline of Interpretive Sociology* (ed.), G. Roth and C. Wittich (Berkeley, CA: University of California Press).

—— (2004), 'Politics as a vocation', in *The Vocation Lectures* (ed.), D. Owen and T. Strong, trans. R. Livingstone (Indianapolis, IN: Hackett).

Wright, C. (2004), 'Consuming lives, consuming landscapes: interpreting advertisements for Cafédirect Coffees', *Journal of International Development* 16(5): 665–80.

Zucker, L. (1977), 'The role of institutionalization in cultural persistence', *American Sociological Review* 42(5): 726–43.

Chapter 6

Voluntarism and Fair Trade

Tim Wilson

Introduction

The notion of fair trade was founded as a consumer-driven, voluntary, social justice alternative to free trade. With standards of living rising across the world, some consumers have altered their concept of value from a focus on the benefits provided by a product against its price to other inherent benefits. Fairtrade was designed to fill a gap in the consumer market for products that delivered a social, environmental and economic dividend in excess of the dividend provided by the free market.

Yet, over recent years, fair trade voluntarism has come under scrutiny. The credibility of voluntary engagement by consumers is under doubt because of increasing questions concerning the 'development' outcomes delivered by Fairtrade as well as rising awareness of unintended consequences of Fairtrade policies. Additionally, lax enforcement of many Fairtrade standards is being revealed, also casting doubt over the alleged welfare benefits offered by the fair trade system. Compounding these dangers still further are the ways in which many activists are undermining the voluntary spirit of fair trade by promoting government regulation at a domestic and international level to codify and enforce the principles underlying Fairtrade's certification standards.

In view of the multiple challenges to voluntarist and free market principles posed by the fair trade movement, this chapter assesses the legitimacy of fair trade as a voluntarist campaign and the capacity for it to exist within a free market system. It also addresses the challenges posed by campaigns that seek to codify and enforce fair trade principles in domestic and international law, and how the absence of voluntarism undermines fair trade's legitimacy.

Drawing primarily on examples from Fairtrade initiatives in the coffee sector, the argument in this chapter is developed in several stages. First, the core concepts of voluntarism and the free market system – which provide the basis for evaluating the legitimacy of the fair trade movement – are introduced. Using this framework for analysis, the chapter then demonstrates that, while Fairtrade has the potential to operate as a voluntary system enabling free exchange between producers and consumers sharing similar values and goals, the actions of many prominent participants in the fair trade movement are currently operating in practice to violate these conditions for legitimacy.

Voluntarism and the Free Market System

The organization of a market economy through the principle of voluntarism lies at the heart of liberal thought and the free market tradition. This underlying philosophical principle is reflected in the kinds of political and economic institutions that have been promoted by liberals committed to maximizing individual, political, social and economic freedom. Voluntarism as a principle implies systems of decision-making that are consensual and free from coercion, generally translating into a strong suspicion of the government's role in the economy and society.

However, liberals do not support voluntarism merely for its capacity to maximize freedom. There are also economic welfare gains from the efficient coordination of capital, which free markets are able to deliver based on price signals and consumer demand. Free markets are also widely regarded as highly effective means of fostering related values of entrepreneurship, dynamism and innovation through reduced limitations on and facilitating the potential of individuals.

Furthermore, the methods and mechanisms of government decisions do not achieve the same level of efficiency due to the complications of democratic decision-making processes, rent-seeking and non-price and non-demand-driven resource allocation. A concern for individual liberty also raises concerns about the dangers to freedom resulting from concentrating power in the hands of the state. Such considerations further add to the appeal of free markets as a foundational form of social and economic organization, since the free market system is itself founded on the notion of voluntary exchange, thereby serving as an important expression of, and vehicle for the protection of, values of individual choice and freedom of association. In this sense, an underpinning principle of free markets is therefore a central belief in the value of the individual engaged in voluntary exchange (Herbert 1978).

In summary, liberals tend to support market-based systems – and correspondingly, a limited role for government – because of a pragmatic desire to promote overall economic and social welfare, and on the basis of a philosophical commitment to freedom founded on voluntarism. Despite the inseparability between these core liberal principles and practices, they are distinct in some important ways. It is therefore useful to outline the content and justification of each, in order to establish a liberal framework upon the basis of which the legitimacy of the fair trade movement can then be systematically evaluated.

The Value of Voluntarism

Voluntary exchange is an ancient concept that has only been fully articulated since the publications of Adam Smith. The principle of voluntary exchange supposes that two or more parties engaging in commerce, without coercion, will achieve mutual benefit. Such a principle need not require both parties to be wholly satisfied with the exchange. Nevertheless, as Ludwig von Mises argued, '[t]he deal is always advantageous both for the buyer and the seller. … If both the buyer and the seller were not to consider the transaction as the most advantageous action they could choose under the prevailing conditions, they would not enter into the deal' (von Mises 1996, 665–6). Similarly, Milton Friedman indicates that the value of an exchange must be weighed against the benefits of a voluntary exchange as well as the cost of not engaging in the exchange at all (Friedman 1962, 13–14).

A commitment to voluntarism is also highly attentive to the historical link between centralized authority and social, political and economic oppression. Such concerns are levied at centralized government because it holds the power of coercion and the potential use of violence over individuals for non-compliance with the decisions of government (Hayek 1944; Friedman and Friedman 1980; Friedman 1962).

The Value of Free Markets

Free market theory suggests that in order to deliver the maximum economic welfare for a society, a society must find the most efficient use of scarce capital and resources. It is strongly believed that the free market is best able to direct scarce capital and resources through price signals. Price signals are designed to reflect the cost of a product's production costs coupled with the overall 'value' a consumer derives from that product. Through the use of price signals, free markets achieve sustainable economic development through the most efficient market-directed use of scarce resources and by discouraging waste, which also has a financial cost and must be factored into the final price of a product. The adoption and success of free markets therefore rests on the apparent economic success it provides. In this sense, free markets and the institutions that support them[1] have been recognized for lifting millions of people out of poverty (Yergin and Stanislaw 2002).

Voluntarism, Free Markets and the Legitimate Roles of Public and Private Actors

Free market principles have important implications for the appropriate delineation of roles between government on the one hand and private firms on the other. Within the framework of a free market system, individuals and enterprises should maximize profit through the efficient use of scarce capital and resources in order to maximize production based on consumer demand. In general, it is therefore assumed that production should take place in the private sector, and resource allocation should be coordinated via markets.

It is often asserted that free markets undermine the capacity for poverty reduction and environmental protection. However, such an argument misunderstands the role of free markets and their capacity to use scarce resources with the most efficiency. Market-based systems are designed to have limited government interference beyond that which is necessary to develop the framework for a functioning market – property rights, enforcement of contracts, a predictable judicial system and so on. Similarly, the non-economic responsibilities of firms are tightly circumscribed within a free market system due to the costs they impose and the involuntary nature of any such obligations compelled by government.

The most prominent assessment of why free market thinkers oppose such forms of 'corporate social responsibility' was written by Friedman in his article, 'The social responsibility of business is to increase its profits' (1970). Friedman's free market argument against corporate social responsibility was premised on the concept of business as an artificial construct and that 'only people can have responsibilities'. Friedman therefore contended that the role of business is to 'make as much money as possible while conforming to the basic rules of the society'.

Such a position is not inconsistent with the objectives of maximizing economic welfare, reducing poverty and improving environmental standards: as outlined above, increasing economic welfare lies at the heart of the free market system. By maximizing the available capital that can be distributed, the greatest number of transactions can be carried out, which in turn optimizes the opportunities for capital to be distributed throughout society. Thus, while governments seek to enhance economic welfare via the forced or non-price signalled allocation of capital, free markets promote overall economic welfare by maximizing the total economic welfare of society.

Moreover, increasing the overall wealth within the community also increases the amount of capital available to address environmental damage, which itself has secondary *economic* impacts in addition to its primary environmental impacts. Environmental damage occurs in both centrally-planned and decentralized, free market economies. Indeed, it is not only inflicted by rich societies; in fact, it can often be worse in poorer countries. However, poor societies cannot afford to address the cost of environmental damage because their limited available capital is predominantly directed towards human security and wellbeing. Further, the concern of individuals regarding their environment tends to improve as societies become more economically developed

---

1   This includes, for example, laws recognizing property rights, a free and fair judiciary to enforce contracts and arguably, democracy.

and are less concerned with the immediacy of their own survival. This relationship has been demonstrated by the environmental Kuznets curve.

Simon Kuznets originally theorized that economic inequality can be graphically demonstrated through a curved graph, with inequality rising and then falling as social wealth rises. In poor societies economic inequality is small, but inequality grows alongside the growth of society and economy until a point is reached after which economic inequality decreases, as wealth is more accessible and society demands a general increase in basic services that enable all citizens to become more economically productive and able to improve their own welfare (Kuznets 1955).

A version of the Kuznets curve also applies to the environment. When a society is poorer, the environment tends to be healthier. As economic welfare rises, the demands on the environment increase and are coupled with a relatively small concern for environmental health. But this lack of concern does peak: as a society becomes wealthier, it demands a higher general standard of living, including a healthier environment through the reduction in pollutants, and it will have the resources to dedicate to it. China has been identified as exemplifying the application of the environmental Kuznets curve (Hayward 2005).

Despite this preference for individually-driven responses to environmental and economic concerns within a free market system, there is some scope for government involvement. Governments have a comparative advantage in performing limited activities in cases where the profit motive can erode long-term foresight, where impartiality in decision-making is required, or where it is necessary to account for the costs of externalities. But the exercise of government power should be limited to only a select few activities to which such comparative advantage applies.[2]

Beyond the activities that governments have a comparative advantage in delivering, free market principles suggest that governments should avoid supplying further services, and should also avoid taxing a population for the provision of those services. Where it is necessary to impose taxes to provide services, these should be directly imposed on individuals rather than levied through alternative taxing mechanisms such as business taxes. A core aim of doing so is to secure government restraint. When taxes are *indirectly* imposed on individuals the impact is typically not fully appreciated. In contrast, taxes imposed directly on individuals are more likely to raise ire. Imposing taxation on individuals therefore ensures that the government is required to exercise a level of restraint, ensuring that taxation levels are acceptable to individuals as, unlike businesses, individuals have voting power.

Similarly, government should limit the extent to which it directly seeks to promote economic, social and environmental goals because of the distance such an approach creates between individuals. *First*, public provision of such social goods can potentially promote resentment and social division between those who provide through taxes or equivalent levies for the costs of economic redistribution and social and environmental programmes, and those who benefit from them.

Second, government intervention discourages individuals from taking responsibility for the society in which they live. A commitment to a limited government does not imply a limited commitment to others and to the society. Quite the opposite: direct government provision of goods and services to a population transfers the obligation of taking care of a society away from individuals and towards the government. In response, individuals believe that the money they pay in taxes enables the government to respond to all their social and environmental concerns. This fosters a culture where individuals absolve themselves of responsibility for the society in which they live. Conversely, limited government requires the voluntary participation of individuals, through direct

---

2   A police force and military are good examples.

personal or financial contributions to charities, to assist others in their society. The motivation for doing so is purely self-interested: to improve the state of the society in which they live.

In a globalized world where national barriers are rarely an inhibiter, the role of the individual is no different. International trade enables individuals to assist those in developing countries directly by empowering privileged consumers in the developed world to buy their products and transfer wealth. The fair trade campaign aims to harness this objective through the use of a comparative sense of value imbued in fair trade products. Utilizing a consumer-driven definition of value, products can be created that provide qualities such as environmental, social or economic production standards, the cost of which is factored into product prices. As long as all participants in the supply chain participate voluntarily, there need be no conflict between the fair trade system and the operation of the free market.

Indeed, such actions have significantly more merit than their government-sponsored alternatives. Such alternatives are pursued via the compulsory acquisition of money for aid and development, which in turn reduces the obligations of individuals to contribute directly. This shifts the burden from individuals to government, as well as promoting a culture of obligation on the part of the donor to the recipient. As a result, governments are often obliged to add criteria to aid funding that outlines the priorities of the donors' value-systems or the government's agenda, regardless of the objectives and priorities of the recipient.

Fair Trade's Voluntarist Potential

The broad aims of the fair trade movement have been to support producers, raise awareness and campaign for 'changes in the rules and practices of conventional international trade' (FLO 2006b) to achieve 'greater equity' (FLO 2006a). Within these broad parameters, the 'Fair Trade' label has been used in a variety of ways, reflecting the multiple philosophies that coexist and, in some cases, compete within the fair trade movement as a whole. This chapter adopts a relatively broad definition of fair trade, focusing on several distinct elements of the movement: the FLO system of product certification; activist campaigns based specifically around the issue of certified Fairtrade purchases; and broader activist campaigns focused on issues of 'trade justice' within the international trading system as a whole.

At the root of the fair trade movement is a voluntary commitment to harness the market forces by targeting consumers who value social, environmental and economic considerations in the products which they buy. In this sense, the origins of fair trade rest in a social justice movement based on principles of voluntarism for both consumers and producers.

Participation in Fairtrade was originally designed as a voluntary, consumer-driven campaign using market forces to promote an alternative economic system. Fairtrade promotes a set of welfarist objectives that prioritize the importance of non-economic goals, such as social, community and environmental objectives, in deciding the best methods for production. These objectives include minimum wage standards, how to distribute the profits from production communally, and the type of materials that can be used in production. However, although the Fairtrade system embraces some of the welfarist goals concerned with protecting the interests of producers that are typically associated with policies of protectionism, it is ultimately not a form of protectionism to the extent that it continues to operate as a non-regulatory system, which is not codified and mandated in national or international trade laws (Zadek, Lingyah and Forstater 1998, 70).

As a result of its voluntary nature, Fairtrade can peacefully coexist with free trade products within the framework of a free market because it does not inhibit consumer choice. As Torsten

Steinrücken and Sebastian Jaenichen (2007, 30, 215) identify, the Fairtrade programme enables consumers to opt into paying 'for social methods of production' whereby those 'who express this willingness in their purchase pattern are charged with the additional expense'. Likewise, while criticizing the *corporate executive* 'insofar as his actions raise the price to customers', Friedman has argued that the *individual* may feel a voluntary responsibility to 'his conscience' and spend wealth accordingly (Friedman 1970). Friedman allows for the possibility that voluntary consumer engagement in Fairtrade may be motivated by the perceived value associated with the ethical dimensions of the product.

Understood in this sense, Fairtrade products can be viewed as a 'bundle' based on the deemed value of the consumer for particular 'social or ecological methods of production' (Steinrücken and Jaenichen 2007, 205). Fairtrade products do not simply operate on the more traditional concept of value based on price. Instead, Fairtrade products rely on 'credence properties' (Steinrücken and Jaenichen 2007, 205) and consumers are required to make further investigations to ascertain the value of the good or service.

Fairtrade Labelling Organizations International (FLO), which manages the standards and certification of Fairtrade products, has achieved voluntary engagement through certification for producers and labelling requirements. The standards and certification process plays a particularly important role in underpinning the possibility of free choice for consumers. Principles of voluntarism require that choice is exercised on the basis of, if not the ideal criterion of 'full information', then at least information sufficiently reliable to ensure that the Fairtrade products which consumers choose to purchase are actually embedded with those production process characteristics that are claimed.

FLO establishes these standards and makes them available to the public at large through its internet site (FLO 2006c). The spirit of these certification standards is also included in the packaging and labelling of many Fairtrade certified goods. As a result of the certification process, only products that are certified to FLO standards can then carry the Fairtrade certification mark. By using labelling to confirm the standards that consumers value in Fairtrade, it provides consumers with choice in their purchasing decisions. Through a voluntary system of labelling, consumers are able to purchase Fairtrade certified goods without hindering their capacity to choose an alternative 'freer trade' product.

Fairtrade is also potentially voluntarist from the perspective of producers. Currently only producers that choose to participate in Fairtrade certification do so. Producers take part in the scheme through the payment of fees for Fairtrade certification and adhering to outlined standards.

As a voluntary certification process, Fairtrade provides both producers and consumers with choice. It provides consumers with a preference for socially-driven economics to buy products that align closely with their values. So long as Fairtrade is rooted in the spirit of voluntarism, it does not directly conflict with the framework of free markets. Instead, it is simply an extension of the value apportioned to products by consumers.

Fair Trade's Violation in Practice of Voluntarist and Free Market Principles

Despite this voluntarist potential of the Fairtrade system, there are several ways in which voluntarist and free market principles are being violated in practice by many elements within the fair trade movement. *First*, some activists are violating principles of voluntarism by attempting to impose Fairtrade products on consumers via coercive, regulatory means. *Second*, principles of both voluntary choice and free market efficiency are being violated by both the fundamental design of and the operational weaknesses within Fairtrade production and certification systems. *Third*, both voluntarist and free market principles are being threatened by fair trade activists' demands to introduce highly interventionist forms of market-distorting regulation at the international level.

Voluntarism Violated by Demands for Coercive Enforcement of Fair Trade Standards

Despite the voluntarist potential of the fair trade movement, efforts to use Fairtrade rules as forms of both domestic and international regulation undermine the voluntarist spirit and its legitimacy. Should Fairtrade standards be entrenched in government regulation as some fair trade activists would like, its enforcement would be achieved through the violence conferred by government compulsion.

In 2002 the Californian activist group Global Exchange introduced a ballot measure to require 'all cups of coffee sold in the city [of Berkeley] to be "fair trade," organic or "shade-grown"' (Burress 2002). This demonstrates an attempt to use regulatory measures to impose Fairtrade certification standards.

In contrast to introducing a ballot-driven measure via government, many of Global Exchange's efforts to impose the adoption of Fairtrade standards have involved placing direct pressure on corporate decision-makers. Global Exchange, as well as many other NGOs, are now forcefully lobbying companies and shareholders to adopt Fairtrade certification standards in their business practices, or lobbying for their businesses to buy Fairtrade certified products. Proctor and Gamble exemplifies this: after significant lobbying by fair trade activists, Proctor and Gamble started selling Fairtrade coffee through its specialist coffee arm (Global Exchange 2007). Successful campaigns have influenced the decisions of large companies such as McDonald's, Starbucks and BP's service station retail coffee outlets.

These campaigns are not equivalent to the use of regulation to secure support for Fairtrade, but they do undermine voluntarism. Lobbying companies forcefully through naming-and-shaming and public protests can force the hand of companies to change tack on how they wish to approach their business practices. While companies may sign up, many do so hesitantly. In the case of Nestlé it has chosen to establish its own 'fair trade' standards rather than buy into the campaigns run by activists. It is clear from these examples that the line between voluntarism and coercion is being blurred.

The primary aim of these activities is to lock in its objectives through the instruments of domestic and international regulation, moving fair trade away from its origins as a voluntary consumer campaign. Fair trade activists seeking to undermine the voluntary nature of Fairtrade do themselves a disservice. Voluntarism is important because it delivers a greater sustainable commitment to solving problems for those disposed towards contributing to the cause. Numerous studies have shown that the compulsion of previously voluntary activities results in resentment and decreased commitment once mandated involvement is removed (Bandow 1999).

More importantly, undermining voluntarism also undermines the coexistence of free markets and Fairtrade as economic alternatives. Free markets, with prices set through voluntary exchange, cannot operate as a labelled alternative under a compulsory Fairtrade regime. Yet free markets can accommodate a labelled Fairtrade alternative. Any effort to undermine the voluntary nature of fair trade affects its legitimacy as a social justice movement. Certainly, consistency with Fairtrade certification requirements necessitate some form of enforcement of the standards imbued in fair trade certification in order to ensure that consumers are receiving the additional value attributed to the product. However, involuntary enforcement imposed through government-sponsored regulation is merely another contribution to the imposition of regulation in a non-voluntarist tradition.

The Inefficiency of Fair Trade Systems of Production and Exchange

Philosophically, the methods adopted by Fairtrade run contrary to the underlying principles of free markets (including free trade), as outlined above. Accordingly, free market thinkers have been traditionally opposed to the concept of Fairtrade. Their opposition is based in Fairtrade's devaluation of the most efficient use of capital in order to prioritize social outcomes. While in the free market system, the market mechanism is regarded as the best vehicle through which social resource allocation can operate. Fairtrade takes a very different approach: instead of using price signals, it actively discourages their use through price floors in order to protect the financial interests of producers. Doing so suffocates price signals to producers that would correspond with consumer demand. Additionally, while Fairtrade may temporarily assist producers by artificially improving their economic welfare, this comes at the expense of improving the economic welfare of their society through efficient application of scarce capital and resources.

Free market advocates are also critical of Fairtrade because it misinterprets the core objectives of market-based systems. Fairtrade neither views profit as a core objective nor believes in the limitation of non-market interference. Instead Fairtrade takes on the spirit of what has commonly become known as 'corporate social responsibility'. In his article 'The social responsibility of business is to increase its profits' (Friedman 1970), Friedman's critique of corporate responsibility initiatives that seek to 'contribute to the social objective of reducing poverty ... at the expense of corporate profits' resonates clearly with a core pillar of Fairtrade that similarly undermines the role of business.

Exclusive and inefficient organizational structures also undermine the Fairtrade system's capacity to promote the welfarist goals advanced as the main justification for demanding broad-based support for the system. One of the most notable criticisms is directed towards the collective nature of Fairtrade organizations, that despite Fairtrade's claim to help improve the lot of individual producers, it actively works against them by promoting coffee purchases exclusively from collectives.

Collectives are designed to be established along democratic lines where individual producers trade their products as a collective. Profits are returned to the collective and distributed according to its decisions, creating significant opportunities for cronyism and preferential deals based on personal and political relationships rather than market signals which would ensure that the best producer gets the best price. Moreover, under the Fairtrade collectives system, Fairtrade suppliers are restricted to small farms; large productive farms that meet Fairtrade requirements, even if they pay their employees good wages, are excluded.

Furthermore, Fairtrade farms are not supposed to be dependent on permanent labour. This certification standard raises an important issue about the intention of Fairtrade's design. Fairtrade is designed to help lift the world's poor out of poverty. Yet a certification standard requiring farms to be run primarily by non-hired labour seems to encourage small, self-sufficient farms. This standard also has the effect of designing the Fairtrade system to support land owners first, at the expense of poor labour. While there is little doubt that many land owners in the developing world are, in fact, poor, the bottom of the food chain is occupied by non-land owning labour. Yet unlike free trade Fairtrade is designed to exclude them from being core beneficiaries in the fair trade scheme.

The Questionable Benefits of Fairtrade Certification

The credibility of voluntarism in Fairtrade requires that consumers and producers buy into Fairtrade with the knowledge that the purchased product delivers the benefits outlined. Free market advocates also criticize individual Fairtrade certification standards, questioning whether consumers are actually receiving the development outcomes promoted. Fundamental flaws within Fairtrade certification systems undermine both welfare goals and principles of voluntarism, which depend to some extent on the availability of reliable information to facilitate informed consumer choices.

Recent studies have shed light on several questionable aspects of Fairtrade certification standards. Colleen Berndt (2007) completed a field study looking at the impact on local communities from Fairtrade, and comparing these against the 'benefits' promoted in Fairtrade literature.

Berndt found that despite perceptions and promotions of Fairtrade coffee as a premium quality product, it was often average grade commodity coffee. From her field studies, she found that many Fairtrade certified producers were selling their premium quality coffee on the free market where they could secure a high price. Fairtrade producers were then selling their remaining product through the Fairtrade system because they were able to secure a higher price than that offered on the free market (Berndt 2007, 212). Instead of actually being a premium quality product, such Fairtrade coffee is securing the brand of a premium coffee while being unable to be sold as such via regular commodity markets.

She also discovered that a large amount of literature misrepresented the gains to communities resulting from Fairtrade. Notably, Berndt discovered that organizations were building schools or health clinics in Fairtrade communities, taking photographs of them and consequently advertising them as a benefit deliverable through the Fairtrade scheme. Yet Berndt discovered in an interview with a Fairtrade manager that these representations were misleading. The Fairtrade manager instead suggested that community facilities were built with other resources and the link with Fairtrade was false (Berndt 2007, 23).

Another study completed by Marc Sidwell (2008) presented comparable conclusions. In addition to reinforcing Berndt's conclusions, Sidwell identified an increasing likelihood that gains from Fairtrade were coming at the expense of non-Fairtrade producers. He connected the suppressed world price of commodity coffee with overproduction. But because Fairtrade is not rooted in market price signals, Fairtrade producers are not encouraged to produce less coffee when there is an oversupply. Accordingly, coffee prices are further suppressed for non-Fairtrade producers (Sidwell 2008, 21). Sidwell's thesis is supported by Berndt's research (2007, 156), which identifies an oversupply of Fairtrade coffee above and beyond market demand. Berndt and Sidwell's research is not isolated. Similar concerns have been raised in other studies (see Howley 2006; Lindsey 2003; Weber 2007; Wilson 2006).

But perhaps the most stinging criticism results from research undertaken by the international newspaper the *Financial Times*. In a 2006 report, the *Financial Times* discovered that beyond questions surrounding the benefits of Fairtrade certification standards, in some cases these standards were not being enforced. The *Financial Times* found for example that Peruvian coffee farm workers were not being paid the Peruvian minimum wage, as required under Fairtrade certification rules (Weitzman 2006).

The extent of lapses in certification standards has even prompted the Australian Competition and Consumer Commission (ACCC) to caution fair trade campaign organization Oxfam Australia about the risks of using 'absolute claims'.[3] In a letter dated 2 July 2008, Bob Weymouth from the ACCC wrote:

---

3   Letter to Tim Wilson from Bob Weymouth from the Australian Competition and Consumer Commission dated 2 July 2008.

> I do recognise that some material exists in the marketplace where Oxfam has repeated Fairtrade
> sentiments that contain absolute claims. I have conveyed my view to Oxfam that absolute claims,
> such as '… guarantees a better deal …', leave it at risk of contravening the Act should the Fairtrade
> certification process not be 100% reliable in the results it delivers.

The advice from the ACCC build upon criticisms concerning the voluntary nature of fair trade; Fairtrade's credibility as a voluntary, consumer-driven campaign can only be intact so long as Fairtrade certification standards are upheld in the interests of producers and consumers alike. Lax certification standards are a clear demonstration of how consumers can be robbed of their voluntary engagement by having the power of their purchasing decisions circumvented.

The extent to which Fairtrade certification standards are not being upheld has resulted in even Fairtrade advocates recently conceding its shortcomings. A Fairtrade certifier publicly conceded that further work must be done to ensure credibility in the Fairtrade system and they have 'already started doing something about it' (Neil 2008).

The cost of questionable development outcomes and poor certification is felt by both producers and consumers. For Fairtrade to have credibility as a voluntary system of certification and socialized production, it must have credibility. Yet producers are being misled about the potential benefits of the scheme when they sign up; consumers are being misled about the scheme they are buying into and the gains that result from their purchasing decisions. This undermines the requirement for full or at least reliable information that underpins the possibility of voluntary choice.

Voluntarist and Free Market Principles Violated by Activist Demands for International Regulation

Despite flaws in the enforcement of certification standards, the design of Fairtrade certification at least has the potential to facilitate a voluntary engagement by producers and consumers alike. However, Fairtrade has evolved beyond FLO certification. Now fair trade campaigns are run independent from the FLO to encourage the absorption of Fairtrade certification objectives into regulation.

The most blatant example is that of the campaign 'Make Trade Fair' (Oxfam International 2006). Make Trade Fair, developed and organized by Oxfam International, is designed as both an activist campaign and a central forum for the discussion of fair trade policy alternatives to free trade. This campaign has been designed to combat trade rules that 'heavily favour the rich nations that set the rules' (Oxfam International 2006). Oxfam argues that international trade rules 'have been developed by the rich and powerful on the basis of their narrow commercial interests … [and that t]rade rules should be judged on their contribution to poverty reduction, respect for human rights, and environmental sustainability' (Oxfam International 2006). The objective of Make Trade Fair is to rig trade outcomes using the instruments of government; this is reflective of their broader approach to fair trade. The campaign attempts to introduce principles of free trade where Oxfam identifies the benefits to developing countries and maintains hostility to the principles of free trade where 'fairer' outcomes are desired.

One of the core focuses of the Make Trade Fair campaign is supporting the voluntary sale and consumption of Fairtrade certified coffee in developed country markets. Oxfam markets Fairtrade products as a consumer-driven campaign to fix the apparent injustices in the international trading system. Slogans and statements on coffee products such as 'Guarantees a better deal for Third World Producers' and 'Fair trade involves paying a fair price, building capacity in producer communities, and developing long-term trading partnerships based on mutual respect' suggest a voluntary scheme for all stakeholders – producers, wholesalers, retailers and consumers.[4] In Oxfam's fair trade reports they similarly argue for consumers to buy more Fairtrade products, ask retailers to stock it and demand that companies adopt Fairtrade standards (Gresser and Tickell 2002).

Yet behind the public efforts to promote voluntary consumption of Fairtrade goods, Oxfam is also advocating for regulation of the international coffee market to achieve compulsory consumption of fair trade products. In its 2002 report, *Mugged: Poverty in Your Coffee Cup*, Oxfam International identifies numerous criticisms against the contemporary international coffee trade that could be addressed through increased consumption of Fairtrade certified coffee (Gresser and Tickell 2002, 49–51). However, of the 48 recommendations listed in the report, five are directed to consumers. The remaining 43 include recommendations such as:

- destroying at least five million bags of coffee,
- organizing producer governments to stop commodities entering the market that cannot be sold, and
- establishing a long-term commodity management initiative.

Such interventions would represent a direct obstruction to the operation of the market mechanism via quantity distortions, in the form of quotas, administered by some kind of international bureaucracy. In this way, not only do Oxfam's proposals in the *Mugged* report contravene principles of voluntarism, they also violate basic principles of a free market system, thus undermining the very social and developmental goals these proposals profess to promote.

The regulations proposed by Oxfam replicate many of the requirements under the United Nations' International Coffee Agreement (ICA), which was administered by the International Coffee Organization. Yet, the ICA was responsible for many of the problems within the coffee market that created the 'need' for fair trade in the first place.

The ICA was used as a development mechanism to assist the developing world; it fell with the collapse of the bipolar architecture of the Cold War. The aim of the Agreement was to stabilize coffee production internationally. It achieved this by controlling the market through quotas and by ensuring that countries withheld supply when it peaked above consumer demand, effectively controlling prices. Agreements were struck for five-year periods with extensions granted while new agreements were negotiated. In the last 15 years, pressure on the international coffee market has been mounting. The ICA as an instrument for controlling prices and production fell in 1989 and with it collapsed the conventional coffee trade that restricted producing countries and limited supply (see Wilson 2006).

An extension to the existing 1983 Agreement was struck but with all quotas and control instruments suspended. When the free market was allowed to operate, the result was a boom in coffee production. Previously locked-out producers were suddenly able to trade on the international market unhindered by multilateral agreements which controlled supply. The explosion in production had an inevitable consequence: a fall in price. By 1992, coffee futures had bottomed and the international supply had clearly outgrown consumer demand. During negotiations for an updated ICA, agreement could not be achieved to control prices and thus the new ICA focused on other avenues of international cooperation. The last ICA was the 2001 Agreement which came into effect in May 2005. Its aims shifted away from regulating coffee supply and demand towards improving coffee consumption and quality (Wilson 2006).

---

4   These are slogans used on some fair trade products by the UK's Fair Trade Foundation.

Under the ICA, it is not surprising that corrupt governments in developing countries allotted quotas to the highest bidder, not the best coffee producer. The fact is that the ICA inflated coffee prices above their natural price. Comparing current prices with ICA annexed prices is unconstructive at best.

Yet in spite of all these demonstrated problems with the ICA system, one of the key platforms being advocated by Make Trade Fair is to re-establish an international coffee quota system in line with the previous ICA that is, to establish a non-price-signalled control of prices and the sale of coffee on to the international market through non-government organization roasters from producer collectives. Re-establishing the ICA concept in this way would artificially increase the price once again, distort the coffee market and directly discourage producers from tying the cost of production to the cost of sale. In such an environment, everybody loses through decreased productivity and limited profit margins and increased prices for consumers, thus likely functioning to reduce consumption.

Moreover, inflating prices beyond their market rate only encourages producers to produce more not less coffee in search of higher profits as the price is guaranteed. Of course, Make Trade Fair has developed a solution to address the over-production of coffee beans: in order to ensure that the price does not fall below the floor price, any over-supplied beans will simply be destroyed. This is a questionable outcome for consumers, producers and the environment (Wilson 2006).

Conclusion

Questions regarding the voluntary nature and legitimacy loom large over fair trade. As a certification system, it is necessary for Fairtrade to have enforced standards in order to ensure that all parties are engaging in the scheme in a credible and voluntary way. It is clear that with FLO establishing poorly enforced standards that deliver questionable development objectives, and activists pushing to turn Fairtrade certification standards from voluntary rules into regulation, the legitimacy of Fairtrade is undermined.

Instead of supporting the codification of Fairtrade's principles and objectives in law, fair trade activists should support Fairtrade products as alternatives in a free market. Doing so both ensures that the product will not be associated with the stigma of compulsion and maintains the flexibility of a system outside of legal frameworks. Meanwhile, fair trade activists should continue vocalizing their opposition to the injustices in international trade caused by developed country subsidy programmes and tariff barriers, while also recognizing that developing countries inflict pain on themselves through tariffs that undermine new industries.

Not surprisingly, not all participants in the debate about addressing global poverty agree on the best means to achieve this important objective. But so long as Fairtrade remains a voluntary, consumer-driven campaign, it has legitimacy in a free market system. To the extent that it utilizes the mechanisms that the free market is able to provide, it cannot be considered antipathetic to the free market.

References

Bandow, D. (1999), 'Voluntarism should be voluntary', *The Freeman: Ideas on Liberty* 49(8).

Berndt, C. (2007), *Does Fair Trade Coffee Help the Poor: Evidence from Costa Rica and Guatemala*, Mercatus Policy Series, Policy Comment No. 11 (Arlington: Mercatus Center, George Mason University).

Burress, C. (2002), 'A great city's people forced to stop drinking swill? Berkeley ordinance would ban all but politically correct coffee', *San Francisco Chronicle*, 21 June, A-1.

Fairtrade Labelling Organizations International (FLO) (2006a), *About Fair Trade*. [Online: FLO]. Available at: http://www.fairtrade.net/about_fairtrade.html [accessed: 19 January 2009].

—— (2006b), *About Us*. [Online: FLO]. Available at: http://www.fairtrade.net/about_us.html [accessed: 19 January 2009].

—— (2006c), *Standards*. [Online: FLO]. Available at: http://www.fairtrade.net/standards.html [accessed: 19 January 2009].

Friedman, M. (1962), *Capitalism and Freedom*, 2nd edition (London: University of Chicago Press).

—— (1970), 'The social responsibility of business is to increase its profits', *The New York Times Magazine*, 13 September, 32–3, 122, 124, 126.

—— and Friedman, R. (1980), *Free to Choose: A Personal Statement*, 1st Harvest edition (San Diego, CA: Harcourt).

Global Exchange (2007), *Advocacy Groups Persuade Procter and Gamble to Offer Fair Trade Certified Coffee: Largest US Coffee Company to Pay Farmers a Fair Price*. [Online: Global Exchange]. Available at: http://www.globalexchange.org/campaigns/fairtrade/coffee/Millstonevictory.html [accessed: 19 January 2009].

Gresser, C. and Tickell, S. (2002), *Mugged: Poverty in Your Coffee Cup*, Make Trade Fair research report (Boston, MA: Oxfam International).

Hayek, F.A. (1944), *The Road to Serfdom*, 2nd edition (Abingdon: Routledge Classics).

Hayward, S. (2005), *The China Syndrome and the Environmental Kuznets Curve*, Environmental Policy Outlook research report (Washington, DC: American Enterprise Institute for Public Policy Research).

Herbert, A. (1978), 'The principles of voluntaryism and free life', in E. Mack (ed.), *The Right and Wrong of Compulsion by the State and Other Essays* (Indianapolis, IN: Liberty Fund).

Howley, K. (2006), 'Absolution in your cup: the real meaning of fair trade coffee', *Reason Magazine*, March. Available at: http://www.reason.com/news/show/33257.html [accessed: 19 September 2009].

Kuznets, S. (1955), 'Economic growth and income inequality', *The American Economic Review* 45(1).

Lindsey, B. (2003), *Grounds for Complaint? Understanding the 'Coffee Crisis'*, Trade Briefing Paper No. 16 (Washington, DC: Cato Institute, Centre for Trade Policy Studies).

Neil, C. (2008), 'Free trade vs fair trade', *ABC Radio National Background Briefing*. [Radio transcript, 13 July 2008]. Available at: http://www.abc.net.au/rn/backgroundbriefing/stories/2008/2297789.htm [accessed: 19 January 2009].

Oxfam International (2006), *About the Campaign*. [Online: Oxfam International]. Available at: http://www.oxfam.org/en/campaigns/trade/about [accessed: 19 January 2009].

—— (2008), *Partnership or Power Play? How Europe Should Bring Development into Its Trade Deals with Africa, Caribbean, and the Pacific Countries*, Oxfam Briefing Paper 110 (Washington, DC: Oxfam International).

Sidwell, M. (2008), *Unfair Trade*, Adam Smith Institute research report (London: Adam Smith Institute).

Steinrücken, T. and Jaenichen, S. (2007), 'The fair trade idea: towards an economics of social labels', *Journal of Consumer Policy* 30(3): 201–17.

Von Mises, L. (1996), *Human Action: A Treatise on Economics*, 4th edition (San Francisco, CA: Fox and Wilkes).

Weber, J. (2007), 'Fair trade coffee enthusiasts should confront reality', *Cato Journal* 27(1): 109–17.

Weitzman, H. (2006), 'The bitter cost of "fair trade" coffee', *Financial Times*, 8 September. Available at: http://www.ft.com/cms/s/2/d191adbc-3f4d-11db-a37c-0000779e2340.html [accessed: 19 January 2009].

Wilson, T. (2006), 'Macchiato myths: the dubious benefits of fair trade coffee', *IPA Review* 58(2): 247.

—— (2007), 'Fair trade no substitute for intellectual property', *IPA Review* 59(1): 234.

—— (2008), 'Flawed focus drove Doha talks to collapse', *ABC News: Opinion* [Online, 1 August]. Available at: http://www.abc.net.au/news/stories/2008/08/01/2321070.htm [accessed: 19 January 2009].

World Trade Organization (WTO) (2008), *The WTO in Brief.* [Online: WTO]. Available at: http://www.wto.org/english/thewto_e/whatis_e/inbrief_e/inbr00_e.htm [accessed: 19 January 2009].

Yergin, D. and Stanislaw, J. (2002), *The Commanding Heights: The Battle for the World Economy* (New York: Touchstone).

Zadek, S., Lingyah, S. and Forstater, M. (1998), *Social Labels: Tools for Ethical Trade*, Final Report, New Economics Foundation (Luxembourg: Office for the Official Publications of the European Communities).

PART II
Responsible Consumers and Corporations

Corporations and Global Justice: Rethinking 'Public' and 'Private' Responsibilities

Terry Macdonald

Introduction

The broad 'global justice' movement – which seeks to promote justice, in part through greater corporate accountability and social responsibility – faces a wide range of political obstacles. Many such obstacles are quite institutionally concrete. These must be overcome through practical political action, by grappling with the complex and context-specific institutional problems that are the focus of many other chapters in this volume. However, another major obstacle to reformist agendas is posed by the *ideological* power of a particular set of liberal ideas about the division of public and private responsibility that designates corporations and other non-state organizations as 'private' political actors lacking any significant 'public' responsibility for advancing global justice.

These ideologically-entrenched liberal ideas involve the proposition that states are 'public' in a special way and should therefore bear primary responsibility for: (a) promoting *social/distributive* justice in its various forms; and (b) instituting decision-making processes that are *accountable* to those affected. In contrast, non-state corporate actors are designated as 'private' entities with distinct social roles (for example, to innovate or to generate profits for owners), which do not include the promotion of social justice or ensuring accountability to 'stakeholders' (see further, Macdonald 2008a). In this familiar liberal model, corporations' responsibilities are limited to compliance with the laws laid down by states or other state-like, international legal agencies (Friedman 1970; Walzer 1995).

An important task facing proponents of global institutional reform is to confront the challenge of theoretical justification effectively: what basis is there for arguing that corporations have responsibilities extending beyond their limited 'private' responsibility to comply with the laws of the territorial jurisdictions in which they operate? In other words, what grounds are there for insisting that corporations should take on some set of direct 'public' responsibilities to uphold principles of global justice and to develop institutional provisions for stakeholder accountability?

In this chapter I explore some theoretical grounds for asserting that corporations *do* have important 'public' responsibilities – both for promoting justice and for ensuring stakeholder accountability. My analysis is firmly grounded within *liberal* theoretical traditions. As such, I begin by endorsing the mainstream liberal view that there are principled and pragmatic grounds for upholding a clear normative distinction between 'public' and 'private' actors in global politics. This liberal view maintains that special ethical responsibilities should be accorded to a subset of political actors deemed to be 'public' and that the responsibilities of other actors designated as 'private' should be more narrowly delimited. However, I depart from many traditional liberal accounts of the public/private distinction by arguing that the category of 'public' actors extends beyond states (and certain state-like international bodies) to encompass powerful corporations operating within a globalized political economy.

I argue that corporations can now be identified as 'public' political actors on two key normative grounds which are linked to two core ethical tenets of public responsibility in liberal thought. First, corporations qualify as 'public' actors due to the function of their *social relationships*: they are 'public' because of their embeddedness in the requisite forms of communities – which we sometimes call 'publics' – constituted through mutual responsibilities for social and political justice. Second, corporations qualify as 'public' actors as a function of their *power*: they are 'public' because their power generates the requisite forms of 'public' *impact* (upon their stakeholder communities), and because it equips them with the requite forms of 'public' *capacity* to promote and uphold 'public goods' shared within the communities in which they operate. As a result, I argue that it is entirely appropriate to accord corporations certain direct 'public' responsibilities (to promote global justice and to exercise accountable decision-making) which extend beyond their 'private' duties to obey the law.

Before proceeding, I should note that this chapter is wholly theoretical in nature. Deeper theoretical concepts and paradigms regarding the concepts of 'fairness', 'justice' and 'accountability' – and about political 'responsibility' for these outcomes more broadly – have important political implications, since they both frame the terms of political debates and structure the underlying ideological discourses that accord some arguments more political potency than others. Theoretical justifications for the proposition that corporations possess a range of 'public' responsibilities for global justice and stakeholder accountability can therefore serve an important role in bolstering global political reform movements by helping to develop firm justificatory foundations for the legitimacy of reformist objectives.

The Division between 'Public' and 'Private' Responsibilities in Liberal-Democratic Thought

The idea that certain liberal norms and responsibilities apply only to a subset of political actors designated as 'public' (rather than *all* political actors) is one with strong liberal foundations; it is a product of what Michael Walzer (1984, 315–30) has called liberalism's 'art of separation'. According to this interpretation of liberal thought, regulatory norms such as 'democracy', 'transparency', 'accountability' and 'social justice' cannot be applied to the regulation of *all* aspects of social life, since such pervasive public regulation would encroach upon the freedom of individuals to direct important aspects of their lives in accordance with their diverse private moral beliefs and behavioural preferences. Instead, liberal thought maintains that such public regulatory norms must have a carefully circumscribed subject in order to protect an appropriately expansive 'private' sphere of individual action.

In keeping with this liberal 'art of separation', 'private' actors (both individuals and organizations) are fundamentally encumbered with the responsibility to obey the law. In practice, this overarching duty can mandate certain 'positive' responsibilities (such as democratic participation or military service) as well as 'negative' restrictions on permissible conduct. But within established liberal legal practice, the range of responsibilities imposed upon 'private' actors is clearly delimited; it does not include requirements to meet the same standards of 'transparency' or 'accountability' that are applied to 'public' actors (paradigmatically, states and their various agencies). In other words, core liberal-democratic norms – such as 'transparency', 'accountability' and so on – are not intended to serve as 'comprehensive' moral principles applying to all social actors in all domains of life, but rather function as norms of distinctively 'public' responsibility, regulating only the special subset of political actors and institutions that are accorded a 'public' status (Rawls 1996).

We can divide these 'public' norms into two broad categories which can be labelled as 'procedural' and 'teleological' norms. The first set of norms can be described as 'procedural' insofar as these norms pertain to the *processes through which decisions should be reached* by 'public' political agencies. These include, for example, norms of participation, inclusiveness, responsiveness, representativeness, transparency and deliberation. These norms are sometimes linked to the notion of 'input' legitimacy, insofar as they focus on the inputs into decisions and the structure of decision-making processes rather than the final outcomes of these decisions (Scharpf 1999).

The second set of 'public' norms can be described as 'teleological', insofar as these norms specify the *goals to which the decisions should be oriented* by 'public' political agencies. These include norms concerned with achieving satisfactory welfare outcomes, individual rights protection and, on some theoretical accounts, social/global 'justice' – the latter serving as the dominant paradigm of 'common good' or 'common interest' in contemporary liberal thought. At some level, these norms can be linked to the notion of 'output' legitimacy, insofar as they focus on the social outcomes advanced by the decisions of public agencies rather than the processes through which they are reached (though the broader concept of 'justice' is sometimes thought to subsume both input and output conceptions of legitimacy).[1]

Associated with these public norms are a range of special public responsibilities, such as those to disclose information of various kinds, to take account of particular interests in decision-making, and to establish certain mechanisms for consultation with wider communities. States and their various government and bureaucratic agencies are generally viewed as the paradigmatic examples of 'public' agencies with corresponding 'public' responsibilities. As such, we are familiar with the idea that state agencies have special responsibilities which do not apply either to individuals or to non-state social institutions designated as 'private'. In liberal-democratic states, state agencies are expected: to disclose information about their finances and decision-making processes; to make decisions in accordance with 'public' or community interests rather than the private interests of groups such as officials, political parties and financial donors; and to adhere to appropriately democratic processes of decision-making, through delegation by elected officials and occasionally through supplementary processes of community consultation. At the level of global politics, various international organizations – for example, the World Trade Organization, the World Bank and United Nations agencies – are also commonly identified as 'public' institutions with such public responsibilities as increasing transparency, accountability and consultative decision-making (Woods 2001).

The special responsibilities accorded to 'public' agencies are generally matched by special sets of rights associated with what is often termed the 'right to rule' (Copp 1999). Public agencies are accorded special sets of powers and privileges – such as the power to make and enforce laws, the associated right to use force and violence (in ways which are prohibited for private individuals and organizations) – and immunities from certain kinds of liabilities – such as some legal liabilities in tort and criminal law to which private individuals and organizations are subject.[2] The arguments I develop here about the public nature of corporate responsibilities may have important implications for corresponding questions of their public *rights and privileges*, and this would constitute an interesting subject for future research on the subject of corporations as public actors. The present chapter, however, will focus its analysis on the special public *responsibilities* of corporations.

---

1   For a helpful discussion of the status of 'justice' norms as procedural or teleological see Pogge (1989).

2   The type and degree of immunity from legal liabilities of this latter kind vary widely between different jurisdictions, but most modern states retain at least some provisions for limited civil and criminal liability for governmental agencies, which has been inherited from the historical 'doctrine of sovereign immunity'. For a discussion of sovereign immunity in an American context (as an example), see Sisk (2005).

What Makes a Political Actor 'Public'?

In a highly influential analysis of the idea that certain core liberal norms have a special 'public' subject, John Rawls (1999, 25) observes that 'the correct regulative principle for a thing depends on the nature of that thing'. Insofar as there is agreement that 'public' liberal norms – such as 'accountability', 'democracy' and 'transparency' – entail the 'correct regulative principles' for delineating public responsibilities, we must next answer the converse theoretical question: what is the 'nature of the thing' for which these are the correct regulative principles? It is necessary to set out some criteria that can be applied to different kinds of globally political actors to assess whether they qualify for 'public' status and thus discharge distinctively 'public' responsibilities.

There are a number of different conceptions of 'publicness' in liberal thought, all of which articulate varying bundles of ideas about how political power can be legitimized in the context of some set of social relationships. In other words, what all major liberal accounts of 'public' responsibility share in common is the articulation and allocation of 'public' responsibilities as fundamentally linked to the legitimation of power within a social order.

Within the parameters of this broad conceptual focus, liberal thought explores two main sets of ideas about what makes political actors 'public' and bearers of 'public' responsibilities. The first set of ideas concerns the kinds of social relationships in which moral imperatives for the legitimation of power, and the corresponding allocation of public responsibility, arise in the first place. This set of ideas articulates the way in which *embeddedness* within certain forms of social relationships serves as a *precondition* for the allocation of public responsibilities. The second set of ideas concerns the *kinds* of political actors (within these social relationships) that can wield power that is *subject to a process of public legitimation*. This set of ideas articulates the forms of power that should count as 'public' power and, accordingly, who or what (within the context of the wider social order) should be marked out as 'public' actors with corresponding public responsibilities.

It is worth noting that in much liberal writing the relationship between these two sets of 'boundary' questions is complex and problematic, and that these two sets of questions are frequently conflated or incompletely distinguished. As a result, there is some degree of overlap between established liberal arguments pertaining to 'external' boundary questions about the 'public' moral community, and those pertaining to 'internal' boundary questions about the delineation of 'public' forms of power *within* liberal communities.[3]

Let us examine conceptions of 'publicness' focused on articulating the nature of *a 'public'*, understood as the community – or set of social relationships – within which there is a moral imperative to legitimize the exercise of political power through the discharge of public responsibility. The question of how to delineate the boundaries of liberal political communities (the 'publics' through which public responsibilities are constituted and in relation to which they must be discharged) is a vexed one, with a long history of theoretical contention. In recent debates, framed in the theoretical language of 'global justice', one of the most central disagreements has focused on whether it is appropriate to conceive of the liberal 'public' (which is the locus for the exercise of 'public' political power and the discharge of 'public' political responsibilities) as subsuming all individuals on a universal global scale, or whether liberal 'publics' should be more narrowly circumscribed – within nations, states, or some other boundaries more exclusive than a 'cosmopolitan' global membership.

---

3   It is beyond the scope of this chapter to tease out the theoretical complexities surrounding the relationship between these two sets of questions in established liberal thought, but readers should be aware that many of the authors cited in what follows do not distinguish these issues as neatly as I do here, for the present analytic purposes.

The most radically cosmopolitan of these interpretations of liberalism maintains that the basis for delineating a liberal 'public' must be a shared moral obligation derived from recognition of the moral equality of autonomous individuals the world over. According to this account, a liberal 'public' (and the boundaries of public responsibility) must be universal or 'cosmopolitan' in scope under all social conditions because the moral claims of individuals upon one another are based on shared humanity rather than upon historically or institutionally contingent social relationships.[4]

In all but this most unconditionally cosmopolitan interpretation of the liberal project, the existence of a 'public' – and, correspondingly, of 'public' forms of political responsibility – is empirically contingent upon certain material conditions being satisfied. That is, it presupposes particular kinds of social relationships whereby people are *materially connected to each other* in certain ways. This material contingency applies not only within various 'communitarian' or 'particularist' accounts of liberalism, which advocate for nationally, culturally, territorially or otherwise delimited liberal polities (see, for example, Rawls 1999; Miller 1995), it also applies within certain 'cosmopolitan' forms of liberalism which claim that there is a global liberal 'public' but see this as contingent upon the existence of certain material institutional relationships between individuals on a global scale (see, for example, Pogge 1989; 2000).

Accounts of what material connections between people are necessary to constitute a 'public' can vary, depending on the underlying theoretical view taken of what kinds of material relationships generate moral responsibility (hence demands for legitimacy) within a group. In particular, we can identify three influential accounts of this within liberal thought, which are developed to greater or lesser degrees within broader arguments about the appropriate scope of public liberal norms such as 'democracy' and 'social justice'.

The first set of underlying moral accounts of this kind can be characterized as 'impact-based' accounts, insofar as they invoke a liberal moral argument based on the value of non-interference with the interests or freedoms of others; that is, they contend that when people harm each other's interests or constrain each other's freedoms, they have a set of responsibilities to one another as a result. According to these accounts, a 'public' exists within social relationships that involve people impacting in some way on each other's interests or freedoms (Macdonald 2008a; Pogge 1992).

The second set of underlying moral accounts of this kind can be characterized as 'benefit-based' accounts, insofar as they invoke a broader moral argument about responsibility which holds that if one benefits from some relationship with another, or from the outcomes of another's actions, then one has a set of responsibilities to the other as a result. Accordingly, a 'public' exists within social relationships that involve some set of people benefiting (either unidirectionally or mutually) from relationships with or the actions of others (see further, Butt 2008). A closely related set of underlying moral accounts of this kind can be characterized as 'cooperation-based', insofar as these accounts invoke a moral argument about the value of reciprocity; that is, when people are engaged in relationships which generate *mutual* benefits, they then have responsibilities to one another to ensure that these collectively generated goods are distributed fairly (see Buchanan and Keohane 1990).

In addition to the material social relationships that are prerequisites for the allocation of moral responsibility in general, the delineation of a liberal 'public' requires that there be some kind of shared *cognitive, communicative and moral framework* within a set of relationships, such that people can communicate meaningfully with one another about the nature of their shared rights and responsibilities, and find some shared values and ways of interpreting the world in relation to these

---

4   Charles Beitz (1983) has defended a version of this view of the moral foundations of a cosmopolitan political order and cosmopolitan public responsibility.

values. Without this kind of shared communicative capacity and moral compass, a group cannot reach agreement on the substance of shared rights and responsibilities, which is a prerequisite for securing any kind of legitimacy. To achieve liberal forms of legitimacy, there must be agreement of the following kinds: agreement that some combination of the above views of the material bases of responsibility are valid; approximate agreement about which groups qualify as members of this 'public' community; and agreement on some shared, liberal moral principles on the basis of which agreement can be reached concerning the substantive content of public responsibilities (see further, Miller 1995; 1999; Rawls 1996).

As established previously, there are two distinct sets of questions and arguments about 'publicness'. Thus far we have only addressed the first: questions concerning the kinds of social relationships in which moral duties to discharge public responsibilities arise. The second set of questions and arguments about publicness concerns the kinds of political actors (within these social relationships) that wield 'public power' and bear corresponding public responsibility. We can identify in particular two influential accounts of this within liberal thought that are developed to greater or lesser degrees within broader arguments about the appropriate scope of public liberal norms.

The first of these can be characterized as an 'impact-based' account, insofar as it identifies political actors as 'public' (and as bearers of public responsibilities) when these actors impact upon others in some morally problematic way which would require special public justification or rectification. These arguments are closely related to the impact-based arguments for delineating 'publics' discussed above and many liberal writers fail to differentiate them clearly. In principle, they can be distinguished, to the extent that liberal thought is able to sustain a *three-tiered* framework of political responsibility in which different categories of responsibility are created *both* across community boundaries (according to a criterion of social membership), *and* across 'public'/'private' boundaries internal to liberal society (according to an additional criterion of 'publicness').

Since social actors routinely impact upon one another in a large variety of ways (including many that we consider morally unproblematic), any impact-based account of this latter kind must clarify *what kind* of impact is required to make a political actor 'public' and thus burdened with special political responsibilities. That is, public responsibilities are allocated to actors who impact on others in a special 'public' way, while social actors who generate impacts of more minimal kinds can retain their 'private' status and so remain unburdened by public responsibilities.

Elsewhere, I have argued that the core liberal value of *individual autonomy* may be an applicable criterion to identify impacts of this special 'public' kind. Since liberal political ideals have the value of individual autonomy at their core, I have argued that the protection of individual autonomy should be the primary consideration in assessing which political impacts should qualify as public and give rise to special public responsibilities. As such, we can specify that political actors should be designated as 'public' when their impact upon others *prospectively limits the autonomy of individuals in some problematic way* (Macdonald 2008a).

This autonomy-based criterion for allocating 'public' status and responsibilities makes a certain set of background assumptions about the underlying *purposes* of a liberal political system: it assumes that individual autonomy is the core value in need of protection through a framework of public institutions. Liberal institutions could, of course, be justified in other ways – for instance, as a framework for protecting certain objectively specified human interests (either at an individual or aggregative level). If we were to think of liberal institutions as justified in some other such way, then the criterion for identifying 'public' impacts and allocating public responsibilities would differ accordingly. For example, if we were to think that the purpose of liberal institutions is to protect certain objective interests, then we would need to designate relevant threats to these interests, rather than threats to individual autonomy, as the basis for identifying public impacts. However, as my purpose here is to explicate the impact-based account of public agency in general terms – rather than to defend a particular normative interpretation of it against other alternatives – it suffices for now just to note these underlying normative issues, and recognize the varying substantive applications that the impact-based criteria may have in practice.

The second major liberal view of what renders some political actors 'public' rather than 'private' within a social order can be characterized as a 'capacity-based' account. This is tied to a conception of moral responsibility that perceives the scope and substance of responsibilities as varying in accordance with the capacities of different actors to achieve specified moral goods. The kinds of moral goods in relation to which an actor must have some special capacities are 'public' goods or 'public interests'; that is, an actor will qualify as 'public' when it has special capacities to advance public goods.

This second liberal account of public agency correlates with one interpretation of the Rawlsian idea that some 'social basic structure' should be assigned as the subject of public (in Rawls' terms, 'political' as distinct from morally 'comprehensive') principles of justice. The first (impact-based) account of public agency can be identified with a rival interpretation of this Rawlsian idea. Rawls (1971) defines the basic structure of a society as premised on the way in which major social institutions distribute fundamental rights and duties in order to determine the distribution of advantages from social cooperation, and he claims that this is the primary subject of 'justice' because its effects are so profound and present from the start. Other commentators invoke broader but related terms to describe the appropriate 'public' subject for a framework of justice: Thomas Pogge (1989) invokes the broader concept of an 'institutional scheme', which he characterizes as any set of basic ground rules of a social system that constitute and constrain interactions so as to produce morally significant 'effects', while others invoke similarly expansive institutional concepts such as 'institutional order' or 'global order'.

There is significant ambiguity here, however, concerning the sense in which the 'basic structure' is supposed to be a *subject* of ('public' or 'political') principles of justice. At times, Rawls (1971) tells us that the basic structure is the subject of public principles of justice because it is 'coercive' and/or has profound 'effects' on people's lives. This invites us to interpret the basic structure as something that exists as a background (pre-theoretical) empirical fact, manifested through its real impacts on people's lives, to which a theory of justice responds through the allocation of special public responsibilities. Yet, at other times, Rawls talks about the basic structure as though it is something to be constituted as a (post-theoretical) fact through the implementation of principles of justice within some population of individuals (presumed to be free and equal). On this latter interpretation, the 'social basic structure' or 'institutional scheme' is the proper subject for public principles of justice insofar as reform of these institutions is the only way of *creating social capacity* to discharge duties of justice effectively (Rawls 1971).[5] While the former interpretation of this basic structure concept seems to invoke a version of the 'impact-based' account of public agency, the latter interpretation resonates strongly with the 'capacity-based' account.

In sum, I have established in this section that to qualify by liberal standards as 'public' and a bearer of special public responsibilities, a political actor must first be able to identify the moral community – the 'public' – within which it is situated and in relation to which its public responsibilities must be discharged. In addition to this, it must qualify as a 'public' rather than

---

5   This latter interpretation is also more consistent with Thomas Pogge's (1989) account of the idea of an 'institutional scheme' as the subject of principles of justice.

'private' actor within this overarching moral community, either by *impacting* on members of the 'public' (moral community) in some especially problematic way, or by possessing some special set of *capacities* to advance important 'public' interests or moral values – such as the discharge of social justice.

Are Corporations 'Public' Actors in Global Politics?

As I have previously noted, it is very common in liberal analyses of political responsibilities for the idea of a 'public' actor, along with the idea of 'public' power, to be linked explicitly to the idea of the state. Sometimes the connection is merely implied by using state-based terminology – for example, terms such as 'governments', 'governance' institutions and political 'authorities' – to characterize public power. But sometimes it is claimed quite explicitly that only states, or state-based political agencies (such as international organizations formed through the cooperative actions of multiple states), can qualify as 'public' actors with corresponding public powers and responsibilities. This final section explores some plausible reasons for rejecting this state-centric account of 'public' actors in the context of a globalized political economy and for attributing some public responsibilities to non-state corporate actors.

The relevance of the normative criteria of 'publicness' set out above can be illustrated by examining how these criteria apply to states, which are generally thought of as the paradigmatic 'public' actors. When we do so, we can readily recognize that the traditional view of states as 'public' actors is entirely appropriate. First, it is easy (at least on somewhat idealized interpretations of statehood) to identify the 'public' communities which generate and are owed the public responsibilities of states. These communities are 'nations' that ideally embody bounded territorial communities with the relevant forms of material interdependence, alongside the requisite shared normative frameworks (based on mutual communication, moral belief and so on), as discussed above.

State agencies also qualify as public rather than private actors *within* bounded nation-state communities insofar as their special powers (such as coercion or law-making) enable them to *impact* on others in ways that sometimes harm the interests and constrain the autonomy of particular individuals and, moreover, equip them with a strong institutional *capacity* to promote public interests and values. As a result of these special 'public' impacts and special 'public' capacities, it is quite appropriate to expect that states have special 'public' responsibilities – for instance, to disclose information, to consult relevant 'publics', to protect certain 'public' interests or to promote justice – corresponding with these powers and capacities (see further, Macdonald 2008b).

Application of the criteria for 'publicness' set out above is here able to provide a straightforward rationale for intuitive and widely-held understandings of why and how state actors should be characterized as 'public'. When applying the same criteria to corporations, there are some strong theoretical grounds for viewing many corporations as 'public' actors alongside states. In the first instance, corporations qualify as *members of communities* that have the characteristics necessary to generate moral relationships and responsibilities among members in general terms. Corporations are members of communities constituted through *material interconnections*, of the kinds discussed above: they impact on others' interests within broad transnational communities affected by the corporations' economic activities; and they benefit from their relationships with other participants in the vast networks of production, exchange and consumption within the globalized economic system. In addition, corporations commonly participate as members of communities constituted by *shared normative institutions*, manifested through their willing compliance with established laws (and the underlying moral principles these reflect) within the territorial communities in which their economic activities are geographically located.

As such, corporations appear to meet the first normative requirement for the designation of 'public' status and responsibility: they are members of broader 'publics' within which general moral responsibilities arise and in relation to which public responsibilities must be discharged. The next question is whether corporations also qualify as 'public' rather than 'private' actors *within* these overarching moral communities, either by *impacting* on members of the 'public' (moral community) in some especially problematic way or by possessing some special set of *capacities* to advance important 'public' interests or moral values.

In many cases, it seems clear that corporations can also meet the criteria that qualify them as 'public' actors within their broader moral communities. In the first instance, corporations sometimes qualify as public insofar as they can *impact* on other members of their communities in ways that constrain the autonomy or harm the fundamental interests of these individuals. The global political power of corporations is primarily a function of their huge economic role within the global economy (Anderson and Cavanagh 2000; Ruggie 2006). As has been widely recognized now, this power can have significant impacts upon populations, especially within the global South. First, corporate activity can impact – sometimes beneficially, but often detrimentally – upon the protection of basic rights within certain communities (such as basic labour standards regarding workers' health and safety). In addition to this, corporate activities often have implications for other important areas of 'public' decision-making, such as how, in particular communities, necessary trade-offs are made between social benefits arising from employment and poverty-reduction for some, and social harms arising from environmental impacts, poor working conditions and increasing social inequalities (see further, Macdonald 2008b).

Corporations can also qualify as public actors to the extent that they possess certain special *capacities* for advancing collective (public) interests or values. The same economic power which enables them to generate significant public *impacts* upon wide global populations also equips them with enormous political *capacities* of the relevant kinds. As noted above, the forms of economic power possessed by corporations do not only lead to impacts upon populations which are morally problematic (through harming individuals' interests or constraining their autonomy). This power can also be wielded to great public *advantage*, such as generating valued social goods and distributing them to those who need them, or organizing systems of global economic production and exchange compliant with principles of distributive justice and human rights standards (see further, Macdonald 2008b).

It seems plausible to claim that corporations can sometimes qualify as 'public' rather than 'private' actors according to both the impact-based criterion and the capacity-based criterion outlined above. This would require corporations to bear some special public responsibilities which they now routinely evade through their insistence of their status as 'private' actors. These most significantly include responsibilities to ensure that their power is subject to appropriate forms of public legitimation – transparency and accountability, participatory decision-making and so on – and responsibilities to comply with principles of justice in exercising their extensive power over workers and broader global populations.

However, the extent to which we can call corporations 'public' is also limited in some important respects. An attempt to apply norms of public responsibility to corporations is undermined by the frequent lack of a single unified 'public' in which a given corporation is embedded and to which its public responsibilities can be said to be owed. Rather, corporations are usually embedded within multiple 'partial' communities, each of which may possess only some but not all of the characteristics of moral 'publics' discussed above. For example, a given corporation may be materially connected to one community of individuals by harming their interests in some way (perhaps by imposing upon them the burdens of environmental 'externalities', such as pollution or other environmental degradation) and, simultaneously, materially connected to a quite different community of individuals by benefiting from their relationships with these people (perhaps by employing these individuals as workers, or selling profitably to them as consumers).

This creates ambiguity concerning how a corporation's responsibilities to these different sets of individuals should be distinguished, given that these two different material grounds for allocating moral responsibilities involve quite different member populations. This moral ambiguity can be further exacerbated if the communities to which the corporation is materially connected are culturally diverse and geographically dispersed and, accordingly, lacking in the shared normative institutions (communicative structures, political values and so on) that generate the third foundation for liberal 'publics', and for the public responsibilities to which they give rise. This disaggregation of the various dimensions of 'public' communities – which are paradigmatically bundled together in the territorially and nationally bounded communities underpinning liberal nation-states – can make the task of connecting corporations (as bearers of public responsibilities) to particular communities (as loci for the discharge of these responsibilities) a very complex and indeterminate undertaking.

Another key problem with attempting to allocate public responsibilities directly to corporations – instead of concentrating these responsibilities within territorial state institutions – is that this increases the *diffusion* of public responsibility throughout the global political system as a whole and, in doing so, creates political confusion surrounding the division or distribution of responsibilities among the many public actors within the system. As I have elaborated in more detail elsewhere, this diffusion of public responsibility can contribute firstly to problems of *responsibility gaps or deficits* – that is, a situation where certain responsibilities (for example, to protect a certain set of human rights) are neglected altogether because it is unclear which public agencies are supposed to discharge them (see further, Macdonald 2008b).

It can also lead to associated difficulties with the *discharge* of certain public responsibilities – in particular, those requiring the establishment of mechanisms for consultative decision-making and accountability to relevant 'publics'. These problems arise since the relevant 'publics' need to know who is responsible for particular decisions or outcomes if they are to know where to direct their democratic input and which actors to hold accountable for particular decisions through appropriate processes of consultation and accountability (see further, Macdonald 2008b).

It is worth remembering, however, that states can run into similar difficulties when attempting to clarify and discharge their public responsibilities. Although the difficulties I have just discussed would not apply to 'states' as public actors if states in practice resembled the 'closed' political communities of ideal liberal theory, they do arise for states operating amidst the political realities of contemporary globalization. In the context of globalization, states too find themselves embedded within many partial and overlapping moral communities and are faced with poorly defined public roles within a pluralist, global political order. Given these contemporary realities, it is plausible to talk about corporations as 'public' – at least in a manner broadly analogous with the 'public' status of states within a globalized order – even though corporations do not satisfy the normative criteria of 'publicness' as neatly as states when viewed within an idealized (nation-state-based) model of liberalism.

Conclusions

In this chapter I have set out some theoretical grounds upon which corporations can be viewed as 'public' actors in the context of a globalized world polity, alongside the state and inter-governmental agencies which are more traditionally viewed as public within liberal analysis. This conclusion is significant; if we accept these reasons for viewing corporations as 'public' actors, then the case for demanding that corporations bear some special public responsibilities – which they now routinely evade through insisting on their status as 'private' actors – is significantly strengthened. Significantly, these corporate responsibilities include those to ensure their power is subject to appropriate forms of public legitimation – such as those of transparency and accountability or participatory decision-making – and compliance with principles of justice in exercising their extensive power over workers and broader global populations.

The conclusion that corporations should bear responsibilities of these kinds is not in itself new or surprising; the novelty of this argument is the application of explicitly *liberal* normative principles and theoretical ideas to arrive at this conclusion. The ideology of 'liberalism' is very commonly associated – at least within discussions of matters of international political economy – with a firm normative commitment to the institutional autonomy of the 'economic' sphere (that is, a commitment to the importance of its ability to function free from undue incursions from 'public' agencies and regulatory standards). Correspondingly, liberal analysis is associated with a strong commitment to the view that corporations, as economic actors, should be cast as 'private' and thus unburdened with any demanding requirements for the discharge of public responsibilities. In contrast, this chapter argues that this mainstream interpretation of the institutional requirements of normative liberalism is mistaken and should be challenged by committed liberals as well as by those already persuaded of the need for corporate responsibility on the basis of other (more illiberal) political ideals.

The other important conclusion to emerge from this analysis is the recognition that casting corporations as 'public' and allocating them direct public responsibilities (for promoting justice and upholding standards of public legitimacy) creates, or at least exacerbates, some serious institutional difficulties associated with the diffusion of public responsibility within the wider global institutional system. A global justice movement concerned with forging the most effective institutional path to greater global justice and legitimacy must make some difficult strategic decisions: should it avoid problems of political pluralism and complexity by establishing more traditional state-like institutions capable of delivering justice and accountable decision-making on a global scale within a more strongly constitutionalized structure of public power and responsibility? Or should it recognize and embrace the reality of institutional pluralism within our increasingly globalized world order, and forge a reform agenda based on redistributing public responsibilities among existing powerful actors, with powerful corporations at the forefront? It is possible that the best and most workable solution for the foreseeable future is to be found through some institutional hybrid of the two approaches. The development of a reform agenda of this kind should be explored and pursued further as a key political priority for advocates of global justice.

References

Anderson, S. and Cavanagh, J. (2000), *Top 200: The Rise of Corporate Global Power* (Washington, DC: Institute for Policy Studies).

Beitz, C. (1983), 'Cosmopolitan ideals and national sentiment', *Journal of Philosophy* 80(10): 591–600.

Buchanan, A. and Keohane, R. (1990), 'Justice as reciprocity versus subject-centred justice', *Philosophy and Public Affairs* 19(3): 227–52.

Butt, D. (2008), *Rectifying International Injustice: Principles of Compensation and Restitution between Nations* (Oxford: Oxford University Press).

Copp, D. (1999), 'The idea of a legitimate state', *Philosophy and Public Affairs* 28(1): 3–45.

Friedman, M. (1970), 'The social responsibility of business is to increase its profits', *The New York Times Magazine*, 13 September, 32–3, 122, 124, 126.

Macdonald, T. (2008a), *Global Stakeholder Democracy: Power and Representation Beyond Liberal States* (Oxford: Oxford University Press).

—— (2008b), 'What's so special about states? Liberal legitimacy in a globalising world', *Political Studies* 56(3): 544–65.

Miller, D. (1995), *On Nationality, Oxford Political Theory* (Oxford: Clarendon Press).

—— (1999), *Principles of Social Justice* (Cambridge, MA: Harvard University Press).

Pogge, T. (1989), *Realizing Rawls* (Ithaca, NY: Cornell University Press).

—— (1992), 'Cosmopolitanism and sovereignty', *Ethics* 103(1): 48–75.

—— (2000), 'On the site of distributive justice: reflections on Cohen and Murphy', *Philosophy and Public Affairs* 29(2): 137–96.

Rawls, J. (1971), *A Theory of Justice* (Cambridge, MA: Harvard University Press).

—— (1996), *Political Liberalism*, new edition (New York: Columbia University Press).

—— (1999), *The Law of Peoples: With, The Idea of Public Reason Revisited* (Cambridge, MA: Harvard University Press).

Ruggie, J. (2006), *Interim Report of the Special Representative of the Secretary-General on the Issue of Human Rights and Transnational Corporations and Other Business Enterprises* (UN Doc. E/CN.4/2006/97) (Geneva: Office of the High Commissioner for Human Rights). Available at: http://www1.umn.edu/humanrts/business/RuggieReport2006.html [accessed: 26 March 2009].

Scharpf, F.W. (1999), *Governing in Europe: Effective and Democratic?* (Oxford: Oxford University Press).

Sisk, G. (2005), 'A primer on the doctrine of federal sovereign immunity', *Oklahoma Law Review* 58(3): 439–68.

Walzer, M. (1984), 'Liberalism and the art of separation', *Political Theory* 12(3): 315–30.

—— (1995), 'The concept of civil society', in M. Walzer (ed.), *Toward a Global Civil Society* (Oxford: Berghahn Books).

Woods, N. (2001), 'Making the IMF and the World Bank more accountable', *International Affairs* 77(1): 83–100.

Chapter 8

Corporate Responsibility and Stakeholder Governance: Relevance to the Australian Garment Sector

Emer Diviney and Serena Lillywhite

Introduction

This chapter argues that the Australian garment industry is lagging behind other OECD countries in its adoption of corporate responsibility (CR) practices and that steps need to be taken to quicken the pace of CR uptake. Research reported in this chapter reveals that the impetus for CR is strong: conditions experienced by workers in the industry, both in Australia and in the international supply chains supplying Australian brands and fashion houses, are often poor, and existing state and non-state CR initiatives are not adequately addressing the problem. In the last 20 years there has been widespread outsourcing of production by Australian garment companies overseas. Simultaneously, like many OECD nations, Australia has experienced a growth in informal, home-based production in the textile, clothing and footwear (TCF) sector characterized by poor wages and conditions as the formal sector has contracted. In response to these worsening labour conditions, a number of innovative 'hard' and 'soft' law initiatives have been developed which may be characterized as corporate responsibility instruments in the sense that they expand the responsibility of Australian TCF 'brands', 'fashion-houses' and manufacturers for the supply chains from which they source their products. However, the state-based labour and supply chain laws and the existing multi-stakeholder initiative – the Homeworkers Code of Practice – do not regulate *international* supply chains. Thus CR international governance occurs only in the private, non-state, domain for Australian companies who outsource production overseas.

This chapter draws upon and adds to research conducted by the Brotherhood of St Laurence (BSL) entitled *Ethical Threads: Corporate Social Responsibility in the Australian Garment Industry* (Diviney and Lillywhite 2007). This study was the first Australian report on corporate responsibility in the garment sector that involved all stakeholders – companies, unions, workers, non-governmental organizations (NGOs), peak industry groups, government and universities. The research found that the Australian garment industry has been slow to embrace either mandatory ('hard') or voluntary ('softer') mechanisms to protect workers in international and local manufacturing supply chains. To address this issue, a key recommendation of *Ethical Threads* was the establishment of a multi-stakeholder platform to promote and implement the global dimensions of corporate responsibility (CR) in the sector. The report further recommended that membership should include small and large companies, NGOs, government, industry associations, unions, suppliers, sourcing agents and workers. This chapter augments the *Ethical Threads* research by providing a deeper analysis of the viability of a multi-stakeholder platform in the Australian garment industry.

The remainder of this chapter is structured as follows: firstly, an overview of the industry in Australia is provided together with an outline of the ways in which Australian CR practices in general – and in the garment industry in particular – are behind other OECD countries in implementing and reporting on CR. Secondly, the chapter reflects on two recent Australian parliamentary inquiries by the Corporations and Markets Advisory Committee (CAMAC) and the Parliamentary Joint Committee on Corporations and Financial Services (PJC)[1] that recommended a continuation of voluntary CR mechanisms. The chapter briefly weighs up the merit of voluntary compared with mandatory CR in the Australian context in which the industry is already regulated by a complex network of voluntary and mandatory laws. Finally, the merits of multi-stakeholder initiatives (MSIs) are discussed in relation to the Australian CR environment.

The Research Methodology

In *Ethical Threads*, the BSL considered three key questions:

1. How do the sourcing and manufacturing practices of Australia's garment sector relate to corporate social responsibility, particularly regarding labour rights?
2. What are the views of agents within the garment industry on the voluntary and regulatory frameworks that exist to protect workers locally and overseas?
3. How can the capacity of the Australian industry to address labour rights in its international and local supply chains be improved?

The research focused on Australian companies sourcing and/or manufacturing garments and apparel both on and offshore for the Australian market. Sourcing and/or production of fabrics, trims, accessories and knitwear were outside the scope of the study. Emphasis was placed on the provision and support of good labour practices and compliance with labour rights and standards throughout the supply chain. The research did not consider environmental issues.

A critical aspect of the research was an assessment of the participating companies' attitudes towards, awareness of, and adherence to the relevant laws, regulations and CR initiatives, including:

- the Australian Workplace Relations Act 1996
- Australian federal and state clothing trades awards
- state and federal Board of Reference requirements
- the Homeworkers Code of Practice (HWCP)

In an international context, the report examined CR initiatives such as:

- the Global Reporting Initiative (GRI)
- SA8000
- the Fair Labor Association
- international standards and conventions such as the ILO Conventions and the OECD *Guidelines for Multinational Enterprises*

---

1 The 2006 Corporations and Markets Advisory Committee (CAMAC) inquiry into corporate responsibility and triple-bottom-line reporting for incorporated entities in Australia, *The Social Responsibility of Corporations*, and the 2006 Parliamentary Joint Committee on Corporations and Financial Services inquiry, *Corporate Responsibility: Managing Risk and Creating Value*.

In-depth interviews were conducted with 37 organizations: 23 companies and 14 industry stakeholders, including business associations, peak bodies, labour rights organizations and trade unions, and key government policy-makers. Interviews were also conducted with 13 garment sector outworkers in two focus groups.

Given the limited engagement with CSR in the Australian industry we could not employ a random sample approach to selecting research participants. Instead we contacted companies, making a concerted effort to select a range that reflects the industry's diversity: large retail brands, sportswear labels, ready-to-wear labels and fashion companies, uniform and work-wear manufacturers and small independent fashion labels. Many companies invited to participate in the research declined.

The research was supported by an advisory committee comprising representatives from companies, industry peak bodies, the Textile Clothing and Footwear Union of Australia (TCFUA), government departments, academics, the CR sector and NGOs. The committee was chaired by an independent CR consultant. This group assisted in the recruitment of research participants and the design and methodology of the research project, and gave feedback on the final document. The advisory committee and researchers formulated the research recommendations collaboratively.

An Overview of the Australian Garment Industry

Reflecting international trends, there has been significant restructuring of the garment industry in Australia since the 1970s. Through the opening of markets to imports and the reduction of trade quotas and tariffs, a global business model has emerged 'based on companies outsourcing production through global supply chains that demand low-cost and "flexible" labour' (Raworth 2004, 17). Foreign investment has contributed to enhanced integration of developing and emerging countries, particularly China, in the global economy. As garment production is very labour-intensive, cut-make-trim processes have moved to competitive locations where labour is plentiful and inexpensive. According to Raworth (2004, 48), 'today, at least 50 countries look to garments for export success, and thousands of manufacturers – both local owners and foreign investors – are vying for a place in big companies' and retailers' supply chains'.

Australia has followed worldwide trends of offshoring and outsourcing. Up to 50 per cent of clothes currently sold in Australia are manufactured overseas (ANZ 2005), mainly in low-wage countries. Complex production chains exist within Australia, and manufacturing processes are commonly outsourced to wholesalers and home-based outworkers. Garments are now rarely produced by the retailer or fashion wholesaler in a company-owned factory. In conversation, Michelle O'Neil asserts that up to 70 per cent of garments manufactured onshore are made by outworkers who are mainly migrant workers working from home. The benefits of outsourcing are that it reduces companies' workforces and thus overheads and oversight costs, as well as allowing greater flexibility in a number of respects. However, the downside is that it weakens the capacity of businesses, unions and NGOs to monitor labour rights (Hale and Shaw 2001). Furthermore, outsourcing does not encourage systematic and sustainable industry investment in human capital and skills development.

Corporate Responsibility – A Growing Trend

Corporate responsibility is a process whereby a company:

- assumes responsibility across its entire supply chain for the social, environmental and economic consequences of its operations;
- reports on these consequences;
- constructively engages with stakeholders (MVO Platform).[2]

Internationally there has been growing recognition of the importance of CR in contributing to sustainable business. This is demonstrated through:

- a rise in the use of CR reporting tools such as the GRI;[3]
- greater support for and synergy amongst CR mechanisms such as the UN Global Compact[4] and the OECD *Guidelines for Multinational Enterprises*;[5]
- the development of new initiatives like the UN *Principles for Responsible Investment*;[6]
- research into business and human rights, notably that by the Special Representative of the UN Secretary-General on the issue of human rights and transnational corporations and other business enterprises (see Ruggie 2007);
- increased multilateral interest in CR, most recently recognition by the European Commission and the 2007 G8 Summit[7] that CR is a key element in the strategy to promote global investment and sustainable growth;
- a rise in business-led initiatives such as the Business Leaders Initiative on Human Rights.[8]

---

2   This is the definition of CSR used by the Dutch CSR Platform (MVO Platform), a coalition of Dutch civil society organizations.

3   Organizations using the GRI Guidelines as the basis for their reporting numbered 750 by December 2005, representing a 24 per cent increase since the 2004 annual review.

4   The United Nations Global Compact was launched in 2000; since then the initiative has grown to almost 5,000 participants, including 3,700 businesses in 120 countries.

5   The OECD *Guidelines for Multinational Enterprises* outline what the 30 OECD member governments and ten non-member countries agree are the basic components of responsible business conduct. They provide voluntary principles and standards for responsible business conduct. They encompass a complaint mechanism which to date has been used by NGOs and trade unions to raise over 100 cases of alleged breaches of the principles by business.

6   The UN *Principles for Responsible Investment* was developed in 2005 to address the growing view among investment professionals that environmental, social and corporate governance issues require appropriate consideration to enhance the performance of investment portfolios. Since its development there has been rapid uptake through a finance sector signatory process.

7   The G8 Summit leaders (in Heilligendamn) in their Declaration, 'Growth and Responsibility in the World Economy', gave detailed attention to CR, firmly placing its value in a policy context. The G8 not only identified its own responsibilities to actively promote internationally-recognized CR and labour standards, but called upon the business community and others to do so as well.

8   The Business Leaders Initiative on Human Rights, introduced in 2003, is a programme designed to lead and develop practical business responses to human rights issues and challenges in the global economy. It has 13 corporate members and is chaired by Mary Robinson, President of Realizing Rights: The Ethical Globalization Initiative.

According to CorporateRegister.com, in 1992 there were only 26 companies producing CR reports; in 2007 that number had grown to 2,460. Australia has also seen a growth in CR reporting. A KPMG study (2005) conducted for the Australian Department of Environment and Heritage documents the number of sustainability reports produced by the top 500 companies in Australia as follows:

- 2005: 119 companies (24 per cent)
- 2000: 65 companies (13 per cent)
- 1995: 6 companies (1 per cent)[9]

However, the 2006 Parliamentary Joint Committee on Corporations and Financial Services review of corporate responsibility stated:

> Despite evidence that Australian companies have shown a greater engagement with the corporate responsibility agenda over the past decade, the committee also heard that, by international standards, Australia lags in implementing and reporting on corporate responsibility. (2006, xiii)

This observation is supported by another KPMG study, which compares trends in sustainability reporting. An assessment of the top 100 internationally listed companies indicates that despite the significant increase in reporting in Australia the rate remains low relative to other OECD countries; for example:

- Australia: 23 per cent
- Japan: 81 per cent
- UK: 71 per cent
- average (16 countries): 41 per cent[10]

The BSL research, *Ethical Threads*, confirms there is limited implementation of CR practices, including reporting, particularly amongst small to medium-sized enterprises (SMEs). When participating company representatives were asked about their CR practices, only six of the 23 had processes in place to map and monitor their supply chains. Further, only five gathered information on outworkers' employment conditions in their companies' Australian supply chains. With the exception of companies producing in excess of one million units annually, most representatives felt that their companies lacked the capacity to implement an ethical supply-chain process.

The issue of limited uptake of CR by SMEs, though not unique to Australia, is of particular concern for the Australian textile clothing and footwear (TCF) sector, as 87 per cent of the industry consists of SMEs. Utting (2007) notes that there is a need to keep the CR trend in perspective. According to UNCTAD (2007) statistics, there are approximately 78,000 transnational corporations and 780,000 affiliates as well as millions of suppliers, let alone other types of enterprises. Utting (2007) also observes that this growing trend is miniscule when taking into consideration the international business community. Most of the international companies engaged in CR are publicly listed multinationals. In the garment sector these include international brands such as Nike, Adidas and GAP.

---

9   Study commissioned by the Department of Environment and Heritage (DEH) into Sustainability Reporting in Australia. Research is undertaken by KPMG Australia, CAER and Deni Green Consulting Services. The most recent survey has just been released and is entitled 'The State of Sustainability Reporting in Australia 2005'.

10   KPMG International's survey of corporate responsibility was issued in 1993, 1996, 1999, 2002 and 2005. The most recent survey is Kolk et al. (2005).

The Origins and Use of Corporate Responsibility

Historically, national governments have had primary responsibility for upholding human rights and ensuring that companies do not breach standards. However, increasing cross-border trade makes this more challenging. Australian garment companies now manufacture goods through complex production networks both on and offshore. Although labour laws exist in most low-wage countries (including China), enforcement is patchy. In the absence of binding international law, workers producing garments for global networks lack protection from exploitation. Labour laws similarly exist in Australia, but enforcement is difficult due to the increasing amount of manufacture performed in unregistered workplaces such as private residences. In this context, there is a need for companies to recognize their social obligations through the development and implementation of credible CR policy and practice.

According to Jenkins et al. (2002) and Justice (2000), the growing CR trend is a result of several factors converging in the 1990s that increased pressure on companies to adopt and implement CR practices and, in particular, voluntary codes of conduct. These factors include:

- the globalization of economic activity
- notions of good governance and an expanding concept of corporate responsibility
- the state's decreasing role in regulating business behaviour
- the failure of national governments to prevent exploitation and to enforce minimum standards and basic human rights
- the significance of brands and corporate reputation, making companies vulnerable to bad publicity
- the international dissemination of information about working conditions
- the proliferation of NGO labour rights campaigns
- the emerging consumer trend to purchase ethically made products

These drivers did not seem as relevant to the BSL research participants, with the exception of some of the larger enterprises. It appears that most organizations interviewed were more concerned with how the CR processes may impact internal operations of their businesses, rather than the broader trends and issues identified by Jenkins and Justice.

The BSL *Ethical Threads* research found that the majority of participating SME garment company representatives could see neither an opportunity for, nor a benefit from, implementing CR processes, due to the following barriers:

- mechanisms only designed for larger companies
- consumers indifferent, and unwilling to pay for 'ethical' garments
- financial sustainability more important than ethical supply
- lack of organizational resources and expertise
- lack of influence due to small size
- difficulty of taking responsibility for workers other than direct company employees

Larger companies and some sportswear/work-wear companies, however, were more inclined to see the benefits of a CR process, for the following reasons:

- demonstrable risk mitigation
- building community confidence in their brand
- positioning the company as an industry leader

The barriers identified by representatives of larger companies related more to the difficulties of implementing a CR process, including:

- driving the process internally
- creating an environment to embed CR in organizational processes
- influencing suppliers as Australia is a small market relative to Europe and the United States
- mapping and understanding complex supply chains

Of the four publicly listed companies that participated in the research, only two representatives indicated that shareholder demand moved them to develop a CR process, and only one business stakeholder said it would motivate companies.

A major disincentive to adopting CR strategies identified by companies interviewed for *Ethical Threads* is the widespread belief that most consumers do not care where or how their garments are sourced, or about the labour conditions under which products are manufactured. Trends in Europe, however, indicate that consumers there are becoming more concerned about the social and environmental impact of their purchases. Recent EU and British polls demonstrate growing community interest in ethical supply, and increased spending on 'ethical' clothing (Co-operative Bank 2006; CSR Europe/MORI 2000). By comparison, research exploring consumer attitudes in New South Wales in 1999 indicated a lack of awareness of outworker exploitation. However, once participants were given information about working conditions, most indicated they would pay 5 per cent more for ethically produced garments (NSW DIR 1999).

Lack of awareness of supply chain issues in Australia can be linked to less visible campaigning regarding sweatshop conditions in Australia, and virtually none focusing on international sourcing practices by Australian-owned companies. One company respondent to *Ethical Threads* noted:

> England has had a strong advocacy platform around sweated labour and conditions in China because NGOs have been huge on this issue. … I don't think this has quite happened in Australia. (Diviney and Lillywhite 2007, 14)

Corporate Responsibility Debate and Practice

The International Debate

Internationally, there is considerable debate as to whether voluntary CR mechanisms have the capacity to impact positively the lives of workers in a company's supply chain (Bendell 2004). Those critical of the voluntary approach are primarily concerned that these initiatives do not guarantee that all corporations will uphold national and international regulations, particularly when operating in developing and transitional economies where national legislation is constrained by a weak enforcement regime. Frequently cited problems are the comparatively small number of companies undertaking monitoring and auditing, and concerns around inadequate disclosure and reporting. There is also a suspicion amongst detractors that those companies that do report tend to include only 'good news' and omit negative or 'high risk' information. Examples given of the latter include the conduct of business in conflict zones or areas of weak governance,[11] and activities with a potential to impact negatively on human rights or the environment. Critics also express the view that voluntary mechanisms cannot be sanctioned, stressing the difficulty of enforcement, and suggest that CR does more to enhance and protect brand reputation than it does to solve labour and environmental problems. Detractors also believe that for voluntary mechanisms to be most effective they need to be underpinned by both national and international law. This, they argue, adds credibility and ensures that stakeholders such as regulators, investors and affected communities can compare data on company performance and encourage greater accountability (O'Rourke 2006; UNEP, KPMG 2006; Justice 2001).

On the other hand, advocates of voluntary mechanisms cite advantages such as greater flexibility, competitiveness and industry relevance. They argue that the voluntary approach results in a greater level of company support and, ultimately, of compliance. Many hold the view that the introduction of national and international mandatory requirements will place an increased burden on companies in particular SMEs, when trading in an increasingly global market, and may disadvantage emerging economies. They further suggest that the introduction of mandatory regulation is premature, as CR is relatively new, complex and evolving (O'Rourke 2006; UNEP, KPMG 2006; Justice 2001).

While the debate is not likely to end soon, emerging thinking – particularly in the area of corporate accountability – suggests that a regulatory environment where voluntary and mandatory mechanisms (including MSIs) coexist is most likely to encourage responsible business conduct in the near future. Nonetheless, as recently suggested by a European Parliament representative, 'the clock is ticking on voluntary mechanisms' (Smith and Partners 2007, 2). This opinion is increasingly shared by NGOs as they lose faith in the potential for voluntary responses to deliver real change and fair and decent labour practices. For example, Solidar[12] has previously asserted that a legislative framework of social and environmental reporting for all EU-based companies is a key step in ensuring transparency of information from companies.[13] The Dutch CSR Platform has identified as an ultimate goal the introduction of internationally binding and enforceable legislation of environmental rights and human rights, including workers rights (Dutch CSR Platform 2007). This will help to achieve a level playing field and limit 'free rider' behaviour.

The Debate in Australia

In Australia, the debate is equally controversial as in the broader international environment. Significant attention has been directed to the mandatory reporting aspects of responsible supply-chain management, particularly in the finance, extractive and manufacturing sectors. The introduction and implementation of regulation to protect local garment workers is one such example. Recently, the Australian Government conducted two inquiries into corporate responsibility, one by the Corporations and Markets Advisory Committee (2006) and the other by the Parliamentary Joint

---

11   The OECD Investment Committee recognizes the added complexity in ensuring responsible business conduct when operating in conflict zones. In response, the OECD has developed the 'OECD Risk Awareness Tool for Multinational Enterprises in Weak Governance Zones'. The tool aims to help companies that invest in countries where governments are unwilling or unable to assume their responsibilities.

12   Solidar is a network of social and economic justice NGOs working in development and humanitarian aid, social policy, social service provision, migration and lifelong learning. With members active in over 90 countries worldwide, Solidar works both in Europe and internationally in alliance with trade unions, the labour movement and civil society.

13   This assertion was on Solidar's website but has since been removed for reasons that are unknown to the authors.

Committee on Corporations and Financial Services (2006). Both inquiries recommended further evolution of voluntary mechanisms, rejecting calls for mandatory regulation that would require directors to consider the interests of stakeholders other than shareholders and to report on their organizations' social and environmental performance.

Regardless of the current state of the international debate on the introduction of mandatory reporting requirements, it is increasingly apparent that Australia is lagging behind Europe and the United States in developing a regulatory CR framework for international supply-chain management and disclosure. Within the EU, changes to the Companies Bill in the UK and a resolution by the European Parliament ('Corporate Social Responsibility: A New Partnership') require corporations to monitor and report on their performance in respect to human and worker rights and the environment. In the United States, the *Decent Working Conditions and Fair Competition Act* (S.3485) was introduced to amend the *Tariff Act* of 1930. The new Act was introduced into the United States Senate on 8 June 2006 as Senate Bill 3485 by Senator Byron Dorgan (D-ND) [1] and was introduced in the House of Representatives on 16 June 2006 as HR 5635 by Rep. Sherrod Brown (D-OH)[2]. If passed, this will prohibit the import, export and sale of goods made with sweatshop labour. In February 2007 the Act was referred to the House Senate Committee on Crime, Terrorism, and Homeland Security,[14] and then on the 25 April 2007 referred to the Sub Committee on Trade,[15] suggesting it is yet to be passed. A recent report by The National Labour Committee (2008), *Nightmare on Sesame Street: Ernie Toy Made in Chinese Sweatshop*, identifies the ongoing issue of excessive overtime, child labour and withheld wages for workers in China makings goods destined for US and European markets. In addition, the government of Sweden (Ministry of Enterprise, Energy and Communications) recently adopted the Guidelines for External Reporting by State-Owned Companies.[16] These Guidelines mandate that state-owned enterprises produce a sustainability report in accordance with the GRI.[17] Reports should include, among other things, issues relating to the environment, human rights, sustainable development, gender equality and diversity. The guidelines are based on the principle of 'comply or explain'.

The findings of the *Ethical Threads* research reflect the international debate concerning mandatory regulation. Overwhelmingly, business organizations and companies felt that voluntary approaches were the appropriate way forward, as suggested by the following company respondent:

> Half the time we try to regulate too much, then people are bucking the trend and they try to do all sorts of things to break the rules because it becomes too rigid and inflexible. (Diviney and Lillywhite 2007, 10)

By contrast, the labour rights advocates interviewed for *Ethical Threads* believed that voluntary mechanisms were useful, but to 'have teeth' they need to be underpinned by both national and international law. According to one respondent:

---

14   Status Updates for S.367, *The Decent Working Conditions and Fair Competition Act*, http://www.washingtonwatch.com/bills [accessed: 31 August 2009].

15   Revisions for the H.R.1910, *The Decent Working Conditions and Fair Competition Act*, http://www.washingtonwatch.com/bils/edits/110_HR_1910.xml [accessed: 31 August 2009].

16   These Guidelines were adopted on the 29 November 2007 and came into effect 1 January 2008. For further information see the Government of Sweden website, www.regeringen.se.

17   The GRI is an internationally developed process for reporting on a company's social, environmental and economic performance that was developed through an MSI.

It would be great if the Australian government required all Australian companies sourcing overseas, and indeed any company exporting to Australia, to source from places where ILO Conventions are respected; but I think we're a long, long way from that. (Diviney and Lillywhite 2007, 10)

The Regulation of Working Conditions in the Australian Garment Sector

Australian labour laws and supply-chain regulation have thus far failed to improve the conditions of garment workers, particularly those working in the informal economy. The Australian system requires companies manufacturing in Australia to adhere to a regulatory framework that covers both factory workers and outworkers. The mandatory regulatory framework includes a complex patchwork of federal and state awards (industry-wide collective agreements) and state supply-chain legislation. It also includes the Homeworkers Code of Practice, which companies can voluntarily sign onto and subsequently submit to a thorough accreditation process. According to Marshall (forthcoming), whilst Australia's regulatory framework is overly complex, it in other respects appears to be a model of regulatory design because it provides a range of regulatory techniques, including incentives in the form of the 'no sweatshop label' which companies, once they have become accredited to the Homeworkers Code of Practice, can display in their garments to attract ethical consumers. However, it also has 'teeth' by providing unions and labour inspectorates with the ability to apply for sanctions in the event of non-compliance. It attempts to address the garment industry's fragmented and complex manufacturing supply chains.

Regardless of the rigour of the regulation, Marshall (forthcoming) argues that countervailing forces and incentives to *non*-compliance must remain stronger than the incentives *to* compliance as there has been no apparent improvement in the conditions experienced by outworkers since new regulatory techniques have been made available. In 1996 the Senate Economic References Committee noted that non-compliance with award wages and conditions was so widespread it was considered normal, and this appears to be no less accurate today. Over the past decade, state and federal inquiries have consistently found that outworkers receive payment and conditions significantly lower than their award and statutory entitlements. These include inquiries by the Productivity Commission (2003) and the Industry Commission (1997). Cregan (2001) found that outworkers' average rate of pay was $3.60 per hour. Most of the participants averaged 12 hours per day, with 62 per cent stating they worked seven days a week. Indeed, the BSL research found that conditions had worsened in the last five years. Thirteen outworkers were interviewed in two focus groups. The first group said they were paid $2.50 for a detailed shirt that took one hour to sew. The second group said they were paid between two to three dollars.

The *Ethical Threads* findings provided some insights into the reasons for non-compliance. The primary reason may simply be lack of legal knowledge. Just over a third of the 23 company representatives interviewed knew of their legal obligation to register with either the state or federal Board of Reference, and none of the small-company representatives was aware of the need to be award-compliant. Both government and business organization respondents commented that a lack of knowledge often resulted in poor industrial practice. According to one government official:

One of the biggest issues for us is people not being aware of relevant awards, Acts and legislation that they are required to comply with when they hire people. (Diviney and Lillywhite 2007, 7)

Companies consistently brought up the need for better industry education regarding regulation and compliance requirements.

Small and medium-sized enterprises in particular felt that the regulation was onerous and confusing, and that they lacked the organizational capacity to manage the legislation when supply chains were so complex. Many of the smaller companies also indicated that due to small production runs they could not exert influence on their supply chains, and most noted how difficult it was to find a manufacturer for small runs, let alone an award-compliant manufacturer.

Labour rights organizations, however, suggested that lack of knowledge of legal obligations and the over-complexity of the laws was only one part of the problem:

> The difficulty for the companies is really lack of knowledge about how they can actually fix the problem and lack of will to do it, because really their priority is competing in the market. (Diviney and Lillywhite 2007, 7)

At the other end of the supply chain, outworkers also lacked knowledge about the regulatory environment. Only a third of the 13 outworkers interviewed knew of their legal status as employees rather than as contractors. They also felt they had no power to exercise their rights, for fear of losing work:

> The law to protect the outworker may be there but it is not useful, because if you ask or complain to the employer they just cut the job to you, and they don't say it's because you complain, they just say they have no work. Even though the law to protect the outworker is there, its protection is no use. That law does nothing for outworkers. (Diviney and Lillywhite 2007, 8)

The Australian Homeworkers Code of Practice

The Homeworkers Code of Practice (HWCP) was developed as a response to the failure of mandatory rules to improve the conditions of outworkers. The *Ethical Threads* study found that the HWCP is failing to achieve its objectives as a CR instrument because it is poorly understood or valued.

Many companies interviewed for the *Ethical Threads* research demonstrated a poor understanding of the technical differences between the award requirements and the voluntary commitment of signing the Code. Support for the Code among business organizations and individual companies was not high. It was not considered a MSI that promoted best practice within the sector. Of particular concern was the perception that the Code was an initiative managed by the TCFUA and a local NGO called FairWear (a community coalition addressing garment outworker conditions). Most companies indicated that they did not feel comfortable signing on to the Code given the union practice of industry prosecutions, and given FairWear campaign actions to highlight unethical practices. Industry respondents also reported concerns, including inadequate monitoring and enforcement of the Code, organizational capacity constraints (such as limited supply-chain influence) on the ability of SMEs to meet the requirements, and prohibitive annual accreditation fees.

The research found that much of the industry criticism was based on misinformation. There was a lack of awareness of the HWCP being a joint business–union initiative governed by a diverse committee of management representing small and large enterprises, business peak bodies and the union. FairWear is not a member of the Homeworkers Code of Practice Committee (HWCPC).

The research recommended that better promotion and resourcing of the HWCP would resolve many of the identified problems. In relation to Australian manufacturing, neither binding regulation nor a voluntary initiative has resolved the poor working conditions in the industry. The challenge for the Australian industry is to better promote both the HWCP and the regulation, and to resource properly these initiatives so that they are effectively monitored and enforced.

The experience and knowledge gained from implementing the HWCP provide numerous lessons that can be applied to any future discussions surrounding the development of an MSI for international sourcing in Australia. An Australian MSI ought to support promotion of the Code, its membership and its aims and objectives. Those involved in a new MSI would need to recognize the traditional adversarial relationships that currently exist within the garment sector and foster new collaborative engagement.

Australian Companies' Private CR Mechanisms

There is now a wide array of instruments aimed at improving the conditions and the rights of workers in global supply chains including: individual company codes of conduct; MSIs; international framework agreements; social labelling; investor initiatives; and governmental regulation (Jenkins 2001; OECD 2001; O'Rourke 2003; Wick 2005). This section of the chapter examines the options for the further development of CR in Australia, drawing on international lessons and reflecting upon engagement with CR by Australian garment companies.

Codes of Conduct

Internationally, the CR mechanisms most commonly adopted by companies are codes of conduct (Utting 2001; Kolk and Van Tulder 2006). The OECD broadly defines codes of conduct as 'commitments voluntarily made by companies, associations or other entities which put forward standards and principles for the conduct of business activities in the marketplace' (Gordon and Miyake 2000, 31). The apparel and footwear sector is often described as one of the leading industries in the development and implementation of such codes (Global Reporting Initiative 2006).

There are a number of qualities of good codes which studies of codes of conduct have identified. These include: (a) supporting freedom of association and the ability of workers to organize and represent themselves, (b) transparency, (c) stakeholder consultation and capacity-building, (d) addressing problems identified in monitoring, and (e) creating greater trust and collaboration between the company and workers. The Australian garment companies' codes are now considered against these qualities.

It was not surprising in light of the absence of an externally generated alternative, six of the 23 companies in the *Ethical Threads* sample with a code of conduct had developed a code of practice unilaterally. One company was also a signatory to the Worldwide Responsible Apparel Production (WRAP) business initiative, a certification process for manufacturers. Five company representatives provided copies of their codes, all of which were limited to the minimum standards in the ILO Fundamental Principles and Rights at Work, with the exception of one company which did not include freedom of association and the right to collective bargaining. Most expanded on the elimination of discrimination by specifically addressing wages and hours of work – both factors considered key issues in the garment sector. Furthermore, three codes addressed issues such as accommodation, toilets and amenities. Two codes mentioned a minimum wage.

Freedom of association

Despite all codes referring to the ILO Conventions, none suggested a way of resolving the legal barriers to freedom of association in countries such as China, despite participating companies actively sourcing from China. The *Ethical Threads* study confirmed that the CR processes adopted by companies participating in the study were not meeting international best practice standards.

Transparency

According to an OECD study:

> A major advantage of the corporate code movement is that it brings corporate responsibility issues out into the open and into the arena of public debate. It does this by increasing the transparency of private commitments. Once in the public domain, the commitments can be evaluated, debated, and at least for the most successful codes, imitated. (Gordon and Miyake 2000, 29)

Most of the companies interviewed for *Ethical Threads*, however, did not make their processes entirely transparent. Only three companies published statements in the public domain regarding ethical supply. Just one company provided a link to its code of conduct on its website – this was also the only company to produce a sustainability report including information about ethical supply and auditing, though only the number of audits undertaken and not the results of the auditing process. Notably, this company's sustainability report was not developed using the GRI, which is recognized internationally as the best existing reporting framework. The other companies interviewed reported progress internally to their boards and/or committees, and via their intranets.

Some companies that had implemented processes to monitor labour conditions in their supply chains did not publicize this, preferring anonymity in order to avoid creating an expectation from consumers and NGOs. This further confirms the need for an MSI to share information and develop a body of knowledge relevant to responsible business conduct in Australia in the garment sector.

Consultation with stakeholders and capacity-building

According to Justine Nolan (2002), former Director Workers Rights Program at the Lawyers' Committee for Human Rights in New York:

> Meaningful engagement with local unions and NGOs – whether they be community-based organizations, legal services organizations, women's groups, labour rights groups, [or] religious groups – with a real interest in bettering working conditions is essential to ensuring the credibility of monitoring procedures.

The BSL research identified that all but one of the companies with a CR strategy had developed and implemented their code without any involvement from process workers, suppliers, unions or NGOs. The exception was a large company whose sustainability report stated that it had conducted supplier consultations. Codes were produced internally or through consultation with an inspection, verification and certification company. However, most indicated they had also referred to intergovernmental standards and MSIs. None had a committee with external stakeholders to offer advice on its ethical procurement and CR strategy.

Another issue raised by the research was how codes were communicated to workers in their supply chains and whether companies had effective grievance processes. Most companies indicated that, as part of their monitoring process, they interviewed workers in private about conditions; some had their codes translated and distributed to workers. However, it was unclear whether the suppliers had effective grievance mechanisms. Two companies had a hotline that employees could call anonymously to report breaches of the code, however, it was unclear whether this service was available to workers in their contracting chains. No company representative mentioned any in-factory training about code requirements. The lack of training and grievance processes could potentially impact on workers' ability to exercise their rights in relation to company code requirements.

Auditing, monitoring and certification

Both labour rights organizations and companies involved in CR agree that audits alone do not improve conditions for workers. A recent review of Britain's Ethical Trading Initiative (ETI)[18] (Barrientos and Smith 2006) found that audits have had some positive impacts, although generally limited to more visible issues such as health and safety. Further, the Clean Clothes Campaign stated that 'an audit, used alone, can never produce change – it can only produce a "shopping list" of items to be remedied' (2005, 74). Another ETI publication, titled *Getting Smarter at Auditing: Tackling the Growing Crisis in Ethical Trade Auditing*, identifies a number of common ways in which ethical trade auditing currently goes wrong. These include:

* unreliability of third party commercial auditing companies
* poor value for money
* multiple audits of the same supplier
* inconsistent corrective action plans
* failure to identify or report serious labour problems
* prevalence of fraudulent practices

Most interviewees whose companies conducted factory audits believed that these ensured satisfactory conditions: this suggested unrealistic expectations amongst Australian garment companies. The one exception was the representative of a large brand who recognized that, with a complex supply chain, change would be incremental: 'We've got 11,000 suppliers. It's not going to be something that is done overnight' (Diviney and Lillywhite 2007, 13).

Creating trust

Finally, the *Ethical Threads* research identified a lack of trust between workers, suppliers, labour rights organizations and principal companies, which do not work collaboratively and often fail to understand each other's circumstances. For example, an overwhelming finding in the BSL research is the lack of awareness amongst respondent companies of, and in some cases the lack of a feeling of responsibility for, the difficult working conditions faced by many garment workers in Australia and overseas. Company perceptions were formed without consultation with workers and, with the exception of a few larger companies, without a process to monitor and evaluate factory conditions. There was also a strong view that 'sweatshops' existed but not in their production chains.

There was also a general feeling from smaller companies that CSR mechanisms such as the HWCP were oriented towards larger businesses and were not designed for SMEs. Furthermore, as demonstrated through the implementation of the HWCP, there is a lack of trust between unions, NGOs and companies. Many companies were not participating in this mechanism due to a misconception about the Code's membership.

---

18   The Ethical Trading Initiative is an alliance of companies, NGOs and trade union organizations. According to the ETI's website (2008), the initiative exists 'to promote and improve the implementation of corporate codes of practice which cover supply chain working conditions. Our ultimate goal is to ensure that the working conditions of workers producing for the UK market meet or exceed international labour standards.'

The Way Forward: A Multi-stakeholder Initiative

One way to foster dialogue and trust is through the creation of mechanisms that allow the exchange of ideas. Multi-stakeholder initiatives are designed to do exactly this. According to Hemmati (2001), the term 'multi-stakeholder' describes processes which:

- aim to bring together all major stakeholders in a new form of communication and decision-finding (and possibly decision-making) structure on a particular issue;
- are based on recognition of the importance of achieving equity and accountability in communication between stakeholders;
- involve equitable representation of three or more stakeholder groups and their views;
- are based on democratic principles of transparency and participation, and aim to develop partnerships and strengthened networks between and among stakeholders;
- can cover a wide spectrum of structures and levels of engagement.

MSIs may assist in the establishment of responsible business policy and practice, contribute to inclusive social policy, and reflect the needs of all constituents by providing a mechanism for consultation amongst both state and non-state actors. Studies of code content, for instance, have overwhelmingly stated that CR mechanisms developed through MSIs are far more comprehensive than those developed unilaterally or through business associations or employer initiatives (Barrientos and Smith 2006; Gordon and Miyake 2005; Wick 2005).

Many commentators question the efficacy of MSIs, as a form of voluntary CR, to deliver improved labour, human rights and environmental practices (Delaney Chapter 14, this voulme; Utting 2007; Wick 2005; Barrientos and Smith 2007). In particular, it is argued that existing MSIs are not delivering on stated objectives, such as improved working conditions. However, critics acknowledge that MSIs are generally considered a more rigorous, transparent, consultative and effective process than codes of conduct developed by individual companies. These criticisms have informed the view, for some, that binding CR regulation is required in place of voluntary mechanisms.[19]

Because MSIs in Europe and the United States have now operated for some time, research, critical evidence and case studies on MSIs exist which identify their strengths and weaknesses and suggest ways in which these mechanisms can be improved. There is no doubt that there are significant limitations to what MSIs can deliver. For instance, it may not be the case that MSIs deliver immediate improvements in working conditions. It is our view that the most significant benefit is the platform for engagement and dialogue that can evolve through a collaborative industry process involving unions, business, NGOs, government and workers, all collectively seeking sustainable business solutions. A 'maturing' of the more established European models, such as ETI and the FairWear Foundation, demonstrate that collaboration is possible. This can be achieved through constructive engagement and without compromising core values. Hughes (2001), in his analysis of the Ethical Trading Initiative, suggests that the ETI has so far been successful in fostering active debate between companies, NGOs and trade unions. The momentum behind much of this debate appears to be the strategic direction afforded by the ETI Secretariat in presenting a central organizational thread around which disparate views and agendas can be woven.

---

19 Corporate accountability relates to mechanisms for increasing the capacity for corporate regulation (Utting 2005; Delaney Chapter 14, this volume).

MSIs may also result in a 'ratcheting up' of so called 'soft laws' such that they become normative in application. This may influence legislative reform or, at least, inspire a greater uptake of CR and improved implementation as well as the reporting of transgressions against voluntary benchmarks and growing community expectations.

Conclusion

The BSL study found that CR is poorly understood and implemented in the Australian garment industry. There appears to be minimal uptake of CR and the companies that are implementing CR strategies are not adhering to international best practice. If we view the international CR movement as a life-cycle, Australia is still in its infancy. There are no industry-wide mechanisms which grapple with improving labour standards in international supply chains, there is no consultation with stakeholders, and companies are not yet making their supply chains transparent. Further, smaller companies participating in the study generally believed that Australian consumers did not care about the conditions under which garments were manufactured, and that no business case existed for developing CR strategies.

In contrast, the CR movement in Britain could be described as progressing towards adulthood, due to: the strong consumer demand for ethical supply; the establishment of industry-wide mechanisms such as the Ethical Trading Initiative to foster and promote ethical supply-chain processes; moves towards binding regulations for CR through changes to the Companies Bill; and robust debate about how to improve companies' performance in this area.

Though not the only contributing factor, the ETI appears to have had an influence on Britain's CR performance. The initiative has brought together key industry stakeholders, including retailers, government, NGOs and unions to work together on ethical supply. Research and evaluation have brought about a greater level of transparency and generated more robust data on the efficacy of CR mechanisms.

Corporate accountability that incorporates binding legal regulation alongside broader mechanisms for corporate self-regulation should be the end goal for the Australian garment industry. The HWCP, as a voluntary mechanism underpinned by legislation, provides an example of corporate accountability in the Australian context. However, such mechanisms need to be further promoted and supported to ensure effectiveness.

In relation to international sourcing, there are still hurdles in our progress towards a robust CR framework. By providing a platform for collaboration, a focal point for education and information, and an industry-wide mechanism that is transparent and can be evaluated, the industry will have more opportunity to mature. An MSI will not provide all the answers to the problems experienced by the Australian garment industry, but it could provide an important initial step towards finding collaborative solutions. Ultimately, the international CR community is likely to adopt mandatory norms and reporting. In support of this, the knowledge gained through an MSI will contribute to regulation that reflects all stakeholders' needs.

According to Nolan (2002):

> The challenge is for all stakeholders to combine forces to continue this momentum so that the progress built up through the development of codes and certification procedures can pave the way for the development of eventual international legally binding norms to govern the behavior of corporations and human rights.

How quickly policy makers, industry and civil society respond remains to be seen. The challenge and opportunity remain for the Australian garment industry to embrace responsible business practices in keeping with growing international expectation.

References

ANZ (2005), *Clothing Wholesalers under Pressure*, ANZ Industry Brief. [Online: ANZ]. Available at: http://www.anz.com/Business/info_centre/economic_commentary/Clothing_Wholesaling_ Industry_Brief_Apr05.pdf [accessed: 4 July 2007].

Barrientos, S. and Smith, S. (2006), *The ETI Code of Labour Practice: Do Workers Really Benefit? Report on the ETI Impact Assessment 2006* (Sussex: Institute of Development Studies, University of Sussex). Available at: <http://www.eti2.org.uk/Z/lib/2006/09/ impact-report/ETI-impact-1-main.get.pdf [accessed: 12 July 2007].

—— (2007), 'Do workers benefit from ethical trade? Assessing codes of labour practice in global production systems', *Third World Quarterly* 28(4): 713–29.

Bendell, J. (2004), *Lifeworth Annual Review of Corporate Responsibility*. [Online]. Available at: http://www.jembendell.com/lw2004 [accessed: 4 July 2007].

Clean Clothes Campaign (2005), *Looking for a Quick Fix: How Weak Social Auditing is Keeping Workers in Sweatshops*. [Online: Clean Clothes Campaign]. http://www.cleanclothes.org/ ftp/05-quick_fix.pdf [accessed: 4 July 2007].

Connor, T. and Dent, K. (2006), *Offside! Labour Rights and Sportswear Production in Asia* (Oxford: Oxfam International). Available at: http://www.oxfam.org.uk/what_we_do/issues/ trade/downloads/offside_sportswear.pdf [accessed: 10 July 2007].

Co-operative Bank (2006), *Ethical Consumerism Report 2006* (UK: Co-operative Bank). Available at: http://www.neweconomics.org/gen/uploads/xtnbbq452mxiiuvshyfhxbn419122005183917. pdf [accessed: 19 July 2007].

CorporateRegister.com (2007), *CorporateRegister.com*. [Online: CorporateRegister.com]. Available at: http://www.corporateregister.com/charts/charts.pl [accessed: 21 May 2008].

Corporations and Markets Advisory Committee (CAMAC) (2006), *The Social Responsibility of Corporations* (Sydney: CAMAC).

Cregan, C. (2001), *Home Sweat Home* (Melbourne: Department of Management, University of Melbourne).

CSR Europe/MORI (2000), *CSR Europe/Mori Poll*. [Online: CSR Europe]. Available at: http:// www.csreurope.org/aboutus/CSRfactsandfigures_page397.aspx#care [accessed: 19 July 2007].

Diviney, E. and Lillywhite, S. (2007), *Ethical Threads: Corporate Social Responsibility in the Australian Garment Industry* (Melbourne: Brotherhood of St Laurence). Available at: http:// www.bsl.org.au/pdfs/Diviney&Lillywhite_ethical_threads.pdf [accessed: 25 March 2007].

Dutch CSR Platform (MVO Platform) (2007), *CSR Frame of Reference* (Amsterdam: MVO Platform).

Ethical Trading Initiative (2006), Getting Smarter at Auditing; Tackling the Growing Crisis in Ethical Trade Auditing: Report from ETI Members' Meeting (London: Ethical Trading Initiative).

—— (2008), *Ethical Trading Initiative*. [Online: Ethical Trading Initiative]. Available at: http:// www.ethicaltrade.org/ [accessed: 13 April 2008].

Global Reporting Initiative (2006), Draft Apparel and Footwear Sector Supplement. [Online: Global Reporting Initiative]. Available at: http://www.globalreporting.org/InDevelopment/ SectorSupplements/ApparelFootwear/ [accessed: 4 July 2007].

Gordon, K. and Miyake, M. (2000), *Deciphering Codes of Corporate Conduct: A Review of Their Contents*, OECD Working Paper on International Investment no. 1999/2. Available at: http:// www.oecd.org/ dataoecd/23/19/2508552.pdf [accessed: 4 July 2007].

Hale, A. and Shaw, L. (2001), 'Women workers and the promise of ethical trade in globalised garment industry: a serious beginning', *Antipode* 33(30): 510–30.

Hemmati, M. (2001), *Multi Stakeholder Processes for Governance and Sustainability: Beyond Deadlock and Conflict* (London: Earthscan).

Hughes, A. (2001), 'Multi-stakeholder approaches to ethical trade: towards a reorganisation of UK retailers' global supply chains?', *Journal of Economic Geography* 2001(1): 421–37.

Industry Commission (1997), *The Textiles, Clothing and Footwear Industries* (Melbourne: Commonwealth of Australia).

Jenkins, R. (2001), *Corporate Codes of Conduct: Self-regulation in a Global Economy*, Technology, Business and Society Programme Paper No. 2 (Geneva: United Nations Research Institute for Social Development).

—— Pearson, R. and Seyfang, G. (2002), *Corporate Responsibility and Labour Rights: Codes of Conduct in the Global Economy* (London: Earthscan).

Justice, D. (2001), *The New Codes of Conduct and the Social Partners*, International Confederation of Free Trade Unions. [Online: ICFTU]. Available at: http://www.icftu.org/ [accessed: 5 April 2008].

Kolk, A., Van der Veen, M. Pinkse, J. and Fortanier, F. (2005), *KPMG International Survey of Corporate Responsibility Reporting 2005* (Amsterdam: University of Amsterdam and KPMG Global Sustainability Services). Available at: http://www.kpmg.it/fmknet/View.aspx?da_ id=2241 [accessed: 1 October 2008].

Kolk, A. and Van Tulder, R. (2006), 'International responsibility codes', in M. Epstein and K. Hanson (eds), *The Accountable Corporation* (Westport, CT: Praeger).

KPMG (2005), Submission by KPMG to Parliamentary Joint Committee on Corporate and Finance Services on Inquiry into Corporate Responsibility. Submission 53 (September 2005).

Marshall, S. (forthcoming), 'Australian textile clothing and footwear supply chain regulation', in C. Fenwick and T. Novitz (eds), *Legal Protection of Workers' Human Rights: Regulatory Change and Challenge* (Oxford: Hart).

Nolan, J. (2002), Holding Multinational Corporations Responsible for Human Rights Abuses, paper presented at the Castan Centre for Human Rights Law (Melbourne: Monash University). Available at: http://www.law.monash.edu.au/castancentre/events/2002/nolan.html [accessed: 30 August 2009].

NSW Department of Industrial Relations (NSW DIR) (1999), *Do Consumers Care about Clothing Outworker Exploitation?* Report prepared by Dangar Research Group. [Online: NSW DIR]. Available at: http://www.industrialrelations.nsw.gov.au/ resources/consumer.pdf [accessed: 1 October 2008].

—— (2006), 'Multi-stakeholder regulation: privatizing or socializing global labour standards?', *World Development* 34(5): 899–918.

OECD (2001), *Corporate Responsibility: Private Initiatives and Public Goals* (Paris: OECD).

O'Rourke, D. (2003), 'Outsourcing regulation: analyzing nongovernmental systems of labor standards and monitoring', *Policy Studies Journal* 31(1): 1–29.

Parliamentary Joint Committee on Corporations and Financial Services (2006), *Review of Corporate Responsibility: Managing Risk and Creating Value*. [Online: Joint Committee]. Available at: http://www.aph.gov.au/senate/committee/corporations_ctte/corporate_responsibility/report/index.htm [accessed: 26 March 2008].

Productivity Commission (2003), *Review of TCF Assistance*, Report No. 26 (Canberra: Australian Government). Available at: http://www.pc.gov.au/inquiry/tcf/finalreport/ index.html [accessed: 30 July 2007].

Raworth, K. (2004), *Trading Away Our Rights: Women Working in Global Supply Chains* (Oxford: Oxfam).

Ruggie, J. (2007), Business and Human Rights: Mapping International Standards of Responsibility and Accountability for Corporate Acts, UNGA, 4th sess., A/HRC/4/035, United Nations Human Rights Council.

Senate Economics References Committee (1996), *Inquiry into Outworkers in the Garment Industry* (Canberra: SERC).

Smith, J. and Partners, J. (2007), 'A model for change: upward harmonisation of OECD guidelines procedures', paper presented at the OECD Watch Multistakeholder Roundtable (Brussels: OECD Watch).

UNCTAD (2007), *World Investment Report 200: Transnational Corporations, Extractive Industries and Development* (New York and Geneva: United Nations). Available at: http://www.unctad.org/en/docs/wir2007_en.pdf [accessed: 2 October 2008].

UNEP, KPMG (2006), 'Carrots and Sticks for Starters: Current Trends and Approaches in Voluntary and Mandatory Standards for Sustainability Reporting' (South Africa: KPMG Global Sustainability Services). Available at: http://www.kpmg.com.au/Portals/0/Carrots_and_Sticksfinal.pdf [accessed: 11 March 2007].

Utting, P. (2001), *Regulating Business via Multi Stakeholder Initiatives: A Preliminary Assessment* (Geneva: United Nations Research Institute for Social Development).

—— (2005), *Rethinking Business Regulation: From Self-regulation to Social Control*, Technology, Business and Society Programme Paper No. 15 (Geneva: United Nations Research Institute for Social Development).

—— (2007), 'CSR and equality', *Third World Quarterly* 28(4): 697–712.

Wick, I. (2005), *Worker's Tool or PR Ploy? A Guide to Codes of International Practice*, 4th edition (Bonn: Friedrich Ebert Stiftung).

Chapter 9

CSR and Policy Incoherence

Peter Utting[1]

Introduction

The rise of the contemporary corporate social responsibility (CSR) agenda is often portrayed as a new approach to development and governance that addresses problems of policy incoherence associated with both neoliberalism and state-centred regulation. Such problems have centred on the tendency for neoliberal policies to neglect social dimensions of development, and the perception that mandatory regulation has been poorly conceived and implemented. New types of corporate self-regulation, voluntary initiatives and 'collaborative governance' (Zadek 2006) have been expected both to nudge business towards social responsibility and to be more effectively implemented than many laws and government policies.

CSR is generally defined as voluntary initiatives that aim to minimize corporate bad practice and continuously improve corporate performance in the domains of the social, the environmental, human rights and corporate governance. CSR instruments typically include: codes of conduct and other sets of principles and guidelines; improvements in environmental management systems, occupational health and safety and company-community relations; triple-bottom line accounting and company sustainability reporting; internal and external monitoring and verification; and stakeholder dialogues. In practice, the CSR agenda, the issues it embraces, as well as the nature and substance of its institutions are fundamentally shaped by the interplay of corporate interests and culture, and the external cognitive, institutional and political environment. Crucial in this latter factor are various forms of contestation, involving civil society actors and heightened social risks that can threaten the reputation of high profile companies and their brands (Levy and Kolk 2002; Levy 2008).

The term 'policy coherence' gained currency during a rethinking of international development policy that took place in the 1990s. This reflection had been prompted by growing recognition of failures and contradictions in structural adjustment programmes, aid delivery and conditionality. However, quite different interpretations of the problem of policy coherence are commonly found. One more technocratic reading is concerned with the gap between policy objectives and outcomes, emphasizing the importance of harmonization, complementarities, synergies and sequencing among policies in order to minimize this gap (Oyejide 2007). Another, more normative interpretation, is concerned with the imbalance between economic and social priorities or dimensions of development. It highlights the need to re-equilibrate economic and social aspects, and proactively address the perverse social effects of neoliberal policies as applied in many developing countries. Yet another is concerned with redressing the institutional deficit or governance gaps that have arisen in the context of globalization and the associated expansion of foreign direct investment (FDI) and global value chains controlled by transnational corporations (TNCs).

---

1   Thanks go to José Carlos Marques and Rebecca Buchholz for research and editorial assistance.

Drawing parallels with Polanyi's analysis of the crisis of early twentieth-century capitalism, scholars and policy advisors warned that, in the contexts of global expansion and liberalization, markets and corporations were becoming increasingly 'disembedded' from societal institutions that could control their perverse effects (Ruggie 2003). Furthermore, regulatory frameworks tend to prioritize the securing of property and other rights demanded by global corporations and foreign investors, and to pay less attention to strengthening corporate obligations commensurate with these rights. The term 'policy incoherence' used in this chapter thus refers to policy and institutional failures and contradictions that manifest themselves in gaps, imbalances or weaknesses associated with some combination of: policy objectives, implementation or outcomes; economic and social policy; institutional unravelling or 'disembedding'; and corporate rights and obligations.

CSR is often described as an important instrument for policy coherence in terms of its managerial, regulatory, institutional and social content or potential. This chapter suggests that the mainstream CSR agenda is itself characterized by chronic problems of policy incoherence that have profound implications for the development model it supports. Not only is there a large gap between policy objectives and implementation, but the CSR agenda typically fails to interrogate several key 'macro' conditions and contexts that render it ineffective as an approach for dealing with externalities. This therefore limits its potential to correct the imbalance between economic and social policy objectives, and deal with problems of institutional deficits.

The two sections that follow this introduction address these aspects. The first describes the operational limits of CSR – that is, weaknesses entrenched in the design and implementation of key CSR instruments including codes of conduct, company sustainability reports and social auditing. The second identifies three sets of conditions or contradictions that seriously limit the potential of CSR. These include imperatives associated with mainstream business preferences or strategy, various developments related to changing patterns and modes of business regulation, and imbalances in power relations between different actors involved in CSR initiatives. Given the crucial role of contestation in defining the scope and substance of the CSR agenda, the chapter then considers the prospects for addressing policy incoherence through an examination of the concerns, demands and proposals associated with two different agendas or 'movements' for change. One of these agendas, more ameliorative in nature, promotes mainstream CSR via standard setting and voluntary initiatives; the other, more transformative in nature, is particularly concerned with controlling corporate power and empowering subaltern stakeholders, in part by creating or strengthening institutions for channelling grievances and seeking redress.

The chapter ends by reflecting on the types of development model that these different forms of activism are implicitly or explicitly supporting. Roughly three different policy approaches or patterns of development have preoccupied scholars and activists, particularly since the 1990s (Utting 2005). The first is neoliberalism, which emphasizes market-led and export-oriented development, the rolling back of certain state functions, securing corporate rights through legal instruments, and so-called trickle-down development; the second is embedded liberalism, which accepts the reality of economic liberalization and 'corporate globalization' but aims to strengthen institutions that protect the vulnerable and mitigate the perverse social and environmental effects that are associated with the freeing-up of markets; and third is 'alter-globalization' – associated in particular with the global justice movement and the World Social Forum – which seeks to transform regulatory systems so as to exert greater social control over markets and corporations, reconfigure the correlation of social forces in favour of labour, communities and small producers, and transform patterns of resource allocation in ways that are redistributive and conducive to social protection. The CSR and corporate accountability agendas relate to these broad approaches in different ways. With its focus on fine-tuning social and environmental aspects of business performance and the legitimization of existing structures of corporate globalization, the CSR agenda straddles both the neoliberal and embedded liberal frameworks. The corporate accountability movement, with its emphasis on giving CSR some teeth, strengthening corporate obligations via legalistic regulation and empowering subaltern groups, straddles both the embedded liberal and alter-globalization frames. The CSR movement may be capable of addressing aspects of policy incoherence related to operational limits of CSR, but it will likely require a consolidated corporate accountability movement to address structural aspects of policy incoherence related to business strategy, regulatory institutions and power relations.

The Operational Limits of CSR

Global corporations have responded to heightened social risk through a range of CSR initiatives and instruments. Initially, such responses were defensive and relied heavily on public relations and window-dressing. This made companies easy prey for those who accused them of 'greenwash' (Greer and Bruno 1996). Many companies have continued in this mode but, with time, some have adopted a more proactive stance in relation to CSR. This is reflected, for example, in less opting for particular voluntary initiatives and instead adopting a more comprehensive approach; applying CSR standards and procedures more systematically throughout corporate structures and the supply chain; relying not only on internal but also external monitoring and verification; not simply reporting on qualitative improvements but actually measuring changes in social and environmental performance; and moving away from self regulation towards participating in multi-stakeholder initiatives such as the Fair Labor Association (FLA), the Ethical Trading Initiative (ETI), the Extractive Industries Transparency Initiative, the Global Reporting Initiative and the United Nations Global Compact.

Despite some advances, the balance sheet emerging after more than two decades of international activity related to CSR illustrates an approach which is heavily flawed in its capacity to deal with issues of corporate power and practice that reproduce and reinforce global inequality and injustice. Key concerns relate to the limited number of companies engaging proactively in the CSR agenda; the quality of CSR interventions; and the issues that remain off-limits.

In quantitative terms, the number of companies actively engaged in CSR is a small fraction of the universe of TNCs, let alone the broader business community. For example, the world's largest CSR initiative, the UN Global Compact, had approximately 3,600 participating companies by the end of 2007, while UNCTAD calculated the total number to amount to 78,000 TNCs and 780,000 affiliates (UNCTAD 2007). Only a few companies were involved in voluntary approaches and corporate self-regulation methods, even though some of them were amongst the world's largest.

The quality of the main CSR instruments remains highly inadequate. By the turn of the millennium, both scholars and activists were taking stock of what CSR had achieved through fairly comprehensive evaluations of particular CSR instruments and industries. Such assessments highlighted the following concerns.

Codes of conduct and other ethical guidelines have increased in number but the gap between rhetoric and practice remains significant. A 2007 survey of US executives found that 60 per cent claim that corporate citizenship is part of their strategy but only 28 per cent had formal policies or statements to substantiate their assertions (BCCCC 2007, 2). For several years following its inception in 2000, the UN Global Compact confronted a barrage of criticism that companies which formally agreed to adhere to the Global Compact principles related to human rights, environmental protection and labour standards could essentially free-ride, that is, gain significant reputational advantages but do very little in return. Indeed, a McKinsey evaluation of the Global Compact carried out in 2004 found that only 9 per cent of participating companies were in fact taking different action to what they would have done anyway (McKinsey and Company 2004).

The range of issues addressed by codes has gradually broadened but still remains narrow, and standards and policy statements are often vague. For example, aspects of human rights are increasingly being addressed by leading 'CSR' companies but 'they do not necessarily recognize those rights on which they may have the greatest impact' (SRSG 2007, 20). A study of 45 leading banks that lend to companies operating in socially and environmentally sensitive sectors such as mining and forestry found that only one (Radobank) had developed a comprehensive human rights policy, 30 had policies that were vaguely worded or aspirational, and 14 had no policy at all (BankTrack 2007).

A similar situation prevails in relation to labour issues. Codes of conduct adopted by TNCs tend to benefit mainly male workers in core enterprises, with far fewer benefits extending to workers in the supply chain, migrant workers and contract workers (Clay 2005; Barrientos and Smith 2006; Pearson 2007). The situation of women workers seems particularly problematic in Export Processing Zones and agriculture. Research by the International Union of Food Workers on working conditions in the cut flower industry in Africa, including on farms involved in CSR initiatives, shows that the sector has brought much needed employment for women workers but that these same workers have paid a heavy price in terms of ongoing problems related to the use of pesticides, repetitive strain injury and sexual harassment. Codes have yielded more benefits in relation to occupational safety and compliance with statutory minimum wages, social security and sick pay for permanent workers, as well as some reduction in excessive overtime, but fewer benefits related to basic labour rights such as freedom of association and collective bargaining (Barrientos and Smith 2006; Rees 2007). They tend to address 'micro' issues related to conditions in and around the workplace, but ignore 'macro' issues related to the broader impacts of firms and the value chains of which they are a part (Kolk and Tulder 2006). This sort of assessment, poor as it is, could well be a best-case scenario, given that the companies studied generally come from the stable of so-called CSR leaders (Ruggie 2007).

With regard to *company reporting and disclosure*, there has been an increase in social, environmental and sustainability reporting, particularly at the level of large TNCs, as well as a strengthening in reporting guidelines and methods through high-profile schemes such as the Global Reporting Initiative. Such initiatives have attempted to overcome the syndrome of 'green glossies' – a prominent feature of company reporting in the 1990s – that were more about public relations than meaningful disclosure. There are, however, serious concerns within some business and inter-governmental bodies such as the UN Conference on Trade and Development that reporting has become unmanageable and excessively costly, leading to initiatives designed to streamline reporting indicators (UNCTAD 2008). NGOs and other stakeholders often find it difficult to use or interpret the information contained in company reports. Many companies are still selective about what they wish to report on, fail to provide meaningful data to measure real progress, or refuse to allow independent verification (Kolk 2004). These concerns emerge from sources such as a study of disclosure related to revenue transparency in the oil and gas industries, which found that only two of 25 companies scored above 30 per cent (Save the Children UK 2005).[2] Therefore, there are concerns about materiality, such as whether reports contain information that really matters

---

2   The scoring system was based on 37 indicators related to revenue payments transparency, other aspects of 'supportive disclosure', anti-corruption measures and whistle-blowing. Indicators were weighted differently (one or two points each) to give a total possible score of 47.

(SRSG 2007, 21). In relation to human rights, a study of 314 companies with CSR credentials, conducted by the UN Special Representative of the Secretary-General for Business and Human Rights, found impact assessment through community consultation processes to be the weakest aspect of corporate accountability (Wright and Lehr 2006, 19), and only one company had placed a human rights impact assessment in the public domain.[3]

The deficiencies that affect reporting are well-illustrated in the case of the UN Global Compact. To address the issue of free-riding and to safeguard the integrity of this scheme, in 2003 the Global Compact introduced a requirement that participating companies must report annually on progress. As a result, a minimalist reporting procedure was established. A significant proportion of companies participating in the Global Compact fail to comply even with these requirements. In 2007, the Global Compact designated one-third of its 3,639 participating companies as either 'inactive' (855) or 'non-communicating' (413) for having failed to comply with the basic reporting procedure. During the first half of 2008, 630 of these companies were actually delisted (UNGC 2008).

In relation to *social auditing*, external monitoring and the verification of code implementation have increased significantly with the growth of the CSR service (including certification) industry and as global firms move from defensive to more proactive approaches to CSR. Social auditing methods have improved in some global brand name companies in sectors such as textiles and athletic footwear. However, major problems persist in relation to giant retailers (CCC 2005). Social audits often assume a 'policing' or top-down character that fails to transform managerial culture or empower workers. Suppliers generally know in advance when audits will occur and prepare accordingly, even to the extent of coaching workers on what to say (Hayter 2007); enlisting the services of consultants who are skilled in 'successful audits'; keeping two sets of records related to pay and overtime (one official, the other not); or operating both 'model' factories where the auditors are taken and clandestine factories that remain in the shadows (see Power 2008).

Reliance on commercial auditors raises serious problems regarding cost, lack of autonomy, skills and methods to assess the situation of workers, and industrial relations (O'Rourke 2003; CCC 2005). For example, instances of sexual harassment and forceful tactics to prevent workers from organizing are unlikely to be discovered by a checklist approach. Some top-tier suppliers find themselves over-audited by the various brand name companies they supply; the FLA reports the case of one supplier, operating in several countries where no labour inspections take place, which had been audited 260 times in one year. Quite rightly, the supplier complained that he was put at a competitive disadvantage *vis-à-vis* his competitors that were rarely audited, if at all.[4]

The Disabling Environment for CSR

Another arena of policy incoherence that undermines the effectiveness of CSR relates to structural conditions. Of particular concern from a strategic perspective is the way in which CSR discourse, as well as practice, has largely failed to interrogate either these conditions or what might be called the 'disabling environment' for CSR. This section focuses on three sets of conditions or contradictions related to business strategy, regulation and power relations which characterize another dimension of policy incoherence.

---

3 John Ruggie, keynote address at the European Commission conference: CSR at the Global Level: What Role for the EU?, Brussels, Belgium, 7 December 2007.

4 Comments by Auret van Heerden, CEO of the Fair Labor Association, at the occasion of the International Labour Organization Multi Forum 07: Better Business: Managing Labour Relations for Productivity and Growth, Geneva, 15–16 November 2007.

Business Strategy

As seen above, inactivity and failing to 'walk the walk' are still prominent features of voluntarism. However, it is not difficult to envisage a scenario where more and more companies will engage in some aspects of CSR. More difficult to foresee is a shift from 'shallow' CSR, which addresses fairly selective aspects of corporate social and environmental performance, to deep CSR, which interrogates the more fundamental features of business strategy and corporate-driven capitalism that have perverse social and environmental impacts. From the perspective of small and medium-sized enterprises in developing countries that form part of global value chains, a key problem relates to the 'Jekyll and Hyde'-like character of their corporate buyers, which often urge suppliers and sub-contractors to simultaneously raise standards (and therefore costs) whilst squeezing them further to reduce prices and lead times (Barrientos and Smith 2006). Someone must pay the cost of CSR. In situations where consumers seem unwilling to change significantly their buying habits, and where CSR does not result in productivity gains, those who pay are likely to be suppliers and/ or their workers. Speaking in December 2007, Neil Kearney of the International Textile, Garment and Leather Workers' Federation pointed out that over the past 12 years – the period when codes of conduct have been forcefully implemented – real wages in the textiles sector have fallen by 25 per cent and working hours increased by 25 per cent.[5]

Other tensions or contradictions between 'CSR logic' and 'commercial logic' include, for example, relocation to countries and regions where labour standards and regulatory environments are weak; improving standards in core enterprises and some top-tier suppliers but ignoring conditions further along the supply chain; and lobbying, either directly or indirectly through business associations, for fiscal and labour policy regimes that are regressive from a social perspective (Jenkins, Lee and Rodgers 2007). On the environmental front, a shift from shallow to deep CSR would involve moving away from a narrow focus on eco-efficiency – that is, altering the ratio of energy use or emissions to growth – to absolute reductions (UNDP 2007). However, there is little evidence that such an approach is gaining ground in the corporate world.

Regulation

One of the reasons why CSR took off internationally in the early 1990s was due to backing by a powerful coalition of business and NGO actors, think tanks and others that were fundamentally distrustful of the state, so-called 'command and control' regulation, and ossified and patriarchal trade union organizations. In reality, state regulation of business did not decline but rather changed its form (Braithwaite and Drahos 2000). Some forms of 'deregulation' did occur, particularly in relation to labour market flexibilization in developing countries and, more specifically, in export-processing zones. In many countries, or at the sub-national level, laws and regulations often remained on the books but a lax attitude was adopted towards enforcement. But globalization and liberalization also requires a new form of 'regulatory' (Braithwaite 2005) or 'competition' state (Cerny 2000) which serves as a facilitator of global insertion, competitiveness and coordination, and delegates certain regulatory responsibilities to private actors.[6]

---

5   Presentations made at the International Labour Organization MultiForum 07: Better Business: Managing Labour Relations for Productivity and Growth, Geneva, 15–16 November 2007 and the European Union Conference on Corporate Social Responsibility: CSR at the Global Level: What Role for the EU?, Brussels, 7 December 2007.

6   The concept of the regulatory state refers to a post-Keynesian state that intervenes less in the economy, does 'less rowing and more steering', does not simply 'de-regulate' but re-regulates to secure the competitive,

Many governments, often under considerable pressure from organized business interests, took steps to restrict increases in real wages and work-related social benefits (Mancuso 2007).[7] Privatization of public services such as drinking water required a complex regulatory infrastructure to avoid an excessive trade-off between efficiency and equity objectives. A new body of law concerned with protecting the rights of TNCs and foreign investors – sometimes referred to as 'New Constitutionalism' (Gill 2008) – expanded rapidly. Laws protecting property rights and corporate profit streams from various forms of state intervention or social unrest proliferated at national, regional and international levels. Bilateral and regional trade agreements sought not only to facilitate market access through 'shallow integration' – that is, by reducing barriers to trade – but also to promote 'deep integration'. This involved synchronizing national policies and encouraging internal factor mobility so that countries could take fuller advantage of international trade (Mejido, Utting and Carrión 2008).

The other historic source of regulatory pressure on big business, namely the labour movement and trade unions, also lost force. In contexts of retrenchment, trade unions often went on the defensive, turning their attention to issues such as retraining and separation benefits. And in regards to increasing casualization and informalization of labour, they saw their traditional social base decline, along with the relevance of conventional strategies for defending workers' rights and conditions.

These developments had profound implications for CSR and corporate accountability. The downsizing of certain state capacities often weakened state labour inspection or environmental regulatory capacity. Deregulation partly underpinned the so-called race to the bottom that has been a feature of FDI in sectors such as apparel. Not only did companies often move to locations where wages and labour standards were low but, notably in the case of China or export processing zones, they moved to locations where certain basic labour rights, such as freedom of association or collective bargaining, were essentially denied.

Some forms of state intervention to protect communities or the environment were deemed illegal under the new legal regime associated with New Constitutionalism. Regional or bilateral trade and investment agreements allow corporations to sue national governments that adopt policies and laws which affect future profit streams. Corporations increasingly resort to institutions such as the International Center for the Settlement of Investment Disputes, an arm of the World Bank group, to seek compensation or some other form of settlement. A recent case involving the activities of Shell, Dole and Dow Chemical in Nicaragua illustrates this point. In the 1990s, agricultural workers who had suffered death, serious ill health and sterility as a result of contact with the pesticide Nemagon, used on banana plantations in the 1970s and the early1980s, commenced legal proceedings against several corporations in the United States. In 2001, the Nicaragua National Assembly passed a law backing the lawsuits against Dole, Dow Chemical and Shell. In 2002, a Nicaraguan court ordered these corporations to pay US$489 million to hundreds of workers. Several cases brought against these companies in the United States were ruled to be inadmissible due to legal irregularities. Following lengthy protests by Nemagon victims, in 2004 the Nicaraguan government eventually agreed to provide legal and social support to those affected and to present the case to the Human Rights Commission in Geneva (Utting 2008). In December 2005, a Nicaraguan judge ordered economic restrictions to be imposed on Shell Oil until it paid part of the US$489 million. In May

---

coordination and social conditions needed for effective privatization, commodification, trade and investment (Braithwaite 2005).

7   In Brazil, for example, there was a concerted and successful campaign by business to urge both the government and parliament to reduce the so-called 'Brazil cost of doing business' (Mancuso 2007).

2006, Shell Brands took the case to the International Center for the Settlement of Investment Disputes, countersuing the Nicaraguan government for the same amount, in compensation for lost profits.

A lax attitude to the enforcement of labour and environmental law was often another feature of the competition state. This was apparent at both national and sub-national levels, particularly in large countries, such as China, Brazil and India, where states competed for investment. With the rise of privatized regulation or corporate self-regulation, some governments experienced an outflow of personnel, skilled in fields such as labour inspection or human resource management, to the private sector. The resultant networks, often involving close informal relations, amounted to a form of institutional capture that could be conducive to slack enforcement. Indeed, the forging of closer relations between public and private sectors, which was both a feature and an objective of the competition state, and the expansion of public–private partnerships facilitated various forms of institutional capture, conflict of interest, and lobbying by organized business interests for government policies or laws that were regressive from a social perspective (Richter 2004; Sawyer and Gomez 2008; Slob and Weyzig 2007; Utting and Zammit 2006).

The regulation of business by trade unions also declined as they became defensive, attempting to survive a neoliberal agenda that brought with it retrenchment, casualization of labour and the associated decline of social benefits and labour rights. Trade unions, for several years at least, resented the largely unaccountable NGOs pushing the CSR agenda and were highly suspicious of CSR itself, which was essentially an oxymoronic strategy for improving working conditions whilst often ignoring instruments and institutions that were key in this regard, namely the self-organization of workers, industrial relations and certain core labour rights. Such tensions, as discussed below, weakened activism concerned with CSR and corporate accountability.

Power Imbalances

The CSR agenda that gathered momentum in the 1980s was partly driven by new thinking within management studies which posited the notion that effective management of modern corporations required engaging more proactively with a broader range of stakeholders to facilitate risk management and organizational learning (Freeman 1984). So-called stakeholder dialogue became a core feature of CSR practice. In the 1990s, the notion that different actors should work collaboratively was further reinforced with the rise of public–private partnerships and multi-stakeholder standard-setting initiatives such as the FLA, the ETI and the UN Global Compact.

To the extent that CSR is essentially concerned with responsiveness to stakeholder concerns and that some key CSR institutions encourage and facilitate dialogue and participation, the CSR agenda would seem to bode well from the perspective of participatory governance and democratic legitimacy. NGOs, in particular, have been able to raise their voices in consultative and decision-making processes associated with new forms of standard-setting and enforcement, most prominently via participation in multi-stakeholder initiatives.

Yet to what extent does this form of collaborative governance or 'deliberative democracy' actually transform power relations? Three major concerns have emerged. First, relationships between the different actors and stakeholders are still characterized by deep imbalances in power. Not only are the voices of civil society participants relatively weak, but certain key stakeholders remain marginal in such processes. The cases of two of the most prominent multi-stakeholder initiatives – the Global Compact and the ETI – are illustrative in this regard.

Since its inception in 2000, civil society organizations have been highly critical of the 'softness' of the Global Compact, that is, the lack of mechanisms to prevent free-riding and ensure that participating companies actually adhere to its ten promoted principles. While the Global Compact projects itself as a multi-stakeholder initiative, the NGOs involved have faced an uphill battle in order to add some teeth to the initiative. Since its launch in 2000, some operational reforms have been introduced.[8] However, a key element underpinning these changes was activism situated outside of the stakeholder dialogue process, either by NGOs and NGO networks engaged in watch-dog activities, 'naming and shaming', critical research and organizing 'counter-summits', or when leading NGOs participating in the Global Compact went public with their concerns (Utting and Zammit 2009). What seems to have been important in this reform process is not only the dual presence of insiders and outsiders, but also insiders organically linked to the 'corporate accountability movement', discussed further below.

The UK-based ETI initiative is generally regarded as a project offering more equitable stakeholder representation and participation. A tripartite governance structure at both central (board) and local (projects) levels ensures that businesses, NGOs and trade unions enjoy equal representation. Furthermore, the UK government also participates as an observer on the board. Nevertheless, the participation of certain key stakeholders, notably Southern workers and suppliers, is quite limited (Schaller 2007). This is a feature of most multi-stakeholder initiatives: they 'show difficulties in integrating representatives from developing countries, and decision-making processes seem to be dominated by Northern experts' (Schaller 2007, 43). Such difficulties may be partly structural in the sense that workers are rarely organized and suppliers change frequently.

The second concern relating to the issue of power imbalances concerns co-optation. NGOs that become part of mainstream CSR networks almost invariably restrain their rhetoric and demands and enter into new sets of more harmonious or collegial social relations which can restrict forms of activism involving confrontation and hard-core criticism. But 'co-optation' is also a two-way street; both sides are required to give and take and empathize with the others' views. Participation in so-called epistemic communities can be an important mechanism for exercising some voice and influence, but when ideas or proposals for progressive reform make some headway through social dialogue, compromise is likely.

Civil society organizations and activists are often obliged to accept voluntary CSR instruments when they confront the reality that the legalistic route to reform is often ineffectual or they see voluntary initiatives as a first step on a long road of regulatory change. This occurred, for example, in the case of the 'Publish What You Pay' campaign which called for mandatory company reporting related to payments to governments but supported the establishment of the voluntary 'Extractive Industries Transparency Initiative' as a next best alternative. Similarly, many NGOs have backed away from the more legalistic proposal put forward by the UN Human Rights machinery for a set of Norms on the Responsibilities of Transnational Corporations and Other Business Enterprises with Regard to Human Rights (UNESC 2003), and have instead supported the mandate of the UN Secretary-General's Special Representative on Business and Human Rights who is exploring a normative framework that has, at the time of writing, emphasized state as opposed to corporate obligations, and voluntary as opposed to legalistic approaches.

A useful analytical frame for understanding the evolution of power relations in the field of CSR draws upon 'radical' political economy, neo-Gramscian perspectives and French regulation theory. Such perspectives suggest that the CSR agenda is being shaped by contestation and hegemonic and counter-hegemonic struggles. Corporate elites have excelled in a hegemonic

---

8   These include, for example, stricter controls on the use of the UN logo by corporations, obliging participating companies to report on their progress in applying the Global Compact's ten principles, delisting and naming companies that do not report, and the introduction of a soft complaints procedure.

strategy in which they do not simply placate the opposition through co-optation or shift position as a defensive reaction to pressure or social risk – they also exercise moral, intellectual and cultural leadership, taking onboard, in a more proactive way, certain concerns of the opposition (Levy and Newell 2002; Utting 2005). This enables them to direct the agenda of change, as well as craft institutions conducive to the longer-term stability of capital. To some extent, this strategy explains the shift from defensiveness to pro-activity that characterized the evolution of CSR since the 1990s. Through this approach, big business interests were able to frame the CSR agenda in such a way that certain crucial issues relating to global injustice remained largely off-limits. Thus the power of big business is, as Doris Fuchs points out, as much 'discursive' as it is structural and instrumental (Fuchs 2005). David Levy observes, that it is difficult to know whether the activism associated with the corporate accountability movement will culminate in 'reformist strategies that lead to co-optation of challengers and the blunting of efforts for more systemic change', or whether 'the shifting terrain of compromise … [can become] the staging ground for another round of contestation' (Levy 2008, 957, 958).

A third issue concerns institutional capture. The participation of corporate interests in multi-stakeholder initiatives and public–private partnerships draws powerful private interests into the domain of public policy at local, national and international levels. Inevitably, such relations enhance the so-called instrumental power of business via: easy access to policy makers; the transfer of knowledge and expertise through participation in epistemic communities; the so-called revolving door syndrome where private sector personnel work in varying capacities and periods of time in public institutions; and collegial social relations, both formal and informal.

Research on private sector influence in the field of global health policy suggests a rise in situations of conflict of interest that are often ignored by international organizations (Richter 2004). However, the problem is not simply ignorance or bureaucratic inaction, but rather a mind-set whereby technocrats, policy-makers and business leaders alike see such interaction as fundamentally pragmatic and positive rather than something that needs to be regulated or managed. Indeed, Richter suggests that such convergence in thinking renders the notion of institutional 'capture' inappropriate:

> One of the most substantive losses resulting from the shift towards the partnership paradigm is the loss of distinction between actors in the international health arena. UN agency, governments, TNCs, their business associations, and public interest NGOs are all indiscriminately called 'partner'. The realisation that these actors have different, possibly conflicting, mandates, goals and roles has, as a result, also been lost. (Richter 2004, 54)

Similar concerns have arisen from research on partnerships at the local or national level. A study, conducted in Kenya and Tanzania, of a United Nations' scheme promoting partnerships for sustainable development found that the influence of private sector interests and mindsets was such that there was little focus on vetting projects from the perspectives of equity and sustainable development; the integration of intended beneficiaries such as farmers in deliberative processes; strengthening the accountability of the proposed partnerships; or promoting consideration of the private sector's relationship to macro and micro development issues (Gregoratti 2007).

The issue of power imbalances relates not only to the processes that characterize concrete collaborations, but also more structural aspects. While CSR is said to reflect the rise of so-called stakeholder capitalism, this agenda has in fact unfolded at a time when so-called shareholder primacy has been consolidated. The management of large corporations has come under far greater pressure to meet the short-term demands of shareholders than those of other stakeholders, and these priorities are internalized in the companies' targets and incentive structures. Similarly, a new generation of government technocrats, many trained in a particular branch of economics and business administration, often uphold a certain worldview that equates development with FDI, privatization, deregulation, economic stabilization and structural adjustment. As such, their assumptions concerning what is required for development in general and private sector development in particular often coincide with the interests of TNCs and foreign investors. Consequently, the structural power of big business has increased tremendously (Farnsworth 2007; Fuchs and Kalfagianni 2009).

The prospects for CSR are further undermined by the rise of new global economic players linked to the emerging market and oil economies, namely state-owned enterprises and sovereign wealth funds. Such entities have remained largely off the radar of civil society organizations, networks and others concerned with CSR and corporate accountability. Furthermore, their relatively low profile and lack of transparency greatly undermine the potency of one of the main traditional drivers of CSR – social risk and the need for companies to protect brand reputation.

Overcoming Policy Incoherence?

The large gaps between policy objectives, implementation and outcomes, and the tensions and contradictions between CSR and other dimensions of corporate and state policy, suggest that both the immediate operational environment of CSR and the broader enabling environment are characterized by 'policy incoherence'.

The challenge of achieving greater policy coherence in the arena of CSR is both technical and political. Technical aspects relate to ways and means of enhancing operational efficacy by refining and ratcheting-up CSR instruments and approaches through, for example: institutionalizing CSR culture and practices throughout corporate structures; internalizing CSR goals in incentive systems; mobilizing the energies not only of business and NGOs but also governments in promoting CSR; more rigorous and systematic disclosure; independent monitoring; investing more resources in training managers; and establishing or activating existing complaints procedures.

The political dimension relates to reasserting social control over markets and big business via various forms of regulation and the reconfiguration of power relations among different actors and stakeholders. It also involves focusing not simply on what companies can do via voluntary initiatives or 'private social policy' but their public policy positions and the ways in which they influence public policy. Furthermore, it entails crafting new modes of 'multi-scalar' activism, spanning local, national, regional and international levels and focusing not only on individual companies in specific countries but sectors, industries and regions (see UNRISD 2008).

Currently the operational limits of CSR both within civil society and business is recognized to a far greater extent. This was apparent during the end-of-year CSR conference season in 2007. The International Labour Organization, European Union and UNRISD conferences, attended by leading players and scholars in the field of CSR, saw CEOs of TNCs[9] talking of the need to go beyond codes of conduct and to place more attention on external monitoring and industrial relations. Trade unionists – traditionally somewhat cautious about CSR discourse – admitted that codes of conduct had in fact managed to achieve what international labour law had largely failed to accomplish over 30 years: to induce companies to think more proactively about labour standards and labour rights.

---

9   In this particular case, Nestlé and Panasonic.

However, they insisted on the need for a new variation of code, quite different in nature to those designed by business or in collaboration with NGOs. Instead, they contended that codes should be the outcome of negotiating processes involving corporations and trade unions, as in the case of more than 50 Global Framework Agreements that have been signed between Global Union Federations and TNCs, or governmental processes and tripartite consultation, as in the case of the OECD Guidelines on Multinational Enterprises. The heads of two of the most prominent multi-stakeholder initiatives – the ETI and the FLA – for their part cautioned against an excessive reliance on voluntary initiatives and, in particular, instruments such as social audits. Instead, they called for stronger public regulatory frameworks, enhanced labour inspection capacity as well as resources for training managers and workers at the factory level.

Other key points to emerge related directly to several of the concerns noted above – namely, the need for enhanced participation of local stakeholders in CSR processes and for greater attention to how business interests influence public policy and their lobbying practices. It was also important for governments to avoid situations where the policies and practices they promote – via Bilateral Investment Treaties, Overseas Development Assistance and export credit agencies – undermine rather than support socially and environmentally responsible business.[10]

The technical and political dimensions of policy coherence are being addressed in differing ways by two somewhat different 'movements' concerned with the role and responsibilities of TNCs in development. Particularly concerned with improving technical aspects is a 'CSR movement' comprised of large corporations, business associations, a burgeoning CSR service industry, NGO think-tanks, government agencies and regional or international organizations. As noted above, this agenda is not static, nor does it simply amount to public relations; it is evolving by embracing an increasing number of issues and concerns. This movement is likely to continue gathering force both in response to societal pressures, government and stock exchange policy and regulations promoting or mandating CSR, and as CSR credentials become an accepted feature of doing business. This movement will focus first and foremost on addressing the first dimension of policy coherence discussed above, namely the operational limits of CSR and the gaps between policy objectives and implementation. Key drivers of technocratic policy coherence are said to be organizational and social learning, and the so-called business case for CSR – that is, establishing a positive relation between improved social and environmental performance and financial performance. In addition to gradually ratcheting-up and fine-tuning CSR initiatives to improve actual CSR performance, corporations and business associations will continue to 'talk the talk', as this has proven to be a highly effective strategy not only to reduce social risk but also to lead the process of reform.

Returning to the three broad approaches to development referred to in the Introduction, there are two ways of reading the purpose and impact of this mainstream CSR movement. For some, it reinforces the neoliberal *status quo*, although explanations as to why this is the case vary. For some it is because CSR amounts to window-dressing, intended to project a certain image when in fact there is little, if any, fundamental change to 'business-as-usual'. Others argue that CSR serves to reinforce the neoliberal approach in a context where key policy and legal instruments have proven wanting. What Ngai-Ling Sum refers to as the 'New Ethicalism' associated with CSR, therefore complements 'New Constitutionalism' in order to shore up the neoliberal paradigm (Sum 2005). Drawing on Polanyi, others argue that CSR represents an attempt to craft a socially-acceptable mode of capitalism or 'embedded liberalism' (Ruggie 2003).

---

10   This point was made by John Ruggie in a keynote address at the 2007 European Commission Conference: CSR at the Global Level: What Role for the EU?, Brussels, Belgium, 7 December 2007.

However, as noted earlier, CSR plays out on a terrain of contestation. This suggests that there is not one overriding logic that characterizes CSR. Neither can the substantive content of this agenda be predetermined with precision as this will depend on the interplay of multiple factors including firm and industry preferences, path dependence and patterns of organizational learning within firms and, crucially, the nature of social risk and societal pressures. In addition to this, the external institutional environment with which firms must interact will also play a part (Levy 2008). For this reason, if generalizations are to be made about the logic of CSR, it is more useful to think of CSR as having a foot in two camps – namely, the approach of neoliberalism and that of embedded liberalism (Utting 2005). Whether one foot is resting more firmly in one or the other camp will depend on the interplay of various conditions.

Another 'movement' is attempting to craft a somewhat different regulatory and political environment for TNCs and global value chains. The myriad concerns, demands and proposals associated with the corporate accountability movement tend to centre on efforts to ensure that voluntary initiatives have some teeth, that legalistic regulation is not crowded out by voluntarism, and that workers and communities are empowered. The corporate accountability movement therefore promotes a variety of regulatory approaches (Broad and Cavanagh 1999; Bendell 2004). One such approach involves ratcheting-up CSR, often through measures that require more systematic disclosure of information and reporting, independent monitoring and verification, and the establishment of complaints procedures. Another involves emphasizing the role of not only companies, business associations, NGOs and international organizations, but also traditional regulatory organizations and institutions – namely, public policy, law, the courts, parliamentary oversight bodies, state enforcement and inspection agencies, trade unions and industrial relations. This approach debunks the view that voluntary initiatives are a preferred substitute for binding legalistic regulation.

In addition to reasserting the role of law in the social, human rights and environmental domains, the corporate accountability movement has expanded the terrain where the so-called voluntary and legalistic approaches merge in ways that are complementary and synergistic. Such forms of 'hybrid' or 'articulated' regulation (Gunningham and Sinclair 2002; McBarnet 2007; Ward 2003; Utting 2005) include, for example, international voluntary initiatives that result in national parliaments internalizing their provisions in national law,[11] or national and international laws which require companies to be more transparent and to report on their social or environmental performance without specifying what that performance should be. If performance standards are found to be low, it is for actors and entities such as civil society organizations, the media, shareholders and public opinion to expose, 'name and shame', or otherwise bring pressure to bear on a company in order to improve its performance.[12]

The corporate accountability movement also emphasizes the importance of international law and draws attention to the need for an expanding body of both 'hard' and 'soft' law that targets corporations. This represents a significant change in the character of international law, which has traditionally focused on the responsibilities and obligations of governments (Clapham 2006; Muchlinsky 2007). Various international codes, declarations, conventions and treaties now also 'fix' on corporations. These include, for example, the Bamako Convention, which controls the international movement of hazardous wastes; the OECD Guidelines on Multinational Enterprises;

---

11   This has occurred in instances such as the Extractive Industries Transparency Initiative (EITI) and, far more widely, with the International Code of Marketing of Breastmilk Substitutes.

12   An example of this is the national and international Pollutant Release and Transfer Registers (PRTRs), which impose reporting obligations on companies producing toxic substances.

the Rotterdam Convention on Prior Informed Consent, which relates to the export of hazardous chemicals; the Aarhus Convention, concerned with facilitating public access to environmental information; and the Framework Convention on Tobacco Control. Further, there has been an attempt to design a comprehensive set of guidelines and monitoring, reporting and redress procedures through UN human rights machinery.[13]

Another arena of law instigated to challenge corporate power and deal with instances of malpractice concerns what has been referred to as 'subaltern legality' or 'counter-hegemonic legality' (Santos and Rodríguez-Garavito 2005; Utting 2008). This involves efforts on the part of social groups, individuals and communities whose livelihoods, identities, rights and quality of life are negatively affected by states and corporations, to use the existing legal apparatus to seek redress for injustice and to participate in struggles and processes associated with accountability. A key feature of such struggles is transnational activism that connects actors at local, national, regional and global levels. Prominent examples of subaltern legality include Public Interest Litigation in India and the approximately 30 cases that have been brought against corporations under the *Alien Tort Claims Act* in the United States.

While the corporate accountability movement is dominated by Northern organizations and networks, it involves a somewhat more representative cross-section of civil society actors, as well as coalitions and alliances that connect actors and organizations that were previously disconnected or wary of each others' agendas. Crucial in this regard is the role of trade union organizations. Weakened by globalization and neoliberalism, and often crowded out by both companies and NGOs promoting CSR, trade unions appear to be reasserting their influence in multi-stakeholder initiatives and processes involving dialogue, bargaining and contestation that aim to improve the social, environmental and human rights performance of global corporations.

What this description of the objectives and actions of the corporate accountability movement suggests, is that it too straddles two of the three approaches to development noted above. But in this case, the focus on ratcheting-up voluntary initiatives, legalistic regulation, more equitable power relations and counter-hegemonic projects suggests that the two approaches involved are those of embedded liberalism and alter-globalization.

Those addressing the injustices linked to corporate globalization face a dual challenge. The first relates to the nature of the forces, players and institutions they confront. Activists and social movements confronting the elite interests that have benefited from the structures, processes and policies associated with globalization and liberalization face not only a giant that can mobilize vast resources to exert power and influence (Reich 2007), but also a medusa. Such interests are extremely adept at working on multiple fronts and employing diverse strategies to frame agendas, shape public policy and craft the rules of the game, including the terms on which civil society actors interact with policy processes. The second challenge relates to the capacity of these activist groups to mobilize, organize and participate; build broad-based networks, coalitions and alliances; find points of entry to the policy process; sustain action; and make demands conducive to ameliorative and transformative reforms. Currently, the corporate accountability movement is a fledgling movement that needs to build technical capacity and political momentum. Yet, unlike the

---

13   This resulted in the adoption of the draft Norms on the Responsibilities of Transnational Corporations and Other Business Enterprises with Regards to Human Rights by the UN Sub-Commission on the Promotion and Protection of Human Rights in 2003 (UN SCPPHR 2003). However, the Norms failed to receive political backing from the UN Commission on Human Rights, which instead mandated the Secretary-General to appoint a Special Representative in order to continue a multi-stakeholder dialogue on the responsibilities of business in relation to human rights and to look into concrete proposals for enhancing business performance in this field.

mainstream CSR movement, it at least recognizes that the challenge of crafting business practices conducive to inclusive development is fundamentally a political one.

From the perspective of policy coherence, the CSR agenda can play a role in sensitizing corporations to social and sustainability issues, organizational learning and the promotion of market-based approaches for dealing with externalities. This agenda can address some of the operational limits of CSR. However, it is likely to take a consolidated corporate accountability movement to bring about policy and institutional change related to both the deepening of CSR and structural aspects of policy incoherence related to business strategy, regulatory institutions and power relations.

References

Alien Tort Claim Act, 28 USC § 1350 (1789).

BankTrack (2007), *Mind the Gap: Benchmarking Credit Policies of International Banks* (Utrecht: BankTrack).

Barrientos, S. and Smith, S. (2006), *The ETI Code of Labour Practice: Do Workers Really Benefit?* (Sussex: Institute of Development Studies).

Bendell, J. (2004), *Barricades and Boardrooms: A Contemporary History of the Corporate Accountability Movement*, Programme Paper (TBS) No. 13 (Geneva: United Nations Research Institute for Social Development [UNRISD]).

Boston College Center for Corporate Citizenship (BCCCC) (2007), *The State of Corporate Citizenship 2007* (Chestnut Hill, MA: Boston College and Hitachi Corporation).

Braithwaite, J. (2005), *Neoliberalism or Regulatory Capitalism*, RegNet Occasional Paper No. 5 (Canberra: ANU).

—— and Drahos, P. (2000), *Global Business Regulation* (Cambridge: Cambridge University Press).

Broad, R. and Cavanagh, J. (1999), 'The corporate accountability movement: lessons and opportunities', *Fletcher Forum of World Affairs* 23(2): 151–69.

Cerny, P. (2000), 'Political globalization and the competition state', in R. Stubbs and G. Underhill (eds), *Political Economy of the Changing Global Order* (Oxford: Oxford University Press), pp. 300–309.

Clapham, A. (2006), *Human Rights Obligations of Non-State Actors* (Oxford: Oxford University Press).

Clay, J. (2005), *Exploring the Links between International Business and Poverty Reduction: A Case Study of Unilever in Indonesia* (Oxford: Oxfam GB, Novib Oxfam Netherlands and Unilever).

Clean Clothes Campaign (CCC) (2005), *Looking for a Quick Fix: How Weak Social Auditing is Keeping Workers in Sweatshops* (Amsterdam: CCC).

Farnsworth, K. (2007), 'Business and social policy in the context of development', paper to the UNRISD Conference: Business, Social Policy and Corporate Political Influence in Developing Countries, Geneva, Switzerland, 12–13 November.

Fuchs, D. (2005), *Understanding Business Power in Global Governance* (Baden-Baden: Nomos).

—— and Kalfagianni, A. (2009), 'Private Food Governance: Implications for Social Sustainability and Democratic Legitimacy', in P. Utting and J.C. Marques (eds), *Corporate Social Responsibility and Regulatory Governance: Towards Inclusive Development?* (Basingstoke: UNRISD and Palgrave Macmillan).

Freeman, R.E. (1984), *Strategic Management: A Stakeholder Approach* (Boston, MA: Pitman).

Gill, S. (2008), *Power and Resistance in the New World Order* (Basingstoke: Palgrave Macmillan).

Greer, J. and Bruno, K. (1996), *Greenwash: The Reality behind Corporate Environmentalism* (Penang: Third World Network).

Gregoratti, C. (2007), 'The growing sustainable business initiative in East Africa: the limits and potential of partnerships for development', paper to the UNRISD Conference: Business, Social Policy and Corporate Political Influence in Developing Countries, Geneva, Switzerland, 12–13 November.

Gunningham, N. and Sinclair, D. (2002), *Leaders and Laggards: Next Generation Environmental Regulation* (Sheffield: Greenleaf).

Hayter, S. (2007), 'Private systems of labour assessment: social auditing and monitoring: a review of the issues', paper to the International Labour Organization MultiForum 07: Better Business: Managing Labour Relations for Productivity and Growth, Geneva, Switzerland, 15–16 November.

Jenkins, H., Lee, E. and Rodgers, G. (2007), *The Quest for a Fair Globalization Three Years on: Assessing the Impact of the World Commission on the Social Dimension of Globalization* (Geneva: International Institute for Labour Studies).

Kolk, A. (2004), 'A decade of sustainability reporting: developments and significance', *International Journal Environment and Sustainable Development* 3(1): 51–64.

—— and Tulder, R. (2006), 'Poverty alleviation as a business strategy? Evaluating commitments of frontrunner multinational corporations', *World Development* 34(5): 789–801.

Levy, D. (2008), 'Political contestation in global production networks', *Academy of Management Review* 33(4): 943–63.

—— and Kolk, A. (2002), 'Strategic responses to global climate change: conflicting pressures on multinationals in the oil industry', *Business and Politics* 4(3): 275–300.

Levy, D. and Newell, P. (2002), 'Business strategy and international environmental governance: toward a neo-Gramscian synthesis', *Global Environmental Politics* 2(4): 84–101.

Mancuso, W.P. (2007), 'Lobbying for reducing the "Brazil cost": political strategies and outcomes of Brazilian entrepreneurs under Cardoso and Lula (1995–2006)', paper to the UNRISD Conference: Business, Social Policy and Corporate Political Influence in Developing Countries, Geneva, Switzerland, 12–13 November.

McBarnet, D. (2007), 'Corporate social responsibility: beyond law, through law, for law: the new corporate accountability', in D. McBarnet, A. Voiculescu and T. Campbell (eds), *The New Corporate Accountability: Corporate Social Responsibility and the Law* (Cambridge: Cambridge University Press).

McKinsey and Company (2004), *Assessing the Global Compact's Impact* (London: McKinsey and Company). Available at: http://www.unglobalcompact.org/docs/news_events/9.1_news_archives/2004_06_09/imp_ass.pdf [accessed: 29 September 2006].

Mejido M., Utting, P. and Carrión, G. (2008), 'The changing coordinates of trade and development in Latin America: implications for policy space and policy coherence', paper to the 12th EADI General Conference: Global Governance for Sustainable Development: The Need for Policy Coherence and New Partnerships, Geneva, Switzerland, 24–8 June.

Muchlinsky, P.T. (2007), *Multinational Enterprises and the Law* (Oxford: Oxford University Press).

O'Rourke, D. (2003), 'Outsourcing regulation: analyzing nongovernmental systems of labor standards and monitoring', *Policy Studies Journal* 31(1): 1–29.

Oyejide, T.A. (2007), *Policy Coherence: Aid, Trade and Investment* (Ottawa: The North-South Institute).

Pearson, R. (2007), 'Beyond women workers: gendering CSR', *Third World Quarterly* 28(4): 731–49.

Power, C. (2008), 'Manufacturing: the burden of good intentions', *Time Magazine*, June 23, 45–8.

Rees, D. (2007), 'Monitoring and social auditing', paper to the International Labour Organization MultiForum 07 Conference: Better Business: Managing Labour Relations for Productivity and Growth, Geneva, Switzerland, 15–16 November.

Reich, R.B. (2007), *Supercapitalism* (New York: Alfred Knopf).

Richter, J. (2004), *Public-Private Partnerships and International Health Policy-making: How Can Public Interests Be Safeguarded?* (Helsinki: Ministry for Foreign Affairs of Finland).

Ruggie, J.G. (2003), 'Taking embedded liberalism global: the corporate connection', in D. Held and M. Koenig-Archibugi (eds), *Taming Globalization: Frontiers of Governance* (Cambridge: Polity Press).

—— (2007), 'Global markets and global governance: the prospects for convergence', in S. Bernstein and L.W. Pauly (eds), *Global Liberalism and Political Order: Toward a New Grand Compromise?* (Albany, NY: State University of New York Press).

Santos, B. and Rodriguez-Garavito, C.A. (eds) (2005), *Law and Globalization from Below: Towards a Cosmopolitan Legality* (Cambridge: Cambridge University Press).

Save the Children UK (2005), *Beyond the Rhetoric. Measuring Revenue Transparency: Company Performance in the Oil and Gas Industries* (London: Save the Children UK).

Sawyer, S. and Gomez, E.T. (2008), *Transnational Governmentality and Resource Extraction: Indigenous Peoples, Multinational Corporations, Multilateral Institutions and the State*, Programme on Identities, Conflict and Cohesion, Programme Paper No. 13 (Geneva: UNRISD).

Schaller, S. (2007), *The Democratic Legitimacy of Private Governance: An Analysis of the Ethical Trading Initiative*, INEF Report 91/2007 (Duisburg: Institute for Development and Peace).

Slob, B. and Weyzig, F. (2007), 'The lack of consistency between corporate lobbying and CSR policies', paper to the UNRISD Conference: Business, Social Policy and Corporate Political Influence in Developing Countries, Geneva, Switzerland, 12–13 November.

Special Representative of the Secretary-General (SRSG) (2007), *Business and Human Rights: Mapping International Standards of Responsibility and Accountability for Corporate Acts*, A/HRC/4/035 (Geneva: Human Rights Council).

Sum, N. (2005), 'From "new constitutionalism" to "new ethicalism": global business governance and the discourses and practices of corporate social responsibility', paper to the European Consortium for Political Research Joint Sessions, Workshop 24: Transnational Private Governance in the Global Political Economy, Granada, Spain, 14–19 April.

United Nations Conference on Trade and Development (UNCTAD) (2007), *Trade and Development Report 2007: Regional Cooperation for Development* (Geneva: UNCTAD).

—— (2008), *Guidance on Corporate Responsibility Indicators in Annual Reports* (New York and Geneva: United Nations).

United Nations Development Programme (UNDP) (2007), *Human Development Report 2007/2008: Fighting Climate Change: Human Solidarity in a Divided World* (New York: UNDP).

United Nations Economic and Social Council (UNESC) (2003), *Norms on the Responsibilities of Transnational Corporations and Other Business Enterprises with Regard to Human Rights*, 55th sess., Agenda Item 4, UN Doc E/CN.4/Sub.2/2003/12/Rev.2 (26 August 2003).

United Nations Global Compact (UNGC) (2008), *630 Companies Delisted as Part of Integrity Measures*. [Online, 25 June]. New York: UNGC. Available at: http://www.unglobalcompact. org/newsandevents/news_archives/2008_06_25.html [accessed: 29 September 2008].

United Nations Research Institute for Social Development (UNRISD) (2006), *Transformative Social Policy: Lessons from UNRISD Research*, UNRISD Research and Policy Brief 5 (Geneva: UNRISD).

—— (2008), *Conference News: Business, Social Policy and Corporate Political Influence in Developing Countries*, Report of the UNRISD Conference, 12–13 November 2007 (Geneva: UNRISD).

United Nations Sub-Commission on the Promotion and Protection of Human Rights (UN SCPPHR) (2003), *Responsibilities of Transnational Corporations and Other Business Enterprises with Regard to Human Rights*, Res 2003/16, 22nd mtg, UN Doc E/CN.4/Sub.2/2003/L.11 (13 August 2003).

Utting, P. (2005), *Rethinking Business Regulation: From Self-regulation to Social Control*, Programme on Technology, Business and Society, Paper No. 15 (Geneva: UNRISD).

—— (2006), *Reclaiming Development Agendas: Knowledge, Power and International Policy Making* (New York: UNRISD and Palgrave Macmillan).

—— (2008), 'Social and environmental liabilities of transnational corporations: new directions, opportunities and constraints', in P. Utting and J. Clapp (eds), *Corporate Accountability and Sustainable Development* (New Delhi: Oxford University Press).

—— and Zammit, A. (2006), *Beyond Pragmatism: Appraising UN-Business Partnerships*, UNRISD Markets, Business and Regulation Programme Paper No.1 (Geneva: UNRISD).

—— (2009), 'United Nations-business partnerships: good intentions and contradictory agendas', *Journal of Business Ethics*.

Ward, H. (2003), *Legal Issues in Corporate Citizenship* (Stockholm and London: Swedish Partnership for Global Responsibility and International Institute for Environment and Development).

Wright, M. and Lehr, A. (2006), *Business Recognition of Human Rights: Global Patterns, Regional and Sectorial Variations* (Geneva: United Nations, Office of the High Commissioner for Human Rights).

Zadek, S. (2006), *The Logic of Collaborative Governance: Corporate Responsibility, Accountability, and the Social Contract*, Corporate Social Responsibility Initiative Working Paper No. 17 (Cambridge, MA: John F. Kennedy School of Government, Harvard University).

Chapter 10

Fair Consumption?
Consumer Action on Labour Standards[1]

Gordon Renouf

Introduction

Consumers in developed countries gain significant benefits from trade with developing countries. Many consumers have seen substantial growth in living standards since the early 1990s, much of which has been derived from imports of an expanding variety of sophisticated consumer and industrial goods at lower and lower prices, particularly from the rapidly expanding economies of Asia.[2] Manufactured goods now make up the majority of imports from developing to OECD countries (World Bank 2005). These changes have coincided with a new wave of concern among many consumers in developing and developed countries about the conditions of production in supplier countries. The rise of the Fairtrade brand and other fair trade schemes are expressions of that concern.

The factories and mines of supplier countries often exploit workers in ways that many people regard as unacceptable. Workers have been denied basic human rights, misled, coerced, exposed to serious risk of injury, illness or death and denied their rights to association and collective bargaining. In agricultural settings, low prices prescribed by terms of trade, harsh contracts and poor or poorly enforced regulatory standards may lead to the exploitation of producers, workers and the environment.

Many fair trade campaigns are founded on a belief that renewed interest in 'ethical consumption'[3] can be harnessed to benefit workers and smallholder producers. This chapter is concerned with the

---

1 Paper based on a presentation to the Fair Trade, Corporate Accountability and Beyond: Experiments in Globalising Justice Conference (2007), sponsored by Govnet and CAPPE (Centre for Applied Philosophy and Public Ethics) and hosted by the Centre for Employment and Labour Relations Law, University of Melbourne, with the support of the Fair Trade Association of Australia and New Zealand. Thanks to Kate Macdonald, Kate Norris, Kate Halliday, Elissa Freeman, Victoria Coleman, Justin MacMullan, Sadie Homer, Julia Lipton and Serena Lillywhite for suggestions and comments on earlier drafts and to Anna Tucker for research assistance. The views expressed are, of course, solely my own other than where attributed.

2 Will Hutton (2008, 10) reports estimates by Morgan Stanley economists that 'Cumulatively American consumers are $100 billion better off ... because China's cheap exports have lowered consumer prices in the United States'.

3 There are numerous ways to define 'ethical consumption'. Crane and Matten (2004) succinctly suggest 'the conscious and deliberate choice to make certain consumption choices due to personal and moral beliefs' whereas the Co-operative Bank proposes 'personal allocation of funds, including consumption and investment, where choice has been informed by a particular issue – be it human rights, social justice, the environment or animal welfare' (Co-operative Bank 2008, 5). Euroconsumer take a different approach – in particular they exclude boycotts: 'Ethical consumerism should be understood as positive buying rather than boycotting: individual consumers' initiative to favor ethical products and businesses that operate on principles based primarily on benefit for the common good (social, environmental, economic) rather than self-interest'

question of the extent to which deliberate actions by consumers can have a positive impact on the conditions of production – through fair trade projects or otherwise – and, if so, under what circumstances.

The chapter first considers the concerned citizen's alternatives to ethical consumption – to pressure corporations or their own or other governments to undertake action. While political action and corporate social responsibility (CSR) offer some prospects for increased fair trade, there are significant barriers to success for each. Further, to the extent that its widespread adoption depends on the corporation benefiting in the market place, CSR is underpinned by ethical consumption.

The second part of the chapter considers the current scope and significance of ethical consumption. The available data suggests that ethical consumption is growing rapidly but that it comprises only a small proportion of total consumption and of total imports. There is evidence that ethical consumption has some impact on the behaviour of brand name corporations, but little evidence of direct impact on unbranded trade.

One of the key questions confronting advocates of ethical consumption is the observed disjuncture between attitudinal surveys that suggest strong support for ethical consumption among consumers but low rates of actual ethical purchasing.[4] The third part of this chapter explores both the reasons for and the implications of the disjuncture and then suggests ways consumers' expressed desire to consume ethically can be more frequently realized. The final section discusses the role of consumer organizations in promoting fair trade through both ethical consumption and political action. Consumer organizations see their role as that of empowering consumers to make better choices. This extends, in varying degrees, to actions intended to increase consumers' awareness of ethical issues and to build social norms that include accepting the responsibility to act. The challenge for consumer organizations is to devise meaningful strategies to assist consumers to meet their ethical aspirations in the face of consumers' reasonable insistence on the availability of functionally equivalent ethical products, as well as their common reluctance to sacrifice their short-term individual interests for longer-term collective benefits.

Alternatives to Ethical Consumption

A person concerned about the exploitation of workers in the production of consumer goods and services has a range of available actions. As consumers they may adopt some form of ethical consumption. As citizens they may seek to influence producers directly, or seek to influence the policies and actions of domestic or foreign governments. They could act individually, together with others or as part of a campaign coordinated by an activist organization. Better integration between consumer focused action and citizen action, and between the role of consumer organizations and that of labour rights NGOs would assist consumers as well as workers and producers in supplier countries.

(Euroconsumers 2008). For my purposes it will suffice to define ethical consumption as referring to any consumption decision made by a consumer which includes attention to an environmental or social dimension of their purchase or investment. Fair trade is one of those dimensions, covering attention to labour standards and rights, human rights associated with production of goods and services, and producer returns. Fairtrade is a particular project that focuses mainly on producer returns but also considers other labour, human rights and environmental issues.

4   The research presented later in the chapter focuses mainly on consumers in OECD countries – but there is clearly interest among consumers in developing countries, who – some developing country consumer organizations note – may have fewer opportunities (Sadie Homer, personal communication).

Governments are ultimately responsible for setting and upholding labour standards and protecting human rights (Ruggie 2008; ILO 1998; 2008). Governments collectively agree international standards and monitoring and enforcement mechanisms. Citizen action might thus be directed at a domestic government to advocate higher labour standards through bilateral or multilateral agreements or to improve compliance with existing standards. Governments regulate commerce within their own borders. Citizens might campaign for government to adopt choice-limiting public policies that exclude particular products[5] from the market or favour particular products; to introduce government purchasing policies which favour particular products or suppliers based on ethical considerations; or seek the introduction of mandated ethical reporting requirements, directors' responsibilities and rights of redress for workers from producer countries in the legal system of the OECD country where the company is based (Corporate Responsibility and Trade Justice Movement 2006).

Citizen action might attempt to directly influence corporations linked to poor labour practices. Citizens might target corporations operating in their home market in ways other than through consumption, for example, by action designed to affect the reputation of those companies or by campaigning for the inclusion of fair trade standards in CSR programmes.[6]

Citizens could campaign for changes in the country where the labour abuses occur. These might directly target particular abuses or include action designed to promote democracy, the rule of law and human rights in those countries in the belief that changes to the political system are essential for progress on labour standards.[7] In turn, this may draw the consumer's ethical attention to the activities of media, internet and other companies alleged to be complicit in restricting the free flow of information and free speech in the target country.[8]

Alternatively, the concerned consumer or citizen may be persuaded by arguments for not acting. Despite their disapproval of unfair labour conditions, consumers might prefer caution arising from an appreciation of the uncertain impact of action and the complexity of global society. Or the consumer might believe that as economic growth has led to increased real incomes in at least some developing countries, this is sufficient reason to leave the resolution of their concerns to the market (Brinkmann and Peattie 2008, 31).

---

5   Examples of choice-limiting action by government include mandatory product safety standards, for example, phasing out incandescent light bulbs and prohibition of imports from countries such as Chile in the 1970s. Examples of government policy favouring countries or products based on human rights records or other social or ethical issues include sanctions imposed on South Africa during the apartheid era and, more controversially, Iraq. Recently the United States and the European Union placed trade sanctions on Burma in response to state crackdowns on pro-democracy demonstrations. These state level sanctions tend to respond to breaches of civil and political rights rather than labour-related rights.

6   As noted below strategies targeting a corporation's reputation or relying on CSR, however, ultimately have a close link to ethical consumption.

7   For example, Amnesty International argues that a fundamental underlying cause of poor labour conditions and human rights abuses in China is the fact that it is not an open society. Among other things, this hinders the ability of the people directly concerned and Chinese activists who support them to stand up for themselves. In response, Amnesty Australia has campaigned to target the Western companies that are complicit in China's efforts to block access to information to its own citizens (Tallay 2007). Consumers International has taken a similar approach in relation to product safety issues. Director Richard Lloyd said after a 2007 visit: '[t]he problem of course is the [Chinese] government does not allow the media to report consumer issues in a way which would promote manufacturer accountability' (personal communication to the author, August 2007).

8   For example, Google, Yahoo and Microsoft have all been named by Amnesty International UK (2006) as complicit in undermining free speech in China.

Limits on Citizen Action

For citizens to pursue action by and through government would be consistent with research that suggests that some consumers are reluctant to take individual 'social responsibility action' as they believe that consumers should act collectively organized by government and not individually (Auger and Devinney 2007). Embracing a self-interested version of this concern – why should I bear the cost of taking socially responsible action if other consumers do not? – leads to a belief that we should all be compelled to act ethically by laws disallowing the unethical choice or favouring the ethical choice in some way.[9] Preferring government action to voluntary ethical consumption is also consistent with reported cynicism concerning frameworks for voluntary corporate action, including CSR (Klempner 2006; Solomon 2008; APCO Worldwide 2004).

Governments' scope for action is, however, limited by international trade agreements. World Trade Organization (WTO) rules, for example, proscribe individual governments from banning goods from other countries on the basis of their (non-)ethical production practices. Gary Sampson (2008), a former Director of the WTO explains the rationale:

> The logic is that while governments should be free to regulate the environment, labour standards, or any other social considerations within their borders, they should not have the right to impose restrictions on the way they are produced outside their borders. For goods produced in WTO countries to be banned in trade there must be agreement to do so by all 152 countries. Such is the case for trade in stolen goods or narcotics.

Sampson's 'pure' fair trade approach perhaps underplays the potential impact of current agreed exemptions such as that which applies to measures 'necessary to protect human, animal or plant life or health (General Agreement on Tariffs and Trade Clause XX(b)), and the relationship between international trade rules and potential future multilateral agreements on 'social considerations'. Nevertheless WTO rules do severely limit the scope for individual governments to ban or impose trade restrictions which favour products on social grounds. They may also inhibit the adoption of government purchasing policies that favour Fairtrade products. A challenge to such a policy by a competitor was rejected by a domestic court in the Netherlands (FLO 2007), though it is not clear whether it would have survived a challenge from another country through the WTO.

Because government action on a scale large enough to make a difference could attract WTO action by an affected trading partner, citizen action would need to pressure successfully their domestic government to press for substantial changes to WTO rules, in the form of a new international agreement allowing countries to modify how they complied with the WTO rules or to leave the WTO altogether. While any of these may be ethically justified (it is difficult to see why a world ban on narcotics trade is qualitatively more important than, for example, a trade ban on the products of child labour), there are many competing political interests as well as practical barriers that would need to be overcome for such a strategy to be successful.

---

9   Auger and Devinney (2007) suggest this consumer attitude is more prevalent in Northern European countries rather than Anglo, Southern European or developing countries, but that there is a degree of support for this approach in all countries studied.

Limits of Corporate Social Responsibility

A fierce debate rages as to the role of corporations in social policy. Advocates for CSR believe that, given the status of corporations as significant modern institutions, corporate action is potentially one of the most effective ways to promote an ethical and sustainable world. Some critics argue that the corporation 'best serves by doing what it does best: generating wealth' and that social and environmental issues should be addressed in other ways. Others observe that voluntary action by some corporations cannot guarantee ethical behaviour by all market players.

These critiques often make optimistic assumptions about the efficiency of the market or the availability and effectiveness of alternatives such as government intervention. Nevertheless, those who advocate CSR as a potentially effective response to fair trade issues need to identify carefully the conditions under which corporations will and will not have sufficiently strong incentives to act in order to develop and implement worthwhile social responsibility standards.

For Martin Wolf (2008), CSR 'mixes up three quite distinct ideas: intelligent operation of a business; charity; and bearing of costly burdens for the benefit of society at large'. The first, he argues, 'is essential; the second is optional; and the third is impossible, unless those obligations are imposed on competitors'. Ethical consumerism provides a way for CSR to be part of the 'intelligent operation of a business'. Where consumers pay ethical attention to an issue, it will very often be in a business's interest to respond to their demands.

But does CSR make any sense without ethical consumers? Perhaps – if we allow for a more complex set of motivations (including institutional and political motivations) for corporate managers than admitted by many critics. Some corporations suggest, for example, that their CSR policies play a role in attracting and retaining staff.[10] Furthermore, CSR can be used to help avoid criticism or unwanted action by government and civil society. The offer of 'good corporate citizenship' by corporate leaders or politicians is often used as part of the public debate in support of avoiding or deferring the introduction of regulation in response to an issue of public concern. Even so, there are few corporations with robust and comprehensive CSR policies and practices on fair trade and ethical sourcing.

It is indeed hard to believe, in the absence of regulation, that private firms will comply with fair trade requirements throughout their entire production network where doing so will place them at a significant competitive disadvantage. As Ian McAuley (2001) concludes, 'in some industries, particularly where there is high investment in brand names and wide consumer choice, firms will be very sensitive about their corporate image, and may invest heavily in corporate social responsibility, but such actions, reasonably, are directed to firms' financial self-interest.' Conversely, industries where brand is less important are much less likely to be influenced by CSR strategies.

This analysis suggests that initiatives founded in (voluntary) CSR will yield only limited and partial success and points to a role for citizen action to campaign for effective incentives to mandate or otherwise promote compliance with certain ethical obligations. The OECD Guidelines for Multinational Enterprises, while voluntary, include a complaint mechanism which has been used by civil society to pressure companies to observe ethical requirements (Brotherhood of St Laurence 2006). Voluntary CSR could be enhanced by actors outside the firm assisting it to identify and act on – or even help to create – socially responsible opportunities that are in its financial interest. Government can assist by identifying and removing barriers or creating incentives for ethical initiatives.

---

10   This is frequently stated as a reason for companies to participate in the Corporate Responsibility Index (personal communication to the author by Julia Lipton then Manager Corporate Responsibility Index, St James Ethics Centre, Sydney).

Citizen action to influence domestic or foreign government policies and CSR form two broad alternatives to ethical consumption as strategies to promote fair trade. Neither are so certain to reduce unfair trade that they leave no role for ethical consumption.

Current Ethical Consumption

How Much Ethical Consumption Is Going On?

Although growing rapidly, measured ethical consumption makes up only a small percentage of total consumption. Compared to total imports (most fair trade ethical choices discriminate in favour of or against certain categories of imports) ethical consumer spending motivated by a concern for fair trade is modest.

Worldwide estimates for total ethical consumption or for ethical spending stimulated by concern for fair trade are difficult to obtain. The Fairtrade Labelling Organizations (FLO) reports that in 2007 consumers spent over €2.3 billion on Fairtrade certified goods, a 47 per cent increase on money spent in 2006 (FLO 2008, 10), and that, overall, the market for Fairtrade certified products has been growing at an average of 40 per cent per year in the last five years (FLO 2008). Of course, spending on Fairtrade certified products makes up only a part of fair trade orientated ethical consumption.

Research by the Co-operative Bank (2007) suggests that UK consumers increased their spending on ethical consumption by 81 per cent in the five years leading to 2006 – yet at less than £33 billion it makes up only around 5 per cent of total UK consumption expenditure. And of ethical consumption expenditure counted in the survey, a considerable proportion is prompted by environmental and animal rights issues; less than a third are related to Fairtrade,[11] ethical clothing purchase or boycotts. Ethical clothing and Fairtrade expenditure did, however, show strong annual growth at 76 per cent and 46 per cent respectively. In addition, ethical investment, which by definition covers a broad range of ethical issues including fair trade, was by far the largest single category at about 22 per cent of all ethical consumption, with an annual growth of 18 per cent.

Fairtrade sales in Australia in 2007 are estimated at AU$18.5 million (€10.8 million) (FLO 2008, 12). While this represents an increase of 59 per cent from 2006, it remains an insignificant part of total final household consumption of AU$606 billion (Australian Bureau of Statistics 2009). Comparisons with the UK suggest that the value of ethical clothing consumption in Australia in 2007 would have been no more than AU$25 million, a tiny fraction (0.7 per cent) of the AU$3.5 billion of clothing imported from China in 2007–2008 (DFAT 2009).

---

11   As noted elsewhere in this volume, there is an overlap but not a coincidence between the concerns of those involved in Fairtrade (which focuses primarily on producer benefit and local environmental sustainability) and those concerned about working conditions. The definition of fair trade adopted by IFAT in 2001 states that: 'Fair Trade is a trading partnership, based on dialogue, transparency and respect, that seeks greater equity in international trade. It contributes to sustainable development by offering better trading conditions to, and securing the rights of, marginalized producers and workers especially in the South. Fair trade organizations ... backed by consumers, are engaged actively in supporting producers, awareness raising and in campaigning for changes in the rules and practice of conventional international trade' (IFAT 2008).

The Impact of Ethical Consumption

Clearly, ethical consumption has some influence on the behaviour of some producer corporations. There are numerous examples of major brand companies seeking brand or product differentiation through association with ethical consumption (Crane 2005). In the UK, Sainsbury's, Tate and Lyle and various coffee chains offer fair trade products exclusively in some lines; in Australia, BP, McDonald's and Gloria Jeans all introduced Fairtrade or Rainbow Alliance coffee in their cafes, BP exclusively so, and Westpac Bank (one of the big four banks in Australia) has heavily marketed its commitment to the Equator Principles.

On the other hand, surveys of manufacturers and importers suggest low levels of interest. In 2003 a survey by Australian consumer organization CHOICE found only two of 45 manufacturers and importers of blue jeans were willing to complete a survey about overseas production practices (CHOICE 2003). In 2008 17 of 61 manufacturers and distributors of toys responded to a similar survey, with the remaining 44 either refusing to participate (eight) or failing to respond. A small number of companies, including Lego and Hasbro, clearly perceived a benefit in taking action and being seen to take action, while many other leading brands, including Mattel and Toys R Us, did not participate (CHOICE 2008c).

Some brands see benefit in differentiation on ethical grounds while many others do not (Crane 2005, 224). Further, there are risks that flow from the fact that major brand motivation is decidedly mixed. Crane (2005, 224) suggests that 'there are few if any markets where differentiation primarily on the basis of ethics is a sustainable business proposition beyond a narrow niche … ethical differentiation is typically just one element in a portfolio of differentiating factors that are necessary to gain significant market share in mainstream markets'. Companies benefit through sales or positive brand characteristics by providing ethical consumption options at the lowest cost: the cost that they are prepared to bear on a commercial basis will be proportional to the perceived benefits of broader brand reputation and/or narrower marketing advantage. In some cases companies with thousands of products introduce a small number of ethical lines and attempt to gain significant brand advantage while most of their products and production processes remain as they were.

Some Conclusions on Current Ethical Consumption

The overview presented above suggests that the level of ethical consumption is currently low, albeit increasing in some markets and often quite rapidly. Ethical consumption has significant impact on some brand name companies, leading to altered marketing, product offering and/or sourcing in response, but it has not compelled many others to act. There is little evidence of any significant impact on sectors where brand is not important to consumers.

Consumers and Ethical Consumption

Consumer Attitudes to Ethical Consumption

What do consumers say about ethical choices? Opinion poll surveys tend to suggest high rates of concern. One survey conducted in the UK found one third of consumers were seriously concerned about ethical issues (Mason 2000, cited in Auger and Devinney 2007, 1); another found that 57 per cent of consumers believed they would change their purchasing behaviour based on ethical considerations (Rogers 1998, cited in Auger and Devinney 2007, 1). A recent survey by CHOICE

(2008b) asked 1,000 Australian consumers about factors important to their purchase decisions in four classes of products – major appliances, hi-tech electronics, baby and children's products, and clothes. Just under 50 per cent of respondents stated that working conditions were very or quite important to their choice in each category of product, with slightly higher levels of concern for human rights in the country of manufacture in each category other than clothing.

But as the relatively low level of ethical purchases suggest, there is a difference between what consumers say they will do and what they actually do. The Co-operative Bank (2007, 6) estimates that only 6 per cent of the adult population in the UK are committed consumers of ethical products.

Part of this gap can be explained by limitations in survey methodologies, especially where there is a 'morally preferred' answer to a survey question. Pat Auger and Timothy Devinney (2007), comparing traditional survey questions of 'intention to purchase' and estimates of an individual's willingness to pay for social attributes in products, concluded that 'simple survey questions are too "noisy" to provide operationally meaningful information and overstate intentions to a considerable extent'.

When consumers are asked to contextualize their concern by comparing it to other factors relevant to their purchase decisions, consumers' responses are more consistent with reported levels of ethical purchasing. The CHOICE survey asked the same consumers to identify their top three purchase criteria from a mix of between nine and 13 product characteristics, including some ethical features. Working conditions were in the top three for only 8 per cent of consumers surveyed for clothes purchases; 4 per cent for baby products and hi-tech goods; and 2 per cent for major appliances. Not surprisingly, respondents were most concerned about aspects of products that directly affect them – performance,[12] quality, price and, for major appliances, energy use (CHOICE 2008b).

Devinney and his colleagues have conducted research into the motivations of a sample of consumers who do make ethical purchases. They divided the characteristics of several products into functional and social features (Auger, Louviere and Devinney 2007). For example, for purchasing a battery, its price, size, voltage and reliability are functional features. Whether or not it contains cadmium or mercury, and the labour conditions under which it was produced are social features. The survey concluded that ethical considerations only come into play once consumers are satisfied that the functional qualities of the product meet their needs.

Some consumers may well be willing to 'pay a few cents more' – or, indeed, quite a lot more (see Auger, Louviere and Devinney 2007, 212) – for an ethical product. But consumers are rarely willing to choose an ethical product that does not perform as required in preference to a non-ethical product that does.

Of course, the division between the functional and social features of a product is not immutably fixed. Functional features include less tangible elements of a product, particularly brand values. Coca-Cola and Pepsi are very similar drinks, but Coca-Cola has acquired a set of brand values that make it the preferred choice for many. The Toyota Prius has in at least some markets managed to include social responsibility in its brand values such that it can compete with alternative vehicles with equivalent functionality bar fuel consumption despite a price premium that far outweighs the fuel costs saved.

---

12   Ease of use for electronics, safety for children's goods and style for clothing.

Barriers to Ethical Consumption

The previous discussion suggests that there is a potential market for functionally equivalent but ethically superior products. Yet there are still a number of other barriers to overcome before consumers' ethical desires can be more readily satisfied. The most important of these are the scarcity of trusted and accurate information concerning ethical issues and the social dimensions of products, and low levels of consumer confidence in the transparency of ethical claims. Concerns have also been expressed about the complexity of the decision-making expected of the ethical consumer.

Understanding and awareness of ethical issues
A consumer cannot act in relation to a denial of labour rights if they are not aware of the problem. In one survey, less than 30 per cent of purchasers of women's clothing recognized the terms 'outworker' or 'home-worker'. Once informed about typical working conditions, a majority expressed outrage and most consumers exhibited some degree of concern (Department of Industrial Relations, NSW 1999).

Information about the social dimensions of products
A consumer motivated to use their consumption behaviour to influence standards will not be able to do so unless they have the information they believe they need concerning the social dimensions of a product and alternatives to it. There is evidence that consumers do not have access to sufficient information and that they may be confused by the range of logos and symbols that are in the market (DTI 2002, 22; Devinney et al. 2008, 18) but that:

> it is clear that part of the attitude-behavior gap when it comes to ethical consumerism can be explained by a lack of knowledge about products. That is, consumers may actually care about social features of the products they purchase but simply don't have the product-specific information required to make more informed decisions. (Auger, Louviere and Devinney 2007, 212; see also Bhattacharya and Sen 2004)

Confidence that an ethical choice will make a difference
How does the consumer know that ethical claims are accurate, and how can a consumer distinguish which claims are important or effective responses to particular social issues? Where does he/she look for guidance? As Consumers International (CI) states: 'consumers want to be sure that the ethical trade initiatives they do support with their purchasing power are credible, [that is] were developed through legitimate processes, actually deliver what they claim to, can demonstrate the impacts achieved and are effective and efficient in doing so' (CI unpublished).

Consumers may also want assurance that their ethical concern is not being exploited through price gouging or misleading marketing. Harford (2007, 33) argues that Fairtrade branding can be used by astute traders to identify those consumers who are willing to part with more money for essentially the same product.[13] Those consumers will not make an optimal contribution to the interests they are aiming to serve (those of coffee producers and their environment) as most of their

---

13   Harford (2007, 33) calculates that the price differential in the quarter ounce of coffee beans required for a cappuccino should translate into less than 1p per cup (in the UK) rather than the 10p demanded. 'Fairtrade coffee allowed Costa [a UK coffee chain] to find customers who were willing to pay a bit more if given a reason to do so'.

extra payment goes to trader profit rather than to producers. Harford argues that it is possible to deliver Fairtrade coffee at a zero price differential. In different circumstances a business may be altruistic or profit-maximizing in doing so.

Just as the marketing of sustainable products to consumers is hampered by a significant incidence of 'green-wash' (CHOICE 2008a; Gillespie 2008, 79), so may marketing claims about ethical offerings designed to appeal to consumer concerns about labour standards, human rights and producer returns do no more than confuse consumers while supporting business as usual.

Consumer responses to complexity

Some argue that asking ethical consumers to base their decision-making on certainty concerning the consequences of their consumption choices 'can be too demanding and abstract for application in everyday life. [It] would presuppose the individual's capacity to make demanding and overly disinterested calculations about what action would produce the most desired aggregate outcomes' (Barnett, Cafaro and Newholm 2005, 24). But consumers are faced with similar dilemmas on a regular basis. It is often too demanding to gather all the information that may in theory be required to make the most utility-maximizing consumption choice. But consumers use various techniques in response to the need to make demanding decisions including the application of heuristics – rules of thumb – and reliance on 'choice editors'. These may or may not provide 'good enough' outcomes to protect the consumer's interests depending on the circumstances.

Consumer rules of thumb include, for example, that they expect prices to be cheaper at a supermarket than a corner store. They develop trust in particular brands, retailers and people they know personally relating to issues of reliability, information and advice. These heuristics may or may not be properly applicable to each new consumer circumstance, and they are constantly modified and negotiated based on the consumer's experience and other information available to them.

Choice editing[14] involves relying on a trusted third party, such as a consumer organization, to narrow the range of options. For example, the Fairtrade logo functions as a choice editor for consumers already committed to consumption decisions in support of fair trade.

Heuristics and choice editing are two techniques that do not require the consumer to assume unreasonably demanding information-gathering tasks. In principle, there is no reason why similar resources would not be available to consumers in order to overcome overly demanding information assessment tasks required of ethical consumption.

The difficulty of accurately assessing the best path among many plausible but not fully convincing options may, of course, lead consumers to feel comfortable with most of them and, instead, make choices on other grounds such as convenience, endorsement or how well they fit with other value systems (such as their role as a citizen). There is thus an important role for leadership by consumer organizations, other NGOs, government and ethical corporations to increase the likelihood that consumer rules of thumb are based on valid assumptions, and that the available choice editing strategies are reliable.

---

14   This term can also be used to refer to mandatory limitation of choice by removing products from the market; I have instead labelled this above as 'choice limiting'.

Ethical Consumerism: Actions and Targets

So far the discussion – and much of the research on which it is based – has explored an ethical consumer's decision to choose one particular good (for example, a brand of coffee, batteries, a car or clothing) over an alternative. In fact, ethical consumption can target goods or services, and range from a specific product to an entire country. Consumer choices – and marketing strategies – might focus on a particular *product* (for example, avoid the Hummer and favour the Prius), particular *brands* (Body Shop, Nestlé) or a *company* to the extent it can be distinguished from a brand, a *sector* (for example, diamond mining), products from a *country* (apartheid era South Africa) or a *market segment* (low price clothing). The consumer may also choose to favour any company, product or brand bearing a particular *certification* (for example, Fairtrade, potentially ISO 26000) or sold by a particular *retailer* (Oxfam).

A consumer with concerns about worker safety in the production of toys might decide not to purchase toys at all; they might purchase toys only where they know they are manufactured in a region or country understood to respect labour and human rights standards; they might try to identify a company which they believe ensures minimum conditions; or they might want to purchase only toys that have been certified to a particular standard. Where a consumer cannot directly determine which products are acceptable, they may use more or less accurate heuristics to make a proxy choice – for example, they may prefer products which are of higher quality and higher levels of safety on the basis that there may be some correlation between product safety standards and labour standards. Alternatively, price may be a guide; according to the Co-operative Bank (2007, 3), '2006 also saw the emergence of a significant number of consumers claiming to avoid budget clothing outlets on the basis that low cost is taken as a likely indicator of poor supplier labour conditions'.

Ethical consumption of services is increasingly important. Consumers in OECD countries spend much more money on services than goods (Productivity Commission 2008, 6). Although most services are produced and consumed locally, this does not mean that there are no labour or producer issues. All service providers use inputs such as food, clothing, stationery and computer and communications equipment. Some use labour located in developing countries (for example offshore processing centres). A significant proportion of consumer expenditure on services is on financial services, including retirement income products and other investments. Ethical investment made up 25 per cent of ethical consumption by value in the UK as measured by the Co-operative Bank for 2006/7 (2008, 5). A consumer could prefer the locally supplied services of a firm that complied with ethical investment and sourcing principles. Some service providers do seek to attract consumers by promoting the ethical aspects of their business (for example, development of the Equator principles by the banking industry).

Ethical consumption choices can be negative (a boycott) or positive. Current promotion of ethical choices often focuses on encouraging consumers to make a positive choice: to buy Fairtrade coffee, animal cruelty-free beauty products or low energy use appliances. Sweatshop-free clothing campaigns have elements of both. Does it matter which kind of action a consumer takes? There is a reasonable amount of evidence that negative information about a product is more likely to result in consumer action – that is, refusal to buy – than positive information is likely to stimulate demand. Auger and Devinney (2007, 45) note that a study conducted by Kimberly Elliott and Richard Freeman (2001) found:

> relatively high elasticities of demand for products made under bad conditions but low elasticities for products made under good conditions. Hence, companies can potentially lose from having their

products identified as being made under bad conditions but have little to gain from marketing their products as being made under good conditions.

Despite this, recent literature has tended to focus on the emergence of 'buycotts' – positive consumer choices in favour of products with ethical characteristics (Euroconsumers 2008) – rather than boycotts. In addition to evidence for effectiveness, boycotts have the potential to be finely targeted and to overcome the problem of assuring the whole supply chain. By examining the supply chain, it may be possible to identify the most vulnerable point for boycott action. Greenpeace was concerned about the destruction of rainforests by soya production: small and medium sized farmers in Brazil grew the soya, then sold it to contractors who ultimately sold it to one of several international wholesalers, the biggest of whom was Cargills. However, Cargills have no direct consumer business. The soya had several uses, but one significant purpose was the feeding of cattle in various countries. Again, this was not a consumer-facing business. However, much of the cattle meat was sold to McDonald's and other burger chains. Here Greenpeace found a target. Direct action produced enough negative consumer sentiment – that is, potential boycott risk – that McDonald's agreed to ensure that they only bought meat from cows fed on soya not grown in newly cleared Brazilian rainforest (Greenpeace International 2006).

While brand name companies have incentives to respond to consumers' ethical concerns, it is their direct and indirect suppliers that are more likely to accept or impose poor working conditions, including those in the agricultural and mining sectors. Long supply chains are often opaque to consumers, making ethical consumption choices difficult. One potentially costly response is certification schemes that consider all inputs that raise potential ethical issues. Another approach centres on independently assured corporate social responsibility performance. If working well, consumers could be reasonably confident the brand name company has in place procedures to ensure ethical sourcing.[15] Finally, rather than focusing on the end of the supply chain (final consumption), a third approach suggests it may be better to follow it from the beginning to determine the most effective potential action to direct at a brand name company (which may be a service company such as a bank rather than a vendor of goods). This suggests a role for activist organizations to marshal consumers to lobby brand name companies and/or boycott brand products with significant 'embedded rights abuses'.

Diversity of Consumer Motivation

Consumers engaged in ethical consumption are likely to have diverse views about the relative value of particular ethical concerns and of particular styles of action in response. Those differing values will affect their motivations and particular ethical consumption options will accordingly have a stronger or weaker appeal to them.

Understanding consumers' diverse motivations may help consumer organizations and others to improve their ability to support consumer action. A comprehensive discussion is outside the scope of this chapter, but the following issues are relevant:

---

15   It is sometimes suggested that those supply chains mean that ethical issues are not visible to the brand name company at the end of the chain. However, DanWatch and Greenpeace International have each demonstrated that it is often easier to follow some supply chains than brand companies would have consumers believe (DanWatch 2008; Greenpeace International 2006).

… among consumers who actually make ethical choices, there are important differences in approach between consumers from different countries and cultures, for example, between approaches focused on individual consumer action and those focused on collective action coordinated by government. (Auger and Devinney 2007)

… perhaps contrary to popular conceptions, few differences in motivation or behaviour have been observed among consumers with differing demographic characteristics (age, gender, class) within a particular country. (Auger and Devinney 2007)

… each individual consumer's ethical consumption decisions involve in varying proportions on one hand a concern for the consequences of the potential action and on the other a 'vehicle for moral self realisation'. (Barnett, Cafaro, and Newholm 2005, 14)

or, put another way,

an aspect of life-style building. (Brinkmann and Peattie 2008, 25)

That these differences are important to consumers suggests that when governments, consumer organizations or activist organizations seek to provide relevant information to consumers, they should explore and respond to consumer diversity, in particular the 'variations in strength, motivations and focus of the ethical concerns of [each and every] consumer' as opposed to identifying and segmenting a subset of consumers as ethical (Brinkmann and Peattie 2008, 29). In a related approach Chris Rose, Pat Dade and John Scott have proposed that research into social values systems be used to develop and fine tune appropriate messages so that they resonate with varying societal beliefs or consumer understandings about 'what makes sense' and how the world works (2008, 75).

Consumer Action on Ethical Issues – Some Conclusions

A consumer concerned about poor labour practices and producer returns can take action as a citizen, choose to make ethical consumption decisions or do both. A strictly rational analysis might conclude that where ethical consumerism is the most effective (or only) way to achieve the relevant social goal, it should be preferred; on the other hand, if achieving the goal through political action would produce more efficient economic outcomes then ethical consumers ought to prefer that approach.

In the real world, however, we can never be completely certain of the consequences of our action for reasons which include the complexity of calculation, inherent uncertainty of cause and effect, and diverging time scales. Given this uncertainty, varying consumer ethical motivations and the often complementary nature of consumption-based and citizen-based approaches, consumers/ citizens and consumer and citizen organizations should support a broad range of citizen-based and consumer-based strategies combined with particular actions targeting specific barriers to ethical consumption.

Consumer choices and citizen action are not distinct; they can often be mutually reinforcing. For example, points of overlap and complementarity can occur where one person explains to another their reasons for boycotting a product or where labelling requirements combine government action to increase information and set ethical consumption norms. Further, increased availability of ethical choices and information about ethical consumption are likely to increase awareness of the underlying issues and build the constituency to compel government action where it can be shown to be more effective than the aggregation of individual consumption choices; in turn, government action is likely to increase the appeal of ethical choices to a greater range of consumers by providing a form of legitimation. As Barnett, Cafaro and Newholm note (2005, 24): '[Ethical consumption practices] must be formulated and reformulated in a continuous and open public debate.'

Consumers whose values motivate them to act on fair trade would be more readily able to use consumption to realize their ethical aspirations if they had greater access to information concerning social issues and the comparative social features of products (including both services and goods) as well as increased confidence in suppliers' ethical claims. More fundamentally, they need ready access to functionally equivalent ethical choices. Enabling such access may be difficult for some products given current technological and social arrangements. However, there will be many areas where some combination of consumers' market pressure, government policies (through incentives or choice-limiting strategies) and corporate decisions can significantly change the mix of products available to consumers. Action by government and corporations is more likely in the presence of pressure from both the market and civil society. There is also likely to be a role for civil society, government and corporations themselves to better identify opportunities for corporations to take socially responsible action that makes business sense.

The notion of 'consumer social responsibility' (Devinney et al. 2006) can be used to expand the capacity of ethical consumption to have a positive impact on labour conditions and producer returns. Consumer ethical motivations may be diverse and the current level of actual ethical consumption low, but provided it is shown to be an effective means to an end, it is in the interests of ethical consumers as well as workers and producers that the pool of consumers motivated and able to make ethical consumption decisions increases. As the demand for ethical products increases, the cost of supplying them will decrease due to economies of scale, not just in production but also in the consumer information and certification processes that are required to support ethical consumption.

Consumer Organizations

As the above discussion has highlighted, in many situations consumers need support to clarify their ethical consumption opportunities, obligations and dilemmas and to have their collective interest in responsible citizenship realized. Consumer organizations have an opportunity to help create a framework that facilitates consumer action in accordance with their values and long-term interests. This framework needs to address each area in which the potential of consumer/citizen action is currently being undermined: consumer information; consumer confidence; availability of functionally equivalent ethical choices; and social norms favourable to fair trade.

Consumer organizations range in their structure, size, orientation and the focus of their activities. They work to empower consumers in direct and indirect ways: they provide information to consumers and seek to increase the amount of accurate and useful information provided by corporations and government. Recognizing that information solutions are often insufficient, they also work to enhance consumers' legal rights and protect them from exploitation through such approaches as advocacy for improved corporate practices, government intervention or the creation of new institutions.

While consumer organizations identify sustainable consumption as a vital issue for consumers, environmental sustainability has received more attention than social sustainability. To date, the key focus has been on consumer confidence in ethical claims, with some attention given to consumer information and social norms. While the need for access to functionally equivalent ethical choices has been recognized (Lloyd 2007), relatively little work has been undertaken in the area.

Consumers International (CI), the international body representing consumer organizations worldwide, has over 220 members in 115 states (Lloyd 2007, 1); many of these are, in turn, national peak consumer organizations. For example, the Consumer Federation of America – a full member of CI – boasts a membership of an estimated 300 non-profit organizations and a combined membership of over 50 million people (CFA 2009).

CI member organizations consider sustainable consumption the primary issue for international collaboration and CI has identified a strong demand for information on ethical consumerism from consumers themselves (Lloyd 2007, 1). In response, CI and its members have targeted consumer confidence in ethical claims, labelling schemes, assurance standards and the ethical behaviour of corporations (Lloyd 2007). CI projects include *From Bean to Cup* (CI 2005), an assessment of fair trade coffee schemes, the *Real Deal* campaign which exposes unethical practices by corporations including unfair labour practices (CI no date), and advocacy for an effective international standard on social responsibility, ISO 26000 – a 'new type of ISO standard' that focuses on 'the social impact of production'. The aim is to give consumers more information about the impact of their purchasing choices (Lloyd 2007).

CI and its members have undertaken some work on social norm building. They have successfully advocated for the adoption of the *Here and Now Education for Sustainable Consumption: Recommendations and Guidelines* (Thoresen 2008) by the OECD and national governments. On 15 October 2008 they celebrated the first annual Global Consumer Action Day with a focus on consumer social responsibility (CI 2008). Research published by CI and AccountAbility (2007) identifies the central importance of building social norms through leading by example and by building consensus on what counts as a sustainable lifestyle.

CI recognizes the gap between consumers' expressed interest in ethical consumption and their consumption actions, and that this discrepancy is not caused solely by information failures. It urges companies to 'link responsibility, quality, service and value for money' to overcome the fact that, for consumers, 'good social attributes rarely outweigh poor functional performance' (Lloyd 2007, 4). CI also supports government action to remove unethical products from consumer markets (Lloyd 2007, 4).

Many other consumer organizations also express a commitment to supporting consumers' ethical consumption choices. In recent years, large 'value for money' consumer organizations such as the Consumers Union in the United States, Which? in the UK and Choice in Australia have adopted many of the agendas of later waves of consumer activism including environmental and other ethical consumption interests (Lang and Gabriel 2005). They are members and major funders of CI, whose ethical consumption agenda is more explicit. Nevertheless, their embrace of ethical consumption has been somewhat tentative. They have been wary of appearing to preach to their paying consumer members by moving too far beyond those consumers' current concerns and have, in recent years especially, focused on green consumption.[16]

International Consumer Research and Testing (ICRT) makes available to its member consumer organizations reports on nearly 200 comparative product tests each year, some of which include ethical criteria (Adriaenssens 2007). By way of example, the four national consumer organizations that make up Euroconsumers published 21 review articles on ethical themes in the five years to 2008, two thirds of them based on ICRT tests (Euroconsumers 2008).

---

16   By September 2008, CHOICE Online – the information web site of CHOICE – had published 46 articles and tests related to green issues (see www.choice.com.au/choicegreen) but less than ten that touch on other ethical issues including fair trade and ethical investing.

Alternative consumer organizations such as the Ethical Consumer Research Association (UK) focus exclusively on 'the promotion of universal human rights, environmental sustainability and animal welfare'; the organization publishes reviews based on the 'ethics' of a product and runs a database with information on the ethics of corporations (Ethical Consumer Research Association no date). The consumer/citizenship education movement has also influenced consumer organizations such as CI. Consumer citizenship is the use of consumerism to engage in political and social issues. Consumer citizenship education is 'interdisciplinary and cross curricular combining civic training, environmental education and consumer education' (Thoresen 2007, 36). It extends beyond providing information to interested consumers to representing views on ethical consumerism in public debate, and encouraging the exchange of ideas on ethical consumerism.

It is likely that mainstream Western consumer organizations could do more to highlight ethical issues in their consumer publications and to undertake increased advocacy to facilitate ethical decision-making by consumers. In doing so, they would contribute to the guidance of consumers' preferences, stimulating demand for ethical products and thus building ethical consumption norms amongst their substantial membership and the many other consumers who have access to their views.

Former CI President Marilena Lazzarini argues that consumer organizations should participate in global consumer campaigning in order to advocate effectively for ethical consumerism. Collaborating internationally with other consumer organizations will, she argues, enable a greater flow of shared information and resources, particularly with those organizations based in developing countries. This will increase campaigning power and provide insight into the impacts of global supply chains on different markets and different consumers (Lazzarini 2007).

Overall, consumer organizations' response to fair trade focuses strongly on providing consumers with information, challenging corporations that mislead consumers and advocating structural solutions to consumers' information and assurance needs, including stronger labelling and certification schemes. Despite some scepticism about CSR, consumer organizations are often willing to work with corporations on social responsibility strategies. Their recognition of a responsibility to educate consumers in sustainable consumption includes social sustainability, albeit less prominently than environmental sustainability. However, there is less evidence of consumer organizations advocating for government action on fair trade, either through international agreement or domestic choice limits. Yet if consumers are to have their desire for ready access to functionally equivalent ethical products realized, stronger government intervention is needed to produce incentives for corporations to play their part. This will likely come at some short-term financial cost to consumers, as some cheaper production options will be eliminated. Consumer organizations, buoyed by stronger levels of consumer interest, have been prepared to provide leadership through advocacy for governmental choice-limiting action in response to climate change, despite similar short-term costs. However, they have not yet conducted a concerted campaign for choice limiting based on fair trade criteria. Similarly, to the extent that consumer organizations have recognized social norm building as a key technique to promote consumers' long-term interests in sustainability, again there has been both more debate and more action concerning environmental issues than fair trade.

In summary, consumer organizations have opportunities to work with consumers, other civil society organizations, multilateral stakeholder organizations (ILO, OECD, ISO), government and corporations on a set of interrelated strategies to assist consumers realize their short- and long-term interest in fairer trade. Potential areas for action include:

- Working to increase both the availability of ethical choices and the proportion of available products which are produced ethically. This may be realized by pressuring corporations to offer ethical alternatives or pushing governments to change incentives or prohibit unethical alternatives. Building support and capacity for government action to exclude non-ethical choices may include action at international as well as national levels – for example, permitting certain types of exclusion under WTO rules.
- Bolstering consumer confidence about the positive impacts on labour and human rights produced by their actions through increased transparency, better standards and certification schemes and the development of effective legal frameworks to eliminate misleading and irrelevant ethical claims.
- Increasing consumer knowledge about social issues relevant to the goods and services they buy, and the social dimensions of those products.
- Publishing more consumer information about the ethical impacts of the companies that produce consumer goods and services.
- Identifying and proposing boycotts of vulnerable brand name products, companies or sectors based on effective and credible research into long supply chains with 'embedded worker exploitation'. Collaboration with labour organizations and use of standard setting and reporting tools are likely to be important parts of this work.
- Supporting the development of consumer behavioural norms consistent with ethical consumption. This may involve a combination of education, examples set by opinion leaders, government or socially responsible corporations, locality based community projects (CI and AccountAbility 2007) and increased media attention.
- Helping identify the business case for corporations to supply products that comply with fair trade standards.
- Developing and promoting a broad consensus on what are considered unethical practices in particular industries.
- Supporting civil society in emerging economies in working to assist governments strengthen and enforce labour standards.
- Supporting civil society campaigns for increased ethical procurement by government.

Conclusion

Ethical consumption is growing rapidly but from a very low base. As a response to concerns about the conditions of production of consumer goods, it faces a number of obstacles. Consumers face significant challenges in identifying ethical consumption choices that they can be confident will deliver improved working conditions or fairer producer compensation. Consumers are unlikely to be persuaded to choose functionally inferior products because they are ethical, although many will choose functionally equivalent ethical products and, in some circumstances, pay a higher price. On the other hand, consumers can be inspired to boycott particular unethical choices where they have suitable alternatives.

Current modest levels of ethical consumption and the barriers identified above may suggest that consumers could achieve more through alternatives such as citizen action directed at corporations, domestic governments or governments in producer countries. However, each of these options has weaknesses from the perspective of promoting fair trade. Moreover, such action may not appeal to all consumers; some consumers' motivation is more likely to derive from personal integrity concerns (not being associated with unethical production) rather than concern for achieving particular consequences (achieving change in a remote location). In fact action as a citizen and action as a consumer will in most circumstances be mutually reinforcing for both the individual and the community. Developing behavioural norms both increases the appeal of ethical consumption choices and builds a constituency to compel political change within the consumer's own political system.

This suggests that there is no single path to increasing fair trade through consumer or citizen action. Instead, consumers, consumer organizations and other NGOs should take action directed at overcoming specific barriers to fair trade-focused ethical consumption. For consumer organizations this may include increasing the amount and range of information on fair trade provided to consumers, advocating the development of tools to help consumers to identify ethical consumption choices that are more likely to have an impact, and building community norms in favour of ethical choices and in support of limiting the availability of unethical choices. It may also include cooperative work with other civil society organizations to provide targeted advice to consumers or to sponsor citizen action initiatives designed to achieve the same underlying ends as ethical consumption.

References

Adriaenssens, Guido (2007), *Comparative Testing for Sustainable Lifestyles*, paper to Consumer International World Congress Sydney. Available at: http://www.slideshare.net/CI.World. Congress.2007/2a-g-adriaenssens-sust-cons [accessed: 22 August 2009].

Amnesty International UK (2006), *Undermining Freedom of Expression in China: The Role of Yahoo!, Microsoft and Google* (London: Amnesty International UK). Available at: http://irrepressible.info/static/pdf/FOE-in-china-2006-lores.pdf [accessed: 26 January 2009].

APCO Worldwide (2004), *Communicating CSR: Talking to People Who Listen*, Global CSR Study (Washington, DC: APCO Worldwide). Available at: http://www.apcoworldwide.com/content/PDFs/Global_CSR_Study.pdf [accessed: 26 January 2009].

Auger, P. and Devinney, T. (2007), 'Do what consumers say matter? The misalignment of preferences with unconstrained ethical intentions', *Journal of Business Ethics* 76(4): 361–86.

Auger, P., Louviere, J. and Devinney, T. (2007), 'Measuring the importance of ethical consumerism: a multi-country empirical investigation', in P. Madsen and J. Hooker (eds), *Controversies in International Corporate Responsibility* (Charlottesville, VA: Philosophy Documentation Center), pp. 207–21.

Australian Bureau of Statistics (ABS) (2007), *2007: Australia at a Glance*, Catalogue 1309 (Sydney: ABS). Available at: http://www.ausstats.abs.gov.au/ausstats/subscriber.nsf/0/3661970ED5DE3830CA25726C007A124C/$File/13090_2007.pdf [accessed: 26 January 2009].

—— (2009), *Australian Economic Indicators, Feb 2009*, Cat 1350.0 Consumption Section. [Online: ABS]. Available at: http://www.abs.gov.au/ausstats/abs@.nsf/Products/BA0D93FB90136B7FCA25754D0022838B?opendocument [accessed: 22 August 2009].

Barnett, C., Cafaro, P. and Newholm, T. (2005), 'Philosophy and ethical consumption', in R. Harrison, T. Newholm and D. Shaw (eds), *The Ethical Consumer* (London: Sage), pp. 11–24.

Bhattacharya, C.B. and Sen, S. (2004), 'Doing better at doing good: When, why, and how consumers respond to corporate social initiatives', *California Management Review* 47(1): 9–24.

Brinkmann, J. and Peattie, K. (2008), 'Consumer ethics research: reframing the debate about consumption for good', *Electronic Journal of Business Ethics and Organisation Studies* 13(1). Available at: http://ejbo.jyu.fi/pdf/ejbo_vol13_no1_pages_22-31.pdf [accessed: 22 August 2009].

Brobeck, S. (2006), 'Defining the consumer interest: challenges for advocates', *Journal of Consumer Affairs* 40(1): 177–85.

Brotherhood of St Laurence (2006), *Detention centres meet NGO demands*. [Online: Brotherhood of St Laurence]. Available at: http://www.bsl.org.au/main.asp?PageId=3857 [accessed: 22 August 2009].

CHOICE (2003), 'They don't want you to know ....', *CHOICE Magazine*, June, 13–17.

—— (2008a), *Green Claims on Supermarket Labels*. [Online: CHOICE Online]. Available at: http://www.choice.com.au/viewArticle.aspx?id=106284 [accessed: 27 January 2009].

—— (2008b), *Consumer Awareness Survey*. [Online: CHOICE Online]. Available at: http://www.choice.com.au/viewArticle.aspx?id=106408 [accessed: 26 January 2009].

—— (2008c), *CHOICE's Toy Industry Survey*. [Online: CHOICE Online]. Available at: http://www.choice.com.au/viewArticle.aspx?id=106376 [accessed: 26 January 2009].

Consumer Federation of America (CFA) (2009), *About CFA*. [Online: CFA]. Washington, DC: CFA. Available at: http://www.consumerfed.org/about.cfm [accessed: 27 January 2009].

Consumers International (CI) (2005), *From Bean to Cup: How Consumer Choice Impacts upon Coffee Producers and the Environment*, research report (London: CI). Available at: http://www.consumersinternational.org/Shared_ASP_Files/UploadedFiles/FDB0EF2D-14FE-4558-B219-A7FD81E089FB_CIcoffeereport.pdf [accessed: 27 January 2009].

—— (2008), *CI Action*. [Online: CI]. London: CI. Available at: http://www.consumersinternational.org/Templates/Internal.asp?NodeID=98256&int1stParentNodeID=89651&int2ndParentNodeID=97688&int3rdParentNodeID=98253 [accessed: 29 January 2009].

—— (no date), *The Real Deal: Exposing Unethical Behaviour*. [Online: CI]. Available at: http://www.consumersinternational.org/Templates/Internal.asp?NodeID=97557 [accessed: 27 January 2009].

—— (unpublished), 'Assuring consumer confidence in ethical standards: fact-finding process'.

—— and AccountAbility (2007), *What Assures Consumers on Climate Change?* (London: CI and AccountAbility). Available at: http://www.consumersinternational.org/shared_asp_files/GFSR.asp?NodeID=96683 [accessed: 29 January 2009].

Co-operative Bank (2007), *The Ethical Consumerism Report 2007* (Manchester: Co-operative Bank). Available at: http://www.goodwithmoney.co.uk/servlet/Satellite/1228203834821,CFSweb/Page/GoodWithMoney [accessed: 26 April 2008].

—— (2008), *The Ethical Consumerism Report 2008* (Manchester: Co-operative Bank). Available at: http://www.goodwithmoney.co.uk/corp/pdf/ECR_2008_Web.pdf [accessed: 26 January 2009].

Corporate Responsibility and Trade Justice Movement (2006), 'Improvements to Companies Bill: movement towards corporate responsibility', joint media release, 18 October. Available at: http://www.tjm.org.uk/news/companies181006.shtml [accessed: 22 August 2009].

Crane, A. (2005), 'Meeting the ethical gaze: challenges for orienting to the ethical market', in R. Harrison, T. Newholm and D. Shaw (eds), *The Ethical Consumer* (London: Sage), pp. 219–32.

—— and Matten, D. (2004), *Business Ethics: A European Perspective* (Oxford: Oxford University Press).

—— (2006), *Business Ethics: Managing Corporate Citizenship and Sustainability in the Age of Globalization* (Oxford: Oxford University Press).

DanWatch (2008), *Bad Connections: How Your Mobile Phone is Linked to Abuse, Fraud and Unfair Mining Practices in DR Congo*, research report (Copenhagen: DanWatch).

Department of Foreign Affairs and Trade (DFAT) (2009), *People's Republic of China Country Brief January 2009: Overview of Australia-China Relations*. [Online: DFAT]. Available at: http://www.dfat.gov.au/geo/china/cb_index.html [accessed: 29 January 2009].

Department of Industrial Relations, NSW (1999), *Behind the Label: The NSW Government Clothing Outworker Strategy*, Issues paper (Sydney: DIR).

Department of Trade and Industry (DTI) (2002), *The Impact of Labelling Schemes* (London: DTI). Available at: http://www.berr.gov.uk/files/file8163.pdf [accessed: 26 January 2009].

Devinney, T., Auger, P., Eckhardt, G. and Birtchnell T. (2006), 'The other CSR: consumer social responsibility', *Stanford Social Innovation Review* 4(3): 30–37.

Devinney T., Auger, P., Louviere, J. and Burke, P. (2008), 'Do social product features have value to consumers?', *International Journal of Research in Marketing* 25(3): 183–91.

Dickinson, R.A. and Carsky, M.L. (2005), 'The consumer as economic voter', in R. Harrison, T. Newholm and D. Shaw (eds), *The Ethical Consumer* (London: Sage), pp. 25–36.

Elliott, K.A. and Freeman, R.B. (2001), *White Hats or Don Quixotes? Human Rights Vigilantes in the Global Economy*, National Bureau of Economic Research Working Paper no. 8102 (Cambridge, MA: National Bureau of Economic Research).

Ethical Consumer Research Association (no date), *About Us*. [Online: Ethical Consumer]. Available at: http://dnn.ethicalconsumer.org/AboutUs.aspx [accessed: 29 January 2009].

Euroconsumers (2008), 'Corporate social responsibility surveys at Euroconsumers' (unpublished paper).

Fairtrade Labelling Organizations International (FLO) (2007), 'Requesting suppliers to meet Fairtrade Standards isn't against free market competition'. [Online: FLO]. Available at: http://www.fairtrade.net/single_view.html?&cHash=51f0f3c408&tx_ttnews[backPid]=168&tx_ttnews[pointer]=2&tx_ttnews[tt_news]=31 [accessed: 26 January 2009].

—— (2008), *An Inspiration for Change: Annual Report 2007* (Bonn: FLO).

Gillespie, E. (2008), 'Stemming the tide of "greenwash"', *Consumer Policy Review* 18(3): 79–83.

Greenpeace International (2006), *McAmazon*. [Online: Greenpeace International]. Available at: http://www.greenpeace.org/international/news/mcamazon-060406 [accessed: 27 January 2009].

Harford, T. (2007), *The Undercover Economist*, Abacus edition (London: Little, Brown).

Hutton, W. (2008), *The Writing on the Wall: China and the West in the 21st Century*, Abacus edition (London: Little, Brown).

International Federation of Alternative Trade (IFAT) (2008), *What is Fair Trade?* [Online: IFAT]. Available at: http://www.ifat.org/index.php?option=com_content&task=view&id=1&Itemid=12 [accessed: 26 January 2009].

International Labour Organization (1998), *Declaration on Fundamental Principles and Rights at Work*. [Online: ILO]. Available at: http://www.ilo.org/declaration/thedeclaration/lang--en/index.htm [accessed: 22 August 2009].

—— (2008), *Declaration on Social Justice for a Fair Globalisation*. [Online: ILO]. Available at: http://www.ilo.org/public/english/bureau/dgo/download/dg_announce_en.pdf [accessed: 22 August 2009].

—— (no date), *Decent Work For All*. [Online: ILO]. Available at: http://www.ilo.org/global/About_the_ILO/Mainpillars/WhatisDecentWork/lang--en/index.htm [accessed: 22 August 2009].

Klempner, G. (2006), 'Philosophy of CSR', *Philosophy for Business* 27. Available at: http://www.businessphilosophy.co.uk/articles/csr_philosophy.pdf [accessed: 26 January 2009].

Lang, T. and Gabriel, Y. (2005), 'A brief history of consumer activism', in R. Harrison, T. Newholm and D. Shaw (eds), *The Ethical Consumer* (London: Sage), pp. 39–53.

Lazzarini, M. (2007), *The Challenge of Being an Ethical Consumer*, presentation at the International Standards Organization Committee on Consumer Policy Workshop: Can Consumers Rely on Fair Trade?, Salvador de Bahia, Brazil, 23 May. Available at: http://www.consumersinternational. org/shared_asp_files/GFSR.asp?NodeID=96623 [accessed: 29 January 2009].

Lloyd, R. (2007), *Industry as a Partner for Sustainable Development: Supply Chain Management in a Globalising World*, presentation to the Commission on Sustainable Development Industrial Development, UN Headquarters, New York, 7 May. Available at: http://www. consumersinternational.org/shared_asp_files/GFSR.asp?NodeID=96577 [accessed: 27 January 2009].

McAuley, I. (2001), *In Defence of Economics Why Public Policy Doesn't Need the Triple Bottom Line*, paper to the National Institute for Governance Seminar: The Triple Bottom Line, Canberra, Australia, 7 November. Available at: http://www.home.netspeed.com.au/mcau/academic/tripbl/ tripbl.pdf [accessed: 26 January 2009].

Productivity Commission (2008), *Review of Australia's Consumer Policy Framework*, Final Report (Canberra: Commonwealth of Australia).

Rose, C., Dade, P. and Scott, J. (2008), 'How social values systems can motivate consumers to act on climate change', *Consumer Policy Review* 18(3): 74–8.

Ruggie, J. (2008), *Protect, Respect and Remedy: A Framework for Business and Human Rights* (Geneva: Human Rights Council).

Sampson, G. (2008), 'WTO should stick to its core mandate', *The Australian Financial Review*, 4 January, 39.

Solomon, M. (2008), *Could Corporate Social Responsibility Destroy Social Business?* [Online: Social Enterprise, Comment]. Available at: http://www.socialenterprisemag.co.uk/sem/ tradingplace/detail/index.asp?id=355 [accessed: 26 January 2009].

Tallay, L. (2007), *Information 'No Through Road'*. [Online: Amnesty International Australia]. Available at: http://www.amnesty.org.au/china/comments/7264/ [accessed: 26 January 2009].

Thoresen, V. (2007), 'The contours of choice: the role of consumer information in social responsibility', in D. Nitsch (ed.), *Consumer Interests Annual* (Milwaukee, WI: American Council on Consumer Interests), pp. 21–37.

—— (2008), *Here and Now Education for Sustainable Consumption: Recommendations and Guidelines*, Working paper, United Nations Environment Programme and the Marrakech Task Force on Education for Sustainable Consumption. Available at: http://www. consumersinternational.org/files/98245/FileName/HereandNowGuidelines.pdf [accessed: 29 January 2009].

Wolf, M. (2008), *Corporate Social Confusion*. [Online: Creative Capitalism: a conversation (blog), 18 August 2008]. Available at: http://creativecapitalism.typepad.com/creative_ capitalism/2008/08/corporate-socia.html [accessed: 26 January 2009].

World Bank (2005), *05 World Development Indicators, Global Links*. [Online]. Available at: http:// devdata.worldbank.org/wdi2005/Section6_1.htm [accessed: 22 August 2009].

PART III
Mobilized Workers

Chapter 11

Corporate Accountability and the Potential for Workers' Representation in China

Anita Chan

In 2007 Chandran Nair wrote in the journal *Ethical Corporation* about the corporate social responsibility (CSR) 'industry' from a corporate insider's perspective. Nair's view is stated unequivocally in the title of his article: 'Corporate responsibility: an industry that has lost its way'. He notes:

> As another year draws to a close it is clear it has been one of countless corporate social responsibility conferences, forums and workshops. The phenomenon is characterised by ever bigger events, more pontification, few original thoughts, less informed debate, more participation by public relations professionals, great earnestness, few actions and an expanding list of 'issues'. (Nair 2007)

The CSR industry has come to a point at which multinationals find themselves stymied in what they are doing. China inevitably looms large in the discussions. In this context, this chapter asks: how is the CSR agenda playing out in China, how much impact is CSR having on the ground and what is the potential for systems of strengthened worker representation to offer more effective means of protecting working conditions in Chinese factories?

CSR and Work Conditions in China's Export Factories

How then has the CSR movement developed in China, and what impact has it had in reality? The region in China most audited by CSR monitors is the Pearl River Delta in Guangdong Province. This area has one of the largest concentrations of export factories (mostly Taiwanese, Hong Kong, Korean and domestic Chinese) and a great many of these factories supply the world's brand-name corporations. The province exports some US$300 billion worth of manufactured products, which constitutes one third of China's total exports (Xu 2007). The Pearl River Delta is important both for the wealthy countries and for China.

A quarter of a century ago the Pearl River Delta region was essentially agricultural. When China began its economic 'opening up' in the early 1980s, it established its first export trade zone, the Shenzhen Special Economic Zone, across from the Hong Kong border. The wages were at least ten times lower than those in Hong Kong. Foreign investors, who were mainly suppliers for transnational corporations (TNCs), quickly moved in, and the entire delta was transformed into the world's workshop in two decades. Almost all of the production-line workers who labour in the Delta toady, numbering about 4.5 million, are from poorer parts of China. The original rural communities have given up farming and have become a *rentier* class, owning all the land and most of the factory buildings. It is in the interest of their local governments to keep wages low in order to attract and retain the foreign-owned factories (see Chan et al. 2009).

The All-China Federation of Trade Unions (ACFTU), which served as a transmission belt between management and workers when China had a socialist economy under Mao, has retained a presence in state-owned enterprises. As an arm of enterprise management, the factory-level union branch performed a welfare function in the Maoist period; the ACFTU had no need to organize trade union branches because they just existed 'naturally', and there was no notion of or necessity for collective bargaining. But the situation became very different for the ACFTU with the sudden introduction of foreign investors who did not want unions in their enterprises, no matter how tame. Unlike Western unions, the ACFTU had never previously experienced hostile management. In vast, newly industrialized regions such as the Pearl River Delta, where all foreign-funded factories stand on greenfield sites, the official trade union is largely absent or, where present, controlled by the local governments and is quiescent. In many cases, the foreign managements are allowed simply to appoint one of the managerial staff to serve as union head. In the early 1990s, as migrant workers flooded in the millions into the world's new industrial frontier, they were totally at the mercy of raw global capitalism (Lee 1998; Chan 2001; Pun 2005a).

As exposés of labour abuses appeared repeatedly in both Chinese and foreign presses, the anti-sweatshop movement began putting pressure on brand-name companies to demand that their suppliers in China comply with corporate codes of conduct. Although initially denying that it was their responsibility to raise labour standards in a supplier company's factories, within the space of a few years many TNCs conceded and, in order to ward off criticism, began to draw up corporate codes of conduct (Bartley 2003).

But how can TNCs compel thousands of supplier factories all over the world to comply with such codes, especially since doing so can be costly to supplier firms? The initial solution was to send in monitors and auditors to spot-check the suppliers' factories. Thus a new, vibrant industry of for-profit agencies emerged that hired themselves out to corporations to monitor factory standards (Tan and Liu 2003).

Nevertheless, supplier firms have quickly developed techniques to circumvent the monitoring. They have developed elaborate methods of double bookkeeping and falsifying time cards and pay-slips (Utting 2005; Clean Clothes Campaign 2005). They have coached workers on what to say to monitors if singled out for interviews. They have set up two factories with two different names in the same factory compound, only one of which was presented to monitors,[1] or they have bribed monitors to overlook transgressions. Many monitors have learned to look the other way, since often the TNCs that hired them were not keen to learn about violations when they were discovered (Pun 2005b). The cheating has become so widespread that some TNCs have openly admitted that their 'policing' policy is in trouble (Henkle 2005; Nike Inc. 2005; Locke et al. 2006).[2]

CSR and Workers' Wages

After one and a half decades of increasingly intensive CSR monitoring in this region, with some factories being 'monitored' regularly by social auditors sent by several different corporate clients, one would have thought that workers' wages today would have reached at least the level of China's minimum legal wage. Yet the fact is that the hourly wage of workers at most of these export

---

1   It is unclear how widespread this is in China, but within a year, while participating in a pilot CSR programme, I came across two such factories.

2   I also learned about this informally from the human rights staff of several large companies at a conference held in Shenzhen, China, in March 2004.

factories is still below the level of China's legal minimum. Workers normally have to work up to three hours of overtime a day during the week and one full day on Saturday paid at below the legal overtime premium. Thus, while on paper workers' monthly wages appear to be substantially higher than the minimum, when all the hours worked for a given month are added up and divided by workers' total monthly earnings, it is evident that workers are normally not paid at the amount they are legally entitled to per hour. Supplier factories violate both the corporate codes of conduct and China's labour laws.

In 2004 China's Ministry of Labor and Social Security announced that 'studies show the real [monthly] salary of a migrant worker in the Pearl River Delta area has grown by a mere 68 yuan [US$8.20] over the last 12 years' (Ministry of Labor and Social Security 2004).[3] This small increase reflects the tendency for even those negligible increases in wages that have taken place to be cancelled out by inflation. The stagnation of inflation-adjusted minimum wages since the early 1990s is further illustrated in Table 11.1 and Figure 11.1.

Table 11.1   Inflation adjustments to minimum wage, Outer Shenzhen, Guangdong Province, 1993–2007

	1993	1994	1995	1996	1997	1998	1999	2000	2001	2002	2003	2004	2005	2006	2007
Minimum wage (Yuan)	286	300	300	310	320	330	330	419	440	460	465	480	580	700	750
Minimum wage adjusted for inflation (Yuan)	238	211	188	180	180	187	189	233	250	258	259	264	314	371	385

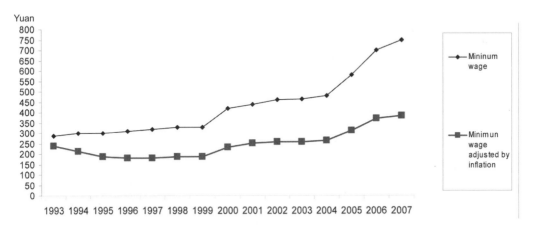

Figure 11.1   Legal minimum wage per month for a 40-hour work week, Outer Shenzhen, Guangdong Province, 1993–2007

---

3   This figure refers to the total wage packages received by workers, adjusted for inflation.

The minimum wage levels in China for the first 40 hours of work per week are set annually by city-level governments, supposedly in accordance with the prevailing wage and the cost of living in the city. The official minimum wage provides a useful basis for calculating how much workers make each month. My research collaborators and I have been to many dozens of factories in this region during the past two decades, and the monthly wage that the migrant workers have received for the first 40 hours per week is invariably the same as the legal minimum wage. But most of these workers labour for far longer than 40 hours per week and, although by law they are required to be paid a higher wage per hour for all overtime and weekend work, in reality most of them are paid at the same rate or marginally more. Some workers make *less* per hour of overtime work than they are paid per hour for their first 40 work hours. Because they are not paid enough for their overtime labour, the overall pay of most of the migrant workers is far less than what is stipulated by law. Yet CSR auditors either do not investigate this or allow themselves to be fooled by supplier factory managers.

There are also systematic violations of both Chinese law and corporate codes of conduct in relation to the amount of overtime hours worked. The legal maximum number of overtime hours per month in China is 36 – that is, on average, 9 hours of overtime work per week. Thus a Chinese worker is not supposed to work for more than 49 hours a week. However, most corporate codes of conduct set the normal work hours at a 60-hour week, which is much longer than China's legal norm. Despite this, few factories in the Pearl River Delta allow a working week with as few as 60 hours. Most workers in the export industries there are required to work 10- to 11-hour days, usually six or seven days a week. During a factory's peak production season, the hours may extend up to 17 or 18 per day.

At almost all the factories, despite slight rises in the minimum wage in recent years, the hourly wage there is still today lower than the legal minimum hourly wage and the amount of overtime hours is at least (and often far in excess of) 30 per cent more than the legal maximum. Yet even though this over-work is undeniably in violation of both the law and CSR codes, again the auditors look the other way.

In what is known as the 'Walmart effect', Western corporations have been forced into competitive price wars to provide products at a lower cost to consumers (Lichtenstein 2006). They have done so by squeezing their suppliers in Asia, relentlessly insisting on depressing the buying price year by year. While willing to spend money on CSR programmes, they are not willing to help suppliers shoulder the costs necessary to raise wages and improve conditions. To counteract this, supplier-factory managements have resorted to squeezing their workers. They have done so by speeding up the pace of production, by increasing the amount of under-paid overtime work, and also, to counteract the very recent rises in the minimum wage, by greatly increasing the deductions they take from workers for food and dormitory fees. There are a hundred and one ways that factories try to cheat the workers and, in turn, the social auditors – and there are numerous reasons that the latter turn a blind eye to the transgressions. These are discussed in other chapters in this volume and need not be repeated here. What can be concluded is that the workers are being exploited, and that social auditing is not working in this part of China.

Reebok's Attempted Solution – Workers' Representation

In the late 1990s and early 2000s, Reebok's Human Rights Compliance Department had the foresight to recognize that, since outside auditing was not working, a better way forward might be to facilitate democratic trade-union elections in suppler factories, so that the workers' own elected representatives could help to ensure that the minimum standards were met. Insisting on workers' empowerment in this way has been the position of many labour NGOs and Western trade unions. These groups argue that empowering workers is the only way to improve labour conditions, not CSR drummed up by corporations. The Reebok programme was an initiative designed to implement the principle of freedom of association – an important element in goals of worker empowerment. This principle is enshrined in almost all codes of conducts developed by corporations; however, it is never truly addressed.

As noted earlier, the so-called 'trade union chairpersons' already in place in these enterprises were actually not trade unionists in any usual sense of the term. They were either sent by the local governments and therefore often prioritized the interests of industrial investment, or the factory itself was allowed to appoint a middle-level manager to serve as the trade union chair. Reebok's programme aimed to replace this type of assigned trade-union leader by democratically elected representatives. To do so, Reebok had to wait until the term of these trade union committees expired and then place strong pressure on its supplier factories to allow elections to take place. Because the local governments were eager to accommodate the demands of investors, they acquiesced in the elections. Reebok's plan was to bring in experienced outside labour NGOs after the elections to assist the newly elected employee committees in organizing to handle trade union affairs and perhaps even to engage in collective bargaining over work conditions.

As pilots, Reebok instigated elections in 2001 and 2002 at two different supplier factories. The first election was held at KTS, a joint Hong Kong-Taiwanese factory in the Pearl River Delta, and the second was at Shunda, a Taiwanese-owned factory in Fujian Province. I secured an opportunity to study both elections and I witnessed workers' enthusiasm during the election process (Chan 2009). After the elections, workers held high hopes that the elected union committees would help to improve their conditions.

In the first year after the elections, the two elected committees encountered different fates. At KTS, during the first few months the committee members held regular committee and sub-committee meetings and then met once a month with the top managers to report on workers' concerns and to present management with requests to rectify the problems. The union was able to extract concessions from factory management in these first few months. For instance, it was able to get the managers to agree to abolish monetary penalties. It was also able to get the factory to agree to pay 75 per cent of the workers' wages when production lines stopped due to the late arrival of materials, whereas previously workers were not paid anything. Third, the factory had not been enrolled in the government's social security system, but from now on workers would be receiving such social security insurance after one year of service. Management also agreed to pay 80–90 per cent of workers' wages during sick leave.

However, this golden period only lasted for about half a year. When the factory underwent an ownership change (the Hong Kong partner bought out his Taiwanese partner), the new owner was not willing to grant any more concessions. He even started axing benefits. Workers soon lost faith in their elected representatives.

The Shunda elected trade union committee did not even have the chance to negotiate with management as its KTS counterpart had. There were two main reasons. Firstly, the district trade union intervened right after the election to curtail any initiatives that might have led to demands on management to implement improvements. Secondly, Shunda management was never willing to accept the legitimacy of the elected committee. No meaningful meetings took place between the two parties. Reebok, having facilitated the election of the union committee, felt it should no longer actively intervene and did not place pressure on management to be cooperative.

Failed Experiments

The pilot programmes at KTS and Shunda ultimately failed. Today the trade unions in KTS and Shunda are under absolute management control. Four problems at the time stood out that would doom Reebok's project to failure.

The first was that, despite all the declarations about social accountability, in practice a Western corporation's human rights department is usually not important within its corporate structure. The staff members in various departments carry on their daily work without much interaction with other departments. Thus Reebok's production department does not know, and does not much care, what its human rights department is doing. For example, during the Shunda factory trade union election – which was causing quite a stir among both workers and Taiwanese managers – I was surprised to find that an American staff member from Reebok's production department, who worked on site to oversee the footwear's quality, had no idea that an election was going on.

Furthermore, Reebok's sourcing department's mission was at odds with that of its human rights department. In fact, one of the main reasons that suppliers are able to persist in violating their clients' corporate codes is because their clients' sourcing practices work against their own codes of conduct: while the TNCs' sourcing departments aim to squeeze as much as they can out of suppliers by paying as little as possible for the products and by imposing short delivery times, the TNCs' human rights departments are supposed to ensure there is no excessive overtime. The production and sourcing departments are important within the TNC, since their responsibility is to ensure that a quality low-cost product is delivered to Western consumers in time to meet a seasonal demand. Failure to coordinate the human rights department functions with other departments in order to make CSR effective is, without doubt, not a simple oversight. Rather, within the broader logic of the situation, the ultimate goals of corporate policy render the CSR programme ineffective.

Secondly, while I observed at the time that the Reebok human rights staff members were serious about helping workers to secure genuine representation, they were inexperienced and made some mistakes in running the pilot programme. One significant misjudgement was in not soliciting the involvement of the top levels of the national union federation. It was a time when the foreign community generally held a very dismissive attitude towards China's national union. While the union leadership in Beijing knew about these elections, it chose not to intervene for two years, which also gave the impression that it silently approved of the programme. In contrast, the district trade union had to be involved because Reebok's initiative was happening in its area. However, because the district union was largely an arm of the district government, it supported the interests of the foreign investors since the local government's revenues depended on the foreign factories. When Reebok demanded an election and pressured the supplier factory to agree, the district union fell into line. It sat in on all the pre-election meetings, but chose to behave as a passive observer.

After the elections, at KTS in Guangdong the union committee under the guidance of Hong Kong NGO staff initially negotiated with management over a variety of issues, not dissimilar to collective bargaining. However, in both the Fujian and Guangdong factories, the district union gradually began to exert its influence and bring the enterprise unions into line, partly through cooptation of their union chairs and committee members. Under the tutelage of the Fujian district union, the Shunda factory union chair and deputy chair gradually allowed themselves to become allies of management, receiving a full-time office from the company and a middle-management staff salary. The enterprise union ultimately did very little to improve workers' conditions (Lee 2007), especially after Reebok was bought by Adidas and its human rights office was disbanded.

Nonetheless, the initial experience of the first year at the KTS factory had been successful, as had the election procedures that involved a self-nomination process, the candidates delivering public speeches, public forums in which workers openly had asked management questions, voting booths and so on. Today, several researchers in the national union federation continue to talk about these elections in a positive way as worthy of emulation, and one is even writing a book about the Shunda experience in order to pass on the experience within Chinese trade union circles.

Conversely, some of the ACFTU leaders were unhappy with this foreign intrusion from its initiation. Had Reebok sought cooperation from the ACFTU from the very beginning, the fate of the enterprise unions might have been different. The elected trade union committee members who initially were serious about their responsibilities might have stood up against management's resistance and the district union's blandishments and intervention. The post-election training of new committee members by Hong Kong labour NGOs, which was cut short as soon as Reebok diverted its attention, might have continued.

A third problem was the programme's failure to insist on the financial independence of the trade union and a right to collective bargaining with factory management, as stipulated by Chinese law. Without a guarantee of these two trade union rights, the ability of the union committees to function independently was very quickly curtailed and they became reliant on management. As noted, at KTS in Guangdong, the newly elected union committee was able to achieve some gains not dissimilar to those from collective bargaining. When the union published its first magazine issue, it read like a workers' magazine. At Shunda in Fujian, the lack of financial independence was felt almost from the start. When the new union committee published its first magazine issue, it had to go to management for funds, which entailed serious compromises[4] and the literature produced was indistinguishable from a factory public relations magazine.

Fourth was the absence of an independent trade union culture among Chinese workers. This takes decades to develop and often emerges out of labour struggles. The workers in these two factories were endowed with a golden opportunity to have their own representatives but the workers did not have much understanding of trade unionism. Workers' consciousness needs time and support to develop. Andrew Walder's findings (1986) about the authoritarian culture of dependency among Chinese state enterprise workers in the Maoist period similarly apply today among Chinese migrant workers. The workers and the elected trade union committee members were grateful to Reebok and relied on the company to continue to help them against management suppression. Reebok itself was caught in a difficult position, however. The head of Reebok's human rights department for China, Jill Tucker, understood that it was not the job of a department of a multinational corporation to run a trade union at a separate company's factory in China. When the national union federation expressed its disapproval, Reebok retreated.

Certainly, it was an odd situation from the beginning. A multinational company is surely not the institution one would expect to assume the task of educating workers in how to organize a functioning trade union – this is normally the job of higher-level trade unions. But short of this, from where will there be any push for an agenda of genuine workers' representation? I argue that we should still try to overcome the dilemma posed here by exploring other solutions.

The Benefits of Foreign Trade Union Involvement

One common feature that ran through these two pilot election programmes was an absence of trade union involvement in training and supporting the workers before and after the elections. Even in societies that have well-established trade unions and trade union cultures, much time and effort is

---

4   One newly elected union committee member told me his article was rejected.

needed to ensure that newly formed workplace trade union branches are competent in bargaining with management. Practical support and continual training by higher-level trade union organs are normally needed; within China's trade environment, support from outside the factory is essential. Reebok initially provided this as best it could and brought in NGOs to help give training, but NGOs cannot take the place of trade unions.

Though collective bargaining – or, in China's preferred expression, 'collective consultation' – is legal and there are some union officials in Beijing who view it as important, it is not a concept widely disseminated at the grassroots. Some small local labour NGOs operate in China, but their focus is on helping workers to seek remedies through the courts when their individual legal rights are violated. Furthermore, as they do not have any officially recognized representative role at the workplace, they cannot represent the workers to bargain collectively with management. At most they can provide advice to labour activists concerning making demands on management.

Even the ACFTU is fully aware that it has little experience working in an environment of hostile management, which is the predominant factory management culture in the export industrial sector, particularly in Guangdong. Under such circumstances, the involvement of foreign trade unions with their wealth of historical experience might become beneficial to the ACFTU if it becomes amenable to organizing real union branches in such factories. If the foreign unions' experience can be 'technically transferred' to the Chinese trade unions it may speed up the process by which China can develop a mature industrial relations system.

Emerging Potential for Strengthened Worker Representation?

In the past few years, signs have emerged indicating that the maturing of China's industrial relations system internally, together with increased support from foreign unions, may be creating a more favourable environment for strengthened worker representation. Developments have been unfolding at a number of levels.

Diffusion of the Direct Trade Union Election Model

In 2003, not long after the Reebok elections, the ACFTU announced that it had implemented direct trade union elections in Zhejiang Province in an effort to show support for trade union democracy (Wang 2003; Howell 2006). The timing and wording of the announcement suggests that this was a reaction prompted by the Reebok elections.[5] The direct election programme has been going on for several years. Whether the process is democratic or not remains to be studied, but the ACFTU now formally recognizes the need for a show of trade union democracy.

ACFTU Support for Grassroots Trade Union Organizing

The ACFTU's first ever grassroots trade union organizing occurred in 2006 at a Walmart store in Fuzhou City, Fujian, followed by similar efforts at a number of other Walmart stores. The union federation and Walmart subsequently signed a five-point memorandum in August 2006 that opens avenues for the emergence of functioning workplace unions (Chan 2007).[6] The Walmart case also

---

    5   However, according to one Chinese media report, direct workplace trade union elections had been trialled for some time at various places (Wang 2003).
    6   Also see ACFTU (2006).

set a precedent as the first time that the union federation has negotiated with a major foreign company. Walmart is a direct employer in China, whereas other multinationals such as Reebok are not, but there is no reason that such a multinational cannot approach the union federation to develop a formula to help workers set up genuine representative bodies inside contractor factories. The union federation today might even welcome this, given that it has difficulty setting up effective union branches in such factories on its own.

Strengthened Collaboration between the ACFTU and Foreign Unions

At the same time, we are also aware that many local trade unions are more pro-management than pro-worker and suppress workers' initiatives. Increased involvement of foreign trade unions would contribute positively to alleviating this problem. Compared to its position six years ago, the ACFTU is now much more willing to reach out to foreign trade unions. For example, trade unions of various European countries with the cooperation of their home country multinationals have been increasingly active in China, especially in these multinationals' supplier factories. As a second example, the Beijing General Trade Union has received training sessions in Canada from Canadian unions on how to bargain collectively.[7]

On the other side of the equation, foreign union engagement is also expanding year by year. The new US trade union federation, Change To Win, established formal links with the ACFTU in 2007 and, half a year later, the International Trade Union Confederation (ITUC, formerly the ICFTU) also passed a resolution that changed its position from no engagement to engagement with the ACFTU (Vandaele 2008).

The growing international contacts can be expected to have a positive impact on the Chinese union federation's conception of what trade unionism entails. This potential is illustrated by consideration of the closely parallel case of Vietnam (which has a political and economic system quite similar to China) and of developments within the Vietnam General Confederation of Labor (VGCL).

With the permission of the Vietnamese Communist Party and government, the Vietnamese union federation has been actively engaging with foreign trade unions for almost two decades. Now, local and foreign labour NGOs are able to function quite openly. The top and middle levels of the Vietnamese union federation are quite pro-labour. The official trade union newspapers report on strikes, with photographs of strikers' demonstrations. The Vietnamese union federation is also willing to participate in CSR programmes. A current CSR programme sponsored by the ILO, 'Improving Industrial Relations at Enterprises in Vietnam', involves the union federation.[8] After a 2006 strike wave at Asian-funded enterprises in southern Vietnam, the Vietnamese government worked closely with the ILO office to revise the law on strikes.

Another relevant initiative is a pilot programme funded by the government of Finland, the Finnish employers' associations and the Finnish trade union federation designed to improve work conditions in two dozen factories. On the ground in Vietnam, the programme has involved both the local union federation and foreign unions: the Vietnamese trade union's participation is coordinated by APHEDA, the foreign aid organization of the Australian trade union federation, the Australian Council of Trade Unions.[9] Admittedly, there are still enormous obstacles. The ultimate problem, be

---

7   Information from Cathy Walker, formerly of the Canadian Auto Workers. She has facilitated a number of exchanges with the ACFTU and its lower level unions and various Canadian trade unions.

8   This programme is funded by the US Department of Labor, the VGCL, the Vietnam Chamber of Commerce and Industry, and the Vietnam Cooperative Alliance.

9   Based on information provided by the APHEDA office in Hanoi 2007.

it in Vietnam or China, is that trade unions are under the control of the ruling Communist parties. For the time being, both these unions are reforming themselves slowly within the space allowed by their governing parties.

Increased Interest in Worker Empowerment among China's CSR Community

At the same time, new developments are stirring among the individuals and organizations that have been engaged in the CSR issue in China. For example, Verité, an organization that conducts social auditing around the world for corporations, held a conference in November 2007 in Shenzhen on 'Worker Engagement and Social Responsibility in China: Ways Forward' (Verité 2007). Verité, like its clients, has been frustrated with the lack of progress in CSR monitoring in China and is open to exploring the possibility of holding democratic trade union elections at TNCs' supplier factories.

Greater Awareness of Labour Rights among China's Migrant Workers

Finally, an important change is taking place among China's migrant workers. They are much more aware of their labour rights and their legal rights today than ever before, especially in Guangdong Province. Compared to half a dozen years ago, their horizons have been expanded by the ease of communication through mobile phones and the internet. Moreover, the Chinese press generally is supportive of labour. The impact has been cumulative. For instance, recently I met an ordinary worker near Shenzhen who said he was very interested in finding out more about how the first Walmart store union had been set up in Fuzhou, having read about it in the Chinese press, because he too wanted to give it a try. The failure of corporate-led CSR has been partly to do with the fact that the workers themselves have been passive players in the process. For example, workers at KTS and Shunda were reliant on Reebok to help them set up a genuine representative system and did not continue to fight to maintain it when the system crumbled. However, with all the changes that have taken place in the past several years, such trade union elections would now have a better base to develop among workers.

References

ACFTU (2006), [Online, 16 August]. Available at: http://www.acftu.org/template/10004/file.jsp?cid=222&aid=41801 [accessed: 29 August 2008]. (An English translation is available at *Chinese Labor News Translations*, http://www.clntranslations.org/article/4/wal-mart).

Bartley, T. (2003), 'Certifying forests and factories: states, social movements, and the rise of private regulation in the apparel and forest products fields', *Politics and Society* 31(3): 433–64.

Chan, A. (2001), *China's Workers Under Assault: The Exploitation of Labor in a Globalizing Economy* (Armonk, NY: M.E. Sharpe).

—— (2007), 'Organizing Wal-Mart in China: two steps forward, one step back for China's unions', *New Labor Forum* 16(2): 87–96.

—— (2009), 'Challenges and possibilities for democratic grassroots union elections in China: a case study of two factory-level elections and their aftermath', *Labor Studies Journal* 34(3): 293–317.

—— Madsen, R. and Unger, J. (2008), *Chen Village: Revolution to Globalization* (Berkeley, CA: University of California Press).

Clean Clothes Campaign (2005), *Looking for a Quick Fix: How Weak Social Auditing is Keeping Workers in Sweatshops* (Amsterdam: Clean Clothes Campaign).

Henkle, D. (2005), 'Gap Inc. sees supplier ownership of compliance with workplace standards as an essential element of socially responsible sourcing', *Journal of Organizational Excellence* 25(1): 18–19.

Howell, J. (2006), *New Democratic Trends in China? Reforming the All-China Federation of Trade Unions*, Centre for the Future State, Institute of Development Studies, Working Paper 263.

Lee, C.K. (1998), *Gender and the South China Miracle: Two Worlds of Factory Workers* (Berkeley, CA: University of California Press).

Lee, P. (2007), 'Democratic trade union election at Shunda factory: five years on', *China Labor News Translations* [Online, 25 August]. Available at: http://www.clntranslations.org/?q=Peter+Lee [accessed: 29 August 2008].

Lichtenstein, N. (2006), 'Wal-Mart: a template for twenty-first-century capitalism', in Nelson Lichtenstein (ed.), *Wal-Mart: The Face of Twenty-First-Century Capitalism* (New York: The New Press), pp. 3–30.

Locke, R., Qin, F. and Brause, A. (2006), *Does Monitoring Improve Labor Standards?: Lessons from Nike*, Corporate Social Responsibility Initiative, Working Paper No. 24.

Ministry of Labor and Social Security (2004), Report [Online, in Chinese]. Available at: http://www.molss.gov.cn/new/2004/0908a.htm [accessed: 2004].

Nair, C. (2007), 'Corporate responsibility: an industry that has lost its way', *Ethical Corporation* [Online, 14 December]. Available at: http://www.ethicalcorp.com/content.asp?ContentID=5582 [accessed: 29 August 2007].

Nike Inc. (2005), *FY04 Corporate Responsibility Report* [Online: Nike Inc.]. Available at: http://nikeresponsibility.com/pdfs/color/Nike_FY04_CR_report.pdf [accessed: 29 August 2007].

Pun, N. (2005a), *Made in China: Women Factory Workers in a Global Workplace* (Durham, NC: Duke University Press).

—— (2005b), 'Global production, company codes of conduct, and labor conditions in China: a case study of two factories', *The China Journal* 54: 101–13.

Tan, S. and Liu, K. (2003), *Kuaguo gongsi de shehui zeren yu Zhongguo shehui* [Corporate Social Responsibility and Chinese Society] (Beijing: Social Science Documentation Press).

Utting, P. (2005), *Rethinking Business Regulation* (New York: United Nations Research Institute for Social Development).

Vandaele, J. (2008), 'International union sets up Chinese links', Inter Press Service [Online, 22 January]. Available at: http://ipsnews.net/news.asp?idnews=40871 [accessed: 29 August 2008].

Verité Inc. (2007), *2007 Verite China Symposium* [Online: Verité Inc.]. Available at: http://verite.org/2007%20Verite%20China%20Symposium [accessed: 19 August 2008].

Walder, A. (1986), *Communist Neo-Traditionalism: Work and Authority in Chinese Industry* (Berkeley, CA: University of California Press).

Wang, J. (2003), 'Zhixuan, zai gueifanzhong pingwen tuijin – quanzong fuzhuxi Suliqing jiu jizeng gonghuizhuxi zhixuan da jizhe wen' [Direct elections: pushing ahead steadily within a framework – ACFTU Vice President Su Liqing's responses to reporters' questions on basic-level trade union chair direct elections], *Workers' Daily*, 25 July.

Xu, L. (2007), 'Chukou tui shui zhengce tiaozheng tui Guangdong chukou jiye de yingxiang fenxi' [An analysis of the impact of adjustment of tax rebates to Guangdong's export enterprises], *Zhujiang Jingji* [South China Review] 193: 32–7.

Chapter 12

The Threat Posed by 'Corporate Social Responsibility' to Trade Union Rights

Jeff Ballinger

Introduction

This chapter examines some of the key factors underlying the current inability of workers in Vietnam to establish and maintain independent trade unions and to force managers to bargain collectively. Discussion attempts to shed light on the complex layers of repressive power relations and legitimating discourses that perpetuate barriers to worker mobilization to demand their rights in the foreign direct investment (FDI) sector of countries such as Vietnam.

The examples analysed in the chapter illustrate how the concentration of economic and political power in a one-party state interacts with the structural power of investors within global supply chains and a broader capitalist economy, enabling enterprise managers to govern the conditions of factory work with little intrusion by political authorities. Workers' rights are undermined not only as a result of the power structures of state-business alliances in the global capitalist system, but also from the discourses and ideologies that support them. Interventions from activists and the growing corporate social responsibility (CSR) movement internationally are shown to have contributed more to legitimizing these power relations than to transforming the underlying power relationships in which these labour practices are grounded. It is partly in this sense that CSR – and the wider practices with which it is associated – operate as a threat to trade union rights: by working within the broader ideological project of global neo-liberalism, the CSR movement plays into and in some ways strengthens this neo-liberal project. CSR and related forms of activism also bring about negative consequences in some cases as a result of their ability to 'crowd out' more traditional forms of worker organizing.

Despite such serious difficulties, it is suggested that prospects for worker empowerment are not altogether bleak. In some cases, self-help strategies by workers appear to offer potential pathways through which the goal of strengthened worker rights may be advanced, by resisting both the power relations and the hegemonic discourses in which worker exploitation is grounded. In some instances, a worker-led self-help approach has delivered some real gains, even where self-regulation, norm-creation and local 'enforcement' efforts have proven unavailing. In other cases, the operation of international activism and CSR appear to operate in a perverse way to create openings through which more traditional forms of grassroots mobilization can operate to build strength. However, the conditions for the success of such self-help strategies are shown to be very stringent, hence in practice few victories have so far been won via such means.

Analysis presented in this chapter is based primarily on the case of Vietnam, particularly on labour conditions in its garment-footwear sector. The author's own field research informs discussion where possible, drawing on survey data with workers, factory managers, and union and non-government organization officials. This material is integrated with findings from other pertinent research (in Vietnam and in other relevant countries such as Indonesia) and insights based on the author's long experience as a labour rights activist in South East Asia and elsewhere.

Following an initial review of the worker rights violations that persist in this sector, and of the failure of state regulators to protect workers against such abuse, the chapter analyses the broad array of interlocking power relations that operate to disempower and exploit workers. Several axes of this matrix of power are identified and discussed in turn: the power of global brands within global supply chains; the associated structures of global capitalism and markets within which these are inserted; and the hostile alliance between business and the state that workers find themselves confronting in the FDI sector. These sources of power are compounded by poor worker awareness and organizing strength.

The chapter then evaluates two major strategies that have been explored to date as potential means of promoting compliance with labour standards: transnational activism; and corporate self-regulation, otherwise known as corporate social responsibility (CSR). Each of these is shown to be seriously flawed in some important respects. Finally, the conditions under which self-help strategies can prove successful are explored. Despite some important and ongoing setbacks, it is shown that there has been some notable progress in relation to worker self-help strategies, and – at least under certain favourable conditions – that these are endorsed as the most effective and legitimate means through which the protection of worker rights can be advanced in globalizing production sectors in Vietnam and other countries facing similar challenges.

The Failings of the Existing Regulatory System

There are over 30 million workers in the apparel, textile and footwear sector worldwide (ILO 2000, 13; Magnusson et al. 2003). Almost every country has at least a small domestic apparel production capacity. The industry serves as a worker rights bellwether as the work is usually quite labour-intensive and subject to Taylorist cost-cutting strategies by management (Fukuyama 1996, 226). The challenges which governments face in trying to regulate the apparel, textile and footwear sector are myriad and quite daunting. Even the Italian city of Prato – the local economy of which historically has been based on the textile industry – is reported to have 4,000 Chinese-run garment shops, most with less than ten employees (Cillis 2001, 24).

During the period following the opening of foreign-invested factories in Vietnam, work in the production-for-export sector was characterized by high levels of physical violence against workers. Though such violence has now been virtually eliminated in the sector, nearly all workers at FDI factories continue to report either high levels of stress or threatening and abusive verbal behaviour by managers (Cameron 2007, 158). Local-investment factories, by contrast, tend to have less contested worker–management relations, though complaints about high production targets are commonly noted. Where physical violence appears, it is often on the workers' side, emerging in the context of strike strategies as a response to low wages or forced overtime policies.[1]

Beyond physical violence, a number of kinds of workers' rights violations are prevalent within the sector. Much academic writing and journalistic reporting advances the 'fact' that FDI factories pay higher wages than the norm in developing countries (Bhagwati 2002, 87–9; Moran 2003, 17; Baldwin and Winters 2004, 317 citing the research of Lipsey and Sjoholm 2004; cf. Locke 2002, 51–2). However findings from the Asian Development Bank's 'Segmentation Survey' are in stark contrast to such claims (Nguyen et al. 2005, 15). FDI workers are the most likely to cite 'low pay' as the highest barrier to finding an acceptable job, with 'bad working conditions' and 'health

---

1   Field research interview with factory management in industrial areas around Hanoi and Ho Chi Minh City, late December 2007.

issues' also emerging as serious concerns (Nguyen et al. 2005, 42). Shoe workers reported the most negative views (compared to apparel and construction). This finding is clearly in disparity to the claims of many observers over the last decade who have maintained that foreign investment shoe factories offer the best jobs in Vietnam (Nguyen et al. 2005, 18).

The Asian Development Bank's report also reveals routine violations of prevailing laws regarding working hours in the for-export sector, citing median working hours per week at 60 for shoe workers (Nguyen et al. 2005, 19). Vietnam once had one of the world's lowest limits on worker overtime at 200 hours per year (Qi et al. 2003, 15). Not long after the arrival of FDI factories in the mid-1990s, this limit was raised to 300. Workers report that common practice is double that limit (Twose and Rao 2003, 19).[2]

Overtime – especially the issue of 'forced overtime' – has been widely debated in the press, policy journals and internet discussion sites for nearly a decade, and it is difficult to believe that such practices have gone unnoticed by public authorities. This suggests that Vietnamese policy-makers consciously ignore these industry contraventions, even as the global labour rights movement debates its implications, academic papers pile up and 'forced overtime' occupies a central focus of CSR discourse.

Overtime is not the only issue of worker abuse systematically neglected by state regulators. The actions of state regulators have operated to undermine workers rights in a number of other areas, both by watering down formal protections and by systematically undermining effective enforcement.

While Vietnam is one of 135 countries to have ratified the International Labour Organization (ILO) Convention No. 81, the *Labour Inspection Convention* 1947, compliance with its reporting requirements has not been forthcoming. This is the norm for all but a handful of countries (ILO 2006, 106–8). In 2001, the Vietnamese government issued 'Directive No 22/2001/CT-TTg of September 11, 2001 on Reorganizing the Work of Inspection and Examination at Enterprises' which notes widespread problems of inspections completed without any consequent decisions; abuse of processes 'for personal benefits'; lack of coordination; and arbitrary prolongation of inspections.

In part such failings can be attributed to the resource deficiencies generated within Vietnam's labour inspectorate, which is seriously under-staffed. According to a representative of the only legal union grouping in Vietnam – the Vietnam General Confederation of Labour (VGCL) – the Ministry of Labour, Invalid and Social Affairs (MOLISA) employs only ten labour inspectors.[3]

The performance of Vietnam's labour inspectorate has also been undermined by features of the labour code as it has evolved. Vietnamese labour rights regimes of trade union and labour relations laws underwent wholesale revisions in the 1990s; a new labour code was adopted in 1994 (amended in 2002) which coincided with a sharp increase in FDI. State-owned enterprises appear to be better employers with respect to issues such as the payment of wages and conditions at work (Fforde 2004), and it is likely that the state paid scant attention to the issue before *Doi Moi* (renovation) opened up the economy to the 'free market' in 1986.

Examining the track record since this time, performance on core labour standards shows little progress, if not outright slippage, in the global context. The erosion of the right to strike, for

---

2   Also from field research interview with production worker (apparel or shoe) in industrial areas around Hanoi and Ho Chi Minh City, late December 2007.

3   Field research interview with non-government entity or union officer in Hanoi and Ho Chi Minh City, late December 2007. While this number seems inordinately low, it suggests that alternative figures – such as a survey conducted by the MOLISA indicating that each factory manager interviewed reported having been inspected by the MOLISA 'recently' – strain credulity. It is worth noting that VGCL staff and officers generally hew to the government line.

example, 'has been severely curtailed … by means of increasingly restrictive legislation' (Harrod and O'Brien 2002, 245). Even the most elementary 'right' to the enforcement of domestic labour laws appears to be losing ground. Vietnamese unions were granted a 'bigger supervisory role … to "check on" (*kiem tra*) the implementation of the labour contract, recruitment, dismissal,' and so on (Chan and Nørlund 1998, 186). However, laws and intentions have a way of wilting under the rapacious demands of foreign capital.

Minimum wages have also remained the subject of serious contention, associated with widespread union mobilization. Even though the minimum wage was overdue for adjustment – before the first strikes in late-2005 – the government postponed the decision repeatedly due to the knock-on effect of requiring adjustments to state workers' salaries and to pensioners' payments.[4]

The strength of the inspection regime has been further weakened by the Vietnamese government's introduction of 'Directive No. 22/2001/CT-TTg of September 11, 2001 on Reorganizing the Work of Inspection and Examination at Enterprises'. Interestingly, the revised decree states that direct inspections 'shall be conducted only when signs of law violation are detected'. How these violations may come to the attention of the inspectorate is not addressed in the decree. In what may portend a new reliance upon 'self-regulation', the decree calls on enterprises 'to enhance the work of internal inspection', suggesting that 'state agencies shall step up the monitoring and guiding of enterprises in their self-inspection and examination' (RoV 2001).

Changing orthodoxy regarding the appropriate regulatory role of the state – associated with the emergence of the CSR agenda – appears to be further compounding the weakened role of state regulation. For example, a 2003 World Bank report focused on 'strengthening developing county governments' engagement with CSR' recommended that inspectors emulate (non- and for-profit) CSR monitoring teams (Twose and Rao 2003, 23). No attention was given to the mandate for inspectors under Decree No. 61/1998/ND-CP for, *inter alia*, inspection procedures, control procedures and responsibility of state agencies in inspection and control activities (Li et al. 2003, 28).

The role of international regulators also appears to be weakening, seemingly reflecting a broader decline in concern for labour rights at the international level (Ross 2004, 282). Even international norms, such as the World Trade Organization (WTO) guidelines – for example, non-discrimination principles of most-favoured-nation (treating other people equally) and national treatment (treating foreigners and locals equally) – while perceived to be amongst the most stringent and well-policed, are ignored with impunity. This can be illustrated by Vietnam's non-compliance with wage guidelines, which set out different tiers of wages by type of investment (local or foreign).[5]

Such trends appear to be compounded further by the increasing fragmentation of international law as reflected, for example, in the ILO Conventions which now number over 200 (Benvenisti and Downs 2007, 610). The 'core standards' approach – developed by progressive forces within the ILO and global labour movements – can play some role in attempting to declutter the international labour rights landscape.[6] Nevertheless, the effectiveness of such standards continues to be

---

4   Field research interview with non-government entity or union officer in Hanoi and Ho Chi Minh City, late December 2007.

5   Field research interview with non-government entity or union officer in Hanoi and Ho Chi Minh City, late December 2007. It should be noted that in some cases non-enforcement can also work to the benefit of workers. For example, while an apparently stringent law was passed recently to hold workers liable for any losses suffered by factories due to strikes, in practice the number of strikes has quadrupled in the last year with no known cases of workers being sued for damages.

6   These standards would 'guarantee freedom of association, the right to collective bargaining, abolition of forced labour, prevention of discrimination in employment and minimum age for employment' (Harrod and O'Brien 2002, 224).

undermined by the capacity of some powerful states to 'creat[e] a world legal order composed of a maze of narrow agreements' which operate in myriad forums and venues in effect to 'sabotage the evolution of a more democratic and egalitarian international regulatory system and to undermine the normative integrity of international law' (Benvenisti and Downs 2007, 610, 596).

Accounting for Failure – A Matrix of Repressive Power Relations

We can gain greater insight into the underlying causes of these failings within existing labour regulatory regimes – particularly those concerning export zones – by conceptualizing such labour relations as situated within a matrix of power relations involving several core axes of power: the power of global brands within a capitalist market economy (encompassing both global supply chains and the associated market institutions in which these are inserted); and the awkward alliance between business and the state that workers find themselves confronting in the FDI sector.

As discussed elsewhere in this volume, large buyers within global supply chains have significant power to define the 'norms' that operate within the supply chain. This power is grounded in such buyers' 'concentrated price-making ability' within the chains: '[w]here there is concentration in a supply (commodity) chain there will be a node of power' (Ross 2004, 145). Such pressure spreads between businesses within the supply chain via a 'cascade effect' in which the explosive 'process of concentration' among the larger buyers (the core 'systems integrators') has affected first-tier suppliers and spilled over to the second and third tiers (Nolan et al. 2008, 43). There is broad agreement among industry analysts and garment industry executives that such bigger buyers therefore have significant culpability for the effects of concessionary pricing on workers (Ross 2004, 144–6); to the extent that buyers are ruthless about outsourcing, workers' wages and conditions thus bend to their will. In this sense, the main problem confronting workers, as explained by one interviewed VGCL official, is the buyers' demand for the lowest price from supplier factories.

Across a wide range of business types, from fast-moving consumer goods to aircraft manufacture, the core systems integrator interacts in the deepest, most intimate fashion with the major segments of the value chain, both upstream and downstream. This constitutes a new form of 'separation of ownership and control', in which the boundaries of the firm have become blurred (Nolan et al. 2008, 43).

Buyers force FDI 'suppliers' in Vietnam to keep costs – including labour costs – low; this predatory relationship yields 'concessionary prices' from suppliers (Ross 2004, 146). The power asymmetries within this relationship were clearly displayed during the recent period of strikes and minimum wage contestation in Vietnam (2004–2007). During this time, companies such as Yue Yuen Industrial Holdings, Ltd[7] sought to downplay the extent of their power and informed shareholders of a tough operating environment since mid-2004: '[w]e expect the footwear-manufacturing sector to continue facing market pricing pressure' (Yue Yuen 2006, 10). Yet Yue Yuen, alongside the company's main buyers, continued to post record profits during this period, reporting the following before-tax profits: Nike $2.2 billion (up 52 per cent); Adidas $1 billion (up 68 per cent); Puma $511 million (up 14 per cent); Yue Yuen $387 million (up 29 per cent) (Maquila Solidarity Network 2008).[8]

---

7   Yue Yuen Industrial Holdings, Ltd is the biggest supplier of sports shoes in the world, employing over 280,000 workers in China, Vietnam and Indonesia.

8   The difficult operating environment faced by Yue Yuen was reflected in a low rating for a bond issue in 2003. A press release by Standard and Poor's commented that the low-cost manufacturing costs, 'are partially offset by increasing pressure on pricing from Yue Yuen's customers and high customer concentration' (Bailey 2003).

The distinctive consequences of these forms of buyer pressure are reflected in the differences in labour practices consistently reported to exist between foreign versus locally oriented firms. Echoing complaints that I had first heard in 1989, one VGCL official remarked that the leading FDI firms (Taiwanese and South Korean suppliers in apparel and footwear) tend to be the most abusive and most resistant to union-invited discussions over workplace issues such as wages.[9] Workers confirmed this, asserting that foreign employers were often more difficult to work for; the only workers who claimed not to know their rights in the workplace were working at Korean FDI factories. Many managers at apparel factories also agreed that price competition has a deleterious effect on workers, one manager reporting that her factory no longer competed for foreign buyers' purchases.[10]

The dynamics of buyer influence over the design of national labour regimes are becoming even more complex, as some big apparel buyers have now begun to acknowledge that states have a key role in protecting workers. This rhetorical position has undergone quite dramatic shifts since the industry's radical makeover since the 1970s, induced by globalization and outsourcing. When first queried about low wages and poor conditions, buyers' response was to declaim any responsibility for what was taking place in supplier factories. As this became untenable in the early 1990s, the focus shifted to supplier 'codes of conduct' insisted upon by buyers and intended to assuage consumer concern over reports of 'sweatshop' exploitation. Only recently (since 2004) has the importance of the host country's application of local labour laws become more widely recognized by influential supply chain actors, perhaps partly in response to increasing recognition that corporate codes and CSR policies are having little impact, as discussed further below.

These dynamics of power within global supply chains can be understood as embedded within the broader dynamics of a global capitalist market economy. Vietnam joined the global capitalist market in the late 1980s with the adoption of *Doi Moi* (renovation) in 1986. Despite a decade or more of rhetoric about widely shared growth under free trade globalization, the result has instead been rising global income inequality, together with unequal power relations (Palley 2004, 21).

These unequal power relations are in turn created and reproduced partially due to the embedding of these market relations within a regulatory and policy environment shaped by what Stephen Gill (1995, 413) has described as 'disciplinary neoliberalism' and a 'new constitutionalism' which expands the influence of global capital at the level of ideas and law. A. Claire Cutler (2003, 199) has similarly identified the multiple ways in which corporations in a globalizing liberal economy 'are working with states in corporatist associations and enhancing state authority and control'.

The purposes and forms of state-business alliances vary significantly across different capitalist states and contexts. In Vietnam, the alliance between business and the state – and their shared role in shaping a repressive labour regime within the country – has played an important part in underpinning the development and growth strategy pursued by the Vietnamese government. In particular, the development of a labour-repressive regime has constituted an important part of the government's strategy for establishing the attractiveness of Vietnam as an investment location, which has crucially underpinned its growth strategies.

Long before Vietnam emerged as an export platform with high rates of growth and an enviable record of attracting foreign investment, it was a key to the burgeoning growth in Asian economies. This was due to the Vietnam conflict which 'provided an economic stimulus for regional states

---

9   Field research interview with non-government entity or union officer in Hanoi and Ho Chi Minh City, late December 2007.

10   Field research interview with factory management in industrial areas around Hanoi and Ho Chi Minh City, late December 2007.

(much as Japan had benefited in the 1950s from the Korean War)' (Marsh et al. 1999, 299). Decades passed, however, before Vietnam belatedly joined the new 'Asian tiger' economies of Thailand, Malaysia and Indonesia.

As part of a development strategy that emerged during these decades, the country emulated the business–government relations exhibited by neighbouring states and the 'State Steering' capacities of the developmental state, wherein 'business interests are well established and organized in most states, [but] the same cannot be said for trade unions' (Marsh 2005, 87).

The lawlessness of the corrupt, one-party state is scorned by numerous scholars as an insuperable impediment to economic development (Rose-Ackerman 1999, xi–xii). Such observers of the global political economy persist in hortatory declarations about the 'rule of law' and its importance to global business. According to Li-Wen Lin (2007, 353), corporations seek accountable legal systems, due process and transparency. More broadly, advocates of the law and economic development theory hold that 'law is an important pillar of economic growth'.

In fact, it appears that several low-skill industries have a marked preference for the opposite type of regime. Vietnam ranks very low in most independent assessments of basic rule of law indicia, yet FDI has been quite strong for over a decade. Indeed, the authoritarian state in Vietnam plays an important role in attracting an influx of FDI. Authoritarian regimes such as Vietnam, China or Indonesia (under Suharto) provide foreign capital with stability in industrial zones that sometimes resemble armed encampments. Ronnie Lipschutz and James Rowe (2005, 175) comment, 'violence is immanent in the market … in terms of the injustices it perpetuates as well as in the threat of punishment (by the state) for those who disturb its order.' Governments, when pressed, rationalize heavy-handed security and the breaking-up of strikes with appeal to 'the utilitarian welfare of populations' and the imperative of 'social stabilization' (Lipschutz and Rowe 2005, 175).

This choice of regime type and development strategy has had a number of important consequences for the shape of the Vietnamese labour regime. Vietnam is now a prime example of:

> Well-known trends associated with the restructuring of the labor-capital relation … [such as] 'downward leveling', deunionization, 'ad hoc' and 'just-in-time' labor supply, the superexploitation of immigrant communities as a counterpart to capital export, the lengthening of the workday, the rise of a new global 'underclass' of supernumeraries or 'redundants' subject to new forms of repressive and authoritarian social control, and new gendered and racialized hierarchies among labor. (Robinson 2004, 104)

The optimism expressed by Chan and Nørlund (1998, 175) – that Vietnam might carve out some political space for trade unions (while remaining short of the 'independent' ideal) – appears less likely now.

Implications for dynamics of conflict over wages within this labour regime are complex, reflecting the messy mix of influence between buyer-led supply chains and the business–state alliance shaping domestic labour regimes, as well as the ongoing negotiation and renegotiation over the terms of this multilevel relationship.

Industrial relations practices in Vietnam today differs from a classic labour–management confrontation in several ways:

1. Two groups of shareholders press for a higher return on investment: the shareholders of the buyers (the 'brands') and those of the manufacturers.

2. The producing factory has conflicting motivations: on the one hand, factory managers must avoid settlements with workers which would increase costs beyond what buyers are prepared to pay, given that there is an available supply from elsewhere; but on the other hand, managers cannot summarily reject worker demands that raise costs in cases where to do so may increase reputational costs for the buyers (Braun and Gearhart 2004).
3. Factory managers may intimidate workers with threats of moving the work elsewhere.
4. Self-regulatory CSR strategies also interact with classic wage-bargaining dynamics between workers and management, with classic worker–management confrontations and bargaining over wages tending to be displaced by 'self-regulatory' models which are used rhetorically as a proxy for worker 'voice' or involvement (a supplier company may fire 20 workers who have led a wage dispute strike; NGOs press buyers for immediate action to get workers rehired; the buyer and supplier agree on rehiring).

In almost no case is a government agency involved and trade union involvement is sporadic.[11]

Workers in Vietnam are left facing a perplexing matrix of power relationships in the FDI sector, which can be understood neither as a coincidence nor as a function of choices made by policy-makers in a vacuum. Rather, they reflect decisions made in the face of a wider system of national and international political economy (Gilpin 2001, 130). Rather than shaping policies that would support values of the rule of law, in seeking to carve out a competitive advantage, policy-makers in Vietnam have accommodated apparel and footwear suppliers, thereby demonstrating that: 'In the world of oligopolistic competition, powerful players can and frequently do use their market power to alter and manipulate the terms of exchange.' These markets 'function differently from the predictions of conventional neoclassical economics' (Gilpin 2001, 132, 132). These considerations determine the way in which an autocratic polity skews economic outcomes by the application of power as investors are favoured and protected. This tendency reflects the perverse incentives enticing policy-makers in the face of wider dynamics and structures in the international political economy. These external pressures in turn interact with changing internal dynamics and pressures, as the local embedding of global capital is accompanied by the globalization of domestic capital, at the same time empowering its national bourgeoisies, as described by Gerard Greenfield (2004, 171). In this context, economic success is not a 'gift from Mother Nature', but rather the deliberate matching of corporate needs with governmental policy choices (Gilpin 2001, 212–13).

The corrosive consequences of these complex patterns of power relations for workers' rights in Vietnam are further compounded by the weakness of worker awareness and organizing strength.

The Vietnam Resident Mission of the Asian Development Bank reports, albeit anecdotally, that workers interviewed were not aware of their rights – especially the internal migrants so prevalent in the garment and footwear for-export sectors (Nguyen et al. 2005, 20). One migrant worker in Beinh Duong found the description of labour legislation (minimum wage, labour contract and collective bargaining) 'very strange'. The interviewer further states of the respondent, 'he says he has never dared to have something like "negotiation" with his master on wages and other working conditions' (Nguyen et al. 2005, 43). While the overwhelming number of workers interviewed expressed confidence that they knew their workplace rights (20 of 27), it is most likely that these rights are particular to that workplace, since many workers suggested that this knowledge had been conveyed from management or trade union officials.

---

11   Field research interview with production worker (apparel or shoe) in industrial areas around Hanoi and Ho Chi Minh City, late December 2007.

The Failings of Prominent Strategies of Intervention

Against this backdrop, a range of different strategies associated with CSR discourses and agendas have presented themselves as possible means of addressing the problems documented above. Strategies of transnational activism have been one important area of activity, as have private regulatory systems including both social auditing and certification schemes and corporate self-regulatory schemes operated by individual companies or groups of companies.

A range of private regulatory schemes articulated through the lens of CSR has emerged in Vietnam, as it has in other producing locations across the world. The expansion of factory certification programmes for labour rights standards has offered the government of Vietnam a partial solution to a nettlesome problem. The prevalence of abusive conditions in foreign investment factories during the 1994–98 period fomented a societal backlash, evidenced by both domestic and foreign press reports. The 'promise' offered by new social regulatory schemes such as SA8000 (now Social Accountability International) was an improvement in conditions without the usual command and control system of the national labour inspectorate.[12] Self-regulatory schemes – operated by individual companies – offer similar promises. A range of self-help strategies have also been attempted.

None of these have proved successful as a means of empowering workers. Of all of these approaches, however, worker self-help holds the most promise. The various reasons for the weakness of such interventions are laid out in the following sections. While each of these interventions presents itself as a way to strengthen workers' rights, analysis shows the effectiveness of such interventions to be seriously limited. Indeed in some respects, each actually contributes actively to *undermining* progressive processes of rights realization by weakening worker-oriented norms, eroding the capacity for grassroots worker organizing and/or diminishing the role of the state in supporting worker-oriented groups.

Outcomes for Workers' Rights – A Persistent Record of Failure

To lay the foundations for an analysis of strategies of intervention, it is first useful to examine the record of similar interventions in terms of outcomes for workers' rights. While there is a distinct lack of direct evidence relating to the effects of interventions within the broad CSR umbrella on worker rights, the patchwork of evidence that is available paints a clear picture of ongoing worker abuse, in spite of the proliferation of CSR schemes and associated rhetoric.

It cannot be denied that the self-regulation edifice is an impressive and costly creation. Some evidence has been presented to suggest that interventions have also had some modest effects. Richard Appelbaum and Nelson Lichtenstein (2006, 118) observe that some poor conditions have been ameliorated since the large brands sought 'the goodwill of the non-governmental organizations' and put in place 'elaborate factory certification program[s]'.[13]

---

12   Evidence of SA8000 involvement was found in most industrial areas in Vietnam in late 2007. For example, during the author's field research conducted in 2007, many factory entrances were adorned with 'SA8000-certified' markings, numerous apparel company brochures alluded to it and it was even found on some garment hang-tags and stencilled onto packaging materials.

13   However, Reebok's estimate that the cost of 'adherence to a legal wage and safety standards' amounted to around four US dollars per pair of shoes (raising the cost of production from seven to 11 dollars a pair) was deemed 'excessive' by the same analysts (Appelbaum and Lichtenstein 2006, 118).

However, the limitations of self-regulation are all too evident in Vietnam today. Richard Locke et al. (2007) have undertaken extensive documentation of actual practices at factories, and compared these against pledges made by firms which have implemented extensive 'certification' and 'code of conduct' compliance programmes. Findings from this research paint a very mixed and complex picture. On some measures, it appeared that improved compliance was associated with more frequent audits. However, looking at 'the *same factories* over time ... a more negative picture emerges' (Locke et al. 2007, 19 [original emphasis]). Nearly half had not changed and over 36 per cent actually received lower compliance scores (Locke et al. 2007, 19). Findings from this research also suggest a negative correlation between better conditions and the length of supplier–buyer relationships – a finding with particular salience given the decades-long collaboration between large suppliers (mainly Taiwan- and Korea-based) and the large 'brand' buyers.

Such findings are broadly supported by a range of other research. One study carried out in Vietnam in 2007 for the ILO found that garment-for-export factories were experiencing 5–20 per cent turnover per month[14] and indicated widespread worker dissatisfaction.[15] In terms of trade union rights and willingness to discuss issues (short of bargaining), the foreign investment factories were declared the worst.[16] Other research has pointed to a range of workers' rights violations carried out by contractors for major brands such as Nike. In one case, workers who led a protest against forced overtime were fired; in another, workers were physically punished for production mistakes (Tran 2007, 435).[17] There is also reported to be ongoing and routine violations of the Vietnamese law on overtime by almost all footwear manufacturers, with infringements ranging from 1.5–2 times the legal limit (Twose and Rao 2003, 19).

Strike activity by workers can also function as an important indicator of workers' personal perceptions regarding the extent of their own exploitation. Examination of strike activity is particularly revealing, with recent strike waves mainly having hit those factories engaged in CSR programmes. Nike reported that, by mid-December 2007 workers in ten of its 35 supplier factories in Vietnam had taken industrial action in the previous year (Rovell 2008). In the immediately following three months, at least 31,000 workers at two additional Nike-producing factories had gone on strike. If monitoring, 'social auditing' and compliance regimes are producing more humane work places, it should be difficult to explain why around 80 per cent of strikes in Vietnam since 2006 have occurred in FDI factories.[18]

Media reports often tend to characterize the dramatic rise in worker activism in Vietnam as being a direct result of inflation (upwards of 14 per cent per annum), especially in food staples (Hasegawa 2008; Hookway 2008; Mitton 2008). In interviews conducted by the author with workers,[19] however, it is clear that other issues loom large. The wage question is in the forefront of workers' minds, although it has tended to be neglected in discussions of corporate responsibility. The main non-wage grievance among workers interviewed was forced overtime. Moreover, the

---

14   E-mail interview with L. Bennington, 4–5 April 2008 (on file).

15   Estimates from Nike are lower, with Nike's Amanda Tucker for example suggesting that turnover in Vietnamese factories producing for Nike was 25 per cent annually (De Ramos 2006).

16   Interview with VGCL officer in Hanoi, 2007.

17   Regarding the 2006–2007 strike wave – a perilous undertaking in a repressive state – Tran states that '[f]rom the workers' perspective, their collective action did not happen overnight but was gradually aggravated by a series of unfulfilled promises made by foreign management' (2007, 435–6).

18   See http://www.atimes.com/atimes/Southeast_Asia/JC18Ae02.html [accessed: 3 September 2009] and http://english.vietnamnet.vn/social/2008/12/816845/ [accessed: 19 May 2009].

19   Field research interview with production worker (apparel or shoe) in industrial areas around Hanoi and Ho Chi Minh City, late December 2007.

FDI factories, according to workers, have a tension-filled work environment with line supervisors frequently yelling and swearing. It was reported that management placed little priority on developing internal systems for mediating work related disagreements. In some factories sexual harassment has been reported to be increasing, with 'local' line supervisors now joining in, whereas earlier it had been only the foreign managers.[20]

Similar problems have been documented in relation to social audit and certification schemes such as SA8000. Managers have complained of 'audit fatigue', with too many buyers sending inspection certification teams. 'Inspection' methodology is also perceived to be flawed, with two managers reporting that workers were interviewed in the workplace, where it is unlikely that the interviewee would be comfortable enough to speak freely.[21]

Overall, despite the extensive development of 'cross-border solidarity' activities, increased consumer consciousness and extensive CSR programme implementation, the workplace abuses in Vietnam today differ little from those in Taiwan and Korea 35 years ago. How then can we make sense of this rather bleak record of progress on worker rights? The following discussion examines several prominent strategies of intervention, identifying key reasons for their relative lack of success.

Transnational Activism and the Weakness of Norm-creation

Analyses on the emergence of the CSR agenda often place strong emphasis on the importance of transnational activism as a means of promoting and diffusing corporate responsibility norms. Norm-creation processes are viewed as being directed partially by guidelines promoted by global civil society – especially international labour rights NGOs which seek to 'bypass their state and directly search out international allies to try to bring pressure … from outside' (Risse and Sikkink 1999, 18).

In contrast to this dominant narrative, analysis of Vietnamese cases suggests that, in fact, transnational activists have played a very limited role in processes of norm-creation in Vietnam. To be effective at promoting processes of norm change, transnational activist strategies need to be backed up by grassroots organizing. Such strategies also benefit from the formation of effective alliances with relevant state actors at the national level and, in some cases, also at the international level; effective timing of campaigns in relation to Northern political agendas can also be a very important factor. In the case of Vietnam, such preconditions for the success of activist strategies have generally not been met.

The timing of Vietnam's growth in the export of consumer goods to more developed countries plays an important role in explaining the relative lack of influence of transnational activism in this case. In the contrasting case of Indonesia, the stories of workplace abuses began to reach the 'consuming' countries in the same timeframe as the development of a general disquiet concerning

---

20 According to several respondents, their factory management has (for more than a decade now) operated in a most disrespectful manner towards line workers, shouting and cursing at mistakes made by workers, slowness of work and other common occurrences. Until 2005, the management employed translators for each department and they could often act as a buffer when disputes arose; the number of these interlocutors has steadily declined from over a dozen to none. Now, it is reported, Korean managers must call up to the main office to deploy a bilingual staff person; usually they just fulminate in a language workers will not understand, or shout the few abusive Vietnamese-language phrases they have learned.

21 Field research interview with factory management in industrial areas around Hanoi and Ho Chi Minh City, late December 2007.

globalization. This latter development occasioned a years-long exposition of the 'sweatshop' issue, in which factories in Indonesia were a prime focus. The attention focused on Indonesian 'sweatshops' was located at the apex of media interest paid to the issue more broadly (Bullert 2000, 6–9; Lipschutz and Rowe 2005, 79–86). By the time Vietnam reached the same point of development, international attention had subsided considerably and CSR programmes had become part of the 'common sense' of marketization (Peterson 2003, 144).

Another reason transnational advocacy networks did not appreciably influence developments in Vietnam is because such networks gain little ground in rights promotion 'without domestic mobilization to provide the necessary pressure from below' (Jetschke 1999, 166). In this sense, trans-border connecting has been more difficult for Vietnamese workers than it was for their Indonesian counterparts a decade earlier when a similar strike wave roiled the foreign-invested factory areas in that country, due in part to the relative lack of local labour rights NGOs or legal assistance groups in Vietnam.

Both the Indonesian and Vietnamese cases illustrate the effectiveness of barriers to norm change, which are constructed by the desire of dominant social interests and actors to retain control of norm setting agendas within important sites of state power, at both national and international levels (Robinson 2003, 219–21). In the presence of a tightly controlled media and a repressive state apparatus in Vietnam, many important processes of norm-creation have taken place at the level of intergovernmental organizations such as the WTO, which dominates prevailing economic policy-making and bureaucratic behaviour. Rights and protections enjoyed by workers where unions are free to operate *could* be part of the 'free trade' and WTO agenda, thus 'for the first time they would become enforceable and not depend on the whims of individual states. Labour wanted the WTO sheriff to include core labour standards on its beat' (O'Brien 2000, 80). Thus far, activists have made little progress in persuading the economically powerful states to join their networks in an effort to change human rights practices in this particular area, despite widespread recognition of the importance of such strategies as means of achieving institutionalized normative change (Risse and Ropp 1999, 238).

In addition to this, to the extent that activist discourses have had an influence on norms regarding worker rights, the willingness of many activist groups to engage extensively with corporate-led CSR discourses has undermined the capacity of activist strategies to authentically articulate stronger workers' rights norms. While some activist groups have attempted to distance themselves from wider CSR agendas, many have contributed to circulating varieties of CSR norms that may contribute to legitimizing exploitative labour–capital relations, as discussed further in the following section. To the extent that activists support the norms being propagated by the CSR movement instead of defending those articulated within intergovernmental labour rights institutions such as the ILO, they tend to contribute to the erosion of international labour rights norms which protect workers' rights.

Private Regulatory Regimes as a Hegemonic Project

The weakness of transnational advocacy networks as a means of strengthening either workers' rights norms or grassroots worker organizing is mirrored in relation to private regulatory regimes and CSR programmes, but to an even more severe degree.

On one level, CSR programmes and associated ideological rhetoric tend to promote norms that legitimize existing forms of corporate power at the expense of stronger norms of worker rights. In this sense, private regulatory regimes operate as a form of hegemonic project, in which the CSR discourses that are increasingly diffused among business elites and in the broader media operate to legitimize corporate-led capitalism and conceal the ongoing forms of worker abuse.

Since 1996, the self-regulatory activities of CSR have drawn a curtain of opacity in front of the world's export processing zones by substituting new normative values for accepted worker rights norms and deploying hundreds of 'certification' monitors into factory areas which host-government labour inspectors rarely, if ever, visit. A growing number of critical management scholars have attempted to draw more widespread attention to such hegemonic strategies of discourse construction. Martin Parker (2002, 93), for example, describes business ethics as 'the managerial colonization of emancipatory projects' with the appropriation of 'the very words that might be used to sponsor radical change … domesticated by managerialism and placed in the service of a globally rapacious capitalism'.

This strategy is labelled by Mark Barenberg (1994, 808–9) as 'universalization' of elite interests – that is, a strategy to portray 'practices that serve the particular interests of some group … as serving the interests of all'. Barenberg proceeds to cite British historian, E.H. Carr: 'any assailant of the interests of the dominant group is made to incur the odium of assailing the alleged common interest of the whole community … an ingenious moral device invoked … to justify and maintain their dominant position.'

These legitimating discourses are then disseminated through management circles via several mechanisms, impacting on ideas among managerial corporate elites. Business schools have played a particularly important role in diffusing norms of this kind. Many code of conduct (CoC) proponents are to be found in Western business schools where curricula have reflected a sharp increase in the importance of international trade and a concomitant rise in the level of interest in 'business ethics'.[22]

The hegemonic nature of CSR discourses being reproduced within business schools has tended to be compounded due to the lack of critical political thinking within the managerialist approaches dominant within business schools. Analysts such as Ken Starkey and Susan Tempest (2005) have commented on the relative absence of interdisciplinary perspectives informing the development of CSR discourse within business schools: '[t]he different discipline groups in the business school struggle to protect their world-view … with their own particular customs and practices which "represent the boundary-consciousness of a hermetic community threatened on all sides with social absorption"' (Starkey and Tempest 2005, 77 citing C. Geertz 1993, 151). Such tendencies run contrary to what analysts such as Starkey and Tempest have identified as a need for stronger critical interdisciplinary approaches to developing agendas around CSR, as a means of preparing business students to become 'critical reflective practitioner[s] who ha[ve] a wider understanding of the social, power and ethical implications of business practice' (Starkey and Tempest 2005, 74).

The assessment of self-regulation's impact has thus been largely an internal discussion amongst practitioners and a small group of (mostly business school) academics. As a result, a 'very particular form of market' is being promoted via dominant business school discourses – this is a market that is hierarchical with an inbuilt preference for 'huge disparities in status and reward' (Parker 2002, 119–201). This leads to a closed and self-referential discussion of business ethics/corporate responsibility, 'concerned to reinforce the moral legitimacy of the business organizations' (Parker 2002, 119–201). This also tends to reproduce a particular form of capitalism, in which the *status quo* of business power and practice is legitimized.

---

22   Jennifer Burns and Deborah Spar (2000) make an object lesson of Nike's tone-deafness on the sweatshop issue in their widely reprinted case study, *Hitting the Wall: Nike and International Labor Practices*. Bartlett et al. (2006) have used it in a popular business school textbook.

Such legitimizing norms are then diffused more widely by a range of other actors. Even institutions that in the past disagreed on how to best regulate international business – such as the United Nations and the Organization for Economic Co-operation and Development – are now foresquare in support of voluntary codes of conduct (Lipschutz and Rowe 2005, 149). Additionally, dozens, if not hundreds, of civil society groups have joined in as 'dialogue' partners; even critics who point out flaws in existing programmes may be viewed as a 'loyal opposition'[23] within self-regulatory projects seeking to acquire social legitimacy. Gérard Fonteneau (2003, 5) writes that unions are pushed aside in such processes as 'companies can choose the partners that suit them. … [T]he many stakeholders become more docile and flexible competitors.' Thus, the NGOs or 'responsible investment' communities provide an apparent check on abuses by displacing government regulatory agencies and workers' organizing struggles. Such discourses have also often been diffused via mainstream media, as 'corporate social responsibility' rhetoric has succeeded in changing the media frame from the earliest depictions of workers' struggles against unfair and often brutal employers – to a praiseworthy attempt by corporate buyers to rein in (by monitoring) their sometimes substandard suppliers (Bullert 2000, 12–13).

Private Regulation as a Means of Crowding Out More Meaningful Forms of Worker Empowerment

Private regulatory systems can also contribute to the erosion of worker rights at the level of grassroots organizing, as the expanded role of monitoring and certification agencies (and NGOs) appears to be 'crowding out' union involvement in settling workplace disputes. Buyer-driven 'freedom of association' policies may appear merely hortatory but these are likely to be disempowering for workers to the extent that they open the doors to an increased role for management-controlled company unions posing as legitimate representatives of worker interests. Workers may express an 'adaptive preference' for the faux participation of 'worker voice' projects (Freeman and Rogers 1999) foisted upon supplier-factory managers by the buyers, which may generate a subtle form of coercion in which alternative forms of independent union organizing may be rendered practically impossible. Barenberg (1994, 811) describes the US Supreme Court view of such company unionism practices in other contexts as 'induc[ing] false descriptive beliefs that blurred the distinction between inside and outside unions'. Further, 'in order to reduce the psychic frustration of not having the independent unionism that they initially preferred, workers' desire for, or valuation of, the attributes of outside unions may have diminished, or their valuation of company unionism and sense of common interest with management may have inflated' (Barenberg 1994, 810).

In this sense, the most deleterious effect of self-regulation may therefore be the 'other side of the coin' of Barenberg's description of company unionism. If workers are deceived, distracted and dispirited by buyer-driven self-regulation schemes, it is possible that the traditional avenues of assistance to nascent independent unions may be similarly affected. Numerous national and international trade union organizations and individual leaders have been drawn into dialogues, partnerships, conferences and pilot programmes with 'multi-stakeholder' groups or with corporations directly. Many of these activities have lent a (as yet undeserved) patina of respectability to corporate self-regulation. In addition, the time-consuming tweaking, critiquing and field assessment of CoC

---

23 'Ballinger … said [that] Eitel's work as vice president for corporate responsibility had rather "marginalized" his group and some others. He said Eitel headed a group of about 90 people who co-opted and partnered with various organizations, while those who didn't go along were called cranks' (Lewis 2009, 5).

practice by unions and labour rights NGOs has diverted precious resources from the challenging task of devising realistic worker empowerment strategies for workers in the autocratic states favoured by global capital.

Meanwhile, these CSR activities have had no discernable impact on altering underlying imbalances of knowledge, power and interest between different groups with a stake in workplace relations – management, shareholders, trade unions, consumers, NGOs and public authorities (Fonteneau 2003, 8–9). For example, a notable feature of the recent debates about minimum wage setting and FDI–VGCL relations – arguably the most important workplace debates in Vietnam in a decade – has been the near-irrelevance of CSR and CoC within this process. Devised and popularized by 'buyers' seeking to protect their companies' expensive brand images, it seems that they are simply not in the line-of-fire when issues of urgent concern to workers (and society) are being directly addressed.

Ultimately, these limitations of private regulatory initiatives can be understood as a product of the intrinsic limitations of distinctively 'private' initiatives as means of constraining market actors within the demands of public interests and norms. According to Lipschutz and Rowe (2005, 174), the 'inadequacy of trying to protect rights through market mechanisms' is attributable to the markets' lack of 'authority or capacity to make the provision and protections of rights a binding obligation on other private parties'. Indeed, corporations which signed onto multi-stakeholder arrangements, such as the Fair Labor Association, were afterwards heard to lament the fact that only a small number of market participants joined with them.[24] Attempts to extend the 'sphere of private law to the detriment of public law' generally tend to enable private bodies to act 'according to their own regulations' in a 'clear inversion of democracy: private companies pretending to know and ensure the common interest instead of the national and international public authorities' (Fonteneau 2003, 5).

Worker Self-help Strategies: Prospects for a Labour-oriented Alliance for Workers' Rights?

Confronted with the extensive weaknesses of a range of external interventions presenting themselves as means of strengthening workers' rights, and the widespread exclusion of workers from direct involvement in such schemes, workers have often relied on a range of 'self-help' strategies. They have attempted to press the government of Vietnam and factory managers for higher standards, challenging both hegemonic discourses and underlying power relations.

In some cases, such strategies have taken the familiar form of strike tactics. Increasing consumer prices in Vietnam since 2006 have led to widespread worker demands for increases to the minimum wage and such demands have often been advanced by means of 'wildcat' strikes. In part as a reaction to such strike activity, the government raised the minimum by 40 per cent in 2007 (Tran 2007, 430) and again by 13 per cent in 2008 (Ellis and Casabona 2008, 8).

In other cases, workers have attempted to harness the media as a means of supporting self-help strategies. While the influence of the trade union newspaper in Vietnam has declined in recent years, the Vietnamese press has not forsaken the workers altogether. Rather, it seems that there has been a shift from the trade union newspaper to the *Touitre* (youth) newspaper as a means of highlighting

---

24   Kevin Sweeney, 'Sweatshops: get more firms to adhere to the code of conduct on working conditions before tackling the salary issue', *Los Angeles Times*, 16 November 1998, Monday, Home Edition.

issues related to worker rights.[25] This is clearly not a substitute for labour law enforcement but it may generate some pressure to address the most egregious cases.

While such worker self-help strategies have not been without effect, they have faced serious challenges and obstacles at several levels. One very direct obstacle is presented by the widespread cooptation of union leadership, resulting from the collision between nascent *laissez-faire* capitalism and what Alfred Stepan (2001, 63–6) describes as a 'unified political community' with a 'monist relationship between the party-state and the citizens'. Because 'the privilege of official recognition' made unions in Vietnam part of the governing apparatus, the trade union apparatus tended to become subservient 'to demands orginating from the state'.

Such weaknesses within the trade union movement itself are underpinned in turn by the broader weakness and vulnerability of workers in Vietnamese society. The Civil Society Index – developed by the South Africa-based CIVICUS organization – ranks workers in Vietnam as the least influential grouping (out of 25), receiving the lowest possible score for social influence within the index (Nørlund et al. 2006, 35).[26]

Such weakness has tended to be reinforced by the disturbing spectre of state repression of trade union activity. Just as China and Indonesia jailed and harassed independent union activists, so Vietnam has sent strong warning signals to workers who have attempted to organize in order to press for meaningful change. The government appears to be particularly anxious to discourage recent strike activities, with the MOLISA issuing a warning that strikes could deter foreign investment (VNB 2008, 4).

In mid-December 2007, four independent union leaders were sentenced to prison. Doan Van Dien, Tran Thi Le Hong, Doan Huy Chuong and Phung Quang Quyen were sentenced for terms ranging from 18 to 54 months for 'spreading distorted information to undermine the state' (RFA 2008). The United Workers-Farmers Organization has campaigned for the right to form independent trade unions since mid-2006. It was banned by the government and, in this case, the activists were found guilty of 'abusing democracy and freedoms to infringe on the interests of the state', under article 258 of the legal code (RFA 2008). Less than two weeks later, workers who led a protest against forced overtime at the Korean San Yang shoe factory near Cu Chi were fired and arrested by local authorities.[27]

The Vietnamese government has also implemented a number of policies that seek to impede worker attempts to organize to demand strengthened worker rights protections. In mid-2006, the labour code was amended to provide sanctions for workers who participate in illegal strikes, while enabling workers who refuse to honour the strike call to be paid full wages. The MOLISA issued another regulation in mid-2007 which authorized village-level authorities to force striking workers back to work. The Committee to Protect Vietnamese Workers – operating from outside the country – suggests that such new power is 'yet another avenue for corruption … willing local authorities can now be bought by employers to act against workers'.[28]

What then does the above analysis suggest might be the prospects for the development of a labour-oriented alliance for worker rights that might underpin genuine improvements in outcomes

---

25   Field research interview with non-government entity or union officer in Hanoi and Ho Chi Minh City, late December 2007.

26   The soaring number of wildcat strikes and government responses – particularly concerning the minimum wage increases – would, however, be likely to lift Vietnamese workers' ranking.

27   Field research interview with production worker (apparel or shoe) in industrial areas around Hanoi and Ho Chi Minh City, late December 2007.

28   Telephone interview with Trung Doan, Chairman of the Committee to Protect Vietnamese Workers, 14 August 2008.

for workers? In part, this depends on the dynamics of interaction between attempted self-help strategies and the wider existence of activist and CSR strategies. We therefore need to consider whether it might be possible for self-help strategies to interact positively with broader strategies of private regulation and norm change, and thereby to lay the basis for a possible counter-hegemonic strategy.

As noted in the above discussion, there is a danger that the tendency of many civil society groups to play into dominant discourses of legitimation diffused via the CSR movement may lead workers' more transformative demands to be discounted, thereby doing more harm than good to the project of building counter-hegemonic resistance to corporate-led globalization. To the extent that civil society actors become stand-ins for the regulatory process and for self-help strategies by workers themselves, there is a real danger that they may 'eliminate the political debate that ought to accompany the regulatory process, thereby ignoring the right of the polity to participate in regulatory decisionmaking' (Lipschutz and Rowe 2005, 54–5). The dominance of legitimizing discourses promoted by business, CSR and activist rhetoric may also undermine worker organization, as discussed in more detail above.

On the other hand, however, the interaction between self-help strategies and broader agendas of CSR and related norm diffusion may play some kind of positive role in creating the underlying conditions for grassroots mobilization. Given the fact that prospects for 're-regulation' are remote, CSR and CoC strategies are deemed by many to be reasonable as an attempt to promote 'best practices' and stem abuses. One NGO interviewee expressed the opinion that 'there is a continuum in CSR practices': while some may be attempts to paper-over grievances, others play a role in helping workers to know their rights, assist in training trade union operatives ('for bottom up pressure') and help in recruitment for the VGCL.[29]

Furthermore, such interactions could potentially lay foundations for strengthened cross-border solidarity in the future, as strategies internationalize. Cross-border solidarity is not currently a factor in Vietnam's industrial relations matrix but, with the number of strikes recently aimed at 'world brand' producers, such multilevel engagements by labour organizations are likely to become an increasingly important feature of labour internationalism in this area (Harrod and O'Brien 2002, 26–7).

In this sense, we may regard the challenge for Vietnam's workers – who are already making some small progress in raising the minimum wage and winning factory-level settlements – as beginning to transnationalize their struggle. Through their efforts, they may help to build 'a new type of redistributive project transposed from the earlier national to the new transnational space' (Robinson 2003, 323).

On the one hand, transnational production chains do not appear to provide a fruitful ground for such a transnationalized form of worker struggle, given their propensity to act instead as a transnational channel for the exercise of unchecked corporate power in the absence of government attentiveness to industrial relations conditions. As William Robinson (2004, 67) highlights: '[t]ransnational production chains provide a much more expansive and fluid material basis for the transnational integration of class groups.' By the same token, however: '[g]lobalization turns the whole world into one giant zone of contestation. Local and global struggles may be linked through transnational alliances that set specific goals ... such as minimum wages in the *maquiladoras*' (Robinson 2004, 176).

---

29   Field research interview with non-government entity or union officer in Hanoi and Ho Chi Minh City, late December 2007.

This is not to say that the wildcat strikes which are now rife in the export-related, foreign-investment factories of Vietnam are organized by workers consciously associated with a resistance to global-capital movement. However, global capital is constrained somewhat in its choice of disciplining measures due to a *de facto* movement for global labour rights. While the political programme of striking shoe and apparel workers may be inchoate, the workers add to an overall sense that a 'crisis of the system's legitimacy' has begun to develop and could lead to a 'transnationally coordinated global justice movement' (Robinson 2004, 169).

Conclusions

In general, what potential is there for leveraging these complex and contradictory dynamics in favour of strengthened worker organizing and labour protection, and what appear to be some of the most important conditions under which such strategies are likely to be successful?

The idea of a worker-oriented alliance seems critically important – the undermining of existing alliances, or at least the failure to contribute to building new strengthened ones, is a major weakness of many of the reviewed initiatives. Such an alliance would need to involve labour-oriented international organizations, activist networks promoting authentic worker-oriented norms, together with strengthened worker organizations on the ground. The importance of linking such alliances to the state apparatus at the national level has also been shown to be very important. In this sense, the contribution of CSR discourses to providing a legitimation for the perpetuation of the business–state alliances that underpin weak regulatory systems at present is of particular concern.

Kevin Kolben (2007, 231) notes the potential of private regulation to '(a) be effective in improving workplace conditions if properly constructed and (b) work symbiotically with public regulation to help develop the capacity of dysfunctional regulatory regimes'. Indeed, the Vietnam/CSR study conducted by the World Bank places heavy emphasis on the capacity-building benefit of CSR and CoC 'monitoring' (Twose and Rao 2003, 9). Such reasoning appears to discount the very real possibility that poor regulatory performance may be attributable to a lack of political will rather than administrative capacity issues.

Kolben's other path – for potential improvements through self-regulation – is predicated on the regime being properly constructed. He goes on to identify the key driver for this task as consumer pressure, suggesting that 'there must be real demand by consumers for workers' rights compliance along supply chains' (2007, 231). The importance of NGOs – while essential in placing pressure on buyers – is severely limited 'without it affecting, or viably threatening to affect consumer behavior' (2007, 231). It seems fair to suggest, unfortunately, that no buyer today feels sufficient consumer pressure to test this hypothesis.

Overall, this chapter has painted a rather bleak picture of the dynamics through which prospective worker mobilization in defence of worker rights is being undermined by a complex matrix of state and corporate power which operates in the facilitating environment of corporate-led globalization. It further maps how these conditions are supported by pervasive hegemonic discourses associated with the contemporary CSR movement that serve to legitimize and reproduce these power structures. Existing efforts to develop worker self-help strategies so far have gained limited ground in the presence of this prevailing matrix of hegemonic power relations.

However, the future emergence of a global worker self-help movement that may operate as a genuinely counter-hegemonic project does not appear out of the question. Via the ongoing development of worker self-help strategies, and a critical awareness of how these power relations operate, it may be possible to develop stronger alliances between the established trade union movement and decision-makers within civil society and the state, taking advantage of emerging vulnerabilities and crises in the legitimacy of the exploitative and inequitable systems of transnational production that currently prevail. To the extent that workers are able to build effectively on such alliances and opportunities, it may be possible to work towards transnational strategies of worker self-help through which both dominant hegemonic discourses and dominant corporate–state power relations may be more effectively resisted.

References

Appelbaum, R. and Lichtenstein, N. (2006), 'A new world of retail supremacy: supply chains and workers' chains in the age of Wal-Mart', *International Labor and Working-Class History* 70(1): 106–25.

Bailey, J. (2003), *S&P Rates HK Yue Yuen's Convertibles BBB-*, press release, 28 November (Hong Kong: Standard and Poor's).

Baldwin, R.E. and Winters, L.A. (2004), *Challenges to Globalization: Analyzing the Economics* (Chicago, IL: University of Chicago Press).

Barenberg, M. (1993), 'The political economy of the *Wagner Act*: power, symbol, and workplace cooperation', *Harvard Law Review* 106(7): 137–9.

—— (1994), 'Democracy and domination in the law of workplace cooperation: from bureaucratic to flexible production', *Columbia Law Review* 94(3): 753–983.

Bartlett, C., Ghoshal, S. and Beamish, P. (2006), *Transnational Management: Text, Cases, and Readings in Cross-Border Management*, 5th edition (New York: McGraw-Hill).

Benvenisti, E. and Downs, G.W. (2007), 'The Empire's new clothes: political economy and the fragmentation of international law', *Stanford Law Review* 60(2): 595–631.

Bhagwati, J. (2002), *Free Trade Today* (Princeton, NJ: Princeton University Press).

—— (2004), *In Defense of Globalization* (Oxford: Oxford University Press).

Braun, R. and Gearhart, J. (2004), 'Who should code your conduct? Trade union and NGO differences in the fight for workers' rights', *Development in Practice* 14(1/2): 183–96.

Bullert, B.J. (2000), *Strategic Public Relations, Sweatshops, and the Making of a Global Movement*, Working Paper Series #2000-14 (Cambridge, MA: Joan Shorenstein Center on the Press, Politics and Public Policy).

Burns, J. and Spar, D.L. (2000), *Hitting the Wall: Nike and International Labor Practices*, Harvard Business School Series, 9-700-047 (Boston, MA: Harvard Business School Publishing).

Cameron, S. (2007), *Trafficking and Related Labour Exploitation in the ASEAN Region*, ICSW Briefing Paper (Utrecht: International Council on Social Welfare).

Chan, A. and Nørlund, I. (1998), 'Vietnamese and Chinese labor regimes: on the road to divergence', *China Journal* 40: 173–97.

Cillis, L. (2001), 'Da immigrati ad artigiani, i cinesi al primo posto' [From immigrants to entrepreneurs: the Chinese on top], *La Repubblica*, 6 August, 24.

Cutler, A.C. (2003), *Private Power and Global Authority: Transnational Merchant Law in the Global Political Economy* (Cambridge: Cambridge University Press).

De Ramos, A. (2006), 'Don't miss Saigon: doing business in Vietnam is better than ever, but still not for the faint-hearted', *CFO Asia*, 21 July. Available at: http://www.ebusinessforum.com/index.asp?layout=rich_story&doc_id=8658&categoryid=&channelid=&search=vietnamese [accessed: 12 June 2009].

Ellis, K. and Casabona, L. (2008), 'Sourcing peril looms from strife over food, energy prices', *Women's Wear Daily* (New York), 21 April,1, 8–9.

Fforde, A. (2004), *State Owned Enterprises, Law and a Decade of Market-oriented Socialist Development in Vietnam*, Working Paper Series 70 (Hong Kong: City University of Hong Kong). Available at: http://www.cityu.edu.hk/searc/WP70_04_Fforde.pdf [accessed: 11 June 2009].

Fonteneau, G. (2003), *Corporate Social Responsibility: Envisioning Its Social Implications*, TLWNSI Issue Essay (Moorpark, CA: Jus Semper Global Alliance).

Freeman, R.B. and Rogers, J. (1999), *What Workers Want* (New York: Cornell University Press).

Fukuyama, F. (1996), *Trust: The Social Virtues and the Creation of Prosperity* (New York: Free Press Paperback).

Geertz, C. (1993), *The Interpretation of Cultures: Selected Essays* (London: Fontana).

Gill, S. (1995), 'Globalisation, market civilisation and disciplinary neoliberalism', *Millennium* 24(3): 399–423.

Gilpin, R. (2001), *Global Political Economy: Understanding the International Economic Order* (Princeton, NJ: Princeton University Press).

Greenfield, G. (2004), 'Bandung redux: anti-globalization nationalisms in Southeast Asia', in L. Panitch and C. Leys (eds), *Socialist Register 2005: The Empire Reloaded* (London: Merlin Press), pp. 166–96.

Harrod, J. and O'Brien, R. (eds) (2002), *Global Unions? Theory and Strategies of Organized Labour in the Global Political Economy* (London: Routledge).

Hasegawa, T. (2008), 'Vietnam's surging inflation seen scaring away foreign money', *Nikkei Weekly* (Japan), 7 July.

Hookway, J. (2008), 'Labour unrest grows as Vietnam struggles to contain inflation', *Globe and Mail* (Canada), 3 June.

International Labour Organization (ILO) (2000), *Labour Practices in the Footwear, Leather, Textiles and Clothing Industries* (TMLFI/2000) (Geneva: ILO).

—— (2006), *Report III (Part 1B): Report of the Committee of Experts on the Application of Conventions and Recommendations (Articles 19, 22 and 35 of the Constitution)*, International Labour Conference, 95th Session (Geneva: ILO).

Jetschke, A. (1999), 'Linking the unlinkable? International human rights norms and nationalism in Indonesia and the Philippines', in T. Risse, S.C. Ropp and K. Sikkink (eds), *The Power of Human Rights: International Norms and Domestic Change* (Cambridge: Cambridge University Press), pp. 134–71.

Kolben, K. (2007), 'Integrative linkage: combining public and private regulatory approaches in the design of trade and labor regimes', *Harvard International Law Journal* 48(1): 203–56.

Lewis, N. (2009), 'Obama's swoosh shot', *Youth Today* (Washington, DC), 1 June.

Li, Q. Taylor, B. and Frost, S. (2003), *Labour Relations and Regulation in Vietnam: Theory and Practice*, Southeast Asia Research Centre Working Paper Series No. 53 (Hong Kong: City University of Hong Kong).

Lin, L.-W. (2007), 'Corporate social accountability standards in the global supply chain: resistance, reconsideration, and resolution in China', *Cardozo Journal of International and Comparative Law* 15(2): 321–70.

Lipschutz, R.D. and Rowe, J.K. (2005), *Globalization, Governmentality, and Global Politics: Regulation for the Rest of Us?* (London: Routledge).

Lipsey, R.E. and Sjoholm, F. (2004), 'Foreign direct investment, education and wages in Indonesian manufacturing', *Journal of Development Economics* 73(1): 415–22.

Locke, R.M. (2002), 'The promise and perils of globalization: the case of Nike', in T.A. Kochan and R. Schmalensee (eds), *Management: Inventing and Delivering Its Future* (Cambridge, MA: MIT Press), pp. 39–74.

—— Qin, F. and Brause, A. (2007), 'Labor standards? Lessons from Nike', *Industrial and Labor Relations Review* 61(1): 3–31.

Magnusson, P., Balfour, F., Shari, M., Kripalani, M., Roberts, D., Smith, G. and Mangi, N. (2003), 'Where free trade hurts: Thirty million jobs could disappear with the end of apparel quotas', *Business Week*, 15 December. Available at: http://www.businessweek.com/magazine/content/03_50/b3862007.htm [accessed: 11 June 2009].

Maquila Solidarity Network (2008), *Clearing the Hurdles: Steps to Improving Wages and Working Conditions in the Global Sportswear Industry*, Play Fair 2008 Campaign. Available at: http://www.playfair2008.org/docs/Clearing_the_Hurdles.pdf [accessed: 11 June 2009].

Marsh, I. (2005), 'Democratization and state capacity in East and Southeast Asia', *Taiwan Journal of Democracy* 2(2): 69–92.

—— Blondel, J. and Inoguchi, T. (1999), *Democracy, Governance and Economic Performance: East and Southeast Asia* (Tokyo: United Nations University Press).

Mitton, R. (2008), 'Vietnam workers fight for better pay; strikes turning violent and factories shut as they strike for wages to keep up with inflation', *Straits Times* (Singapore), 20 May.

Moran, T.H. (2003), *Reforming OPIC for the 21st Century* (Washington, DC: Peterson Institute for International Economics).

Nguyen, T.K.D., Nguyen, M.H., Tran, T.H. and Tran, K.C. (2005), *Making Markets Work Better for the Poor: Labor Market Segmentation in Vietnam: Survey Evidence* (Hanoi: Asia Development Bank).

Nolan, P., Zhang, J. and Liu, C. (2008), 'The global business revolution, the cascade effect, and the challenge for firms from developing countries', *Cambridge Journal of Economics* 32(1): 29–47.

Nørlund, I. et al. (ed.) (2006), *The Emerging Civil Society: An Initial Assessment of Civil Society in Vietnam*, CIVICUS Civil Society Index Shortened Assessment Tool, CSI-SAT Vietnam (Hanoi: CIVICUS).

O'Brien, R. (2000), 'The World Trade Organization and labour', in R. O'Brien, A.M. Goetz, J.A, Scholte and M. Williams (eds), *Contesting Global Governance: Multilateral Economic Institutions and Global Social Movements* (Cambridge: Cambridge University Press), pp. 67–108.

Palley, T. (2004), 'The economic case for international labour standards', *Cambridge Journal of Economics* 28(1): 21–36.

Parker, M. (2002), *Against Management: Organization in the Age of Managerialism* (Oxford: Wiley-Blackwell).

Peterson, V.S. (2003), *A Critical Rewriting of Global Political Economy: Reproductive, Productive and Virtual Economies* (London: Routledge).

Qi, L., Taylor, B. and Frost, S. (2003), *Labour Relations and Regulation in Vietnam*, South East Asia Research Centre Working Paper Series, No. 53 (Hong Kong: City University of Hong Kong).

Radio Free Asia (RFA) (2008), *Vietnam Upholds Dissident Jail Terms*. [Radio broadcast, 27 February]. Distributed by Radio Free Asia, Vietnam. Available at: http://www.rfa.org/english/news/vietnam/vietnam_dissident-20080227.html [accessed: 12 June 2009].

Republic of Vietnam (RoV) (2001), 'On reorganizing the work of inspection and examination at enterprises', Directive No. 22/2001/CT-TTg. Available at: http://laws.dongnai.gov.vn/2001_ to_2010/2001/200109/200109110004_en/lawdocument_view [accessed: 4 June 2009].

Risse, T. and Ropp, S.C. (1999), 'International human rights norms and domestic change: conclusions', in T. Risse, S.C. Ropp and K. Sikkink (eds), *The Power of Human Rights: International Norms and Domestic Change* (Cambridge: Cambridge University Press), pp. 234–78.

Risse, T. and Sikkink, K. (1999), 'The socialization of international human rights norms into domestic practices: introduction', in T. Risse, S.C. Ropp and K. Sikkink (eds), *The Power of Human Rights: International Norms and Domestic Change* (Cambridge: Cambridge University Press), pp. 1–38.

Robinson, W.I. (2003), *Transnational Conflicts: Central America, Social Change, and Globalization* (London: Verso).

—— (2004), *A Theory of Global Capitalism: Production, Class and State in a Transnational World* (Baltimore, MD: Johns Hopkins University Press).

Rose-Ackerman, S. (1999), *Corruption and Governments: Causes, Consequences, and Reform* (Cambridge: Cambridge University Press).

Ross, R. (2004), *Slaves to Fashion: Poverty and Abuse in the New Sweatshops* (Ann Arbor, MI: University of Michigan Press).

Rovell, D. (2008), *Swoosh! Inside Nike*. [Television broadcast, 12 February]. Distributed by CNBC, US (news transcript on file).

Starkey, K. and Tempest, S. (2005), 'The future of the business school: knowledge challenges and opportunities', *Human Relations* 58(1): 61–82.

Stepan, A. (2001), *Arguing Comparative Politics* (New York: Oxford University Press).

Tran, A.N. (2007), 'Alternatives to the "race to the bottom" in Vietnam: minimum wage strikes and their aftermath', *Labor Studies Journal* 32(4): 430–51.

Twose, N. and Rao, T. (2003), *Strengthening Developing Country Governments' Engagement with Corporate Social Responsibility: Conclusions and Recommendations from Technical Assistance in Vietnam: Final Report* (Washington, DC: World Bank).

Vietnam News Briefs (VNB) (2008), 'Wave of labor strikes surge in Vietnam', *Vietnam Panorama* (Hanoi), 18 January, 4.

World Bank (2005), *Local Governance, Transparency and Anti-Corruption in Community-Driven Development in Vietnam* (Hanoi: Rural Development and Natural Resources East Asia and Pacific Region).

Yue Yuen Industrial (Holdings) Limited (2006), *2006 Annual Report* (Hong Kong: Yue Yuen Industrial (Holdings) Limited). Available at: http://www.yueyuen.com/hk/annual/2006/E_ Yue%20Yuen%20AR-1754.pdf [accessed: 11 June 2009].

Chapter 13

Can CSR Help Workers Organize?
An Examination of the Lessons Learnt
and an Exploration of a New Way Forward

Andrea Maksimovic

Introduction

Labour activists have had an uneasy relationship with the corporate social responsibility (CSR) movement since its birth. They have greeted it with a mixture of support, cynical engagement and opposition: sometimes attempting to gain leverage from existing initiatives; at other times sidestepping existing initiatives and generating their own. This chapter first examines instances in which labour activists and labour unions have attempted to use CSR instruments to gain greater control for workers over their working and living conditions. Two main examples will be used to illustrate the relative difficulties of utilizing international mechanisms by trade unions and civil society organizations: the OECD Guidelines on Multinational Enterprises and the Palm Oil Roundtable. The work of various organizations such as the Clean Clothes Campaign, and a range of initiatives in the clothing sector will also be critically examined in order to discern lessons for civil society, including the dangers associated with the burgeoning social audit industry.

Next, the chapter examines instances in which labour activists have generated their own corporate accountability (CA)[1] initiatives. As a result of the shortcomings of existing CSR instruments and/or as a particular consequence of the lack of sustainable instruments, civil society has been involved in developing home-grown strategies. Such strategies utilize a mixture of cross-border trade union organization, links between consumers and producers, and local community involvement. These new strategies will be examined with a view to their potential for increasing the scope of civil society's role in supply-chain governance.

The Birth of the CSR Industry

In the debate over the effectiveness of corporate social responsibility, and particularly its global dimension, it is worth remembering how we came to be at this point in time – a time in which CSR terminology rolls off the tongues of corporate executives and governments alike with such ease that one could be forgiven for thinking that the dynamics of the global supply chain have changed significantly.

The origins of CSR are to be found somewhere in the realization of the early 1980s that more and more of the world's workplaces existed in transnational supply chains which were often

---

1   See Peter Utting in this volume for an explanation of the difference between the terms 'corporate social responsibility' and 'corporate accountability'.

immune to local labour laws and practices. It further stems from the belief that business can solve problems. CSR was never intended to empower workers to take an active role in defining the management practices of their workplaces. Rather, it has almost always been conceived of as a unilateral management response to the growing criticism of and public distrust of business, driven by stories of relocation, greed, corporate scandals and frequent reporting in the global North of the exploitation of workers and environmental destruction in countries of the global South. Most of these scandals relate to the failure of national governments to fulfil their role or the failure to develop rules governing the behaviour of business at the international and intergovernmental level.

Furthermore, many CSR initiatives emerged from the campaigns of the environmental movement, thus leading to the notion of making the 'business case for CSR' which emphasized that strategies such as eco-efficiency can, in fact, save money.

The rise of CSR has given birth to a CSR industry which advises companies and many governments and intergovernmental organizations, including the European Union and the OECD, creating their own policies on CSR. Multi-stakeholder initiatives (MSIs) have also proliferated, one of which will be addressed further below. With a few notable exceptions, most codes of conduct and standard-setting initiatives[2] make no mention of trade unions or collective bargaining, preferring instead to include freedom of association in a longer list of human rights and qualified with 'where lawful'. MSIs largely include some form of civil society representation. Yet while NGOs may have good policy intentions, they do not directly represent those affected by a company's behaviour. The dimensions of this dilemma will be further explored below.

The Least Worst Option: The OECD Guidelines for Multinational Enterprises

In international labour movement circles, when asked to identify a reasonable model of the regulation of transnational company behaviour, the OECD Guidelines for Multinational Enterprises are often pointed to as a standard-setting initiative. Originally adopted in 1976, the Guidelines were updated in 2000 to include all of the human rights incorporated in the 1998 International Labour Organization (ILO) Declaration on the Fundamental Principles and Rights at Work, often referred to as Core Labour Standards. They are the authoritative guidelines for government and, although recommendations and thus not legally binding, they are applicable to all enterprises that fall within their scope. It is not necessary for companies to sign up to the Guidelines: all companies based in the territories of adhering governments (the OECD countries as well as Argentina, Brazil, Chile, Estonia, Latvia, Lithuania, Slovenia, Romania and Israel) are expected to observe the Guidelines wherever they operate.

The follow-up procedures stipulate that every country is expected to set up a National Contact Point (NCP) which is responsible for promoting the Guidelines and contributing to the resolutions of problems concerning their application. Trade unions and other concerned parties can raise complaints under the Guidelines, which focus on dialogue and problem resolution.

The role of NCPs is crucial: they decide whether to take the complaint forward – that is, they determine admissibility. Many trade unions and labour organizations which have attempted to use the OECD Guidelines have found this to be a major stumbling block. In a June 2007 meeting of OECD Watch – a group set up in 2005 to evaluate the effectiveness of the Guidelines – all

---

2   Standard-setting initiatives involve some form of 'certification' that companies can use to publicize their product's compliance to a particular standard.

participants emphasized that there was a great need to improve NCP policies and procedures. According to OECD Watch, out of the 60 OECD Guidelines cases filed by trade unions and NGOs in the last seven years, only three have ended satisfactorily (Smith and Partners 2007). Activists attempting to use the Guidelines are further obstructed by confidentiality regulations. According to NCP rules, while matters are being addressed the details of the complaint are not to be made public. This means that if a dispute erupts while the process is underway, the regular campaigning techniques labour organizations might use to attempt to resolve the dispute are restricted.

This was recently highlighted in a complaint filed through the Guidelines by the Clean Clothes Campaign (CCC) against G-Star. The CCC is an international campaign, involving 11 European member countries, focused on improving working conditions in the global garment and sportswear industries. The CCC and the India Committee of the Netherlands (another NGO working to inform the Dutch public about the impact of Western policies on Indian people) have been publicly urging the Indian garment companies Fibres and Fabrics (FFI), Jeans Knit (JKPL) and companies currently sourcing from them to address workers' rights violations in India, including an attempt at silencing the local trade union, the Garment and Textile Workers' Union (GATWU). In July 2006, FFI/JKPL had taken out a court order gagging the local union on the basis of a libel complaint. By October 2006, most of the companies had stopped sourcing from this supplier with the exception of G-Star. The CCC filed a complaint against them with the Dutch NCP.

In a significant move which will have significant consequences for international labour campaigning, in January 2007, the CCC, the India Committee and their two Dutch internet providers were accused of 'indulging in a systematic, planned conspiracy to malign and cause harm and damage to the business, image and reputation of our clients by deliberately publishing false information' by FFI/JKPL's lawyers. They were informed that they would be charged with 'offences including cyber crime' unless they, firstly, withdrew all references to the case from their website and, secondly, stopped bullying companies buying from FFI/JKPL into demanding that they drop charges against the local trade union (Pramila Associates 2007).

In June 2007, the two campaign organizations were summoned to appear in a Bangalore court. As they failed to appear, on September 2007, a warrant was issued for their arrest. At this point, the international implications of this case became apparent and a number of organizations including Amnesty International and the International Trade Union Confederation issued statements in support of the activists. These statements had no evident impact. In a further twist, during a state visit by the Dutch Queen to India in the same month, the Indian Minister of Economic Affairs, Sri Kamal Nath, confronted the delegation with the issue, accusing the Dutch government of funding labour rights organizations which threatened India's sovereignty and labelling their interference a 'non-tariff trade barrier'. This accusation was widely interpreted as a veiled threat to use the WTO dispute mechanism on the basis of anti-competitive behaviour. Ironically, the CCC had requested that the Queen raise the issue with the Indian government, however, the Queen's delegation had refused. Nath subsequently held a press conference in which he revealed that he had also written to the Finnish government and the EU Trade Commissioner, Peter Mandelson, to make similar allegations.

Despite repeated calls by a growing number of organizations for the Indian government to intervene in the dispute and prevent its further escalation, on 1 December 2007, the Bangalore court issued an international arrest warrant for the seven Dutch activists and the director of their internet provider, Antenna, calling on the Indian Ministry of Home Affairs to request their extradition.

The confidentiality requirements attached to making complaints through the Guidelines had, throughout this period, prevented the labour activists from employing their normal channels of campaigning – naming and shaming – against G-Star as the last client of the suppliers in question.

Frustrated by the lack of NCP progress, they subsequently chose to abandon the process and continued to the pressure G-Star to withdraw its orders from FFI by urging their supporters to write to the company.

Whilst G-Star publicly acknowledged that the gag order on the local unions under Indian law was a hindrance to freedom of association, this did not lead the company to abandon ties with its supplier companies. Instead, it commissioned the company SGS to execute an audit to assess compliance with freedom of association elements of its clauses. After extensive lobbying by Clean Clothes and their supporters, many MSIs, including the Ethical Trading Initiative (ETI) and the Social Accountability International (SAI), expressed concerns that the gag order on local organizations was a fundamental barrier to assessing compliance. They voiced further concerns that there was evidence that workers had been coached for the audit and pointed to the SGS's conflict of interest as the company involved in issuing FFI/JKPL with a SA8000 certificate for meeting SAI social accountability standards (this certification was subsequently withdrawn). Despite the concerns raised by credible MSIs, G-Star supported the findings of the audit report, which confirmed that FFI/JKPL were in compliance with the right of freedom of association. However, G-Star refused to make the report publicly available.

Following the issue of international arrest warrants, G-Star attempted to distance itself from the scandal. On 4 December 2007, it withdrew its orders with the two Indian suppliers. The CCC had repeatedly asked G-Star to withdraw orders within the framework of a strategy which would transfer the orders to other local factories and ask those factories to employ the FFI staff who would be rendered jobless by this action. G-Star did not comply with this demand. Eventually, on 29 January 2008, the parties to the court case came to an agreement and the charges were dropped.[3]

This case study reveals a number of emerging issues concerning the use of CSR to defend labour rights: the rise of the power of sub-contractors; the threat of using WTO dispute mechanisms to stop international labour campaigning; and the virtual impotence of the OECD Guidelines in resolving disputes. The traditional model of CSR-type initiatives has relied on utilizing consumer and labour activist pressure to convince sourcing companies to require adherence to fair labour standards by their sub-contractors. Whilst the CCC is accustomed to brands threatening to sue them for defamation, in this case the sub-contractor has been the most aggressive by pursuing both lobbying action and legal action against activists in a local court. Although all the brands sourcing from the company had severed their contracts with FFI/JKPL over the duration of the dispute, this did not stop the supplier from continuing its chosen train of action. The dispute was resolved not by G-Star's action, but by a massive mobilizing effort involving the Dutch government.

The trend of mid-level suppliers gaining and wielding power in their own right is one that will challenge the traditional model of labour rights campaigning. No consumer in the United States or Europe has ever heard of FFI or JKPL, which made mobilizing pressure once the brands had pulled out all the more difficult. The involvement of internet provider Antenna in legal proceedings is a further blow to the promise of global North–global South CSR collaboration, as it relies heavily on the ability of Northern consumers to target the companies in question through cyberspace. This case also points to an emerging issue that labour campaigners need to address: it is no longer just a question of taming Northern capital; increasingly, it is a question of taming local (Southern) capital, to which all those struggling with the challenge of Asian MNCs can attest.

The intervention of the Indian government is also unprecedented, particularly with regards to its threat to employ WTO mechanisms. It is clear that the case has become a *cause célèbre* for the

---

3   For more background information concerning the case, see www.cleanclothes.org.

Indian government, which has traditionally been reticent about combining the issues of labour rights and trade, as evidenced by its refusal in the WTO – as well as numerous bilateral agreements – to include any clauses or references to the issue. The fact that the Indian government considers the exploitative practices of their citizens by TNCs as a competitive advantage is of considerable concern. It is the opinion of labour activists that this view will only be changed through insistence that local labour laws are strengthened and applied more rigorously.

This case study exposes the limits of even the best CSR mechanisms. Because of the failure of the OECD Guidelines to deliver improved labour standards in this case, as in others, the Guidelines, along with other CSR mechanisms, are likely to be increasingly circumnavigated by labour activists in future. The ineffectuality of the complaint brought against G-Star under the OECD Guidelines points to the inability of the process to respond in a timely fashion to a fast-moving, concerted campaign against trade unions and their supporters.

In March 2007, the European Parliament passed a resolution calling for an improvement in the functioning of NCPs and it is currently considering how the Guidelines can be applied in a binding manner through EU trade agreements. These movements signal a wide recognition that the clock is ticking on voluntarism and, moreover, that there are serious concerns being raised by stakeholders about the effective delivery of the OECD Guidelines as a voluntary instrument.

Codes of Conduct, Multi-stakeholder Initiatives and the Supply Chain

Codes of conduct have been implemented most prominently by companies in the clothing, footwear and toy industries, with relatively recent additions in the agriculture industry. While some trade unions sought to be involved, this raised the issue of trade unions from 'host' countries participating in the negotiation of codes on behalf of workers in developing countries where trade unions were weak or non-existent. As a result, local unions had no control over the management policy they were trying to influence and the mechanisms established are unsustainable as they are difficult to enforce without locally organized workers. Many of the codes adopted by companies operate in locations where national laws are prohibitive to freedom of association and collective bargaining. Use of the codes allows companies to make public claims that they operate without violating human rights. For example, trade unions have attempted numerous times to push for a greater presence in China through the CSR initiatives of friendly companies such as IKEA and Heineken. However, the limits of this strategy have been quickly recognized. While this strategy may afford some opportunities, as soon as a small number of workers begin organizing and pushing beyond the accepted norms, they are quickly pulled into line.

A further danger for trade unions in 'host' countries relying upon or endorsing the use of company codes is that they are typically cited by companies as a justification for operating in countries with repressive regimes. It has been argued that through codes of conduct or social auditing initiatives, companies can ensure the workers in their particular supply chain are not exploited. In reality, however, local labour activists are unable to associate or organize freely due to the countervailing pressures of local legislation. The hollowness of this justification used by companies was exposed recently when the US and EU Chambers of Commerce lobbied the Chinese government heavily over its intention to reform labour laws in order to give workers increased protection, yet still denied them the right to join the union of their choice and bargain collectively.

Verification is one issue for companies in relying on codes. How does a company know that its supplier or sub-contractor is observing the code? A further difficulty is determining what action the company should take if the code has been breached. In response to these difficulties, a new industry of 'social auditors' – who act as private labour inspectors – has emerged, as well as numerous 'multi-stakeholder' initiatives.

The social auditing industry has caused considerable cynicism about code implementation. Companies generally assert that the monitoring required by codes is ongoing and independent, but recent research has cast a shadow over these claims (see Pruett 2005). More often than not, the sheer volume of resources that trade unions and NGOs have devoted to monitoring the monitors has been a drain on their capacity. The most high-profile failure of social auditing in recent times led to 64 dead and 80 injured workers in a clothing factory collapse in Bangladesh in April 2005. Many of the companies sourcing from this factory were members of the Business Social Compliance Initiative, an industry-controlled code-monitoring mechanism, which had repeatedly failed to detect not only that there were serious labour rights violations (like the minimum one day off), but also that the factory was in violation of its construction permit.

The limits of social auditing have now been recognized by some of the largest brands in the clothing industry. In fact, Nike, the company we used to love to hate, has admitted that problems which are identified and appear to be resolved simply recur once auditors have left. This is why they have instead made public their entire supply chain. They have also encouraged the organization of trade unions as the only permanent system of verification of compliance to labour standards. This example gives rise to some hope that companies may adopt better practices. History suggests that they need to go through a series of failed social audits to come to this understanding. The Nike case is unique simply due to the company's long-time position as a high-profile target.

Other benefits have come from codes. The most important of these is an acceptance by companies that what happens in their supply chain is 'their business'. Recently, many companies have incorporated ILO standards into their codes. This must be seen as the result of constant pressure by organizations such as the CCC, which has sought to promote transparent mechanisms that require direct input from workers and their organizations. A number of such procedures exist[4] and are increasingly being adopted, both by companies as a means of solving problems and by labour rights activists as another avenue for pressuring companies to make improvements.

In most cases where code compliance mechanisms are invoked, governmental bodies are also approached in order to maximize pressure and draw attention to the broader, systemic issues. An examination of the organizational level at which complaints are made revealed that local workers' organizations do so directly to local management, whereas labour activists and international organizations raise complaints to sourcing companies and relevant MSIs (see Ascoly and Zeldenrust 2003). The MSIs have themselves developed mechanisms to receive complaints and, in some cases, provisions for their member companies to handle complaints, with attempts to solve problems made firstly at the workplace level. For example, as a condition of certification, the SAI requires that suppliers have a mechanism in place to handle complaints raised to management by workers.[5] The SAI's procedures are the most developed CSR instruments, however, they lack clarity regarding where workers are expected to take their complaint. If they must lodge their complaint with the same body which initially certified the company, conflicts of interest may arise

---

4   These are mostly used by clothing and footwear multi-stakeholder initiatives and include the Worker Rights Consortium (WRC), the Fair Labour Association (FLA), the ETI, the SAI and the FairWear Foundation (FWF).

5   SAI-certified companies must appoint a management representative responsible for ensuring there is a confidential, accessible system for workers to lodge complaints. Furthermore, workplaces must have an elected SA8000 representative who can be contacted by workers for more information or assistance in raising the complaint. An appeals mechanism must also involve the certification body and SAI directly, with a requirement of protecting the complainant's identity.

and, in some cases, this has frustrated the inquisitorial process. For instance, in the Indonesian case of PT Kasrie in 2002, the certification auditor restated the conclusions reached in its original audit, essentially creating delays in uncovering the problems and incurring unnecessary expenses.

The Workers Rights Consortium (WRC) initiative calls for maximum participation of local and regional actors in the complaints process as it seeks concurrently to empower and strengthen the investigative capacity of local and regional actors. This raises an often recurring important question of how the capacity of workers can be increased where, initially, the skills needed for workers and local actors to be involved in auditing processes often do not exist. Their involvement is often seen as prolonging the auditing process or complaint mechanism, rendering it less efficient. However, this investment is crucial if we are to be serious about developing better functioning and more sustainable complaints mechanisms.

Workers involvement in auditing entails additional issues, such as the protection of local workers' identities, and addressing the risk that management-controlled workers' organizations will be the main workers' body involved in auditing rather than independent workers' organizations.

Other issues which arise during the course of making a complaint include addressing the limited capacity of workers to file a complaint and gather the required evidence, as well as ensuring that the complaint is filed with workers' agreement. The time delay involved in investigating a complaint may also make the process unpalatable to workers. In the garment industry, workers fired illegally for organizing for a minimum wage frequently spend several months demanding back pay, reinstatement or severance benefits; eventually these workers need to continue working elsewhere to support themselves. As many garment workers are migrants, they return to their hometowns when blacklisting prevents them from being hired elsewhere, thus making the complaint 'disappear'. Furthermore, the mechanisms do not deal comprehensively with the operations of short-term suppliers.

Other identified risks include the possibility that brands will 'cut and run' following a negative audit. Increasingly, this is not a brand-driven strategy; in a number of recent incidences, suppliers have refused to cooperate with any suggested changes (for example, Tarrant in Mexico and PT Kahatex in Indonesia 2003). Given the increasing number of large supplier conglomerates in these sectors – often multinational corporations themselves, built with or controlled by Asian capital – it is possible that the power dynamics in supply networks are such that a supplier can readily afford to lose a client. On the other hand, sourcing companies may be using the refusal of suppliers to cooperate as a convenient excuse to avoid exploring all the available options, such as the promise of long-term relations and/or investments.

Multi-stakeholder Initiatives and the Potential for Division

MSIs are most prevalent in the clothing and footwear industries, however, such mechanisms are becoming widespread in other industry sectors, most notably agriculture. While many years of experience and hard work in the clothing industry have led to an agreed way of working amongst key stakeholders, including trade unions at both local and global levels and NGOs, the lessons learnt have not necessarily been transposed to other industries. Further knowledge transfer concerning MSIs is needed from industry to industry – the larger international organizations are committed to participating in this process.

A recent incident in the agriculture industry points to the need for such learning to occur. Many NGOs campaign within this industry and a range of initiatives exist as a response to the social and environmental impacts of agricultural practices. The palm oil industry is particularly key in many of the renewable fuel targets set by governments and the EU in particular as they seek to combat climate change. Palm oil is also an essential ingredient in many processed foods, detergents and personal care products. However, the expanding cultivation of palm oil has not been mirrored by expanding rights for palm oil workers. The work remains hard and dangerous as production techniques have hardly changed in 150 years, and large amounts of toxic herbicides are sprayed during cultivation. One initiative in this sector, the Roundtable on Sustainable Palm Oil (RSPO), was set up in 2004 by a number of palm oil producers (growers and processors), banks/investors and retailers such as Sainsbury's, as well as manufacturers such as Unilever and the NGO, the WWF. It emerged out of environmental concerns linked to deforestation as well as social conflicts arising from land disputes between plantation owners and local communities.

The RSPO sought to develop criteria for sustainable production and use of palm oil, promote best practices and communicate with consumers regarding the value of sustainable palm oil production. In 2005, Oxfam UK and the Netherlands joined the initiative. Organizations can become members by simply filing an application to the Executive Board and committing themselves to the RSPO's objectives. Until very recently no codes or verification systems were involved in the Roundtable processes.[6]

It is perhaps not surprising that the Roundtable came under fire in 2005 following the actions of one of its prominent Indonesian member companies, PT Musim Mas. Despite the fact that KAHUTINDO PT Musim Mas – a legally registered trade union – represented 1,183 workers out of a total workforce of 2,000, the company systematically refused to recognize the union or negotiate with them regarding the implementation of minimum legal standards for plantation workers required under Indonesian law. Instead, the company's response was to: dismiss trade union officers; simultaneously sack 701 union members; refuse to renew the contracts of an additional 300 unionized contract workers; forcibly evict 700 workers and their families from their plantation housing; and expel their children from school. In order to destroy the union, the company finally orchestrated the arrest and conviction of key union officers, who were detained in the presence of the company manager after being invited by the local police to enter the refinery office on the pretext of initiating negotiations (see further, International Union of Foodworkers 2006).

During their trial, the prosecution argued that the six union leaders 'and 1,000 other workers' pushed down the gates of the refinery, which in turn caused minor injuries to two people. Rather than arrest and prosecute the 1,000 workers, the Public Prosecutor held the six union leaders individually responsible. In February 2006, two union leaders received sentences of two years, and the remaining four received 14 months.

The case was brought to the attention of the RSPO, which, at its 24 November 2005 meeting in Singapore, watched a presentation by three Musim Mas representatives in response to the concerns expressed by the International Federation of Building and Wood Workers (IFBWW) (now Building Workers' International – the global trade union federation for construction, woodworking and forestry workers) concerning gross human rights violations by Musim Mas in Pelawan.

In their presentation, the Musim Mas representatives claimed that local police had initiated the arrests and convinced the RSPO board that the events were unworthy of investigation or fell comfortably within the Roundtable's remit of promoting 'socially beneficial' palm oil. The minutes of the meeting show that the discussion concluded with the WWF being mandated to respond to the IFBWW that both parties were proceeding through appropriate legal channels (RSPO Secretariat 2005, 3).

---

6   For more information see the RSPO website, http://www.rspo.org.

Despite the support of the Building Workers' International and the International Union of Foodworkers (IUF), the global trade union for foodworkers, the sacked workers had come under considerable pressure to give up their legal rights in return for compensation. By 7 June 2006, the remaining 200 workers who had been holding out agreed to accept financial compensation in return for dropping all claims against the company. The compensation amounts to US$123 per week – the equivalent of six weeks wages. The six prisoners were also compelled to renounce their legal right to appeal (IUF 2006).

The company praised the 'mutual agreement' by announcing that the matter had been resolved in compliance with Indonesia's labour laws, and the government, under fire at the ILO in Geneva for serial violations of international conventions, praised this agreement 'which will contribute to more positive industrial relations in the palm oil industry' (World Rainforest Movement 2006).

This case is not unique, but it illustrates quite sharply some of the divisions that MSIs can cause between trade unions and NGOs. During the dispute, the FNV, the national trade union centre in the Netherlands, called on their government to cut off financial support to the Roundtable. This put them at odds with their some-time friends and often collaborators, Oxfam Novib and Oxfam UK, both of which have a strong record of working on labour rights. For example, one of the most successful collaborations between trade unions and NGOs on the issue of labour rights was the Play Fair at the Olympics 2004 campaign, which arose from collaboration between these groups.[7] In contrast, during the Musim Mas dispute, the relations between Oxfam and the IUF in particular broke down significantly, reflecting some of the wider differences of opinion between NGOs and trade unions around the benchmark or threshold criteria for engagement in a stakeholder process.

The IUF publicly challenged both Oxfams to withdraw from the Roundtable on the grounds that their participation on the Executive Board lent credibility to a scheme which had no direct labour representation. The Oxfams called for improvement in the RSPO's governance and communications; they decided to remain on the board and re-establish participation on behalf of Oxfam International. PT Musim Mas was not re-elected to the Board and the case led to the adoption of a code of conduct for members, and complaints and grievances procedures. Oxfam International also commissioned a review of the RSPO's members' progress reporting to support this, which is yet to be released.

Only time will tell whether either the approach of IUF or Oxfam was justified. An argument could be made for the distinct division of labour between NGOs and trade unions, under which one body builds pressure on the outside and the other challenges the stakeholders in such initiatives on the inside. However, as far as the livelihoods and human rights of workers at Musim Mas are concerned, it is clear that any gains are a very long way off.

Using Corporate Accountability Tactics to Achieve Regulation

The above cases serve to illustrate some of the contemporary dilemmas associated with codes of conduct and MSIs. One important outcome of the exhaustion of attempts to gain leverage from existing CSR instruments is the growth out of these initiatives of civil society-driven hybrid schemes for the improvement of labour conditions in supply chains.

---

7   The campaign was led by the International Confederation of Free Trade Unions (ICFTU, now the ITUC), the International Textile, Garment and Leather Workers' Federation (ITGLWF), Oxfam International and the CCC. See the contribution in this collection by Apo Leong, Chan Ka-wai and Anna Tucker for a less flattering account of the campaign.

One such new and promising initiative is the Asia Wage Floor Alliance (AWFA). A number of Asian and international organizations, led by trade unions but including labour rights, women's and other civil society organizations, have recognized that the garment industry is possibly the most integrated international industry today and that Asian countries account for over 70 per cent of the global garment trade, creating a fertile ground for an innovative regional industrial strategy. Researchers have established that the garment industry has, for the most part, bottomed out or, rather, completed its restructuring with regard to its production locations (Tuwari 2006). In the global North, so-called big box multi-goods retail chains such as Walmart, Carrefour and Tesco are becoming the primary channels for marketing, gradually taking away this function from big brands.

The pioneering work around the global garment industry from both the production and retail ends laid the groundwork for a campaign which would deliver an enforceable Asia Floor Wage for Tier 1 workers in the Asian garment industry, as well as fair pricing. Through careful analysis of the strengths and limitations of corporate monitoring and accountability mechanisms, AWFA has identified that despite creating a wealth of public outrage and, most importantly, awareness amongst consumers in the North, initiatives overall have not been able to build worker collectivity with bargaining power.

Although many of the initiatives have forced employers to recognize the right of workers to organize, this has not necessarily led workers to organize, nor has organizing necessarily led to increased bargaining power. While many workers have taken courageous action, their attempts to get companies to enter into bargaining have been undermined by the threat of or actual re-location and loss of jobs. AWFA believes the best response to these limitations is hence an industry-wide bargaining strategy. Research has shown that the wages of garment workers are comparable internationally and that despite the fact that labour laws, definitions of statutory wages and government regulations vary considerably from country to country, so called 'Tier 1' workers are paid at the higher end of the production chain in all of the countries (Asia Floor Wage 2005). A significant part of the strategy is also derived from the demand for larger and larger volumes of goods following the consolidation of retail companies. This in turn requires predictable relationships with large, stable and advanced manufacturers.

This campaign hopes to utilize the work already conducted by labour activists on the big brands or Tier 1 companies and combine it with a global South union-led international campaign that demands a living wage for Asian garment workers. In the process, AFWA has identified that it needs to build alliances with a range of actors (hence the involvement of SOLIDAR, a European-based network of social and economic justice NGOs) but that it also needs to stay focused on one clear objective. China has been identified as a priority country. If the campaign is successful it will then hopefully put pressure on Tier 2 companies to raise their wages. Ultimately, the model could be spread to other industries and regions. The singular emphasis on pricing is also important as it entails recognition that retailers are often, in effect, squeezing suppliers. It is anticipated that this will be a very interesting test of the capacity of international campaigning to achieve realizable objectives.

The campaign is in its initial research phase and will not be publicly launched until the beginning of 2009. In its current setup, it is an experiment which warrants close attention, as it promises to escape the normal business-shifting paradigm that other campaigns have faced. It utilizes the lessons learnt from campaigns that have given us CSR, but emphasizes the importance of regulation.

Another interesting national example of a campaign with international consequences is the work carried out by the Corporate Responsibility Coalition (CORE) in the UK. Unlike many global

North labour rights campaigns which focus on changing individual companies or industry-wide behaviour, this campaign mobilizes consumers to focus on the business environment in which companies operate and seeks to influence government regulation of these companies. It also seeks to mobilize shareholders, including pension trustees, to use their influence to change company behaviour. This version of shareholder activism differs from most in that it has a more public face, backed by a strong commitment to influencing government policy. With the highest concentration of supermarket chains in the world, the UK provides fertile ground for challenging the public to think about who makes their food and how it is made. Since the UK government launched its review of company law in 2001, organizations involved in CORE, including SOLIDAR member War on Want, have been mobilizing citizens to call for regulation of companies.

Their campaign focuses on three main demands:

1. transparency – calling for companies to be legally required to report on their social and environmental impacts to both shareholders and the public;
2. responsibility – ensuring companies and directors have direct legal responsibility in law to manage their impact;
3. accountability – giving people overseas the right to take action against companies who have harmed their well-being in a UK court where local remedies are inadequate or unavailable.

The new Companies Act 2006 came into force in 2007 and links director's duties to a company's reporting obligations and requires them to consider the company's impacts in decision-making. The new Act also requires the company to report annually on a number of specific issues including its impact on the company's employees.

As this is a new Act, its effectiveness is yet to be tested and, as with many of these scenarios, it is not until there is a large volume of case law that we will be able to assess the results.

Conclusions

This paper has argued that the attempts made thus far by labour rights' advocates to utilize CSR as a tool for improving working conditions have revealed a number of weaknesses in popular instruments. CSR was born out of the assumption that there was a business case for ensuring socially responsible conduct by companies, as opposed to their moral and legal obligation to do so. The potential of CSR, in its myriad incarnations, to support workers' organizations is still largely unfulfilled. Some improvements have been realized, however. In many instances, work conducted by labour activists to draw attention to the limitations of these initiatives has led to their improvement and to greater appreciation by some companies that quick-fix schemes that fail to contend properly with labour-rights violations are not in their interest. Important improvements have been witnessed in China. There, labour activists have long encountered hurdles to gaining information concerning labour rights violations. Recently, though, due to a combination of work carried out by state and non-state actors, activists are gradually having more success in realizing change.

On the whole, however, CSR instruments have failed to mediate basic conflicts of interest between capital and labour. This problem has been demonstrated in this chapter by examining the OECD Guidelines for Multinational Enterprises. As this is one of the strongest CSR instruments, its failure is particularly damning of the CSR movement. Only two complaints raised in the last seven years regarding labour rights abuses have resulted in a resolution by an OECD Guidelines 'Point of Contact'. The recent case of the complaint filed under the Guidelines by the Clean Clothes

Campaign against G-Star betrays the Guidelines' ultimate impotence in resolving disputes within a timeframe that would benefit workers and their organizations. Significant investments were made in their 2000 revision by governments, companies and civil society, yet, the Guidelines' ultimate impotence has led labour rights advocates to question the efficacy of attempting to use them in light of the time and energy required for engaging in the process of their re-evaluation.

Similarly divertive of scarce resources is the monitoring of numerous codes of conduct and MSIs that have arisen in the last 20 years. Their proliferation has given birth to an auditing industry which seeks to replace labour inspections normally undertaken by government departments with a private system of audits. MSIs have some positive consequences: they bring together NGOs, trade unions and companies to discuss various issues and have at times had a positive impact on companies' behaviour. However, their major weakness remains how removed they are from the workers whose interests they claim to be representing. The case of the mass sackings at Musim Mas in Indonesia and the subsequent lack of response from the Roundtable on Sustainable Palm Oil reveals a potential for significant division between various civil society actors. In particular, it raises problems with NGOs on the one hand seeking to advocate workers' rights and on the other hand wishing to maintain constructive engagement with companies. Current multi-stakeholder models fail to grapple with the question of 'representation': that is, who legitimately speaks for workers.

Perhaps the greatest benefit of labour activist engagement with CSR initiatives is their use as a springboard for seeking greater government intervention and regulation of companies and industries. CSR has undeniably strengthened labour's capacity to analyse and understand capital's interests and corporation behaviour, and it has created a tradition of consumer solidarity with workers in producing countries, utilizing 'naming and shaming' techniques. This is fertile ground for new and innovative approaches to labour organization, such as the imminent AFWA campaign. The new corporate accountability (CA) campaigns explored briefly in this paper would not be possible without the groundswell that created CSR in the first instance and the subsequent awareness-raising of the limits of these initiatives. Their main thrust involves the push for governments to reclaim their responsibility for regulating business for the benefit of all. At the same time, the growing number of producers in the global South catering for the domestic market is likely to give CSR a second wind as consumer awareness in those markets grows and becomes an important force influencing the behaviour of Southern companies.

Any hope of governing supply chains in the interest of labour can only occur through the interaction between regulation, pioneering private sector involvement with CA and increased capacity of workers and their organizations in the global North and the global South to organize effectively and represent the interests of workers. CSR initiatives have by and large been unable to fix labour's problems in the age of globalization, but have allowed labour advocates to sharpen the tools they need for being able to do so.

References

Ascoly N. and Zeldenrust, I. (2003), *Considering Complaint Mechanisms* (Amsterdam: Centre for Research on Multinational Corporations [SOMO]).

Asia Floor Wage (2005), *First Discussion Paper on Asia Floor Wage 2005*. [Online]. Available at: http://www.asiafloorwage.org/Asset/PDF/AFW_First_Discussion_Note.pdf [accessed: 6 October 2008].

International Union of Foodworkers (IUF) (2006), *Musim Mas Starves Union into Defeat*. [Online, 13 June]. Available at: http://www.iuf.org/cgi-bin/dbman/db.cgi?db=default&ww=1&uid=default&ID=3547&view_records=1&en=1 [accessed: 7 October 2008].

Pramila Associates (2007), Letter to the Clean Clothes Campaign, 11 January. Available at: http://www.indianet.nl/br070111.pdf [accessed: 7 October 2008].

Pruett, D. (2005), *Looking for a Quick Fix: How Weak Social Auditing is Keeping Workers in Sweatshops* (Amsterdam: Clean Clothes Campaign).

Roundtable on Sustainable Palm Oil (RSPO) Secretariat (2005), *EB 04–05: Minutes of Executive Board Meeting, 22 November 2005* (Singapore: RSPO). Available at: http://www.rspo.org/resource_centre/EB200405.pdf [accessed: 7 October 2008].

Smith, J. and Partners, J. (2007), 'A model for change: upward harmonisation of OECD guidelines procedures', paper to the OECD Watch Multi-stakeholder Roundtable: A Model for Change: Upward Harmonisation of OECD Guideline Procedures, Brussels, 15 June.

Tuwari, M. (2006), *Targeting Global Supply Chains: Innovations in Labor Organizing in the Indian Garment Industries*. Paper to the University of North Carolina conference: Workshop on Multinational Production and Labor Rights, Chapel Hill, NC, 22–3 September. Available at: http://www.unc.edu/~lmosley/Tewari2006.doc [accessed: 7 October 2008].

World Rainforest Movement (2006), *Indonesia: From Oil Palm Plantations, with Repression ...*, Bulletin No. 109. [Online: World Rainforest Movement]. Available at: http://www.wrm.org.uy/bulletin/109/Indonesia.html [accessed: 7 October 2008].

Chapter 14

Corporate Accountability through Community and Unions: Linking Workers and Campaigning to Improving Working Conditions across the Supply Chain

Annie Delaney

Introduction

As corporate social responsibility and fair trade movements mature, greater emphasis is being placed on achieving improvements in the wages and working conditions of the workers producing goods. However, the focus often remains on broad standards or rights. Whilst instruments often recognize the right to freedom of association, they rarely involve workers in their processes or enhance the agency, empowerment and organization of workers. This case study proposes that linking corporate accountability initiatives to campaigning and grassroots worker activities can increase corporate accountability and suggests that broader policy and legislative initiatives can stem from such activities. The chapter argues that 'corporate accountability' – rather than corporate social responsibility (CSR) – strategies are more suitable for the inclusion of homeworkers in organizing, policy and ethical supply chain regulation issues. The chapter uses the FairWear campaign in Australia and the role of community-union alliances in monitoring supply chains where informal work-relations are the norm as a case study. It explores the participation of homeworkers in this campaign, the nature of their participation, and how this contributes to the organizing capacity of these most marginalized workers.

The early years of the twenty-first century have witnessed a growing awareness that different forms of informal work are increasing in both developed and developing countries, with the consequence that many millions of workers are living in poverty without any forms of legal or social protection. The ILO defines informal work as work which is unprotected legally and socially or where some protection exists but cannot be accessed (ILO 2000; ILO 2002a). Whilst economic literature has previously treated informality as an 'either/or' condition – either a worker is formal or not – new work on informality suggests that the condition is far more fluid. A 'continuum approach' to informal employment suggests that most unregulated work exists on a continuum of extremes; that work performed by the one worker may sometimes be regulated and not at other times; that it is invariably linked to formal work, enterprise and economic activities (Trebilcock 2006). This view considers production and employment relations that define workers and employers intersecting across various sectors and economic activity, and is therefore more likely to incorporate all workers regardless of having any protection or formal recognition.

The heterogeneity and informal nature of homework presents significant challenges for the ways in which social protection, employment law and supply-chain regulation policies are conceived and implemented (Trebilcock 2006). Because homeworkers are situated at the extreme (least regulated) end of the informal spectrum but are often deeply interlinked with workers and firms at other points in a supply chain, the idea of a continuum of informality is a particularly useful tool for better comprehending and generating policy relevant to informal workers.

This more complex understanding of the informal economy also brings into relief the extent to which conventional CSR approaches are failing the most vulnerable workers. CSR has been defined as 'policies or actions that identify companies as being concerned with society-related issues' (Roberts 1992, 595), such as employee rights, the environment and poverty. The term is also used to mean 'the degree of (ir)responsibility manifested in a company's strategies and operating practices as they impact stakeholders and the natural environment' (Waddock 2004, 10). Waddock (2004, 10) further suggests that CSR is the 'subset of corporate responsibilities that deals with a company's voluntary and discretionary relationships with its societal and community stakeholders'. The literature on CSR currently suggests that the vast majority of organizations do not take CSR seriously and that most firms use their resources to defend their non-compliance and to avoid regulation (Jonker and Marberg 2007). Even those firms which are genuinely committed to improving the ethical standards of their sourcing, and have adopted the best available practices, are still generally failing to improve the conditions of homeworkers. The failure of CSR has led to the emergence of the concept of 'corporate accountability' which relates to mechanisms for increasing the capacity for corporate regulation (Utting 2005).

This chapter argues that the collective organization of homeworkers, and community-union alliances combined with corporate accountability features – legislative and voluntary mechanisms to regulate the supply chain – increase the likelihood of codes being relevant to informal and formal workers. The chapter starts with a discussion of homework in the global context, examines informal employment, and contrasts CSR to the emergent theme of corporate accountability. It includes a detailed case study of the FairWear campaign, an example of an Australian community-union campaign with links to grassroots organizing through the campaign partners Textile, Clothing and Footwear Union of Australia (TCFUA) and Asian Women at Work (AWATW). The lessons learned from this case are significant for unions and labour rights groups. Understanding how corporate accountability relates to homework is critical to the overall effectiveness of supply-chain regulation, and to the capacity to enable broader worker empowerment, collective organizing and the improvement of work standards in informal economies.

Homework in the Global Informal Work Context

This section of the chapter contextualizes homework within the informal continuum. The aim here is to explain the impetus for concerted efforts to improve labour protections and provide a framework for assessing corporate accountability options for extending labour protections to a wider range of workers.

Homeworkers constitute a significant proportion of informal workers globally, yet are the least organized and most marginalized. Homeworkers are commonly found at the bottom rung of supply chains and face the most exploitative conditions (Fernandez-Kelly and Garcia 1989; HWW 2004; Staples 2006). Homework is a typical form of unprotected and informal work performed across globalized supply chains. The significant changes that have occurred over the last 20 years with the rise of neoliberal policies, trade liberalization, increased mobility and lack of regulation of transnational corporations also contribute to the rise in informal work conditions in developing and developed economies (Beneria 2003; Portes, Castells and Benton 1989).

Homeworkers are commonly rendered invisible to regulators, labour enforcement departments and unions and marginalized from their activities. The nature of the work performed in the home and carried out predominantly by women, though often assisted by other family members, leaves homeworkers particularly disadvantaged in social, economic and legal terms. Since women often perform homework to survive, they regularly take whatever work is available to them regardless of the conditions on offer, combining it with their child rearing and household responsibilities (Balakrishnan 2002; Beneria 2001a).

Homework is generally defined as having two distinct types. Homework located within the supply chain is often referred to as 'industrial homework' or 'dependent homework' (ILO 2002b). 'Own account homework', the second category, typically concerns homeworkers initiating work and then selling their products either to middle people or directly in their local neighbourhood at street stalls, markets and other locations (ILO 2002b). Economic and social forces associated with globalization have rendered the distinction between own account and dependent homeworker categories less distinct. Workers may concurrently conduct work that fits into either category. For instance, compared with 20 years ago, it is now more common to find a homeworker who produces traditional embroidery of a predetermined pattern onto the bodice of a fashion dress or shirt that will sell in retail outlets in Europe, the United States, Japan and Australia (dependent work). This homeworker may also weave carpets or embroider pieces for a middle person (dependent work). This work may be seasonal or intermittent and, when finished, the worker may sell her work where she can (own account work). Dependent work is paid per piece and subject to tight deadlines, and the homeworker may need friends and family members to help her complete the work. This example illustrates the commonly occurring movement of homeworkers between dependent and own account work (HWW 2004).

The blurring of the employee (dependent)/self-employed (own account) distinction has exacerbated problems regarding legal recognition and coverage by labour law and social protections (Burchielli, Buttigieg and Delaney 2008; HWW 2004) which have simultaneously become more precarious due to changes in government policy. Many governments around the world in the last 20 years have adopted neoliberal policies of privatization, deregulation and over-reliance on markets as regulators (Beneria 2003). At the same time they have removed legal protections that define workers as employees (Trebilcock 2004). In developing countries, also, the tendency to define workers as self-employed and micro-entrepreneurs is promoted by international micro-credit schemes administered by governments and development organizations in the name of poverty alleviation.[1] Furthermore, unions are reluctant to engage in organizing activities that fall outside the traditional worker definition, despite unorganized informal workers growing as a proportion of workers in many countries in both the North and the South. These combined factors contribute to the increasing gap in protections afforded by conventional labour laws and social protections.

In instances where laws do exist to protect homeworkers, few workers can access such rights and the laws rarely extend to protect own account work arrangements. Regulatory reconceptualization is required to allow greater inclusiveness, providing recognition and rights beyond the traditional employee–employer relationship of old. This stands out as a critical issue with implications towards forms of CSR and the regulation of workers conditions across supply chains, as well as the need for unions and labour groups to be permitted freely to exist, organize and represent workers.

---

1   International financial institutions, governments, policy makers and some development agencies have promoted micro-credit schemes in order to develop individual entrepreneurs. However, many individuals are in fact workers, and would benefit from collective 'unionization' strategies to improve their income and legal and social protection.

Moving from CSR to Corporate Accountability

In this section CSR is contrasted with Corporate Accountability, which, it is argued, is a preferable approach to improving informal workers' rights and conditions. Corporate accountability is an emerging approach that is critical of CSR programmes. It incorporates the capacity for corporate legal regulation alongside broader mechanisms for corporate self-regulation (Garvey and Newell 2005; Utting 2005).

> Rather than seeing corporate self-regulation and voluntary approaches as a superior alternative
> to governmental and international regulation, the corporate accountability agenda suggests a
> re-articulation of voluntary and legal approaches. (Utting 2005, 12)

These governance issues outlined in the previous section present significant hurdles to the overall improvement in homeworkers' work conditions and protection. Governance issues extend to the substantial role of transnational corporations: how accountable they are through supply-chain monitoring and regulation, and other mechanisms that could contribute to inclusion and improved protection of workers, especially homeworkers. This challenge is of particular significance when global financial and trade institutions' macro-economic policy trends and directives have been responsible for the dissolution of national laws and institutional frameworks to provide laws, policies and programmes to deliver services and protection to persons in specific countries, many of whom are engaged in informal employment (Fernandez-Kelly and Shefner 2006).

The CSR movement has grown significantly over the last ten to 15 years. This has occurred at the same time as the use of subcontracted labour has contributed to increasing informalization in developed and developing countries (Beneria 2003; Sassen-Koob 1989). In addition, the squeeze on suppliers by 'buyer-driven' supply chains creates cost pressures for producers further down the chain (Gereffi 1999; Hale and Opondo 2005). Corporations are often involved in codes (either company codes or externally generated codes) in an attempt to reduce public pressure and salvage their reputations. They may simultaneously place 'ethical' conditions on their suppliers while leaning on them for the lowest price and imposing tight deadlines. These factors leave suppliers to assume that nothing has changed and it is 'business as usual', since unless principal companies change buying practices, little can change along the supply chain (Barrientos and Smith 2007).

A key problem associated with CSR is its voluntary and discretionary nature (Jonker and Marberg 2007). The CSR movement has traditionally been a top-down approach. It is commonly negotiated in buyer countries and associated with terms such as 'positive engagement' and 'partnerships', as well as a plethora of NGOs, unions and monitoring businesses eager to highlight 'best practice' corporation behaviour (Chang and Wong 2005; Garvey and Newell 2005; Utting 2005). However, anti-sweatshop activists have become increasingly vocal about the poor outcomes of CSR and, in particular, the lack of focus at the bottom – the workers – compared to being a consumer-focused movement. In addition, global unions have shifted emphasis away from CSR towards International Framework Agreements in order to address the failure of codes to affect workers access to core labour standards.

Increasing doubts and questions surrounding CSR programmes raise concerns about the authenticity and effectiveness of these mechanisms for workers at all levels to enable rights, but particularly for workers engaged in informal employment. CSR efforts to date have rarely been linked to informal workers positioned along the supply chain. Informal workers – such as day labourers, temporary or short-term contract workers and homeworkers – remain invisible in most instances. They are rarely mentioned in 'codes'[2] and seldom gain any benefits. While there is some available evidence that codes support improvement in outcome standards such as occupational health and safety and working hours, these developments have only been relevant to formal workers, not the workers at the lower reaches of the chain (Barrientos and Smith 2007). Generally, studies conclude that very few workers benefit from codes, suggesting that codes fail to deliver any improvement in core labour standards such as the right to organize and bargain collectively (Barrientos and Smith 2007). It appears that codes have little relevance to workers located at the first tier and no consequence for workers beyond the first tier supplier (factory level). The failure to recognize workers across the informal continuum operates as an effective measure of exclusion. Ultimately, it ignores the majority of workers engaged in the provision of the majority of local and global commodities and services.

Understanding how CSR programmes might incorporate homework is critical to the future effectiveness of supply-chain regulation. Very few examples of CSR exist which successfully extend regulation to homeworkers. The Australian FairWear campaign is an exception. The informal continuum approach demonstrates the importance of a multi-layered approach to work and enterprise regulation – at the national and international level – and is critical to incorporating a broader and inclusive perspective across the supply chain context. The following section provides detail on the Australian homework context and the FairWear campaign's role in promoting homeworker rights through campaigns to maintain legal protection and supply-chain regulation. The case illustrates how homeworker involvement in campaign activities has led to increased legal rights and empowerment for these workers, and how these have impacted on corporate accountability activities.

Garment Homeworkers in Australia

The nature of homework in the garment industry in Australia typifies global trends. The workforce has shifted from being factory-based to predominantly home-based (Rowbotham 1999; TCFUA 1995; Weller 1999). The home-based workforce is largely unorganized and despite the existence of legal protection for garment homeworkers, few access such protections and then only rarely. Similarities regarding the organization and conditions of homework exist whether workers are located in Australia, the UK, Chile, the United States, Mexico, India or China. Work is given out at low piece rates with unrealistic deadlines, commonly with links to national and global supply chains and brand names (Cregan 2001). Predominantly, women perform the work at home while responsible as carers for childrearing and often for the livelihood of the family. For a range of reasons it is difficult for informal workers such as homeworkers to self-identify as workers. This is one reason they face greater challenges than workers in formal workplace arrangements to organize collectively, join a union and secure legal and social protection. Unions have traditionally organized 'employees' (dependent workers) but not 'contractors' or 'self-employed workers'. Even where homeworkers are dependent, in many instances, homeworkers cannot identify their direct employer. Furthermore, as outlined earlier in this chapter, many homeworkers are own account workers or may move across the dependent/own account divide depending on the work they are conducting at any particular time.

---

2   Codes refer to the broad range of voluntary instruments from multi-stakeholder agreements, to individual corporate codes, and industry sector standards that may not include core ILO labour standards.

The Homework Campaign outlined in the next section of this chapter has attempted to overcome problems created by the legal distinction between 'employees' and 'contractors' and generated a new model of union organizing which extended the scope of union membership beyond formal workers.

The Homework Campaign in Australia

The FairWear campaign, established in Australia in 1996 as an anti-sweatshop movement, has used innovative campaign tactics such as media-friendly creative stunts to highlight injustices against workers in the garment industry, and has focused on homeworkers in the supply chain (Delaney 2004; Nash 2001). The campaign works with key partners to combine information, industry knowledge, homeworker involvement, and to include a broad network of supporters to maintain a critical voice around the garment industry. FairWear campaign partners are typically drawn from unions, churches and student, women and community organizations. Campaign endorsement includes a wide range of organizations and individuals that participate at different levels and capacities across the campaign activities.

The FairWear campaign grew out of the long-term TCFUA involvement with outworker or homeworker[3] issues in the textile, clothing and footwear industry. The TCFUA clothing division, previously CATU, has a history of involvement in campaigning for the inclusion of homeworkers in the Clothing Award (Rowbotham 1999). CATU won a historic case before the Industrial Relations Commission in 1987 that improved the 'outwork clauses' of the *Clothing Trades Award 1982* (Cth).[4] The improved clauses were intended to ensure that homeworkers receive the same pay and conditions as factory workers performing the same work. These clauses prescribed the ways in which companies could outsource work outside their premises, and the conditions under which the principal company or the subcontractor could engage homeworkers. The union conducted general information campaigns, in a number of community languages, directed towards homeworkers (predominantly migrant and refugee women) across Australia, rather than union members. The first was conducted in 1989, closely following the Industrial Relations Commission decision to amend the Clothing Trades Award to provide improved entitlements for homeworkers and reporting requirements for employers of homeworkers.

This approach was successful in improving award protection but failed to translate into homeworkers joining the union. Other reasons for lack of organizing success could be attributed to the fact that companies or brands that profited from homeworker exploitation were not made the focus of campaign activities. Moreover, there was little support within the union for prioritizing homeworkers in the day-to-day work of union officials.

Incentives for the union to address homeworkers in the clothing industry originated from the drastic effects of industry restructuring. At the time, the union organizer experience was increasingly about visiting factories, where there were only a handful of workers but thousands of racks of clothes. This suggested that the work and location of the workers had shifted from the factory to the home. This presented the union with questions regarding how to find and contact this new workforce, and even greater problems concerning how to organize them. The other primary motivation for union

---

3   The term 'outwork' is used interchangeably with 'homework'. In Australia, the term outwork is used in awards and legislation; homework is generally used across the international context. Refer, for example, to the ILO Homework Convention No. 177.

4   See *Re Clothing Trades Award 1982* [1987] 19 IR 416.

intervention was an awareness that homeworkers were being exploited and that the union was the only organization likely to intervene on the workers' behalf (Delaney 1995).

In 1994 the union implemented a federal government-funded information campaign. The campaign focused on explaining award entitlements and the union's role and health and safety issues. As the union was faced with increased factory closure and the shift of production to the home, it agreed to a broader approach to contacting homeworkers. The 1994 campaign included a national, multilingual phone-in. Initial contact with homeworkers, predominantly from Indo-Chinese communities, resulted through homeworkers calling bilingual workers to discuss work-related issues.

The union estimated that the phone-in and community meetings led to contact with approximately 4,000 homeworkers. The information collected was compiled in a report, *The Hidden Cost of Fashion* (TCFUA 1995). The report generated considerable interest: it was the first time that the nature of subcontracting and homework in the industry had been documented through primarily the use of information gathered directly from homeworkers (Delaney 1995; TCFUA 1995). The information was then used to develop ongoing strategies for targeting companies responsible for poor working conditions; for the development of the FairWear campaign, and for ongoing initiatives to establish direct links with homeworkers.

Getting a Community Union Campaign Started

The TCFUA reached the view that a national community campaign was necessary for the issues affecting homeworkers to be fully addressed (Delaney 1995). The union was aware that it would need to be a community campaign to have credibility and, coincidently, this would ensure that the union remained publicly accountable. The Australian Government Senate Economics References Committee inquiry into outwork in the garment industry 1996–1997 and 1998 (Senate Economics Committee 1997), required industry and employer groups to make submissions to the committee, and therefore to put on the public record their defence of homework employment practices. This placed the garment industry, employers and employer groups under considerable pressure. Public interest generated by this inquiry exposed the clandestine and invisible nature of homework in the industry.

The TCFUA submission to the inquiry stated that national legislation was necessary to curb the exploitation that was rife across the garment industry,[5] and to regulate retailers and brand owners. The union also recommended that the federal government promote ethical agreements amongst retailers to guarantee national labour laws and that award entitlements under the Clothing Trades Award be provided to homeworkers[6] (TCFUA 1996). These recommendations, amongst others, focused on methods to deliver existing legal protections to homeworkers along-side additional regulatory and voluntary mechanisms that would obligate companies to ensure that minimum award conditions were applied to homeworkers down the supply chain (Delaney 1995). The publicity

---

5   The union strongly favoured legislative mechanisms. It also promoted supplementary non-legal regulatory mechanisms to support the implementation of any legislative measures concerning homework. The TCFUA submission to the Outwork Senate inquiry recommended a Sale of Clothing Act be enacted to ensure that clothing outworkers receive 'fair' conditions of employment, and to apply penalties for noncompliance.

6   The TCFUA also recommended that the Federal Government promote Ethical Sourcing Agreements by linking any government corporate subsidies to companies providing homeworkers legal wages and other entitlements. In addition, they proposed ethical sourcing agreements for government departments and similarly award contracts from companies that follow ethical practices through entering into ethical agreements.

surrounding the *Hidden Cost of Fashion* and the Senate inquiry not only increased the union's profile on the homework issue, but contributed to a broad range of community organizations taking up the homeworker cause. The inquiry also assisted the union to identify potential community allies with which they could discuss the establishment of a national community anti-sweatshop campaign: FairWear. The early work of the TCFUA on homework, and later in combination with FairWear, has contributed to the existence of improved homeworker protection. These issues are further explored below.

Linking Supply-chain Regulation to Campaigning for Homeworkers

Homeworkers in the Australian garment industry have been included in industry sectoral awards, and have been awarded equivalent wage and work conditions as factory-based workers. In the past, this has been subject to a case-by-case basis of legal determination that the homeworker is in fact an employee. The employment rationale of homework has long been contested in Australian courts and legislation at federal and state levels has settled this dispute: homeworkers (in the garment industry) are defined as employees for the purpose of labour laws (FairWear 2005b; Rawling 2007; TCFUA 1995).[7]

However, Australian garment homeworkers face a dilemma in that they are likely to lose their work or be excluded from receiving work when they attempt to access legal rights and conditions. Overall, homeworkers remain outside minimum labour conditions despite the range of mechanisms in place to promote access to the minimum labour standards. This case study will now examine the various regulation mechanisms and how they combine to improve supply-chain regulation.

There exist three types of mechanisms that regulate the supply chain and, in particular, homeworkers' work entitlements:

1. Clothing Trades Award 1999;
2. Homeworkers Code of Practice 1996 (a voluntary industry code);
3. homework-specific state legislation – for example, the *Industrial Relations (Ethical Clothing Trades) Act 2001* (NSW), and the *Outworkers (Improved Protection) Act 2003* (Vic).[8]

These mechanisms of regulation have different points of focus, degrees of sanctions, and levels of effect across the supply chain. The range of regulatory mechanisms are consistent with a 'regulatory pyramid' approach that includes punitive sanctions positioned at the top end and educational and 'soft' approaches at the bottom (Marshall forthcoming).[9] The net of homework regulatory mechanisms is essential to enable supply-chain regulation, and combines to give effect to the legislation and, most important, improve homeworkers' capacity to access such protections.

The TCFUA plays a pivotal role in monitoring the supply chain, initiating legal prosecutions or 'sanctions', taking complaints and information from homeworkers and providing key information to the FairWear campaign to initiate consumer pressure on individual brands and corporations. The involvement of homeworkers through the AWATW network and the union is a key source of information for this ongoing monitoring.

---

7   See, for example, the *Industrial Relations (Ethical Clothing Trades) Act 2001* (NSW).

8   For other examples of homework-specific legal protection in state legislation, see the *Industrial Relations and Other Acts Amendment Act 2005* (Qld); and the *Industrial Law Reform (Fair Work) Act 2005* (SA).

9   For further explanation of homework regulatory mechanisms, see Marshall (forthcoming) and Rawling (2007).

In the next section, these legislative and voluntary mechanisms are considered in greater detail in order to explore the benefits of their mutual re-enforcement.

The Clothing Trades Award (CTA) and the Homeworkers Code of Practice (HWCP)

The CTA provisions include minimum conditions and requirements for wages and conditions of homeworkers. The provisions prescribe requirements by corporations and their suppliers in regard to record keeping, lists of suppliers and registration with a registration board. Prescribed contract details include a requirement for manufacturers, fashion houses or contractors to record parties to whom they provide work, how much they are paying, how many hours work is involved and the total volume of work. The contract and record-keeping requirements of the CTA allow for work to be traced to the next level of the contracting chain, and to track the cascading levels of obligation from employer to employer in regard to the conditions under which the work is performed by homeworkers.

The HWCP was developed out of the Senate inquiry process of 1996–97, when employers lobbied against legislation. This industry code, a voluntary mechanism, led to the development of an accreditation scheme and to the use of a 'no sweatshop' label as the sign of compliance to the code (Homeworkers Code Committee 2001). The code has also been amended to reflect legislative changes. The HWCP, as the name indicates, focuses on homeworkers in the supply chain, requiring corporations to make their whole supply chain transparent in order to secure accreditation. Through the code, a corporation can seek accreditation by providing evidence of compliance with the award, or lose its accreditation in the event that it fails to remedy a complaint made against it. The code mirrors the standards and requirements of the CTA and therefore, as corporations seek accreditation they also fulfil conditions to become award compliant. Most importantly, the code has become the public face of industry standards and compliance for homework. FairWear issues an ethical shopping guide to consumers which lists the corporations or brands meeting these minimum conditions. The corporations that become the subjects of campaigning are encouraged to become accredited by the code and thus promotable as ethical suppliers (FairWear 2006).

Campaigning to Maintain Garment Industry Award Conditions

The CTA (1999) outwork clauses underwent a number of union-initiated amendments throughout the 1980s and early 1990s. Further changes occurred in 1999 as a consequence of Federal Government Award simplification legislation under the *Workplace Relations Act 1996* (Cth). The role of FairWear and its campaign-based focus has provided the union with the public face to campaign for such legislative reforms or, in some instances, to protect the current standards from being further eroded. Law reform in regard to homework has been a union priority both historically and in recent times. The activities of FairWear have been critical in determining how these regulatory mechanisms have come into being, how they have been maintained and protected under threat of removal and, in some instances, how they have been improved upon.

The CTA simplification case of 1999 and the campaign around WorkChoices in 2005 are recent examples of activities to maintain homework legal protection and preserve legislation and award provisions that enable regulation of the supply chain. The validity of the CTA outwork clauses were assessed by the full bench of the Industrial Relations Commission, which upheld the clauses as valid and consistent with the *Workplace Relations Act 1996* (Cth). This positive outcome can be largely attributed to the effective community campaigning conducted by FairWear and coordinated with the union responsible for issuing the legal claim (FairWear 1999; HomeNet 2000; TCFUA 1998).

The FairWear WorkChoices campaign argued that homeworkers should be considered as special cases and thus afforded greater protection than other classes of workers. Lobbying, letter writing and other organized events emphasized how WorkChoices would legalize exploitation. Homeworkers from AWATW and FairWear campaigners travelled to Canberra to address a Senate inquiry on the legislation. The evidence of homeworkers and others highlighted the fact that homeworkers remain one of the most marginalized and vulnerable groups in Australia (FairWear 2005a). In addition, FairWear highlighted the fact that WorkChoices would make homeworkers more vulnerable and render the award, state legislation, and the HWCP inoperable and, at worst, irrelevant (FairWear 2005c). The *Workplace Relations Amendment (WorkChoices) Act 2005* (Cth) reduced all Australian workers' conditions and rights to bargain collectively, but did maintain the homeworker protection that existed in various state laws and the Clothing Award (1999) prior to its

Table 14.1   Summary of homework regulation mechanisms to promote supply-chain regulation and homework protection

Regulatory mechanisms	Key features of mechanisms to promote supply-chain regulation	Activities to support homeworker collective organizing and participation in corporate accountability activities
Clothing Trades Award	Prescribes employer record-keeping, lists of suppliers, contracts and annual registration, and promotes transparency of supply chain; Cascading obligations – principle corporation responsible for pay and conditions of homeworkers; Penalties apply. Union or government may initiate prosecutions.	*Asian Women at Work:* Homeworkers' network; Homeworkers' advocacy group; Homeworkers' training, leadership, English language classes and radio programme; Participates in FairWear activities; Supports union in monitoring supply chain and negotiating with corporations.
State homework-specific legislation	Prescribes employer record-keeping, lists of suppliers, contracts and annual registration, and promotes transparency of supply chain; Cascading obligations concerning pay and conditions of homeworkers; Penalties apply. Union or government may initiate prosecutions; promotes award conditions and compliance.	*TCFUA:* Initiates prosecution for Award and legislative breaches; Monitors supply chain and code compliance; Participates in FairWear activities; In some states, has contact with homeworkers via-English classes and other training.
Homeworkers Code of Practice (HWCP) (Voluntary Industry Code)	Accredited corporations keep records and contracts; promotes transparency of supply chain; Accredited company responsible for pay and conditions of homeworkers for suppliers; Promotes award conditions and compliance.	*FairWear:* Community campaigning on regulatory mechanisms; Initiates community action, protests and activities; Ethical shopping list; Liaises with and supports homeworker radio group; Supports union to monitor supply chain and negotiate with corporations; Brings FW partners together to develop proactive responses to corporate and government inaction over homeworker exploitation.

introduction (FairWear 2005b). FairWear successfully campaigned to secure legal protection for garment homeworkers by campaigning against the anti-worker national labour laws. The inclusion of homeworkers in the *WorkChoices Act* (2005) as employees – *not* as contractors – was a significant win, as was the retention of existing protections in state jurisdictions as well as maintaining the HWCP. The FairWear campaign was successful in securing the protections that had been won over the previous decade and, importantly, in maintaining the ongoing role of the union in monitoring the supply chain.

Table 14.1 provides a summary of the homework regulation mechanisms, and lists key features and activities to support homework participation and protection.

Work with Homeworkers

The TCFUA, AWATW and FairWear have developed joint activities, along the lines of a 'community-union collaboration' model, in regard to homework. This community-union collaboration is a particularly innovative model. The ongoing participation of homeworkers has contributed to the FairWear campaign to hold corporations accountable for their supply-chain labour conditions. The role of each of these organizations is now considered.

TCFUA

The union has been the main link to homeworkers through traditional union representation and servicing of members for such issues as under-payments and other industrial matters. Since the 1990s, the union has broadened this notion of representation to include general rights information, such as 'know your rights' and 'what to do if you are underpaid'. The union approach to contacting and establishing networks with homeworkers (often not as union members) has varied in each state and been dependent on external funding sources. English classes for homeworkers were trialled in Victoria and found to be an effective way to bridge contact. Moreover, the English classes address homeworker needs to learn English as well as their interest to meet with others, brought on by the isolation and marginalization they experience as migrant and refugee women homeworkers. The union became a registered training provider and conducts classes in Melbourne and Sydney. In Melbourne, the union branch directly employs English teachers to run the classes. In Sydney, contact with homeworkers has occurred mainly outside the union, through AWATW, which contacts and recruits homeworkers to classes and employs English teachers. This union branch has maintained its role of advocacy and representation of homeworkers at state and national policy levels, but little contact is made directly with homeworkers unless AWATW links them directly to the union office.

AWATW

The role of AWATW has evolved from a contact point for Asian women workers in marginalized, informal work arrangements – such as homework and sweatshop work – to the main organization in Sydney that addresses such workers needs. AWATW was established as a New South Wales-based NGO in 1994 and adapted the community-union coalition work that evolved from Korea in the 1980s (Carstens 2003). This model focuses on collaborating with unions and aims to assist and promote trade unionism through a range of activities with targeted workers. AWATW has worked specifically with Asian women workers in the garment industry. Members and bilingual workers of AWATW participated in the first national homework phone-in and have played a key role in the development of homeworker initiatives since the early 1990s. As previously mentioned, AWATW recruited and carried out a range of training courses and programmes for garment homeworkers in Sydney. Some of these were contracted by the TCFUA, others were funded by the state government.

AWATW has played a pivotal role in the NSW Government's 'Behind the label' strategy and has supported information dissemination to consumers, training programmes for homeworkers and initiatives in the garment industry. The 'Behind the label' strategy resulted in companies agreeing to become accredited under the homeworkers code of practice and the passing of the *Industrial Relations (Ethical Clothing Trades) Act 2001* (NSW) (Sutherland 2007).

The methods used by AWATW to establish and maintain contact with homeworkers stand out as innovative pro-homeworker activities. For example, AWATW has ongoing links with Chinese community organizations and employs bilingual staff. It thus provides an effective way to communicate with homeworkers if they cannot communicate in English. AWATW established a Chinese homeworkers' network in the 1990s and successfully set up a Vietnamese homeworkers network in 2000–2001 (AWATW 2001). AWATW has also established an advocacy group that has surveyed homeworkers, targeted companies and made direct representation to companies whose products have been identified as homeworker-made. Moreover, group members have improved their own skills and confidence. The method of contacting homeworkers embraces issues beyond women's employment and adopts a 'whole person' approach with the effect of increasing homeworker confidence and visibility (Hill 2005). AWATW has supported and been a key participant of the FairWear campaign in Sydney, and the FairWear campaign office is located at the AWATW office.

FairWear

The FairWear campaign's main contact with homeworkers is through campaigning. While focused on broader consumer campaign activities, the FairWear offices in Melbourne and Sydney are in regular contact with homeworkers through AWATW in Sydney. In other states, FairWear representatives work with the TCFUA and community organizations. FairWear has relied upon campaign partners to provide information about homework in order to resource campaign activities. The FairWear Sydney office has day-to-day contact with homeworkers through AWATW English classes or meetings at their office. In Melbourne, FairWear organizes contact with homeworkers directly, or through the TCFUA-run training and English classes. Since 2003, FairWear has supported 'Outworkers Voice' a Vietnamese homeworker radio programme, through which homeworkers are trained to be radio announcers and produce a weekly radio programme. The link between AWATW, the TCFUA and FairWear provides the opportunity for homeworkers to participate in FairWear activities and for FairWear to have direct contact with homeworkers.

Implications of the FairWear Community–Union Approach, Does it Benefit Homeworkers?

The FairWear community–union alliance involves organizations in contact with homeworkers utilizing information collected from homeworkers to regulate the supply chain, monitor workers conditions, target companies for community campaigning and to prosecute companies for breaches of the *Clothing Trades Award 1999* (Vic) and other legislation. The AWATW model provides a model of union–community homeworker organization, and this combined with FairWear activities enables homeworker participation in maintaining relevant regulatory mechanisms and corporate accountability activities. The FairWear activities have focused on bridging the net of regulatory mechanisms to make strong links between homeworker conditions and unethical corporate behaviour. The strength of this approach has been that the emphasis has shifted from reliance upon an individual worker complaints process to a broader approach of corporate accountability through the maintenance of regulatory mechanisms and implementation through suppliers across the supply chain to provide minimum conditions to homeworkers. The promotion of minimum standards collectively for homeworkers has meant that homeworkers are not singled out and therefore face less risk for participation in FairWear activities, thus facilitating homeworker involvement in campaign activities. Furthermore, the FairWear campaign provides a space for key organizations to develop strategies and effective activities to organize homeworkers in relation to corporate accountability. Such organization would otherwise be difficult to arrange on an individual basis.

Benefits from the FairWear strategy still elude the majority of homeworkers. Homeworker legislative and award conditions are rarely implemented, despite the extent of regulatory mechanisms in place and campaign activities that have occurred over the last ten years. Recent evidence indicates that garment homeworker piece rates have declined over the last five years (Diviney and Lilywhite 2007). Arguably, the small number of homeworkers that are collectively organized remains a barrier to homeworkers accessing their legal entitlements. Homeworkers remain isolated and lack the industrial strength and capacity to change their individual circumstances. Making contact with homeworkers and establishing a level of trust has been critical in building ongoing links with them. The union's involvement in homeworker activities has not led to an increase in union membership, and while there remain real obstacles to unionization – such as limited resources, homeworkers' irregular work and fear of losing work – unions need to address the reasons for the lack of homeworker inclusion. In addition, union prioritization policy and regulatory activities over organizing strategies has contributed to fewer homeworkers being collectively organized. Organizing dependent homeworkers worldwide has met mixed success (HWW 2004). Positive examples of organization of dependent homeworkers come from less traditional union approaches (Delaney 2004; HWW 2004). Despite the gap in organizing activities, the Australian example appears consistent with those internationally; AWATW and FairWear as labour rights groups have prioritized homeworker activities, and the TCFUA focus on supply-chain monitoring remains instrumental to the success of other aspects of homework campaigns by FairWear.

In regard to corporate accountability, one method of measuring the effectiveness of this strategy is through the range of regulatory mechanisms in place. At this level, the FairWear strategy can be considered a success. However, the extent to which corporations comply with these regulatory standards and therefore provide homeworkers with minimum wages, legal and social protection remains limited. A corporate culture of non-compliance continues despite high union presence around supply chain issues, the FairWear campaigning and homeworker participation in these activities. Government initiatives have varied: until recently, federal government actions were hostile to unions; and while state governments have passed homework-specific legislation, little has been done to hold corporations to account. Governance issues remain critical to the implementation of laws and other initiatives relevant to homework.

Conclusion

This case study has shown that whilst great efforts have been made through grassroots organizing to mobilize homeworkers, real obstacles remain to broader collective organizing of informal workers in the Australian garment industry. Of the estimated hundreds of thousands of homeworkers working in the industry, the number of homeworkers that are members of AWATW, the TCFUA, and involved in FairWear activities remains relatively small. Although collectively organizing homeworkers in the garment industry in Australia has had limited success, what has been achieved to date indicates how important such strategies are to holding corporations accountable. The community–union alliance through FairWear has shifted the focus from corporate self-regulation onto corporation accountability through a net of regulatory mechanisms that emphasize accountability along the supply chain. Further, the alliance has shown the importance of a corporate accountability approach that prioritizes worker participation, social movement campaigning and a combination of legal and voluntary mechanisms.

While regulatory mechanisms have been secured through extensive campaigning, this has not yet led to improvements in homeworkers' working conditions. Rather, homeworkers' conditions continue to decline. There is a large gap between the formal rights of homeworkers on the one hand and the actual piece rates received and homeworkers' inability to access other legal and social entitlements in practice on the other. This highlights the need for a continued multi-pronged tactic that features legislative measures combined with voluntary mechanisms in order to improve homeworkers access to their rights and protection.

Homeworker organization and making homework visible in the supply chain remains a serious challenge worldwide. Informal employment is increasing and it is necessary for unions and labour rights groups to support worker empowerment organizing models in order to increase global corporate accountability. The injustices experienced by garment homeworkers in Australia are mirrored by unjust sourcing practices in the garment industry internationally, even where CSR programmes are operating. Lessons from the Australian FairWear example can be applied to anti-sweatshop campaign activities broadly. The case study indicates that a more inclusive approach to dealing with informal workers, including workers that do not fit the traditional worker definition, is imperative. There needs to be a refocus on building worker organization through unions and worker groups, in particular amongst informal workers, for corporate accountability to increase. Unions who are accustomed to working with formal sector, 'traditional' workers have often been ill-equipped and slow to organize informal workers. However, this case study has shown that when unions join together in partnerships with like-minded community groups, NGOs or those with links to informal workers they can potentially strengthen the capacity for workers to mobilize and to participate in corporate accountability activities.

A move towards national and global formal legal mechanisms may give teeth to voluntary mechanisms and multi-stakeholder agreements so that corporations become more accountable and trade becomes fairer for workers. A first step in this process must involve increasing the visibility of homeworkers in the supply chain and must be taken by all parties involved in governing supply chains: companies, unions and NGOs, industry bodies and so on. Corporate accountability activities which are consistent with the informal continuum approach may strengthen union and labour rights groups' right to exist and organize homeworkers and other workers across the supply chain. This case study has shown that once this has occurred, there still remains a significant challenge in translating increased agency into concrete access to formal protections and improved livelihoods.

References

Asian Women At Work (AWATW) (2001), *Dare to Act: A Report on the Establishment of a Vietnamese Women Outworkers Network* (Sydney: AWATW with the Vietnamese Womens Association of NSW).

Balakrishnan, R. (ed.). (2002), *The Hidden Assembly Line: Gender Dynamics of Subcontracting in a Global Economy* (Bloomfield, CT: Kumarian Press).

Barrientos, S. and Smith, S. (2007), 'Do workers benefit from ethical trade? Assessing the codes of labour practice in global production systems', *Third World Quarterly* 28(4): 713–29.

Beneria, L. (2001a), *Changing Employment Patterns and the Informalization of Jobs: General Trends and Gender Dimensions* (Geneva: International Labour Organization).

—— (2001b), 'Shifting the risk: new employment patterns, informalization, and women's work', *International Journal of Politics, Culture and Society* 15(1): 27.

—— (2003), *Gender, Development and Globalization: Economics as if All People Mattered* (New York and London: Routledge).

Burchielli, R., Buttigieg, D. and Delaney, A. (2008), 'Organizing homeworkers: the use of mapping as an organizing tool', *Work, Employment and Society* 22(1): 167–80.

Cagatay, N. (2003), 'Gender and international labor standards in the world economy', in E. Mutari and D. Figart (eds), *Women and the Economy: A Reader* (Armonk, NY: M.E. Sharpe).

Carstens, D. (2003), 'Community unionism: the Asian women at work model', unpublished (AWATW).

Chang, D. and Wong, M. (2005), 'After the consumer movement: toward a new international labour activism in the global garment industry', *Labour Capital and Society* 38(1 and 2): 126–56.

Cregan, C. (2001), *Home Sweat Home: Preliminary Findings of the First Stage of a Two-part Study of Outworkers in the Textile Industry in Melbourne Victoria. January-June 2001* (Melbourne: Department of Management, Melbourne University).

Delaney, A. (1995), 'Outwork coordinator: work notes April 1994–May 1995', unpublished personal notes.

—— (2004), *Campaigns at Work: A Guide to Campaigning for Homeworker Organisations, Unions, Campaign Groups and Activists* [Online: HomeWorkers Worldwide]. Available at: http://www.homeworkersww.org.uk/files/resources/campaign-manual.pdf [accessed: 7 July 2004].

Diviney, E. and Lilywhite, S. (2007), *Ethical Threads: Corporate Social Responsibility in the Australian Garment Industry* (Melbourne: Brotherhood of St Laurence).

FairWear (1999), '20 good reasons to stop the changes to the industrial relations laws', unpublished briefing document.

—— (2005a), *FairWear Submission to Senate Employment, Workplace Relations and Education References Committee Inquiry into Workplace Agreements* (Melbourne: FairWear).

—— (2005b), 'Outworkers protections maintained after sustained lobbying', unpublished report on Workchoices (FairWear Campaign).

—— (2005c), *WorkChoices Changes Sew Unfair*. [Online: FairWear]. Available at: http://www.fairwear.org.au [accessed: 16 March 2006].

—— (2006), *Ethical Shopping Guide*. [Online: FairWear]. Available at: http://www.fairwear.org.au/media/client/November_walletcard_2006.pdf [accessed: 16 November 2006].

Fernandez-Kelly, P. and Garcia, A. (1989), 'Informalization at the core: Hispanic women, homework, and the advanced capitalist state', in A. Portes, M. Castells and L.A. Benton (eds), *The Informal Economy* (Baltimore, MD and London: Johns Hopkins University Press).

Fernandez-Kelly, P. and Shefner, J. (eds) (2006), *Out of the Shadows: Political Action and the Informal Economy in Latin America* (University Park, PA: Pennsylvania State University Press).

Garvey, N. and Newell, P. (2005), 'Corporate accountability to the poor? Assessing the effectiveness of community-based strategies', *Development in Practice* 15(3 and 4): 389–404.

Gereffi, G. (1999), *A Commodity Chains Framework for Analyzing Global Industries*. [Online]. Available at: http://www.yale.edu/ccr/gereffi.doc [accessed: 6 Feb 2007].

Hale, A. and Opondo, M. (2005), 'Humanising the cut flower chain: confronting the realities of flower production for workers in Kenya', *Antipode* 37(2): 301–23.

Hill, E. (2005), 'Organising "non-standard" women workers for economic and social security in India and Australia', paper presented at the Association of Industrial Relations Academics of Australia and New Zealand (AIRAANZ)19th Conference Reworking Work, Sydney.

HomeNet (2000), *HomeNet: The Newsletter of the International Network for Homebased Workers* 13 (Spring) (Leeds: HomeNet International).

Homeworkers Code Committee (2001), *Changing Fashion: The Story of the No Sweatshop Label* (Melbourne: Homeworkers Code of Practice Committee).

HWW (2004), 'Organising for change: women homebased workers in the global economy', unpublished final mapping report, Homeworkers Worldwide.

International Labour Organization (ILO) (2000), *Employment in the Informal Sector: Challenges and Future Agenda* (Geneva: International Labour Office).

—— (2002a), *Decent Work and the Informal Economy: Report VI* (Geneva: International Labour Office).

—— (2002b), *Women and Men in the Informal Economy: A Statistical Picture* (Geneva: International Labour Office).

Jonker, J. and Marberg, A. (2007), 'Corporate social responsibility quo vadis? A critical inquiry into a discursive struggle', *Journal of Corporate Citizenship* 27(Autumn): 107–19.

Katz, C. and Perez, C. (2001), 'The manifesto and globalization', *Latin American Perspectives* 28(6): 5–16.

Marshall, S. (forthcoming), 'Australian textile clothing and footwear supply chain regulation', in C. Fenwick and T. Novitz (eds), *Legal Protection of Workers' Human Rights: Regulatory Change and Challenge* (Oxford: Hart).

Nash, A. (2001), *people.dot.com:munity* (Geelong West: Villamanta Legal Service).

Portes, A., Castells, M. and Benton, L.A. (eds) (1989), *The Informal Economy* (Baltimore, MD: Johns Hopkins University Press).

Rawling, M. (2007), 'The regulation of outwork and the federal takeover of labour law', *Australian Journal of Labour Law* 20(2): 189.

Roberts, J. (1992), 'Determinants of CSR disclosures', *Accounting, Organizations and Society* 17(6): 595–612.

Rowbotham, S. (1999), *New Ways of Organising in the Informal Sector: Four Case Studies of Trade Union Activity* (Leeds: HomeNet).

Sassen-Koob, S. (1989), 'New York City's informal economy', in A. Portes, M. Castells and L.A. Benton (eds), *The Informal Economy* (Baltimore, MD: Johns Hopkins University Press).

Senate Economics Committee (1997), *Outworkers in the Garment Industry, December*. [Online]. Available at: http://www.aph.gov.au/senate/Committee/economics_ctte/completed_inquiries/1996-99/outworkers/report/contents.htm [accessed: 14 April 2008].

Staples, D.E. (2006), *No Place Like Home: Organizing Home-Based Labor in the Era of Structural Adjustment* (New York and London: Routledge).

Sutherland, E. (2007), 'An epidemic of community, union and government induced reform? Mapping the "tipping point" for ethical governance of homebased apparel work in NSW, Australia', in D. Buttigieg et al. (eds), *Trade Unions in the Community: Values, Issues, Shared Interests and Alliances* (Heidelberg: Heidelberg Press).

Textile, Clothing and Footwear Union of Australia (TCFUA) (1995), *The Hidden Cost of Fashion: Report on the National Outwork Information Campaign* (Sydney: TCFUA).

—— (1996), *Outwork: TCFUA Report to the Senate Economics Reference Enquiry February 1996* (Sydney: TCFUA).

—— (1998), 'Outline of award simplification and outwork clauses issues and strategy', unpublished briefing document.

Trebilcock, A. (2004), 'Decent work and the informal economy', paper presented at the EGDI-WIDER Conference on Unlocking Human Potential – Linking the Informal and Formal Sectors, Helsinki.

—— (2006), 'Using development approaches to address the challenge of the informal economy for labour law', in G. Davidov and B. Langille (eds), *Boundaries and Frontiers of Labour Law: Goals and Means in the Regulation of Work* (Oxford and Portland, OR: Hart).

Utting, P. (2005), 'Corporate responsibility and the movement of business', *Development in Practice* 15(3 and 4): 375–88.

Waddock, S. (2004), 'Parallel universes: companies, academics, and the progress of corporate citizenship', *Business and Society Review* 109(1): 5–42.

Weller, S. (1999), 'Clothing outwork: union strategy, labour regulation and labour market restructuring', *Journal of Industrial Relations* 41(2 June): 203–27.

Chapter 15

Triangular Solidarity as an Alternative to CSR and Consumer-based Campaigning

Apo Leong, Chan Ka-wai and Anna Tucker[1]

Introduction

This chapter argues that the two interrelated 'private' (non-state based) methods of improving labour conditions – corporate social responsibility (CSR) and consumer based labour campaigns – have failed to improve the conditions of workers. This is due primarily to their reliance upon and reproduction of the power dynamics that capital generates through international supply chains. In this current climate, it is necessary to respond by fostering new campaign methods.

Since 2002, the Asia Monitor Resource Centre (AMRC) and other organizations have been developing 'triangular solidarity' as a method of strengthening the effectiveness of labour rights campaigning. This chapter will first highlight some of the problems with CSR and consumer-based campaigns before describing the development of triangular solidarity. In this chapter, we focus on China, using the conditions and experience of workers in Southern China as a key example, but also drawing on other countries in the region in which we work. While there are limits to analysing CSR in relation to labour issues alone, labour issues are amongst the most critical and difficult problems that CSR and consumer-based campaigns attempt to address and thus serve to illuminate underlying contradictions and weaknesses of these two models of social action.

'Triangular' Patterns of Global Production and Trade

Much of the world's production now occurs through 'triangular' trade. Increasing numbers of export-manufacturers in newly developed countries are investing in overseas production plants or moving production to less developed countries while maintaining headquarters – that is, their export office – in their own country. They do so in order to take advantage of lower production costs (lower labour and material costs) as well as lower, if not entirely abolished, import tariffs. Under the triangular trade arrangement, generally, two buyer–seller relationships co-exist. The buyer (Northern importer) buys from a seller (exporter) based in a newly developed country. The seller (exporter) in turn buys from a third party (supplier), usually a manufacturer. The seller and the third party enter into a buyer–seller relationship. The third party ships the goods directly to the buyer, rather than to the seller.

Companies from Hong Kong and Taiwan are now the world's largest 'organizers' or 'sellers' of production. They obtain contracts from Europe, the United States and elsewhere in the global North, and manufacture products in developing countries. In the province of Guangdong alone

---

1   The authors thank Shelley Marshall, Peter Lee, Xu Xiao Hong, Diana Beaumont and Doris Lee for their contributions to this chapter.

(which is now known as the biggest production powerhouse in the world), corporations from Hong Kong, Macau and Taiwan have recruited 1.055 million labourers, nearly two and a half times greater than the total number of labourers (463,700) employed in other foreign enterprises (Qiang 2004, 19–20).

CSR and consumer-based labour campaigns seek to address problems arising from both the increasing scope and flow of capital and the increasing international division of labour which has accompanied this phenomenon. As globalization and free trade have accelerated the flow of capital, so too has capital's flow become more boundless. This has, in turn, caused conflict between labour in the global North and South. Many Northern corporations have closed their production capacities in their home countries, dramatically reducing production costs by subcontracting (for instance, by having their subsidiaries open manufacturing factories in developing countries), resulting in mass unemployment in their countries of origin. This has given rise to complaints from workers and their representatives in developed countries that workers from developing countries are taking their jobs. At the same time, however, workers in developing countries are increasingly objecting to the harsh conditions experienced. Although it was expected that labour standards would increase in time, improvements have rarely been realized due to a combination of local and international factors (Chang and Wong 2005, 149). This chapter is mainly concerned with the impact of the downward pressure resulting from international subcontracting practices.

Whether supply chains take a 'triangular' form or some different configuration, multinational corporations (MNCs) which subcontract internationally generally do not play a direct role in production. However, they may still draw upon various means to keep production under their control. Employing a stylized account of supply-chain governance, we might say that there are two major models of international subcontracting. In original equipment manufacturing, MNCs, as buyers, exercise control over all skills, materials and design, while manufacturers simply make semi-finished products from raw materials, or assemble parts together. Under this system, relations between buyers and manufacturers are neither equal nor stable. Buyers can, at any time, change suppliers, and manufacturers must follow buyers' every instruction in order to obtain and retain contracts. The second type of international subcontracting is original design manufacturing. In this production process, manufacturers are responsible for product research and design. Relations between buyers and manufacturers are more akin to that of partners, since buyers have to rely on manufacturers' research and design. Although they are not equal in status, manufacturers still have a certain amount of bargaining power. Under the original design manufacturing system, manufacturers can even develop their own brands and sales network (see Chen and Wong 2002 at Chapter 8).

Therefore, to varying degrees in international subcontracting, buyers and manufacturers are in an unequal relationship. S. Prakash Sethi (2003) calls this a new kind of 'neo-mercantilism', which results in a more or less monopolistic position allowing the MNCs to receive all of the benefit. As Sethi (2003, 7–12) points out, there are several ways to control the price of a product:

1. MNCs can monitor a manufacturer's production structure from time to time in order to exercise control over production costs.
2. MNCs can coordinate with different manufacturers to avoid the increase of labour cost that would result from competing with one another in the employment market.
3. Manufacturers can employ migrant workers from rural areas to work in the city, especially young female workers, as most of these workers know very little about their own rights.

4. Manufacturers can collaborate with local governments in order to contravene labour legislation regarding wages, working hours and other labour conditions.
5. MNCs can exercise control over manufacturers in setting workers' wages and working conditions in the production processes.

This final method of controlling prices (5) occurs as a consequence of a downwards pressure on prices. Buyers seek to lower prices in order to earn greater profits. They do so by forcing their supplying companies to be increasingly more competitive in terms of pricing and lead-time. Many manufacturers have very little bargaining power; they have no choice but to accept harsher contracts. Contract prices are driven down so far that workers become the victims (see HKCIC 2001; see also Chan 2003, 41–9), with the resultant proliferation of 'sweatshops' (Sethi 2003 at Chapter 2). Our analysis of the problems with CSR and consumer-based labour campaigns flow from this understanding of the nature of international subcontracting, triangular trade and the international division of labour which has developed as a consequence of its proliferation.

Problems with CSR

In this section we underline a major paradox facing labour activists in the Asia region: why have multinational corporations (MNCs) suddenly become the promoters and defenders of labour rights when they are frequently identified as the perpetrators of labour exploitation? The globalization of the world economy has entailed, along with a myriad of other influences, a push by MNCs for national and local governments to weaken labour standards in order to avoid capital outflow and to attract foreign direct investment, resulting in a squeeze on wages and welfare. However, at the same time, through the vessel of the CSR movement, MNCs now serve as role models of good conduct and have become prestigious 'corporate citizens' and 'caring corporations'. Nearly every week there are numerous fora, talks and seminars presenting different viewpoints and case studies on this issue. In corporate environments such as China, CSR is a booming industry.

This section considers three primary problems with CSR, although many have been raised elsewhere (including in other chapters in this book). While there is no clear definition of CSR, definitions generated by the business sector place emphasis on the economic benefits of CSR and the positive impact of adopting CSR on profits. However, if genuinely implemented, efforts to improve labour conditions ought to result in a redistribution of profits away from business in favour of workers. The second concern raised relates to the discretionary nature of CSR. Not only does this mean that businesses may implement CSR in an *ad hoc* fashion, but also that where CSR is seen as a replacement for weak labour laws, it entails the privatization of labour regulation. Both of these problems are exacerbated by our third and primary concern with CSR, which is its reliance upon and re-enforcement of international supply chain power dynamics instead of redistributing power from North to South. We focus on these issues because they inform both our concerns with consumer-based campaigns and our views about the appropriate strategies which ought to be adopted by labour organizations in order to improve the conditions of workers in the global South in a sustained manner.

There is no commonly agreed definition of CSR – corporations adopt different aspects of a range of possible CSR techniques. These may include: compliance with the law and local moral codes; observance of codes of business ethics; accountability to shareholders and the public; support for philanthropic work and donations to charities; and promotion of the corporation's social participation. This is in addition to protecting the environment, promoting occupational safety, safeguarding labour laws and rights, showing respect to the community, and protecting the disadvantaged (see Schilling et al. 2003). Furthermore, corporations interact with different groups in different CSR areas. For example, they may have to deal with organizations for environmental protection and local communities; or they may need to work with labour organizations, workers and labour unions (Qiang 2004, 16).

Differences in the definition of CSR reflect the diversity of concerned parties' views. Some researchers attempt to distinguish between a corporation's social and economic responsibility, contending that corporate economic responsibility lies in pursuing the interests of shareholders, while social responsibility requires corporations to satisfy the generally acceptable demands of the public in social sustainability and social justice issues (see Zheng 2004, 33). Other business consultants and researchers actively 'selling' the concept of CSR believe that aligning the social and the economic elements of a company's responsibility can bring huge profits to the business. A great deal of evidence shows that the implementation of CSR can:

1. boost the sales of their products and increase their market share;
2. help the brand attain a good reputation;
3. improve the image of the corporation;
4. attract and retain talent, and promote employee productivity;
5. reduce production costs; and
6. attract more investment and achieve more positive credit ratings (Kotler and Lee 2005, 10–18).

In short, CSR can increase profits and is thus of great economic significance.

As a consequence, for many corporations CSR is not an obligation, but rather a competitive business strategy (Kotler and Lee 2005, 4–10). For example, Business for Social Responsibility, an American pro-business organization, interprets CSR as the attainment of business achievements by respecting ethical values and protection of the community and environment (BSR 2003), thus recasting it as a method of achieving a corporation's final goal of profit-making.

However, if MNCs genuinely pursue ethical practices, this should result in at least some redistribution of profits along the supply chain to suppliers and, ultimately, to workers. There may be benefits to MNCs in terms of an increased consumer market share resulting from a heightened ethical reputation, yet profit margins ought to be reduced unless MNCs make up for the loss of profits normally reaped from cheap production through increased efficiency in managing the supply chain or reducing advertising costs.

An alternative definition of CSR can be used to analyse the nature of CSR itself. Philip Kotler and Nancy Lee point out that CSR is a self-commitment made by the corporation to improve community well-being through 'discretionary' business practices and 'discretionary' contributions of corporate resources to society, where the well-being of the community includes human happiness and protection of the environment (2005, 4–10). They emphasize the discretionary nature of this commitment – these business activities go beyond ethics, law, normal business operation or even the expectations of the public (Kotler and Lee 2005, 3).

This 'discretionary' nature of CSR has been heavily critiqued by non-government labour rights organizations. The critique has been targeted at codes of conduct in particular, which are the most common embodiment of CSR. A code of conduct is a commitment made by a corporation to regulate the labour and environmental protection standards practised in its production process or that of its supplier companies or manufacturing and business partners. While many corporations maintain their own codes of conduct, which state that both they and their partners in production must follow the local labour laws, most of these local labour laws fall far below international labour standards.

Even in areas where comprehensive labour legislation exists, if the local government is powerless or unwilling to enforce the legislation, in practice the stipulated legal regulations function as a 'discretionary' guide to proper behaviour. In other words, the corporation can decide 'at its discretion' how to implement the codes of conduct, which articles they should follow, and which ones they can temporarily suspend. We see this as enacting the privatization of labour law itself.

Problems with the discretionary nature of CSR are borne out, in particular, in the self-monitoring of corporations. For example, Nike's recent CSR China report admitted that the top three management issues arising from Nike's audit in China are an inadequate system to enforce compliance with Nike's code of conduct, lack of knowledge and training around compliance, and insufficient communication internally and externally (Nike Inc. 2008, 13). Without the ability to enforce CSR instruments they may amount to a mere publicity strategy (see Sethi 2003, 82).

This example also indicates that problems of poor labour conditions cannot be dealt with in a technical manner. While most corporations prefer to pursue technical measures to fulfil CSR duties – for example, in the decrease of pollution,[2] in the protection of workers' health, and in the reduction of industrial accidents – labour issues involve the management of a corporation and as such involve sensitive power relations between employers and employees, including the right of workers to speak out on factory affairs where their interests are involved.

The real targets of codes of conduct are manufacturers, as the MNCs themselves are now rarely involved in production – production activities generally being outsourced. Although most MNCs employ social auditors to monitor their suppliers, the MNCs themselves are rarely under scrutiny. Further, the fact that only manufacturers are targeted limits the coverage of codes of conduct considerably. For example, in the course of the monitoring activities conducted by the AMRC, we have noticed that very few other labour activists or monitors pay attention to labour conditions inside Disney's amusement park in China – most only concentrate on the labour standards of the suppliers who manufacture Disney's products.

Whilst codes of practice are nominally aimed at acting as a countervailing pressure against the strong downwards pressure produced by supply-chain management, they may, in some instances, further exacerbate price pressures on suppliers. For instance, in most cases suppliers must pay for auditing and CSR expenses. In one example, a 200-worker garment supplier had to spend US$20,000 in order to acquire certification and a further US$40,000 to 'clean up' the factory before the brand would place the order, but had no guarantee that the brand would continue to place fresh orders. The operation of codes of conduct reinforces and strengthens the bargaining power of MNCs in international subcontracting. For supplying manufacturers, harsh contracts combined with codes of conduct are something which MNCs 'force' them to accept in order to consolidate their unequal relationship (Chang and Wong 2005, 149–50).

Codes have often been adopted in order to address problems created by state failure, yet this state failure undermines their efficacy. In production areas there are often grave defects in laws, or the government enforces the laws poorly. The former can be illustrated by wage legislation in Indonesia where, according to the minimum salary, workers can hardly feed themselves, let alone their families.[3] The best example of the latter is in China, where the labour law is quite

---

2 In *Global Reporters*, a SustainAbility project in partnership with the United Nations Environment Programme (UNEP), efforts initially focused on the monitoring of environmental protection. From 2002, it started to produce reports on CSR – these recognize that in cases of purely technical issues, things can usually be settled easily (SustainAbility and the UNEP 2000, 6–7).

3 There is now considerable evidence to show that most Asian countries – including developed and developing countries – tend to weaken labour laws and make workers more vulnerable (Asia Monitor Resource Centre 2003).

comprehensive and advanced but enforcement by local governments is weak. Codes of conduct seek to redress the lack of well-written legislation, strong legal systems, proper enforcement of laws, and labour unions truly representing workers. However, all the codes of conduct we have examined in the course of our work as monitors state clearly that the manufacturer should strictly observe the local labour law. This creates a major hitch in the enforcement of codes as they either ask supplying companies to adhere to defective labour laws or, alternatively, to good laws which have never been enforced.

A further problem, which codes of conduct were designed to address, is the absence of representative or strong labour organizations. If there was a powerful labour union in the production area, workers could reach a collective contract with manufacturers or even with the contracting multinational corporations, through the assistance of a labour union safeguarding their rights. Yet in many developing countries labour unions are too feeble or, in the cases of China and Burma, are suppressed or corporatist. Once again, the codes of conduct we have examined in the course of our work state that they will respect labour unions organized by the workers and the rights of collective negotiation. However, the sad truth is that these two things rarely exist in the areas in which the effective enforcement of codes of practice is most needed. These two flaws in codes of practice underline the deeply contradictory nature of CSR.

Western-based Consumer Campaigns

Although, as we saw in the previous section, MNCs reap great benefits from international subcontracting, subcontracting is also a double-edged sword: a corporation can earn exorbitant profits by controlling prices but, as they cannot supervise the whole production process directly, this brings new risks in management – especially in the quality of the product, labour issues and pollution in the manufacturing processes. All these risks may expose the corporation to criticism and damage its public image (Chang and Wong 2005, 149–50, note 35).

In many countries in the North, from the late 1980s onwards news of labour exploitation in sweatshops has resulted in indignation and the formation of strong consumer campaigns (also known as Action Alert Brand Targeting Campaigns). The voice of consumers is very clear: MNCs should be held responsible for the labour conditions of their supplying companies. In this sense, consumer campaigning jeopardizes the profits of the corporation: the greater the pressure from the consumer campaigning, the more pressure is placed on the corporation to assume further social responsibilities. The proliferation of company codes of conduct has been largely in order to 'please' or 'pacify' consumers, and, simultaneously, to protect MNC's interests in international subcontracting. On the one hand, codes of conduct are part of business public relations in response to accusations made by consumer campaigning. On the other hand, the codes formally acknowledge that corporations should be primarily responsible for the workers that they do not directly employ in the manufacturing process, and that the labour rights of these workers should be protected (Labour Rights in China 1999). These also serve as the basis for non-governmental organizations (NGOs) to monitor and intervene in the manufacturing processes of multinational corporations.

One of the major criticisms directed at consumer campaigns is that they rely upon and reproduce the power dynamics of North/South supply chains. That there are good reasons for this tendency is undeniable: consumer-based campaigns operate where they have most leverage. Given the reputation-sensitivity of Northern- (and generally Western-) based MNCs, it makes sense for campaigning activities to occur at the place of consumption, where MNCs are most susceptible to 'naming and shaming' techniques. In the absence of strong labour movements in the place of production, MNCs have the most leverage over suppliers who are seen to be directly responsible for poor working conditions. Indeed, unless MNCs can be made responsible for the conditions of workers further down the supply chain and, hopefully, relieve some of the downwards price and time pressure which leads suppliers to pass on pressure to workers, the conditions of workers will never improve.

However, the power of these campaigns lies with the Northern-based consumer campaign group, not with the Southern-based workers' organization: workers are the objects rather than the subjects of the campaign. This is not to say that consumer-based campaigns do not involve or begin from the premise of solidarity – for instance, many Northern consumer-based campaigns take a particularly egregious labour abuse in a factory or a shocking external monitor's report as their impetus. However, campaigns will have difficulty overcoming this essential power dynamic as long as the decision-making and greatest point of leverage remains in the global North.

A further problem with this method of campaigning, which is shared with CSR in general, is its focus on single enterprises, such as, for example, a Taiwanese-owned garment factory employing 2,000 workers producing for Nike. Nike may exercise considerable power over that factory, and efforts to improve the conditions of those 2,000 workers are important, however, given the scale of labour abuses suffered throughout this region and in the global South in general, it is not an effective or efficient campaigning method. This problem is exacerbated by the low success rate of campaigns, even with regard to single enterprises.

As Dae-oup Chang states, '[t]he problem with [consumer-based campaigns] is that there is no room for "class", either capital or labour' (Chang 2005, 22). The very limited success of consumer-based campaigns in encouraging solidarity between workers in the South shows that building a campaign framework on individual success stories cannot be the foundation of a 'movement'. Therefore, it is our view that the strategies of consumer movements must be revised in order to address the question of how to promote the sustainable organization of workers in producing countries *during* and *after* the campaign. The conditions of workers in the South will not improve in a widespread manner until workers are able to form permanent, independent workers' organizations which extend their reach beyond factories which produce goods for Northern consumption. Those workers who produce for local consumption, those who are in service-oriented employment, and also those who are unwaged ought to be involved in sustained campaigns.

The Road Ahead

Based upon this analysis, we believe that there are three avenues of progress for labour organizations, although only one will be focused upon in this chapter. The first, which flows from the analysis presented in this chapter, is that we must attempt to demystify CSR through whatever forums are at our disposal in order to demonstrate its flaws and discourage reliance upon it as a mechanism for improving labour conditions. The second is that we need to generate our own, common standards, which we will enforce during negotiations with corporations, instead of monitoring standards which corporations themselves have generated.[4] The third avenue, which we will focus on for the remainder of this chapter, involves reconfiguring our campaign methods so as to overcome a range of problems thus far outlined in this chapter.

---

4   See the chapter in this volume by Andrea Maksimovic for a development of this theme.

Triangular Solidarity

Our focus over the last two years has been on fostering triangular solidarity as an organizing method. The parties involved in this triangle are: (a) worker organizations (including unions and other NGOs) in the South in the place of production; (b) non-government organizations in the place where the company organizing production (the 'organizer' or 'seller') is based; and (c) consumer-based campaigning organizations and unions in the North. The structure of the campaigns thus mirrors the structure of triangular trading, which, as outlined earlier in this chapter, has become the most dominant configuration of supply chains for production carried out in Asia. Triangular solidarity differs from consumer-based campaigns in a number of respects. It involves building campaigns at all nodal points at which triangular trading occurs, it is initiated by organizations which work directly with workers, and it is aimed at building sustainable workers' movements which involve all affected parties (waged and unwaged workers in the communities where production *and* consumption occurs) and which can challenge capital as a class.

We became convinced of the efficacy of this campaign configuration for achieving change after experiencing success in various campaigns. For instance, in the autumn of 2006, a Hong Kong-owned Thai Gina Form garment factory laid off all its workers in Bangkok (Plaiyoowong and Robertson Jnr 2004, 1; CCC 2006). After exhausting all possible channels in Bangkok, union leaders came to Hong Kong to seek support from Hong Kong-based NGOs and unions. Hong Kong-based groups responded by staging a series of actions outside the company headquarters and outside outlets in major shopping centres for one week. This strategy brought the employer to the bargaining table and, finally, more compensation was paid to the workers. In another case concerning a Hong Kong-owned Cambodian garment factory, a face-to-face dialogue took place between the employer and unions in the presence of a Hong Kong-based labour organization. Subsequently, a collective bargaining agreement was concluded.

Our experience in these as well as past campaigns has highlighted various risks entailed in triangular solidarity which mirror those of traditional consumer-based campaigns. For instance, there remains the risk of unforeseen consequences, such as factory closures. However, triangular solidarity has the benefit of strengthening communication and the power-base of each of the parties involved in the campaign. Perhaps because the Thai Gina Form factory campaign involved only Southern-based organizations, we managed to avoid some of the pitfalls experienced in triangular solidarity campaigns, in which Northern-based campaigns hold considerable bargaining power. These hazards were evident during the more ambitious Play Fair at the Olympics 2004 campaign.

Play Fair at the Olympics 2004 Campaign

The Play Fair at the Olympics Campaign (PFOC) was devised as a limited duration campaign for the six months leading to the 2004 Athens Olympic Games and was the biggest international workers' rights mobilization of its kind. The steering committee for the campaign was comprised of the AMRC, the Clean Clothes Campaign (CCC), Global Unions, Oxfam and the Thai Labour Campaign. Worldwide, hundreds of other organizations participated in PFOC. The campaign was initiated by Oxfam and the CCC, and this may have had an impact on campaign planning and the consistency of participant goals.

The campaign was targeted at 'B-Brand' companies: those that did not receive the same critical exposure of their production and purchasing policies as 'A-brand' companies such as Nike, Adidas and Reebok. The campaign rationale was that if these companies began to place a greater emphasis on working conditions when contracting with factories and suppliers, there would be a greater impetus for factories to adjust their practices. The companies targeted were ASICS, Fila, Kappa, Lotto, Mizuno, Puma and Umbro.

Campaigners in each country were encouraged to target at least one of these companies as well as any other sportswear companies, especially if their Olympic team was supplied by a company not in the target group. In addition to these specific targets, the campaign aimed to instigate recognition and action from sportswear suppliers, the sportswear industry as a whole, the Olympics movement (particularly the International Olympic Committee [IOC]) and the public.

The actions taken in the campaign were varied and included petitions, street actions, worker tours, media-actions and picketing aimed at individual companies (Merk 2005, 11). In Asia, the Thai Labour Campaign and AMRC held a Workers' Solidarity Olympics and Workers' Exchange, with sportswear and garment workers from different countries in the region as participants (Oxfam International 2004). This was a key event which included workers in the wider campaign.

The outcomes of the campaign were mixed and, as we shall see, the evaluations of campaigns conducted by European organizations compared with Asian organizations diverged greatly in emphasis and, thus, the conclusions they reached. The issue of worker participation in the campaign figured little in the official CCC evaluation and other European reports of the campaign.

The CCC produced three reports evaluating the effectiveness of the campaign on sportswear companies, the sportswear industry body and the IOC. Oxfam and Labour Behind the Label, both European organizations running the PFOC, evaluated the campaign against the same indicators (Labour Behind the Label 2004; 2005; Oxfam International 2004). The CCC did acknowledge that organizations in producer countries needed a more central role in future campaigns (Clean Clothes Campaign 2005).

The many concerns regarding triangular solidarity raised by Asian organizations involved in the PFOC did not feature in the evaluations made by European organizations. The two Asian organizations highlighted here, the Asian Transnational Corporation Monitoring Network (ATNC) and the Thai Labour Campaign, in contrast, placed great emphasis on worker solidarity and creating a strong labour movement at grass roots level through the PFOC.

In evaluations of the campaign by European organizations, success was assessed largely in terms of the response of the sportswear companies. The campaign led to greater dialogue between companies and campaigners. For instance, Asics, Mizuno, Lotto, Umbro and Puma all entered into some degree of dialogue with campaigners (Merk 2005, 12). Fila responded negatively to the campaign, choosing to act independently, and Kappa failed to respond at all.

The official campaign evaluation cited the development of a dialogue between PFOC organizers and several of the sportswear companies as one of the key outcomes of the campaign (Merk 2005). Five of the seven companies revised their policies or codes of conduct following the campaign (Clean Clothes Campaign 2005). Commitments were made by four companies to support freedom of association, and two companies committed to enter into a dialogue with trade unions and labour rights groups in Europe and Asia (Merk 2005, 22). None of the companies committed to altering purchasing practices, with only two companies responding to this recommendation, both of whom maintain that it is not an issue (Merk 2005, 22).

Despite concerted efforts to gain official recognition by the IOC, no official recognition was given to the PFOC. The IOC refused to accept a 500,000 signature petition on the rights of sportswear workers presented in Athens (Oxfam International 2004). Some national Olympic Committees gave limited recognition to the PFOC but did not take any action. The British Olympic Association said that they would consult campaigners in relation to contracting for the London Olympics in 2012 (Labour Behind the Label 2005).

The views of Northern-based PFOC organizations regarding the success of the campaign differed significantly from those of Southern-based organizations. The ATNC felt that the campaign did not adhere to the triangular solidarity premise as, despite involving regional organizations such as the Thai Labour Campaign, ATNC and AMRC, the PFOC was based on a consumer campaign strategy (an Action Alert Brand Targeting Campaign). This was felt to be ineffective as it was another discussion between 'consumers/western NGOs-TU [trade unions] and commercial capital', thus excluding the workers and employers directly implicated in the poor labour practices which the campaign was intended to target (ATNC 2006). However, the ATNC did feel that its efforts, and those of other Asian organizations, had succeeded in insisting that workers' voices were heard in the campaign. This changed the dynamic of the campaign to some extent, at least at the level of process.

The dialogue that was opened between PFOC organizers and some of the targeted companies was the chief achievement for many of the Northern campaigning organizations. The ATNC, however, felt that this was an indicator of the Campaign's failure to engage with its Southern participants, and with the more ideal goal of 'systematized, empowered negotiation between labour representatives and their employers in the sector of the region' (ATNC 2006). They noted that under the consumer campaign strategy no efforts were made to build a powerful labour movement in the affected regions, and that this reduced its relevance to the workers it was intended to benefit. Indeed, workers' inclusion in the campaign was lacking at a grass roots level, with worker involvement limited to those involved in existing workers' organizations.

The Thai Labour Campaign coordinated the Workers' Solidarity Olympics and a Workers' Exchange where the experience and outcomes of the PFOC were discussed. The Workers' Exchange involved workers from the garment and sportswear industries in India, Pakistan, Bangladesh, Indonesia, Philippines, Sri Lanka, Hong Kong, Taiwan, China, Cambodia and Thailand. The responses varied, but overall participants agreed the value in the campaign and its events was that it helped increase regional solidarity and understanding in the sportswear sector, and gave participants a more consistent expectation of what the likely outcomes of such a campaign would be (Arnold 2004, 29). For example, there was a sentiment expressed that national campaigns, such as the 'Bed & Bath' campaign in Thailand, were more likely to gain concrete improvements for workers, whereas international campaigns such as the PFOC, which focused on changing purchasing policies, were longer term and unlikely to have quantifiable results (Arnold 2004).

The benefits of an international campaign were seen to be the information gathered which could be used for local and national campaigns and negotiations. The Workers' Exchange participants also pressed for their own input into campaigns, including the selection of which brands or MNCs to target, and which results to push for, such as agreements between large brands and trade unions or for national commitments to freedom of association (Arnold 2004, 30).

Overall, the failures of the campaign in Asia were seen to lie in the lack of regional coordination and communication. This meant that campaigns were run on a national or local basis, and did not have the consistency of message or means to achieve true regional solidarity. Some of the contributing factors to this were seen to be the lack of any campaign funding which could have been used for coordination – instead, individual organizations ran their own campaigns at their own cost. The difficulty of coordinating campaigns by email was also noted (Arnold 2004).

In sum, the evaluations of the PFOC by Northern and Southern campaigns used vastly different measures of success. The concerns over triangular solidarity raised by Asian organizations involved in the campaign were not present in the evaluations of Northern-based organizations such as the CCC. Indeed, the issue of worker participation in the campaign figured far less in the official CCC report and other European evaluations of the PFOC. The ATNC and Thai Labour Campaign envisioned the PFOC increasing the regional solidarity of workers in Asia and affecting labour union organization at the worker/factory level. This was not a focus for European organizations, for whom the primary focus was consumer campaigning and results at the level of the individual sportswear company or sportswear industry body.

2008 Play Fair Campaign

In the lead-up to the 2008 Beijing Olympics a Play Fair campaign was once again initiated, which targeted the IOC, the National Olympics Committees and sportswear brands. The campaign involved an even broader range of organizations than the 2004 Athens campaign and was primarily organized by the CCC, the International Trade Union Confederation and the International Textile, Garment and Leather Worker's Federation. Supporters from 35 countries pledged support to the following statement:

> We believe that sportswear and athletic footwear companies, the International Olympic Committee (IOC), National Olympics Committees, as well as national governments must take steps to eliminate the exploitation and abuse of workers in the global sporting goods industry.
>
> We urge them to take inspiration from the spirit of the Olympics and demonstrate to the world how the principles of *fair play* can be extended to the workplace … (PlayFair2008.org 2008)

Early in the campaign, Chinese organizations withdrew on the basis that they were not genuinely being consulted and, thus, the campaign entailed too many risks for Chinese workers. Only the Clothing Industry, Clerical and Retail Trade Employees General Union, Hong Kong remained involved. The IOC refused to concede to Fair Play demands. On a more positive note, at the beginning of July 2008 a group of sportswear companies agreed to form a working group to address some of the root causes of bad labour conditions in the sector. There were some additional successes in negotiating with National Campaign Committees: for instance, the Chinese National Campaign Committee agreed that official Olympic products should be produced under strict codes of conduct. For the AMRC, however, this outcome simply raised all the issues examined in this chapter, including who monitors the codes of conduct. Whilst it is too early to conduct a full assessment of the campaign, it appears that the primary organizers have not learnt from the failures of the 2004 Fair Play campaign.

Conclusion

This chapter has argued that triangular solidarity campaigns are the most effective method for dealing with challenges thrown up by the increasingly triangular trading patterns of international supply chains. There are now three main pressure points in supply chains: (a) the producers based in developing countries; (b) the organizers or sellers, now often located in newly developed countries in Asia such as Taiwan and Hong Kong; and (c) the buyers or 'brands'. Campaigns should be built at all three points of the triangular trading chain not just in order to gain greater leverage and cover all pressure points, but also to ensure that all parties affected are genuinely involved in decision-making and campaign actions. Consumer-based campaigns have mirrored the power relations of international subcontracting supply chains, with the balance of power located within Northern organizations. As this chapter has argued, they have generally sought to enforce CSR instruments that position MNCs as the promoters and defenders of labour rights and enact the privatization of labour law.

Ideally, triangular solidarity campaigns will have a more even distribution of power amongst campaign organizations, with workers' organizations from the areas in which production occurs initiating and guiding the campaign direction. This may not overcome attendant risks involved in campaigns of this type. For example, factories may still close as a result of campaigns. However, workers may more readily accept this risk when they have been involved in decision-making.

It is regrettable that the largest mobilizations of workers' organizations in recent years – the 2004 Fair Play at the Athens Olympics Campaign and the 2008 Fair Play at the Beijing Olympics Campaign – have not overcome the perils incumbent in consumer-based campaigns. Evaluations carried out by Asian workers' organizations after the 2004 Athens campaigns complained that the main dialogue had occurred between Northern NGOs and unions and Northern capital, thus marginalizing the workers and employers directly implicated in the poor labour practices which the campaign was intended to target. Presently, it appears that similar assessments are likely to be made of the 2008 Fair Play at the Beijing Olympics campaign.

References

Amnesty International (2004), *The UN Human Rights Norms for Business: Towards Legal Accountability* (London: Amnesty International Publications).

Arnold, D. (2004), *Worker's Exchange Report: Play Fair at the Olympics* (Bangkok: Play Fair at the Olympics). Available at http://www.fairolympics.org/background/Play_Fair_Olympics_Bangkok.pdf [accessed: 9 October 2008].

Asia Monitor Resource Centre (2003), *Asia Pacific Labour Law Review: Workers' Rights for the New Century* (Hong Kong: Asia Monitor Resource Centre).

—— (2006), 'Multi-stakeholder initiatives in China: spotlight on ethical trade initiative', *Asian Labour Update* 60: 16.

Asian Transnational Corporation Monitoring Network (ATNC) (2006), *About Us.* [Online: ATNC]. *Asian Transnational Corporation Monitoring Network: Building a Labour Movement.* Available at: http://atnc.org/html/aboutus [accessed: 9 October 2008].

Business for Social Responsibility (BSR) (2003), *Overview of Corporate Social Responsibility: Issue Brief.* [Online: BSR]. Available at: http://www.bsr.org/research/issue-brief-details.cfm?DocumentID=48809 [accessed: 9 October 2008].

Chan, A. (2003), 'A "race to the bottom": globalisation and China's labour standards', *China Perspectives* 46: 41–9.

Chang, D. (2004), 'Demystifying codes of conduct', in T. Tiwari et al. (eds), *A Critical Guide to Corporate Codes of Conduct: Voices from the South* (Hong Kong: Asia Monitor Resource Centre).

—— (2005), 'Asian TNCs, labour, and the movement of capital', in D. Chang and E. Shepherd (eds), *Asian Transnational Corporation Outlook 2004: Asian TNCs, Workers, and the Movement of Capital* (Hong Kong: Asia Monitor Resource Centre).

—— and Wong, M. (2005), 'FDI and labour in China: the actors and possibility of a new working class activism', in D. Chang and E. Shepherd (eds), *Asian Transnational Corporation Outlook 2004: Asian TNCs, Workers, and the Movement of Capital* (Hong Kong: Asia Monitor Resource Centre).

Chen, Y. and Wong, M. (2002), *New Bondage and Old Resistance: Realities and Challenges of the Labour Movement in Taiwan* (Hong Kong: Hong Kong Christian Industrial Committee).

Clean Clothes Campaign (CCC) (2005), *Still Seeking Fair Play the Olympics Campaign Moves On*, Newsletter 19. [Online: CCC]. Available at: http://www.cleanclothes.org/news/newsletter19-12.htm [accessed: 9 October 2008].

—— (2006), *Gina Form Bra Closed Down: Action Needed Today!* [Online: CCC]. Available at: http://www.cleanclothes.org/companies/55 [accessed: 29 August 2009].

Connor, T. and Dent, K. (2006), *Offside! Labour Rights and Sportswear Production in Asia* (Oxford: Oxfam International).

Global Principles Steering Group (2003), *Principles for Global Corporate Responsibility: Bench Marks for Measuring Business Performance* (Marshalltown, RSA: Bench Marks Foundation). Available at: http://www.bench-marks.org/downloads/Bench Marks – full.doc [accessed: 9 October 2008].

Hong Kong Christian Industrial Committee (HKCIC) (2001), *How Hasbro, McDonald's, Mattel and Disney Manufacture Their Toys: Report on the Labor Rights and Occupational Safety and Health Conditions of Toy Workers in Foreign Investment Enterprises in Southern Mainland China* (Hong Kong: Hong Kong Christian Industrial Committee).

Jonsson, B. (2006), 'EU-Asia corporate responsibility research agenda', *EurAsia Bulletin* 10(11–12): 17–19.

Kotler, P. and Lee, N. (2005), *Corporate Social Responsibility* (Hoboken, NJ: John Wiley and Sons).

Labour Behind the Label (2004), *Play Fair at the Olympics: A Progress Report*. [Online: Labour Behind the Label]. Available at: http://www.labourbehindthelabel.org/campaigns/playfair/archive/94-playfair2004/59 [accessed: 9 October 2008].

——(2005), *Play Fair at the Olympics: An Evaluation*. [Online: Labour Behind the Label]. Available at: http://www.labourbehindthelabel.org/campaigns/playfair/archive/94-playfair2004/64 [accessed: 9 October 2008].

Labour Rights in China (1999), *No Illusions: Against the Global Cosmetic SA8000* (Hong Kong: Labour Rights in China).

Merk, J. (2005), *The Play Fair at the Olympics Campaign: An Evaluation of the Company Responses*, Clean Clothes Campaign, ICFTU and Oxfam. Available at: http://www.cleanclothes.org/ftp/05-07-pfoc_evaluation.pdf [accessed: 9 October 2008].

Nike Inc. (2008), *Innovate for a Better World: Nike China 2008 Corporate Responsibility Reporting Supplement* (Beaverton, OR: Nike Inc.).

Oxfam International (2004), *Campaign Update*. [Online: Make Trade Fair – Oxfam International]. Available at http://www.maketradefair.com/en/index.php?file=campaign_update.htm [accessed: 9 October 2008].

Plaiyoowong, S. and Robertson Jnr, P.S. (2004), *The Struggle of the Gina Workers in Thailand: Inside a Successful International Solidarity Campaign*, Working Papers Series No. 75 (Hong Kong: Southeast Asia Research Centre).

PlayFair2008.org. (2008), *Play Fair 2008 Supporters*. [Online: Play Fair 2008]. Available at: http://www.playfair2008.org/ [accessed: 9 October 2008].

Qiang, Z. (2004), 'Guangdong at the frontier of CSR', paper presented at the Panyu Migrant Worker Documentation Center Seminar: Monitoring of Corporate Social Responsibility, Guangdong, 6 December.

Schilling, D. et al. (2003), *Principles for Global Corporate Responsibility: Bench Marks for Measuring Business Performance*. [Online]. Available at: http://www.bench-marks.org/ [accessed: 29 August 2009].

Sethi, S.P. (2003), *Setting Global Standards: Guidelines for Creating Codes of Conduct in MNCs* (Hoboken, NJ: John Wiley and Sons).

Students and Scholars Against Corporate Misbehaviour (SACOM) (2005), *Looking for Mickey Mouse's Conscience: A Survey of the Working Conditions of Disney's Supplier Factories in China* (Hong Kong: SACOM). Available at: http://www.sacom.hk/html/uploads/disney.pdf [accessed: 9 October 2008].

—— (2006), *A Second Attempt at Looking for Mickey Mouse's Conscience: A Survey of the Working Conditions of Disney's Supplier Factories in China* (Hong Kong: SACOM). Available at: http://www.sacom.hk/html/uploads/Disney_Research_Report_2006_ENG [accessed: 9 October 2008].

SustainAbility and the United Nations Environment Programme (UNEP) (2000), *The Global Reporters*, 1st edition (London: SustainAbility).

Wells, D. (2007), 'Too weak for the job: corporate codes of conduct, non-governmental organizations and the regulation of international labour standards', *Global Social Policy* 7(1): 51–74.

Yu, H.Q. (2006), 'Monitoring the monitors: observations of CSR in action', *Asian Labour Update* 60: 10.

Zheng, G.H. (2004), '"Consumers" response to CSR: an observation on the relation between nations and societies', paper presented at the Panyu Migrant Worker Documentation Center Seminar: Monitoring of Corporate Social Responsibility, Guangdong, 6 December.

Zhihuan, L. (ed.) (2004), *SA8000 and the Establishment of CSR in China* (Beijing: China Economic Publication).

PART IV
A Strengthened and Transformed Role for the State

Chapter 16

Regional Trade Agreements in the Pacific Islands: Fair Trade for Farmers?

Nic Maclellan

Introduction

As fair trade marketing expands in Europe, Australia, New Zealand and other developed countries, small businesses and farmers' associations in the Pacific islands are developing small-scale initiatives to promote fair trade products from the region. From organic coffee grown in the highlands of Papua New Guinea to coconut products from Samoa or the Solomon Islands, there are fledgling attempts by island producers to develop fair trade exports. These initiatives come at a time when rural farmers are also seeking to diversify from traditional cash crops into niche agricultural exports, with products like vanilla, noni juice, spices, exotic forest products and kava.

But can fair trade initiatives really flourish in this era of 'free trade'? At a time of multilateral and bilateral trade negotiations, small developing countries in the Pacific face particular problems in creating opportunities for new exports from the rural producers who make up the vast majority of people in the region. This chapter argues that it is difficult to create fair trade opportunities in the Pacific without addressing the trade policy and non-tariff trade barriers created in regional trade negotiations.

In recent years, Pacific island countries have increasingly focused on trade liberalization as a central pillar of efforts to promote regional integration and cooperation, with trade policy developed through the Pacific Islands Forum (the regional inter-governmental body that links Australia, New Zealand and 14 independent island states).[1] A growing debate over 'free trade' in the islands region has been framed by principles from the World Trade Organization (WTO) and the Asia Pacific Economic Co-operation (APEC) forum. In recent government policy statements, increased trade and 'open economies' are often presented as a panacea to address the lack of economic growth and social development in island nations. Duncan Kerr, formally Australia's Parliamentary Secretary for Pacific Islands Affairs has argued:

> Trade is good. Open markets do matter. In the long term, it is trade more than development assistance that will reduce poverty. Open trade opens doors. Making trade easier and removing excessive regulations can have enormous benefits. ... More trade will result in economic growth in the Pacific and for its people. It will reduce dependency and lead to more prosperity and sustainability. (Kerr 2008)

---

1   The Pacific Islands Forum membership includes Australia, Aotearoa/New Zealand and the independent island states of Papua New Guinea, Solomon Islands, Vanuatu, Fiji, Kiribati, Tuvalu, Cook Islands, Tonga, Samoa, Marshall Islands, Federated States of Micronesia, Palau, Niue and Nauru. Tokelau and Timor Leste have observer status with the Forum, while New Caledonia and French Polynesia are associate members. The other US and French colonies in the region are not Forum members. At time of writing, Fiji has been suspended from Forum membership after the 2009 abrogation of its constitution by the military.

The 2000 Cotonou Agreement, which links the European Union and the African, Caribbean and Pacific (ACP) grouping, likewise proposes that further integrating Pacific economies into the global market is compatible with reducing and eventually eradicating poverty in the context of sustainable development.[2]

But the automatic connection between open markets, economic growth and sustainable human and environmental development has been challenged; neo-liberal ideology on free trade has been debated within and without multilateral and regional trade fora. The notion that the Doha Development Round will contribute to sustainable development in the Pacific has left many islanders unconvinced, as Professor Jane Kelsey has noted:

> Whether the WTO can deliver net gains to such small, isolated and vulnerable island states is a litmus test for the Doha 'development' round. Experience to date suggests the WTO is failing that test and potentially setting the price of membership beyond what the Pacific Islands can afford. The prevailing orthodoxy, based on neoclassical trade theory and backed by econometric modelling, suggests that full trade liberalisation is intrinsically beneficial for every country. Empirically based assessment of the economic and social prospects for the Islands under such a regime suggest otherwise. (Kelsey 2004c)

Current negotiations for regional free trade agreements (FTAs) have highlighted an unequal playing field in which island states do not have the economic and political weight to strike equitable trade deals with larger powers like Australia, New Zealand and the EU. The rhetoric that links free trade, economic growth and social development suggests coherence between different arms of government – as if trade officials and development assistance experts work hand-in-glove to forge 'whole of government' policies that benefit the poorest members of the community in developing island nations. But recent negotiations for an economic partnership agreement (EPA) between the EU and Pacific nations have shown the opposite.

As discussed below, rhetoric about 'sustainable development' is not evident in negotiating drafts put forward by EU trade negotiators who have rejected proposals advanced by Pacific governments to address their specific needs and who look at the Pacific agreements in the context of global multilateral trade objectives. The EU has tried to use the EPA process to open the way for European corporations to access the services sector and to introduce provisions through the regional EPAs – on services, intellectual property rights, government procurement and investment – that were rebuffed in the multilateral Doha negotiations by larger developing countries such as Brazil, South Africa and India.

The potential to expand fair trade initiatives in the Pacific will be hampered by this clash between the interests of major corporations and those of marginal trading nations. The 'free trade' mantra, which implies that all developing countries have the same opportunities for growth through trade, downplays the particular difficulties faced by small island developing states (SIDS) as they attempt to negotiate with major trading partners like Australia, New Zealand, Japan or the EU. As one New Zealand official has noted, '[w]hen it comes to trade, there is no "special relationship" with the Pacific. The negotiators do a group hug, then put their Geneva hats on' (Kelsey 2004b, 23).

---

2   The main objective of the Cotonou Agreement, signed in 2000, is 'reducing and eventually eradicating poverty consistent with the objectives of sustainable development and the gradual integration of the ACP countries into the world economy' (Cotonou Agreement, Art. 1).

In response, many community groups, indigenous organizations and trade unions have begun questioning 'free trade', arguing that the balance in trade negotiations must be shifted to reflect the needs of the poorest sectors of the community in the rural areas of small island states. Some Forum island countries are attempting to develop trade policies more relevant to their economic and social standing as SIDS, creating opportunities that are relevant for countries with populations numbered in the thousands rather than the millions.[3]

This chapter begins with a brief summary of Pacific trade, outlines some new fair trade initiatives, and then details current negotiations on regional trade liberalization through the Pacific Island Countries Trade Agreement (PICTA), the Pacific Agreement on Closer Economic Relations (PACER), PACER-Plus and the EU-ACP EPA. The chapter then presents a case study on kava exports from the Pacific as an example of the development rhetoric of major economic powers failing to match trade reality. It outlines a campaign by a coalition of farmers' and growers' organizations, research scientists and indigenous rights NGOs to reverse European and Australian bans on kava imports which have damaged a booming industry for the islands. The imposition of bans on kava in order to protect the health of developed countries' citizenry has sparked anger in the region, as the restrictions come at a time when developed nations have used the international trade regime aggressively to maintain their own exports of mutton flaps and junk food to the islands, regardless of the consequences for nutrition, health and social development.

When policies on public health, social development and free trade conflict in this way, it raises questions about the ways in which fair trade and social development can be integrated. As negotiations between Australia, New Zealand and island states commence over a new regional trade agreement (dubbed PACER-Plus), it will be important to reflect upon how the regional trade agenda will affect people engaged in farming and fishing in rural and outer island communities in the Pacific.

Fair Trade for Farmers?

Pacific trade patterns are characterized by narrow export sectors, dominated by natural resources such as minerals, timber, agricultural products or the fisheries in island Exclusive Economic Zones. Exports include both processed and unprocessed commodities, such as: palm oil from the Solomon Islands and Papua New Guinea; sugar from Fiji; and canned fish from the Solomon Islands, Papua New Guinea, American Samoa and Fiji. Papua New Guinea and the Solomon Islands have been the largest exporters of forestry products, notably round logs.

The region faces significant constraints to increase trade opportunities, such as: distance from the main global trading centres; vulnerability to external economic or environmental shocks; limited foreign investment; and small domestic markets. Forum island countries have an unusually high dependence on imports, including oil and diesel fuel, foodstuffs and a wide range of manufactured products. Only a few of the larger island nations – Papua New Guinea, Fiji, Samoa and the French territories – have a significant manufacturing sector and are often reliant on a few key industries (such as garments and mineral water in Fiji or the Yazaki automotive assembly plant in Samoa). Some countries are seeking to develop their services sector, including educational services, finance and banking, the establishment of call centres in Fiji or the sale of internet domain names (such

---

3 Only Papua New Guinea, with six million people, has a population greater than one million. The smaller island nations (such as Palau and the Cook Islands with 15,000 people, Tuvalu with less than 10,000, Niue with 2,000 or Tokelau with 1,500) will never compete with major Asian trading nations.

as Dot.tv from Tuvalu or Dot.tk from Tokelau – the internet-era equivalent of Tuvalu's philately industry that brought in significant earnings from the sale of stamps until the 1970s).

Another key Pacific export is people. Development options for some communities are limited by the realities of geography and demography, thus policy on labour mobility takes on increasing importance (Luthria et al. 2006). Pacific workers today are international and mobile: i-Kiribati and Tuvaluan seafarers staff the global shipping trade; Samoan and Tongan labourers work in factories and building sites in Sydney and Auckland or pick fruit in Australia's Murray Valley (often as 'illegal' or undocumented workers); more than two thousand Fijians have worked in Iraq and Kuwait as security guards, truck drivers and labourers, while Fijian soldiers and police officers serve in peace-keeping operations around the globe. Meanwhile Indo-Fijian and Tongan computer technicians, nurses, accountants and teachers migrate to seek a better life, in the face of political turmoil and limited career opportunities in their homeland.

These patterns of migration provide benefits such as the transfer of remittances, the repatriation of skills and education, the promotion of tourism and the seeding of funds for small business development. Remittances sent home play a vital part of the economy of countries like Tonga, Samoa, Niue, Tuvalu, Kiribati, the Cook Islands, the Territory of Wallis and Futuna Islands and Fiji. But overseas migration or seasonal work also create a series of problems related to loss of human capital, family separation and the social consequences of the three Ms – mobile men with money.

Although many Pacific countries are reliant on remittances from overseas workers, Mares and Maclellan (2007) have argued that Australia's migration policies place significant restrictions on labour mobility for unskilled workers from the Pacific – the labour market is open for skilled workers such as teachers, nurses, accountants and rugby players, but it is constrained for people engaged in farming and fishing who make up the vast bulk of island populations. These constraints are significant as farmers seek extra money for basic needs (for example, payment of school fees, housing improvements and fuel for outboard motors).

Rural villagers rely on their gardens for daily subsistence, but many are also involved in cash cropping for domestic or international markets. However, prices for traditional commodity exports face significant fluctuations: Fiji's sugar industry is waning as prices drop and EU subsidies are removed under WTO pressure; palm oil faces new challenges with NGOs seeking to end forest clearing to combat global warming; the transport costs for copra cannot compete with larger producers like the Philippines. Therefore, Pacific exporters have been encouraged to seek new niche markets, through the export of coconut products (for example, coconut oil and cream), vanilla, noni juice, spices, exotic forest products or kava.

Beyond lobbying and advocacy, some NGOs and small businesses are working to promote trade with 'just and equitable development at their heart' (CSO Forum 2007, 6). With fluctuating prices for traditional products, there have been a number of attempts to develop fair trade marketing of Pacific agricultural and forest products, such as the Solomon Western Islands Fair Trade (SWIFT) timber initiative.

Fair Trade Initiatives in the Region

Today there are a number of initiatives in the Pacific which claim a fair trade component and a focus on women and rural development. These small-scale initiatives are developing niche markets locally and overseas and providing cash for rural communities that can be used, like remittances, for improved housing and school fees. Recent examples of fair trade marketing include Kokonut Pacific, WIBDI, Coffee Connections and FRIEND.

Kokonut Pacific

Kokonut Pacific is a foundation member of the Fair Trade Association of Australia and New Zealand. The Australia-based company began in 1994 and established operations in Solomon Islands in 2005, teaching villagers about organic and pesticide-free growing. Their 'Direct Micro-Expelling' (DME) process presses coconut flesh to produce extra-virgin coconut oil, allowing for the manufacture of coconut oil soap and coconut oil biodiesel fuel. The company claims a significant development role from its initiative, arguing that the product is:

- produced by small village units with easy-to-use DME hand-operated presses;
- produced where coconuts grow, empowering local families in their own business in remote areas;
- reversing the trend of youth moving into the cities to look for work;
- gender-neutral, family 'cottage industry' processing – not factory conditions.[4]

Women in Business Development Incorporated (WIBDI)

Samoan-based WIBDI utilizes the DME technology and small business programmes to build a network of women's cooperatives:

> The Virgin Coconut Oil project now involves more than 200 organically-certified farmers and their extended families. Women involved in the project are experiencing increased status in their villages with their new economic power. The income is vital to their families' livelihoods and security. For some this has enabled them to pay for their children's education, for others it has reduced their dependence on remittances from family members working overseas. (Oxfam New Zealand 2008)[5]

Coffee Connections

Coffee Connections in Papua New Guinea exports organic and specialty coffee assessed by members of the International Federation of Organic Agriculture Movements (IFOAM).[6] The company draws on organically certified coffee producers such as Highlands Organic Agriculture Co-operative Ltd, which represents over 2,500 farmers from 32 village communities spread over the Purosa Valley of Papua New Guinea's Eastern Highlands Province. Coffee is the only cash crop for these communities and the cooperative growers support about 12,000 family members.

The Foundation for Rural Integrated Enterprises N Development (FRIEND)

FRIEND is a non-governmental organization in Fiji which supports community programmes for unemployed and rural women. It is particularly focused on poverty alleviation and creating gender equity in rural and underserved communities in Fiji and has established a brand to sell locally produced chutneys, pickles, jams and handicrafts.[7]

---

4   For further information, refer to the Kokonut Pacific website: http://www.kokonutpacific.com.au/.

5   For information on WIBDI, see the Oxfam New Zealand website: http://www.oxfam.org.nz/whatwedo.

6   For further information, refer to the Coffee Connections website: http://www.coffeeconnections.biz/.

7   See the FRIEND website for further details: http://www.fijifriend.com/index.html.

Pacific producers face many challenges to develop fair trade in products like kava and coconut due to the limitations of intellectual property rights legislation, which sometimes prohibits the granting of products rights for generic products (PCRC 1995; Mead and Ratuva 2007). The coconut products exporter Kokonut Pacific has noted:

> Criteria or protocols have been set up for a wide range of commodities (eg Coffee, tea, cocoa, vanilla, certain handicraft products etc.) to confirm their Fair Trade status in export markets. At the present time, no criteria have been established for Fair Trade with coconuts, so, strictly speaking, nobody trading in any coconut products can claim internationally recognised Fair Trade status for this commodity. (Kokonut Pacific 2007)

In spite of initiatives such as these, efforts to promote fair trade and niche markets for Pacific goods have foundered on the rocks of changing trade policies in Australia, New Zealand and the EU. At a time when island farmers and small businesses are trying to promote a fledgling 'fair trade' industry and develop niche export markets for agricultural products, trade and quarantine policies of major states have seriously damaged the interests of rural producers.

Regional Trade Negotiations

Even with increased global awareness of environmental and trade justice issues, truly fair trade products make up a tiny amount of global commodity trade. Any discussion of fair trade for the island states of the Pacific must be framed within the realities of the international trading system.

WTO policies affect the whole region, even though most states of the 16-member Pacific Islands Forum are not WTO members; only Australia, New Zealand, Fiji, Papua New Guinea, Solomon Islands and Tonga are full members of the WTO, while Samoa and Vanuatu have applied to join. In some countries this accession process has been contested by civil society groups due to the onerous conditions being placed on small island states (Kelsey 2004a; Oxfam New Zealand 2005).

With the failure to complete the Doha Development Round in the WTO, the trade agenda in the Pacific is largely being played out through negotiations over regional FTAs. Forum member countries are engaged in the negotiation and implementation of three key regional agreements.

Pacific Island Countries Trade Agreement (PICTA)

PICTA covers trade in goods for Pacific Island Forum countries except Australia and New Zealand. PICTA was endorsed at the Forum Heads of Government meeting in Nauru in August 2001 and provides for the phased elimination of tariffs between island countries. It provides for the abolition of most tariffs by 2010 for the larger island economies and by 2016 for the smaller ones. The phasing in of the agreement over this period is to be accompanied by strategies to help governments adopt alternative taxes and economic reform measures to compensate for the revenue they will lose from tariff reductions.[8]

---

8   By September 2008, 11 countries had ratified PICTA which came into force on 13 April 2003, but only six countries are already trading under the FTA – the Solomon Islands, the Cook Islands, Fiji, Samoa, Vanuatu and Niue. Kiribati, Nauru, Papua New Guinea, Tuvalu and Tonga are in the process of completing their domestic requirements prior to announcing their trading under PICTA. The Federated States of Micronesia are yet to ratify PICTA while Palau and the Republic of Marshall Islands are yet to make a decision on their accession to PICTA. The French territory of New Caledonia is investigating the option of joining the regional agreement.

Pacific Agreement on Closer Economic Relations (PACER)

PACER was also endorsed at the Forum meeting in Nauru in 2001. It sets out a broader umbrella agreement for all Forum members, including Australia and New Zealand. In August 2009, Forum leaders meeting in Cairns agreed to move beyond the current arrangements for closer regional economic relations covered by PACER, towards a more comprehensive free trade agreement, which has been dubbed PACER-Plus. Pacific trade ministers stressed

> that any PACER-Plus arrangement (i.e. moves beyond PACER for deepening regional trade integration), must be much more than a simple trade agreement if it is to succeed in providing a workable framework for deepening regional trade and economic cooperation among the Members, covering such issues as temporary movement of natural persons and fisheries management. (Pacific Islands Forum Secretariat 2007)

Economic Partnership Agreement (EPA)

An EPA is currently being negotiated between the EU and Pacific members of the African, Caribbean and Pacific grouping (PACP) under the 2000 Cotonou Agreement. The EU has maintained that one of the objectives of an EPA is to get each of the six ACP regions under a single trade regime to encourage regional integration, growth of regional markets and creation of supply chains. The EPA was scheduled to be finalized by 31 December 2007, but Pacific (and wider ACP) resistance to EU negotiating proposals resulted in only the Caribbean agreeing to a regional EPA by that deadline (Kelsey 2007). At the time of writing, only Fiji and Papua New Guinea have signed interim EPAs in the Pacific and regional negotiations are currently floundering.

These three trade processes are interlinked (and were intended to fit into the broader global framework set by the Doha 'development' round). For example, under the 2001 PACER agreement, Pacific countries are obliged to begin consultations on negotiating arrangements with Australia and New Zealand if they enter free trade agreement negotiations with another developed country, so that Australia and New Zealand are not disadvantaged. Thus PACER requires that Australia and New Zealand be treated at least on the same negotiating basis as the European Union. It is believed that some provisions agreed to by Pacific island nations under the EPA will have a flow on effect for trade agreements with their more immediate neighbours.

On the eve of the July 2007 meeting of Pacific Trade Ministers in Vanuatu, NZ trade minister Phil Goff said the Pacific Island Forum should 'advance their vision of a single market in the Pacific. What is needed is a comprehensive agreement much broader than simply free trade in goods' (*The National* 2007). Warren Truss, the then Australian Trade Minister, echoed these objectives, stating:

> The new so-called 'PACER Plus' will foster economic opportunities and competitiveness for countries in the region and help Pacific Island countries secure the benefits from liberalisation and integration while operating within WTO rules. It will also ensure that Australia and New Zealand maintain market access to the Pacific Island countries that are likely to conclude an Economic Partnership Agreement with the European Union. (Truss 2007)

The trade negotiations are a key element in Forum plans for increased regional integration, highlighted by the signing of the Pacific Plan for Strengthening Regional Co-operation and Integration in 2005, which includes four central pillars of regional security, economic growth, good governance and sustainable development.

In publications such as *Embarking on a Global Voyage: Trade Liberalisation and Complementary Reforms in the Pacific* (Duncan et al. 2002), World Bank researchers have argued that the larger and more comprehensive the trade liberalization, the greater the aggregate welfare gains. But the new trade liberalization agenda is part of a broader programme of 'good governance' and 'public sector reform', promoted by multilateral agencies such as the World Bank and Asian Development Bank (ADB) since the early 1990s.

Around the Pacific, the ADB has financed structural adjustment programmes in a process coordinated through donors' meetings and the Forum Economic Ministers' Meetings (FEMM). The FEMM Action Plan, adopted by the Forum leaders meeting in Nauru in 2001, has been used to promote these policies to Pacific elites. The bundle of policies which are promoted include: liberalization of trade and removal of tariffs; reduction of staffing in the public sector; flexible labour markets; corporatization and privatization of public utilities in transport, communications, energy, water and other sectors; introduction of 'Value Added' or GST consumption taxes; and removal of some controls on the finance sector.

The ADB has long been advocating cuts in public sector employment throughout the Pacific, with structural reform programmes leading to massive job losses in the mid-1990s, ranging from 33 per cent of public sector jobs in the Marshall Islands to 57 per cent in the Cook Islands (Knapman and Saldanha 1999). There has been significant debate over the social impacts of these cuts, as public sector employment is one of the few sources of income for people in many small island states, and job cuts in sectors like nursing and teaching have a disproportionate effect on women, who have limited opportunities for paid employment.

Key donor governments are also beginning to push for land reform or 'land mobilization' in the region, seeking changes to customary land tenure to promote growth, open the way for new resource or tourism projects and guarantee security of investment for overseas corporations (Fingleton 2005). The EU has included a call for greater foreign ownership of land in its requests to Papua New Guinea and the Solomon Islands during WTO GATS negotiations, while the April 2006 White Paper on Australian Aid notes that '[t]he aid program will encourage growth by improving the policy environment for private sector growth. Initiatives include a collaborative and demand-driven Pacific Land Mobilisation Program to explore the major land tenure constraints to growth in the region' (AusAID 2006a, xii).

Free Trade or Fair Trade?

The adverse effects of the regional trade agenda have been critiqued by community groups such as the Pacific Network on Globalisation (PANG), the South Pacific and Oceanic Council of Trade Unions (SPOCTU) and trade justice activists like Professor Jane Kelsey from Auckland University Law School (see Kelsey 2004b; Kelsey 2005). Of key concern has been the way that the EPA negotiations have been marked by a refusal by EU states to seriously address issues raised by Pacific countries in their status as SIDS, in contrast to the larger African nations that are at the centre of EU trade policy.

The realities of the Pacific have slowed the move towards trade liberalization. The Forum Secretariat is concerned that many smaller island states are not engaging with PICTA as it provides limited opportunities for trade. A 2007 study of PICTA presented to the Forum Secretariat suggests that current trade proposals will not necessarily benefit all small island states (IITPTC 2007). Fijian journalist Samisoni Pareti has noted:

> Islands of the Pacific have the unenviable task of striking a PACER ... that ensures the benefits of free trade with Australia and New Zealand will not only accrue for the exclusive pleasure of their two Trans-Tasman neighbours, a report commissioned by the Secretariat of the Pacific Islands Forum has warned. By its own calculations, some islands countries stand to lose up to US$10 million annually in revenue due to trade liberalisation. Such a loss may spell disaster for economies that currently impose high import tariffs. (Pareti 2007a)

Even so, Australia and New Zealand are pushing a broader agenda of trade liberalization. PICTA currently covers trade in goods, but the Forum leaders' meeting in 2005 agreed on the need for 'integration of trades in services, including temporary movement of labour' (PIFS 2005, 10). Australian and New Zealand officials want to start moving on PACER-Plus, under pressure from corporate interests which see European companies moving in sectors that have long been dominated by the Oceanic powers.

The agenda of trade liberalization is sparking debate in the region, with civil society organizations beginning to question the impacts on indigenous land, resource owners and poorer sections of the community. Trade unions, community groups, churches and other non-government organizations are slowly beginning to coordinate regionally to develop a coherent critique of the new free trade agenda. USP academic Elise Huffer (2007) has critiqued the Pacific Plan process for its failure to address gender and cultural issues. Other NGOs have argued that the limited econometric modelling conducted on PICTA, PACER and the EPA has largely focused on economic impacts, without detailed studies on social, cultural or environmental effects. At its 2006 regional meeting on trade negotiations, the Pacific Civil Society Organisations Forum stated:

> As civil society groups meeting in Nadi, Fiji, we believe that trade agreements must have just and equitable development at their heart. Genuine sustainable development – including economic, social, cultural, gender and environmental dimensions – must be the central pillar of these agreements. We are concerned that the proposed EPA in its current form will not fulfil these development objectives. ... There are areas which should not be liberalised as part of trade deals, including our land, ownership and use of customary land, cultural heritage, key public services, food security and farmers' livelihoods. (Pacific Civil Society Organisations Forum 2006)

Current proposals for trade liberalization will involve major economic and political challenges. Many smaller Pacific countries are reliant on tariffs and import duties for significant levels of government revenue – which can reach more than 30 per cent, as in the case of Tonga – and the alternatives are regressive user charges, sales tax or consumption taxes. These options raise questions of equity and just development, particularly in countries where up to 80 per cent of the population are subsistence farmers whose income is derived largely from remittances or small-scale cash cropping.

Throughout the ongoing EPA negotiations, the EU has been reluctant to budge on most rules of origin or phyto-sanitary regulations, and Pacific exporters are fearful that trade promotion efforts will fail due to lack of awareness about the development benefits for rural producers. Developed nations' trade policy is not well coordinated with development assistance programmes, and domestic trade regulations can cripple export markets for small island states reliant on one or two products.

The current impasse over the EU-PACP trade negotiations has highlighted the uneven playing field for small island states, even as these same states seek to develop niche trade markets. As the following case study on kava exports from the Pacific suggests, the expansion of niche exports can be devastated by trade bans from developed countries' markets. A seven-year Pacific campaign has also focused attention upon the way that European and now Australian bans on kava imports has damaged the welfare of rural producers, causing over US$1 billion in losses to an industry that creates employment opportunities and much needed cash for rural communities.[9]

The Ban on Kava

Yaqona, 'ava, sakau, kava – kava is a popular brew in all of its derivations. In many Pacific countries, kava is consumed regularly as a social drink, far beyond its traditional role in ceremony and medicine; from the nakamals of Vanuatu to the grog bowls of Suva and the sakau drinkers of Pohnpei, kava is the drink of choice.

Kava is the popular name for the plant known botanically as *piper methysticum*. It is most commonly consumed as a drink made from the roots and stems of the plant – chewed or crushed and mixed with water. For generations, Pacific islanders have been developing new hybrids of kava and growing it as a cash crop, as well as for ceremonial, medical or social use.

Recently, kava has gained popularity in Europe, the United States and Australia, as people seek more natural medicines to alleviate stress, anxiety and insomnia. Major pharmaceutical companies, recognizing the valuable properties of the drug, have started producing kava pills and capsules. In the 1990s, this interest in the pharmaceutical properties of *piper methysticum* contributed to a growing kava export trade for countries like Fiji, Vanuatu, Tonga and Samoa, amounting to nearly US$200 million per annum (PANG 2007, 3).

As a result of this boom in the late 1990s, many farmers started planting more kava – this was largely an initiative of small-scale farming rather than agri-business (Prasad 2006). Prices at the farm level initially increased, providing significant cash earnings for rural farming communities in Fiji and Vanuatu, and the development of small business opportunities as local agents worked between growers and overseas purchasers.

However, this valuable overseas trade from the Pacific was badly damaged in 2001 by reports from Germany and other European countries that the consumption of kava could be linked to liver damage. In 2001, the Federal Institute for Drugs and Medicinal Devices in Germany withdrew product licences for all products containing kava, and other EU countries subsequently introduced restrictions on the sale of kava-based food supplements and herbal medicines (Gruenwald et al. 2003). The European bans compounded problems for the kava industry at a time when the small island nations were coming to terms with the complexities of inter-island free trade under PICTA – for example, a trade dispute between Fiji and Vanuatu over biscuit manufacture under PICTA, with Vanuatu seeking to protect a local manufacturer of cabin crackers against cheaper Fijian imports, led to retaliatory Fijian trade bans on Vanuatu kava exports in 2005.

The drop in income for small-scale farmers hit quickly after the November 2001 announcement of health warnings by the EU. In the last three months of 2001, Fiji earned nearly F$1.4 million from kava exports. In the first three months of 2002, the amount dropped to just F$323,000 – a 75

---

9   This case study draws on my reporting for Radio Australia (Maclellan 2002) and, with thanks, a study by Wesley Morgan for the Pacific Network on Globalisation (PANG 2007).

per cent reduction. Vanuatu's kava earnings fell from 174 million vatu to 42 million vatu in the same period (Maclellan 2002).

Exports to Australia have also been affected, after the Australian government issued cautionary advice on the consumption of kava-based products in 2001, worried over the excessive consumption of kava by young Aboriginal men in northern Australia. In June 2007, Australia also moved to ban commercial imports of kava, even though a 2004 study by Food Standards Australia states: 'the available data does not suggest any specific health problems associated with the moderate use of kava' (FSANZ 2004). According to the Fiji Kava Council, the Australian ban could cost Fijian growers an estimated F\$32 million (A\$24 million) per annum (*Fiji Times* 2007a).

The effect of kava bans extends beyond the economic loss for farmers, hitting the Fijian and Tongan communities living in Australia. Kava clubs (*kalapu kava* or *faiokava*) are an important place for people to meet in the migrant diaspora, a venue to share political and social information as well as for socializing and entertainment. These grassroots structures promote identity and reinforce cultural links across international boundaries:

> There are in existence in Australia more than a 100 Tongan Kava Clubs. … Membership of these clubs are usually based on home village/island blood ties, or church/ religious denomination affiliations, such that every Tongan Church Parish/Diocese/Congregation in Australia has a Kava Club and almost every village and island in Tonga has a corresponding Kava Club in Australia … [T]hese Kava Clubs serve to reinforce social cohesion within the Tongan community in Australia and to cultivate positive behaviour traits appropriate for living in a multi-ethnic environment … Through the Kava Clubs the youth are taught about Tongan culture and traditions using the Tongan language. … A secondary objective of these Clubs is to raise money for community development projects in their home villages/islands in Tonga. (Senituli 2007)

Together with churches and sporting groups, these kava clubs provide important community links between villagers at home and the diaspora in Australia, as the overseas associations often raise funds for local community development projects in areas such as water and roads.

A coalition of concerned groups, mobilizing government and non-government representatives, farmers associations, research scientists and indigenous rights NGOs, have mounted a campaign to reverse the bans on kava imports in order to protect an industry that produces many multiplier effects in the economy and contributes to alleviation of rural poverty (PANG 2007). This response highlights the importance of joint community campaigns to raise awareness of the economic and social cost of developed countries' trade policies.

Forum countries began political lobbying to encourage European, Australian and US authorities to review their restrictions on kava, drawing on research from the Pacific Health Research Council, the Fiji School of Medicine and the University of the South Pacific (USP). Pacific researchers such as Subramaniam Sotheeswaran, a USP Professor of Organic Chemistry, analysed and critiqued the available medical studies on liver toxicity, arguing that the proportion of kavalactones – the active ingredient in the drug – is a crucial difference between kava pills and kava dissolved in water, and that many reported cases of liver damage in Europe involved contributing factors such as alcohol abuse or co-medication.

In November 2005, over 120 participants from 16 countries met in Fiji to discuss the current state of research on kava and the social and economic effects of the kava bans, leading to the July 2007 publication of a major report from the World Health Organization (WHO), which assessed the potential hazards of liver toxicity. The WHO report declares kava to be a safe product and provides guidelines on how kava could be re-introduced into overseas markets (WHO 2007).

Non-governmental organizations and growers' groups have condemned the failure of EU states to address the bans seriously. The damage to a trade which benefits small farmers and rural communities highlights the lack of accountability towards farmers in small island states, according to PANG:

> It is hard to imagine that this barrier to trade wouldn't have been overcome much earlier, had the roles of the EU and the PICs [Pacific Island Countries] been reversed. Given that the EU economy is 1,400 times bigger than the PIC economies (and that the EU has a massive pharmaceutical industry), it seems certain that European growers and producers would quickly eliminate trade barriers of this kind, if a significant percentage of their export earnings were to be affected. The experience of trade bans and kava exports highlights the fact that there is no such thing as a 'level playing field' in international trade. The experience the kava export industry to Europe also indicates the significant barriers to trade with Europe which are hurting Pacific producers in other areas. Stringent sanitary requirements make it virtually impossible for small-scale agricultural producers in the Pacific to export to the EU. (PANG 2007, 7)

According to Ratu Josateki Nawalowalo, Pacific chair of the International Kava Executive Council, Pacific island countries – and rural producers – have lost an estimated US$1.4 billion in export earnings as a consequence of the bans over the last seven years:

> This is a lot of money for small island states like us. For Fiji, we were the major exporters of kava. Our farmers have suffered immensely as a result. 90 per cent of our kava farmers are indigenous people living in the villages across the country, who are dependant on kava income for their livelihood and sustenance. (*Fiji Times* 2007b)

There is certainly a need to study potential health impacts from kava use in Australia and Europe and develop public health responses to cases of abuse. But the kava bans have sparked anger in the Pacific as they have come at a time when developed nations have condemned the use of trade policy by Pacific countries to achieve public health outcomes.

Trade, Health and Obesity

At the same time as developed countries are purporting to protect the health of their citizens through kava bans, they are aggressively lobbying to maintain their market share for export of agricultural and manufactured foodstuffs to the Pacific, despite the concerns of public health officials in the islands over the impact of these imports on nutrition.

In recent years, some Pacific governments have mounted public health campaigns against poor nutrition, attempting to combat the increasing rates of diabetes, hypertension and other health impacts from obesity. They have supplemented public education initiatives by utilizing trade and taxation policy – for example, under the *Excise Act 1986*, Fiji added excise duties on sugar, chocolate, instant noodles and other snack foods and introduced a 10 per cent tax on soft drinks in 2006. However these imposts must be phased out under PICTA and PACER as they are designed not only to contribute to public health policies but also to protect fledgling industries in Fiji.

As noted in a study in the *Bulletin of the World Health Organization*:

Given recent initiatives towards trade liberalisation and the creation of the World Trade Organization (WTO), tariffs or import bans may not serve as alternative measures to control consumption [of poor quality food]. This presents significant challenges to health policy-makers serving economically marginal populations and suggests that some population health concerns cannot be adequately addressed without awareness of the effects of global trade. (Evans et al. 2001, 856)

The market of poor quality meat exported to Fiji, Tonga, Samoa and other Pacific nations such as turkey tails from the United States or mutton flaps from New Zealand – the fatty waste meat from the sheep's belly which is high in saturated fat – provides a further example (Gewertz and Errington 2007). In its 2000 budget, the Coalition government led by the then Prime Minister Mahendra Chaudhry imposed a ban on mutton flaps through a prohibition order issued under s.102 of the *Fair Trading Decree (1992)* to address its concerns about the health consequences of poor quality sheep meat imports. However, New Zealand threatened to take Fiji to the WTO disputes process, arguing that a ban on NZ products could be seen as effective trade discrimination in favour of the United States, which also exports junk meat to Fiji (Government of Fiji 2001).

A similar issue arose in Tonga, where healthier options such as locally caught fish are between 15 and 50 per cent more expensive than mutton flaps or imported chicken. Researchers such as Professors Mark Lawrence and Boyd Swinburn have studied the impact of mutton flaps on the health of Tongans and the policy options for reducing their contribution to the food supply (Swinburn et al. 1999; Rush et al. 2004). In 2004, their research was developed as a Cabinet paper for the Minister of Health to place a quota restriction on mutton flap imports. However, because Tonga was in the process of acceding to the WTO at the time, it was reluctant to put these trade restrictive practices in place and the proposal was shelved. Tonga's 2007 accession to the WTO has come with so many concessions that there is widespread public concern that the country will not be able effectively to regulate foreign corporations moving into the health sector and other service industries (Oxfam New Zealand 2005).

The debate over trade and development objectives is brought sharply into focus by concern that public health initiatives in the islands could be compromised by regional and international free trade agreements like PACER-Plus. As Clarke and McKenzie (2007, 11) note in a 2007 WHO report:

Many of the foodstuffs which contribute to the obesity epidemic in the Pacific are imported from outside the region. In theory, increasing tariffs and duties on them could reduce their intake in local populations. ... [T]he volume of high fat foods imported into the Pacific means that import duties could be useful in restricting consumption of foods contributing to obesity. However import controls also present difficulties under trade agreements.

Article 16(1b) of PICTA allows countries to claim a trade restriction necessary to protect human health. Under article XX (b) of the General Agreement on Tariffs and Trade (GATT), countries may also adopt trade measures necessary to 'protect human, animal or plant life or health'. But these provisions place onerous burdens on the country to prove that no other measures are possible and that the regulations do not constitute a 'disguised restriction on international trade'. Poor island nations do not have the human or financial resources to utilize effectively the WTO disputes procedure, and will be under significant pressure under PACER-Plus to abstain from measures that will hinder Australia- and New Zealand-based exporters.

Sustainable Development Outcomes?

The purpose of regional trade agreements is to improve the social and economic development of the SIDS of the Pacific. But as Pacific farmers and local communities begin to develop fair trade marketing, there is a need for broader engagement with governments on the trade policy which frames market opportunities.

The conduct of EU officials at the recent EU–Pacific trade negotiations raise major concerns about the future development benefits for rural producers in small island states (Kelsey 2007). The draft trade agreements between the EU and Pacific ACP countries explicitly state that sustainable development is at the centre of trade policy. For example, the *EU-Pacific Interim FTA* agreement with Papua New Guinea, initialled on 23 November 2007, notes:

- The Parties reaffirm that the objective of sustainable development shall be an integral part of the provisions of this agreement … and especially the general commitment to reducing and eventually eradicating poverty in a way that is consistent with the objectives of sustainable development; (Art. 3(1)).
- The application of this Agreement shall fully take into account the human, cultural, economic, social, health and environmental best interests of their respective population and of future generations; (Art. 3(2a)).
- The Parties agree to work cooperatively towards the realization of a sustainable development centred on the human person, who is the main beneficiary of development; (Art. 3(3)).

However, the rhetoric does not match the reality. In June 2006, Pacific trade negotiators made well-researched and specific proposals that would have built development benefits into the EPA agreement (such as proposals for funds to finance small business and strengthen export programmes, new assistance to overcome barriers to exports and the creation of job opportunities for temporary workers in the EU). Almost all of these proposals were rejected by the EU. Widespread resistance to the EU's counter-proposals has resulted in EU negotiators seeking interim agreements on goods rather than a full agreement, and individual country agreements rather regional ones. As noted by activists from PANG:

> Interim deals on goods-trade were made necessary because of a stalemate in the negotiations for a more comprehensive EPA. ACP countries maintain fundamental opposition to key EU demands in those wider negotiations. … The EU has marked its shift in policy by seeking market access reciprocity and WTO compatibility under the Cotonou Agreement, but also by extending the scope of trade relationships to include services, competition and investment policy and intellectual property rules. Clearly the EPA negotiations are in part a 'market grab' for the EU to gain market access to ACP countries not extended to other developed countries under the WTO. (Sami and Morgan 2007)

With the end of WTO waivers in December 2007 and no agreement on a final EPA, EU officials set a 23 November deadline for ACP nations to sign interim deals on trade, threatening to increase tariffs on imports from ACP countries. The conduct of EU negotiators has angered Pacific officials. According to media reports, Peter Mandelson, the Commissioner for Trade at the EU, personally threatened to impose duty on Pacific exports if no transitory agreement was signed by 31 December (Pareti 2007b). Mandelson was also accused of insulting behaviour to Pacific representatives: according to reports in *Islands Business* magazine, when Papua New Guinea's foreign and trade minister Samuel Abal called on him in his Brussels office, Mandelson pulled out an atlas, stating that he wanted to see where exactly Papua New Guinea was (Pareti 2007b).

Under pressure due to concern over potential job losses in the sugar and tuna export industries if they did not concede, the Pacific's largest countries, Fiji and Papua New Guinea, finally split ranks with other Pacific nations to sign an interim deal on trade-in-goods with the EU. The Interim Partnership Agreement allows for 100 per cent liberalization by value by the EU as of 1 January 2008, with transition periods for rice and sugar. It allows for 88 per cent liberalization by value by Papua New Guinea and 80 per cent liberalization by Fiji over a time period of 15 years (European Commission 2007). The interim agreement also includes a non discrimination (most favoured nation) clause that means if either party subsequently offers better market access to a third party, that access must be extended within this agreement – of vital importance given that EPA concessions will flow on to Australia and New Zealand in the forthcoming PACER negotiations, and Australian and European corporations will compete for market access in the small Pacific economies.

Under the proposed EPA, domestic producers in Fiji and Papua New Guinea are likely to face stiff competition from the EU, an advanced region that is more than 1,400 times the economic size of the Pacific. The interim deal has been criticized by Forum trade officials and Pacific trade justice activists (PANG 2008), with development NGO Oxfam New Zealand noting that the two Pacific nations only signed the interim agreement because of

> an immediate threat to thousands of workers' livelihoods from the apparently imminent tariff hike. This threat by the EU is directly contrary to its undertakings in the Cotonou Agreement that they would not disadvantage countries that did not choose to sign an EPA. It makes a mockery of the EU's rhetoric about the EPA agreements supporting the processes of regional integration. (Oxfam New Zealand 2007)

A leaked email from a Forum trade official lamented:

> The ministers gave in on virtually every issue to whatever the EU wanted and the EPA negotiations are in effect over. The only issue that remains square bracketed is the non-execution clause which would allow trade sanctions for political violations – unheard of at the WTO and possibly illegal. In effect, we have abandoned almost all forms of traditional trade policy. In return, we got nothing. (Pareti 2007b)

Conclusion

Fair trade initiatives are a vital example of how trade initiatives can contribute to sustainable human development. However, fair trade can only flourish in a context that links economic, social and environmental development in a coherent way. But coherence involves more than government departments coordinating policy (although this is a vital step in bringing development and poverty issues to the forefront of the trade debate). NGOs are beginning to critique the links between Poverty Strategy Reduction Programs, aid and trade negotiations as the tools of coherence driven in the interests of the major powers across the IMF, World Bank and WTO.

Throughout the 1990s, Pacific governments and NGOs were represented at a series of international summits – in Rio, Vienna, Barbados, Copenhagen and Beijing – which started to map out global visions for a post-Cold War world. But the 1994 Barbados Program of Action, with its vision of sustainable development in SIDS, is rarely discussed in contemporary analyses of Pacific regionalism. What is needed is the integration of the perspectives derived from a series of meetings since the Rio Environment and Development Summit, which meet the special and differential needs of small states in a large ocean. The current push for regional economic integration and open economies does not include any discussion of these perspectives,[10] and a first need is for small, vulnerable countries to maintain policy space and genuine flexibility in developing economic strategies.

Community sector involvement is central to this change. The EU Cotonou agreement with the developing countries of ACP has provisions regarding the involvement of 'non-state actors' in development. These non-state actors include the private sector, economic and social partners including trade union organizations, and civil society in all its forms according to national characteristics (Cotonou Agreement, art. 6(1)(b)). But the debate over kava and the damage to Pacific interests in ongoing EPA negotiations both highlight the tension between government commitment to civil society engagement and the reluctance of state officials to accept critical advocacy on trade and development issues. There is concern that government and donors regard NGOs as simply a mechanism to deliver services that government cannot or will not provide.

The Pacific Islands Forum Secretariat has unveiled a policy on NGO consultation – a major change as the Forum was the one regional body that had initially resisted formal engagement with the non-government sector. A series of parallel fora, as regional NGO, church and union organizations meet alongside the annual Forum leaders meeting, has slowly sparked an engagement on issues of accountability and development. In practice, government and non-government representatives in the Pacific have often formed uneasy alliances to lobby the governments of developed nations, as shown with the ongoing campaign around kava bans. But the forthcoming negotiations on PACER-Plus will test those relationships, as Australia and New Zealand develop their regional policy.

References

Australian Agency for International Development (AusAID) (2006a), *Australian Aid: Promoting Growth and Stability – A White Paper on the Australian Government's Overseas Aid Program* (Canberra: AusAID).

—— (2006b), *Pacific 2020: Challenges and Opportunities for Growth* (Canberra: AusAID).

—— (2008), *Pacific Economic Survey 2008* (Canberra: AusAID).

Clarke, D. and McKenzie, T. (2007), *Legislative Interventions to Prevent and Decrease Obesity in Pacific Island Countries* (Manila: WHO Western Pacific Regional Office).

CSO Forum (2007), *Pacific Regional CSO Forum Nuku'alofa Communiqué*, Tonga Civil Society Organisations Forum, Nuku'alofa, Kingdom of Tonga, 15 October 2007.

Duncan, R. et al. (2002), *Pacific Islands – Regional Economic Report – Embarking on a Global Voyage: Trade Liberalization and Complementary Reforms in the Pacific*, Report No. 24417-EAP, World Bank. Available from: http://www-wds.worldbank.org/external/default/WDSContentServer/WDSP/IB/2002/09/27/000094946_02091804042860/Rendered/PDF/multi0page.pdf [accessed: 15 September 2009].

---

10   For example, AusAID's *Pacific 2020* study (AusAID 2006b) and subsequent *Pacific Economic Survey 2008* (AusAID 2008) make no mention of the Barbados Program of Action or a range of initiatives by SIDS to leverage their small size onto the international stage, through the Alliance of Small Island States (AOSIS), the programmes of the Commonwealth Secretariat and SIDSNet.

European Commission (2007), 'Update: interim economic partnership agreements', *Trade Policy in Practice: Global Europe*, 13 December (Brussels: Directorate General for Trade, European Commission).

Evans, M. et al. (2001), 'Globalization, diet, and health: an example from Tonga', *Bulletin of the World Health Organization* 79(9): 856–62.

Fiji Times (2007a), 'Aussie ban costs \$32m: kava body', *Fiji Times*, 22 August, 11.

—— (2007b), 'Europe, Australia to review kava bans', *Fiji Times*, 22 October, 5.

Fingleton, J. (2005), *Pacific 2020 Background Paper: Land* (Canberra: AusAID).

Food Standards Australia New Zealand (FSANZ) (2004), *Kava: A Human Health Risk Assessment*, Technical Report Series No. 30, FSANZ. Available at: http://www.foodstandards.gov.au/_srcfiles/30_Kava.pdf [accessed: 15 September 2009].

Gewertz, D. and Errington, F. (2007), 'The alimentary forms of the global life: the Pacific-Island trade in lamb and mutton flaps', *American Anthropologist* 109(3): 496–508.

Government of Fiji (2001), 'Health of Fijians more important than NZ threats', press release, issued 15 March.

Gruenwald, J. et al. (2003), *Kava Report 2003: In-depth Investigation into EU Member States Market Restrictions on Kava Products*, Centre for the Development of Enterprise. Available at: http://www.analyze-realize.com/Papers/Phytopharm_Consulting.de.pdf [accessed: 15 September 2009].

Huffer E. (2007), 'Regionalism and cultural identity: putting the Pacific back into the plan', in S. Firth (ed.), *Globalisation and Governance in the Pacific Islands* (Canberra: ANU E Press).

Institute for International Trade and Pacific Trade Consult (IITPTC) (2007), *The Potential Impact of PICTA on Smaller Forum Island Nations: Final Report*, IITPTC. Available at: http://www.forumsec.org/_resources/article/files/PICTA%20Impact%20Study%20Final%20Report%2028 0507.pdf [accessed: 15 September 2009].

Kelsey, J. (2004a), 'Acceding countries as pawns in a power play: a case study of the Pacific Islands', *Focus on the Global South*. [Online: Focus on the Global South]. Available at: http://www.focusweb.org/content/view/442/36/ [accessed: 22 September 2008].

—— (2004b), *A People's Guide to PACER: The Implications for the Pacific Islands of the Pacific Agreement on Closer Economic Relations (PACER)* (Suva: Pacific Network on Globalisation).

—— (2004c), 'Sink or swim: Pacific Islands in the WTO', paper presented at the Kansas Symposium on Trade, Kansas.

—— (2005), *A People's Guide to the Pacific's Economic Partnership Agreement: Negotiations between the Pacific Islands and the European Union Pursuant to the Cotonou Agreement 2000* (Suva: World Council of Churches Office in the Pacific).

—— (2007), 'Going nowhere in a hurry: the Pacific's EPA negotiations with the EU', *Victoria University of Wellington Law Review* (VUWLR) 38: 81–103.

Kerr, D. (2008), 'Launch of Pacific Economic Survey 2008', speech presented at the Pacific Economic Survey 2008, Vanuatu.

Knapman, B. and Saldanha, C. (1999), *Reforms in the Pacific: An Assessment of the Asian Development Bank's Assistance for Reform Programs in the Pacific*, Pacific Studies Series No.17 (Manila: Asian Development Bank).

Kokonut Pacific (2007), 'Full and fair trade'. [Online: Kokonut Pacific]. Available at: http://www.kokonutpacific.com.au/Index.html?production/fair_trade.html [accessed: 15 September 2009].

Luthria, M. et al. (2006), *At Home and Away: Expanding Job Opportunities for Pacific Islanders through Labour Mobility* (Manila: World Bank).

Maclellan, N. (2002), 'Unhealthy criticisms of kava', [Radio] Radio Australia Pacific Beat, 23 November.

Mares, P. and Maclellan, N. (2007), 'Pacific seasonal workers for Australian horticulture: a neat fit?', *Asian and Pacific Migration Journal* 16(2): 271–88.

Mead, A. and Ratuva, S. (eds) (2007), *Pacific Genes and Life Patents: Pacific Indigenous Experiences and Analysis of the Commodification and Ownership of Life* (Wellington: Call to the Earth Llamando de la Tierra and the United Nations University Institute of Advanced Studies).

National (2007), 'Pacific free trade idea is misguided', *The National*, 3 August 2007. Available at: http://www.bilaterals.org/article.php3?id_article=9231 [accessed: 15 September 2009].

Oxfam New Zealand (2005), *Proposed WTO Accession: Key Issues for Tonga* (Auckland: Oxfam New Zealand). Available at: http://www.oxfam.org.nz/imgs/pdf/wto%20key%20issues%20for%20tonga.pdf [accessed: 15 September 2009].

—— (2007), 'European trade deal undermines Pacific integration', press release, issued 7 December.

—— (2008), 'Trading coconuts with the Body Shop'. [Online: Oxfam New Zealand]. Available at: http://www.oxfam.org.nz/whatwedo.asp?s1=What%20we%20do&s2=Where%20we%20work&s3=Pacific&s4=Samoa&s5=Trading%20coconuts [accessed: 15 September 2009].

Pacific Civil Society Organisations Forum (2006), 'Final communiqué', Pacific Civil Society Meeting on Trade Negotiations, 13–16 June 2006, Nadi.

Pacific Concerns Resource Centre (PCRC) (1995), *Proceedings of the Indigenous Peoples' Knowledge and Intellectual Property Rights Consultation, April 1995* (Suva: PCRC).

Pacific Islands Forum Secretariat (PIFS) (2005), *Thirty-sixth Pacific Island Forum: Papua New Guinea, 25–27 October 2005: Forum Communiqué*, PIFS(05)12 (Madang: PIFS).

—— (2007), 'Forum members consider studies on further trade liberalisation in the region', press statement (98/07), issued 13 August.

Pacific Network on Globalisation (PANG) (2007), *Lift the Kava Ban Now: Provide an Economic Lifeline for the Pacific!* (Suva: PANG).

—— (2008), *Social Impact Assessment of the Economic Partnership Agreement (EPA) Being Negotiated between the European Community and Pacific ACP States* (Suva: PANG).

Pareti, S. (2007a), 'Trade/PACER: a plus or negative? Islands could lose $10m annually in revenue: report'. [Online: Island Business International]. Available at: http://www.islandsbusiness.com/islands_business/index_dynamic/containerNameToReplace=MiddleMiddle/focusModuleID=17625/overideSkinName=issueArticle-full.tpl [accessed: 15 September 2009].

—— (2007b), 'Fiji, PNG "turncoat" spells doom for region: EPA a sellout', *Islands Business*, December.

Prasad, N. (2006), 'Perils of unmanaged exports growth: Fiji's kava sector', *Journal of Business and Entrepreneurship* 19(4): 381–94.

Rush, E. et al. (2004), 'Body size, body composition, and fat distribution: a comparison of young New Zealand men of European, Pacific Island, and Asian Indian ethnicities', *New Zealand Medical Journal* 117(1207): 1203–10.

Sami, R. and Morgan, W. (2007), 'Why the EU is far from the level with the EPAs', *Fiji Times*, 24 November.

Senituli, L. (2007), 'Security, stability and governance in the Pacific: where the "kava" still has meaning', paper presented at the 10th Pacific Island Political Studies Association Conference, Port Vila. Available at: http://rspas.anu.edu.au/papers/melanesia/ conference_papers/pipsa/4PIPSApaperKEYNOTELopetisenituli.pdf [accessed: 15 September 2009].

Swinburn, B. et al. (1999), 'Body size and composition in Polynesians', *International Journal of Obesity* 23(11): 1178–83.

Truss, W. (2007), 'Liberalised trade for a more prosperous Pacific region', media release, issued 14 June.

World Health Organization (WHO) (2007), *Assessment of the Risk of Hepatotoxicity with Kava Products* (Manila: WHO Press).

Chapter 17

Crowding Out or Ratcheting Up?
Fair Trade Systems, Regulation and New Governance

Orly Lobel

Introduction

The corporate social responsibility (CSR) movement and fair trade systems have grown in the past decade, reflecting a belief that corporations operating at a global level must voluntarily assume the role of raising production and trade standards and that consumers should play a role in pressuring industry to behave responsibly. This chapter discusses the multi-level interaction of corporate social responsibility (CSR) and fair trade regimes with state-based legal systems. It opens with an analysis of the potential problems arising when multiple systems are overlaid upon each other. In particular, the chapter explores two conflicting arguments concerning how regulatory approaches coincide with 'softer' private efforts: first, that regulation can crowd out voluntary private efforts, thereby diminishing their effectiveness and legitimacy; and the second, countervailing argument that fair trade systems and regulation can be complimentary and mutually reinforcing. It then discusses ways to better synthesize state and non-state governance initiatives, analysing the examples of highly visible multinational corporations (MNCs) such as Nike and Walmart, as well as examples from recent policy developments in the United States in the areas of safety, discrimination and environmental regulation.

The Promise and Limits of Fair Trade Mechanisms

As countries vie over their share in global production chains, competition threatens social and environmental standards. The CSR movement demands that corporations, because of their dominance as global institutions, address these standards and ensure responsible production and trade practices. Multinational firms increasingly face pressures from consumer groups and activists to demonstrate their social responsibility efforts, including more environmentally safe production, improved labour conditions and fair trade among transnational subsidiaries. The fair trade movement is located among the efforts to increase transnational social responsibility. The term 'fair trade' – implying that some practices are unfair – is usually used to contrast with 'free trade,' calling for higher standards of production and protection to be afforded to developing countries (Moore 2004). These efforts are prevalent at both local and international levels, motivated by the fear that international competition will precipitate a race to the bottom (Trebilcock and Howse 2005). While, as one commentator has articulated, 'our corporate law, paradoxically, tells managers that to be good managers they must be bad citizens' (Greenwood 2004), the CSR and fair trade movements ask corporate actors to become 'good citizens'. In other words, while managers are guided by traditional corporate law doctrine to maximize profits for their shareholders, regardless of the effects of their growth on other stakeholders, these recent accountability movements urge corporations to embrace a broader view of their interests and responsibilities.

In the past three decades, the CSR and fair trade movements have grown dramatically and witnessed various successes. While, during the 1980s, firms routinely responded to challenges by human rights activists with dismissal, recent years have seen a change in attitude and a broadening of legitimate claims over corporations. It is no longer legitimate for a MNC to dismiss critiques about the labour standards practised by its subsidiaries simply by claiming that it has no knowledge about, or responsibility for, the manufacturing companies. In response to public pressure from consumers, investors, unions and NGOs, MNCs have adopted corporate codes of conduct. Campaigns that demand consumers' and investors' 'Right to Know' have increased economic transparency and have established non-governmental organizations that monitor and compare MNCs. In turn, multinationals increasingly make demands for regulatory compliance from their suppliers.

However, the main criticisms of these responses are ineffective implementation, absence of monitoring, and lack of incentives to comply. Similarly, today there are dozens of fair trade programmes and labelling initiatives. Although during the early 1990s many of the fair trade initiatives were *ad hoc* and dispersed, in 1997 many of the different labelling organizations united to create the 'Fairtrade Labelling Organizations International' (FLO) as an umbrella body that sets standards for, inspects and certifies producers. In 2002, the FLO launched its international certification mark, which is now used in over 50 countries on a range of products (FLO 2008).[1] According to the FLO, in 2006 consumers spent approximately 2.2 billion dollars on certified products, a 42 per cent increase over the previous year. The products certified by the FLO include coffee, cocoa and cotton, tea, a number of fruits, wine and flowers. Farms are certified when they can show that they meet socially and environmentally high standards, such as the absence of child labour or harmful chemicals.

Even major retailers which have made aggressive cost reductions through their trademark business techniques are reacting to the fair trade and CSR movements. Recently, Walmart, the reigning 'nemesis' of social activists (Lobel 2007a), launched an expensive public relations campaign to signal its willingness to improve its social responsibility in the regions where it operates. For social activists, the campaign against Walmart serves three distinct purposes. First, Walmart – the largest employer in the United States and, according to some measures, the largest employer in the world – is an effective target, serving as a deep pocket for policy reform, litigation and social activism. Second, Walmart, as a familiar, visible and brazen corporation, emblematizes the dilemmas regarding the costs and benefit distribution of global for-profit enterprises. Third, Walmart serves as a model for strategically exploring the efficacy of alternatives in legislation, litigation, non-governmental strategies and political struggles for social reform. Walmart has been the target of substantial grassroots and transnational activism, including organizations devoted entirely to addressing Walmart standards, such as Wake Up America, funded by the United Food and Commercial Worker International Union, and Walmart Watch, funded by the Service Employees International Union. Walmart symbolizes unapologetic bottom-line profit management and vigilant price slashing, exerting intense pressures on its managers, partners, and sub-contractors to lower costs on every front (Lobel 2007a). In fact, social activists regularly use Walmart as an example of the 'low road' taken by some corporations as opposed to high road options – entailing higher social and environmental standards – which can result in similar or even better returns. For instance, a study by *Business Week* compared the two large retailers Walmart's and Costco's wage and compensation practices, arguing that despite Costco's significantly better compensation packages,

---

1   In the United States and Canada, however, a different fair trade certified mark is used.

Costco has been able to contain labour costs and even reduce those costs below those of Walmart's Sam's Club (Lobel 2006). Nevertheless, as part of Walmart's efforts to overhaul its image, it is attempting to target consumers that care about factors other than low prices. Chief executive Lee Scott describes this new business philosophy being utilized by Walmart as 'Doing Well by Doing Good' (Mui 2006a).

Walmart's Sam's Club, similar to popular chains such as Dunkin' Donuts, McDonald's and Starbucks, already sells fair trade coffee, paying above-marker price for coffee beans that meet certain social and environmental standards. Walmart is now seeking to work directly with South American bean farms to create a new, less expensive line by controlling the supply chain, 'direct-to-the-farmer,' from the ground up (Mui 2006a). Walmart has already forged partnerships with hundreds of social and environmental groups to develop sustainability initiatives. TransFair USA, the only independent fair trade certifier of farms in the United States, is working with Walmart on fair trade coffee acquisitions. The company is also working with the Rocky Mountain Institute in efforts to reduce the fuel consumption of its trucking fleet. Employing approximately 1.8 million people in the United States alone, Walmart has the resources to experiment with other socially responsible practices as well; in addition to the fair trade interest, Walmart recently introduced its plans to construct 'green stores,' supercentres with environmentally responsible features designed to reduce energy and water usage. The stores will include solar cells embedded in skylights and recycled water and heat. Walmart announced that it will request independent assessment of these efforts by outside monitors and vows to extend the 'best practices' of the experimental stores to its other 'big box' (mega retailers) stores (Lobel 2007a).

The inclusion of Walmart on the fair trade bandwagon raises several questions. The company is well known for exerting downward pressures on manufacturers around the world. Because of its impact on its subcontractors, Walmart should also be understood as one of the world's largest manufacturers. In other words, it is more accurate to understand Walmart as both a retailer and a maker of goods, which employs tens of thousands of workers around the world through subcontracting to manufacture goods at a specified low cost. The company's management dictates outsourcing and is responsible for lowering labour and environmental standards, eliminating jobs, avoiding unionization, increasing work hours and decreasing pay and benefits (Cleeland, Iritani and Marshall 2003). As one commentator put it, 'supporting fair trade presents a paradox for Walmart. It is a tacit admission that there is a point at which no more efficiencies can be squeezed out of the system without harming the people who make it work' (Mui 2006a).

Despite Walmart's efforts, activists have been sceptical of the corporation's mixed signals of aiming to achieve both an economic bottom line and ethical and social accountability. The Organic Consumers Association has urged shoppers to patronize independent cafés and roasters rather than buy Walmart's fair trade labelled products (Mui 2006b). In addition to suspicions concerning Walmart's contradictory 'Do Good' efforts in a small subset of products, and harsh management and retail practices for most of its operation, fair trade activists worry about the effect of these developments on the fair trade movement in general. Some commentators suggest that once the 'Fair Trade' label is sold by mass-market big box retailers, its retail value will decrease as consumers will cease to view these products as offering something unique.

These concerns indicate the general limitations of CSR and fair trade strategies. Despite some success, the CSR and fair trade mechanisms and developments have been the subject of critique from both left and right. On the left, such regimes are viewed as too weak and cosmetic to actually bring fairness to a globalized market. On the right, critics perceive these efforts as distorting the comparative advantage of developing countries in selling their products and labour for competitive prices (Espstein 2007). One commentator writes:

those who … advocate various half-baked schemes to prop up prices may have the best intentions, but they are not really helping. At best they are diverting time and energy into dead ends; at worst they could end up making the situation even worse. It may feel good to ignore market realities, but it won't do any good. (Lindsey 2004)

Fair trade regimes are 'soft law' in the sense that they consist of a range of mechanisms but rely on corporations, consumers and investors to create their value (Freeman 1994). These private instruments include social labelling, voluntary corporate codes of conduct, private accreditation and certification by non-government actors. There is no governmental standard for either fair trade certification or corporate codes of conduct. From the consumer's perspective, the logic of paying a premium on certified products is two-fold: first, it ensures that the products themselves have been produced with certain criteria; furthermore, it signifies that for future products, the premium will filter down through the chain of production all the way to local producers in the developing country as well as fund the certifying fair trade organizations. In other words, fair trade labelling seeks to identify goods that have generated a premium above market prices for the original producer (Meidinger 2002–2003) and it relies on consumers to be willing to pay that premium.

A growing body of empirical work demonstrates that consumers have preferences not only about the quality of the product or service they are purchasing, but also about the process, including the social standards and environment in which they were developed (Kysar 2004). However, while empirical studies indicate that many consumers are indeed willing to pay to support fair labour standards and corporate environmental responsibility (International Communications Research 1999), such willingness is limited in both depth and breadth. Consumer willingness is primarily significant for certain consumption products and when consumers are able to process information about production and corporate processes. Fair trade efforts have focused on only a small fraction of overall production and trade. These efforts have identified a number of industries or even specific companies where standards are thought to fall low. There is also great variance of opinion on what constitutes the substance of 'fair,' such as which labour standards should be considered core standards that should be followed and how compliance is to be monitored. Relying on consumers to monitor trade standards through their willingness to pay is fraught with collective action and data processing problems, and, most basically, uncertain preferences problems. Focus on the end sale at the importing country as a mechanism of regulating production processes in the exporting country indicates the weakness of such a strategy. The percentage of products actually affected by certification efforts is very low. Even in coffee, fair trade certified products consist of a miniscule percentage of trade; only 3.3 per cent of coffee sold in the United States in 2006 was certified fair trade (TransFair USA 2008, 19). Indeed, a fundamental limitation is that many violations of core labour standards occur not in the production of export goods but in the informal or local production sectors. As such, relying on consumer taste for responsible production will not affect labour standards in these contexts.

Similarly, while CSR campaigns that focus on paradigmatic MNCs such as brand-name apparel and big box retailers have seen positive effects, these efforts are limited in their scope and possibilities. Using iconic corporate symbols to attain larger goals also has its disadvantages. Activists risk reducing the message of human rights to the single context of a specific firm (Lobel 2006). Social responsibility campaigns that single out the icon into an exceptional target may lose sight of the greater goal of widespread social responsibility. For example, during the 1990s, Nike often became the sole focus of consumers in the apparel industry. While Nike products were often produced under exploitative conditions, other corporations, remaining below the consumers' radar, were also producing under similar conditions. The World Bank Group commented on these limitations to CSR practices, stating:

[W]hile meaningful progress has been made in apparel, and to a lesser degree in agriculture, the existing 'system' of implementation may be reaching its limits in terms of its ability to deliver further sustainable improvements in social and environmental workplace standards. This in some ways is natural when one considers that current approaches are not the result of a systematic effort to marshal the forces of the public and private sectors, trade unions and NGOs, and workers. Instead, it is clear from the consultations that current efforts are the result of a series of steps often taken through ad hoc and isolated decisions. (World Bank Group 2003, 2)

In sum, while responsible investment and ethical consumption can have significant effects on the behaviour of corporations, the potential of fair trade mechanisms to alleviate poverty is limited at best. This chapter suggests that it is rather the type and continuing role of state regulation which remains key.

Regulatory Crowding Out and New Governance Ratcheting Up

Just as the private processes of encouraging corporation accountability are limited in their reach, the limits of the legal process are numerous. In recent years, activists have moved to private standard setting in part as a result of scepticism concerning the ability of legal systems to bring about significant results (Lobel 2007b). Regulatory failures have been at the centre of legal study for several decades. In the United States, regulation has been described as having become 'the Stalingrad of domestic political warfare' (Schuck 2000, 117). Traditional regulation has been criticized as rigid, inefficient and suppressive of innovation and competition. It has also been characterized as secretive and hostile to public participation. In the absence of an encompassing governance approach, regulation also risks regressive taxation when its costs are passed on to consumers. Similarly, many social activists view litigation, either as a method of regulation or to enforce existing regulations, as an ineffective path to bring social reform. Litigation is most often expensive, time consuming and resource draining. Moreover, even when a social movement undergoes successful litigation, there are post-victory struggles for award collection and for enduring structural changes.

Social activists have posited a particularly acute critique of the legal system that under the traditional regulatory model, groups and individuals are perceived as the passive object of regulation without room for dynamic input and participation (Roberts 1998). This in turn communicates a message of adversarial behaviour, mutual distrust and conflict. These concerns coincide with behavioural studies which suggest that external interventions, such as regulatory sanctions or monetary incentives can have the effect of crowding out intrinsic or moral motivation. The theory, supported by empirical evidence, argues that the introduction of such external mechanisms may undermine any internal willingness to follow ethical paths (Akerlof 1982). Formal incentives may thus in fact adversely impact upon informal, private norms (Frey and Jegen 2001).

Another concern about using the regulatory system to promote social responsibility is that, in a command and control approach, information flows selectively and corporations may be reluctant to examine and retain data about their own practices (Farber 1993). This is particularly problematic due to the informational asymmetries existing between government regulators and private industry. An example of this concern arose in the late 1990s, when Nike was sued in California by an activist named Kasky for false advertisement under California consumer protection laws. The suit was enabled by Nike's response to grassroots activism through a CSR public relations campaign. In reaction to the law suit, the Nike Corporation removed manufacturing information from its website, to protect itself from increased challenges by consumers. The removal of such information reveals the weakness of regulation strategies in their potential to halt both positive cooperation between civil society and businesses and practices of transparency by MNCs.

A countervailing thesis about the potential of overlaying private initiatives with more structural, formal interventions arises from new approaches to regulation which attempt to reconcile the tension between government intervention and market self-regulation. Archon Fung, Dara O'Rourke, and Charles Sabel (2001) have argued that fair trade strategies will 'ratchet labour standards', through a process of information gathering and distribution, systematic monitoring and comparing of peers – firms will compete on labour standards performance, generating a race-to-the-top (Fung, O'Rourke and Sabel 2001). When standards are developed collaboratively by civil society organizations, industry representatives, scientific experts and government representatives, they receive input from a range of interests. However, as described above, relying merely on decentralized voluntary decisions of individual consumers is limited in its reach. Market failures include: collective action and free rider problems; information asymmetries; cognitive biases; and scale inefficiencies. Markets also frequently lack adequate spaces for the public exchange of ideas and the identification of best practices.

In recent years, both in practice and in scholarly endeavours, a new approach to regulation has emerged, often referred to as 'New Governance.' This new vision of regulatory governance attempts to reconcile the tension between the fear of regulatory inefficiency by big government and the need for a public response to social challenges. New Governance scholarship is an effort to bring together insights from the empirical field of regulatory research and the changes in the new economy (Lobel 2004). In particular, New Governance approaches rely more on collaborative efforts between government and industry to continuously develop the best practices and increase compliance through preventative and multi-level efforts rather than through traditional top-down command and control regulation. New Governance scholars illuminate the wide range of regulatory possibilities, defying a purely dichotomized notion of command and control government regulation and non-governmental private ordering. Ayres and Braithwaite (1992) argue for 'enforced self-regulation,' where a regulatory agency negotiates particularized regulations with individual firms, while retaining the threat of less tailored rules if the firm fails to self-enforce and cooperate. This increases commitment on behalf of the company more so than if the standards are imposed by an external body. It also allows for better tailoring of the risks and solutions to specific companies and encourages innovation by allowing the company to choose the least costly solutions.

New Governance approaches, committed to collaboration between state and non-state actors, promise the encouragement of discussion and spaces for dialogue and mutual accountability. They promote the identification of shared goals and the abandonment of entrenched positions that construct other actors as the problem rather than partners to a solution (Lobel 2004). A central critique of traditional regulation is its 'one-size-fits-all' methodology, for example, imposing the same safety rules for diverse workplaces, without regard to the nature and real risks at each production site. New Governance approaches recognize the legitimacy of private economic interests while appealing to public values. Thus, New Governance assumes a harder definition of 'soft law,' preserving an active role for both the state and the legal regime. It offers a framework that enables us to view the three sectors – state, market and civil society – as part of a comprehensive, interlocking system. The focus of New Governance is on how government interacts with and facilitates the involvement of private actors in public action and policy.

Exemplary of the synergy between private standardization, monitoring efforts and government agencies is the use of information and disclosure regimes as policy tools which allow for choice and participation (Pedersen 2001). In areas as diverse as securities regulation, banking and loan management, environmental safety, health care, pharmaceuticals and consumer protection, regulatory agencies require information on performance, rates and quality to be available for the use of interested stakeholders in order to generate better practices. For example, the European Union has formalized social and environmental reporting and disclosure obligations as a matter of corporate law (Kysar 2005). Even when imposed by regional or national law in this manner, corporate social and environmental reporting still constitutes a significant departure from conventional command and control mechanisms. In a disclosure regime, the state mandates nothing beyond the provision of information to interested non-state actors who, in turn, are encouraged to utilize the information in ways that will promote collectively desirable behaviour. Thus, even when formalized and adopted by state regulation, this approach offers 'a vibrant, alternative ethos to two oppositional orthodoxies – regulation and deregulation' (Lobel 2004).

New Governance mechanisms also call for inter-jurisdictional competition through decentralization and privatization, promoting experimentation and the evaluation of multiple approaches before selecting a particular solution. Private codes of conduct and non-governmental fair trade standards can thus serve as a benchmark for state codification and enforcement. Indeed, under a New Governance framework, government can designate private standard-setters; as a result, formal process-oriented state rules co-determine actions in conjunction with a range of other norms. Importantly, New Governance approaches blur the line between following the law and going beyond it, thereby reducing the relative advantage of CSR in which the law goes 'beyond compliance' to ethical behaviour beyond the confines of codified regulation. New Governance also builds on the principle that law has an expressive value in addition to its direct control over individuals and corporations. The law offers principled reasons and justifications for action in addition to its direct, tangible prohibitions and results (Anderson and Pildes 2000) and declaration of a formal rule influences prevailing social norms (Sunstein 1996). In fact, the existence of mandatory law can itself be norm generating: the regulatory regime creates a relational contract between government and industry that supports the generation of private norms (McMaster and Sawkins 1996). Conversely, when efforts remain in the realm of civil society and mechanisms are understood as purely voluntary, the frameworks perpetuate a conservative notion that the state no longer has any role to play in ensuring fairness and welfare in market relations (Lobel 2007b).

New Governance can direct CSR efforts by setting external substantive norms and providing a check on levels of enforcement, as well as setting the processes by which they are enforced. As such, the state can ask corporations to take initiatives and additionally hold them accountable for their own self-regulation. Christine Parker has referred to this as 'meta-regulation' – where the law sets out to constitute corporate consciences by 'getting companies to want to do what they should do' (Parker 2007). In other words, the law becomes more process-oriented to ensure that the substance presented as CSR or fair trade claims has legitimacy. In this process, government, industry and civil society groups all share responsibility for achieving policy goals. Industry is expected to participate in a search for common goals rather than rigidly asserting its narrow economic or political interests. The role of government changes from regulator and controller to facilitator and coordinator. Law becomes a process of shared problem-solving rather than an ordering activity (Freeman 1997).

Experiments in Private–Public Synergies

Corporations have always been immersed in both legal and non-legal norms. In the following section, several examples of New Governance efforts emerging at the national level in the United

States are described. These areas of experimentation exemplify the particular synergy between private efforts and public administration. These cases test the possibility of building upon and supporting privately generated norms by adopting them into the administrative or jurisprudential process (Rubin 1994). The section concludes with several observations on the connection between national levels and transitional and international efforts.

A prime example of New Governance shifts is in the area of occupational safety and health. The Occupational Safety and Health Administration (OSHA) has a broad power to regulate workplace safety across all industries. Partly due to this administrative power, OSHA has been commonly understood as a paradigmatic case study of bureaucratic regulatory failure, accused of gross regulatory unreasonableness and portrayed as exemplifying all the pathologies of the legal-bureaucratic regime (Handler 1988). Yet, even in its first years, OSHA was directed by the legislature to adopt existing private industry standards by reference to associational safety codes. At OSHA's foundation, the agency entered in contractual relations with the non-governmental American National Standards Institute (ANSI) for the provision of technical support in the development and application of safety standards. ANSI sets standards through collaboration with corporations, professional organizations and trade associations. It oversees the processes of private standard setting organizations and recommends the incorporation of their conclusions into the standards promulgated by OSHA. In spite of this attempt to generate standards which were responsive to industry need through partnership with ANSI, the standards were criticized as being inflexible; OSHA was critiqued for being too focused on the promulgation of substantive rules which established rigid universal standards for issues such as exposure to toxins. At the implementation stage, again the agency operated in an adversarial top-down manner *vis-à-vis* the private sector. The agency enforced these rules by random inspections of worksites and prosecution where violations were discovered. At the beginning of the 1980s, major litigation resulted in judicial decisions striking down several of OSHA's central top-down promulgated rules. The extensive litigation by private industry reflected the controversy triggered in the business community by OSHA's regulatory activity.

In recent years OSHA has shifted its emphasis from extensive elaboration of standards and high rates of inspection to conducting fewer inspections and more programmes of collaborative, semi-voluntary compliance. At the state and federal levels, agencies are experimenting with innovative governance approaches to occupational health and safety. For example, California's Occupational Health and Safety Administration has adopted the California Cooperative Compliance Program, which authorizes unions and employers to develop and implement safety requirements, delegating governmental inspection and enforcement roles to joint labour/management safety committees. As long as this programme of audited self-regulation proves to reduce accidents effectively, the agency does not intervene in the process. The auditing process is non-adversarial and is performed by periodic corporate submissions of reports on self-monitoring and prevention activities as well as accident rates to the compliance agency. This gives firms and industries incentives to learn, improve, and share information dynamically with others. Similarly, the federal OSHA has established cooperative programmes, such as the Voluntary Protection Program (VPP), allowing companies with exemplary safety records to take over the role of OSHA inspectors themselves and be exempt from regular inspections. According to OSHA's reports, injuries and illnesses have been cut by 47 per cent at worksites engaged in cooperative relationships with the agency. OSHA also aims to foster relationships with other civil society organizations in order to address critical safety and health issues, expanding collaborative partnerships, voluntary programmes and assistance in outreach, education and compliance.

In 2004, the Government Accountability Office (GAO) completed a study on OSHA's cooperative programmes. It found that participation in the programmes has considerably reduced injury and illness rates, improved relationships with OSHA, increased productivity and decreased worker compensation costs. While the study emphasizes that OSHA does not currently collect complete and comparable data that would enable full evaluation of the programmes, the report suggests that the new cooperative strategies have improved safety and health practices by allowing OSHA to play a 'collaborative, rather than a policing, role with employers' (GAO 2004). These findings are consistent with a number of studies: OSHA self-reports the reduction of injury rates and lost workday incidence at a VPP when compared to a traditionally regulated worksite (OSHA 2005; Spieler 1994; Rees 1988). A derivative benefit of VPP participation seems to be the reduction of production costs, explained by increased worker productivity and decline in worker compensation costs (GAO 2004). Finally, less tangible benefits reported by programme participants include increased trust between management and government and between management and workers (GAO 2004).

This report echoes findings of comparative studies on the significance of maintaining a culture of safety in organizations. John Braithwaite (1985), surveying 39 coalmining accidents in Australia, the United States, Britain, France, Belgium and Japan, found that fatal accidents were attributable to defects in various areas: planning, internal communication, definition of responsibilities and authority, deficiencies in training, inadequate supervision and an overarching culture of safety. In an Australian-based study, Fiona Haines (1997) studied 37 firms responsible for workers' deaths at a multi-employer worksite, observing that responses by firms were attributable to differences in corporate culture. Haines found two opposing safety cultures that corresponded with different levels of risk prevention activities. She describes the 'virtuous culture' as one which views safety as integral to organizational processes. The 'non-virtuous culture' pushes safety into the background in order to focus on short-term demands.

New employment anti-discrimination strategies are another example of the adoption of the New Governance model. Employment discrimination policies in the United States have largely been based on a regulatory and adversarial regime. Its main strategy was the direct prohibition of certain practices, including illegal consideration of gender and race in hiring and promotions, followed by top-down implementation and enforcement. The regulatory model was founded on the assumption that employment discrimination is an intentional act and thus the best response is usually a lawsuit for damages or an injunction. While this approach has brought significant changes by eliminating the most obvious and direct occurrences of discrimination, it is limited in its ability to deal with more complex and subtle discriminatory practices taking place in more dynamic and multi-faceted workplaces. Discriminatory practices are frequently not the result of a distinct and direct decision to discriminate but are rather the consequence of complex practices, including corporate culture, informal norms, networking, training, mentoring and evaluation. The complex nature of this type of discrimination 'resists definition and resolution through across-the-board, relatively specific commands and an after-the-fact enforcement mechanism' (Sturm 2001, 469). The boundaries between legal and illegal conduct are blurred, although the consequences of discrimination are no less harmful.

New Governance approaches to discrimination focus upon continual problem-solving efforts, involving workers as key participants in anti-discrimination efforts. It emphasizes the explicit articulation and specification of decision-making criteria and goals in order to allow comparison, learning and continuous improvement. As with multinational CSR practices, the voluntary adoption of ethical codes of conduct in the workplace is common practice for corporate America. Similarly, many corporations have implemented voluntary diversity training programmes. These private efforts have been integrated into policy through New Governance strategies primarily as liability defences in traditional litigation. The US Supreme Court established a defence to punitive damages in discrimination suits based on the ability of managerial agents to demonstrate good faith efforts to comply with Title VII (*Kolstad v ADA*, 527 U.S. 526 (1999)). Employers may show good faith efforts through the implementation of internal compliance structures, including self-adopted equal employment policies, codes and diversity training programmes. It is worth noting that this shift to reliance on internal monitoring and prevention practices was reactive to voluntary private industry efforts and courtroom litigation strategy, rather than an active, planned programme adopted by either legislature or administrative agencies.

Empirical studies show that these private efforts in the discrimination context are highly varied. While corporate America often appears to be doing more than it is required by law to promote workplace diversity, new studies indicate that only some types of private approaches are effective and the legal system must be more sensitive to these variances (Dobbin, Kalev and Kelly 2007). Similar to CSR and fair trade programmes, these new efforts have been mostly voluntary initiatives, albeit in the shadow of a litigation threat. The Equal Employment Opportunity Commission has recently initiated more systematic study, support and guidance on these private, internal self-governance efforts. It appears that the threat of litigation is often the trigger for corporations to rethink their internal governance practices (Estlund 2005).

Here, the example of Walmart is particularly illustrative: recently, a class of women has been certified to bring a class action against the corporation. This is the largest civil rights class action in the United States' history and has prompted managerial changes in promotion processes at Walmart (*Dukes v Wal-Mart, Inc.*, 509 F.3d 1168 (9th Cir. Cal. 2007); Greenhouse 2007). Before the class action, Walmart did not publicize openings for management positions. This contributed to the disparities among men and women who applied and were promoted to higher paid jobs. According to the lawsuit, Walmart had ignored internal warnings about discriminatory practices for years, including dismissing the 1998 recommendations of a diversity task force. Only in reaction to the employment discrimination litigation did the corporation take action. Walmart formalized some of its promotion processes, using technology to ensure notice on job openings reaches a broader subset of its employees. In 2003, Walmart founded its 'Office of Diversity' and adopted a new job classification and promotion system. The corporation has also adopted reforms, including a new information technology and a 'corporate compliance team' in response to wage and hour litigation (Lobel 2007a). The Walmart example demonstrates that there can be a positive synergy between the background rules of command and control regulation and *ex post facto* reactions – triggered either by litigation or settlement – by private industry adopting more preventative self-monitoring and dynamic solutions.

Another example can be found in environmental law. As early as the late 1960s, the emergence of an environmental social movement 'coincided with the decline of an older dream – the image of an independent and expert administrative agency creatively regulating a complex social problem in the public interest' (Ackerman and Hassler 1981). Environmentalists have long been frustrated by impasses and deadlocks and have sought more collaborative approaches to environmental law. Frequently, the nature of ecological resource management calls for intergovernmental coordination, learning and adjustment (Karkkainen 2003). In New Governance approaches to environmental management, public authorities provide cooperative implementation, relying on private groups to help interpret, implement and enforce applicable rules. Government provides incentives for self-implementation programmes and encourages private participation by disseminating information to the public. For example, environmental information disclosure initiatives such as the federal Toxic Release Inventory Program require firms to report their environment-related activities to the

Environmental Protection Agency, which then posts the data on the internet for use by industries, consumers and non-governmental groups.

Over a decade ago, the US Congress endorsed ideas of collaborative rule-making by standardizing regulatory negotiation in the *Negotiated Rulemaking Act of 1990*, which was permanently reauthorized in 1996. Negotiated rule-making is a process through which stakeholders come together to negotiate and reach consensus as to the substance of regulation. A particular example of negotiated planning collaborative experimentation in the environmental area is the development of Habitat Conservation Planning under the *Endangered Species Act of 1973 (ESA)*. Until the mid-1980s, the *ESA* established a rigid, prohibitive regulatory regime, imposing a near-absolute ban on land development in areas of wildlife conservation. This rigidity was criticized not merely by businesses, which were barred from developing conservationist areas, but also by activists and scientists for its uncompromising nature. The binary endangered/not endangered listing led to strategic behaviours and, as a result of local negotiation efforts between environmentalists and developers to allow more flexibility, government was presented with consensus agreements that included some taking of habitat in return for guarantees of sufficient open space for long-term specie survival (Thomas 2003).

Subsequently, Congress amended the *ESA* to encourage such multi-party planning. Habitat Conservation Plans must provide detailed information on monitoring and funding strategies as well as alternative actions considered during the negotiations. Although the federal agency is designated to give its final approval of the plan, the roles of subsequent supervision and coordination can be delegated to a private intermediary, such as a non-profit land conservation environmental organization (Breckenridge 1999). Just as within the context of labour and employment standards, environmental regulation through collaborative public–private efforts reveals mixed results.

Experiments in the areas of labour and environmental standards indicate that in order fully to realize the potential synergies between private efforts for corporate accountability and government oversight, there is a need for more data and learning, as well as coordinated pooling and sharing of information. One of the lessons of New Governance approaches is that the more these collaborative, reflexive elements of the governance methods are given teeth by the threat of litigation or penalty, the more likely they are to be effective. Good governance requires both private participation and the support of a centralized legal system. The internet offers a new frontier for social responsibility, both by allowing greater transparency and by reducing barriers of access into social activism. The greatest challenge remains that of sustainability, ensuring that cooperative initiatives have long-term effectiveness and staying power in a global setting.[2] If the *raison d'être* of voluntary initiatives such as CSR is to avoid accountability, then New Governance efforts – which require a promise of hard law in the case of non-compliance – are incompatible with purely privatized systems.

---

2   The problems of a regulatory background in the case of non-compliance and sustainability are most pronounced when we move into an international setting. In 2003, the United Nations Sub-Commission on the Promotion and Protection of Human Rights adopted the *Norms on the Responsibilities of Transnational Corporations and Other Business Enterprises with Regard to Human Rights*, seeking to coordinate many of the existing voluntary initiatives. For MNCs it remains to be seen whether the CSR movement can have sustainable effects on accountability and transparency. A promising aspect of fair trade initiatives, which separates them from one-sided CSR initiatives by corporations, are their consumer and investor driven processes involving a multitude of stakeholders and intrinsically allowing for external monitoring. This brings them closer to the New Governance model.

Conclusion

Philip Selznik (1949) described the democratic process as the means, instruments and tools 'which define the relation between authority and the individual.' Traditionally, a narrow vision of the regulatory system inhibited stakeholders from participating in the process of standard setting and enforcement. In recent years, activists and policy-makers have been shifting their attention to the work of private parties in ensuring ethical and socially responsible market behaviour. Both in their compliance with and in their resistance to regulatory standards and enforcement, firms display motivations that go beyond costs and monetary incentives, behaving in ways that are far more complex than the demands of simple rational calculations of cost avoidance. The merits of private regulation are that good-faith firms will focus on effective improvement of their labour, environmental and social standards rather than on ineffective liability avoidance. Thus, a broader repertoire of regulatory tools that includes private standard setting, monitoring and enforcement is desirable.

Nevertheless, the lessons from recent experiments in New Governance approaches serve as a cautionary tale for advocates of CSR and fair trade regimes. Governments, strapped for resources and facing both shrinking budgets and regulatory resistance, can benefit from using private actors to complement standard setting and enforcement activities. Moreover, law can gear these complex motivations and incentives of firms to the improvement of their practices by expanding non-conventional, governance-based policies. At the same time, private efforts cannot serve as a substitute for government oversight in all instances because there are significant limits in the scope and depth of private industry interest to improve standards. The need for both public coercive and cooperative public–private policies remains. Under certain conditions, economic enterprises can be engaged in ethical and socially responsible behaviour without hard law. The task of regulatory agencies and public policy remains to identify these conditions and support them, as well as to recognize the instances in which they are absent.

References

Ackerman, B.A. and Hassler, W.T. (1981), *Clean Coal/Dirty Air: or How the Clean Air Act Became a Multibillion-Dollar Bail-Out for High-Sulfur Coal Producers and What Should Be Done About It* (New Haven, CT: Yale University Press).

Akerlof, G.A. (1982), 'Labor contracts as partial gift exchange', *Quarterly Journal of Economics* 97(4): 543–69.

Anderson, E.S. and Pildes, R.H. (2000), 'Expressive theories of law: a general restatement', *University of Pennsylvania Law Review* 148(5): 1503–75.

Ayres, I. and Braithwaite, J. (1992), *Responsive Regulation: Transcending the Deregulation Debate* (Oxford: Oxford University Press).

Blackett, A. (2001), 'Global governance, legal pluralism and the decentered state: a labor law critique of codes of corporate conduct', *Industrial Journal of Global Legal Studies* 8(2): 401–47.

Bradley, K.C. (2003), 'Toward ecologically sustainable democracy?', in A. Fung and E.O. Wright (eds), *Deepening Democracy: Institutional Innovations in Empowered Participatory Governance* (London: Verso), pp. 208–19.

Braithwaite, J. (1985), *To Punish or Persuade: Enforcement of Coal Mine Safety* (Albany, NY: State University of New York Press).

Breckenridge, L.P. (1999), 'Nonprofit environmental organizations and the restructuring of institutions for ecosystem management', *Ecology Law Quarterly* 25(4): 692–706.

Brooke Group v Brown & Williamson Tobacco, 509 US 209, (1993).

Cleeland, N., Iritani, E. and Marshall, T. (2003), 'The Wal-Mart effect: scouring the globe to give shoppers an $8.63 polo shirt', *Los Angeles Times*, 24 November, A1.

Crane, D.A. (2005), 'The paradox of predatory pricing', *Cornell Law Review* 91(1): 1–66.

Dobbin, F., Kalev, A. and Kelly, B. (2007), 'Diversity management in corporate America', *Contexts* 6(4): 21–8.

Endangered Species Act of 1973, 16 USC (2004).

Epstein, E.M. (2007), 'The good company: rhetoric or reality? Corporate social responsibility and business ethics redux', *American Business Law Journal* 44: 207–22.

Estlund, C.E. (2005), 'Rebuilding the law of the workplace in an era of self-regulation', *Columbia Law Review* 105: 319–404.

Fairtrade Labelling Organizations International (FLO) (2008), 'Explanation of Fairtrade certification'. [Online]. Available at: http://fairtrade.net/sites/certification/explanation.html [accessed: 29 September 2008].

Farber, D.A. (1993), 'Revitalizing regulation', *Michigan Law Review* 91(6): 1278–96.

Fishman, C. (2003), 'The Wal-Mart you don't know', *Fast Company.com* 77. [Online: Fast Company.com]. Available at: http://www.fastcompany.com/magazine/77/walmart.html [accessed: 23 September 2008].

Freeman, J. (1997), 'Collaborative governance in the administrative state', *UCLA Law Review* 45(1): 1–98.

Freeman, R. (1994), 'A hard-headed look at labour standards', in W. Sengenberger and D. Campbell (eds), *International Labour Standards and Economic Interdependence* (Geneva: International Institute for Labour Studies), pp. 79–92.

Frey, B.S. and Jegen, R. (2001), 'Motivation crowding theory: a survey of empirical evidence', *Journal of Economic Surveys* 15(5): 589–611.

Fung, A., O'Rourke, D. and Sabel, C. (2001), 'Realizing labor standards', in J. Cohen et al. (eds), *Can We Put an End to Sweatshops?* (Boston, MA: Beacon Press), pp. 3–42.

General Accounting Office (GAO) (2004), *Workplace Safety and Health: OSHA's Voluntary Compliance Strategies Show Promising Results, but Should Be Fully Evaluated before They Are Expanded*. GAO-04-378. (Washington, DC: GAO). Available at: http://www.gao.gov/new.items/d04378.pdf [accessed: 20 September 2008].

Goetz, S. and Swaminathan, H. (2006), 'Wal-Mart and county-wide poverty', *Social Science Quarterly* 87(2): 211–26.

Gorgemans, A. (2005), 'Addressing child labor: an industry approach', *eJournal USA* 10(2): 32–4.

Greenhouse, S. (2005), 'How Costco became the anti-Wal-Mart: company has succeeded with generous employee compensation', *New York Times*, 17 July. Available at: http://www.nytimes.com/2005/07/17/business/yourmoney/17costco.html [accessed: 23 September 2008].

—— (2007), 'Court approves class-action suit against Wal-Mart', *New York Times*, 7 February.

Greenwood, D. (2004), 'Enronitis: why good corporations go bad', *Columbia Business Law Review* 2004(3): 773–848.

Grossman, J. (2003), 'The culture of compliance: the final triumph of form over substance in sexual harassment law', *Harvard Women's Law Journal* 26: 3–75.

Haines, F. (1997), *Corporate Regulation: Beyond 'Punish or Persuade'* (Oxford: Clarendon Press).

Handler, J. (1988), 'Dependent people, the state, and the modern/postmodern search for the dialogic community', *UCLA Law Review* 35(6): 999–1113.

Holmes, S. and Zellner, W. (2004), 'The Costco way: higher wages mean higher profits, but try telling Wall Street', *Business Week* 12 April, 76–7.

International Communications Research (1999), *The Consumer and Sweatshops*. [Online: Arlington: Marymount University Center for Ethical Concerns]. Available at: http://www.marymount.edu/news/garmentstudy [accessed: 16 September 2008].

Kaimat, W. (1996), 'Labor and lemons: efficient norms in the internal labor market and the possible failures of individual contracting', *University of Pennsylvania Law Review* 144(5): 1953–70.

Karkkainen, B.C. (2003), 'Toward ecologically sustainable democracy?', in Archon Fung and Erik Olin Wright (eds), *Deepening Democracy: Institutional Innovations in Empowered Participatory Governance* (London and New York: Verso).

Kasky v Nike, Inc., 27 Cal.4th 939 (2002).

Kysar, D.A. (2004), 'Preference for processes: the process/product distinction and the regulation of consumer choice', *Harvard Law Review* 118(2): 526–642.

—— (2005), 'Sustainable development and private global governance', *Texas Law Review* 83(7): 2109–66.

Lindsey, B. (2004), *Grounds for Complaint London: 'Fair Trade' and the Coffee Crisis* (London: Adam Smith Institute). Available at: http://www.adamsmith.org/images/stories/groundsforcomplaint.pdf [accessed: 16 September 2008].

Lobel, O. (2004), 'The renew deal: the fall of regulation and the rise of governance in contemporary legal thought', *Minnesota Law Review* 89(2): 342–470.

—— (2006), 'Sustainable capitalism or ethical transnationalism: off-shore production and economic development', *Journal of Asian Economics* 17(1): 56–62.

—— (2007a), 'Big boxes benefits: the targeting of giants in a national campaign to raise work conditions', *Connecticut Law Review* 39(4): 1685–712.

—— (2007b), 'The paradox of 'extra-legal' activism: critical legal consciousness and transformative politics', *Harvard Law Review* 120(4): 937–88.

McMaster, R.S. and Sawkins, J.W. (1996), 'The contract state, trust distortion, and efficiency', *Review of Social Economy* 54(2): 145–67.

Meidinger, E.E. (2002–2003), 'The new environmental law: forest certification', *Buffalo Environmental Law Journal* 10(1–2): 211–300.

Miller, G. (2004), *Everyday Low Wages: The Hidden Price We All Pay for Wal-Mart*. Report by the Democratic Staff of the Committee on Education and the Workforce (Washington, DC: US House of Representatives). Available at: http://edlabor.house.gov/publications/WALMARTREPORT.pdf [accessed: 23 September 2008].

Moore, G. (2004), 'The fair trade movement: parameters, issues and future research', *Journal of Business Ethics* 53(1–2): 73–86.

Mui, Y.Q. (2006a), 'For Wal-Mart, fair trade may be more than a hill of beans: retail giant looks at link with coffee farmer', *Washington Post*, 12 June, A01.

—— (2006b), 'Change brewing at Wal-Mart? Giant retailer turns to fair trade coffee', *Washington Post*, 18 June.

Negotiated Rulemaking Act of 1990, 5 USC § 561 (1992).

Occupational Safety and Health Administration (OSHA) (2005), *Voluntary Protection Programs: An OSHA Cooperative Program*. [Online: OSHA]. Available at: http://www.osha.gov/dcsp/vpp/index.html [accessed: 20 September 2008].

Parker, C.E. (2007), 'Meta-regulation: legal accountability for corporate social responsibility', in Doreen McBarnet, Aurora Voiculescu and Tom Campbell (eds), *The New Corporate Accountability: Corporate Social Responsibility and the Law* (Cambridge: Cambridge University Press).

Pedersen, W.F. (2001), 'Regulation and information disclosure: parallel universes and beyond', *Harvard Environmental Law Review* 25(1): 151–211.

Ramseyer, M.J. (1987), 'Takeover in Japan: opportunism, ideology and corporate control', *UCLA Law Review* 35(1): 1–64.

Rees, J. (1988), *Reforming the Workplace: A Study of Self-Regulation in Occupational Safety* (Philadelphia, PA: University of Pennsylvania Press).

Roberts, R.G. (1998), 'Environmental justice and community empowerment: learning from the civil rights movement', *American University Law Review* 48: 229–69.

Rock, E.B. and Wachter, M.L. (1996), 'The enforceability of norms and the employment relationship', *University of Pennsylvania Law Review* 114: 1913–52.

Rubin, P.H. (1994), 'Growing a legal system in the post-communist economies', *Cornell International Law Journal* 27(1): 1–47.

Sabel, C.F., O'Rourke, D. and Fung, A. (2000), *Ratcheting Labor Standards: Regulation for Continuous Improvement in the Global Workplace*, Social Protection Discussion Paper No. 0011. (Washington, DC: Social Protection Advisory Service, World Bank).

Schuck, P.H. (2000), *The Limits of Law: Essays on Democratic Governance* (Boulder, CO: Westview Press).

Selznick, P. (1949), *TVA and the Grass Roots: A Study in the Sociology of Formal Organization* (Berkeley, CA: University of California Press).

Spieler, E.A. (1994), 'Perpetuating risk? Workers' compensation and the persistence of occupational injuries', *Houston Law Review* 31(1): 119–264.

Sturm, S. (2001), 'Second generation employment discrimination: a structural approach', *Columbia Law Review* 101(3): 458–568.

Sub-Commission on the Promotion and Protection of Human Rights (2003), *Norms on the Responsibilities of Transnational Corporations and other Business Enterprises with Regard to Human Rights*, Res 2003/16, UN Doc E/CN.4/Sub.2/2003/L.11 (13 August 2003).

Sunstein, C.R. (1996), 'On the expressive function of law', *University of Pennsylvania Law Review* 144(5): 2021–53.

Thomas, C.W. (2003), 'Habitat conservation planning', in A. Fung and E.O. Wright (eds), *Deepening Democracy: Institutional Innovations in Empowered Participatory Governance* (London: Verso), pp. 144–74.

TransFair USA (2008), *Almanac: 2007* (Oakland, CA: TransFair USA).

Trebilcock, M.J. and Howse, R. (2005), 'Trade policy and labor standards', *Minnesota Journal of Global Trade* 14(2): 261–300.

World Bank Group (2003), *Strengthening Implementation of Corporate Social Responsibility in Global Supply Chains* (Washington, DC: World Bank Group).

Chapter 18

The Regulatory Impact of Using Public Procurement to Promote Better Labour Standards in Corporate Supply Chains

John Howe[1]

Introduction

This chapter examines the potential of government procurement as a mechanism for improving job quality and alleviating poverty, and suggests some ways in which this approach can be rendered more effective. The promotion of higher labour standards through government procurement is a 'soft' law mechanism that may appeal to governments at a time when economic globalization has, among other things, reduced the political willingness and ability of governments to safeguard the welfare of workers and communities through the maintenance of conventional labour law systems. In many developed economies, governments have reduced their traditional legal protection of labour rights and standards. Many developing countries maintain strong labour laws 'on paper' but lack resources, adequate institutional frameworks and, at times, the will to enforce labour standards properly. This chapter assumes, however, that governments have a crucial role to play in promoting and enforcing labour standards. The difficulties of enforcement and the high disincentives to compliance with labour laws for businesses mean that governments must find innovative ways to create inducements for more widespread compliance with labour standards. It is the contention of this chapter that promotion of existing labour standards or higher than existing legal standards through government procurement may be effective because it is responsive to existing power and resource distribution among economic and social actors (Ayres and Braithwaite 1992; Teubner 1983).

Poor job quality and labour abuses continue to be major causes of poverty and human degradation around the world. This is especially so in developing countries. It is widely accepted that improvements in internal labour standards can assist the reduction of poverty in developing countries significantly (see, for example, DFID 2004). One response to the 'ossification' of labour law and enforcement (Estlund 2002) has been the proliferation of private or non-governmental labour regulation and governance. This has been exemplified by the actions of NGOs and trade unions to persuade and/or pressure multinational corporations to sign on to codes of conduct or other voluntary standards as forms of supply-chain regulation, often within the rubric of 'corporate social responsibility' (CSR). As well as functioning to enhance domestic observance of better labour practices, these non-governmental approaches are commonly used to supplement international labour regulation of the operations of transnational corporations in developing countries.

1   I would like to thank Ingrid Landau for research assistance and discussion of ideas. I am also grateful to Shelley Marshall and Kate Macdonald for helpful comments and discussions.

Questions have been raised about the desirability and effectiveness of non-governmental regulation and CSR as a strategy for improving labour standards in the absence of state regulation (see, for instance, Heeks and Duncombe 2003, 1; Utting in this volume). The challenge facing state and non-state actors willing to locate and hold businesses accountable to labour standards – whether these are enshrined in law, are above the floor of minimum standards, or are more aspirational goals – is the actual or perceived conflict between these standards and the main drivers of corporate business activity: profit-seeking and shareholder value (Parker 2007, 224–229). This conflict is not easily overcome.

One mechanism by which governments can leverage corporate responsibility for labour standards without using mandatory legal regulation is through public procurement: making government purchases of goods and services conditional upon contractors and supply chains observing desired labour practices linked to job quality criteria. The significant role of governments as purchasers of goods and services provides the necessary economic leverage against corporate resistance, while being more politically palatable by avoiding the use of law to mandate broadly applicable standards. Procurement can be used to promote better labour standards domestically as well as allow governments of developed countries to influence the observance of labour standards by businesses operating in developing countries.

Government procurement is an interesting site for analysis of labour regulation, as expansion in government purchasing is itself a symptom of the transformation of the state from 'public provider' of goods and services and direct regulator of corporate activity to a phase of 'regulatory capitalism' (Braithwaite 2005), where the state plays more of a role in enabling or facilitating economic activity and self-regulation. Examining government procurement as a technique of labour regulation is also an opportunity to reflect on the maintenance and extension of the notion of government as 'model employer' (McCrudden 2007).

The *potential* impact of government procurement as a mechanism for improving job quality and alleviating poverty is the focus of this chapter. While government procurement initiatives which seek to promote better labour practices in a domestic context will be considered, greater emphasis is placed on the actual and possible use of procurement to promote better labour standards in developing countries. This chapter will examine various instances in which developed countries are linking procurement with supply-chain governance mechanisms in order to reach suppliers in developing countries with lower living standards. One issue considered is the tension between social objectives and economic efficiency values inherent in any attempt to use government purchasing to address social concerns. This may bring procurement mechanisms into tension with multilateral and bilateral 'free trade' agreements. Further, this chapter investigates the extent to which these mechanisms of regulation are likely to be legitimate and effective means of bringing about greater organizational commitment to better labour standards. In doing so, the chapter also analyses the actual and potential interaction between procurement and other strands of regulation and governance, including traditional state labour regulation and non-governmental approaches.

Government Procurement as Regulatory Technique

Government procurement can be characterized as a specific regulatory technique or approach available to the state. It can be distinguished from direct legal and private regulation or voluntary CSR. This chapter adopts a broad understanding of regulation,

... as any process or set of processes by which norms are established, the behaviour of those subject to the norms monitored or fed back into the regime, and for which there are mechanisms for holding the behaviour of regulated actors within the acceptable limits of the regime (whether by enforcement action or by some other mechanism). (Scott 2001, 331)

The focus of this chapter is on the role of the nation state in regulating labour standards. Regulation may, of course, occur 'above and beyond the state' (Morgan and Yeung 2007). The promulgation of labour standards by the International Labour Organization (ILO) is an example of such international regulation. Some consideration will be given to the interaction between state regulation and regulation by the ILO later in the chapter.

In seeking to influence behaviour through the establishment, monitoring and enforcement of norms, the state has a number of regulatory techniques and approaches available to it. Of these alternative techniques, 'soft' or 'light touch' approaches to regulation are distinguished from 'hard' legal or centred 'command and control' regulation – in which formal rules are created, monitored and enforced by the state through orders and sanctions – on the basis that the former are less reliant on government imposition of generally applicable mandatory legal standards as a means of regulating behaviour (Ogus 2001; Howe and Landau 2007). Moreover, it is recognized that regulation is 'multifaceted, differentiated and increasingly "shared" by a range of public and private actors' (Lucio and Mackenzie 2004, 78).

Approaches vary and are rarely mutually exclusive across this spectrum of labour regulation. Many initiatives rely on government deployment of its wealth resource to secure behavioural change in order to avoid the use of 'hard' law. Such initiatives include attaching conditions to procurement contracts and offering financial incentives or rewards in return for desired behaviour (Howe 2006). Some approaches employ 'meta-regulation' – in other words, facilitation of 'co-regulation' or corporatist arrangements and/or 'self-regulation' by requiring or encouraging firms and stakeholders to develop standards of behaviour which are better than state sanctioned minima (Parker 2007). Another broad area of government action is use of information and education strategies designed to encourage the adoption of decent work practices by presenting socially responsible or ethical practices in a way which suggests consistency with ideals of good corporate (self-)governance (Weiss 2002). Information strategies include those which impose public disclosure requirements on firms, including 'triple bottom line' reporting, as well as dissemination of voluntary codes of practice, and 'best practice guidelines' or 'case studies'.

There is a growing interest in alternatives to command and control regulation, including public procurement, as government 'drivers' of CSR (Moon 2004; Barnard, Deakin and Hobbs 2004). This extends to consideration of the role that some of these regulatory approaches might take in influencing the labour practices of multinational corporations beyond the borders of the host state (Cooney 2004). CSR tends to encapsulate voluntary initiatives, or at least initiatives adopted by companies as a result of pressure from social movements rather than as a result of government regulation. The basic assumption of CSR campaigns is that enterprises will respect labour standards if this respect is shown to be a relevant factor in maintaining or enhancing competitiveness and higher productivity. However, while command and control regulation frequently fails to ensure that corporations comply with important social policy goals, it is also true that many corporations, when left to their own devices, fail to take CSR seriously (for example Cooney 2006; Jones, Marshall and Mitchell 2007; McBarnet 2007, 14). This failure is exacerbated when it comes to corporate responsibility to employees, where studies have suggested that employers will often conceive of CSR as 'incorporating a set of external issues concerning the image and reputation of the company rather than the issue of its employment conditions' (Barnard, Deakin and Hobbs

2004, 30). The difference between voluntary CSR and light touch regulation, such as the use of targeted monetary incentives, is the role the state plays in seeking to steer or leverage corporate governance to internalize public policy goals. An example of this is the goal to procure better labour standards through the different tools at its disposal.

Soft or light touch approaches to state regulation have become increasingly popular with governments in the era of regulatory capitalism. It is arguable that this is because, in the context of economic globalization and increased competition among nation states for private investment, governments are either fearful of, or ideologically opposed to, the use of command and control regulation, for fear of causing corporate flight. Light touch regulation is seen as more consistent with the 'business case' for social responsibility. Moreover, soft forms of regulation are not always subject to the same jurisdictional and/or constitutional limitations as more formal law. However, they do represent a continuing role for government in the establishment of norms and mechanisms for securing compliance with those norms. The key issue here is whether these alternative forms of regulation are *effective*. Do they induce the desired responses from firms?

Evaluating Procurement as Regulation

There are a number of different criteria by which different regulatory techniques and systems can be evaluated. In this chapter, the potential impact of procurement as a technique for promoting better labour standards will be assessed in terms of the overlapping concepts of effectiveness and legitimacy.

We can anticipate that asking contractors to ensure that their transnational supply chains comply with specified labour standards might meet some resistance. While the incorporation of labour standards into government procurement programmes will have at least some symbolic significance, empirical studies of regulation have consistently established that it cannot be assumed that state promulgated standards will be effective, even where they are backed by penalties and other sanctions for non-compliance. It is therefore worthwhile thinking about ways in which procurement might be designed in order to maximize effectiveness.

Regulatory scholars and scholars influenced by discourse incorporating systems theory argue that regulation is more likely to be effective if used in a manner which is reflexive or responsive to existing power and resource distribution among economic and social actors (Ayres and Braithwaite 1992; Teubner 1983). These discourses reflect some common themes. One of the most significant of these is the contention that state regulation is simply one of a number of interacting and competing regulatory systems (Cooney 2006). Many scholars have argued that states should be seeking to harness or enlist these non-state systems in order to achieve public policy objectives, rather than seeking to interfere with or override those systems, because the latter approach is frequently ineffective in changing non-state behaviour. In other words, government should 'work with the grain of things', seeking to shape and steer forms of private ordering or self-regulation, such as corporate governance. It should not demand change through mandatory legal regulation or 'command and control', which is prone to avoidance (Braithwaite 2005; Cooney 2004; Arup 2001).

In doing so, regulation should be designed to facilitate or encourage 'de-centred' models of regulation, whereby non-state actors are responsible, empowered participants in norm creation, implementation and monitoring and enforcement (Black 2001). Indeed, it has been argued that an important criteria of effectiveness in any regulatory regime is its legitimacy, in the sense that it is 'worthy of public support' (Baldwin and Cave 1999). While this can be assessed in a number of ways, I will argue in this chapter that the legitimacy and therefore the effectiveness of any government policy will be influenced by the quality of public deliberation and participation by various stakeholders when determining regulatory objectives and the mechanisms for achieving those objectives (Vincent-Jones 2006, 107–109).

Some models which draw on these ideas are based on 'enforced self-regulation' or 'co-regulation', where 'instead of insisting on corporate compliance with state-mandated rules, governments can instead require corporations to institute internal systems designed to promote socially desirable outcomes', often with the mandatory involvement of stakeholders (Cooney 2006, 194–5).

It is important to note that theories of responsive or reflexive regulation do not necessarily leave development of these internal systems entirely in the hands of non-state actors. Barnard, Deakin and Hobbs have argued that '[a] crucial aspect of reflexive law is that it involves not simply an attempt to delegate rule-making authority to self-regulatory mechanisms such as collective bargaining, but also an effort to use legal norms, procedures and sanctions to "frame" or "steer" the process of self-regulation' (Barnard, Deakin and Hobbs 2004, 4).

This would not necessarily require legislation. It has also been suggested that states can facilitate development of internal systems, involving multiple stakeholders, by deploying their wealth resource as an incentive to corporations to internalize public policy norms, or more democratic decision-making processes (Parker 2002, 29; Cooney 2004).

What else is likely to be effective in convincing an organization to embrace public policy goals and values such as improvement of labour standards? Johnstone and Jones suggest that the answer to the more general question of regulatory effectiveness lies in regulation which is constitutive at the level of the firm (Johnstone and Jones 2006). Their study of occupational health and safety (OHS), dismissal, discrimination and sexual harassment regulation suggests that constitutive regulation exists where 'demands are placed on employers to discover and understand regulatory requirements, engage appropriate personnel (including advisers), establish and implement appropriate policies and procedures, and monitor and evaluate the implementation of those procedures to ensure that the organization complies with these regulatory requirements' (Johnstone and Jones 2006, 501).

Finally, it must be born in mind that pluralism in regulation will not necessarily be productive and effective. The overlaying of procurement or other alternative regulatory approaches over existing mechanisms of labour regulation may lead to 'regulatory collision' which undermines the objective of using procurement in this way (Johnstone and Mitchell 2004). Design of regulation must take account of the potential for unproductive regulatory conflict if it is to be legitimate and effective.

Procurement as a Form of Labour Regulation

Government procurement is an extremely significant area of government economic activity. The OECD estimates that globally, public procurement expenditure accounts for 15 per cent of the world's Gross Domestic Product (OECD 2005, 35). In Australia alone, it has been estimated that the Commonwealth Government annual procurement budget is in excess of $16 billion dollars, a figure which does not take into account state and local government procurement expenditure (Cooney 2004, 340). In larger economies, the government procurement budget is of course even more significant. For example, while annual central government expenditure in the UK amounts to £15 billion, total public sector procurement exceeds £150 billion (Bell and Usher 2007). The extent of public procurement is in itself a sign of the transformation in government. Governments have moved away from direct provision of many goods and services, and are instead purchasing those services from the private sector.

While it might be argued that the immediate purpose of procurement is the purchase of goods and services necessary for government administration, and that this is largely an economic purpose which should be subject to evaluation by economic efficiency criteria, government procurement, as a form of social regulation has a long history. Particularly since the early twentieth century, if not earlier, governments have used procurement to regulate labour practices, and in many countries continue to do so, including in Australia, Canada, the United States and the UK (McCrudden 2007).

The ILO has promoted the inclusion of labour considerations within public procurement contracts since the late 1940s. *The Labor Clauses (Public Contracts) Convention 1949* (No. 94) provides that all public procurement contracts awarded by central public authorities must include clauses ensuring wages, hours of work and other conditions of labour which are no less favourable than those established for work of the same character in the trade or industry concerned, in the district where the work is carried out (ILO 1949; ILO 2008).

This latter requirement begs the question of the *reach* of labour regulation through procurement. Given that this chapter is concerned with the use of procurement as a tool for achieving better labour standards and alleviating poverty, it will distinguish between procurement used to achieve better labour conditions in the 'home' country, and procurement seeking to influence labour standards in other countries where labour and living standards are poorer than in the home country. For this reason, the chapter will focus on developments in Australia, the United States and the UK.

This chapter presents evidence that public procurement is not extensively used as a form of labour regulation (see also ILO 2008). Before examining the way in which procurement is used to regulate labour practices, it is first necessary to consider some of the different forms and geographies of procurement, as well as how it might be used to achieve social objectives. Government procurement can be categorized according to whether it is public works, goods or services that are purchased (McCrudden 2007, 3). This categorization will be relevant to whether procurement can be used to influence labour standards, and the extent of regulation possible. For example, procurement of public works such as construction will normally be limited to domestic companies and workers. In this context, linking labour criteria to procurement will only impact on the conditions of domestic workers. Procurement linkages with labour standards concerning the purchase of public works and services are relatively common. However, where governments purchase goods such as equipment, clothing, stationary and so on, suppliers of those goods may have sourced products or components from overseas. It is within this context that governments of developed economies can influence labour conditions in developing countries most strongly. Yet, as will be shown, this is also a difficult proposition for governments, and examples of linkages between goods procurement and labour standards are relatively rare.

There are two ways in which governments can procure goods so that they promote better labour standards. First, governments can simply procure goods which are certified as 'fair trade' or 'ethically produced' by a recognized certification agency. Fair trade certification would normally require compliance with at least the core labour standards (Bell and Usher 2007, 9). Of course, there is only a limited range of goods attracting fair trade or some other recognized certification and governments are also significant purchasers of services. Second, governments can require contractors supplying goods to comply with specified labour standards, in the same way that they might regulate the supply of services.

Assuming that a government takes the latter approach to achieving social objectives through goods and services procurement, there are three stages at which governments can impose labour standards: qualification or eligibility to tender for a government contract; the tender assessment process; and the contractual requirements imposed on the successful tenderer (McCrudden 2007).

By imposing standards as 'qualification' criteria, government can restrict the tendering process to those companies that already comply with social objectives such as labour standards, thus providing an incentive for companies wishing to obtain government contracts to observe the desired minimum standards. There are various ways in which governments can integrate labour standard considerations into the tender assessment process. A programme could identify a quota of contracts which are 'set aside' for contractors of a particular type. There may be a 'price preference' for certain types of contractor, where, for example, the bid submitted by bidder A, although higher than that of bidder B, is regarded as equal to that of B if A undertakes to implement a particular social policy. The past practice or the willingness of a past bidder to implement the social objectives may be taken into account as a 'tie-breaker' where otherwise equal bidders are in competition. Alternatively, the social criteria may be either just one set of considerations to take into account, or determinative where tenders are otherwise equal. Another approach may be to 'offer back' to preferred tenderers, allowing them to match the lowest bid of the non-preferred tenderer.

However, the approach of many Australian governments, for example, is to include labour standards as one of a number of different criteria, including value for money, upon which tenders will be assessed, without clear weighting given to each element of the criteria (Howe and Landau 2007). Such an approach leaves considerable space for labour-related considerations to be subsumed within, or overlooked by, government administrators under pressure to secure best value for money, which is assessed narrowly in terms of the cheapest available price.

Alternatively, governments and their procuring agencies can require successful tenderers to demonstrate ongoing compliance with labour standards as a performance condition of the contract. Contracts might provide a mechanism for monitoring of compliance, such as contractor reporting, and termination of the contract can be used as a penalty for non-compliance, thus aiding enforcement of any labour-related conditions.

Of course, the effectiveness of all of these approaches will depend on the veracity of information provided to procuring authorities and on the adequacy and effectiveness of monitoring mechanisms. This issue will be discussed later in the chapter, as it is a consideration which also arises in relation to non-governmental mechanisms for promoting better labour standards.

Another consideration here is the role of law in relation to public procurement and labour standards. ILO *Convention 94* assumes that ratifying states would enact legislation to regulate the social aspects of public procurement. However, in the jurisdictions examined for the purpose of this chapter, including Australia, the United States and the UK, it is apparent that where social criteria are incorporated into public procurement, this is often achieved through administrative action and contract rather than through legislation.

Assuming that labour standards are included in public procurement tender assessment and contractual performance criteria, there are two broad types of labour standard which may be linked to public procurement programmes (Howe 2006). Firstly, procurement may be used as a method of enforcing *existing* legal obligations either domestically or in a supplier's host country; that is, as a supplement to existing mechanisms for enforcement of minimum rights and standards set by legislation and/or applicable industrial instruments, including ILO conventions or the ILO's Core Labour Standards (CLS). Secondly, procurement may be used to advance desired modes of labour relations *above and beyond* those required by applicable laws. Thus, for example, while a country may not have a legally enforceable right to collective bargaining, recognition of trade unions and the practice of collective bargaining may be encouraged through procurement.

Incidence of Public Procurement as a Form of Transnational Labour Regulation

In Australia, public procurement by the Commonwealth and the various state governments and their agencies is governed by a complex web of policies, frameworks, codes and guidelines (see generally Howe and Landau 2007, 373–80). In each jurisdiction, there is a broad procurement policy or framework that sets out general principles applying to government procurement contracts. Both Commonwealth and state governments include at least some labour conditions in their procurement criteria. In the case of Victoria, one of the broad policies requires all businesses that tender for government contracts to adhere to an 'ethical employment standard' (Victorian Government Purchasing Board 2003). Queensland and Victoria also have codes of best practice that set out specific labour standards and industrial relations practices with which all businesses in particular industries that tender for government contracts must comply. For example, Queensland has codes of practice for the building and construction industry, call centres and the clothing industry (Howe and Landau 2007, 336–337). In NSW, since 2005, there has been a single code of practice governing all types of government procurement which sets out standards of behaviour expected of government agencies, tenderers, service providers, employer and industry associations, and unions (Howe and Landau 2007, 337).

While both Commonwealth and state governments in Australia use public procurement as a means of promoting labour standards, their policies differ according to the type of contract or firm to which the policy applies, the precise standards promoted, the sanctions imposed for breach, and the use of monitoring mechanisms (Howe and Landau 2007). In the case of state governments, compliance is limited to onshore businesses – participation in procurement is not made dependent on offshore suppliers meeting labour standards. The recently elected Rudd Labor Government has committed to an 'ethical procurement policy' which will require major suppliers to the Commonwealth 'to ensure compliance with [ethical] procurement policies by all sub-contractors involved in the principal's supply chain to the Commonwealth' (ALP 2007). At the time of writing, the Rudd Government is yet to provide details of how this policy will work in practice.

Beyond this commitment, there have been only isolated examples of procurement policies in Australia which have extended to offshore labour used in the production of goods. In the lead-up to the Sydney Olympic Games in 2000, the Sydney Olympic Games Organizing Committee (SOCOG), the NSW Labor Council and the Australian Council of Trade Unions (ACTU) agreed to a 'Code of Labour Practice for Production of Goods Licensed' for the Games (SOCOG 1998; Webb 2001). The Code required all manufacturers or suppliers of licensed products to certify that they and their contractors and subcontractors (not limited to 'onshore' businesses) met specified minimum labour standards. These standards included not only core labour standards such as prohibition of child labour and respect for freedom of association and collective bargaining, but also required payment of 'fair wages' (at least complying with legal or industry minimum standards, and 'sufficient to meet basic needs and provide some discretionary income'), that hours of work were not excessive, and that a 'safe and hygienic working environment … be provided' (SOCOG 1998). The Victorian Government agreed to similar guidelines to ensure that official clothing and other merchandise for the 2006 Commonwealth Games in Melbourne was sourced ethically (ACTU 2006).

Queries have been raised about how far even these rare examples went in terms of ensuring that goods sourced for the respective Games were produced in conditions which met the agreed minimum standards. After the SOCOG Code was agreed to, unions raised concerns about whether all licensees' overseas manufacturers (mainly in China and Fiji) had been inspected for compliance. SOCOG initially refused ACTU permission to send a representative to inspect conditions in overseas factories, or even to provide information regarding contractors and subcontractors of licensees (Webb 2001, 213). While SOCOG eventually withdrew its objections and provided unions with a list of known contractors and subcontractors, unions lacked necessary resources to carry out on-site monitoring.

More innovative developments have taken place in other developed countries. The incorporation of social policy goals including labour standards within public procurement has long been a matter of debate within the European Union (McCrudden 2007). Several countries have legislation which requires or allows government purchasers to include labour clauses in government contracts. Belgium, Finland and Austria have especially strong requirements regarding these labour clauses (ILO 2008, 37). However, these requirements are largely concerned with domestic labour conditions. There is also evidence of some European countries reducing their commitment to attach labour criteria in procurement contracts. For example, a recent ILO study found that France had ceased to apply the ILO Convention in relation to procurement (ILO 2008, 19).

In terms of the use of procurement to regulate labour standards across transnational supply chains, the most significant developments have been in relation to legal changes allowing government purchasing of certified fair trade products in several European countries, including Belgium, Italy and the UK (Fairtrade Foundation 2007; European Fairtrade Association 2007).

There is a growing interest in the incorporation of labour standards into procurement by all levels of government in the UK (Bell and Usher 2007; Fairtrade Foundation 2007). The Office of Government Commerce provides guidance to UK purchasing authorities on the incorporation of social criteria including the ILO CLS and other 'employment issues' into different stages of the procurement process (Office of Government Commerce 2006). Actual implementation of labour standards through procurement in the UK still seems to be largely at the discretion of individual government departments and agencies. While some departments and some local governments have committed to purchasing fair trade certified products (Fairtrade Foundation 2007), there is less evidence of more widespread inclusion of labour criteria in the purchase of goods and services.

Use of procurement to regulate labour standards beyond the borders of the purchasing country appears to be more common in the United States, where federal legislation requires labour clauses to be included in federal contracts for services and manufactured goods (*McNamara-O'Hara Service Contract Act* 41 U.S.C. 351; *Walsh-Healey Public Contracts Act* 41 U.S.C. 35). However, it is at state and local government level where innovation in relation to transnational labour regulation has occurred. Many of these innovations are a result of the activist network Sweatfree Communities persuading many US state and local governments to adopt 'sweatfree' procurement policies in relation to garment purchasing. Sweatfree Communities recommends that states and cities in the United States require suppliers of apparel, footwear and laundry services to comply with some basic labour standards. These include the ILO's core labour standards, but also any 'applicable local laws' in the country where the manufacturing takes place, whether the United States or another country (Sweatfree Communities 2006). Sweatfree Communities argues that, if possible, procurement contracts should also require compliance with a 'non-poverty wage' rather than the legal minimum wage. This is because legal minimum wages in many countries do not necessarily provide sufficient income to allow workers and their families to avoid poverty. Sweatfree Communities suggests that in countries other than the United States, this would be the wage and benefit level required to raise a family of three out of poverty based on the national standard of living index for that country.

According to Sweatfree Communities, six states and 38 cities in the United States have adopted some form of sweatfree procurement policy (Sweatfree Communities 2007). While the content of each state's and city's policy varies, most require that contractors at least comply with legal minima. Some states (including California, Illinois, New Jersey and Pennsylvania) and cities have adopted the non-poverty wage standard. The city of Los Angeles' Sweatfree Procurement Ordinance (Ordinance No 176291, adding Article 17 to the Los Angeles Administrative Code, Div. 10, Ch. 1) applies to all contracts for material, supplies, equipment and laundry services where the value of the contract exceeds US$25,000 and the term of the contract is in excess of three months. Under the Ordinance, contractors with the city must sign a City Contractors Code of Conduct, whereby the contractor promises to ensure compliance with 'all human and labor rights and labor obligations that are imposed by treaty or law on the country in which the equipment, supplies, goods or materials are made and assembled'. In addition, for contracts involving the procurement of 'garments, uniforms, foot apparel and related accessories', contractors must ensure that contractors are paid a 'procurement living wage' (Sec. 10.43.3.D, Los Angeles Administrative Code, Div. 1, Ch. 1). For countries outside the United States, the relevant city agency 'shall establish a procurement living wage which is comparable to the wage for domestic manufacturers as defined above, adjusted to reflect the country's level of economic development by using the World Bank's Gross National Income per capita Purchasing Power Parity index' (Sec. 10.43.3.D, Los Angeles Administrative Code, Div. 1, Ch. 1). Successful contractors are required to 'take good faith measures to ensure that, to the best of the contractor's knowledge, the contractors' subcontractors also comply with the City's Contractors Code of Conduct'. The City of Los Angeles has also entered into an agreement with an NGO, the Workers Rights Consortium, to carry out monitoring of compliance with the Code. This arrangement will be discussed in more detail later in the chapter.

Thus it appears that there is a growing interest in the use of procurement by governments in developed countries to influence labour standards in developing countries. However, as discussed in the following section of the chapter, there is a lack of empirical evidence regarding the impact of these policies. Are these policies merely aspirational statements by governments in developed countries under pressure from labour and fair trade activists, or are they designed and resourced to be legitimate and effective forms of regulation?

Studying the Impact of Procurement as Labour Regulation

In this section, consideration is given to whether procurement is or can be an effective mechanism for promoting better labour standards. In doing this, it is necessary to outline some of the obstacles to successful use of procurement as labour regulation. Drawing on the regulation and governance literature and assessments of non-government labour regulation, this chapter then outlines some possible strategies for the effective and legitimate use of procurement to promote better labour standards in developing countries.

Possible Barriers and Limitations to Use of Procurement

Any study of the impact of procurement as labour regulation must take account of any relevant barriers or limits to this approach, whether legal, political or economic. The first limitation is a powerful conventional wisdom that procurement is a commercial function of government which must be carried out efficiently in order to ensure 'value for money' for taxpayers (McCrudden 2007, 115). Value for money is often assessed in narrow cost-benefit terms, that is, choosing the contractor that will provide the best service at the lowest cost to the public purse, thus excluding consideration for social concerns. Even where governments adopt an ethical purchasing policy, purchasing officers may give such policies very little weight compared to value for money criteria.

From the perspective of contractors, if procurement imposes too great a cost on a business in terms of compliance with labour standards then legitimacy of the procurement criteria will be undermined. Businesses may agree to labour standards, yet fail to comply with those standards in practice, especially if there is inadequate monitoring and enforcement by government or its agents.

Another (related) potential restriction arises from the promotion of competition and free trade, both at domestic and international regulatory levels. For example, in Australia the *Trade Practices Act 1974* (Cth) ('*TPA*') has been identified as a potential restriction on the capacity of a state government to use procurement to impose social obligations on businesses supplying goods or services to the government (Queensland Government 2006, 8.4). A number of commentators, however, have suggested that the *TPA* does not apply to public procurement (for example Seddon 2004, Ch. 6). Nevertheless, doubts about the extent of the *TPA*'s application may be a reason for state government hesitation to strengthen labour conditions attached to public procurement policies.

Perhaps more significant, both multilateral and bilateral free trade agreements and regulatory frameworks have been identified as restrictions on the use of procurement to 'discriminate' between businesses on the basis of labour standards, such as the World Trade Organization's Government Procurement Agreement (GPA). Once again, the restrictions posed by such rules may be more perceived than real. In the EU, both the EU Treaty and the EU Public Procurement Directive 2004 are intended to assure free movement of goods and services and non-discrimination against contractors on grounds of national origin. This has not prevented national governments of member states from including labour standards as part of public procurement processes (Bovis 2007).

Another possible difficulty with the use of procurement as labour regulation pertains to the potential for regulatory complexity which may undermine the legitimacy and effectiveness of procurement as a mechanism for promoting better labour standards. Where used domestically to improve labour standards by requiring firms to adopt labour standards and/or employment practices 'above the floor' of standards set by statute, labour criteria in procurement contracts add another layer of regulation to what is, in Australia at least, an already complex area.

The use of procurement as a form of transnational regulation of labour standards in developing countries also raises a number of concerns. Some of these barriers are legal, in the sense that there may be constitutional or other jurisdictional limitations on some levels of government seeking to influence labour standards in another country. Other challenges relate to possible unintended consequences of a relatively developed country seeking to raise labour standards in a developing country. Many of these have been canvassed in relation to non-government regulatory mechanisms – for example, that any standards set through procurement contracts must be sensitive to local conditions. Governments must be sensitive to the possibility that requiring supplier businesses to observe higher labour standards than is their customary practice could lead to a loss of jobs by workers in developing countries, resulting in those workers being 'squeezed' into worse jobs as a result (Heeks and Dunscombe 2003; Doorey 2005, 386–7).

Further concern expressed with respect to private regulation such as supply-chain regulation through codes of conduct is that such initiatives crowd out or undermine domestic labour law and labour regulation institutions in developing countries (Heeks and Duncombe 2003). The same concern could be raised in relation to attempts to use procurement as a form of inter-state labour regulation.

Many of these challenges can be overcome through appropriate regulatory design and implementation. The next section provides an evaluation of some existing procurement policies and includes an assessment of how procurement processes could be designed to enhance legitimacy and effectiveness. This requires an extensive combination of public and private regulatory approaches and mechanisms.

Procurement Strategies for the Legitimate and Effective Promotion of Better Labour Standards

Accepting the desirability of public procurement as a tool for promoting better labour standards, it is important to give careful consideration to its design and implementation. Failure to do so may cause it to be ineffective or have unintended consequences, such as where the intended beneficiaries of these initiatives end up worse off than they were beforehand (Doorey 2005, 358). This has been discussed above. Moreover, the literature on regulation canvassed earlier emphasizes that unless policy places demands on organizations to take compliance seriously, these approaches are likely to be nothing more than window dressing.

There are a number of elements that must be considered in the design of a legitimate and effective procurement process which has the potential to be constitutive of compliance by firms and their supply chains: first, agreement on appropriate labour rights and standards to be enforced through the procurement process; second, the disclosure of information; and third, an adequate system of monitoring and enforcement of the agreed norms and standards. This last element of regulatory design may be reformed by the experience of non-governmental mechanisms of international supply chain regulation and 'ethical trade' initiatives.

Firstly, to ensure the legitimacy of any use of procurement to promote or secure better labour rights and standards, government must work responsively with their own financial officers, trade unions and their international affiliates, the ILO, relevant NGOs and potential contractors to agree on appropriate labour rights and standards to be incorporated into eligibility criteria, tender assessment processes and the actual contracts themselves. These standards must be adaptive to local regulation and labour market conditions.

There have been a number of different approaches to this challenge incorporated into voluntary codes of conduct or firm/industry-level CSR initiatives (for example Nike and Reebok) and 'multi-stakeholder' non-government regulatory schemes. Many of these initiatives are prepared in consultation with business, trade unions and NGOs, and thus reflect the core ILO Conventions. An example of such a scheme is the OECD Guidelines for Multinational Enterprises (for an overview, see Cooney 2004) Some require compliance with the labour law of the country where work is performed, however, minimum labour standards, especially wages, in developing countries may not be sufficient to serve as a mechanism for poverty alleviation. Thus, while there is concern that labour standards in codes of conduct are not so high as to have unintended consequences, they should not be so low as to be ineffective in improving working conditions.

The City of Los Angeles Sweatfree Procurement Ordinance discussed above is an example of a responsive approach to this aspect of the procurement challenge. Where it addresses labour standards of sub-contractors in countries other than the United States, the Ordinance requires compliance with local minimum standards. However, it also requires payment of a 'procurement living wage' assessed on the basis of local conditions.

The second element of a legitimate and effective procurement regime is a mechanism to ensure information disclosure by contracting companies regarding the companies and factories in their supply chains, as well as information concerning compliance with set labour standards down the supply chain (Doorey 2005; Cooney 2004). If government is to ensure that only companies with suppliers observing the minimum standards are considered for government contracts, there must be some mechanism by which companies must provide this information, and where it is subjected to some sort of monitoring and accountability process. Such a process would prompt firms to give consideration to the regulatory purposes behind such a requirement, which might encourage the internalization of these norms. Furthermore, it allows for verification of compliance by independent monitors. Returning to the example of the Sweatfree Procurement Ordinance, it appears that contractors with the city must provide a list of their suppliers and the location of any worksites used in the supply of goods and materials (WRC 2008). The city can then require that contractors ensure that monitors can access those businesses and sites to monitor compliance with the labour standards set under the procurement Ordinance.

This last point brings us to monitoring and enforcement of labour conditions in procurement contracts. Once again, the legitimacy and effectiveness of procurement processes to promote better labour standards would be enhanced by the involvement of stakeholders in the monitoring and enforcement of standards (Vincent-Jones 2006). Evidence suggests that the procurement process must incorporate specifications regarding monitoring and enforcement of compliance with the agreed labour rights and standards in order to maximize effectiveness. Such a monitoring regime is built into the Sweatfree Communities procurement 'Toolkit' (Sweatfree Communities 2006). Monitoring might take the form of an audit of factory compliance with specified standards as part of the tender assessment process, or monitoring of ongoing compliance with labour standards agreed to in procurement documentation. Ideally, these processes should supplement or complement private monitoring by trade unions and NGOs, ILO and local labour regulation in order to maximize the legitimacy of monitoring activity (Kolben 2007). Specifications must also ensure that firms take responsibility for implementing internal planning and management processes which emphasize the importance of compliance with labour criteria in procurement contracts (Graham and Woods 2006, 878). In other words, although governments cannot be expected to devote significant resources to monitoring compliance with labour standards as part of their procurement functions, they can encourage development of self-regulatory mechanisms and draw on non-government monitoring and evaluation mechanisms by requiring contractors to agree to monitoring by trade unions, local government agencies or independent auditing bodies.

Again, the Sweatfree Procurement Ordinance provides an excellent example of this approach in the context of procurement initiatives. By engaging the Workers Rights Consortium (WRC) as an independent monitor of compliance with the Ordinance, the City has adopted an innovative model of private monitoring. The approach of the City also provides the most detailed assessment of the impact of procurement as mechanism for transnational labour regulation, as the WRC has recently completed a monitoring report in relation to compliance with the Ordinance by a major supplier of garments to the City.

The WRC is a non-government organization formed in the United States in 2000 as a result of protests by students that official university apparel in the United States was being produced in sweatshop conditions (for a detailed explanation and analysis of the WRC, see Barenberg 2007). The WRC both develops and monitors codes of practice designed to ensure that participating universities and colleges source their official garments from 'sweatfree' global supply chains. Mark Barenberg has argued that 'the WRC has developed the most effective, transparent, and "participatory" model of transnational labour monitoring' (Barenberg 2007, 38). According to Barenberg, this is largely because the WRC maintains its independence from employer and trade union interests in the apparel industry in terms of its governance structure and funding sources, and by engaging to the greatest possible extent with local workers and communities in carrying out factory monitoring in developing countries (Barenberg 2007).

By engaging the WRC to carry out monitoring of compliance with its Ordinance, the City of Los Angeles has implemented this model in a procurement context (WRC 2008; City of Los Angeles undated). In late 2007, the WRC carried out an 'assessment' of an apparel factory in Phnom Penh, Cambodia, owned by a Taiwan-based multinational corporation, New Wide Garment (NWG). Williamson-Dickie, a major supplier of 'Dickies' brand garments to the City of Los Angeles, had named NWG as one of its suppliers, and as a result NWG was subject to the city's

Sweatfree Ordinance. According to the WRC, NWG employs approximately 1,400 workers at its Cambodian factory, more than 90 per cent of them women.

The WRC's assessment was based on interviews with the management and the company's 'code of conduct' compliance officer, 'in-depth' interviews with 31 NWG production employees, review of factory documentation including payroll records, employment contracts and personnel policies, and a physical inspection of the factory. Unfortunately, the WRC's assessment report does not provide much information on the composition of the team used to conduct the assessment. Previous analysis of the WRC's activities in relation to the monitoring of the WRC code for university purchasing suggests that the WRC is intended to maximize local participation in the assessment. In addition to including locals in the assessment team, the WRC would normally engage with local labour ministries, tribunals and other officials, as well as building the capacity of local NGOs (Barenberg 2007, 41).

WRC found that the factory was not complying with the Los Angeles Sweatfree Ordinance in a number of respects. Some of these were instances of non-compliance with Cambodia's own labour legislation, including unlawful discrimination against pregnant workers, unlawfully long probationary periods, failure to provide sick leave and breach of Cambodia's freedom of association protections. The WRC also found that while NWG paid workers the minimum salary permitted by Cambodian law, this was below the Procurement Living Wage required by the Ordinance. The WRC estimated the Cambodian living wage at US 63c per hour, or roughly $130 per month under the terms of the Ordinance. Workers were being paid $50–62 per month.

Under the terms of its agreement with the City of Los Angeles, the WRC held discussions with NWG and it agreed to address some of the violations identified in the assessment. For example, the company agreed to adopt a policy of non-discrimination against pregnant workers. Unresolved issues were addressed by the WRC in the form of recommendations to the City of Los Angeles. Interestingly, the WRC was careful not to recommend that the City of Los Angeles require NWG (through Williamson-Dickie) to increase wages to meet the Procurement Living Wage. The WRC recognized that a wage increase could only be achieved if NWG's customers were willing to pay significantly higher prices for its product. Instead, it resolved to hold discussions with the city regarding this issue.

This discussion of the ways in which procurement mechanisms are implemented and enforced suggests that there are risks associated with the use of procurement as a mechanism for the alleviation of poverty and the promotion of higher labour standards. The first is that even after contractors have agreed to ensure compliance with specified labour standards throughout their global supply chains, many are still likely to be non-compliant as the NWG example shows. The second is that in the absence of monitoring, this non-compliance is likely to continue notwithstanding that the head contractor has legal obligations to the contrary. However, when combined with independent and rigorous monitoring of compliance by contractors' supply chains, procurement can have an impact on labour standards in developing countries. The WRC assessment report suggests that workers at the NWG factory would enjoy improved working conditions as a result of the assessment, including, at the very least, a higher level of employment security. At least some of the employees of NWG may enjoy a less precarious existence as a result of the Los Angeles Ordinance.

The Los Angeles Ordinance appears to represent a rigorous and comprehensive model combining public and private regulatory mechanisms which could be applied more widely within the procurement context. It involves a mechanism which is not reliant on self-regulation, but rather relies on the Ordinance and Code to force contractor companies to engage with the sweatfree norms not only within the contractor company, but also across that company's global supply chains.

The appointment of a well-resourced, independent monitor ensures that demands can be placed on contractors and their suppliers to engage with the relevant labour standards. It also seems that the WRC is able to work closely with local groups, thus maximizing legitimacy and effectiveness of the relevant code or policy by ensuring that extensive evidence of compliance is collected. However, the approach of engaging with local workers, communities and officials also ensures that monitors are sensitive to local conditions and perspectives in terms of the course of action which is recommended.

A report by the City of Los Angeles's City Administrative Officer to the Chair of the Housing, Community and Economic Development Committee estimates that the annual cost to the City of engaging the WRC would be in the sum of $50,000 (City of Los Angeles 2003). It is therefore an approach which requires the expenditure of significant resources. As noted earlier, it is questionable whether many governments would be willing to commit such resources to monitoring sweatfree procurement policies. In Australia, the Sydney Olympics example reveals that even where a policy is agreed upon, resourcing for adequate monitoring and enforcement does not form part of the arrangement. That role is left to NGOs and trade unions which have many different limitations on their resources. The alternative is to rely on self-monitoring of supply chains by contracting companies, which on its own has also proved to be unreliable (Barenberg 2007; Graham and Woods 2006; Locke, Qin and Brause 2007).

What happens when contractors and their suppliers are found to be non-compliant with labour standards in procurement contracts? One of the advantages of government procurement over non-government supply-chain regulation with respect to labour standards is the extent to which effective sanctions are available. In most cases where government procurement contracts impose labour standards, a basic sanction for non-compliance will be cancellation of future contracts and ineligibility for future government contracts (see, for example, the Los Angeles Sweatfree Procurement Ordinance). For many businesses, especially those dependent on government buyers to provide a market for their goods, exclusion from government contracts on the basis of failure to comply with labour standards may be a significant penalty. This nevertheless requires a commitment from governments to enforce sanctions where breaches are discovered in relation to suppliers who have been long-term, preferred contractors, or where suppliers are few and far between.

Procurement must be used to supplement existing forms and processes of regulation and avoid overriding or conflicting with existing mechanisms. A combination of public and private regulation has been shown to be effective in securing actual outcomes in terms of better labour standards (Weil and Mallo 2007). Thinking about effective strategies for promotion of labour standards through procurement also requires engagement with the literature on private regulation and monitoring in this area. To some degree, when considering government purchasers as supply-chain regulators, there is a significant overlap with supply-chain regulation by private purchasers in terms of the issues which must be confronted.

In concluding this discussion, I am not suggesting that effective and legitimate use of procurement to promote better labour standards is a technocratic process of optimal regulatory design. The barriers and challenges laid out in the previous section of this chapter – whether real or perceived – present a significant obstacle to the development and implementation of procurement policies linked with labour standards. In some contexts, especially in Australia where the use of procurement to secure better labour standards is relatively under-developed, an incremental approach to the implementation of these ideas is most likely the best that can be expected.

A relatively straightforward option for governments to implement in the short term is to require factory list disclosure as a condition of eligibility and as a tender condition for procurement contracts. That is, companies wishing to tender for government work could be required to disclose a list of the names and addresses of the factories which form part of the corporation's supply chain (Doorey 2005; see also Kolben 2007). This proposal does not require that companies provide information regarding the labour standards observed by supplier factories, or that contractors allow monitoring of compliance down their supply chains. However, Doorey, the proponent of this approach, argues that the factory list disclosure proposal could address some of the barriers to enforcement of labour standards. It is an important first step which helps overcome some of the expenses of collecting compliance information. Doorey argues that disclosure of both supplier factories *and* their level of compliance can in fact lead to some of the harmful unintended consequences for workers described earlier (Doorey 2005, 384–8). By limiting disclosure to the list of supplier factories, there is a lower cost to both the potential contractor and the government because of the relative ease of providing this information and the reduction in monitoring requirements. The information can nevertheless empower the state and local workers and institutions in a way which does not force workers to be involved in something which may ultimately disadvantage them.

Conclusion

This chapter has outlined several ways in which government procurement can be used to achieve better labour standards and alleviate poverty in developing countries. Governments in developed countries can use public wealth to leverage greater compliance with labour standards by contractors using suppliers in developing countries. Achieving greater compliance with standards, including the payment of a 'living wage', will hopefully contribute to poverty reduction in those countries.

There are, however, a number of obstacles to the effective use of public procurement as a mechanism for the improvement of labour standards. The first is to persuade governments to think beyond 'value for money' in the context of procurement, or at least to see good labour practices in supply chains as an economic benefit rather than a cost. However, even where governments have incorporated labour standards into their procurement policies, there is very little evidence to show that these policies are actually effective in ensuring compliance. Only by having adequate disclosure and monitoring arrangements will it be possible to ensure that procurement policies are having any effect.

It is important to place public procurement as labour regulation in perspective. There are natural limits to the reach of procurement as a regulatory tool – it only has the potential to impact on workers employed by companies which choose to contract with government, and their suppliers. Even where the challenges facing this particular approach to labour regulation are overcome, it is important that procurement be seen as a step along the way in the achievement of better labour standards in developing countries and not as the ultimate goal.

References

Arup, C. (2001), 'Labour law as regulation: promise and pitfalls', *Australian Journal of Labour Law* 14: 229.

Australian Council of Trade Unions (ACTU) (2006), 'Commonwealth Games souvenirs may breach labour standards', media release, 3 March. Available at: http://www.actu.asn.au/ Archive/MediaandCommunication/ACTUNews/Commonwealth GamesSouvenirMayBreach LabourStandards.aspx [accessed: 9 April 2007].

Australian Labor Party (ALP) (2007), *National Platform: Chapter Five – Fostering Competitive and Innovative Australian Industries*. Available at: http://www.alp.org.au/platform/chapter_05.php#5government_procurement [accessed: 17 April 2007].

Ayres, I. and Braithwaite, J. (1992), *Responsive Regulation: Transcending the Deregulation Debate* (New York: Oxford University Press).

Baldwin, R. and Cave, M. (1999), *Understanding Regulation: Theory, Strategy and Practice* (Oxford: Oxford University Press).

Barenberg, M. (2007), 'Toward a democratic model of transnational labour monitoring', in B. Bercusson and C. Estlund (eds), *Regulating Labour in the Wake of Globalization: New Challenges, New Institutions* (Oxford: Hart).

Barnard, C. Deakin, S. and Hobbs, R. (2004), 'Reflexive law, corporate social responsibility and the evolution of labour standards: the case of working time', Working Paper No. 294, ESRC Centre for Business Research, University of Cambridge.

Bell, S. and Usher, A. (2007), *Labour Standards in Public Procurement: Background Paper for DFID Labour Standards and Poverty Reduction Forum, 23 May 2007* (London: Ergon Associates).

Black, J. (2001), 'Decentring regulation: understanding the role of regulation and self-regulation in a post-regulating world', *Current Legal Problems* 54: 103.

Bovis, C. (2007), *EU Public Procurement Law* (Cheltenham: Edward Elgar).

Braithwaite, J. (2005), 'Neoliberalism or regulatory capitalism?', Occasional Paper No. 5, Regulatory Institutions Network, Research School of Social Sciences, Australian National University.

City of Los Angeles (2003), *Report of the City Administrative Officer: Sweat-Free Procurement Ordinance and Amendment to Contractor Responsibility Ordinance*. Available at: http://www.sweatfree.org/policies/lacitysweatfreereport.pdf [accessed: 11 April 2008].

—— (undated), 'Sweat Free Ordinance Independent Monitor Agreement with Workers Rights Consortium'. Available at: http://www.sweatfree.org/policies/Sweatfree_Contractv2.10_Final.pdf [accessed: 11 April 2008].

Cooney, S. (2004), 'A broader role for the Commonwealth in eradicating foreign sweatshops', *Melbourne University Law Review* 28: 290–342.

—— (2006), 'Exclusionary self-regulation: a critical evaluation of the AMMA's proposal in the mining industry', in Arup C. et al. (eds), *Labour Law and Labour Market Regulation* (Sydney: Federation Press).

Department for International Development (UK) (DFID) (2004), *Labour Standards and Poverty Reduction* (London: DFID).

Doorey, D. (2005), 'Who made that? Influencing foreign labour practices through reflexive domestic disclosure regulation', *Osgoode Hall Law Journal* 43: 353–405.

Estlund, C. (2002), 'The ossification of American labor law', *Columbia Law Review* 102: 1527.

European Fair Trade Association (2007), *Fair Trade 2007: New facts and Figures from an Ongoing Success Story* (Culemborg: Dutch Association of Worldshops).

Fairtrade Foundation (2007), *Buying into Fairtrade: Procurement in the Private and Public Sector* (London: Fairtrade Foundation).

Graham, D. and Woods, N. (2006), 'Making corporate self-regulation effective in developing countries', *World Development* 34(5): 868–83.

Heeks, R. and Duncombe, R. (2003), 'Ethical trade: issues in the regulation of global supply chains', Working Paper Series, No. 53, Centre on Regulation and Competition, University of Manchester.

Howe, J. (2006), '"Money and favours": government deployment of public wealth as an instrument of labour regulation', in C Arup et al. (eds), *Labour Law and Labour Market Regulation* (Sydney: Federation Press).

—— (2008), 'The role of light touch labour regulation in advancing employee participation in corporate governance: the case of partners at work', in S. Marshall, R. Mitchell and I. Ramsay (eds), *Varieties of Capitalism, Corporate Governance and Employees* (Melbourne: Melbourne University Press).

—— and Landau, I. (2007), '"Light touch" labour regulation by state governments in Australia', *Melbourne University Law Review* 31.

International Labour Organization (ILO) (1949), *The Labour Clauses (Public Contracts) Convention 1949*, opened for signature 29 June 1949, ILO C94, art. 2(1) (entered into force 20 September 1952). Available at: http://www.ilo.org/ilolex/cgi-lex/convde.pl?C094 [accessed: 28 August 2009].

—— (2008), *Labour Clauses in Public Contracts: Integrating the Social Dimension into Procurement Policies and Practices*, General Survey Concerning the Labour Clauses (Public Contracts) Convention 1949 (No. 94) and Recommendation (No. 84), Report of the Committee of Experts on the Application of Conventions and Recommendations, Report III (Part 1B) for the International Labour Conference, 97th Session, 2008.

Johnstone, R. and Jones, J. (2006), 'Constitutive regulation of the firm: occupational health and safety, dismissal, discrimination and sexual harassment', in C. Arup et al. (eds), *Labour Law and Labour Market Regulation* (Sydney: Federation Press).

Johnstone, R. and Mitchell, R. (2004), 'Regulating work', in C. Parker et al. (eds), *Regulating Law* (Oxford: Oxford University Press).

Jones, M., Marshall, S. and Mitchell, R. (2007), 'Corporate social responsibility and the management of labour in two Australian mining companies', *Corporate Governance: An International Review* 15(1): 56.

Kolben, K. (2007), 'Integrative linkage: combining public and private regulatory approaches in the design of trade and labor regimes', *Harvard International Law Journal* 48: 203–56.

Locke, R., Qin, F. and Brause, A. (2007), 'Does monitoring improve labour standards? Lessons from Nike', *Industrial and Labor Relations Review* 61(1): 3.

Lucio, M. and Mackenzie, R. (2004), '"Unstable boundaries?" Evaluating the "new" regulation within employment relations', *Economy and Society* 33: 77.

McBarnet, D. (2007), 'Corporate social responsibility beyond law, through law, for law: the new corporate accountability', in D. McBarnet, A. Voiculescu and T. Campbell (eds), *The New Corporate Accountability: Corporate Social Responsibility and the Law* (Cambridge: Cambridge University Press).

McCrudden, C. (2007), *Buying Social Justice* (Oxford: Oxford University Press).

Moon, J. (2004), 'Government as a driver of corporate social responsibility', No. 20-2004, International Centre for Corporate Social Responsibility Research Paper Series, University of Nottingham, Nottingham.

Morgan, B. and Yeung, K. (2007), *An Introduction to Law and Regulation: Text and Materials* (Cambridge: Cambridge University Press).

Office of Government Commerce (UK) (2006), *Social Issues in Purchasing* (London: Office of Government Commerce).

Ogus, A. (1995), 'Rethinking self-regulation', *Oxford Journal of Legal Studies* 15: 97.

—— (2001), 'New techniques of social regulation: decentralisation and diversity' in H. Collins et al. (eds), *Legal Regulation of the Employment Relation* (London: Kluwer Law International).

Organisation for Economic Cooperation and Development (OECD) (2005), *DAC Guidelines and Reference Series: Harmonising Donor Practices for Effective Aid Delivery, Volume 3: Strengthening Procurement Capacities in Developing Countries* (Paris: OECD).

Parker, C. (2002), *The Open Corporation* (Cambridge: Cambridge University Press).

—— (2007), 'Meta-regulation: legal accountability for corporate social responsibility', in D. McBarnet, A. Voiculescu and T. Campbell (eds), *The New Corporate Accountability: Corporate Social Responsibility and the Law* (Cambridge: Cambridge University Press).

Queensland Government, Department of Public Works (2006), *State Purchasing Policy Review: Policy Paper – November 2006.*

Salamon, L.M. (2002), 'The new governance and the tools of public action: an introduction', in L.M. Salamon (ed.), *The Tools of Government: A Guide to the New Governance* (New York: Oxford University Press).

Scott, C. (2001), 'Analysing regulatory space: fragmentary resources and institutional design', *Public Law* 329.

Seddon, N. (2004), *Government Contracts: Federal, State and Local*, 3rd edition (Sydney: Federation Press).

SOCOG (1998), *Code of Labour Practice for Production of Goods Licensed by the Sydney Organising Committee for the Olympic Games and the Sydney Paralympic Organising Committee* (Sydney: SOCOG).

Sweatfree Communities (2006 and 2007), *Sweatfree Policy Toolkit*, Sweatfree Communities and Global Exchange. Available at: www.sweatfree.org [accessed: 12 December 2007].

Teubner, G. (1983), 'Substantive and reflexive elements in modern law', *Law and Society Review* 17: 239.

Victorian Government Purchasing Board (2003), *Ethical Purchasing Policy*, Victorian Government Purchasing Board. (Copy held on file by author).

Vincent-Jones, P. (2006), *The New Public Contracting: Regulation, Responsiveness, Relationality* (Oxford: Oxford University Press).

Webb, T. (2001), *The Collaborative Games: The Story Behind the Spectacle* (Sydney: Pluto Press).

Weil, D. and Mallo, C. (2007), 'Regulating labour standards via supply chains: combining public/ private interventions to improve workplace compliance', *British Journal of Industrial Relations* 45(4): 791–814.

Weiss, J. (2002), 'Public information', in L.M. Salamon (ed.), *The Tools of Government: A Guide to the New Governance* (New York: Oxford University Press).

Workplace Rights Consortium (WRC) (2008), *WRC Assessment Re New Wide Garment (Cambodia): Findings, Recommendations and Status Report, March 6 2008* (Washington, DC: WRC).

Chapter 19

CSR is Not the Main Game: The Renewed Domestic Response to Labour Abuses in China

Sean Cooney

Introduction

The difficulties faced by labour law in ensuring decent work in contemporary developed economies are widely recognized (for example, Davidov and Langille 2006; Stone 2004; Estlund 2002; Supiot 2001). We are now quite familiar with the proliferation of non-standard employment, the decline of collective institutions in many countries, and widespread political hostility – encouraged by several international agencies – to various forms of labour market regulation. In the developed world, labour law scholars, governments and non-governmental actors have devised innovative forms of regulation – frequently 'decentred' (Black 2001) – to address this new environment (Arup et al. 2006; Lobel 2005; Conaghan et al. 2002). This has included many private sector initiatives, often advertised as corporate social responsibility (CSR) measures.

Whatever the success of these new forms of labour regulation in advanced economies, the obstacles they confront in the developing world are far more formidable. They include: low educational levels; poverty; ineffective institutions; and inadequate enforcement resources. For countries that are in a process of fundamental economic transition and/or are governed by authoritarian regimes the difficulties are even greater. China is perhaps the most prominent of developing countries facing the full gamut of obstacles. Its extraordinary entry into global trade over the last 30 years has seen a proliferation of manufacturing enterprises around the country; there are currently in excess of 30 million (Kanamori and Zhao 2004, 24). While many of these manufacturing firms are producing increasingly sophisticated products and require a high-skilled workforce, there remains an ongoing demand for low-skilled labour. This demand is often met by workers migrating from China's rural areas. Notoriously, these *nongmingong* (rural workers) frequently suffer from very poor working conditions (see, for example, Lee 2007). These conditions have led many organizations in developed countries to accuse China of unfair trade (for perhaps the best know example, see the AFL-CIO's application to the US Trade Representative in 2004) (Becker 2004).

This chapter outlines a number of regulatory responses to the failure of many enterprises to observe labour standards. I begin by outlining the initial stage of labour legislation – legislation which quickly proved to be based on obsolescent assumptions about China's labour market. I then briefly note how CSR initiatives emerged, in part to compensate for regulatory failures at the state level that were alleged to lead to unfair trade. The later part of the chapter focuses on a number of recent *domestic* developments in China's labour law and labour institutions, both formal and informal. These address, admittedly in a limited way, many of the shortcomings in the initial state of law-making. I suggest that the recent developments are potentially of much greater consequence than CSR measures. Insofar as 'fair trade' means trade involving decent working conditions, then it can be said that these measures are contributing towards fairer international trade. Central to this chapter, however, is the argument that the primary impetus for these measures remains domestic.

The 1990s: Law Fails to Keep Pace with the Transforming Economy

This section contextualizes how China's Labour Law became obsolete and ineffective shortly after it was enacted. This situation created regulatory space for CSR measures and ultimately led to the recent major overhaul of the law pertaining to work. In order to understand how the Labour Law could be outdated so soon after it was enacted, it is necessary to bear in mind that China has transitioned from a command economy to what is largely a market system in a relatively short period of time.

Prior to the 1980s, employment relations in the People's Republic of China were radically different from those in liberal capitalist societies. Labour transactions were organized largely by means of administrative assignment (see Josephs 2003, 11–41; Zhu 2002). That is, under a 'unified placement system', workers, especially those in urban areas, were allocated to particular enterprises on a permanent basis. These enterprises were owned by the state or by collectives. The larger enterprises operated as 'mini-welfare states', providing housing, health care, pensions and other benefits to permanent workers in the *danwei*, or work units. The role of the official trade union, the All China Federation of Trade Unions (ACFTU), was essentially to assist in the administration of this welfare system and to help resolve intra-firm conflicts. There was little or no bargaining as wage rates and conditions were determined largely by state agencies. Apart from the privileged permanent workforce, there was also a category of 'temporary workers' whose job status and entitlements were far less secure.

Following the death of Mao Zedong and the victory of the Chinese Communist Party faction associated with Deng Xiaoping in the late 1970s, China undertook a series of incremental reforms which reoriented the country's economic structure along market lines. A legal framework was gradually developed to support market-based economic relations. In accordance with this programme, the shift from administrative allocation of labour to allocation through a labour market was buttressed by a series of temporary legal measures introduced in the 1980s.

The first phase of developing a legal framework for a Chinese labour market culminated in the Labour Law of 1994, the first employment law of general application in the 'socialist market economy' of contemporary China. The Law contractualized work relations and ended, at least on paper, the practice of permanent employment. The Law also provided basic labour protections by setting out a range of labour standards in relation to pay, working hours, leave and other conditions. These standards are broadly consistent with ILO Conventions. In addition, the Labour Law established a legislative basis for a labour dispute resolution system. It was complemented by the Trade Union Law enacted two years earlier.

However, while key features of the Labour Law are not dissimilar to those found in the statutes of liberal capitalist societies, many aspects of the Law continued to reflect concepts more appropriate to conditions under the command economy. Even though the Law was intended to apply to both state and private sector enterprises, it fundamentally reflected a focus on state-owned enterprises (this was even more true of the Trade Union Law). At the time of drafting, such a focus was a reasonable orientation since state-controlled enterprises were still a dominant feature of the Chinese economy. However, this dominance was rapidly lost as the number of domestic and foreign private-sector enterprises exploded during the 1990s. Furthermore, state-owned and collective enterprises were privatized, corporatized or closed and the Chinese mini-welfare state function dismantled. The premises upon which the Labour Law and Trade Union Law were based, characteristic of an early stage of economic transition, were therefore increasingly at odds with the realities of most Chinese workplaces.

As the turn of the millennium approached, conditions in China were becoming challenging for any form of labour regulation. Chinese enterprises engaged in progressively fiercer domestic and international competition and the flow of rural workers to industrialized areas provided, at least for a time, a plentiful supply of cheap labour. These structural problems which were creating poor working condition were exacerbated by the failure of the legal system to provide appropriate forms of regulation for a vastly more complex economy than originally anticipated. This failure led to a 'free-for-all' in many workplaces (Chan 2001).

Three key problems with the legal infrastructure can be mentioned here. Firstly, while the labour law system enjoyed some degree of compliance in large enterprises still under state ownership and among higher skilled urban workers, it largely failed rural workers. Appalling conditions in textile, footwear, toy-making, electronics, mining and construction industries have often been highlighted in international debates. Some of these have been the result of flagrant breaches of law. However, during the 1990s, entrepreneurs increasingly engaged in hiring practices designed to render difficult both the detection of breaches and the application of law (Cooney 2007, 1058–60). Such practices included: engaging workers without formal documentation; using labour dispatch companies, thereby obscuring which firm was the effective employer of workers; using complex subcontracting chains; and/or the designation of workers as independent contractors (*laowu guanxi*), regardless of the substantive nature of the relationship (Zhou 2007, 266–304).

Secondly, dispute resolution institutions were (and, to a large extent, still are) highly bureaucratic and ill-suited to dealing with adversarial relations in private enterprises (Ho 2003; Zheng 2003; Cooney 2007; Halegua 2008). When disputes occur between people in employment relationships, the Labour Law sets out a procedure involving intra-firm mediation, arbitration and then litigation. The Labour Law *requires* parties to undergo labour dispute arbitration prior to accessing courts (Article 79). This position may be contrasted with self-employed workers who can sue a person who engages them directly in a court. In principle, the idea that workplace disputes can be resolved by a process separate to general commercial litigation is attractive. However, the unresponsive nature of labour arbitration has meant that it has tended to become a mere stepping stone to the court system, adding to the cost and delay for claimants. Thus, although the number of labour arbitrations greatly increased from the mid-1990s, many if not most cases continued on to the courts (Gallagher 2005).

Many of these defects lie in the history of the mediation and arbitration processes: they were constructed to deal with state-owned enterprises. This is particularly apparent from the provisions in the Labour Law dealing with intra-firm mediation, where the tripartite mediation committee consists of representatives of the employer, the staff and the union, which is evidently perceived as having a neutral role rather than that of representing employees. However, at the arbitration stage, the union *is* conceived of as representing staff. This structure is not conducive to resolving disputes where there is a sharp delineation between the employer and the employees, as is the case in many private enterprises. In such enterprises, a union must have a consistent function throughout the process if it intends to engage the confidence of employee disputants.

Furthermore, some disputants are denied access to labour dispute resolution outright. Many arbitration committees have tended to dismiss cases for want of jurisdiction, especially when confronted with unusual or undocumented forms of employment relations. Since such arrangements have proliferated, particularly among rural workers, remedies have been denied to large categories of workers.

Thirdly, the official trade union movement ACTFU has been intertwined with enterprise management and has lacked capacity in bargaining, advocacy and in enforcing the law (Taylor et al. 2003; Chen 2003; Lee 1999). Again, this stems from its experience in the command economy, where it exercised a welfarist and mediating role rather than one potentially in conflict with management. Indeed, union leaders have often held very senior roles in enterprise management whereas, in most liberal democracies, this would be considered unlawful management interference in union affairs. A harmonious, welfarist, conception of Chinese trade unions has been reflected in the Trade Union Law which, during the 1990s indicated little awareness that unions and management could come into conflict. For example, prior to 2001, the Law did not contain any substantive provisions that prevented a private sector employer from discriminating against union members or attempting to undermine a union.

Furthermore, during this period Chinese unions did not organize migrant labour, ostensibly because they were considered to be rural workers (Cooney 2007, 1076). The lack of union assistance to migrant workers, coupled with the ineffectiveness and/or expense of arbitration and litigation, meant that those workers' main formal channel of redress has been through the inspection arms of labour bureaux. Unfortunately, in many localities, local inspectorates have often developed corrupt links with businesses, rendering this last formal option ineffective as well (for a comprehensive analysis which focuses on environmental law, see Van Rooij 2006).

In summary, both the state and the state corporatist institution which is the ACFTU were slow to respond legally to the rise of sweatshop conditions in new manufacturing firms and to the tactics used by employers to avoid their legal responsibilities. Despite the rising level of unrest – reflected both in formal labour disputes and informal protest actions – there was little legal innovation in labour law until after the turn of the millennium.

The Diffusion of CSR Initiatives

The declining relevance of domestic law for many enterprises and the difficulties with compliance institutions (the mediation and arbitration committees, courts, labour inspectors and official trade unions) opened the way for CSR initiatives to assume great importance as an alternative form of regulation. The timing was propitious. CSR practices were expanding globally during the same period: for example, codes of conduct were being devised by many multinational corporations (MNCs) with supply chains anchored in developing countries. As is now well known, the archetypal arrangement arose as a result of major Western MNCs facing pressure from consumer organizations and NGOs to engage in fair trade. A frequent response from MNCs was to impose a code of conduct regulating production processes on the suppliers linked to it through contracting arrangements (Gereffi and Korzeniewicz 1994). The code of conduct mandated that certain labour standards – and often other standards such as those pertaining to the environment – were to be observed by the suppliers, failing which a sanction (sometimes including termination of contract) might be imposed. Other forms of private sector initiatives, which could either be complements or alternatives to codes of conduct, included engagement strategies such as providing worker training.

In principle, private sector initiatives are a powerful device for improving working standards and thereby achieving fair trade; the sophisticated methods practised by major corporations to control product quality and production schedules through logistical arrangements in supply chains could be adapted to the enforcement of labour standards. The market power held by major international retailers might be deployed to punish recalcitrant suppliers. In addition, the availability of advanced information technology and production techniques might enable major corporations to assist suppliers in improving occupational health and safety standards and other working conditions.

A comparatively early example of a code of conduct operating within a Chinese context was implemented in 1996 by the British Toy and Hobby Association and subsequently the International Council of Toy Industries. The effectiveness of this initiative was dubious, with little evidence of changes in working conditions (Murray 1998). In the following years, codes of conduct and other CSR measures became increasingly common in industries such as apparel and footwear. The impact, and the limitations, of CSR measures at the beginning of this decade can be gauged from empirical work led by the ILO's Ivanka Mamic (see Mamic 2002). This research involved visits to 20 MNEs and 74 factories worldwide, many of the latter based in China. This nuanced report focusing on footwear, apparel and retail noted that the MNEs had become strongly committed to CSR, at least in the abstract, with several relatively promising initiatives. However, the report also noted the very wide diversity in codes and implementation practices across and within industrial sectors, and continuing problems such as stakeholder involvement, intra-firm commitment to the codes and monitoring.

In the last few years, CSR discourse has moved beyond Western MNEs to firms and organizations based in China and other East Asian states.[1] The change – in rhetoric, if not actual practice – can be illustrated by observing the behaviour of the Taiwanese firm Pou Chen, a huge footwear manufacturer (which is currently expanding into areas such as electronics). Pou Chen has hundreds of thousands of employees, many located in mainland China. In a 2004 study, Anita Chan and Wang Hong-zen, two leading sociologists of East Asian labour practices, noted that Pou Chen felt little pressure to raise labour standards because Western MNCs constituted a 'buffer' diverting potential scrutiny away from its operations. However, by 2008, Pou Chen sought to demonstrate its own observance of social responsibility, including in its employment practices. Indeed, it managed to win an award for its labour practices in CSR rankings undertaken by *Global* magazine, an award highlighted by Taiwan's Ministry of Economic Affairs CSR division (MOEA 2008).

Nonetheless, while CSR initiatives have produced new methods of improving labour standards in China, greater information about working conditions in supply chains and, in some instances, greater compliance with the law, their overall effectiveness has always been subject to doubt. Despite attempts to address flaws in earlier CSR measures, they continue to be viewed with scepticism. There is a substantial amount of literature pointing to several shortcomings of private sector initiatives (see, for example, Blackett 2001; Pearson and Seyfang 2001; Liubicic 1998; Cooney 2004). Some of the main objections can be outlined here – they are explored in greater detail elsewhere in this book, particularly in the chapter by Anita Chan.

First, consumer pressure does not operate evenly across all industries in developed countries and therefore codes tend to be more prominent in those industries that are more exposed to public criticism (such as the clothing or toy manufacturing industry) as opposed to those that are not as directly in the public eye (such as the chemicals or electronics industry).

A second, related criticism is that private sector initiatives based in Western countries may have little effect on workers engaged in industries which are not directly connected to, or do not greatly depend on, international product market chains. Thus, while working conditions in the mining, transport and construction sectors are notoriously poor in many developing countries, including China, employers in these sectors often do not need to respond rapidly to international pressure. Moreover, even where employers are exposed to such pressures, the increasing size of domestic

---

1   For regular accounts of CSR in Asia, including the position of actors based in the region, see the CSR Asia website: http://www.csr-asia.com. For one of many examples of an organization based in China which promotes CSR, see the Corporate Social Responsibility Alliance website: http://www.csr.org.cn/.

markets in countries like China may reduce the influence of Western consumers over time. Demand for 'no sweat-shop' products in developing countries is in an embryonic state.

Third, even the carefully devised monitoring systems in those industries closely connected to international markets struggle to supervise accurately the conditions in supplier firms. This is especially the case with small-scale manufacturers which benefit from larger firms outsourcing parts of the production process. These smaller firms often have the worst labour conditions. But even larger firms are frequently skilful at deceiving monitors, adopting a formulaic rather than substantive approach to compliance.

Fourth, major corporations in the developed world often send out mixed messages: on the one hand, they require adherence to labour standards, whether from fear of consumer pressure or ethical commitments or both; on the other hand, the demands of market competition mean that they are highly concerned about price and production time. Firms in China and other developing countries can often correctly claim that Western corporations place irreconcilable obligations on them, without any willingness to provide resources for satisfying those obligations. This is reflected in the observation made by Mamic about the tenuous intra-firm relationship between MNC personnel responsible for CSR on the one hand and product sourcing on the other (Mamic 2002, 246). Anita Chan makes a similar comment about firms specifically operating in China in her chapter of this book.

This list of concerns is by no means exhaustive. Other problems, which may be present to greater or lesser extent depending on the nature of the initiative, include: failure to consult the workers, or their representatives, covered by the codes; failure to coordinate with domestic governmental agencies; selectivity in choice of labour standards (collective bargaining being a common omission); and counterproductive sanctions (for example, shutting down firms causing worker unemployment).

All of these difficulties are compounded in the authoritarian political system of the People's Republic of China. Randall Peerenboom, a pre-eminent scholar of Chinese law, has expressed considerable scepticism concerning the feasibility of private actors displacing the functions of an effective regulatory state in China. He points to a long list of impediments to the operation of private sector initiatives (Peerenboom 2002, 428–31; see also the discussion in Cooney 2007, 1084–6). These include the Chinese polity's adherence to top-down democratic centralism; the absence of strong, autonomous, civil society organizations; the lack of independent vehicles for diffusing and critiquing information; low education and literacy levels; the likely bureaucratic hostility to alternative approaches; the probable resistance of local governmental institutions to requirements of information disclosure and external monitoring and evaluation (vital to the effectiveness of codes of conduct); the prevalence of corruption among both state and private actors; and weak judicial institutions.

In light of the recent growth of NGOs in China (discussed below), this assessment, produced in 2002, may be overly pessimistic. Nonetheless, Peerenboom's emphasis on the severely constrained capacity of private sector measures accords with empirical realities. The inability of CSR measures to deliver widespread, demonstrable and sustained improvements in working conditions even in the high-profile footwear and apparel industries in China (let alone in China's construction, mining and chemical industries) suggests it cannot be the sole or most significant vehicle for securing compliance with labour standards in China.

This is aptly illustrated by the fate of one of the more creative and initially promising CSR experiments: the organization of direct and fair union elections in several of Reebok's Fujian supplier firms, which were controlled by Hong Kong and Taiwanese entrepreneurs. As Anita Chan's chapter in this volume shows, this carefully conceived experiment largely seems to have failed for a variety of reasons. These reasons include the failure to bring all relevant Chinese institutions on side (especially the ACFTU) and a possible reduced commitment from the MNC management following Adidas's takeover by Reebok. By 2008, the *Sunday Times* (Sheridan and Newell 2008) was reporting that Adidas' Fujian suppliers paid workers poorly, required them to engage in long hours of unpaid overtime and systematically discriminated against male workers due to their perceived propensity to strike. The allegations in this report, and claims that union elections are no longer fair were denied by Adidas (Adidas Group 2008). But at the very least, it can be said that even in the clothing and footwear industry, claims of CSR success by high profile MNCs continue to be seriously doubted.

Fortunately, while problems with CSR persist, new developments in China, driven largely by domestic forces, have produced forms of labour regulation that may be more effective than both the 1990s legal framework and the MNC-led CSR movement.

The Renewal of Chinese Labour Law

In the last few years, there have been major changes in labour law and practice in the People's Republic of China. This may be connected with the change of leadership; under President Hu Jintao and Premier Wen Jiabao, focus has shifted to balancing economic growth with social and environmental considerations. This goal is expressed in the slogan 'harmonious society', promoted by the Chinese Communist Party since 2004. The rhetorical change may reflect the fact that social issues such as poor working conditions, environmental pollution and compulsory acquisition of land are increasingly leading to widespread unrest – sometimes even violent rioting – and so must be addressed by the leadership of the Chinese party-state. How directly this change of rhetoric by the leadership has in fact contributed to accelerated labour law reforms is unclear; many of the reforms have their genesis prior to Hu and Wen taking office. Nonetheless, at the least it can be said that there is now, apparently, significant political impetus to implement them.

The renewal of Chinese labour law is occurring in multiple ways. As will be discussed below, new major laws have been enacted; new enforcement methods are being trialled; there is sporadic evidence of greater activism by official unions in favour of workers; and the non-governmental sector is starting to play a very important role. Again, while some reforms are nation-wide, innovation is often taking place at a local level. For example, there are very great differences between the behaviour of the ACFTU branches from city to city.

While CSR in China continues to arouse considerable debate internationally, the institutional changes instigated domestically are, in my opinion, far more significant. Collectively, they affect all industries, not just those exposed to international consumer scrutiny. They engage primarily not the market power of major corporations and moral suasion but the enforcement power of the state, exercised through legal, political and party institutions. They are largely the product of Chinese actors, rather than being devised in North America and Europe.

These labour law changes may not necessarily fundamentally change the nature of work relationships in China (such as by greatly reducing the number of sweatshops). Nevertheless, they augment substantially the potential avenues for addressing labour problems and create the possibility of systemic change. Four recent developments will now be considered.

Legislative Change

The Labour Contract Law of the People's Republic of China came into force on 1 January 2008. Its enactment followed very extensive public debate and consultation with domestic actors and international groups such as the ILO. Indeed, it was subject to more public submissions than any other legal instrument in China apart from the Constitution. Earlier drafts aroused the vociferous opposition of business groups, in particular the American Chamber of Commerce in Shanghai, yet much of that early content was maintained in the final law. As I have examined the genesis and content of the Labour Contract Law in more detail elsewhere, together with my colleagues Sarah Biddulph, Li Kungang and Zhu Ying (Cooney et al. 2007), I will refer only briefly to some major provisions here.

The importance of the Labour Contract Law lies in addressing fundamental regulatory gaps in the Labour Law of 1994. For example, it has created specific legal norms to deal with the rapidly spreading 'irregular' forms of employment, such as labour hire (*laowu paiqian*) and undocumented work. While there are genuine grounds for using labour hire and for engaging employees informally in some situations, both forms of working arrangements were being increasingly used by substantive employers to deny contractual and statutory obligations to workers.

The Law contains an extensive section regulating labour hire. It includes provisions that, *inter alia*, specify the minimum capital requirements of labour hire agencies, provide for minimum levels of remuneration for the employees of labour hire agencies, and require firms hiring labour from the agencies to provide working conditions to hired labour comparable to those enjoyed by their regular workforce.

Similarly, in order to restrict the proliferation of undocumented working arrangements, the Law casts an onus on employers to enter into written contracts with all workers except casual employees working no more than 24 hours per week. Failure to do so triggers deeming provisions and an obligation to pay double remuneration.

The Law also clearly prohibits abuses such as bonded labour and places limits on wage deductions (which have sometimes been unreasonable and/or capricious). The use of fixed term and casual contracts is regulated in much greater detail than previously, and rules of termination have been clarified. Further, unions and other employee representatives have been given greater rights to examine and (depending on how the law is interpreted) reject employer changes to working arrangements.

Even after the enactment of the Labour Contract Law, there are still many ambiguities and shortcomings in the legal framework. But while one can debate whether the Law is too prescriptive, or insufficiently prescriptive, it is clear that the fundamental framework for labour relations has been greatly improved.

Change in Union Behaviour

The ACFTU has long been criticized for its failure to adapt to a market economy. As indicated above, in many firms it has carried over its role as mediator and welfare provider in state-owned enterprises to the private sector and it is not at all uncommon to find union officials holding senior management positions in private enterprises.

Yet along with significant legislative change, there is also some evidence of organizational dynamism. Certainly, at the national level, the ACFTU has continued to avoid taking positions which might render it more relevant to many workplaces, such as endorsing recourse to industrial action. On the other hand, its legislative interventions have been crucial in driving positive change to the law. In 2001, the Trade Union Law was amended to include protections for unionists against employer retaliation. The amended Law also prohibited close relatives of senior managers from standing for election to union committees, although it stopped short of preventing senior management *themselves* from holding such positions. The ACFTU was one of the most powerful Chinese institutions promoting drafts of the Labour Contract Law and opposing the attack on earlier drafts by business interests (Cooney et al. 2007).

On the ground, the ACFTU has also taken practical action to enforce union and employee rights. Since 2003, it has begun to recruit migrant workers. It has also proactively attempted to organize private firms. The best known instance concerns the unionization of Chinese Walmart outlets. The struggle between the ACFTU and Walmart was resolved in the ACFTU's favour partly through the intervention of President Hu Jintao. In 2006, President Hu directed the ACFTU to improve its efforts to organize foreign firms in China (*China Daily* 2006). But it would appear that some of the most significant change is occurring at the grass roots level: many of the Walmart stores were organized not by government fiat or the ACFTU hierarchy but by activist workers on the ground, who approached workers away from their union-hostile management (see Anita Chan's chapter in this book).

Moreover, although the ACFTU has not been known for its capacity to engage in meaningful workplace bargaining (Clarke et al. 2004), this may be changing in some parts of the country, such as the prosperous areas at the eastern end of the Yangtse. Chinese labour law provides for collective negotiation (*xieshang*) rather than bargaining (*tanpan*) and this has usually occurred, rather ineffectually, at the enterprise level. The integration of union leadership and management has meant that even negotiation is of little substance. However, in some cities in Zhejiang Province, for example, the local ACFTU has engaged in sectoral bargaining and concluded multi-employer collective agreements regulating the wages and conditions of thousands of workers in industries such as hairdressing and transportation (*Zhejiang Ribao* 2005).

None of these developments suggest that an effective trade union movement, independent from management and government, is about to appear in China. However, it does suggest that there has been a considerable shift since the 1990s and that parts of the ACFTU, at least, are having a tangible impact on Chinese industrial relations.

Dispute Resolution and Enforcement

State dispute resolution and enforcement institutions are also undergoing changes. In May 2008, a new Labour Disputes Mediation and Arbitration Law (LDMAL) came into effect. This law is a response to criticisms surrounding the outmoded processes for dealing with employer–employee disputes noted above, criticisms pressed in China by scholars such as Zheng (2003). However, the LDMAL is in some ways disappointing as it does not make fundamental changes to the previous structure. For example, it would seem that in most cases arbitration will still be a precondition of litigation.[2]

Yet the Law makes a number of important procedural changes, many of which are directed at preventing employers from defeating employee claims on technicalities or through prolonging litigation. These include: confirming the broad jurisdiction of labour disputes settlement bodies; restricting employer appeals on factual findings; requiring employers to disclose evidence under their control, where failure to do so will lead to adverse inferences being drawn; extending the time

---

2   There are limited exceptions to this, including enforcement of a mediation settlement.

limits for employee actions; and allowing for interim enforcement orders against employers – for example, where wages have not been paid.

Reforms to enforcement agencies are perhaps even more important. This is because a local labour bureau's compliance system is the point at which migrant workers – who bear the brunt of abuses – are most likely to enlist the help of the state in pursuing a labour claim. The innovation here is essentially local in nature and thus there are wide variations around the country (see Cooney 2007). In current research, conducted with my colleagues Sarah Biddulph and Zhu Ying, involving interviews with labour bureau inspectors at several different sites in China, we have found that some agencies, such as those in Shenzhen, have very substantially revised their enforcement strategies. For example, some have located many more staff in local communities rather than in central offices.[3]

These measures are complemented by local regulations which clarify employer obligations and expand the remedies available to labour bureau staff dealing with recalcitrant employers. For instance, in Guangdong Province and more particularly in Shenzhen, there are now clear rules requiring employers to keep, and furnish to employees, detailed wage records. The rules further clarify when wages must be paid, overcoming gaps in national-level laws. In relation to remedies, provincial-level rules make some contractors liable for the wage arrears owed by their sub-contractors. Similarly, they make corporate officers personally liable for wages in egregious circumstances. They also provide for labour officers to set up public warning systems identifying employers who breach the law.

The potential improvements effected by some of these initiatives may be belied by their implementation. However, they cannot be dismissed as simply cosmetic; our investigations to date suggest that, in some cases at least, agencies are engaged in dynamic and serious attempts to put them into practical operation.

NGOs

In a ground-breaking empirical study of channels used by workers to pursue claims for wages, Aaron Halegua (2008) has shown that non-governmental migrant worker advice centres have developed enforcement tactics in recent times that are frequently more effective than the formal dispute resolution process, involving inspection and/or mediation and arbitration through the labour bureaux. For example, he describes the 'Little Bird' mediation service in Beijing, which involves over 100 registered volunteer lawyers, coordinated by a smaller group of activists. Through the media, connections with government agencies and sophisticated negotiation strategies, the service has facilitated the payment of many millions of *yuan* owing to migrant workers.

He also references the Beijing Migrant Workers Legal Aid Office which, staffed by full-time lawyers, operates similarly to a legal aid organization in developed countries. The Office adopts a more litigious approach to recovering wages than the 'Little Bird' mediation service, with greater preparedness to engage in the formal dispute resolution and court systems. According to my discussions with staff in 2008, the Office is expanding its operations around China.

Elsewhere in China, other forms of migrant advice centres are emerging, often linked with universities. For instance, law schools at Suzhou University and Northwestern Polytechnic University in Xi'an are establishing clinical legal programmes in which law students, under the supervision of qualified lawyers, provide legal assistance to migrant workers, and assist in organizing cases for arbitration and litigation.

---

3   This research was published in 2009.

Conclusion

This account of the interplay between domestic and international measures designed to improve working conditions in China suggests that domestic measures are ultimately the more significant, although conclusive empirical evidence is, as usual in the Chinese context, hard to come by. Much community energy in developed countries has been directed towards pressing MNCs to use their market power in order to ameliorate labour abuses in the supply chain. I do not argue that these attempts are misplaced but their limitations must be clearly recognized. In this chapter I have pointed to matters such as the limited coverage of CSR (to consumer sensitive, export-based industries) and the difficulty of monitoring smaller firms, in which the worst labour abuses occur. At the end of the day, there is, even for those enterprises amenable to public campaigns, a basic conflict between CSR aspirations and production and sales requirements. Consumer pressure and campaigning can only be so effective in offsetting the greater weight of the latter. The adverse reaction of the American Chamber of Commerce in Shanghai – an enthusiastic proponent of CSR – to the Labour Contract Law demonstrates that labour costs are frequently a dominant consideration.

On the other hand, many regulatory developments in China gain insufficient attention. This is partly because, obviously enough, they are often accessible only to people able to read Chinese. It is also because it is frequently difficult for overseas organizations to liaise with Chinese counterparts, for political as much as linguistic reasons. Nonetheless, if domestic developments are proving more consequential than the MNC-focused ones, then they should be comprehended and integrated into international campaigns to improve labour rights.

References

Adidas Group (2008), 'Adidas Group's comments on the Shunda union election', press release, issued 19 March. Available at: http://www.reports-and-materials.org/adidas-comments-on-Shunda-Union-Election-15-Apr-2008.pdf [accessed: 1 November 2008].

Alston, P. and Henan, J. (2004), 'Shrinking the international labor code: an unintended consequence of the 1998 ILO declaration on fundamental principles and rights at work?', *New York University Journal of International Law and Policy* 36(2–3): 221–64.

Arup, C. et al. (eds) (2006), *Labour Law and Labour Market Regulation* (Sydney: Federation Press).

Ayres, I. and Braithwaite, J. (1992), *Responsive Regulation: Transcending the Deregulation Debate* (New York: Oxford University Press).

Becker, E. (2004), 'Bush rejects labor's call to punish China', *New York Times*, 29 April.

Black, J. (2001), 'Decentring regulation: understanding the role of regulation and self-regulation in a post-regulating world', *Current Legal Problems* 54: 103–47.

Blackett, A. (2001), 'Global governance, legal pluralism and the decentered state: a labor law critique of codes of corporate conduct', *Indiana Journal of Global Legal Studies* 8: 401–47.

Chan, A. (2001), *China's Workers Under Assault: The Exploitation of Labor in a Globalizing Economy* (Armonk, NY: M.E. Sharpe).

—— (2006), 'Made in China: Wal-Mart unions', *YaleGlobal Online*. [Online: 12 October 2006]. Available at: http://yaleglobal.yale.edu/display.article?id=8283 [accessed: 1 November 2008].

Chen, F. (2003), 'Between the state and labour: the conflict of Chinese trade unions' double identity in market reform', *China Quarterly* 176: 1006–28.

China Daily (2006), 'Hu's order led to Wal-Mart unions', *China Daily*, 17 August. Available at: http://www.chinadaily.com.cn/china/2006-08/17/content_666706.htm [accessed: 1 November 2008].

Clarke, S., Lee, C.-H. and Li, Q. (2004), 'Collective consultation and industrial relations in China', *British Journal of Industrial Relations* 42(2): 235–54.

Conaghan, J., Fischl, R. and Klare, K. (eds) (2002), *Labour Law in an Era of Globalization: Transformative Practices and Possibilities* (Oxford: Oxford University Press).

Cooney, S. (2004), 'A broader role for the Commonwealth in eradicating foreign sweatshops?', *Melbourne University Law Review* 28(2): 290–342.

—— (2007), 'Making Chinese labor law work: the prospects for regulatory innovation in the People's Republic of China', *Fordham International Law Journal* 30: 1050–97.

—— Biddulph, S., Zhu, Y. and Li, K. (2007), 'China's new labour contract law: responding to the growing complexity of labour relations in the PRC', *University of New South Wales Law Review* 30(3): 788–803.

Corporate Social Responsibility Alliance (no date), *Corporate Social Responsibility Alliance*. [Website]. http://www.csr.org.cn/ [accessed: 19 August 2008].

CSR Asia (no date), *CSR Asia – Corporate Social Responsibility in Asia*. [Website]. http://www. csr-asia.com [accessed: 19 August 2008].

Davidov, G. and Langille, B. (2006), *Boundaries and Frontiers of Labour Law* (Oxford: Hart).

Estlund, C. (2002), 'The ossification of American labor law', *Columbia Law Review* 102(6): 1527–612.

Fenwick, C., Howe, J., Marshall, S. and Landau, I. (2006), *Labour and Labour-related Laws in Micro- and Small Enterprises: Innovative Regulatory Approaches* (Melbourne: Centre for Employment and Labour Relations Law, University of Melbourne).

Gallagher, M. (2005), '"Use the law as your weapon!" Institutional change and legal mobilization in China', in N. Diamant, S. Lubman and K. O'Brien (eds) (2005), *Engaging the Law in China: State, Society and Possibilities for Justice* (Stanford, CA: Stanford University Press).

Gereffi, G. and Korzeniewicz, M. (eds) (1994), *Commodity Chains and Global Capitalism* (Westport, CT: Greenwood Press).

Greenfield, G. and Pringle, T. (2002), 'The challenge of wage arrears in China', in M.S. Velasco (ed.), *Paying Attention to Wages: Labour Education 2002/3*, Report No. 128 (Geneva: International Labour Organization).

Halegua, A. (2008), 'Getting paid: processing the labor disputes of China's migrant workers', *Berkeley Journal of International Law* 26(1): 254–322.

Ho, V.H. (2003), *Labor Dispute Resolution in China: Implications for Labor Rights and Legal Reform* (Berkeley, CA: Institute of East Asian Studies, University of California).

Josephs, H. (2003), *Labor Law in China* (Huntington, NY: Juris Publishing).

Kanamori, T. and Zhao, Z. (2004), *Private Sector Development in the People's Republic of China* (Tokyo: Asian Development Bank Institute).

Lee, C.K. (1999), 'From organized dependence to disorganized despotism: changing labor relations in Chinese factories', *China Quarterly* 157: 44–71.

—— (2007), *Against the Law: Labor Protests in China's Rustbelt and Sunbelt* (Berkeley, CA: University of California Press).

Liubicic, R. (1998), 'Corporate codes of conduct and product labeling schemes: the limits and possibilities of promoting international labor rights through private initiatives', *Law and Policy in International Business* 30(1): 111–58.

Lobel, O. (2005), 'Interocking regulatory and industrial relations: the governance of workplace safety', *Administrative Law Review* 57: 1071–151.

Mamic, I. (2002), *Business and Code of Conduct Implementation: How Firms Use Management Systems for Social Performance* (Geneva: International Labour Organization).

Ministry of Economic Affairs (MOEA), Department of Investment Services (2008), 'The best corporate social responsibility award', *CSR in Taiwan*, 28 March. Available at: http://csr.moea. gov.tw/en/articles/articles_content.asp?ar_ID=B2wAN1BjCTc%3D [accessed: 1 November 2008].

Murray, J. (1998), *Corporate Codes of Conduct and Labour Standards* (Geneva: ILO, Bureau for Workers' Activities).

Pearson, R. and Seyfang, G. (2001), 'New hope or false dawn: voluntary codes of conduct, labour regulation and social policy in a globalizing world', *Global Social Policy* 1(1): 49–78.

Peerenboom, R. (2002), *China's Long March Toward the Rule of Law* (Cambridge: Cambridge University Press).

Sheridan, M. and Newell, C. (2008), 'Adidas workers on £11 a week in China: staff complain of terrible conditions in the Olympic sponsor's factories', *Sunday Times*, 30 March.

Stone, K.W. (2004), *From Widgets to Digits: Employment Regulation for the Changing Workplace* (Cambridge: Cambridge University Press).

Supiot, A. (2001), *Beyond Employment: Changes in Work and the Future of Labour Law in Europe* (Oxford: Oxford University Press).

Taylor, B., Chang, K. and Li, Q. (2003), *Industrial Relations in China* (Cheltenham: Edward Elgar).

Van Rooij, B. (2006), *Regulating Land and Pollution in China: Lawmaking, Compliance, and Enforcement; Theory and Cases* (Leiden: Leiden University Press).

Wang, H. and Chan, A. (2003), 'States and the anti-sweatshop movement: evidence from China and Vietnam', *Hong Kong Journal of Social Sciences* 26(1): 103–26.

Zhejiang Ribao (2005), 'Laozi Shuangfang de Lüse Tongdaohang Dansheng Shoufen Hangye Jiti Hetong' [劳资双方的绿色通道 杭诞生首份行业集体合同], *Zhejiang Ribao* [浙江日报], 23 December.

Zheng, S. (2003), *Laodong Zhengyi Chuli Chengxufa de Xiandaihua* [*The Modernisation of Labour Adjustment Procedure Law*] (Beijing: Fazheng Press).

Zhou, C. (ed.) (2007), *Laodong Paiqian de Fazhan yu Falü Guizhi* [*The Development and Legal Regulation of Labor Dispatch*] (Beijing: China Labour and Social Security Publishers).

Zhu, Y. (2002), 'Economic reform and labour market regulation in China', in S. Cooney, T. Lindsey, R. Mitchell and Y. Zhu (eds) (2002), *Law and Labour Market Regulation in East Asia* (London and New York: Routledge).

CONCLUSION

Chapter 20

Experiments in Globalizing Justice:
Emergent Lessons and Future Trajectories

Kate Macdonald and Shelley Marshall[1]

Introduction

Civic, corporate and state-based governance initiatives that seek to promote norms of social or global 'justice' are achieving steadily rising levels of reach and influence in the global economy. More seem to be emerging every day, and their legitimacy as mechanisms of local, national and transnational regulation is achieving increasing acceptance in many quarters. They perform a range of functions – from delivering social services and facilitating economic redistribution and poverty reduction, to establishing, monitoring and enforcing social and labour standards within global production systems across large parts of the industrialized and developing worlds. Although the patterns of their diffusion are still limited and highly uneven, it is important to understand the forces that drive them, the mechanisms and actors through which they operate, and the factors that condition their success or failure.

This book has examined a broad range of these emerging experiments in transnational governance through the lens of several central questions:

- What are the core problems of injustice or governance failure that these initiatives seek to respond to, and how are these problems evolving?
- How are these initiatives themselves developing through an ongoing process of experimentation and adaptation?
- What outcomes are the initiatives achieving, in relation to both direct facilitation of rights fulfilment and the promotion of institutional transformation to create the structural conditions for rights fulfilment at a broader and sustained level?
- What factors determine the relative success of different initiatives in promoting these outcomes?

Contributors to this book, who have each added to our collective understanding of these issues, have based their analyses on a broad range of case studies from a number of geographical and sectoral contexts. In this concluding chapter, we search for sources of differences and similarity between the cases examined, considering both the strategies used and the outcomes achieved. In particular, we seek to evaluate the extent to which initiatives of different kinds have succeeded in promoting forms of institutional transformation more compatible with increasing the social and political agency of workers and, ultimately, creating the conditions for longer term rights fulfilment.

1   The authors would like to thank Sanjay Pinto and John Howe for their thorough and insightful comments on an earlier draft of this chapter. We are also grateful to Kamillea Aghtan and Anna Tucker for their research assistance.

We first present a review and synthesis of the differing approaches taken by the transnational governance initiatives examined in this collection, and then offer an assessment of the relative strengths of these different approaches.

In the introductory chapter to this volume we described the process by which, in the 1980s and 1990s, capital took on new organizational forms, making it more difficult to regulate in many respects. At the same time, often due to shifting ideological influences, most liberal market economy states[2] significantly curtailed their responsibility for the decommodification of social relations and the stable cooperation of capital and labour at the point of production. The governments of coordinated market economies also loosened their grips on these roles.[3] The states of developing countries came under normative pressure to give capital a freer rein, with a variety of responses. We are again witnessing a further change in the role of the state as it grapples with the 2007–2009 financial crisis. While the exact nature of this change will take some time to emerge, it seems clear that there is now an increasing willingness to underwrite and integrate capitalist systems in a way that has been absent for the last two decades.

Our analysis in this chapter seeks to identify links between the strengths and weaknesses of the governance strategies and the structure and dynamics of the underlying governance challenge, which was discussed at length in the introduction to this volume. Our resulting view is that while these initiatives seek *directly* to address perceived problems of poverty, socioeconomic underdevelopment, distributive injustice and the underrealization of substantive rights, they are, *in the process*, grappling with a set of deeper institutional dynamics in which these more visible problems are grounded: the disembedding of capitalist systems of production and exchange from many norms and institutions that contribute to maintaining a broadly acceptable balance between competing social values and interests, and thereby promote and facilitate goals of system stability and social justice.

Governance Responses to Evolving Economic and Political Dynamics

As we suggested in the introduction, new transnational governance systems are commonly characterized as strategies for (re)embedding capitalist economic systems of production and trade within systems of public governance which seek to promote principles of global social and economic justice (as defined in Chapter 1 of this volume). The goal of this book has been not only to document and flesh out this central idea but also to illustrate the ways in which specific strategies of social embedding are evolving in relation to changing economic and political conditions.

Part of the evolution of governance strategies has been driven by responses to systemic changes in patterns of disembedding, as significant changes have taken place within regimes of production and accumulation as well as within wider economic and political institutions. In this sense, the governance initiatives examined in this book can be understood as part of a struggle between

---

2   The varieties of capitalism literature generally groups the national capitalist systems into two stylized models: the liberal market model (these economies are also referred to as 'market/outsider' systems), which include countries such as the United States, the United Kingdom, Canada, Australia and New Zealand; and the coordinated market model (also referred to as 'insider/relational' systems), which includes countries such as Germany, Sweden, Japan and so on (Hall and Soskice 2001). It is mooted that there are other broad varieties of capitalist economies – for example, an Asian model (Wailes et al. 2008).

3   There is disagreement in the surrounding literature concerning the extent to which coordination is being loosened in coordinated market economies. Some argue that deregulation has occurred selectively and unevenly across industries, for instance Hall (2007).

rival pressures. On one side, there are strong pressures for the expansion of markets and the commodification of social relations, with the increased uncertainty and social instability that these often entail. On the other side are social demands for political stabilization of relative prices, for the de-commodification of social relations and for 'decent' working conditions. (Polanyi 1944). The governance initiatives examined in this book seek to redirect distributions of risk and create greater stability for workers and their communities. To do this, they have continued to adapt to new power dynamics and organizational structures.

Many strategies which appeared appropriate in the early development of CSR and fair trade soon confronted significant barriers. Significant frustration often resulted not only from ongoing barriers to more far-reaching change but also from the perceived disconnection between discourses and realities; this often led to further experimentation with new strategies, giving rise to a proliferation of instruments and methods. In more recently developed initiatives, we can often observe a tactical shift towards governance strategies directed at deeper levels of institutional transformation, as the gains from more collaborative strategies are perceived by many to diminish. Such strategies seek to challenge the social power relations and ideologies that underpin prevailing distributional outcomes.

In the discussion that follows, we trace some of the important ways in which the initiatives have evolved, and highlight their major strengths and weaknesses in terms of their capacity to promote rights fulfilment directly and to support processes of institutional transformation towards stronger systems of transnational social governance.

Different Responses to Global Injustice

In the introduction to this volume we suggested that governance initiatives seek to transform the system to varying extents based on their differing perceptions of the nature of the problem. In this section, we focus on the means by which initiatives undertake such transformation. As we shall see in the concluding comments to this chapter, the kinds of strategies adopted have some important implications for the potential of governance initiatives to bring about deep forms of institutional transformation that not only tackle inequitable distributional outcomes directly, but also challenge the social power relations and ideologies that underpin them.

Targets of the Governance Initiatives

Following from our analysis of the economic and policy problems that governance initiatives are attempting to address – presented in the introductory chapter to this book – we suggest that differing strategic approaches focus their attention on different aspects of this perceived problem:

a. *economic aspects of global capitalism* such as markets and global production and trading systems; and
b. *political aspects of global capitalism*, including a range of state and non-state decision-making agencies, institutions and regimes.

In relation to the *economic aspects of capitalism*, the governance initiatives analysed in this book have adopted a range of strategies that have sought to promote in differing ways what we broadly refer to as 'economic re-embedding'. Strategies in relation to economic dimensions of capitalism include:

1. *Broadly accepting existing economic structures and dynamics*: some initiatives attempt to harness the economic dynamics of global capitalism for social purposes. They largely accept the legitimacy of structures of global production and trading systems but seek to alter distributive social outcomes; in some but not all cases they also seek to make minor adjustments to the social power relations that underpin prevailing distributive outcomes. They generally attempt to create collaborations between capital, labour and other stakeholders.

2. *Reforming economic structures and dynamics*: some initiatives attempt to transform the institutions of capitalism at a deeper constitutive level, seeking to reshape allocations of rights and duties and associated understandings of legitimate distributions of welfare and power. They therefore seek to reshape the structure of local and global production and trading systems concretely in ways that more deeply challenge established relations of power and associated systems of ideas.

3. *Creating alternative economic structures and dynamics*: some initiatives attempt to sidestep existing global production systems and instead create alternative trading systems that are based on radically different productive relations, with workers and producers controlling or utilizing capital for their own benefit and having greater power throughout the trading system.

In relation to *political aspects of capitalism*, we also see governance initiatives adopting a range of strategies which we broadly refer to as 'political re-embedding':

1. *Enhancing the state and other policy regimes*: some initiatives seek to augment the role of state and non-state policy regimes by increasing the effectiveness of enforcement, strengthening incentives to comply with laws, policies and standards, and so on. Strategies of this kind seek to strengthen the operation of the existing system while accepting existing norms of state responsibility and the power relations that underpin them.

2. *Pressuring the state to reinsert itself*: some initiatives aim at compelling the state and other multilateral or international institutions to reinsert themselves in roles of social and system integration from which they have withdrawn or otherwise become increasingly disembedded. Strategies of this kind are motivated by a desire to reconfigure understandings and practices of state responsibility and to create new sources of legal or social power to achieve this.

3. *Replacing the state and other policy regimes*: some initiatives are going beyond enhancing state and non-state policy regimes, instead acting as alternatives to these institutions. They aim to act as agents of social integration (the protection and stabilization of social relations against the unpredictability of fluctuating prices) and system integration (providing for the stable cooperation between capital and labour at the point of production) by creating their own systems for political organization; such systems attempt to re-embed systems of production, accumulation and exchange within transformed values and power relations, and associated allocations of rights, roles and responsibilities.

With respect to both economic and political aspects of contemporary capitalism, we therefore see existing governance strategies aimed at: (i) working within; (ii) reforming and (iii) creating alternatives to and/or radically transforming existing frameworks.

While to some extent these categories can be used as a means of classifying existing governance initiatives, in some cases it may be more accurate to represent these as depicting *strategic dilemmas* which governance initiatives face as they try to transform and socialize global production and trading systems and associated policy regimes. These strategic dilemmas correspond with broader arguments within governance literatures concerning the effectiveness of non-state governance and voluntary systems of fair trade and CSR on the one hand; and, on the other hand, the potential legitimacy and effectiveness of introducing new forms of state-based regulation and law to interact with and strengthen voluntary approaches.

In practice, it is therefore common for initiatives to move between these strategies or adopt more than one at a time. FairWear in Australia, for example, broadly accepts the existing structures of capitalism through its more cooperative mechanisms such as the Homeworkers Code of Practice, but also attempts to reform production chains (as discussed further below).

In the following section, the advantages and disadvantages of these strategies are examined in relation to the underlying structures and dynamics of the governance problems to which they respond.

Economic Re-embedding

Broadly Accepting Existing Economic Structures and Dynamics of Capitalism

The fact that many CSR initiatives are perceived as working 'with the grain' of existing economic structures and power relations has drawn considerable criticism from those who wish to see these relations challenged to a greater extent (such as Ballinger, Chapter 12 in this volume). On the other hand, it may be the more 'ameliorative' or 'collaborative' (Utting, Chapter 9) characteristics of these types of initiatives that have allowed their spread to be so pervasive and have perhaps created a normative space in which to question the role of business. As a number of authors in this volume have suggested, there is also a chance that these types of initiatives may have contributed to creating a foothold for more deeply transformative mechanisms, in part by providing an entry point around which to build more sustainable social alliances. As such, ameliorative and collaborative initiatives may contribute to goals of 'globalizing justice' in a number of ways.

First, some have been able to offer forums that facilitate improved stakeholder dialogue and participation, thereby enabling processes of communication and shared learning around areas of potentially common interests, and enabling NGOs and affected groups to participate directly in consultative and decision-making processes associated with new forms of standard-setting and enforcement. As Emer Diviney and Serena Lilywhite show in their chapter in this volume (Chapter 8), in a number of cases around the world multi-stakeholder forums have contributed to promoting trust and collaboration in which multi-party planning could encourage communication and shared information, thereby helping to build systems that are flexible and suitable for different business and broader contexts.

Delaney (Chapter 14) likewise stresses the benefits of a multipronged strategy in her case study of the FairWear campaign. The campaign employs collaborative strategies through the Homeworkers Code of Practice Committee, on which both employer and union representatives sit. At the same time, however, it often runs campaigns against companies in order to cajole them into signing the Code of Practice. While Delaney sees this dual role as a source of strength, Diviney and Lilywhite highlight the risks that also confront such approaches, pointing to the ways in which weak communication and trust between workers, suppliers, unions, NGOs and companies have operated on one level to undermine the success of the Homeworkers Code of Practice labelling scheme.

Other authors highlight the role of collaborative processes in promoting normative change in favour of the idea that businesses ought to accept more extensive responsibilities for certain social impacts of their activities. Orly Lobel's chapter (Chapter 17) points to examples where the CSR movement's promotion of broader views of corporate interests and responsibilities has been diffused to even 'laggard' firms such as Walmart. Peter Utting similarly highlights the acknowledgement among many that CSR discourses have managed to achieve what international labour law had largely failed to accomplish over 30 years: to induce companies to think more proactively about labour standards and labour rights. Processes of engagement and socialization entrenched and embraced at the micro-level of organizational culture were shown to be particularly important. This was especially the case in relation to subtle and complex features of organizational culture such as discrimination and health and safety regulatory systems, where normative change and participatory engagement are often important prerequisites for effectiveness.

Tim Wilson (Chapter 6) argued that the voluntary status of such governance initiatives plays an important role in strengthening processes of normative diffusion at the level of individual consumers and firms, in particular by protecting underlying sources of intrinsic motivation for responsible conduct. Wilson is highly critical of what he characterizes as attempts by activists to undermine the voluntary spirit of fair trade, suggesting that voluntarism can foster individual responsibility for promoting important social goals and that attempts to impose fair trade systems on unwilling participants ultimately erode intrinsic motivation and compliance.

Second, in some cases collaborative approaches were able to contribute to the building of new *institutional capabilities* for effective compliance. Following involvement in CSR processes, corporate actors were able to deploy constructively both existing institutional capabilities and those created or learnt through the CSR process towards goals of monitoring, capacity-building and compliance. Major corporations typically have sophisticated methods of controlling product quality and production schedules through logistical arrangements in supply chains. These have sometimes been deployed as a means of assisting suppliers in improving occupational health and safety standards and other working conditions. To the extent that collaborative approaches have been associated with transparent dialogue and learning between stakeholders, they have in some cases generated further information about working conditions in supply chains, contributing to improved compliance with certain aspects of the law.

Such supply-chain capabilities by no means have translated directly into improved performance. Even in those cases where corporate managers were highly motivated to engage with CSR processes, persistent capacity weaknesses continued to present obstacles. Significant barriers often arose as a result of weak internal corporate auditing systems, underpinned by capacity weaknesses such as lack of knowledge and training of management around compliance, inadequate internal systems to enforce compliance, and insufficient communication internally and externally. Such problems were often particularly pronounced in the case of small and medium-sized enterprises suffering from organizational constraints, a lack of supply-chain power and insufficient financial resources to either cover accreditation fees for multi-stakeholder initiatives or employ specialized internal staff to discharge compliance responsibilities. This is a particular problem given the dominance of small and medium-sized firms in certain sectors, such as clothing and footwear in Australia as noted by Diviney and Lillywhite. Nevertheless, the potential strength of collaborative approaches as means of bridging such capacity deficits where they exist emerged as an important lesson.

'Working within the system' has also offered an important means of strengthening the capacity of the system to promote goals of rights fulfilment in the case of the fair trade system. By developing business models that can compete successfully in competitive retail markets and engage mainstream corporate buyers and retailers in the distribution and marketing of Fairtrade certified products, recent mainstream approaches to fair trade have succeeded in extending opportunities to sell products via fair trade markets to a rapidly increasing number of individual farmers and communities.

In addition to the forms of capacity-building enabled by provision of a fair trade price and social premium, the fair trade system has contributed in many cases to grassroots capacity building and empowerment among member cooperatives, thereby bolstering the potential for the exercise of transformative collective agency at the local level. This, in turn, can help producers leverage their ability to provide directly some social services, infrastructure and technical assistance to farmers and their communities, to support monitoring of fair trade standards, and to enable farmers to access broader markets. Organizational strengthening at this level can also play a role in the monitoring and enforcement of fair trade standards, though as Tim Wilson's chapter (Chapter 6) emphasizes, significant capacity limits in all these regards continue to exist. Such grassroots forms of capacity-building often receive greater priority within more 'alternative' and transformative fair trade models, although they are also indirectly supported by Fairtrade mainstreaming approaches.

The kinds of collaborative methods discussed are certainly not neutral in their impact on power relations, though there is some disagreement between authors regarding the nature of this impact. Several authors highlight ways in which the operation of voluntary CSR initiatives has strengthened labour's capacity to analyse and understand business interests and behaviour and provided the basis for increased identification and organization linking consumers with workers in producing countries, thereby creating new forms of awareness and social mobilization. Voluntary initiatives can also feed into underlying changes to social power relations via their spill-over into campaigning activities which, in many contexts, have used CSR programmes and voluntary corporate codes as a basis for more adversarial forms of campaigning. On the other hand, there is a risk that instead of strengthening new norms of global social justice, such initiatives may instead serve to legitimize ideologies and interests more closely aligned with prevailing business interests than with norms of social justice – as argued by Jeff Ballinger (Chapter 12).

Reforming Economic Structures and Dynamics

The development of more deeply transformative campaigns and initiatives has, at times, grown out of the softer CSR movement and, at other times, in opposition to it. Increased emphasis on the creation of social alliances through collaborative approaches has paved the way for a number of initiatives to develop organizing techniques aimed at promoting more far-reaching agendas of reform. In particular, it has opened up a greater role for the involvement of worker organizations in the management of labour supply chain issues.

The chapter by Anita Chan (Chapter 11), for instance, charts the experiment by one corporation – Reebok – with new approaches in response to widely acknowledged failures in their social auditing methods. Such forms of worker participation – especially when based in strengthened grassroots organizational capacity – were consistently shown to be extremely important as a basis for effective code functioning. In the few and often short-lived cases in which worker organization or representation has been established, positive outcomes for workers have often been achieved, both in factory settings and among homeworkers. Conversely, the effectiveness of dominant models of social auditing operating without such participation was shown to be significantly limited. Several chapters in this volume, including those by Chan (Chapter 11) and Leong, Ka-wai and Tucker (Chapter 15), highlight the ways in which supplier firms have developed sophisticated techniques to circumvent the monitoring systems for supplier codes imposed upon them, developing elaborate methods of double bookkeeping and the falsification of time cards and pay slips, as well as coaching workers on what to say to monitors.

A number of groups in Asia have developed campaigning strategies that reject traditional consumer-based campaigns in view of their dependence on and reproduction of Northern-dominated power relations within global supply chains. They have instead based their strategies around the aim of building sustainable workers' movements that attempt to involve all affected parties. Maksimovic (Chapter 13) tracks one such campaign in her discussion of the Asian Wage Floor Alliance. Such campaigns have, in some cases, sought to involve not only trade unions but also labour rights, women's and other civil society organizations, sharing a commitment to building stronger regional alliances to promote sustainable and worker-led systems of compliance. These strategies also seek to reflect changes in the regional clustering of production and the rising power of first tier suppliers in East Asia. This shift is reflected in campaign strategies discussed by Leong, Ka-wai and Tucker, where worker organizations seek to mirror the structure of triangular trading which has become the dominant configuration of supply chains for production carried out in Asia. Such campaigns include worker organizations in the place of production, NGOs in the place where the company organizing production is based, and consumer-based campaign organizations in the North. These campaigns have at times used innovative methods in order to build solidarity among workers based in different production areas. For instance, a Workers' Solidarity Olympics and Workers' Exchange, with sportswear and garment workers from different countries in Asia as participants, was held at the same time as the Athens Olympics (Leong et al., Chapter 15).

A similar approach to grassroots capacity building and collaboration has been developed by Australian unions seeking to strengthen compliance with labour standards among homeworkers, documented by Delaney in Chapter 14. They have developed innovative forms of community engagement such as community-based English language courses and a community radio station, as means of establishing and strengthening contact with homeworkers and encouraging the involvement of migrant workers in campaigns and monitoring. These techniques have been particularly important when confronting patterns of informalization.

New approaches to grassroots organizing have often operated alongside more conventional forms of worker mobilization and self-help. In the Australian case documented by Delaney, new forms of community engagement, such as offering English classes, are coexisting alongside traditional forms of union representation and servicing. In the Vietnamese case examined by Ballinger (Chapter 12), worker self-help strategies have involved traditional tactics such as strikes as well as attempts to mobilize the media in support of worker demands.

While we conclude that there is a clear trend towards recognition of the importance of worker involvement, the question of how to actually achieve worker participation is much more difficult, in light of entrenched power imbalances and significant institutional barriers to worker empowerment. In some cases, unions remain extremely weak or lack independence, suffering from financial dependence and/or a co-opted leadership, while in other instances such as the important case of China, several authors, including Chan and Cooney, have documented a gradual shift in the strategies of the All-China Federation of Trade Unions (ACFTU) towards more active engagement in adversarial processes at the enterprise level. Among homeworkers employed under informal conditions, workers' lack of legal literacy and fear of repercussions by employers/outworker bosses remains a serious barrier to collective organization.

Several authors also highlight the significant resource and capacity limitations facing NGOs and worker groups, who in many cases have been called upon to participate in supply chain monitoring systems without the provision of any financial or organizational resources that would enable them to do so effectively. Conflicts between stakeholder groups can further complicate attempts to increase grassroots participation within social governance systems, as illustrated by Maksimovic's discussion of tensions between trade unions and NGOs within the Roundtable on Sustainable Palm Oil.

Furthermore, achieving worker participation at the enterprise level often requires addressing not only power relations within the firm but also broader relationships of power beyond the enterprise. Chan's chapter, for example, highlights the difficulties of sustaining systems of enterprise-level worker representation in the absence of the engagement of broader social and institutional systems – in this case, the national and district union leadership. Ballinger similarly points to entrenched and powerful barriers coming from broader sources such as dominant public discourses by CSR agendas seeking to legitimize state–business alliances and ongoing repression of workers by the state.

Within mainstream approaches to fair trade, the goal of prioritizing grassroots participation has similarly proved problematic in many cases. Several authors highlight the limits to producer participation in FLO governance,[4] as well as ongoing tensions between the goal of developing a competitive and flexible global business model for the fair trade system and that of enabling strengthened grassroots participation. Such challenges are not insurmountable. Anna Hutchens (Chapter 4) documents some cases of fair trade brands based on co-ownership models with producers, in which producers are able to acquire increased power within the terms of mainstream market relations and participate in the governance of the system. Nevertheless, the attempt to scale up the fair trade system via increased engagement with mainstream markets and associated development of business models more suited to this purpose continues to present significant strategic dilemmas for the movement in relation to balancing the goals of a successful business model and a participatory governance structure.

The central lesson that emerges across all these examples is that while effective and sustainable systems of supply-chain governance clearly require enhanced grassroots participation, enabling such participation is less a simple institutional solution, and more another institutional challenge in its own right. There is clearly a problem with presenting participation as a means of overcoming entrenched power relations when, in many ways, overcoming such power relations is a precondition for enhancing meaningful participation in the first place. This tension is certainly not intractable, but it does underscore the deeply political nature of such an endeavour and, correspondingly, the need for more sophisticated approaches to supply chain governance than have been developed in most cases to date.

The rising emphasis among some governance initiatives on the politics of underlying social alliances and power relations is certainly not new; many groups have long expressed deep scepticism about the pursuit of collaborative approaches to the governance of liberal production and trading systems. As Maksimovic emphasizes in her contribution to this volume (Chapter 13), labour activists have had an uneasy relationship with the CSR movement since its birth, greeting it with a mixture of support, cynical engagement and opposition. We should also be careful not to overstate the increased emphasis on deeper transformation, as the dominant view in many quarters is still in favour of voluntarist and collaborative approaches to CSR. Nevertheless, the cases and arguments documented by many contributors to this volume illustrate a clearly discernible – if gradual and rather embryonic – shift in emphasis towards recognition of the importance of such strategies.

---

4   See the description of the FLO in the introductory chapter to this volume and in Steve Knapp's chapter (Chapter 2).

Creating Alternative Economic Structures and Dynamics

Some initiatives have sought to develop their own systems of production and exchange and, as much as possible, to sidestep mainstream capitalist relations. As Hutchens highlights in her chapter, there are a number of distinct strains within the fair trade movement (also described in the Introduction to this volume). For traditional, 'alternative' approaches to fair trade, the goal of empowering producers is placed at the centre of the system's design and operation. This goal is supported by establishing a central role for capacity-building and organizational strengthening among producers in the operation of the trading system. Existing organizational capacity at the local level – enabled by the central role of member cooperatives in the system – provides the basis for producer participation in fair trade governance systems at the international level.

To some extent, the fair trade system has attempted to isolate itself from the disempowering consequences of broader systems of power relations by creating an autonomous and self-sustaining system of production and trade. However, this system is only able to operate autonomously from wider relations of social power up to a certain point. Despite its creation of an alternative 'vertical' supply chain system, producers and fair trade businesses are still deeply embedded in systems of power at local and international levels; this constrains the scope and depth of what the system is able to achieve. The more transformative elements of the fair trade movement certainly seek to challenge these wider institutions and ideologies via the broader campaigning activities also encompassed by the movement. Additionally, capacity-strengthening at the local level facilitated by the central role in the fair trade system for producer cooperatives or worker organizations can, in some cases, enable fair trade producers to form alliances in order to make demands on governments at the local level, thereby challenging power relations and macro-policy regimes at this level. Nevertheless, the current achievements of the fair trade movement in producing wider transformations in entrenched power relations have been limited.

Political Re-embedding

Strategies reliant on non-state actors and mechanisms as instruments of transnational governance often attract criticism on the grounds that voluntary CSR initiatives commonly enable corporations to decide at their own discretion how to implement codes of conduct, which codes to follow and which elements to discount or suspend where they involve trade-offs or costs. In view of such concerns, many groups have expressed rising dissatisfaction and scepticism towards voluntary approaches to CSR, often calling for the increased utilization of law to generate harder incentives for compliance, thereby countering power asymmetries between business and labour. A range of traditional regulatory organizations and institutions have been engaged by those seeking to develop a stronger legal underpinning for the social justice goals of transnational governance systems. Some seek to strengthen existing legal and policy regimes which are seen to be consistent with the goal of de-commodifying social relations. Others go further, as we shall see in the second part of this section of the chapter.

The case studies presented in this volume suggest that effective use of policy regimes and legal instruments can rebalance the strength of competing incentives in favour of greater social protection and provide a means by which such inevitable tensions may be resolved on a normatively principled and consistently applied basis. Such findings support the view that law can play an important role in reshaping power relations.

Enhancing the State and Other Policy Regimes

A number of the initiatives examined in the chapters of this book aim to augment state and non-state laws and policy regimes via an approach that endeavours to be reactive to actors, social facts and norms within a given regulatory space. These reflect what have often been termed as 'reflexive' or 'responsive' forms of regulation (Black 2002; Shearing 1993), or 'New Governance' (see Lobel, Chapter 17 in this volume). Regulatory theory that explores reflexive or responsive forms of regulation stresses that there are modes and forms of regulation other than command and control varieties of formal law enforced by public bodies that may prove more effective in achieving public policy objectives in a given social context. Private bodies may also be involved in regulation, either alone or in concert with public bodies. Ideally, the regulatory design should seek to 'harness and develop the dispersed resources which would be likely to support the public policy objectives of the regulatory regime' (Scott 2001, 330). Some advocates of responsive regulation have emphasized the importance of retaining both institutional structures which regulate substantive ends *and* sanctions for enforcing those ends as the apex of an 'enforcement pyramid', which is necessary to ensure that other techniques are effective (Ayres and Braithwaite 1995).

There are several examples of the state intervening to strengthen private initiatives. In some cases, national parliaments have internalized voluntary codes in national and international laws which require companies to be more transparent and report on social or environmental performance, thus enabling enhanced social monitoring and sanctioning (Vogel 2005). In other cases, the existing legal apparatus has been 'creatively' deployed – often in ways that go beyond the original intentions of relevant provisions – as a means of providing harder measures of enforcement for norms of corporate responsibility. Administrative agencies, parliamentary oversight bodies and state enforcement and inspection agencies have at times also played important roles in providing stronger legally-backed imposition of social responsibility norms.

Lobel presents several case studies of mechanisms in the United States which have been developed by state agencies to enhance existing laws. These initiatives are born from a reluctance to enforce social justice norms through command and control mechanisms, partly due to the failure of that style of regulation. One example of reflexive regulation on behalf of a state agency presented in Lobel's chapter is the California Cooperative Compliance Program adopted by California's Occupational Health and Safety Administration which retains the opportunity for litigants to enforce standards.

The government procurement mechanisms presented in John Howe's chapter (Chapter 18) operate according to a similar logic: that is, they involve a governance strategy aimed at increasing the incentives for compliance with existing legally established labour standards. When governments offer contracts for services or trade, private companies are required to demonstrate that they are complying with national labour standards in order to have their tender considered. These procurement mechanisms may be extended to production processes carried out overseas, though offshore production has rarely been regulated via such means, perhaps due to the difficulties of monitoring and enforcing systems of rules applied outside the regulator's own jurisdiction. Nevertheless, such problems are not insurmountable, as demonstrated by Howe's analysis of the City of Los Angeles Sweatfree Procurement Ordinance. Where it addresses labour standards of subcontractors in countries other than the United States, the Ordinance requires compliance with local minimum standards and the payment of a 'procurement living wage' assessed on the basis of local conditions, engaging the Workers Rights Consortium as an independent monitor of compliance. According to the available evidence presented by Howe, this auditing mechanism has proven quite effective.

In addition to such 'reflexive' initiatives led by state actors, some mechanisms have been developed by private actors to augment under-performing laws. The Homeworkers Code of Practice, discussed in the chapters by Diviney and Lillywhite and Delaney, operates as a voluntary industry code but mirrors the standards and requirements of the legally-entrenched Clothing Trades Award. The Code seeks to offer a number of extra incentives for compliance beyond the penalties offered by command and control style regulation.

By embedding themselves within existing legal structures and, in turn, attempting to further reinforce those legal structures, such mechanisms seek to overcome some of the motivational conflicts experienced by both businesses and consumers. In relation to businesses, the mechanisms aim to overcome countervailing competitive pressures to cut costs in order to increase profits. The tension between private profit-making incentives and broader social justice imperatives also exists at the level of individual consumer choices, giving rise to a persistent disjuncture between expressed sentiment in support of social justice norms and actual purchasing behaviour. This is a consequence of the fact that purchasing decisions operate on a range of product features, of which social dimensions is a single factor weighed against others. Such tensions limit the extent to which voluntary, consumer-driven systems of social governance can be relied upon to promote social justice norms on a consistent and principled basis, although – as Gordon Renouf highlights in his chapter (Chapter 10) – ethical consumerism interacts in important and generally complementary ways with broader forms of ethically-motivated citizen engagement, including engagement with legal and governmental forms of regulation. This underscores the inability of voluntary approaches to *substitute* for legal mechanisms, but also highlights their important contribution to supporting wider social norms and power relations that in turn underpin the effective functioning of law.

Pressuring the State to Reinsert Itself

Rising dissatisfaction and scepticism among many groups towards voluntary approaches to CSR has also resulted in continuing pressure on the state to reassert its power *vis-à-vis* capital. To the extent that voluntary CSR instruments can be accessed and effectively utilized – which has varied across instances, as demonstrated in a number of case studies presented in the chapters of this volume – they can play an important role in rebalancing the extreme power asymmetries that often exist between workers and business. The chapters in this volume have shown, however, that even within non-state initiatives, such improvements are frequently achieved only at the cost of resource intensive forms of top-down monitoring and enforcement, with all the attendant problems criticized by those who believe collaboration is more effective (see Chan, Chapter 11). In such cases, a significant tension arises between the desire to avoid command and control forms of social regulation and the necessity to reproduce them in privatized forms.

This tension is a product of the constant battle between incentives supportive of compliance promoted by CSR (such as labelling, brand promotion and potentially higher price premiums) and incentives to non-compliance driven by more short-term considerations of cost reduction and profit maximization. Many advocating voluntary approaches to corporate responsibility play down the significance of these tensions, most notably by advancing the concept of the 'business case' for socially responsible conduct, as opposed to a legal or moral obligation that overrides business logics and imperatives. Nevertheless, many authors have illustrated examples of such conflicts persisting, with extremely problematic consequences for the effectiveness of social governance systems. Such disjunctures exist at the level of individual companies, where human rights or compliance departments often operate at cross-purposes to procurement departments. The latter place demanding price and delivery requirements on suppliers, leading to what Utting describes as the 'Jekyll and Hyde' character of Northern corporate buyers in their dealings with Southern producers. Major conflicts also exist between corporate attempts to promote socially sustainable supply chain management on the one hand, and, on the other hand, their attempts to lobby for socially regressive fiscal and labour policy regimes and/or to relocate to regions where standards are relatively weak.

Recognition of the need to establish incentives for compliance that are sufficient to combat countervailing incentives to lower labour standards has given rise to practical questions about the efficacy of private bodies employing command and control techniques of social control without access to the kinds of penalties that public bodies are able to impose. For instance, there is little indication that new outworker legislation in Australia has resulted in improvements in labour conditions for outworkers. This is largely due to problems of enforcement. States have not matched new legal clout with resources for the departments and unions responsible for monitoring and prosecution (Marshall forthcoming). It is also partly due to the same factors which undermine the effectiveness of other forms of corporate responsibility enforcement: the incentives for non-compliance amongst businesses outweigh the risk of being caught and penalized in some way. Some argue that states are simply better placed to carry out the role of enforcing labour standards (see the chapters by Cooney and Chan in this volume).

Others have raised normative questions about private bodies assuming roles normally assigned to the state without the attendant democratic control, right of administrative review or other checks and balances that have evolved in liberal democratic states (Haufler 2001; Keohane 2003). The absence of these characteristics is inimical to the rule of law, which requires at a minimum that (Tamanaha 2004):

* everyone is subject to the law, including governments;
* laws are not arbitrary; that is, they can only be made by parliament (and, in common law countries, by independent courts);
* laws are transparent and readily available to all citizens;
* independent court systems interpret and apply the laws.

It is because of these conflicts that many social alliances which promote corporate accountability have pressured the government to resume the task of de-commodifying social relations and promoting social justice. The case studies in this volume show that, far from seeking a return of the post-war state, these organizations are pressuring for the return of state power in ways that reflect new formations of capitalism.

A number of campaigns of this kind were examined in the chapters of this book. The FairWear Campaign is one such example: this alliance between churches, community organizations and unions has, for many years, pressured state and federal Australian governments to strengthen the regulation of homeworking. In particular, FairWear has pressured governments to enact innovative styles of regulation extending beyond the regulation of the standard 'employer/employee' relationship associated with Fordist models of production. The campaign has encouraged governments to expand the definitions of 'employer' and 'employee' so as to cover business entities which do not themselves manufacture but, rather, organize and outsource production, and workers who are many steps removed from those who design and procure production. Successful campaigning in this case has led to the introduction of a range of highly innovative instruments of supply chain regulation (Fenwick et al. 2008).

The Asia Wage Floor Alliance, of which Maksimovic (Chapter 13) provides an account, demonstrates another instance of the insistence by corporate accountability campaigns upon new regulatory techniques on behalf of states. This campaign is based upon three significant premises with regards to the operation and structure of global capitalism: (i) that the garment industry is highly internationally integrated; (ii) that Asian countries account for over 70 per cent of the global garment trade; and (iii) that the garment industry has completed its restructuring with regard to its production locations, which has most likely led to the bottoming out of prices. The Asian Wage Floor Alliance is thus campaigning for an enforceable Asia Floor Wage for workers in the Asian garment industry and fair pricing for suppliers across Asia. It is insistent upon both the role of the state in mediating labour standards and production prices and consistent transnational standards across borders, reflecting the structure of the global industry.

It therefore appears that social justice governance initiatives have not only sought to 'bring the state back in' but also wish to see the state reconfigure itself and its methods of regulation in such a way as to regulate more effectively mobile capital and post-Fordist social relations. Whilst there are strong arguments in favour of these strategies, they have not thus far had great success either in terms of resulting government reform or concrete benefits for workers.

Replacing the State and Other Policy Regimes

Voluntary forms of CSR have at times been criticized for replacing the role of the state and thus contributing to undermining state authority and legitimacy. However, in their defence, advocates of non-state governance initiatives have pointed to the weakness of state capacity or the absence of laws upholding international standards. For example, such weaknesses commonly arise in instances in which CSR instruments seek to promote independent workers' organizations in countries where a corporatist relationship exists between unions and the state. In newly industrialized regions of China such as the Pearl River Delta which now conduct a large proportion of production for export, official trade unions are largely absent or, where present, controlled by the local governments. Anita Chan (Chapter 11) suggests that, in many cases, foreign management is permitted to appoint one of the managerial staff to serve as union head.

Until the recent labour law reforms charted by Cooney in his chapter (Chapter 19), CSR instruments which operated in China often promoted representation by independent workers' organizations in a manner which was inconsistent with existing labour laws. Chan's chapter describes one such instrument in some detail. In the late 1990s and early 2000s, Reebok's Human Rights Compliance Department experimented with facilitating independent union representation in order to overcome the limitations of relying upon auditing as the primary mechanism for union enforcement. Ultimately, these experiments failed, although not without small successes along the way. One reason for this outcome was Reebok's failure to properly comprehend and adapt to the local and national union setting. Critically, it failed to solicit the involvement of the top levels of the national union federation. When the ACFTU flexed its muscles in order to express its disapproval at being undermined, Reebok retreated.

Those sections of the fair trade movement that seek to avoid engaging with mainstream corporate and market structures often also aim to sidestep the state in certain respects. Some fair trade organizations in developing countries have collectively employed their social premium – sometimes augmented by aid or funds from political allies – to advance designated goals of social justice. Where self-organization is most developed, cooperatives play many of the roles normally associated with the state, contributing among other things to provision of health care and schools. Even where these collectivized services are not provided, fair trade initiatives often enable democratic control for producers over price-setting in a way that is not generally offered by the state.

Assessment of the Transformative Potential of New Governance Initiatives

What can be said about the relative strengths and weaknesses of different fair trade and corporate accountability initiatives? Because the chapters in this book have adopted different methodologies and examined varying types of initiatives, the evidence they offer regarding the effect of the initiatives on the welfare and rights of workers is somewhat inconsistent in its scope and emphasis. Viewed together, however, the chapters have painted quite a detailed picture of the *types of institutional engagement* made possible by the adoption of different strategies, as we have discussed in the previous section. In this section we draw some overarching – if somewhat tentative – conclusions concerning the *potential transformative impact* of different types of initiatives.

Our focus here is on the contribution of each type of initiative to:

a. strengthening institutional capacities to promote and protect worker and producer wellbeing directly;
b. increasing opportunities for worker and producer influence over business decision-making;
c. strengthening the capacity of institutions to promote trust and cooperation; and
d. promoting definitions of business, consumer and state rights and responsibilities – as embodied in and promoted by institutional arrangements – that are supportive of social justice norms.

In Table 20.1 we present a graphic depiction of this assessment. The top horizontal row denotes categories of initiatives or vehicles for transformation. These categories were discussed in some detail in the introductory chapter to this volume, and we will not repeat this discussion here. Very few initiatives fit neatly into these categories; rather, most draw on some combination of these 'ideal type' strategic vehicles. The illustrative examples we point to below in relation to each category simply reflect our selection of those that seem to fit most neatly into individual categories. Nevertheless, the categories are useful for exploring the potential benefits and trade-offs associated with differing strategies.

The reason we label the table 'contribution to institutional transformation' (rather than simply extent of institutional transformation) is because the tangible effect of specific initiatives on institutional change depends upon much more than can be taken account of here: the characteristics of the individuals involved; the organizations' material attributes; the business environments in which they are operating; and so forth. We can, however, make some generalizations from the case studies considered here (and in other research that we have referred to in our discussion) regarding the structural limitations presented by certain strategies and their general aims, strengths and weaknesses. These have informed the ratings given to initiatives based upon whether their contribution to institutional transformation is low (L), medium (M), medium to high (M/H) or high (H).

Such evaluations clearly require a significant dose of subjective judgement. Transparency with respect to the criteria used in assigning such rankings is therefore of particular importance. We generated these rankings by considering several criteria that each attempt to get at a measure of the significance of the initiatives' contribution to relevant kinds of institutional transformation: intensity of impact (the degree to which it contributed to changed outcomes); scope of impact (the breadth of impact across workers/producers/workplaces/sectors); and apparent sustainability of impact over time. Where contributions were difficult to assess empirically (for example, in those cases where processes of change were especially gradual or diffused), we attempted to infer likely impacts by means of reference to: the objectives of the initiatives; the processes through which they operate; and/or the capabilities they embody.

Table 20.1 Extent of contribution to institutional transformation

Type of initiative: Dimensions of institutional transformation supportive of social justice norms	Business-led CSR, e.g. corporate code of conduct	Mainstream fair trade, e.g. FLO	Collaborative multi-stakeholder initiatives, e.g. ETI	Alternative fair trade, e.g. IFAT	Corporate accountability, e.g. Olympic campaign
1. Strengthening technical capabilities of governance institutions and key players within them	M/H	M/H	H	H	L
2. Contribution to underlying productive capabilities of the economic system being regulated	L	M/H	L	M/H	L
3. Increased information and understanding for workers'/producers' organizations regarding business decisions	M/H	M/H	H	H	M
4. Increased right of consultation for workers'/producers' organizations regarding business decisions	L	M/H	M	H	L
5. Increased right of veto for workers'/producers' organizations over business decisions	L	M	L	H	L
6. Direct opportunities for affected individuals to exercise choice/agency over business decisions	L	M	L	H	L
7. Promotion of coordination, communication and trust between labour/producers and capital	H	H	H	H	L
8. Promotion of coordination, communication and trust between labour/producers, capital and government	H	H	H	L	L
9. Promotion of sustainable social alliances between labour/producers' organizations	L	M	L	H	H
10. Challenging ideas relating to rights and responsibilities of business	M	H	M	H	H
11. Challenging ideas relating to rights and responsibilities of workers/producers	L	H	M	H	H
12. Challenging ideas relating to rights and responsibilities of consumers	M	H	M	H	H
13. Challenging ideas relating to rights and responsibilities of states	L	L	M	M	M

Notes: High (H), medium to high (M/H), medium (M), low (L).

Our analysis shows that different vehicles have very different strengths and weaknesses. Overall, however, the mix of strategic approaches embodied most closely by alternative fair trade initiatives appear to offer the greatest transformative potential. In practice, their limited scale may undermine this potential but, in structural terms, they present great opportunities for institutional transformation.

Institutional Capacities to Promote and Protect Worker and Producer Wellbeing Directly (rows 1–2 in Table 20.1)

Even in the absence of any contribution to changing the 'terms of the system' in which global economic relations are 'embedded', institutional qualities of a governance system may contribute to realizing justice aims simply by strengthening the functional qualities of the governance system within its existing terms, and thereby enhancing the direct contribution of these initiatives to desired outcomes for individuals and communities. This may take the form of managerial capacity-building within both supply chains and individual companies, strengthened means of communication and negotiation between corporate, governmental and civil society actors and/or strengthened institutional and human resources to support self-help activities among workers and producers themselves. As discussed above, fair trade systems have contributed importantly to producers' capacities, both via organizational strengthening at the grassroots level, and by supporting sustainable alliances between producers at the local, national and international levels. While many observers consider fair trade bodies such as IFAT to have a stronger record of performance than FLO with respect to goals of institutional strengthening, the performance of both elements of the fair trade system has been relatively strong in this regard. Some collaborative corporate and multi-stakeholder initiatives have also contributed importantly to building skills and capabilities required to support more responsible approaches to doing business.

   This category also encompasses consideration of the impact of the governance initiatives on the productive capacity of the economic processes they seek to regulate. Little evidence has been presented to suggest that the initiatives have a decisive impact one way or another; the fair trade system has been analysed most extensively from this perspective, but the evidence is mixed: on one hand some suggest that the system suffers from significant efficiency losses as a result of its costly certification processes and limited economies of scale; others point in contrast to the long-term productivity gains achieved via investment in capacity-building and improved productive technologies among disadvantaged farming communities.

Opportunities for Worker and Producer Influence over Business Decision-making (rows 3–6 in Table 20.1)

Fair trade initiatives produce significantly better results with regards to participation in decision-making than do CSR initiatives, though there is also some variation within the fair trade system itself. Alternative fair trade systems, in particular, endeavour to prioritize grassroots control throughout the supply chain; while the democratic and producer-oriented credentials of the FLO system have been significantly strengthened in recent years, many consider the weakness of worker and producer empowerment in Fairtrade supply chains dominated by corporate buyers of Fairtrade certified products to remain a significant weakness within the mainstream Fairtrade system.

   More collaborative or ameliorative CSR vehicles are able to provide workers and producers with access to certain kinds of information regarding business decisions. However, this does not translate into high levels of influence over those decisions with regards to prices of labour or production, and other aspects of managerial prerogative. More confrontational corporate accountability campaigns such as the Olympics Campaign described in the chapter by Leong et al. (Chapter 15) may aim, in the long term, to provide workers with greater control over business decision-making at a system wide level. However, the case studies presented in this volume suggest that, perhaps because their aims are more ambitious in scope, this potential is usually extremely limited in the short term: such strategies seem to contribute more to giving credence to the *idea* of workers' influence over decision-making than to *realizing* it in practice.

C) Capacity of Institutions to Promote Trust and Cooperation (rows 7–9 in Table 20.1)

Generally speaking, the potential strength of CSR instruments such as company codes of practice lies in their ability to create greater trust and cooperation between workers/producers, capital and the state. Participants in such schemes may at times become disenchanted and policy incoherence within businesses and supply chains may reduce the effectiveness of many initiatives in practice. Nevertheless, these types of initiatives offer significant potential to build cooperation and trust across actors and institutions that otherwise may find it difficult to work effectively together. In many cases the more confrontational tactics adopted by relatively more combative corporate accountability vehicles contribute to an erosion of trust between business and worker/producer groups, though this is by no means always the case; it is also possible for confrontational tactics to result in the opening of new channels of communication, which may subsequently enable more collaborative relationships to develop.

On the other hand, corporate accountability campaigns such as the Olympic Campaign hold far greater potential to create sustainable social alliances between workers and producers than more ameliorative CSR initiatives. CSR vehicles such as corporate codes of conduct tend to downplay the differences in interests between workers and capital, and correspondingly de-emphasize the value of building movements around those differing interests. Multi-stakeholder initiatives may provide a forum for the creation of better working relationships between workers and producer organizations, but this is not their aim and not what they are structurally set up to achieve. In contrast, a number of the corporate accountability movements examined in the chapters of this book embraced as a foundational aim the building of alliances and solidarity between workers in different regions. By emphasizing commonalities between workers in different countries, and confronting capital as a united front, these campaigns seek to build trust between workers and their representative organizations across countries.

The fair trade system (encompassing both the FLO system and a diverse range of 'alternative' fair trade organizations) contributes importantly to the promotion of trust and cooperation between the various players in the system. These initiatives promote trust and cooperation between producers at a local level, and also between producers at a regional (South–South) level, as we saw in some of the chapters of this book. By providing a strong framework for decision-making and a fairer distribution of profits throughout the supply chain, fair trade systems also seek to ameliorate conflicting interests and promote institutionalized cooperation between producers and buyers.

Definitions of Business, Consumer and State Rights and Responsibilities that the Institutional Arrangements Embody and Promote (rows 10–13 in Table 20.1)

Here, once again, more ameliorative vehicles for CSR offer less potential for *profound* transformation at the level of ideas than more confrontational corporate accountability initiatives. There is no doubt that these vehicles seek to promote social purposes for business and augment rights of certain limited types for workers. Indeed, because ideas generated by CSR initiatives around business responsibilities are often framed in accordance with a 'business case' for corporate responsibility, they appeal to a wider audience than would otherwise be the case. However, these discourses do not challenge the functions and responsibilities of business at a deeper level. Institutionalized recognition of the 'public' functions and impacts of business – as conceptualized by Terry Macdonald (Chapter 7) – remains limited. Within arenas of public debate, corporate accountability initiatives often propose far greater shifts in the roles and responsibilities of business actors. In practice, however, such initiatives are often constrained in their promotion of such norms, due to limited resources and in some cases also a lack of agreement regarding what specific form such responsibilities should take.

   None of the vehicles rate highly with regard to their potential to challenge the role of the state. Some of the more confrontational corporate accountability campaigns agitate for a renewed role for the state in the regulation of labour standards, as have some fair trade alliances at meetings of inter-governmental bodies such as the WTO.[5] As seen in the case of the FairWear campaign and the Asia Floor Wage campaign, such initiatives sometimes advocate for the state to transform its regulatory framework to take into account new, post-Fordist, capitalist formations. However, they rarely argue for a radically reconfigured state in territorial terms. While many argue for reconfigurations of the state's role in mediating power relations and embedding social justice norms, the majority accept that state responsibilities should remain nationally bounded in most important respects. Yet, the territorial boundedness of the state places significant limits on what the state can achieve, both because of limits to existing state powers to address the increasingly global workings of economic relations, and because of the disproportionate power of Northern states and their unwillingness in most cases to use this power to address the problems of Southern workers and populations, given that their own constitutional and democratic responsibilities remain tied to national populations. With a small number of exceptions – such as in relation to crimes against humanity, or the introduction of limited social clauses in inter-governmental agreements (Vandaele 2005) – few campaigns have argued for the introduction of more expansive 'cosmopolitan' (Held 1995) forms of regulation that would harness the resources and regulatory capacities of Northern governments in support of marginalized workers and producers in the global South, and in turn hold Northern governments accountable to Southern constituencies for the exercise of such power.

---

   5   The fair trade movement developed a joint position towards the Sixth WTO Ministerial Conference in Hong Kong, and it was decided to step up efforts for coordinated advocacy work on areas such as CSR, the Economic Partnership Agreements and other bilateral and regional trade arrangements. At the Fair Trade Fair and Sustainable Trade Symposium, participants included over 70 producers, representing 20 countries. More than 600 people attended one or more of the 20 panels that made up the Symposium and Policy Forum, which was the first ever of this kind at an official international meeting (Fair Trade Advocacy Office 2004).

Conclusion

In this chapter we have examined a range of civic, corporate and state-based governance initiatives that seek to promote global justice from a number of different perspectives by attempting to re-embed capitalism in social justice norms. In doing so, such initiatives endeavour to counter a range of perceived deficiencies in the contemporary international political economy, which the chapter has also reviewed. The interaction between the background structures of the international political and economic system and these emergent governance initiatives was shown to be unfolding along highly dynamic and interactive pathways. The background institutional terrain is continually shifting and in response, CSR and fair trade initiatives are, like capital, constantly on the jump as they attempt to adapt to new capitalist formations, anticipate future configurations and dynamics and assert their legitimacy within the emerging institutional system.

On a practical level, these initiatives perform a range of functions – from delivering social services and facilitating economic redistribution and poverty reduction to establishing, monitoring and enforcing social and labour standards within global production systems across large parts of the industrialized and developing worlds. They attempt to transform existing economic and political institutions to different extents. Some see great benefits in working with the grain and largely accepting the market and policy structures they insert themselves within. Others wish to transform these political and economic institutions more deeply. We also saw that some initiatives seek to sidestep existing institutions and create new market and social relations.

Our overarching assessment, presented in Table 20.1, highlights the contrasting strengths and weaknesses characterizing alternative vehicles for the re-embedding of capitalism. In practice, specific initiatives often combine a range of strategies in an attempt to counterbalance the deficiencies of one tactic with the strengths of another. Whether such mixed approaches ultimately achieve this intended balance is an issue over which no consensus emerged in this book.

More ameliorative vehicles are generally better at promoting trust, cooperation and the sharing of information, whereas more confrontational vehicles challenge more deeply the rights and responsibilities of business, consumers and workers/producers, and hold greater potential to shift the relations of power among these sets of actors. Initiatives across this spectrum failed to press for a territorial reconfiguration of the role of the state in a way that might appropriately counterbalance the challenge to the efficacy of state regulation presented by transnational capital. As we discussed in the introduction to this volume, this appears to reflect a deeper ambiguity among initiatives of this kind regarding the extent to which they are willing to question norms of national sovereignty and bounded state responsibility, and embrace a more expansive cosmopolitan notion of global social justice. Resolving such ambiguity would demand the resolution of a range of difficult and complex normative dilemmas, which it is perhaps not realistic to expect the global justice movement to resolve any time soon. Nevertheless, the persistence of such ambiguity does appear to imply ongoing constraints to the scope of what such initiatives can be expected to achieve.

Moreover, most of the initiatives we have examined continue to operate within a rather fragmented universe of governance arrangements, which lacks system level coherence and coordination. Many contributors to this volume have highlighted the various ways in which these initiatives interact in practice at the systemic level – with each other and with wider national and global arrangements. However, the initiatives themselves are rarely conceived with these external interactions and impacts clearly in view. This can lead to problems of duplication, poor engagement with state-based regulatory instruments, and a lack of effective coordination across initiatives and jurisdictions.

How concerned should we be about limitations of these kinds as we pull together the pieces of the puzzle to craft a final assessment of the contribution and significance of these initiatives to the broad project of globalizing justice? In considering this, we find ourselves encountering an apparent tension in the tone of the book's analysis. On the one hand, many of the chapters within the volume adopt very critical positions in relation to the contribution and potential of these initiatives. Indeed, one of the central objectives of the book has been to gain insight into the nature of such enduring challenges with which these initiatives continue to struggle, and of new challenges that are emerging. In seeming contrast to such a critical stance, the tone of much of our own analysis above – within both our concluding and introductory chapters – seems infused with a greater spirit of optimism.

We suggest that this apparent tension may be reconciled via the interpretation of these processes of social change and political struggle as 'experiments' in social transformation. Viewing these initiatives as one moment in a broader, forward-reaching process of systemic change can justify an optimistic interpretation of their achievements and potential, in spite of the existing limitations that have been clearly detailed above. As we have emphasized, to view these initiatives as static institutional arrangements would be to misunderstand their purpose and impact – as both experimental, learning devices in specific governance contexts, and as broader vehicles for social transformation via their provision of ongoing sources of knowledge and pressure that can leverage processes of progressive change within wider social and political institutions.

Despite the range of lessons regarding both successes and failures documented in this volume, much uncertainty remains and a great deal more experimentation will be needed as such processes continue. But we suggest that it is only through continuing to navigate these experimental pathways of social change that we may continue to consolidate and advance our understanding of how the resources and energies devoted to these initiatives by those attempting to globalize principles of social justice can best be deployed. And it is perhaps through experiments of this kind, grounded in the combined efforts of responsible consumers, businesses, activists and governments – working sometimes cooperatively and sometimes in constructive tension, but always with the shared goals of globalizing norms of social justice in view – that the entrenched challenges of injustice within a globalizing political economy may most effectively be confronted.

References

Ayres, I. and Braithwaite, J. (1995), *Responsive Regulation: Transcending the Deregulation Debate* (New York: Oxford University Press).

Black, J. (2002), 'Critical reflections on regulation', *Australian Journal of Legal Philosophy* 27: 1–35.

Fair Trade Advocacy Office (2004), Newsletter (December). [Online: Fair Trade Advocacy Office]. Available at: http://www.fairtrade-advocacy.org/documents/NewsletterDecember2004.pdf [accessed: July 2006].

Fenwick, C., Howe, J., Marshall, S. and Landau, I. (2008), 'Labour and labour related laws in small and micro enterprises: innovative regulatory responses' (ed.), SEED (Geneva: International Labour Organization).

Hall, P.A. (2007), 'The evolution of varieties of capitalism in Europe', in B. Hancke, M. Rhodes and M. Thatcher (eds), *Beyond Varieties of Capitalism: Conflict, Contradictions and Complementarities in the European Economy* (Oxford: Oxford University Press).

—— and Soskice, D. (eds) (2001), *Varieties of Capitalism: The Institutional Foundations of Comparative Advantage* (Oxford: Oxford University Press).

Haufler, V. (2001), *A Public Role for the Private Sector: Industry Self-Regulation in a Global Economy* (Washington, DC: Carnegie Endowment for International Peace).

Held, D. (1995), *Democracy and the Global Order: From the Modern State to Cosmopolitan Governance* (Stanford, CA: Stanford University Press).

Keohane, R.O. (2003), 'Global governance and democratic accountability', in D. Held and M. Koenig-Archibugi (eds), *Taming Globalization: Frontiers of Governance* (Cambridge: Polity Press).

Marshall, S. (forthcoming), 'Australian textile clothing and footwear supply chain regulation', in C. Fenwick and T. Novitz (eds), *Legal Protection of Workers' Human Rights: Regulatory Change and Challenge* (Oxford: Hart).

Polanyi, K. (1944), *The Great Transformation: The Political and Economic Origins of Our Time* (Boston, MA: Beacon Press).

Scott, C. (2001), 'Analysing regulatory space: fragmented resources and institutional design', *Public Law* (Summer): 329–53.

Shearing, C. (1993), 'A constitutive conception of regulation', in P. Grabosky and J. Braithwaite (eds), *Business Regulation and Australia's Future* (Canberra: Australian Institute of Criminology).

Tamanaha, B.Z. (2004), *On the Rule of Law: History, Politics, Theory* (Cambridge and New York: Cambridge University Press).

Vandaele, A.D.A. (2005), *International Labour Rights and the Social Clause: Friends or Foes* (London: Cameron May).

Vogel, D. (2005), *The Market for Virtue: The Potential and Limits of Corporate Social Responsibility* (Washington, DC: Brookings Institution Press).

Wailes, N., Kitay, J. and Lansbury, R. (2008), 'Varieties of capitalism, corporate governance and employment relations under globalisation', in S. Marshall, R. Mitchell and I. Ramsay (eds), *Varieties of Capitalism, Corporate Governance and Employees* (Melbourne: Melbourne University Publishing).

Index